OTHER BOOKS BY PETER GAY

The Bridge of Criticism: Dialogues on the Enlightenment (1970)
The Enlightenment: An Interpretation. Volume II, The Science of Free-
   dom (1969)
Weimar Culture: The Outsider as Insider (1968)
A Loss of Mastery: Puritan Historians in Colonial America (1966)
The Enlightenment: An Interpretation. Volume I, The Rise of Modern
   Paganism (1966)
The Party of Humanity: Essays in the French Enlightenment (1964)
Voltaire's Politics: The Poet as Realist (1959)
The Dilemma of Democratic Socialism: Eduard Bernstein's Challenge to
   Marx (1952)

Modern Europe (with R. K. Webb) (1973)

TRANSLATIONS WITH INTRODUCTIONS

Voltaire: Candide (1963)
Voltaire: Philosophical Dictionary, 2 vols. (1962)
Ernst Cassirer: The Question of Jean Jacques Rousseau (1954)

ANTHOLOGIES

Deism: An Anthology (1968)
John Locke on Education (1964)

The Enlightenment

A Comprehensive Anthology

EDITED BY PETER GAY

Simon and Schuster · New York

SBN 671-21465-9 Casebound
SBN 671-21707-0 Touchstone paperback edition
Library of Congress Catalog Card Number: 72-87947
Designed by Irving Perkins
Manufactured in the United States of America

1 2 3 4 5 6 7 8 9 10

❀ Contents

The Enlightenment

A Comprehensive Anthology

❧ Preface

An anthology is both an appetizer and an argument. It is, first, an appetizer: it cannot achieve, nor should it simulate, completeness. It seeks to be informative and representative, but if it leaves the reader with the comfortable sense that he need read no further, it has been a failure. Its true function is not to satisfy, but to arouse and sharpen, appetite. While the present anthology is long, and ranges widely, I have compiled it with the purpose of incitement in mind. Inevitable limitations of space have compelled me to be selective and self-denying; I could not include some of my favorites because they were simply too long or did not lend themselves to my editorial scissors. I particularly regret the absence of such masterpieces as Voltaire's *Candide* or Hume's *Dialogues Concerning Natural Religion;* I can only hope I can persuade the reader to discover them for himself. Like these tantalizing omissions, the passages I did include should stimulate inquiry. To facilitate such inquiry, I have appended lists for further reading to the Introduction and to the headnotes, which commend other works by the author anthologized, and secondary works that should prove helpful in the closer study of the Enlightenment.

In the second place, an anthology is an argument. As I have suggested, it should seek to be representative, to supply a dependable sketch map of the terrain. But the anthologist should have his sense of what that terrain is, and in reflecting that sense an anthology is a personal statement. Only the professional may know just whom the anthologist is debating with, but this much should be clear to all from the outset: by including some authors and excluding others, by giving much space to some and little space to others, the anthologist is offering his interpretation of the past. So it is here. I have written extensively on the Enlightenment, and attempted in these writings to redraw the map of a controversial, though much traveled, tract of the past. I have designed my Introduction and my comments on other books to orient the reader among the polemics. But, in addition, he should take the very shape of this anthology to be more than a perfunctory or accidental collocation of texts: it testifies to what I think the Enlightenment really was. This means that while most of the familiar names and titles are here, I have also included some less familiar texts which, together, should make my argument for me.

In compiling this anthology, I have had much generous aid. I have made specific acknowledgments to publishers for their permissions to reprint. In addition, I want to thank Paul D. Neuthaler for suggesting this enterprise and sustaining it through its vicissitudes. Above all, I want to thank my wife, Ruth, who collaborated with me in every way, from the inception of this book to its completion.

PETER GAY

✿ *Introduction*

I

The career of the name "Enlightenment" is almost as complex as
the historical reality it designates. The first to have applied the
term to a distinct period were the Germans; as early as the
eighteenth century itself, they spoke, not always appreciatively, of
the *Aufklärung.* One of the most revealing texts of the age is,
appropriately enough, a popular essay by the German philosopher
Immanuel Kant, entitled "Answer to the Question: What Is Enlightenment?" Kant's answer was brief and clear: "Enlightenment
is man's emergence from his nonage." Man has failed to reach his
majority not through "lack of intelligence" but from "lack of
determination and courage to use that intelligence without another's guidance. *Sapere aude!* Dare to know! Have the courage to
use your own intelligence!"* While Kant was offering this striking
definition of Enlightenment, other countries had the thing, but not
the word. The English did not import it from Germany until the
nineteenth century. The French, who regarded themselves as international headquarters for the movement, sometimes praised their
century as a *siècle des lumières,* or, even more significantly, as a
"philosophic century." While the French, then, did not supply the
age with its name, they did supply it with the name for its dominant intellectual type: "philosophe."† "Philosopher" was, of course,
a time-honored epithet, but in eighteenth-century France it meant a
philosopher of a new sort: a man of and in the world, a lucid and
persuasive writer, and an adept in the new sciences. In his last book,
the *Essay on the Reigns of Claudius and Nero,* Denis Diderot,
himself perhaps the most characteristic of philosophes, ambitiously
defined this new philosopher as a kind of universal guide:

* "Beantwortung der Frage: Was ist Aufklärung?," *Werke,* ed. Ernst Cassirer
et al. (11 vols., 1912–22) , IV, 169. For a selection from Kant's essay, see below,
selection 30.

† Since this is a word of French origin, it has been customary to italicize it;
I have, in my own writings, naturalized it as a loan word and thus dropped the
italics. I have adopted the same usage here; it will, I hope, underscore the
international quality of the Enlightenment.

The magistrate deals out justice; the philosopher teaches the
the magistrate what is just and unjust. The soldier defends his
country; the philosopher teaches the soldier what a fatherland is.
The priest recommends to his people the love and respect of the
gods; the philosopher teaches the priest what the gods are. The
sovereign commands all; the philosopher teaches the sovereign
the origins and limits of his authority. Every man has duties to his
family and his society; the philosopher teaches everyone what
these duties are. Man is exposed to misfortune and pain; the
philosopher teaches man how to suffer.

In a word, the philosopher is "the preceptor of mankind."* Most of
Diderot's contemporaries, whether friendly or hostile, compatriots
or foreigners, were certain that this paragon must be French. When
Horace Walpole, fastidious observer of humanity and brilliant
letter writer, visited Paris in 1765, he limited the term to Frenchmen—to a few Frenchmen. "The *philosophes*," he wrote to a friend,
"are insupportable, superficial, overbearing, and fanatic: they
preach incessantly."† Whether the waspish English visitor was right
in his description—and one can see why he should have gained his
impression—he was wrong to narrow the term in this way. There
were preachers of reasonableness, humanity, secularism spread
across Europe and into the American colonies: while the Frenchmen Voltaire, Diderot, Holbach were the most celebrated of the
philosophes, there were philosophes in Great Britain (notably
David Hume, Adam Smith, Edward Gibbon), in the German states
(one thinks of Gotthold Ephraim Lessing, Christoph Martin
Wieland, Immanuel Kant), in northern Italy (chiefly the Verri
brothers and Cesare Beccaria), in the British colonies of North
America (Benjamin Franklin, Thomas Jefferson and James Madison come immediately to mind), in the Scandinavian countries, in
the Iberian Peninsula, even, as will appear in these pages, in remote
Russia.‡

It is only fair to add that the French philosophes knew this well
and acknowledged it freely. As good cosmopolitans they set no
national boundaries to reason, and felt themselves part of an inter-

* *Essai sur les règnes de Claude et de Néron,* in Diderot, *Oeuvres complètes,*
eds. Jules Assézat and Maurice Tourneux, 20 vols. (1875–77), III, 248, 176.
† To Thomas Gray, Nov. 19, 1765 in, Walpole, *Letters,* ed. Mrs. Paget Toynbee,
16 vols. (1904–5), VI, 352.
‡ For brief biographies of these and other philosophes, see the appropriate
selections.

national movement, no matter by what name philosophes were called elsewhere. The philosophes were an international family; quarrelsome like most families, and, like most families, united mainly in times of emergency. Jean-Jacques Rousseau, the stormiest of them, came to be regarded as an enemy within the camp, but while his estrangement from the others ran deep and proved permanent, Rousseau remained a member of the philosophic family, though hardly in good standing: a black sheep is still a sheep. As late as 1766, after Rousseau had repudiated his old friend Diderot and his much admired Voltaire, Diderot found it possible to include his errant friend in some ultimate philosophical community. In a letter to his mistress, Sophie Volland, he imagined someone showing Voltaire a "shocking page which Rousseau, citizen of Geneva, has just scribbled against him." He gets furious, he loses his temper, he calls him villain, he foams with rage; he wants to have the miserable fellow beaten to death. "Look," says someone there, "I have it on good authority that he's going to ask you for asylum, today, tomorrow, perhaps the day after tomorrow. What would you do?" "What would I do?" replies Voltaire, gnashing his teeth. "What would I do? I'd take him by the hand, lead him to my room, and say to him, 'Look, here's my bed, the best in the house, sleep there, sleep there for the rest of your life, and be happy.' "* Actuality proved a little less pleasing than this: neither Voltaire nor Diderot ever forgave Rousseau for what they regarded as Rousseau's treacheries. But the very persistence and vehemence of their denunciations shows the long, unpleasant imbroglio to be what it was—a family quarrel.

Generally, relations among the philosophes were in any event rather less stormy. Some, like Holbach and Diderot, were long-standing friends; others, like Voltaire, appeared to the rest as respected, if not always respectable, teachers. The philosophes' mutual commerce was social and intellectual, and their sociability served the intellect. The Scottish Enlightenment was a small and cohesive group of friends—David Hume, Adam Smith, Adam Ferguson, and others—who knew one another intimately and talked to one another incessantly. In France, what their enemies called a coterie, or even a conspiracy, was a collection of friends visiting and corresponding with one another. D'Alembert for a time worked with Diderot on the *Encyclopédie,* and went to see Voltaire on a fateful visit by which he unintentionally precipitated a crisis in the

* Jan. 27, 1766, Diderot, *Correspondance,* ed. Georges Roth (1955–   ), VI, 34.

Enlightenment.* When Hume went to France after the end of the
Seven Years' War, he consorted with the Parisian philosophes as a
matter of course; he might disagree with them about the theory of
knowledge, but he saw them as brothers in the fight against superstition and fanaticism. When the philosophes did not know one
another as friends, they learned from one another as writers. Kant
was a disciple of the Englishman Isaac Newton, the Scot David
Hume, and the Genevan Jean-Jacques Rousseau. The Scottish
Enlightenment was deeply indebted to the Frenchman Montesquieu. Beccaria, the great Italian theorist of legal reform, explicitly
attributed what he called his "conversion to philosophy" to one
Scottish and several French philosophes: to Hume, to Montesqueiu,
d'Alembert, Diderot, Helvétius, and Buffon. These writers, he told
his French translator Morellet, were his "constant reading matter,"
daily and "in the silence of night."† The intellectual traffic did not
flow all one way: Beccaria amply repaid his teachers with his *Essay
on Crimes and Punishments,* which had as much influence on
French philosophes as they had had on him. The philosophes
embodied the cosmopolitan ideal without question and without
straining; it was a natural mode of thinking for them. They were
convinced—in the words of Wieland, whom many contemporaries
called "the German Voltaire"—that "only the true cosmopolitan
can be a good citizen"; he alone can "do the great work to which we
have been called: to cultivate, enlighten, and ennoble the human
race."‡

The first step toward a definition of the Enlightenment, then, is
to see it as a congenial and informal movement of literary men—of
philosophers, critics, playwrights, essayists, storytellers, editors, all of
them articulate and prolific men of words—"called," in Wieland's
striking religious word, to do their great work. I must add that by
no means all of them felt this sense of mission with equally burning
intensity. The passion of Voltaire, who wrote literally millions of
words in behalf of a humane code, in defense of victims of legal
injustice, in criticism of cruelty, bellicosity, and superstition, contrasts with the philosophic calm of Hume, who was glad to persuade
others to his views, but lost no sleep over a world in which stupidity
was master and, it seemed, fairly well entrenched. In their tempera-
ments, as in their prescriptions, the philosophes differed widely. To

---

* See below, page 293.

† Jan. 26, 1766, in *Illuministi Italiani,* ed. Franco Venturi, III (1958), 203.

‡ *Gespräche unter vier Augen,* in *Sämmtliche Werke,* ed. J. G. Gruber, 50
vols. (1824–77), XLII, 127–28.

speak of them as one movement is not to speak of them as a disciplined troop, or even as members of a school. What united them was the common experience of shedding their inherited Christian beliefs with the aid of classical philosophers and for the sake of a modern philosophy. They were by and large agreed that Christianity, in company with all other supernatural religions, was wrong,* and that science, with its dependable results and its principled modesty before the eternal mysteries of mind and matter, was the way to truth and (to the extent that such was at all attainable) to happiness. And what united the philosophes above all was confidence in the critical method.

Here we have reached the core of the eighteenth-century Enlightenment as a movement. The philosophes of all countries and all persuasions were lyrical in their single-minded praise of criticism. They likened it to the surgeon's knife that cuts away the cancer of superstitions, to the fresh breeze that blows down the screen of tradition, to the beam of light that penetrates the gloom of accepted nonsense, to the blow that levels the grim citadel of unreason. Immanuel Kant, defending his age against the charge of shallowness, pointed to its accomplishments in mathematics and the natural sciences, but principally to its cleaning vigor. The century, he insisted—and it was the highest praise he could bestow—was "the very age of criticism."†

For the philosophes, criticism, as their metaphors amply make plain, was an act of aggression. The Christian centuries through which Western civilization had passed, and the Christian faith in whose grip the civilization still found itself, had erected protective walls around the most important areas of human activity, notably religion, politics, and sexual morality. Now criticism impartially claimed the right to criticize everything; if there was one thing it refused to recognize, it was privileged sanctuaries. "Everything must be examined," Diderot wrote in the *Encyclopedia*, "everything must be shaken up, without exception and without circumspection."‡

But while the philosophes' criticism was a form of aggression, it was far from being undisciplined. They did not merely lash out at what seemed to them outmoded, mendacious, or doubtful; they

---

* Though even on this point the agreement among the philosophes was less than complete: Lessing constructed a kind of ethereal religion of his own; a few others, like Jefferson, after bouts with unbelief, returned to a tepid, liberal religiosity later in life.

† "Vorrede," *Critik der reinen Vernunft,* in *Werke,* III, 7.

‡ Article "Encyclopédie," in *Oeuvres complètes,* XIV, 474.

systematically inquired into the faculty of criticism itself, and into the relation of criticism to the activity of philosophizing. It is not an accident that they were addicted to psychology, that in their hands philosophy turned from metaphysics to epistemology, or that the towering philosophical work of the century, Kant's trilogy, should have been a critique of human faculties, consisting of Critiques of Pure Reason, of Practical Reason, and of Judgment. This too is why they devoted so much energy investigating the systems of metaphysicians and the methods of scientists. Their conclusion, as will emerge in the course of this anthology, was that next to theological speculations metaphysical systems were the most useless of intellectual enterprises. Metaphysicians built vast constructions trembling on tiny foundations of fact, made unjustifiable mental leaps, wasted their time debating the "essence" of matter and the "nature" of the soul. It was far more profitable to find out what could be dependably known and then discover how to know it. The philosophes deified Isaac Newton* for his antimetaphysical pronouncements quite as much as for his laws of gravitation.

The philosophes' passion for criticism has led historians to charge them with a passion for destruction, with equating negative criticism with good thinking. Alfred North Whitehead observed about Voltaire, "If men cannot live on bread alone, still less can they do so on disinfectants."† His felicitous image has been widely accepted. But the philosophes would have found the charge incomprehensible; we, who can understand it, must reject it as inappropriate. The philosophes were destructive because they thought one must clear the ground before one can build; one cannot construct the city of man under fire from the enemy, on rubbish, or on a swamp. The world that religion had shaped for so long was—in the philosophes' language—prey to the wild beasts of fanaticism and enfeebled by the poisonous fruits of the tree of superstition. What else could one do with "l'infâme" but to crush it? But beyond this, criticism had its positive function: it permitted man not merely to clear the ground, but to concentrate his energies. "All that men have been," Gibbon wrote in his first book, "all that genius has created, all that reason has weighed, all that labor has gathered up—all this is the business of criticism. Intellectual precision, ingenuity, penetration, are all necessary to exercise it properly."‡ There is yet more to be said:

---

* See below, selections 6 and 13.
† Whitehead, *Science and the Modern World* (1925), 87.
‡ *Essai sur l'étude de la littérature,* in Gibbon, *Miscellaneous Works,* ed. John, Lord Sheffield, 5 vols., 2nd edn. (1814), IV, 38.

while most of the philosophes enjoyed the disinterested love of knowledge—the sheer pleasure of discovering truths for their own sake—they sought knowledge above all for the sake of its utility. That is why they were so intent on improving, and, if necessary, even inventing, sciences of man. Their work in psychology, sociology, political economy, had this practical aim: these were disciplines that, once mastered, would help to make humanity freer, richer, more civilized than before. David Hume, himself a pioneer not merely in the theory of knowledge but also in political science, economics, and demography, spoke for the philosophic family in his first book. A sensible "moral philosophy" (by which he meant what we mean by applied social science) may be difficult to establish. But, once established, this "science" will "not be inferior in certainty, and will be much superior in utility to any other of human comprehension."* The Age of Criticism was also an Age of Philosophy, and by philosophy the philosophes meant an activity that would change the world—for the better.

I I

If this definition seems a little elusive, the elusiveness is deliberate. I have already said that the philosophes differed widely. Across time and from place to place, their political, religious, and social ideas ranged across a generous spectrum. Their reputation to the contrary, most of them did not accept the political ideal of "enlightened despotism";† at the same time, they did not agree on the

* Introduction, *A Treatise of Human Nature* (1739–40), ed. L. A. Selby-Bigge (1888), xxiii. See below, selection 38.

† It is worth emphasizing that the much used name "enlightened despotism" is essentially meaningless. Joseph II of Austria, Frederick II of Prussia, Catherine II of Russia, normally put forward as prototypes of the "enlightened despot," differed drastically in their personalities and their policies. If we extend the term to include Leopold of Tuscany and Charles III of Spain, as is often done, confusion becomes total. Besides yoking together rulers who do not belong together beyond their common desire to rule effectively, the term burdens them with the unsavory epithet "despot," which is at best a partial truth. But worst of all, the term conjures up philosophes eagerly sitting at the elbows of power and guiding the hands of the mighty through sinister personal influence. Sinister or not, this kind of influence was at best a passing fantasy in some of the philosophes; it was not a deliberate policy, let alone a political philosophy. In short, "enlightened despotism" is a nineteenth-century cliché we would do well to discard. For a polemical bibliographical survey, see Peter Gay, *The Enlightenment: An Interpretation*, II, *The Science of Freedom* (1969), 682–89,

virtues of political liberalism. Again, only some of them were atheists; many of them were deists, postulating a god who had made the world with all its unbreakable physical and moral laws and then withdrew from it. A handful clutched the security blanket of reasonable Christianity, while others professed themselves skeptics, as reluctant to adopt atheist dogmatism as they were hostile to the Christian superstition. This does not make it impossible to define them as a single group; I have used the metaphor of the family largely because it describes this informal and often tense intimacy, their fundamental philosophical affinity and their spirited debates. They were all, as I have said, devotees of criticism; they believed in decency, humanitarianism, freedom from censorship, a loosening up of the moral code. Their world was, in the positive sense of the word, disenchanted: they were willing to believe almost anything but a miracle.

Remembering this mixture of essential agreement and vigorous disagreement, we can plot the evolution of the Enlightenment on the scale of time, and map the Enlightenment on the terrain of Western civilization. To begin with, time. It is convenient to limit the Enlightenment within the hundred-year span staked out by the dates 1689 and 1789. These are approximate, like all terminal markers enclosing a period. But they are evocative: the first recalls the triumph of the English Revolution and the birth of Montesquieu, the second the outbreak of the French Revolution and the death of Holbach. Obviously, the roots of the Enlightenment go far back; they reach down to classical antiquity, the Renaissance, the scholars, scientists, and philosophers of the seventeenth century. But the intellectual and religious world of their forebears was far different from the world of Montesquieu and of Voltaire. The Enlightenment was not the last act of the Renaissance, important though the Renaissance was to the Enlightenment; it was not merely the working out of seventeenth-century thought, decisive though *that* was to the Enlightenment. The lineaments of the Enlightenment emerge most plainly if we treat Locke and Newton as its precursors.* The Enlightenment proper, then, was the collaborative

---

and, despite its title, John G. Gagliardo, *Enlightened Despotism* (1967), a brief and reasonable treatment of the field.

* For these and earlier precursors, see Part I below. I should comment that the notion of precursors has validity only from a particular perspective, in this case the perspective of the eighteenth century. Obviously, the thought of the seventeenth century has its own validity; to regard Locke and Newton as travelers toward the Enlightenment who, from some inner limitation, did not quite reach their destination is to be unhistorical.

product of three closely linked generations. The towering figures of the first of these were Montesquieu and Voltaire, who was born five years after Montesquieu, in 1694. With their magisterial writings and their long lives—Montesquieu died in 1755, Voltaire in 1778— the two loomed over the second generation of philosophes, which came to maturity before mid-century. Yet this new generation was too talented, and too independent, to remain in the shadow even of giants; it struck out in untried directions, assimilating and extending the ideas of its masters for new and larger purposes. The mere catalogue of their names reminds us that this generation could not have been simply a clutch of disciples. Benjamin Franklin, scientist, publicist, statesman, was born in 1706; Buffon, whom many called the Newton of natural philosophy, in 1707; La Mettrie, who, among the materialist philosophers, was the most scandalous and the most amusing, in 1709. Hume was born in 1711, Rousseau in 1712, Diderot in 1713, Condillac in 1714, Helvétius in 1715, d'Alembert in 1717. By 1750 or shortly after, these writers had made their mark with philosophical, psychological, ethical, and scientific polemics or formal treatises. Yet they left the third generation much to do: Holbach (born in 1723) and Kant (born in 1724) worked out the implications of scientific thought, the first to move into materialism, the second into his complex Critical philosophy; Turgot (born in 1727) emerged as one of the few statesmen among the philosophes, idealized by the others for joining thought and action; Lessing and his friend Moses Mendelssohn (both born in 1729) and Wieland (born in 1733) did much to spread the ideas of *Aufklärung* among a still small but increasingly receptive public.

The younger generations, as younger generations will, rejected some of their forerunners' work, but they also profited from that work—enormously. The tentative and lighthearted social criticism of Montesquieu, the brilliant and impudent religious satire of Voltaire, gave way to full-fledged assaults on every facet of traditional dogma. By the 1760s, and more extensively by the 1770s, there were philosophes preaching naturalism, democracy, sexual reform, even socialism. And the daring later philosophes stood on the shoulders of their elders, with genuinely felt and publicly acknowledged gratitude.

The internal history of the Enlightenment, then, is a history of radicalization and of the spreading of its ideas to new quarters. The geography of the Enlightenment shows a similar diversity, especially in the field of political thought. The philosophes were practical men, far more practical than hostile historians, detecting what they consider the philosophes' "Utopianism," have acknowledged, though perhaps rather less practical than they themselves liked to think they were. Yet, with all their lapses, they were practical enough to recognize that political positions and programs realistic in one country were unrealistic in another: the principled relativism implicit in Montesquieu's sociological writings becomes explicit in the political views of most philosophes. This relativism, I should emphasize, was never complete: all the philosophes rejected some forms of government, as they rejected some types of punishment as unworthy of human and humane polities. Yet their relativism was more extensive than has often been recognized, and it was a relativism born of experience. Voltaire, an avid participant or, if participation proved unsafe, shrewd observer of the political scene across Europe, offers a splendid instance of the impress that experience left on enlightened political conviction. In England, Voltaire thought the rising power of the House of Commons appropriate and praiseworthy; in the Dutch Republic, he singled out for commendation the democratic bearing of the ruling elite; in France, faced with the choice between a powerful monarchy and a powerful nobility, he chose the monarchy, not because he was a principled monarchist, but because he detested the French nobility as incurably self-seeking and consistently reactionary. In the Genevan Republic, which he came to know intimately after years of residence in its territory and on its borders, he observed the local political parties closely and shifted his allegiance twice. He began by supporting his natural allies, the Genevan plutocracy, the French-educated families who came to his dinners and admired his dramas, who ran the little republic by influence, shrewd marital alliances, and occasional violence; he moved to the middle group, the Genevan bourgeoisie, which sought a larger share in political affairs than the exclusive old families would grant them. At the end he championed the cause of the so-called Natifs, the disenfranchised local craftsmen whose class, and whose tastes, certainly were not his own, but whose case seemed to him irrefutable. Not even Rousseau, the principled democrat, had found it possible to move as far as Voltaire in support of the "people." In other political climates, in Prussia (which he knew well) and in Russia (which he knew only through the correspondence with Catherine and her paid agents), he did not hesitate to applaud royal attempts at absolutism. Faced with an illiterate, overwhelmingly agricultural populace, he thought that rulers had no choice but to make "their" subjects happy through fiat; to advocate popular participation in the political process seemed to him nothing short of madness. One could insist—as Voltaire insisted—that rulers in such a state be humane and deceive their people, if deceive they must, only for the people's own good. But beyond this, and beyond calls for gradual widening of education, a practical political thinker like Voltaire was not prepared to go.

Few of the philosophes were prepared to go further: the spectrum of Voltaire's political opinions, which shades toward enlightened absolutism the farther east he moved, accurately represents the spectrum of political opinion in the Enlightenment in general. In the American states, in England, in the Dutch Republic, perhaps in France, one could hope for widening education and spreading enlightenment, and thus hope for widespread manhood suffrage. But the German states, the Hapsburg and Russian Empires, had no political institutions for open debate, no habits of political expression. They were ridden by ignorance and stifled by censorship. "A heavy tax rests, at least in Germany, on the windows of the Enlightenment." This was the gloomy view of the German *Aufklärer,* the physicist and essayist Georg Christoph Lichtenberg, in the 1790s.* It is not surprising, then, that as the philosophe moved from west to east, the more intent he became, not to broaden the base of popular discussion and prepare the way for participation, but to improve the machinery of government. While in the west the Enlightenment mainly sought ways of teaching people to take affairs into their own hands, in the east it mainly sought ways of lightening their burdens through benevolent and efficient intervention from above. The widespread charge of Utopianism would have been justified only if the philosophes had thought in any other way.

III

The divergences within the Enlightenment that time and space produced point to another essential element in its definition. They show that the philosophes were intimately involved in the life of their age. The philosophes responded to its possibilities and to its problems; their ideas, far from being the facile generalizations of coffeehouse gossips or the abstract results of isolated academics,

---

* Aphorism L 88, in Lichtenberg *Aphorismen* (1793–99) , ed. Albert Leitzmann (1908) , 26.

reflect reality, often in the most tough-minded way. The philosophes have often been charged with being shallow optimists, a
charge as off target as the allied charge that they were Utopians.
The famous, or notorious, theory of progress, which holds that life
must improve, whether through divine decree, biological conflict, or
historical necessity, is not at all characteristic of the Enlightenment.
True, some of the philosophes, like Turgot, Kant, and, at the end of
the century, Condorcet,* developed genuine theories of progress,
though, if closely examined, even their optimism seems moderate
indeed. But in general the philosophes thought that while improvement was now more likely than ever before, it was by no means
inescapable, and was in any event often temporary. Most of the
philosophes were convinced that civilizations are cyclical affairs,
rising and falling through a life cycle much as individuals do, and
that all improvement has to be paid for, somehow and somewhere.
"No advantages in this world," David Hume noted, "are pure and
unmixed."† As so often, Hume spoke for most of the philosophes.
Kant even made a ponderous joke at the expense of the prophets of
progress: they reminded him, he said, of a physician who persisted
in finding his patients getting better every day. One day, himself ill,
the physician received the visit of a friend to inquire, "How is your
illness?" And the professional optimist replied, "How should it be
going? *I'm dying from sheer improvement!*"‡
    Of course, the philosophes were men of hope. But they were men
of hope because the age forced hope upon them. Progress was
less a theory for them than an experience. In their own professional
lives, as writers, they saw their status improve, their income rise,
their freedom grow. In international affairs, though the Seven
Years' War was savage enough, they saw the scourge of war grow
more remote. In medicine they saw (or thought they saw) a distinct
improvement in the prospect for better health and longer life. In
government they saw growing attention to reasonable methods and
increasing humanity. Best of all, the philosophes had a sense that
their civilization, though still overwhelmingly religious, was on
their side in many things. It is instructive to compare the convictions of philosophes with those of a devout Protestant like Samuel
Johnson or of a host of moderate and modern Roman Catholics on

---

* See below, selection 56.
    † "Of the Rise and Progress in the Arts and Sciences," in *The Philosophical
Works of David Hume,* ed. T. H. Green and T. H. Grose, 4 vols. (1882 edn.),
III, 191.
    ‡ *Der Streit der Fakultäten,* in *Werke,* VII, 406–7.

the Continent.* None of these was even remotely a philosophe, most of them were deeply suspicious and openly hostile to the philosophes; but they too ridiculed superstition, deplored fanaticism, extolled humanitarianism, admired science. The philosophes, in other words, were in no way alienated from their culture; they shared many of its presuppositions and enjoyed the unwilling and unwitting support of many respectable people. That is why the name Enlightenment stands ultimately for something broader than a great movement. It is appropriately the name for an age.

FURTHER READING

Carl Becker, *The Heavenly City of the Eighteenth Century Philosophers* (1932). A brilliantly written, impressively brief, and fatefully influential book arguing that the philosophes merely restated medieval thought in up-to-date language. Wrong but charming.

Ernst Cassirer, *The Philosophy of the Enlightenment* (tr. 1951). An often profound analysis, making the vital distinction between seventeenth-century rationalism and eighteenth-century empiricism. Though too much oriented toward German thought, a very valuable work.

Alfred Cobban, *In Search of Humanity: The Role of the Enlightenment in Modern History* (1960). The book mixes lucid exposition of enlightened thought with thoughtful reflections on the meaning of the Enlightenment for our time.

Lester G. Crocker, *An Age of Crisis: Man and World in Eighteenth Century Thought* (1959). A massive reading of French ethical treatises, and useful mainly for that; its history is deplorable and its insistence on the importance of the Marquis de Sade modish.

———, *Nature and Culture: Ethical Thought in the French Enlightenment* (1963). As massive as its predecessor, but more restrained in interpretation and hence more usable than *An Age of Crisis*.

Robert Darnton, "Reading, Writing, and Publishing in Eighteenth-Century France: A Case Study in the Sociology of Literature," *Daedalus*, December 1970.

———, "The High Enlightenment and the Low-Life of Literature in Pre-Revolutionary France," *Past and Present*, No. 51 (May 1971). Two articles that shed much-needed light on the lower echelons of Enlightened propaganda.

Peter Gay, *The Enlightenment: An Interpretation*, Vol. I, *The Rise of Modern*

* To offer at least a sampling of this "other Enlightenment," I have included selections from Swift, Pope, and Johnson below.

Paganism (1966), Vol. II, *The Science of Freedom* (1969). A comprehensive interpretation of the Enlightenment in Europe and America, attempting to link the philosophes' ideas to their experience; I have drawn on these volumes in this anthology.

————, *The Party of Humanity: Essays in the French Enlightenment* (1964). A series of studies concentrating on France; it contains, along with eight other pieces, a critique of Carl Becker's *Heavenly City* (see above).

————, *The Bridge of Criticism: Dialogues among Lucien, Erasmus, and Voltaire on the Enlightenment* (1970). An attempt to state in brief compass in dialogue form the arguments and conclusions of the longer books cited above.

Norman Hampson, *A Cultural History of the Enlightenment* (1969). An intelligent and clear introduction.

George R. Havens, *The Age of Ideas: From Reaction to Revolution in Eighteenth-Century France* (1955). Scholarly, dependable biographies of the greatest among French philosophes; little interested in history and a shade too admiring of its subjects.

Paul Hazard, *The European Mind: The Critical Years, 1680–1715* (tr. 1953). A famous interpretation that sees the transition to enlightened thought rather too abruptly; worth reading.

————, *European Thought in the Eighteenth Century from Montesquieu to Lessing* (tr. 1954). An ambitious survey that does not quite manage to make the age clear. Like the earlier volume, though, worth reading for the information alone.

Kingsley Martin, *French Liberal Thought in the Eighteenth Century: A Study of Political Ideas from Bayle to Condorcet* (1962 edn.). As its title implies, confined to France and to politics; vigorous, always interesting, though not always acceptable.

Harold Nicholson, *The Age of Reason: The Eighteenth Century in Reason and Violence* (1961). Worthless. Interesting only as typical of its anecdotal and superficial genre, from which the Enlightenment has suffered so badly.

Preserved Smith, *A History of Modern Culture*, Vol. II, *The Enlightenment, 1687–1776* (1934). Rather dated now and conventional, but an intelligent survey.

Fritz Valjavec, *Geschichte der abendländischen Aufklärung* (1961). Chronological, well argued, a little too compressed. Deserves translation.

Franco Venturi, *Utopia and Reform in the Enlightenment* (1971). A brilliant summing up by a great historian of eighteenth-century Europe.

I

The Making of the Enlightenment Mind

The learning of many centuries went into the making of the Enlightenment mind, and a sampling of some of the material the philosophes absorbed and transformed tells much of that mind, not only in the making but in its essence. The immediate and in many ways most potent ancestor of the Enlightenment was the scientific philosophy of the seventeenth century. The philosophers were trinitarians, and their trinity consisted of Bacon, Newton, and Locke, whom they regarded as the pioneers in the construction of the new world view—their own. But they had other ancestors in the recent past as well, notably Bayle, whom they read as the very embodiment of skepticism, and Descartes, whose physics they felt bound to reject, but whose questioning of all traditional authority they applauded and to some measure imitated. Yet the philosophes found more in the recent past that was usable: the growth of reasonable religion, the emergence of a Christianity as hostile—well, almost as hostile—to the ravages of "superstition" and the effusions of religious "enthusiasm" as the philosophes themselves were to be. If we need some evidence for the impression that the philosophes were at home in their world, a sermon by Archbishop Tillotson will supply it.

But the ancestry of the philosophes also goes back much further; it makes a kind of leap across the Christian Middle Ages to classical antiquity. As the English aesthetician Lord Shaftesbury advised a young correspondent: "If the Antients, in their Purity, are as yet out of your Reach; search the Moderns, that are nearest to them. If you cannot converse with the most Antient, use the most Modern. For the authors of the middle Age, and all that sort of Philosophy, as well as Divinity, will be of little advantage to you."* To be sure, the philosophes, like all educated men and women in the eighteenth century, had undergone classical schooling, and most of them loved the classics for their own sake. Their Latin was better than their Greek, and they tended (at least from our perspective) greatly

---

* Shaftesbury to Michael Ainsworth, May 5, 1709, in *Life, Unpublished Letters, and Philosophical Regimen*, ed. Benjamin Rand (1900), 400.

to overvalue the Romans at the expense of the Greeks; some of them ranked Vergil above Homer; most of them thought Cicero, whom we now treat somewhat disdainfully as a fine speechmaker and a diligent compiler of older philosophical ideas, as the most remarkable mind that their beloved antiquity had produced. Only lack of space prevents me from demonstrating how far the cult of Cicero went; the reader may discover it for himself by seeing the philosophe David Hume paying the supreme compliment, an Imitation, to his favorite ancient thinker, "Tully": nothing is more instructive than to read Cicero's dialogue on religious systems, De natura deorum, side by side with Hume's splendid Dialogues Concerning Natural Religion. Hume designs his debate, conducts his argument, and imports certain jokes as open and deliberate reminiscences of Cicero's work. I have had space for a briefer demonstration of this kind of tribute: if one compares the passages from Tacitus printed below with Gibbon's description of Augustus' power,* one will see the later writer doing little more than paraphrasing the earlier one.

Why? For the Enlightenment, the beloved classical past was also an immensely useful one. Gibbon called Tacitus, his model, "the first of the historians who applied the science of philosophy to the study of facts," and thought him perhaps the only ancient historian to deserve the epithet "philosophic historian."† These phrases give us the clue we need. Eager to leap out of the circle of Christian faith, the philosophes found aid and comfort in selected classical writers. Their favorite ancients, they found, had moved from myth to thought—a direction that Christianity, unfortunately, had reversed. The "philosophes" of antiquity had exposed the gods to be a response to psychological needs, mortal heroes lent immortality by the credulous, or symbols for natural forces and seasonal rhythms. They had more or less banished supernatural powers from the course of human events; they had, one might say, laid the foundation for the first Enlightenment, the antique Enlightenment, by training and expanding man's capacity for critical thinking. The philosophes could not, of course, remain content with the ancients; they were not antiquarians. Indeed, just as their reading of the ancients taught them independence from Christians, so their read-

---

* See below, pp. 38 and 621–622.

† See *The History of the Decline and Fall of the Roman Empire*, ed. J. B. Bury, 7 vols. (1896–1902), I, 213, and *Essai sur l'étude de la littérature*, in *Miscellaneous Works*, ed. John, Lord Sheffield, 5 vols., 2nd edn. (1814), IV, 66.

ing of science taught them independence from the ancients. Classicism plus science is perhaps an overly brief but far from misleading definition of the Enlightenment mind.

FURTHER READING

R. R. Bolgar, *The Classical Heritage and Its Beneficiaries*, 2nd edn. (1964). A thorough survey of classical writings and their fortunes down into the Renaissance.

E. M. Butler, *The Tyranny of Greece over Germany* (1935). Vehement, brilliant, but overstated assault on German scholarship and literature since the eighteenth century for its presumed fatal infatuation with ancient Greece (see Hatfield, below).

M. L. Clarke, *Classical Education in Britain, 1500–1900* (1959). An informative essay.

Henry Hatfield, *Aesthetic Paganism in German Literature: From Winckelmann to the Death of Goethe* (1964). Judicious and intelligent, this volume serves as corrective to the hostility of E. M. Butler (see above) and the unreasoning worship of Greek *Kultur* endemic among German scholars.

Frank Manuel, *The Eighteenth Century Confronts the Gods* (1959). An important survey of the Enlightenment's theories of the origin of religion, theories that drew heavily on classical authors.

Erwin Panofsky, *Renaissance and Renascences in Western Art*, 2nd edn. (1969). A brilliant account of the reintegration of antique themes and viewpoints into European civilization.

Jean Seznec, *The Survival of the Pagan Gods* (tr. 1953). Indispensable to an understanding of the transmission of the mythological tradition into the Renaissance.

———, *Essais sur Diderot et l'Antiquité* (1957). Immensely illuminating and suggestive study of one of the most learned of philosophes and his love affair with Greece and Rome. Of great importance.

Augustin Sicard, *Les Études classiques avant la Révolution* (1887). Old but by no means out of date.

J. A. K. Thomson, *The Classical Background of English Literature* (1948). One of three volumes Thomson wrote on the classical influences that informed English prose and poetry.

I ❁ LUCRETIUS

De rerum natura

[From *Lucretius, His Six Books of Epicurean
Philosophy* . . . , translated by Thomas Creech
(1700), Book I, lines 84–121, Book II,
lines 1–63.]

*The roman poet Titus Lucretius Carus (c.99 B.C.–c.55 B.C.) remains
mysterious; the Church Father Saint Jerome, appalled at Lucretius'
Epicurean philosophy and antireligious diatribes, suggested that
Lucretius was insane and had committed suicide. The philosophes,
who admired Lucretius for the very reasons that the early Christians
feared him, dismissed the story as an insignificant slander. Lucretius' great poem,* De rerum natura, *is in six books; it begins with an
invocation to the "mighty one of Greece," Epicurus, who dared to
free men from the oppression of religion and the fear of death.
"Tantum religio potuit suadere malorum," the famous line which
our translation renders "Such Devilish Acts Religion could persuade," reappears in strategic places throughout Lucretius' poem; it
was a line that the philosophes knew by heart. In the course of his
exposition, Lucretius offers a materialistic account of the body and
the mind, and assails religion (which, to him, is practically synony-
mous with superstition) for enslaving men with tales of terror. It
was said that Frederick the Great of Prussia took Book III of* De
rerum natura *into battle with him; the young Voltaire wrote a
Lucretian poem,* Épître à Uranie, *that rejects the wrathful God of
Christianity, and later stated the position of the Enlightenment
toward this great philosophical poet: "Lucretius," he wrote, "is
admirable in his exordiums, in his descriptions, in his ethics, in
everything he says against superstition. That beautiful line,
'Tantum religio potuit suadere malorum,' will last as long as the*

world lasts."* *The excerpt here reproduced (though it sounds a little archaic in its eighteenth-century dress) gives an idea of Lucretius' force.*

THE FIRST BOOK

... Long time Men lay opprest with slavish Fear,
Religion's Tyranny did domineer,
Which being plac'd in Heaven look'd *proudly* down,
And frighted abject Spirits with her Frown.
At length a mighty one of *Greece* began
T'assert the natural Liberty of Man,
By senseless Terrors and vain Fancies led
To slavery; streight the conquer'd Fantoms fled,
Not the fam'd stories of the Deity,
Not all the Thunder of the threatning Sky
Could stop his rising Soul; thro all he past
The strongest Bounds that powerful Nature cast:
His vigorous and active Mind was hurl'd
Beyond the flaming limits of *this* World
Into the mighty Space, and there did see
How things begin, what can, what cannot be;
How all must die, all yield to fatal force,
What steddy limits bound their natural course;
He saw all this and brought it back to us.
Wherefore by *his* success *our* Right we gain,
Religion is *our* Subject and *we* Reign.
    If you shall start at these bold Truths, and fly
These Lines as Maxims of Impiety,
Consider, that Religion did, and will
Contrive, promote and Act the greatest Ill.
By that, *Diana*'s cruel Altar flow'd
With innocent and Royal Virgins Blood.
Unhappy Maid! With Sacred Ribbands bound,
  (Religion's Pride,) and holy Garlands crown'd,

___

* *Lettres de Memmius à Cicéron,* in Voltaire, *Oeuvres complètes,* ed Louis Moland, 52 vols. (1877–85) , XXVIII, 439.

To meet an undeserv'd untimely Fate,
Led by the *Grecian* Chiefs in Pomp and State;
She saw her Father by, whose Tears did flow
In streams, the only pity he could show:
She saw the crafty Priest conceal the Knife
From him, bless'd and prepar'd against her Life;
She saw her Citizens with weeping Eyes
Unwillingly attend the Sacrifice;
Then dumb with Grief her Tears did pity crave,
But 'twas beyond her Father's power to save;
In vain did Innocence, Youth and Beauty plead,
In vain the first Pledge of his Nuptial Bed;
She fell, e'en now grown ripe for Nuptial joy,
To bribe the Gods, and buy a Wind for Troy:
So dy'd the innocent, the harmless Maid,
Such Devilish Acts Religion could persuade! ...

THE SECOND BOOK

'Tis pleasant, when the Seas are rough, to stand
And view another's danger, safe at Land:
Not 'cause he's troubled, but 'tis sweet to see
Those Cares and Fears, from which our selves are free;
'Tis also pleasant to behold from far,
How Troops engage, secure our selves from War.
But above all, 'tis pleasantest to get
The top of high *Philosophy,* and sit
On the calm, peaceful, flourishing head of it;
Whence we may view, deep, wondrous deep below,
How poor mistaken *Mortals* wandring go,
Seeking the path to *Happiness:* Some aim
At Learning, Wit, Nobility, or Fame;
Others with Cares and Dangers vex each hour,
To reach the top of Wealth, and Sovereign Power,
    Blind, *wretched* Man! In what dark paths of strife
We walk this little journey of our Life!
Whilst frugal *Nature* seeks for only ease,
A *Body* free from pains, free from disease,

A *Mind* from cares and jealousies at peace.
Now little is required to maintain
The Body found in health, and free from pain;
Not Delicates, but such as may supply
Contented *Nature*'s thrifty *Luxury;*
She asks no more. What tho no *Boys* of Gold
Adorn the Walls, and sprightly Tapers hold;
Whose beauteous rays scattering the gawdy Light,
Might grace the sweats and revels of the Night?
What tho no Gold adorns, no Musick's sound
With doubled sweetness from the roofs rebound?
Yet underneath a *loving Myrtle*'s shade,
Just by a purling Stream supinely laid,
When *Spring* with fragrant flowers the Earth hath spread,
And sweetest Roses grow around our Head,
Envied by wealth and power, with small expence
We may enjoy the sweet delight of Sense.
Who ever heard a *Fever* tamer grown
In Cloths *Embroider'd* o'er, and beds of Down,
Than in coarse Rags? Since then such toys as these
Contribute nothing to the *Body*'s ease,
As honour, wealth, and nobleness of blood;
'Tis plain, they likewise do our *Mind* no good.
If when thy fierce imbattell'd Troops at Land
Mock-fights maintain, or when the Navies stand
In graceful ranks, or sweep the yielding Seas;
If then before such Martial shows as these,
Disperse not all black Jealousies and Cares,
Vain dread of Death, and superstitious fears,
Nor leave thy Mind: but if all this be vain,
If the same cares and dread, and fears remain,
If Traytor-like they seize on e'en the Throne,
And dance within the *Circle* of a Crown;
If noise of *Arms,* nor *Darts* can make them flie,
Nor the gay sparklings of the Purple Die;
If they on *Emperours* will rudely seize;
What makes us value all such Things as these,
But *Folly* and dark *Ignorance* of Happiness?
For *we,* as *Boys* at *Night,* at *Day* do fear
Shadows, as vain too and senseless as those are.

Wherefore that darkness that o'erspreads our Souls
Day can't disperse, but those *Eternal* Rules,
Which from *Premises* true Reason draws,
And a deep insight into *Nature*'s Laws. . . .

FURTHER READING

Wolfgang Bernard Fleischmann, "The Debt of the Enlightenment to Lucretius,"
Studies on Voltaire and the Eighteenth Century, XXV (1963), 631–43. A useful
summary.
———, *Lucretius and English Literature, 1680–1740* (1963). Specializes, as the title
shows, on Lucretius' influence on one country.
George Depue Hadzsits, *Lucretius and His Influence* (n.d. [1925]). Has a short
chapter on his later impact.
Gustav R. Hocke, *Lukrez in Frankreich von der Renaissance bis zur Revolution*
(1935). Does for France what Fleischmann does for England.
George Santayana, *Three Philosophical Poets* (1910). The first of these three
essays is a beautiful evocation of the poet.

2 ❧ TACITUS

Annals

[From *The Annals,* translated by A. J. Church
and W. J. Brodribb (1876), Book I, 1–3.]

*While Lucretius was the undisputed favorite among the philo-
sophes, Tacitus (c.55–c.117), though enormously influential,
aroused some skepticism. Voltaire, for one, thought him too gloomy
to be wholly reliable. But the historians of the Enlightenment used
Tacitus' work freely and with undisguised admiration; David
Hume called him "that fine historian," and "the greatest and most
penetrating genius, perhaps, of all antiquity,"* while Gibbon's
debt to him, as I have noted, is direct and vast.† Tacitus was, of
course, a Roman of his time, but what mattered to his eighteenth-
century admirers was his realism and his essential secularism. Tacitus was well connected—Agricola, the conqueror and for a time the
governor of Roman Britain, was his father-in-law—and he was
lucky: he survived the terror imposed by the emperors of the late
first century to become proconsul of Asia under Nerva. His historical writings have come down to us incomplete: the* Histories *and
the* Annals *cover the reigns of Tiberius, Claudius, Nero, Galba, and
Vespasian, though with tantalizing gaps. They are grave and laconic accounts of viciousness in high places and of the decay of
Roman virtue. Like these histories, Tacitus' early treatise on rhetoric, the* Dialogus, *his famous account of the German tribes, known
as the* Germania, *and his admiring biography of his father-in-law,
the* Agricola, *were favorite reading in the eighteenth century.
Tacitus' style was then, and is now, the despair of the translator;*

---

* *Enquiry Concerning Human Understanding,* in *The Philosophical Works of
David Hume,* ed. Green and Grose (1882), IV, 100.
† See above, page 30.

among the philosophes, Rousseau, Diderot, and d'Alembert all tried their hand. Tacitus is witty, economical, epigrammatic—in a word, inimitable.

BOOK I

A.D. 14, 15

1. ROME at the beginning was ruled by kings. Freedom and the consulship were established by Lucius Brutus. Dictatorships were held for a temporary crisis. The power of the decemvirs did not last beyond two years, nor was the consular jurisdiction of the military tribunes of long duration. The despotisms of Cinna and Sulla were brief; the rule of Pompeius and of Crassus soon yielded before Caesar; the arms of Lepidus and Antonius before Augustus; who, when the world was wearied by civil strife, subjected it to empire under the title of "Prince." But the successes and reverses of the old Roman people have been recorded by famous historians; and fine intellects were not wanting to describe the times of Augustus, till growing sycophancy scared them away. The histories of Tiberius, Caius, Claudius, and Nero, while they were in power, were falsified through terror, and after their death were written under the irritation of a recent hatred. Hence my purpose is to relate a few facts about Augustus—more particularly his last acts, then the reign of Tiberius, and all which follows, without either bitterness or partiality, from any motives to which I am far removed.

2. When after the destruction of Brutus and Cassius there was no longer any army of the Commonwealth, when Pompeius was crushed in Sicily, and when, with Lepidus pushed aside and Antonius slain, even the Julian faction had only Caesar left to lead it, then, dropping the title of triumvir, and giving out that he was a Consul, and was satisfied with a tribune's authority for the protection of the people, Augustus won over the soldiers with gifts, the populace with cheap corn, and all men with the sweets of repose, and so grew greater by degrees, while he concentrated in himself the functions of the Senate, the magistrates, and the laws. He was wholly unopposed, for the boldest spirits had fallen in battle, or in the proscription, while the remaining nobles, the readier they were

to be slaves, were raised the higher by wealth and promotion, so that, aggrandized by revolution, they preferred the safety of the present to the dangerous past. Nor did the provinces dislike that condition of affairs, for they distrusted the government of the Senate and the people, because of the rivalries between the leading men and the rapacity of the officials, while the protection of the laws was unavailing, as they were continually deranged by violence, intrigue, and finally by corruption.

3. Augustus meanwhile, as supports to his despotism, raised to the pontificate and curule aedileship Claudius Marcellus, his sister's son, while a mere stripling, and Marcus Agrippa, of humble birth, a good soldier, and one who had shared his victory, to two consecutive consulships, and as Marcellus soon afterward died, he also accepted him as his son-in-law. Tiberius Nero and Claudius Drusus, his stepsons, he honored with imperial titles, although his own family was as yet undiminished. For he had admitted the children of Agrippa, Caius and Lucius, into the house of the Caesars; and before they had yet laid aside the dress of boyhood he had most fervently desired, with an outward show of reluctance, that they should be entitled "princes of the youth," and be consuls-elect. When Agrippa died, and Lucius Caesar as he was on his way to our armies in Spain, and Caius while returning from Armenia, still suffering from a wound, were prematurely cut off by destiny, or by their stepmother Livia's treachery, Drusus too having long been dead, Nero remained alone of the stepsons, and in him everything tended to center. He was adopted as a son, as a colleague in empire and a partner in the tribunitian power, and paraded through all the armies, no longer through his mother's secret intrigues, but at her open suggestion. For she had gained such a hold on the aged Augustus that he drove out as an exile into the island of Planasia, his only grandson, Agrippa Postumus, who, though devoid of worthy qualities, and having only the brute courage of physical strength, had not been convicted of any gross offense. And yet Augustus had appointed Germanicus, Drusus' offspring, to the command of eight legions on the Rhine, and required Tiberius to adopt him, although Tiberius had a son, now a young man, in his house; but he did it that he might have several safeguards to rest on. He had no war at the time on his hands except against the Germans, which was rather to wipe out the disgrace of the loss of Quintilius Varus and his army than out of an ambition to extend the empire, or for any adequate recompense. At home all was tranquil, and there were magistrates with the same titles; there

was a younger generation, sprung up since the victory of Actium, and even many of the older men had been born during the civil wars. How few were left who had seen the republic! . . .

FURTHER READING

M. L. W. Laistner, *The Greater Roman Historians* (1947). Has two informative chapters on Tacitus.

Clarence W. Mendell, *Tacitus: The Man and His Work* (1957). A sound survey.

Jürgen von Stackelberg, "Rousseau, D'Alembert et Diderot traducteurs de Tacite," *Studi Francesi*, No. 6 (September–December 1958), 395–407. A pioneering essay on eighteenth-century attempts to render Tacitus into modern French.

————, *Tacitus in der Romania: Studien zur literarischen Rezeption des Tacitus in Italien und Frankreich* (1960). An ambitious general account of Tacitus' later influence; see especially Chapter 13.

Ronald Syme, *Tacitus*, 2 vols. (1958). A masterpiece of interpretation and scholarship, written in a Tacitean style, a device that works—almost.

3 ✿ MONTAIGNE

Essays

[From "Apology for Raimond de Sebonde," in
Montaigne's Essays in Three Books, translated by Charles Cotton, 3 vols. (6th edn.,
1743), II, 216–18.]

*The historic reorientation of mind and feeling that the philosophes
hailed, a little vaguely, as "the revival of the arts and of learning,"
and that Jacob Burckhardt has taught us to call "the Renaissance,"
had obvious and immense significance for the Enlightenment. But
most of that significance was indirect: it consisted mainly of the
Humanists' rediscovery of classical manuscripts neglected for centuries in monastic libraries, their passion for antique learning and
admiration of antique style, and their vehement, partisan criticism
of the "Dark Ages" that had preceded them. But, just as the
Humanists were not philosophes at an early stage of development,
the philosophes were not latter-day Humanists. Most Renaissance
scholars and writers were Christians—often unorthodox, often given
to complicated religious systems that included elements of Greek
and Alexandrian thought and occult learning drawn from the Jews
and the Arabs, but Christians still. It was the liberating effect of
their labors, their opening of new windows on the world, that made
their effect on European culture and thus ultimately prepared the
ground for the work of the Enlightenment.*

*In the late Renaissance, in the sixteenth century, the rediscovery
of antiquity took on special form. The so-called "Platonism" and
"Aristotelianism" of their predecessors had been exceedingly im-
precise and partial; in the sixteenth century, antique doctrines,
especially the Roman versions of Stoicism, Epicureanism, and Skepticism, reemerged as potential if still rather timid rivals to Christian-*

ity. *Antique realists like Niccolò Machiavelli (1469–1527) or
equally antique skeptics like Montaigne (1533–92) thus became
useful as well as delightful reading for philosophes. It is significant
that the men of the Enlightenment rejected as groundless Machiavelli's terrible reputation as the advocate of lying and murder for
political reasons.* He was, David Hume insisted, "a great genius";*
*the men of the Enlightenment were convinced that Machiavelli's
notorious* Prince *was not a handbook for tyrants but a satire on
tyranny. The philosophes had a special gift for using the past and
protecting their admired ancestors from criticism.*

*This tendency is especially noticeable with Michel Eyquem de
Montaigne. A French grand seigneur and tepid but lifelong Catholic, Montaigne in his earlier years was active in public service—for
some years he was mayor of Bordeaux—but most of his days he
spent in his château, reflecting on his vast classical reading, and on
himself. The result was a magnificent and unprecedented voyage of
self-discovery, which he relates in the most leisurely fashion in his
celebrated* Essays. *In the course of his ruminations, Montaigne
traversed three distinct stages, beginning with Stoic resignation,
moving into a prolonged period of skepticism, and entering at last
into a positive humanism which took Socrates for its model and
"living appropriately" for its ideal. If Montaigne had one persistent
conviction it was that fanaticism is the supreme evil. In the midst of
the religious wars that ravaged France from the early 1560s to the
mid-1590s, he belonged to a small group of farseeing men, the*
Politiques, *who put public peace above the triumph of this or that
religious sect. For the philosophes, who found his horror of fanaticism immensely attractive, Montaigne's skeptical phase was of central importance. "He bases his ideas on the ideas of great men,"
Voltaire wrote. "He judges them, he fights them, he talks with
them, with his reader, with himself. He is always original in his
manner of presentation, always full of imagination, always a
painter, and he always (and I love that!) he always knows how to
doubt."† This was the phase in which he coined his motto,* Que sais-
je?—*"What do I know?"—and wrote the longest of his essays, the
"Apologie de Raimond Sebond," from which our extract is taken.
Note that it ends with that passage from Lucretius we have already
encountered:* "Tantum religio potuit suadere malorum."

---

* "Of Civil Liberty," in *The Philosophical Works of David Hume*, ed. Green
and Grose (1882), III, 156.

† Voltaire to Comte de Tressan, Aug. 21, 1746, *Voltaire's Correspondence*, ed.
Theodore Besterman, 107 vols. (1953–65), XV, 119–20.

. . . We cannot say, that Man suffers much when the Worms feed upon his Members, and that the Earth consumes them:

> *Et nihil hoc ad nos, qui coitu conjugioque*
> *Corporis atque animæ consistimus uniter apti.*

> What's that to us, who longer feel no Pain,
> Than Body and Soul united do remain?

> [Lucretius]

Moreover upon what Foundation of their Justice can the *Gods* take notice of, or reward Man after his Death for his good and virtuous Actions, since it was themselves that put them in the Way and Mind to do them? And why should they be offended at, or punish him for wicked ones, since themselves have created him in so frail a Condition, and when with one Glance of their Will, they might prevent him from falling? Might not *Epicurus* with great Colour of human Reason object that to *Plato,* did he not often save himself with this Sentence, *That it is impossible to establish any Thing certain of the immortal Nature by the Mortal? She [reason] does nothing but err throughout, but especially when she meddles with Divine Things.* Who does more evidently perceive this than we? For altho' we have given her certain and infallible Principles; and tho' we have enlightened her Steps with the Sacred Lamp of Truth, that it has pleas'd *God* to communicate to us; we daily see nevertheless, that if she swerve never so little from the ordinary Path; and that she strays from, or wander out of the Way, set out and beaten by the *Church,* how soon she loses, confounds and fetters herself, tumbling and floating in this vast, turbulent and waving Sea of Human Opinions, without Restraint, and without any determinate End. So soon as she loses that great and common Road, she enters into a Labyrinth of a thousand several Paths. Man cannot be any thing but what he is, nor imagine beyond the Reach of his Capacity: *'Tis a greater Presumption, says Plutarch, in them who are but Men, to attempt to speak and discourse of the* Gods *and* Demi-Gods, *than it is in a Man, utterly ignorant of* Musick, *to judge of* Singing; *or in a Man who never saw a* Camp, *to dispute about* Arms *and* Martial Affairs, *presuming by some light Conjecture to understand the Effects of an* Art *he is totally a Stranger to.* Antiquity, I believe, thought to put a Compliment upon, and to add something to the Divine Grandeur, in assimilating it to Man, investing it with his Faculties, and adorning it with his ugly Humours, and more shameful Necessities: Offering it our *Aliments* to eat, presenting it with our *Dances, Masquerades,* and *Farces* to divert it; with our *Vestments* to cover it, and our *Houses* to inhabit, caressing it with the Odours of Incense, and the Sounds of Musick, Festoons and Nosegays: And to accommodate it to our vicious Passions, flattering its Justice with inhuman Vengeance, that is delighted with the Ruin and Dissipation of Things by it created and preserv'd: As *Tiberius Sempronius,* who burnt the rich Spoils and Arms he had gained from the Enemy in *Sardinia,* for a Sacrifice to *Vulcan:* And *Paulus Æmilius,* those of *Macedonia* to *Mars* and *Minerva:* And *Alexander* arriving at the *Indian* Ocean, threw several great Vessels of Gold into the Sea, in honour of *Thetes;* and moreover loading her *Altars* with a Slaughter, not of innocent Beasts only, but of Men also; as several Nations, and ours among the rest, were commonly used to do: And I believe there is no Nation under the Sun, that has not done the same.

> *Sulmone creatos*
> *Quatuor hic juvenes, totidem quos educat Ufens*
> *Viventes rapit, inferiis quos immolet umbris.*
>
> At *Sulmo* born he took of young Men four;
> Of those at *Ufens* bred, as many more;
> Of these alive in most inhuman wise,
> To offer an infernal Sacrifice.
>
> *[Aeneid]*

The *Getes* hold themselves to be immortal, and that their Death is nothing but a Journey towards *Zamolxis.* Once in five Years they dispatch some one among them to him, to entreat of him such Necessaries as they stand in need of: Which Envoy is chosen by Lot, and the Form of his Dispatch, after having been instructed by Word of Mouth what he is to deliver, is, that of the Assistants, three hold out so many Javelins, against the which the rest throw his Body with all their Force. If it happen to be wounded in a mortal Part, and that he immediately dies, 'tis reported a certain Argument of Divine Favour; but if he escapes, he is look'd upon as a wicked and execrable Wretch, and another is dismiss'd after the same manner, in his stead. Amestris, the Mother of *Xerxes,* being grown old, caus'd at once fourteen young Men, of the best Families of *Persia,* to be buried alive, according to the Religion of the Country, to gratify some infernal Deity. And even to this Day, the Idols of *Temixtitian* are cemented with the Blood of little Children, and they delight in no Sacrifice but of these pure and infantine Souls; a Justice thirsty of innocent Blood.

Tantum Religio potuit suadere malorum.

Such impious Use was of Religion made,
So many Ills and Mischiefs to persuade. . . .

FURTHER READING

M. Dréano, *La Renommée de Montaigne en France au XVIIIe siècle* (1952). A useful study of Montaigne's influence in the age of the Enlightenment.

Donald M. Frame, *Montaigne's Discovery of Man: The Humanization of a Humanist* (1955). Ably develops Montaigne's three phases without being rigid or schematic.

———, "Did Montaigne Betray Sebond?," *Romantic Review*, XXXVIII (December 1947), 297–329. An analysis of Montaigne's longest essay.

Fortunat Strowski, *Montaigne: Sa Vie publique et privée* (1938). An excellent biography.

4 ❧ BACON

The Great Instauration

[From Francis Bacon, preface to *The Great
Instauration* (1620), in *Works*, 14 vols.
(1857–74), IV, 13–21.]

*With Francis Bacon, Viscount St. Albans (1561–1626), we enter the
prehistory of the Enlightenment proper. It is notorious that Bacon,
the great poet and prophet of the scientific revolution, was not a
scientist himself and failed to appreciate some of the most brilliant
scientific achievements of his own day. It is true, of course, that his
public life was not that of a natural philosopher but that of a
lawyer and statesman: he began his rise under Queen Elizabeth and
consummated it under James I; in 1621 he became Lord Chancellor
and was created Viscount St. Albans. But in the same year, his
career suddenly collapsed with his plea of guilty to charges of
bribery. While he wrote much in the midst of his busy political life,
his disgrace brought him leisure, and in the last five years of his life
he continued to write his speculative accounts about a great renova-
tion of the human mind, long overdue and now at last possible,
that would give man power over nature. Bacon was a visionary of
the practical: he advocated empirical investigation, collaboration
among scientists, and a firm concentration on human improvement.
"The true and lawful goal of the sciences," he wrote, "is none other
than this: that human life be endowed with new discoveries and
powers." As several of our selections will make clear, it was this
vision of the "kingdom of man, founded on the sciences," that made
him into a culture hero for the Enlightenment. A superb stylist,
Bacon coined memorable metaphors and laconic aphorisms that
reverberate in the writings of the philosophes.*

PREFACE

That the state of knowledge is not prosperous nor greatly advancing; and that a way must be opened for the human understanding entirely different from any hitherto known, and other helps provided, in order that the mind may exercise over the nature of things the authority which properly belongs to it.

It seems to me that men do not rightly understand either their store or their strength, but overrate the one and underrate the other. Hence it follows, that either from an extravagant estimate of the value of the arts which they possess, they seek no further; or else from too mean an estimate of their own powers, they spend their strength in small matters and never put it fairly to the trial in those which go to the main. These are as the pillars of fate set in the path of knowledge; for men have neither desire nor hope to encourage them to penetrate further. And since opinion of store is one of the chief causes of want, and satisfaction with the present induces neglect of provision for the future, it becomes a thing not only useful, but absolutely necessary, that the excess of honour and admiration with which our existing stock of inventions is regarded be in the very entrance and threshold of the work, and that frankly and without circumlocution, stripped off, and men be duly warned not to exaggerate or make too much of them. For let a man look carefully into all that variety of books with which the arts and sciences abound, he will find everywhere endless repetitions of the same thing, varying in the method of treatment, but not new in substance, insomuch that the whole stock, numerous as it appears at first view, proves on examination to be but scanty. And for its value and utility it must be plainly avowed that that wisdom which we have derived principally from the Greeks is but like the boyhood of knowledge, and has the characteristic property of boys: it can talk, but it cannot generate; for it is fruitful of controversies but barren of works. So that the state of learning as it now is appears to be represented to the life in the old fable of Scylla, who had the head and face of a virgin, but her womb was hung round with barking monsters, from which she could not be delivered. For in like manner the sciences to which we are accustomed have certain general positions which are specious and flattering; but as soon as they come to particulars, which are as the parts of generation, when they should produce fruit and works, then arise contentions and barking disputations, which are the end of the matter and all the issue they can yield. Observe also, that if sciences of this kind had any life in them, that could never have come to pass which has been the case now for many ages—that they stand almost at a stay, without receiving any augmentations worthy of the human race; insomuch that many times not only what was asserted once is asserted still, but what was a question once is a question still, and instead of being resolved by discussion is only fixed and fed; and all the tradition and succession of schools is still a succession of masters and scholars, not of inventors and those who bring to further perfection the things invented. In the mechanical arts we do not find it so; they, on the contrary, as having in them some breath of life, are continually growing and becoming more perfect. As originally invented they are commonly rude, clumsy, and shapeless; afterwards they acquire new powers and more commodious arrangements and constructions; in so far that men shall sooner leave the study and pursuit of them and turn to something else, than they arrive at the ultimate perfection of which they are capable. Philosophy and the intellectual sciences, on the contrary, stand like statues, worshipped and celebrated, but not moved or advanced. Nay, they sometimes flourish most in the hands of the first author, and afterwards degenerate. For when men have once made over their judgments to others' keeping, and (like those senators whom they called *Pedarii*) have agreed to support some one person's opinion, from that time they make no enlargement of the sciences themselves, but fall to the servile office of embellishing certain individual authors and increasing their retinue. And let it not be said that the sciences have been growing gradually till they have at last reached their full stature, and so (their course being completed) have settled in the works of a few writers; and that there being now no room for the invention of better, all that remains is to embellish and cultivate those things which have been invented already. Would it were so! But the truth is that this appropriating of the sciences had its origin in nothing better than the confidence of a few persons and the sloth and indolence of the rest. For after the sciences had been in several parts perhaps cultivated and handled diligently, there has risen up some man of bold disposition, and famous for methods and short ways which people like, who has in appearance reduced them to an art, while he has in fact only spoiled all that the others had done. And yet this is what posterity like, because it makes the work short and easy, and saves further inquiry, of which they are weary and impatient. And if any one take this general acquiescence and consent for an argument of weight, as being the judgment of Time, let me tell him that the reasoning on which he relies is most fallacious and weak. For, first, we are far from knowing all that in the matter of sciences and arts has in various ages and places been brought to light and published; much less, all that has been by private persons secretly attempted and stirred; so neither the births nor the miscarriages of Time are entered in our records. Nor, secondly, is the consent itself and the time it has continued a consideration of much worth. For however various are the forms of civil polities, there is but one form of polity in the sciences; and that always has been and always will be popular. Now the doctrines which find most favour with the populace are those which are either contentious and pugnacious, or specious and empty; such, I say, as either entangle assent or tickle it. And therefore no doubt the greatest wits in each successive age have been forced out of their own course; men of capacity and intellect above the vulgar having been fain, for reputation's sake, to bow to the judgment of the time and the multitude; and thus if any contemplations of a higher order took light anywhere, they were presently blown out by the winds of vulgar opinions. So that Time is like a river, which has brought down to us things light and puffed up, while those which are weighty and solid have sunk. Nay, those very authors who have usurped a kind of dictatorship in the sciences and taken upon them to lay down the law with such confidence, yet when from time to time they come to themselves again, they fall to complaints of the subtlety of nature, the hiding-places of truth, the obscurity of things, the entanglement of causes, the weakness of the human mind; wherein nevertheless they show themselves never the more modest, seeing that they will rather lay the blame upon the common condition of men and nature than upon themselves. And then whatever any art fails to attain, they ever set it down upon the authority of that art itself as impossible of attainment; and how can art be found guilty when it is judge in its own cause? So it is but a device for exempting ignorance from ignominy. Now for those things which are delivered and received, this is their condition: barren of works, full of questions; in point of enlargement slow and languid; carrying a show of perfection in the whole, but in the parts ill filled up; in selection popular, and unsatisfactory even to those who propound them; and therefore fenced round and set forth with sundry artifices. And if there be any who have determined to make trial for themselves, and put their own strength to the work of advancing the boundaries of the sciences, yet have they not ventured to cast themselves completely loose from received opinions or to seek their knowledge at the fountain; but they think they have done some great thing if they do but add and introduce into the existing sum of science something of their own; prudently considering with themselves that by making the addition they can assert their liberty, while they retain the credit of modesty by assenting to the rest. But these mediocrities and middle ways so much praised, in deferring to opinions and customs, turn to the great detriment of the sciences. For it is hardly possible at once to admire an author and to go beyond him; knowledge being as water, which will not rise above the level from which it fell. Men of this kind, therefore, amend some things, but advance little; and improve the condition of knowledge, but do not extend its range. Some, indeed, there have been who have gone more boldly to work, and taking it all for an open matter and giving their genius full play, have made a passage for themselves and their own opinions by pulling down and demolishing former ones; and yet all their stir has but little advanced the matter; since their aim has been not to extend philosophy and the arts in substance and value, but only to change doctrines and transfer the kingdom of opinions to themselves; whereby little has indeed been gained, for though the error be the opposite of the other, the causes of erring are the same in both. And if there have been any who, not binding themselves either to other men's opinions or to their own, but loving liberty, have desired to engage others along with themselves in search, these, though honest in intention, have been weak in endeavour. For they have been content to follow probable reasons, and are carried round in a whirl of arguments, and in the promiscuous liberty of search have relaxed the severity of inquiry. There is none who has dwelt upon experience and the facts of nature as long as is necessary. Some there are indeed who have committed themselves to the waves of experience, and almost turned mechanics; yet these again have in their very experiments pursued a kind of wandering inquiry, without any regular system of operations. And besides they have mostly proposed to themselves certain petty tasks, taking it for a great matter to work out some single discovery;—a course of proceeding at once poor in aim and unskilful in design. For no man can rightly and successfully investigate the nature of anything in the thing itself; let him vary his experiments as laboriously as he will, he never comes to a resting-place, but still finds something to seek beyond. And there is another thing to be remembered; namely, that all industry in experimenting has begun with proposing to itself certain definite works to be accomplished, and has pursued them with premature and unseasonable eagerness; it has sought, I say, experiments of Fruit, not experiments of Light; not imitating the divine procedure, which in its first day's work created light only and assigned to it one entire day; on which day it produced no material work, but proceeded to that on the days following. As for those who have given the first place to Logic, supposing that the surest helps to the sciences were to be found in that, they have indeed most truly and excellently perceived that the human intellect left to its own course is not to be trusted; but then the remedy is altogether too weak for the disease; nor is it without evil in itself. For the Logic which is received, though it be very properly applied to civil business and to those arts which rest in discourse and opinion, is not nearly subtle enough to deal with nature; and in offering at what it cannot master, has done more to establish and perpetuate error than to open the way to truth.

Upon the whole therefore, it seems that men have not been happy hitherto either in the trust which they have placed in others or in their own industry with regard to the sciences; especially as neither the demonstrations nor the experiments as yet known are much to be relied upon. But the universe to the eye of the human understanding is framed like a labyrinth; presenting as it does on every side so many ambiguities of way, such deceitful resemblances of objects and signs, natures so irregular in their lines, and so knotted and entangled. And then the way is still to be made by the uncertain light of the sense, sometimes shining out, sometimes clouded over, through the woods of experience and particulars; while those who offer themselves for guides are (as was said) themselves also puzzled, and increase the number of errors and wanderers. In circumstances so difficult neither the natural force of man's judgment nor even any accidental felicity offers any chance of success. No excellence of wit, no repetition of chance experiments, can overcome such difficulties as these. Our steps must be guided by a clue, and the whole way from the very first perception of the senses must be laid out upon a sure plan. Not that I would be understood to mean that nothing whatever has been done in so many ages by so great labours. We have no reason to be ashamed of the discoveries which have been made, and no doubt the ancients proved themselves in everything that turns on wit and abstract meditation, wonderful men. But as in former ages when men sailed only by observation of the stars, they could indeed coast along the shores of the old continent or cross a few small and mediterranean seas; but before the ocean could be traversed and the new world discovered, the use of the mariner's needle, as a more faithful and certain guide, had to be found out; in like manner the discoveries which have been hitherto made in the arts and sciences are such as might be made by practice, meditation, observation, argumentation,—for they lay near to the senses, and immediately beneath common notions; but before we can reach the remoter and more hidden parts of nature, it is necessary that a more perfect use and application of the human mind and intellect be introduced.

For my own part at least, in obedience to the everlasting love of truth, I have committed myself to the uncertainties and difficulties and solitudes of the ways, and relying on the divine assistance have upheld my mind both against the shocks and embattled ranks of opinion, and against my own private and inward hesitations and scruples, and against the fogs and clouds of nature, and the phantoms flitting about on every side; in the hope of providing at last for the present and future generations guidance more faithful and secure. Wherein if I have made any progress, the way has been opened to me by no other means than the true and legitimate humiliation of the human spirit. For all those who before me have applied themselves to the invention of arts have but cast a glance or two upon facts and examples and experience, and straightway proceeded, as if invention were nothing more than an exercise of thought, to invoke their own spirits to give them oracles. I, on the contrary, dwelling purely and constantly among the facts of nature, withdraw my intellect from them no further than may suffice to let the images and rays of natural objects meet in a point, as they do in the sense of vision; whence it follows that the strength and excellency of the wit has but little to do in the matter. And the same humility which I use in inventing I employ likewise in teaching. For I do not endeavour either by triumphs of confutation, or pleadings of antiquity, or assumption of authority, or even by the veil of obscurity, to invest these inventions of mine with any majesty; which might easily be done by one who sought to give lustre to his own name rather than light to other men's minds. I have not sought (I say) nor do I seek either to force or ensnare men's judgments, but I lead them to things themselves and the concordances of things, that they may see for themselves what they have, what they can dispute, what they can add and contribute to the common stock. And for myself, if in anything I have been either too credulous or too little awake and attentive, or if I have fallen off by the way and left the inquiry incomplete, nevertheless I so present these things naked and open that my errors can be marked and set aside before the mass of knowledge be further infected by them; and it will be easy also for others to continue and carry on my labours. And by these means I suppose that I have established for ever a true and lawful marriage between the empirical and the rational faculty, the unkind and ill-starred divorce and separation of which has thrown into confusion all the affairs of the human family.

Wherefore, seeing that these things do not depend upon myself, at the outset of the work I most humbly and fervently pray to God the Father, God the Son, and God the Holy Ghost, that remembering the sorrows of mankind and the pilgrimage of this our life wherein we wear out days few and evil, they will vouchsafe through my hands to endow the human family with new mercies. This likewise I humbly pray, that things human may not interfere with things divine, and that from the opening of the ways of sense and the increase of natural light there may arise in our minds no incredulity or darkness with regard to the divine mysteries; but rather that the understanding being thereby purified and purged of fancies and vanity, and yet not the less subject and entirely submissive to the divine oracles, may give to faith that which is faith's. Lastly, that knowledge being now discharged of that venom which the serpent infused into it, and which makes the mind of man to swell, we may not be wise above measure and sobriety, but cultivate truth in charity.

And now having said my prayers I turn to men; to whom I have certain salutary admonitions to offer and certain fair requests to make. My first admonition (which was also my prayer) is that men confine the sense within the limits of duty in respect of things divine: for the sense is like the sun, which reveals the face of earth, but seals and shuts up the face of heaven. My next, that in flying from this evil they fall not into the opposite error, which they will surely do if they think that the inquisition of nature is in any part interdicted or forbidden. For it was not that pure and uncorrupted natural knowledge whereby Adam gave names to the creatures according to their propriety, which gave occasion to the fall. It was the ambitious and proud desire of moral knowledge to judge of good and evil, to the end that man may revolt from God and give laws to himself, which was the form and manner of the temptation. Whereas of the sciences which regard nature, the divine philosopher declares that "it is the glory of God to conceal a thing, but it is the glory of the King to find a thing out." Even as though the divine nature took pleasure in the innocent and kindly sport of children playing at hide and seek, and vouchsafed of his kindness and goodness to admit the human spirit for his playfellow at that game. Lastly, I would address one general admonition to all; that they consider what are the true ends of knowledge, and that they seek it not either for pleasure of the mind, or for contention, or for superiority to others, or for profit, or fame, or power, or any of these inferior things; but for the benefit and use of life; and that they perfect and govern it in charity. For it was from lust of power that the angels fell, from lust of knowledge that man fell; but of charity there can be no excess, neither did angel or man ever come in danger by it.

The requests I have to make are these. Of myself I say nothing; but in behalf of the business which is in hand I entreat men to believe that it is not an opinion to be held, but a work to be done; and to be well assured that I am labouring to lay the foundation, not of any sect or doctrine, but of human utility and power. Next, I ask them to deal fairly by their own interests, and laying aside all emulations and prejudices in favour of this or that opinion, to join in consultation for the common good; and being now freed and guarded by the securities and helps which I offer from the errors and impediments of the way, to come forward themselves and take part in that which remains to be done. Moreover, to be of good hope, nor to imagine that this Instauration of mine is a thing infinite and beyond the power of man, when it is in fact the true end and termination of infinite error; and seeing also that it is by no means forgetful of the conditions of mortality and humanity, (for it does not suppose that the work can be altogether completed within one generation, but provides for its being taken up by another) ; and finally that it seeks for the sciences not arrogantly in the little cells of human wit, but with reverence in the greater world. But it is the empty things that are vast: things solid are most contracted and lie in little room. And now I have only one favour more to ask (else injustice to me may perhaps imperil the business itself) —that men will consider well how far, upon that which I must needs assert (if I am to be consistent with myself), they are entitled to judge and decide upon these doctrines of mine; inasmuch as all that premature human reasoning which anticipates inquiry, and is abstracted from the facts rashly and sooner than is fit, is by me rejected (so far as the inquisition of nature is concerned), as a thing uncertain, confused, and ill built up; and I cannot be fairly asked to abide by the decision of a tribunal which is itself on its trial.

FURTHER READING

F. H. Anderson, *The Philosophy of Francis Bacon* (1948). An orderly and reasonable survey.

C. D. Broad, *The Philosophy of Francis Bacon* (1926). Though suggestive, the book is important mainly as an example of the now dated disparagement of Bacon's scientific thinking.

Benjamin Farrington, *Francis Bacon: Philosopher of Industrial Science* (1949). A Marxist view.

R. F. Jones, *Ancients and Moderns: A Study of the Background of the Battle of the Books* (1936). A splendid investigation of the impact of Bacon's ideas on his century.

5 ❀ DESCARTES

Discours de la méthode

[From René Descartes, *The Method, Meditations
and Selections from the Principles*, translated
by John Veitch (1887), 59–65, 75–76.]

*It has long been customary to confront Bacon, the philosopher of
experimentalism and induction, with Descartes, the philosopher of
speculation and deduction. In some degree, this absolute and
inaccurate contrast stems from the way in which the philosophes—
especially in France—treated Descartes. In their more dispassionate
moments they recognized, as d'Alembert did in the* Encyclopédie,
*that Bacon and Descartes together fostered "the spirit of experi-
mental science."* While eighteenth-century philosophes read Descartes extensively, and admired his bold assault on "Scholastic"
metaphysics and his equally bold attempt to reconstruct human
knowledge, they found his physics unacceptable; his respectability
among Catholic philosophical circles made him, in any case, unwelcome as a model. Consequently, the influence of Descartes on the
men of the Enlightenment went at least partially unacknowledged,
though we can see it emerging in the materialist speculations of
Holbach† and his associates. As Diderot put it, the Enlightenment
saw Descartes as an "extraordinary genius born to mislead and to
lead."‡*

*Born in 1596, René Descartes spent most of his adult life away
from his native France, in the Dutch Republic and, at the end of*

---

* "Expérimental," in *The Encyclopédie of Diderot and d'Alembert: Selected
Articles* (in French), ed. John Lough (1954), 73.

† See below, pages 372ff.

‡ Quoted by Aram Vartanian, *Diderot and Descartes: A Study of Scientific
Naturalism in the Enlightenment* (1953), 2.

his life, in Sweden, where he died in 1650. Despite his many debts to his predecessors, Descartes was profoundly original; his enterprise was nothing less than to prove the existence of the outside world and of God by depending solely on what he could know with certainty. He wrote extensively and fruitfully on the passions, on optics, and on cosmology, but for the intellectual history of Europe his strictly philosophical writings are of the greatest importance. It is noteworthy that he wrote his intellectual autobiography, the Discours de la méthode *(1637), in lucid French—a significant departure in a field in which Latin had so far reigned almost unchallenged. The passage below shows him, much like Bacon, rapt in a vision of a better life founded on the sciences.*

PART VI

Three years have now elapsed since I finished the Treatise containing all these matters; and I was beginning to revise it, with the view to put it into the hands of a printer, when I learned that persons to whom I greatly defer, and whose authority over my actions is hardly less influential than is my own Reason over my thoughts, had condemned a certain doctrine in Physics, published a short time previously by another individual [Galileo], to which I will not say that I adhered, but only that, previously to their censure, I had observed in it nothing which I could imagine to be prejudicial either to religion or to the state, and nothing therefore which would have prevented me from giving expression to it in writing, if Reason had persuaded me of its truth; and this led me to fear lest among my own doctrines likewise some one might be found in which I had departed from the truth, notwithstanding the great care I have always taken not to accord belief to new opinions of which I had not the most certain demonstrations, and not to give expression to aught that might tend to the hurt of any one. This has been sufficient to make me alter my purpose of publishing them; for although the reasons by which I had been induced to take this resolution were very strong, yet my inclination, which has always been hostile to writing books, enabled me immediately to discover other considerations sufficient to excuse me for not undertaking the task. And these reasons, on one side and the other, are such, that not only is it in some measure my interest here to state them, but that of the public, perhaps, to know them.

I have never made much account of what has proceeded from my own mind; and so long as I gathered no other advantage from the Method I employ beyond satisfying myself on some difficulties belonging to the speculative sciences, or endeavoring to regulate my actions according to the principles it taught me, I never thought myself bound to publish anything respecting it. For in what regards manners, everyone is so full of his own wisdom, that there might be found as many reformers as heads, if any were allowed to take upon themselves the task of mending them, except those whom God has constituted the supreme rulers of his people, or to whom he has given sufficient grace and zeal to be prophets; and although my speculations greatly pleased myself, I believed that others had theirs, which perhaps pleased them still more. But as soon as I had acquired some general notions respecting Physics, and beginning to make trial of them in various particular difficulties, had observed how far they can carry us, and how much they differ from the principles that have been employed up to the present time, I believed that I could not keep them concealed without sinning grievously against the law by which we are bound to promote, as far as in us lies, the general good of mankind. For by them I perceived it to be possible to arrive at knowledge highly useful in life; and in room of the Speculative Philosophy usually taught in the Schools, to discover a Practical, by means of which, knowing the force and action of fire, water, air, the stars, the heavens, and all the other bodies that surround us, as distinctly as we know the various crafts of our artisans, we might also apply them in the same way to all the uses to which they are adapted, and thus render ourselves the lords and possessors of nature. And this is a result to be desired, not only in order to the invention of an infinity of arts, by which we might be enabled to enjoy without any trouble the fruits of the earth, and all its comforts, but also and especially for the preservation of health, which is without doubt, of all the blessings of this life, the first and fundamental one; for the mind is so intimately dependent upon the condition and relation of the organs of the body, that if any means can ever be found to render men wiser and more ingenious than hitherto, I believe that it is in Medicine they must be sought for. It is true that the science of Medicine, as it now exists, contains few things whose utility is very remarkable: but without any wish to depreciate it, I am confident that there is no one, even among those whose profession it is, who does not admit that all at present known in it is almost nothing in comparison of what remains to be discovered; and that we could free ourselves from an infinity of maladies of body as well as of mind, and perhaps also even from the debility of age, if we had sufficiently ample knowledge of their causes, and of all the remedies provided for us by Nature. But since I designed to employ my whole life in the search after so necessary a Science, and since I had fallen in with a path which seems to me such, that if anyone follow it he must inevitably reach the end desired, unless he be hindered either by the shortness of life or the want of experiments, I judged that there could be no more effectual provision against these two impediments than if I were faithfully to communicate to the public all the little I might myself have found, and incite men of superior genius to strive to proceed farther, by contributing, each according to his inclination and ability, to the experiments which it would be necessary to make, and also by informing the public of all they might discover, so that, by the last beginning where those before them had left off, and thus connecting the lives and labors of many, we might collectively proceed much farther than each by himself could do.

I remarked, moreover, with respect to experiments, that they become always more necessary the more one is advanced in knowledge; for, at the commencement, it is better to make use only of what is spontaneously presented to our senses, and of which we cannot remain ignorant, provided we bestow on it any reflection, however slight, than to concern ourselves about more uncommon and recondite phænomena: the reason of which is, that the more uncommon often only mislead us so long as the causes of the more ordinary are still unknown; and the circumstances upon which they depend are almost always so special and minute as to be highly difficult to detect. But in this I have adopted the following order: first, I have essayed to find in general the principles, or first causes, of all that is or can be in the world, without taking into consideration for this end anything but God himself who has created it, and without educing them from any other source than from certain germs of truths naturally existing in our minds. In the second place, I examined what were the first and most ordinary effects that could be deduced from these causes; and it appears to me that, in this way, I have found heavens, stars, and earth, and even on the earth, water, air, fire, minerals, and some other things of this kind, which of all others are the most common and simple, and hence the easiest to know. Afterward, when I wished to descend to the more particular, so many diverse objects presented themselves to me, that I believed it to be impossible for the human mind to distinguish the forms or species of bodies that are upon the earth, from an infinity of others which might have been, if it had pleased God to place them there, or consequently to apply them to our use, unless we rise to causes through their effects, and avail ourselves of many particular experiments. Thereupon, turning over in my mind all the objects that had ever been presented to my senses, I freely venture to state that I have never observed any which I could not satisfactorily explain by the principles I had discovered. But it is necessary also to confess that the power of nature is so ample and vast, and these principles so simple and general, that I have hardly observed a single particular effect which I cannot at once recognize as capable of being deduced in many different modes from the principles, and that my greatest difficulty usually is to discover in which of these modes the effect is dependent upon them; for out of this difficulty I cannot otherwise extricate myself than by again seeking certain experiments, which may be such that their result is not the same, if it is in the one of these modes that we must explain it, as it would be if it were to be explained in the other. As to what remains, I am now in a position to discern, as I think, with sufficient clearness what course must be taken to make the majority of those experiments which may conduce to this end: but I perceive likewise that they are such and so numerous, that neither my hands nor my income, though it were a thousand times larger than it is, would be sufficient for them all; so that, according as henceforward I shall have the means of making more or fewer experiments, I shall in the same proportion make greater or less progress in the knowledge of nature. This was what I had hoped to make known by the Treatise I had written, and so clearly to exhibit the advantage that would thence accrue to the public, as to induce all who have the common good of man at heart, that is, all who are virtuous in truth, and not merely in appearance, or according to opinion, as well to communicate to me the experiments they had already made, as to assist me in those that remain to be made.

But since that time other reasons have occurred to me, by which I have been led to change my opinion, and to think that I ought indeed to go on committing to writing all the results which I deemed of any moment, as soon as I should have tested their truth, and to bestow the same care upon them as I would have done had it been my design to publish them. This course commended itself to me, as well because I thus afforded myself more ample inducement to examine them thoroughly, for doubtless that is always more narrowly scrutinized which we believe will be read by many, than that which is written merely for our private use (and frequently what has seemed to me true when I first conceived it, has appeared false when I have set about committing it to writing), as because I thus lost no opportunity of advancing the interests of the public, as far as in me lay, and since thus likewise, if my writings possess any value, those into whose hands they may fall after my death may be able to put them to what use they deem proper. But I resolved by no means to consent to their publication during my lifetime, lest either the oppositions or the controversies to which they might give rise, or even the reputation, such as it might be, which they would acquire for me, should be any occasion of my losing the time that I had set apart for my own improvement. For though it be true that everyone is bound to promote to the extent of his ability the good of others, and that to be useful to no one is really to be worthless, yet it is likewise true that our cares ought to extend beyond the present; and it is good to omit doing what might perhaps bring some profit to the living, when we have in view the accomplishment of other ends that will be of much greater advantage to posterity. And in truth, I am quite willing it should be known that the little I have hitherto learned is almost nothing in comparison with that of which I am ignorant, and to the knowledge of which I do not despair of being able to attain; for it is much the same with those who gradually discover truth in the Sciences, as with those who when growing rich find less difficulty in making great acquisitions, than they formerly experienced when poor in making acquisitions of much smaller amount. Or they may be compared to the commanders of armies, whose forces usually increase in proportion to their victories, and who need greater prudence to keep together the residue of their troops after a defeat than after a victory to take towns and provinces. . . .

If some of the matters of which I have spoken in the beginning of the Dioptrics and Meteorics should offend at first sight, because I call them hypotheses and seem indifferent about giving proof of them, I request a patient and attentive reading of the whole, from which I hope those hesitating will derive satisfaction; for it appears to me that the reasonings are so mutually connected in these Treatises, that, as the last are demonstrated by the first which are their causes, the first are in their turn demonstrated by the last which are their effects. Nor must it be imagined that I here commit the fallacy which the logicians call a circle; for since experience renders the majority of these effects most certain, the causes from which I deduce them do not serve so much to establish their reality as to explain their existence; but on the contrary, the reality of the causes is established by the reality of the effects. Nor have I called them hypotheses with any other end in view except that it may be known that I think I am able to deduce them from those first truths which I have already expounded; and yet that I have expressly determined not to do so, to prevent a certain class of minds from thence taking occasion to build some extravagant Philosophy upon what they may take to be my principles, and my being blamed for it. I refer to those who imagine that they can master in a day all that another has taken twenty years to think out, as soon as he has spoken two or three words to them on the subject; or who are the more liable to error and the less capable of perceiving truth in very proportion as they are more subtle and lively. As to the opinions which are truly and wholly mine, I offer no apology for them as new,—persuaded as I am that if their reasons be well considered they will be found to be so simple and so conformed to common sense as to appear less extraordinary and less paradoxical than any others which can be held on the same subjects; nor do I even boast of being the earliest discoverer of any of them, but only of having adopted them, neither because they had nor because they had not been held by others, but solely because Reason has convinced me of their truth. . . .

In conclusion, I am unwilling here to say anything very specific of the progress which I expect to make for the future in the Sciences, or to bind myself to the public by any promise which I am not certain of being able to fulfill; but this only will I say, that I have resolved to devote what time I may still have to live to no other occupation than that of endeavoring to acquire some knowledge of Nature, which shall be of such a kind as to enable us therefrom to deduce rules in Medicine of greater certainty than those at present in use; and that my inclination is so much opposed to all other pursuits, especially to such as cannot be useful to some without being hurtful to others, that if, by any circumstances, I had been constrained to engage in such, I do not believe that I should have been able to succeed. Of this I here make a public declaration, though well aware that it cannot serve to procure for me any consideration in the world, which, however, I do not in the least affect; and I shall always hold myself more obliged to those through whose favor I am permitted to enjoy my retirement without interruption than to any who might offer me the highest earthly preferments.

FURTHER READING

Albert G. A. Balz, *Cartesian Studies* (1951). Useful essays.

Peter Gay, *The Enlightenment: An Interpretation,* Vol. II, *The Science of Freedom* (1969), 617–19. Surveys briefly the controversy over Descartes' influence over the Enlightenment.

Alexandre Koyré, "Newton and Descartes," *Newtonian Studies* (1965), 53–114. A searching comparison.

Norman Kemp Smith, *New Studies in the Philosophy of Descartes: Descartes as Pioneer* (1952). Illuminating essays on a variety of themes.

Aram Vartanian, *Diderot and Descartes: A Study of Scientific Naturalism in the Enlightenment* (1953). Suggestive, intelligent, but somewhat too insistent on its thesis that Cartesianism was very powerful in the eighteenth century but largely clandestine.

6 ❀ NEWTON

Letters

[From J. Edleston, *Correspondence of Sir Isaac Newton and Professor Cotes* (1850), 154–56, and *Four Letters from Sir Isaac Newton to Doctor Bentley Containing Some Arguments in Proof of a Deity* (1756), 1–11.]

If the Enlightenment was ready to deify anyone, it was Newton; for the philosophes he was, in Voltaire's view, the greatest man who ever lived. What impressed the philosophes so immensely was the combination of qualities that Newton possessed, as much as the qualities themselves. He was an unsurpassed observer of nature, a synthesizer of unprecedented powers, as well as an impressive philosopher of scientific method. The Age of the Enlightenment was filled with biologists, mathematicians, psychologists, aspiring to become the Newton of their discipline. When Beccaria's friends sought to call him by an affectionate name, they called him "Little Newton." While for some decades French academic scientists resisted the Newtonian laws of attraction in favor of Descartes' theory of vortices, that resistance collapsed by the middle of the eighteenth century. In 1776 Voltaire could state the matter quite calmly: "We are all his disciples now."*

Even so sober a commentator as David Hume found the strongest language in his vocabulary when he came to Newton in his History of England. *"In Newton," he wrote, "this island may boast of having produced the greatest and rarest genius that ever rose for the ornament and instruction of the species. Cautious in admitting no principles but such as were founded on experiment; but resolute to*

---

* Voltaire to the Académie Française, in *Oeuvres complètes*, ed. Louis Moland, 52 vols. (1877–85), VII, 335.

*adopt every such principle, however new or unusual: from modesty, ignorant of his superiority above the rest of mankind; and thence less careful to accommodate his reasonings to common apprehensions: more anxious to merit than acquire fame: he was, from these causes, long unknown to the world; but his reputation at last broke out with a lustre which scarcely any writer, during his own lifetime, had ever before attained."**

Sir Isaac Newton was born in 1642, and made his decisive discoveries early; between 1665 and 1667 he worked out a rudimentary version of the calculus, discovered the essential optical law that white is a composite color, and grasped the fundamental principle of the law of gravitation. He published this last, his greatest contribution to science, with some reluctance in 1687, in his Latin treatise Philosophiae naturalis principia mathematica. It established him overnight as the greatest scientist of the age. His second masterpiece, the Opticks, was published in English in 1704. He was a strange man, given to isolation and excessive suspiciousness, but he had something of a public career as Master of the Royal Mint and, from 1703 on, as president of the Royal Society. His contribution to the natural sciences is as immense as it is obvious, but to the Enlightenment his curt slogan Hypotheses non fingo—"I feign no hypotheses"—had a special attraction. It meant methodical inquiry, concentration of intellectual effort on matters that could be known, and an unwearied attention to nature. The first two letters printed below, to Roger Cotes, give a suggestion of this methodological principle. The last, to Bentley, shows Newton the scientific revolutionary as the good if somewhat eccentric Christian. The philosophes were to adopt Newton's science, copy Newton's method, invoke Newton's name, and discard Newton's God.

For the Reverend Mr. Roger Cotes, Professor of Astronomy, at his Chamber in Trinity College in Cambridge.

SIR,

I had yours of Feb 18th, & the Difficulty you mention which lies in these words *"Et cum Attractio omnis mutua sit"* is removed by

* *The History of England,* 5 vols. (1864 edn.) , V, 481.

considering that as in Geometry the word Hypothesis is not taken in so large a sense as to include the Axiomes & Postulates, so in Experimental Philosophy it is not to be taken in so large a sense as to include the first Principles or Axiomes which I call the laws of motion. These Principles are deduced from Phaenomena & made general by Induction: which is the highest evidence that a Proposition can have in this philosophy. And the word Hypothesis is here used by me to signify only such a Proposition as is not a Phaenomenon nor deduced from any Phaenomena but assumed or supposed without any experimental proof. Now the mutual & mutually equal attraction of bodies is a branch of the third Law of motion & how this branch is deduced from Phaenomena you may see in the end of the Corollaries of ye Laws of Motion, pag. 22. If a body attracts another body contiguous to it & is not mutually attracted by the other: the attracted body will drive the other before it & both will go away together with an accelerated motion in infinitum, as it were by a self moving principle, contrary to ye first law of motion, whereas there is no such phaenomenon in all nature. . . .

I have not time to finish this Letter but intend to write to you again on Tuesday.

I am
Your most humble Servant

London. 28 March [Saturday] 1713   Is. NEWTON

SIR,   London. 31 Mar. 1713.
On Saturday last I wrote to you, representing that Experimental philosophy proceeds only upon Phenomena & deduces general Propositions from them only by Induction. And such is the proof of mutual attraction. And the arguments for ye impenetrability, mobility & force of all bodies & for the laws of motion are no better. And he that in experimental Philosophy would except against any of these must draw his objection from some experiment or phaenomenon & not from a mere Hypothesis, if the Induction be of any force. . . .

To the Reverend Dr. Richard Bentley, at the Bishop of Worcester's House in Park-street, Westminster.

SIR,

When I wrote my Treatise about our System, I had an Eye upon such Principles as might work with considering Men, for the Belief of a Deity, and nothing can rejoice me more than to find it useful for that Purpose. But if I have done the Public any Service this way, it is due to nothing but Industry and patient Thought.

As to your first Query, it seems to me that if the Matter of our Sun and Planets, and all the Matter of the Universe, were evenly scattered throughout all the Heavens, and every Particle had an innate Gravity towards all the rest, and the whole Space, throughout which this Matter was scattered, was but finite; the Matter on the outside of this Space would by its Gravity tend towards all the Matter on the inside, and by consequence fall down into the middle of the whole Space, and there compose one great spherical Mass. But if the Matter was evenly disposed throughout an infinite Space, it could never convene into one Mass, but some of it would convene into one Mass and some into another, so as to make an infinite Number of great Masses, scattered at great Distances from one to another throughout all that infinite Space. And thus might the Sun and fixt Stars be formed, supposing the Matter were of a lucid Nature. But how the Matter should divide itself into two sorts, and that Part of it, which is fit to compose a shining Body, should fall down into one Mass and make a Sun, and the rest, which is fit to compose an opaque Body, should coalesce, not into one great Body, like the shining Matter, but into many little ones; or if the Sun at first were an opaque Body like the Planets, or the Planets lucid Bodies like the Sun, how he alone should be changed into a shining Body, whilst all they continue opaque, or all they be changed into opaque ones, whilst he remains unchanged, I do not think explicable by mere natural Causes, but am forced to ascribe it to the Counsel and Contrivance of a voluntary Agent.

The same Power, whether natural or supernatural, which placed the Sun in the Center of the six primary Planets, placed *Saturn* in the Center of the Orbs of his five secondary Planets, and *Jupiter* in the Center of his four secondary Planets, and the Earth in the Center of the Moon's Orb; and therefore had this Cause been a blind one, without Contrivance or Design, the Sun would have been a Body of the same kind with *Saturn, Jupiter*, and the Earth, that is, without Light and Heat. Why there is one Body in our System qualified to give Light and Heat to all the rest, I know no Reason, but because the Author of the System thought it convenient; and why there is but one Body of this kind I know no Reason, but because one was sufficient to warm and enlighten all the rest. For the *Cartesian* Hypothesis of Suns losing their Light, and then turning into Comets, and Comets into Planets, can have no Place in my System, and is plainly erroneous; because it is certain that as often as they appear to us, they descend into the System of our Planets, lower than the Orb of *Jupiter,* and sometimes lower than the Orbs of *Venus* and *Mercury,* and yet never stay here, but always return from the Sun with the same Degrees of Motion by which they approached him.

To your second Query, I answer, that the Motions which the Planets now have could not spring from any natural Cause alone, but were impressed by an intelligent Agent. For since Comets descend into the Region of our Planets, and here move all manner of ways, going sometimes the same way with the Planets, sometimes the contrary way, and sometimes in cross ways, in Planes inclined to the Plane of the Ecliptick, and at all kinds of Angles, 'tis plain that there is no natural Cause which could determine all the Planets, both primary and secondary, to move the same way and in the same Plane, without any considerable Variation: This must have been the Effect of Counsel. Nor is there any natural Cause which could give the Planets those just Degrees of Velocity, in Proportion to their Distances from the Sun, and other central Bodies, which were requisite to make them move in such concentrick Orbs about those Bodies. Had the Planets been as swift as Comets, in Proportion to their Distances from the Sun (as they would have been, had their Motion been caused by their Gravity, whereby the Matter, at the first Formation of the Planets, might fall from the remotest Regions towards the Sun) they would not move in concentrick Orbs, but in such eccentrick ones as the Comets move in. Were all the Planets as swift as *Mercury,* or as slow as *Saturn* or his Satellites; or were their several Velocities otherwise much greater or less than they are, as they might have been had they arose from any other Cause than their Gravities; or had the Distances from the Centers about which they move, been greater or less than they are with the same Velocities; or had the Quantity of Matter in the Sun, or in *Saturn, Jupiter,* and the Earth, and by consequence their gravitating Power been greater or less than it is; the primary Planets could not have revolved about the Sun, nor the secondary ones about *Saturn, Jupiter,* and the Earth, in concentrick Circles as they do, but would have moved in Hyperbolas, or Parabolas, or in Ellipses very eccentrick. To make this System therefore, with all its Motions, required a Cause which understood, and compared together, the Quantities of Matter in the several Bodies of the Sun and Planets, and the gravitating Powers resulting from thence; the several Distances of the primary Planets from the Sun, and of the secondary ones from *Saturn, Jupiter,* and the Earth; and the Velocities with which these Planets could revolve about those Quantities of Matter in the central Bodies; and to compare and adjust all these Things together, in so great a Variety of Bodies, argues that Cause to be not blind and fortuitous, but very well skilled in Mechanicks and Geometry.

To your third Query, I answer, that it may be represented that the Sun may, by heating those Planets most which are nearest to him, cause them to be better concocted, and more condensed by that Concoction. But when I consider that our Earth is much more heated in its Bowels below the upper Crust by subterraneous Fermentations of mineral Bodies than by the Sun, I see not why the interior Parts of *Jupiter* and *Saturn* might not be as much heated, concocted, and coagulated by those Fermentations as our Earth is; and therefore this various Density should have some other Cause than the various Distances of the Planets from the Sun. And I am confirmed in this Opinion by considering, that the Planets of *Jupiter* and *Saturn,* as they are rarer than the rest, so they are vastly greater, and contain a far greater Quantity of Matter, and have many Satellites about them; which Qualifications surely arose not from their being placed at so great a Distance from the Sun, but were rather the Cause why the Creator placed them at great Distance. For by their gravitating Powers they disturb one another's Motions very sensibly, as I find by some late Observations of Mr. *Flamsteed,* and had they been placed much nearer to the Sun and to one another, they would by the same Powers have caused a considerable Disturbance in the whole System.

To your fourth Query, I answer, that in the Hypothesis of Vortices, the Inclination of the Axis of the Earth might, in my Opinion, be ascribed to the Situation of the Earth's Vortex before it was absorbed by the neighbouring Vortices, and the Earth turned from a Sun to a Comet; but this Inclination ought to decrease constantly in Compliance with the Motion of the Earth's Vortex, whose Axis is much less inclined to the Ecliptick, as appears by the Motion of the Moon carried about therein. If the Sun by his Rays could carry about the Planets, yet I do not see how he could thereby effect their diurnal Motions.

Lastly, I see nothing extraordinary in the Inclination of the Earth's Axis for proving a Deity, unless you will urge it as a Contrivance for Winter and Summer, and for making the Earth habitable towards the Poles; and that the diurnal Rotations of the Sun and Planets, as they could hardly arise from any Cause purely mechanical, so by being determined all the same way with the annual and menstrual Motions, they seem to make up that Harmony in the System, which, as I explained above, was the Effect of Choice rather than Chance.

There is yet another argument for a Deity, which I take to be a very strong one, but till the Principles on which it is grounded are better received, I think it more advisable to let it sleep.

I am,

Your most humble Servant
to command,

Cambridge,   Is. NEWTON.
Decemb. 10, 1692.

FURTHER READING

Charles C. Gillispie, *The Edge of Objectivity: An Essay in the History of Scientific Ideas* (1960). An important and original evaluation of Newton and of science in the Enlightenment.

Alexandre Koyré, *Newtonian Studies* (1965). Profound essays.

Frank E. Manuel, *A Portrait of Isaac Newton* (1968). An interesting psychoanalytical biography.

L. T. More, *Isaac Newton, A Biography* (1934). The standard biography, though somewhat old-fashioned and not wholly reliable.

7 ❧ LOCKE

A Letter Concerning Toleration

[From *A Letter Concerning Toleration* (1689),
in *The Works of John Locke,* 9 vols. (1824), V,
5–19, 23–25, 32–37.]

*John Locke (1632–1704) requires more extensive excerpting than
our earlier authors. This is so not because Locke was a greater
mind than Newton—a thinker to whom Locke, though ten years
older, always looked up—but because his influence on enlightened
thought was pervasive in many areas. A physician and philosopher,
Locke made the empiricist pronouncements of Bacon and the
empiricist practice of Newton into a coherent philosophy of mind.
His most important philosophical work is doubtless the* Essay
Concerning Human Understanding *(1690), which attacks the notion of innate ideas and insists instead that all our knowledge comes
from our sensations and reflection on those sensations. As we shall
see below, Locke was also an influential and reforming publicist in
the field of education, and a political theorist who left his mark on
eighteenth-century speculation.**

Locke's four Letters Concerning Toleration *grew from his liberal
political thought and Latitudinarian Protestantism. A supporter of
that group of politicians who in 1680 sought to exclude the future
James II from the throne for his Catholicism, he was compelled to
flee to the Netherlands, where he composed the essay from which
excerpts follow. Its central ideas had been in Locke's mind since the
1660s. Locke's plea is distinctly modern: it is not dissenters who
threaten society, but society which by suppressing dissenters produces threats for itself; whatever restriction on toleration the state
may logically apply must be justified on political, not on religious,*

---

* See below, pages 89ff., 199f., 303.

*grounds. Roman Catholics may be denied toleration because they
serve a foreign power; atheists, because their oath cannot be
trusted; rebels on religious principle, because they are rebels.*

HONOURED SIR,

SINCE you are pleased to inquire what are my thoughts about the
mutual toleration of christians in their different professions of religion, I must needs answer you freely, that I esteem that toleration
to be the chief characteristical mark of the true church. For whatsoever some people boast of the antiquity of places and names, or of
the pomp of their outward worship; others, of the reformation of
their discipline; all of the orthodoxy of their faith, for every one is
orthodox to himself: these things, and all others of this nature, are
much rather marks of men's striving for power and empire over one
another, than of the church of Christ. Let any one have ever so true
a claim to all these things, yet if he be destitute of charity, meekness, and good-will in general towards all mankind, even to those
that are not christians, he is certainly yet short of being a true
christian himself. "The kings of the gentiles exercise lordship over
them," said our Saviour to his disciples, "but ye shall not be so,"
Luke xxii. 25, 26. The business of true religion is quite another
thing. It is not instituted in order to the erecting an external pomp,
nor to the obtaining of ecclesiastical dominion, nor to the exercising
of compulsive force; but to the regulating of men's lives according
to the rules of virtue and piety. Whosoever will list himself under
the banner of Christ, must, in the first place and above all things,
make war upon his own lusts and vices. It is in vain for any man to
usurp the name of christian, without holiness of life, purity of
manners, and benignity and meekness of spirit. "Let every one that
nameth the name of Christ, depart from iniquity," 2 Tim. ii. 19.
"Thou, when thou art converted, strengthen thy brethren," said
our Lord to Peter, Luke xxii. 32. It would indeed be very hard for
one that appears careless about his own salvation, to persuade me
that he were extremely concerned for mine. For it is impossible that
those should sincerely and heartily apply themselves to make other
people christians, who have not really embraced the christian religion in their own hearts. If the gospel and the apostles may be
credited, no man can be a christian without charity, and without

that faith which works, not by force, but by love. Now I appeal to the consciences of those that persecute, torment, destroy, and kill other men upon pretence of religion, whether they do it out of friendship and kindness towards them, or no: and I shall then indeed, and not till then, believe they do so, when I shall see those fiery zealots correcting, in the same manner, their friends and familiar acquaintance, for the manifest sins they commit against the precepts of the gospel; when I shall see them prosecute with fire and sword the members of their own communion that are tainted with enormous vices, and without amendment are in danger of eternal perdition; and when I shall see them thus express their love and desire of the salvation of their souls, by the infliction of torments, and exercise of all manner of cruelties. For if it be out of a principle of charity, as they pretend, and love to men's souls, that they deprive them of their estates, maim them with corporal punishments, starve and torment them in noisome prisons, and in the end even take away their lives; I say, if all this be done merely to make men christians, and procure their salvation, why then do they suffer "whoredom, fraud, malice, and such like enormities," which, according to the apostle, Rom. i. manifestly relish of heathenish corruption, to predominate so much and abound amongst their flocks and people? These, and such like things, are certainly more contrary to the glory of God, to the purity of the church, and to the salvation of souls, than any conscientious dissent from ecclesiastical decision, or separation from public worship, whilst accompanied with innocency of life. Why then does this burning zeal for God, for the church, and for the salvation of souls; burning, I say literally, with fire and faggot; pass by those moral vices and wickednesses, without any chastisement, which are acknowledged by all men to be diametrically opposite to the profession of christianity; and bend all its nerves either to the introducing of ceremonies, or to the establishment of opinions, which for the most part are about nice and intricate matters, that exceed the capacity of ordinary understandings? Which of the parties contending about these things is in the right, which of them is guilty of schism or heresy, whether those that domineer or those that suffer, will then at last be manifest, when the cause of their separation comes to be judged of. He certainly that follows Christ, embraces his doctrine, and bears his yoke, though he forsake both father and mother, separate from the public assemblies and ceremonies of his country, or whomsoever, or whatsoever else he relinquishes, will not then be judged an heretic.

Now, though the divisions that are among sects should be allowed

to be ever so obstructive of the salvation of souls; yet nevertheless
"adultery, fornication, uncleanness, lasciviousness, idolatry, and
such like things, cannot be denied to be works of the flesh;" concerning which the apostle has expressly declared, that "they who do
them shall not inherit the "kingdom of God," Gal. v. 21. Whosoever
therefore is sincerely solicitous about the kingdom of God, and
thinks it his duty to endeavour the enlargement of it amongst men,
ought to apply himself with no less care and industry to the rooting
out of these immoralities than to the extirpation of sects. But if any
one do otherwise, and whilst he is cruel and implacable towards
those that differ from him in opinion, he be indulgent to such
iniquities and immoralities as are unbecoming the name of a christian, let such a one talk ever so much of the church, he plainly
demonstrates by his actions, that it is another kingdom he aims at,
and not the advancement of the kingdom of God.

That any man should think fit to cause another man, whose
salvation he heartily desires, to expire in torments, and that even in
an unconverted state, would, I confess, seem very strange to me,
and, I think, to any other also. But nobody, surely, will ever believe
that such a carriage can proceed from charity, love or good-will. If
any one maintain that men ought to be compelled by fire and sword
to profess certain doctrines, and conform to this or that exterior
worship, without any regard had unto their morals; if any one
endeavour to convert those that are erroneous unto the faith, by
forcing them to profess things that they do not believe, and allowing them to practise things that the gospel does not permit; it
cannot be doubted indeed, that such a one is desirous to have a
numerous assembly joined in the same profession with himself; but
that he principally intends by those means to compose a truly christian church, is altogether incredible. It is not therefore to be
wondered at, if those who do not really contend for the advancement of the true religion, and of the church of Christ, make use of
arms that do not belong to the christian warfare. If, like the captain
of our salvation, they sincerely desired the good of souls, they would
tread in the steps and follow the perfect example of that prince of
peace, who sent out his soldiers to the subduing of nations, and
gathering them into his church, not armed with the sword, or other
instruments of force, but prepared with the gospel of peace, and
with the exemplary holiness of their conversation. This was his
method. Though if infidels were to be converted by force, if those
that are either blind or obstinate were to be drawn off from their
errors by armed soldiers, we know very well that it was much more

easy for him to do it with armies of heavenly legions, than for any son of the church, how potent soever, with all his dragoons.

The toleration of those that differ from others in matters of religion, is so agreeable to the gospel of Jesus Christ, and to the genuine reason of mankind, that it seems monstrous for men to be so blind, as not to perceive the necessity and advantage of it, in so clear a light. I will not here tax the pride and ambition of some, the passion and uncharitable zeal of others. These are faults from which human affairs can perhaps scarce ever be perfectly freed; but yet such as nobody will bear the plain imputation of, without covering them with some specious colour; and so pretend to commendation, whilst they are carried away by their own irregular passions. But however, that some may not colour their spirit of persecution and unchristian cruelty, with a pretence of care of the public weal, and observation of the laws; and that others, under pretence of religion, may not seek impunity for their libertinism and licentiousness; in a word, that none may impose either upon himself or others, by the pretences of loyalty and obedience to the prince, or of tenderness and sincerity in the worship of God; I esteem it above all things necessary to distinguish exactly the business of civil government from that of religion, and to settle the just bounds that lie between the one and the other. If this be not done, there can be no end put to the controversies that will be always arising between those that have, or at least pretend to have, on the one side, a concernment for the interest of men's souls, and, on the other side, a care of the commonwealth.

The commonwealth seems to me to be a society of men constituted only for the procuring, preserving, and advancing their own civil interests.

Civil interest I call life, liberty, health, and indolency of body; and the possession of outward things, such as money, lands, houses, furniture, and the like.

It is the duty of the civil magistrate, by the impartial execution of equal laws, to secure unto all the people in general, and to every one of his subjects in particular, the just possession of these things belonging to this life. If any one presume to violate the laws of public justice and equity, established for the preservation of these things, his presumption is to be checked by the fear of punishment, consisting in the deprivation or diminution of those civil interests, or goods, which otherwise he might and ought to enjoy. But seeing no man does willingly suffer himself to be punished by the deprivation of any part of his goods, and much less of his liberty or life,

therefore is the magistrate armed with the force and strength of all
his subjects, in order to the punishment of those that violate any
other man's rights.

Now that the whole jurisdiction of the magistrate reaches only to
these civil concernments; and that all civil power, right, and dominion, is bounded and confined to the only care of promoting these
things; and that it neither can nor ought in any manner to be
extended to the salvation of souls; these following considerations
seem unto me abundantly to demonstrate.

First, Because the care of souls is not committed to the civil
magistrate, any more than to other men. It is not committed unto
him, I say, by God; because it appears not that God has ever given
any such authority to one man over another, as to compel any one
to his religion. Nor can any such power be vested in the magistrate
by the consent of the people; because no man can so far abandon
the care of his own salvation, as blindly to leave it to the choice of
any other, whether prince or subject, to prescribe to him what faith
or worship he shall embrace. For no man can, if he would, conform
his faith to the dictates of another. All the life and power of true
religion consists in the inward and full persuasion of the mind; and
faith is not faith, without believing. Whatever profession we make,
to whatever outward worship we conform, if we are not fully satisfied in our own mind that the one is true, and the other well-
pleasing unto God, such profession and such practice, far from
being any furtherance, are indeed great obstacles to our salvation.
For in this manner, instead of expiating other sins by the exercise of
religion, I say in offering thus unto God Almighty such a worship as
we esteem to be displeasing unto him, we add unto the number of
our other sins, those also of hypocrisy, and contempt of his Divine
Majesty.

In the second place, The care of souls cannot belong to the civil
magistrate, because his power consists only in outward force: but
true and saving religion consists in the inward persuasion of the
mind, without which nothing can be acceptable to God. And such is
the nature of the understanding, that it cannot be compelled to the
belief of any thing by outward force. Confiscation of estate, imprisonment, torments, nothing of that nature can have any such
efficacy as to make men change the inward judgment that they have
framed of things.

It may indeed be alleged, that the magistrate may make use of
arguments, and thereby draw the heterodox into the way of truth,
and procure their salvation. I grant it; but this is common to him

with other men. In teaching, instructing, and redressing the erroneous by reason, he may certainly do what becomes any good man to
do. Magistracy does not oblige him to put off either humanity or
christianity. But it is one thing to persuade, another to command;
one thing to press with arguments, another with penalties. This the
civil power alone has a right to do; to the other, good-will is authority enough. Every man has commission to admonish, exhort, convince another of errour, and by reasoning to draw him into truth:
but to give laws, receive obedience, and compel with the sword,
belongs to none but the magistrate. And upon this ground I affirm,
that the magistrate's power extends not to the establishing of any
article of faith, or forms of worship, by the force of his laws. For
laws are of no force at all without penalties, and penalties in this
case are absolutely impertinent; because they are not proper to
convince the mind. Neither the profession of any articles of faith,
nor the conformity to any outward form of worship, as has been
already said, can be available to the salvation of souls, unless the
truth of the one, and the acceptableness of the other unto God, be
thoroughly believed by those that so profess and practise. But
penalties are no ways capable to produce such belief. It is only light
and evidence that can work a change in men's opinions; and that
light can in no manner proceed from corporal sufferings, or any
other outward penalties.

In the third place, The care of the salvation of men's souls cannot
belong to the magistrate; because, though the rigour of laws and the
force of penalties were capable to convince and change men's
minds, yet would not that help at all to the salvation of their souls.
For, there being but one truth, one way to heaven; what hope is
there that more men would be led into it, if they had no other rule
to follow but the religion of the court, and were put under a
necessity to quit the light of their own reason, to oppose the dictates
of their own consciences, and blindly to resign up themselves to the
will of their governors, and to the religion which either ignorance,
ambition, or superstition had chanced to establish in the countries
where they were born? In the variety and contradiction of opinions
in religion, wherein the princes of the world are as much divided as
in their secular interests, the narrow way would be much straitened;
one country alone would be in the right, and all the rest of the
world put under an obligation of following their princes in the
ways that lead to destruction: and that which heightens the absurdity, and very ill suits the notion of a deity, men would owe their
eternal happiness or misery to the places of their nativity.

These considerations, to omit many others that might have been urged to the same purpose, seem unto me sufficient to conclude, that all the power of civil government relates only to men's civil interests, is confined to the care of the things of this world, and hath nothing to do with the world to come.

Let us now consider what a church is. A church then I take to be a voluntary society of men, joining themselves together of their own accord in order to the public worshipping of God, in such a manner as they judge acceptable to him, and effectual to the salvation of their souls.

I say, it is a free and voluntary society. Nobody is born a member of any church; otherwise the religion of parents would descend unto children, by the same right of inheritance as their temporal estates, and every one would hold his faith by the same tenure he does his lands; than which nothing can be imagined more absurd. Thus therefore that matter stands. No man by nature is bound unto any particular church or sect, but every one joins himself voluntarily to that society in which he believes he has found that profession and worship which is truly acceptable to God. The hope of salvation, as it was the only cause of his entrance into that communion, so it can be the only reason of his stay there. For if afterwards he discover any thing either erroneous in the doctrine, or incongruous in the worship of that society to which he has joined himself, why should it not be as free for him to go out as it was to enter? No member of a religious society can be tried with any other bonds but what proceed from the certain expectation of eternal life. A church then is a society of members voluntarily uniting to this end.

It follows now that we consider what is the power of this church, and unto what laws it is subject.

Forasmuch as no society, how free soever, or upon whatsoever slight occasion instituted (whether of philosophers for learning, of merchants for commerce, or of men of leisure for mutual conversation and discourse), no church or company, I say, can in the least subsist and hold together, but will presently dissolve and break to pieces, unless it be regulated by some laws, and the members all consent to observe some order. Place and time of meeting must be agreed on; rules for admitting and excluding members must be established: distinction of officers, and putting things into a regular course, and such like, cannot be omitted. But since the joining together of several members into this church-society, as has already been demonstrated, is absolutely free and spontaneous, it necessarily follows, that the right of making its laws can belong to none but the society itself, or at least, which is the same thing, to those whom the society by common consent has authorised thereunto.

Some perhaps may object, that no such society can be said to be a true church, unless it have in it a bishop, or presbyter, with ruling authority derived from the very apostles, and continued down unto the present time by an uninterrupted succession.

To these I answer. In the first place, Let them show me the edict by which Christ has imposed that law upon his church. And let not any man think me impertinent, if, in a thing of this consequence, I require that the terms of that edict be very express and positive.— For the promise he has made us, that "wheresoever two or three are gathered together in his name, he will be in the midst of them," Matth. xviii. 20 seems to imply the contrary. Whether such an assembly want any thing necessary to a true church, pray do you consider. Certain I am, that nothing can be there wanting unto the salvation of souls, which is sufficient for our purpose.

Next, pray observe how great have always been the divisions amongst even those who lay so much stress upon the divine institution, and continued succession of a certain order of rulers in the church. Now their very dissension unavoidably puts us upon a necessity of deliberating, and consequently allows a liberty of choosing that, which upon consideration we prefer.

And, in the last place, I consent that these men have a ruler of their church, established by such a long series of succession as they judge necessary, provided I may have liberty at the same time to join myself to that society, in which I am persuaded those things are to be found which are necessary to the salvation of my soul. In this manner ecclesiastical liberty will be preserved on all sides, and no man will have a legislator imposed upon him, but whom himself has chosen.

But since men are so solicitous about the true church, I would only ask them here by the way, if it be not more agreeable to the church of Christ to make the conditions of her communion consist in such things, and such things only, as the Holy Spirit has in the Holy Scriptures declared, in express words, to be necessary to salvation? I ask, I say, whether this be not more agreeable to the church of Christ, than for men to impose their own inventions and interpretations upon others, as if they were of divine authority; and to establish by ecclesiastical laws, as absolutely necessary to the profession of Christianity, such things as the Holy Scriptures do either not mention, or at least not expressly command? Whosoever requires those things in order to ecclesiastical communion, which Christ does not require in order to life eternal, he may perhaps indeed constitute a society accommodated to his own opinion, and his own advantage; but how that can be called the church of Christ, which is established upon laws that are not his, and which excludes such persons from its communion, as he will one day receive into the kingdom of heaven, I understand not. But this being not a proper place to inquire into the marks of the true church, I will only mind those that contend so earnestly for the decrees of their own society, and that cry out continually the CHURCH, the CHURCH, with as much noise, and perhaps upon the same principle, as the Ephesian silversmiths did for their Diana; this, I say, I desire to mind them of, that the Gospel frequently declares, that the true disciples of Christ must suffer persecution; but that the church of Christ should persecute others, and force others by fire and sword to embrace her faith and doctrine, I could never yet find in any of the books of the New Testament.

The end of a religious society, as has already been said, is the public worship of God, and by means thereof the acquisition of eternal life. All discipline ought therefore to tend to that end, and all ecclesiastical laws to be thereunto confined. Nothing ought, nor can be transacted in this society, relating to the possession of civil and worldly goods. No force is here to be made use of, upon any occasion whatsoever: for force belongs wholly to the civil magistrate, and the possession of all outward goods is subject to his jurisdiction.

But it may be asked, by what means then shall ecclesiastical laws be established, if they must be thus destitute of all compulsive power? I answer, they must be established by means suitable to the nature of such things, whereof the external profession and observation, if not proceeding from a thorough conviction and approbation of the mind, is altogether useless and unprofitable. The arms by which the members of this society are to be kept within their duty, are exhortations, admonitions, and advice. If by these means the offenders will not be reclaimed, and the erroneous convinced, there remains nothing farther to be done, but that such stubborn and obstinate persons, who give no ground to hope for their reformation, should be cast out and separated from the society. This is the last and utmost force of ecclesiastical authority: no other punishment can thereby be inflicted, than that the relation ceasing between the body and the member which is cut off, the person so condemned ceases to be a part of that church.

These things being thus determined, let us inquire in the next place, how far the duty of Toleration extends, and what is required from every one by it.

And first, I hold, that no church is bound by the duty of Toleration to retain any such person in her bosom, as after admonition continues obstinately to offend against the laws of the society. For these being the condition of communion, and the bond of society, if the breach of them were permitted without any animadversion, the society would immediately be thereby dissolved. But nevertheless in all such cases care is to be taken that the sentence of excommunication, and the execution thereof, carry with it no rough usage, of word or action, whereby the ejected person may any ways be damnified in body or estate. For all force, as has often been said, belongs only to the magistrate, nor ought any private persons, at any time, to use force; unless it be in self-defence against unjust violence. Excommunication neither does nor can deprive the excommunicated person of any of those civil goods that he formerly possessed. All those things belong to the civil government, and are under the magistrate's protection. The whole force of excommunication consists only in this, that the resolution of the society in that respect being declared, the union that was between the body and some member, comes thereby to be dissolved; and that relation ceasing, the participation of some certain things which the society communicated to its members, and unto which no man has any civil right, comes also to cease. For there is no civil injury done unto the excommunicated person by the church minister's refusing him that bread and wine, in the celebration of the Lord's supper, which was not bought with his, but other men's money.

Secondly: no private person has any right in any manner to prejudice another person in his civil enjoyments, because he is of another church or religion. All the rights and franchises that belong to him as a man, or as a denison, are inviolably to be preserved to him. These are not the business of religion. No violence nor injury is to be offered him, whether he be christian or pagan. Nay, we must not content ourselves with the narrow measures of bare justice: charity, bounty, and liberality must be added to it. This the Gospel enjoins, this reason directs, and this that natural fellowship we are born into requires of us. If any man err from the right way, it is his own misfortune, no injury to thee: nor therefore art thou to punish him in the things of this life, because thou supposest he will be miserable in that which is to come.

What I say concerning the mutual toleration of private persons differing from one another in religion, I understand also of particular churches; which stand as it were in the same relation to each other as private persons among themselves; nor has any one of them any manner of jurisdiction over any other, no not even when the civil magistrate, as it sometimes happens, comes to be of this or the other communion. For the civil government can give no new right to the church, nor the church to the civil government. So that whether the magistrate join himself to any church, or separate from it, the church remains always as it was before, a free and voluntary society. It neither acquires the power of the sword by the magistrate's coming to it, nor does it lose the right of instruction and excommunication by his going from it. This is the fundamental and immutable right of a spontaneous society, that it has to remove any of its members who transgress the rules of its institution: but it cannot, by the accession of any new members, acquire any right of jurisdiction over those that are not joined with it. And therefore peace, equity, and friendship, are always mutually to be observed by particular churches, in the same manner as by private persons, without any pretence of superiority or jurisdiction over one another.

That the thing may be made yet clearer by an example; let us suppose two churches, the one of arminians, the other of calvinists, residing in the city of Constantinople. Will any one say, that either of these churches has the right to deprive the members of the other of their estates and liberty, as we see practised elsewhere, because of their differing from it in some doctrines or ceremonies; whilst the Turks in the mean while silently stand by, and laugh to see with what inhuman cruelty christians thus rage against christians? But if one of these churches hath this power of treating the other ill, I ask which of them it is to whom that power belongs, and by what right? It will be answered, undoubtedly, that it is the orthodox church which has the right of authority over the erroneous or heretical. This is, in great and specious words, to say just nothing at all. For every church is orthodox to itself; to others, erroneous or heretical. Whatsoever any church believes, it believes to be true; and the contrary thereunto it pronounces to be errour. So that the controversy between these churches about the truth of their doctrines, and the purity of their worship, is on both sides equal; nor is there any judge, either at Constantinople, or elsewhere upon earth, by whose sentence it can be determined. The decision of that question belongs only to the Supreme Judge of all men, to whom also alone belongs the punishment of the erroneous. In the mean while, let those men consider how heinously they sin, who, adding injustice, if not their errour, yet certainly to their pride, do rashly and arrogantly take upon them to misuse the servants of another master, who are not at all accountable to them. . . .

. . . Let us now consider what is the magistrate's duty in the business of toleration: which is certainly very considerable.

We have already proved that the care of souls does not belong to the magistrate: not a magisterial care, I mean, if I may so call it, which consists in prescribing by laws, and compelling by punishments. But a charitable care, which consists in teaching, admonishing, and persuading, cannot be denied unto any man. The care therefore of every man's soul belongs unto himself, and is to be left unto himself. But what if he neglect the care of his soul? I answer, what if he neglect the care of his health, or of his estate; which things are nearlier related to the government of the magistrate than the other? Will the magistrate provide by an express law, that such an one shall not become poor or sick? Laws provide, as much as is possible, that the goods and health of subjects be not injured by the fraud or violence of others; they do not guard them from the negligence or ill-husbandry of the possessors themselves. No man can be forced to be rich or healthful, whether he will or no. Nay, God himself will not save men against their wills. Let us suppose, however, that some prince were desirous to force his subjects to accumulate riches, or to preserve the health and strength of their bodies. Shall it be provided by law, that they must consult none but Roman physicians, and shall every one be bound to live according to their prescriptions? What, shall no potion, no broth, be taken, but what is prepared either in the Vatican, suppose, or in a Geneva shop? Or, to make these subjects rich, shall they all be obliged by law to become merchants, or musicians? Or, shall every one turn victualler, or smith, because there are some that maintain their families plentifully, and grow rich in those professions? But it may be said, there are a thousand ways to wealth, but one only way to heaven. It is well said indeed, especially by those that plead for compelling men into this or the other way; for if there were several ways that lead thither, there would not be so much as a pretence left for compulsion. But now, if I be marching on with my utmost vigour, in that way which, according to the sacred geography, leads straight to Jerusalem; why am I beaten and ill-used by others, because, perhaps, I wear not buskins; because my hair is not of the right cut; because, perhaps, I have not been dipt in the right fashion; because I eat flesh upon the road, or some other food which agrees with my stomach; because I avoid certain by-ways, which seem unto me to lead into briars or precipices; because, amongst the several paths that are in the same road, I choose that to walk in which seems to be the straightest and cleanest; because I avoid to keep company with some travellers that are less grave, and others that are more sour than they ought to be; or in fine, because I follow a guide that either is, or is not, cloathed in white, and crowned with a mitre? Certainly, if we consider right, we shall find that for the most part they are such frivolous things as these, that, without any prejudice to religion to the salvation of souls, if not accompanied with superstition or hypocrisy, might either be observed or omitted; I say, they are such like things as these, which breed implacable enmities among christian brethren, who are all agreed in the substantial and truly fundamental part of religion. . . .

But it will here be asked: If nothing belonging to divine worship be left to human discretion, how is it then that churches themselves have the power of ordering any thing about the time and place of worship, and the like? To this I answer; that in religious worship we must distinguish between what is part of the worship itself, and what is but a circumstance. That is a part of the worship which is believed to be appointed by God, and to be well pleasing to him; and therefore that is necessary. Circumstances are such things which though in general they cannot be separated from worship, yet the particular instances or modifications of them are not determined; and therefore they are indifferent. Of this sort are the time and place of worship, the habit and posture of him that worships. These are circumstances, and perfectly indifferent, where God has not given any express command about them. For example: Amongst the Jews, the time and place of their worship, and the habits of those that officiated in it, were not mere circumstances, but a part of the worship itself; in which if any thing were defective, or different from the institution, they could not hope that it would be accepted by God. But these, to christians under the liberty of the Gospel, are mere circumstances of worship which the prudence of every church may bring into such use as shall be judged most subservient to the end of order, decency, and edification. Though even under the Gospel also, those who believe the first, or the seventh day to be set apart by God, and consecrated still to his worship; to them that portion of time is not a simple circumstance, but a real part of divine worship, which can neither be changed nor neglected.

In the next place: As the magistrate has no power to impose by his laws the use of any rites and ceremonies in any church, so neither has he any power to forbid the use of such rites and ceremonies as are already received, approved, and practised by any church: because if he did so, he would destroy the church itself; the end of whose institution is only to worship God with freedom, after its own manner.

You will say, by this rule, if some congregations should have a mind to sacrifice infants, or, as the primitive christians were falsely accused, lustfully pollute themselves in promiscuous uncleanness, or practise any other such heinous enormities, is the magistrate obliged to tolerate them, because they are committed in a religious assembly? I answer, No. These things are not lawful in the ordinary course of life, nor in any private house; and therefore neither are they so in the worship of God, or in any religious meeting. But indeed if any people congregated upon account of religion, should be desirous to sacrifice a calf, I deny that that ought to be prohibited by a law. Meliboeus, whose calf it is, may lawfully kill his calf at home, and burn any part of it that he thinks fit. For no injury is thereby done to any one, no prejudice to another man's goods. And for the same reason he may kill his calf also in a religious meeting. Whether the doing so be well-pleasing to God or no, it is their part to consider that do it.—The part of the magistrate is only to take care that the commonwealth receive no prejudice, and that there be no injury done to any man either in life or estate. And thus what may be spent on a feast may be spent on a sacrifice. But if peradventure such were the state of things that the interest of the commonwealth required all slaughter of beasts should be forborn for some while, in order to the increasing of the stock of cattle, that had been destroyed by some extraordinary murrain; who sees not that the magistrate, in such a case, may forbid all his subjects to kill any calves for any use whatsoever? Only it is to be observed, that in this case the law is not made about a religious, but a political matter: nor is the sacrifice, but the slaughter of calves thereby prohibited.

By this we see what difference there is between the church and the commonwealth. Whatsoever is lawful in the commonwealth, cannot be prohibited by the magistrate in the church. Whatsoever is permitted unto any of his subjects for their ordinary use, neither can nor ought to be forbidden by him to any sect of people for their religious uses. If any man may lawfully take bread or wine, either sitting or kneeling, in his own house, the law ought not to abridge him of the same liberty in his religious worship; though in the church the use of bread and wine be very different, and be there applied to the mysteries of faith, and rites of divine worship. But those things that are prejudicial to the commonwealth of a people in their ordinary use, and are therefore forbidden by laws, those things ought not to be permitted to churches in their sacred rites. Only the magistrate ought always to be very careful that he do not misuse his authority, to the oppression of any church under pretence of public good.

It may be said, what if a church be idolatrous, is that also to be tolerated by the magistrate? In answer, I ask, what power can be given to the magistrate for the suppression of an idolatrous church, which may not, in time and place, be made use of to the ruin of an orthodox one? For it must be remembered, that the civil power is the same every where, and the religion of every prince is orthodox to himself. If therefore such a power be granted unto the civil magistrate in spirituals, as that at Geneva, for example; he may extirpate, by violence and blood, the religion which is there reputed idolatrous; by the same rule, another magistrate, in some neighbouring country, may oppress the reformed religion; and in India, the christian. The civil power can either change every thing in religion, according to the prince's pleasure, or it can change nothing. If it be once permitted to introduce any thing into religion by the means of laws and penalties, there can be no bounds put to it; but it will in the same manner be lawful to alter every thing, according to that rule of truth which the magistrate has framed unto himself. No man whatsoever ought therefore to be deprived of his terrestrial enjoyments, upon account of his religion. Not even Americans, subjected unto a christian prince, are to be punished either in body or goods for not embracing our faith and worship. If they are persuaded that they please God in observing the rites of their own country, and that they shall obtain happiness by that means, they are to be left unto God and themselves. Let us trace this matter to the bottom. Thus it is: an inconsiderable and weak number of christians, destitute of every thing, arrive in a pagan country; these foreigners beseech the inhabitants, by the bowels of humanity, that they would succour them with the necessaries of life; those necessaries are given them, habitations are granted, and they all join together and grow up into one body of people. The christian religion by this means takes root in that country, and spreads itself; but does not suddenly grow the strongest. While things are in this condition, peace, friendship, faith, and equal justice, are preserved amongst them. At length the magistrate becomes a christian, and by that means their party becomes the most powerful. Then immediately all compacts are to be broken, all civil rights to be violated, that idolatry may be extirpated: and unless these innocent pagans, strict observers of the rules of equity and the law of nature, and no ways offending against the laws of the society, I say unless they will forsake their ancient religion, and embrace a new and strange one, they are to be turned out of the lands and possessions of their forefathers, and perhaps deprived of life itself. Then at last it appears what zeal for the church, joined with the desire of dominion, is capable to produce: and how easily the pretence of religion, and of the care of souls, serves for a cloak to covetousness, rapine, and ambition.

Now whosoever maintains that idolatry is to be rooted out of any place by laws, punishments, fire, and sword, may apply this story to himself. For the reason of the thing is equal, both in America and Europe. And neither pagans there, nor any dissenting christians here, can with any right be deprived of their worldly goods, by the predominating faction of a court-church; nor are any civil rights to be either changed or violated upon account of religion in one place more than another.

But idolatry, say some, is a sin, and therefore not to be tolerated. If they said it were therefore to be avoided, the inference were good. But it does not follow, that because it is a sin it ought therefore to be punished by the magistrate. For it does not belong unto the magistrate to make use of his sword in punishing every thing, indifferently, that he takes to be a sin against God. Covetousness, uncharitableness, idleness, and many other things are sins, by the consent of all men, which yet no man ever said were to be punished by the magistrate. The reason is, because they are not prejudicial to other men's rights, nor do they break the public peace of societies. Nay, even the sins of lying and perjury are no where punishable by laws; unless in certain cases, in which the real turpitude of the thing and the offence against God, are not considered, but only the injury done unto men's neighbours, and to the commonwealth. And what if in another country, to a mahometan or a pagan prince, the christian religion seem false and offensive to God; may not the christians for the same reason, and after the same manner, be extirpated there?

FURTHER READING

Richard I. Aaron, *John Locke,* 3rd edn. (1971). A lucid survey of Locke's life and thought.

Maurice Cranston, *John Locke, A Biography* (1957). Uses unpublished papers, but is weak on Locke's ideas.

John W. Yolton, *John Locke and the Way of Ideas* (1956). An important analysis of Locke's radical reputation.

8 ❀ LOCKE

Some Thoughts Concerning Education

[From *The Works of John Locke,* 9 vols. (1824),
VIII, 6–12, 35–38.]

*John Locke returned to England in the wake of the successful
Glorious Revolution of 1688–89 which expelled the Catholic King
James II and brought to the English throne the Protestant pair
William and Mary.* Some Thoughts Concerning Education *(1693)
was one result of these later years of his life. It is a vivid expression
of the new philosophy that Locke was doing so much to foster. The
idea that children should be treated as children rather than as little
adults seems obvious now, but it was a drastic departure from
accepted doctrine in its time. Its way had been prepared by
Rabelais and Montaigne in the sixteenth century and by a handful
of seventeenth-century reformers, but Locke brought to it his customary good sense and ease of style. It is important to recognize that
Locke developed his pedagogical program in close conjunction with
his general philosophy: the* Essay Concerning Human Understanding, *which had appeared three years before the* Thoughts, *is its
epistemological and psychological counterpart. In both he stresses
the need to moderate one's expectations concerning knowledge in
the world, the significance of experience in shaping the child, a
general and still rather novel humaneness toward children, a flexible, undogmatic attitude to education as a transaction larger than
mere formal schooling, and the clear recognition of the need to
awaken the child's interest. "Where there is no desire, there will be
no industry." Jean-Jacques Rousseau, the great educational theorist
of the Enlightenment, would learn a great deal from this philosophy.*

§ 1.   A sound mind in a sound body, is a short but full description of a happy state in this world: he that has these two, has little more to wish for; and he that wants either of them, will be but little the better for any thing else. Men's happiness or misery is most part of their own making. He whose mind directs not wisely, will never take the right way; and he whose body is crazy and feeble, will never be able to advance in it. I confess, there are some men's constitutions of body and mind so vigorous, and well framed by nature, that they need not much assistance from others; but, by the strength of their natural genius, they are, from their cradles, carried towards what is excellent; and, by the privilege of their happy constitutions, are able to do wonders. But examples of this kind are but few; and I think I may say, that, of all the men we meet with, nine parts of ten are what they are, good or evil, useful or not, by their education. It is that which makes the great difference in mankind. The little, or almost insensible, impressions on our tender infancies, have very important and lasting consequences: and there it is, as in the fountains of some rivers, where a gentle application of the hand turns the flexible waters into channels, that make them take quite contrary courses; and by this little direction, given them at first, in the source, they receive different tendencies, and arrive at last at very remote and distant places.

§ 2.   I imagine the minds of children as easily turned, this or that way, as water itself; and though this be the principal part, and our main care should be about the inside, yet the clay cottage is not to be neglected. I shall therefore begin with the case, and consider first the health of the body, as that which perhaps you may rather expect, from that study I have been thought more peculiarly to have applied myself to; and that also which will be soonest despatched, as lying, if I guess not amiss, in a very little compass.

§ 3.   How necessary health is to our business and happiness, and how requisite a strong constitution, able to endure hardships and fatigue, is to one that will make any figure in the world, is too obvious to need any proof.

§ 4.   The consideration I shall here have, of health, shall be, not what a physician ought to do, with a sick or crazy child; but what the parents, without the help of physic, should do for the preservation and improvement of an healthy, or, at least, not sickly constitu-

LOCKE: *Some Thoughts Concerning Education* 91

tion, in their children: and this perhaps might be all despatched in this one short rule, viz. that gentlemen should use their children as the honest farmers and substantial yeomen do theirs. But because the mothers, possibly, may think this a little too hard, and the fathers, too short, I shall explain myself more particularly; only laying down this, as a general and certain observation for the women to consider, viz. that most children's constitutions are either spoiled, or at least harmed, by cockering and tenderness. . . .

§ 9. Another thing, that is of great advantage to every one's health, but especially children's, is to be much in the open air, and very little, as may be, by the fire, even in winter. By this he will accustom himself also to heat and cold, shine and rain; all which if a man's body will not endure, it will serve him to very little purpose in this world: and when he is grown up, it is too late to begin to use him to it: it must be got early and by degrees. Thus the body may be brought to bear almost any thing. If I should advise him to play in the wind and sun without a hat, I doubt whether it could be borne. There would a thousand objections be made against it, which at last would amount to no more, in truth, than being sun-burnt. And if my young master be to be kept always in the shade, and never exposed to the sun and wind, for fear of his complexion, it may be a good way to make him a beau, but not a man of business. And although greater regard be to be had to beauty in the daughters, yet I will take the liberty to say, that the more they are in the air, without prejudice to their faces, the stronger and healthier they will be; and the nearer they come to the hardships of their brothers in their education, the greater advantage will they receive from it, all the remaining part of their lives. . . .

§ 42. Thus much for the settling your authority over children in general. Fear and awe ought to give you the first power over their minds, and love and friendship in riper years to hold it: for the time must come, when they will be past the rod and correction; and then, if the love of you make them not obedient and dutiful; if the love of virtue and reputation keep them not in laudable courses; I ask, what hold will you have upon them, to turn them to it? Indeed, fear of having a scanty portion, if they displease you, may make them slaves to your estate; but they will be nevertheless ill and wicked in private, and that restraint will not last always. Every man must some time or other be trusted to himself, and his own conduct; and he that is a good, a virtuous, and able man, must be made so within. And therefore, what he is to receive from education, what is to sway and influence his life, must be something put into him betimes: habits woven into the very principles of his nature; and not a counterfeit carriage, and dissembled outside, put on by fear, only to avoid the present anger of a father, who perhaps may disinherit him.

§ 43. This being laid down in general, as the course ought to be taken, it is fit we come now to consider the parts of the discipline to be used, a little more particularly. I have spoken so much of carrying a strict hand over children, that perhaps I shall be suspected of not considering enough what is due to their tender age and constitutions. But that opinion will vanish, when you have heard me a little farther. For I am very apt to think, that great severity of punishment does but very little good; nay, great harm in education: and I believe it will be found, that, cæteris paribus, those children who have been most chastised, seldom make the best men. All that I have hitherto contended for, is, that whatsoever rigour is necessary, it is more to be used, the younger children are; and, having by a due application wrought its effect, it is to be relaxed, and changed into a milder sort of government.

§ 44. A compliance, and suppleness of their wills, being by a steady hand introduced by parents, before children have memories to retain the beginnings of it, will seem natural to them, and work afterwards in them, as if it were so; preventing all occasions of struggling, or repining. The only care is, that it be begun early, and inflexibly kept to, till awe and respect be grown familiar, and there appears not the least reluctancy in the submission and ready obedience of their minds. When this reverence is once thus established, (which it must be early, or else it will cost pains and blows to recover it, and the more, the longer it is deferred) it is by it, mixed still with as much indulgence as they made not an ill use of, and not by beating, chiding, or other servile punishments, they are for the future to be governed, as they grow up to more understanding.

§ 45. That this is so, will be easily allowed, when it is but considered what is to be aimed at, in an ingenuous education; and upon what it turns.

1. He that has not a mastery over his inclinations, he that knows not how to resist the importunity of present pleasure or pain, for the sake of what reason tells him is fit to be done, wants the true principle of virtue and industry; and is in danger of never being good for any thing. This temper, therefore, so contrary to unguided nature, is to be got betimes; and this habit, as the true foundation of future ability and happiness, is to be wrought into the mind, as

early as may be, even from the first dawnings of my knowledge or apprehension in children; and so to be confirmed in them, by all the care and ways imaginable, by those who have the oversight of their education.

§ 46. 2. On the other side, if the mind be curbed, and humbled too much in children; if their spirits be abased and broken much, by too strict an hand over them; they lose all their vigour and industry, and are in a worse state than the former. For extravagant young fellows, that have liveliness and spirit, come sometimes to be set right, and so make able and great men: but dejected minds, timorous and tame, and low spirits, are hardly ever to be raised, and very seldom attain to any thing. To avoid the danger that is on either hand is the great art: and he that has found a way how to keep up a child's spirit, easy, active, and free; and yet, at the same time, to restrain him from many things he has a mind to, and to draw him to things that are uneasy to him; he, I say, that knows how to reconcile these seeming contradictions, has, in my opinion, got the true secret of education.

§ 47. The usual lazy and short way by chastisement, and the rod, which is the only instrument of government that tutors generally know, or ever think of, is the most unfit of any to be used in education; because it tends to both those mischiefs; which, as we have shown, are the Scylla and Charybdis, which, on the one hand or the other, ruin all that miscarry.

§ 48. 1. This kind of punishment contributes not at all to the mastery of our natural propensity to indulge corporal and present pleasure, and to avoid pain at any rate; but rather encourages it; and thereby strengthens that in us, which is the root, from whence spring all vicious actions and the irregularities of life. From what other motive, but of sensual pleasure, and pain, does a child act, who drudges at his book against his inclination, or abstains from eating unwholesome fruit, that he takes pleasure in, only out of fear of whipping? He in this only prefers the greater corporal pleasure, or avoids the greater corporal pain. And what is it to govern his actions, and direct his conduct, by such motives as these? what is it, I say, but to cherish that principle in him, which it is our business to root out and destroy? And therefore I cannot think any correction useful to a child, where the shame of suffering for having done amiss does not work more upon him than the pain.

§ 49. 2. This sort of correction naturally breeds an aversion to that which it is the tutor's business to create a liking to. How obvious is it to observe, that children come to hate things which were at first acceptable to them, when they find themselves whipped, and chid, and teazed about them? And it is not to be wondered at in them; when grown men would not be able to be reconciled to any thing by such ways. Who is there that would not be disgusted with any innocent recreation, in itself indifferent to him, if he should with blows, or ill language, be hauled to it, when he had no mind? or be constantly so treated, for some circumstances in his application to it? This is natural to be so. Offensive circumstances ordinarily infect innocent things, which they are joined with: and the very sight of a cup, wherein any one uses to take nauseous physic, turns his stomach; so that nothing will relish well out of it, though the cup be ever so clean, and well-shaped, and of the richest materials.

§ 50.   3. Such a sort of slavish discipline makes a slavish temper. The child submits, and dissembles obedience, whilst the fear of the rod hangs over him; but when that is removed, and, by being out of sight, he can promise himself impunity, he gives the greater scope to his natural inclination; which by this way is not at all altered, but on the contrary heightened and increased in him; and after such restraint, breaks out usually with the more violence. Or,

§ 51.   4. If severity carried to the highest pitch does prevail, and works a cure upon the present unruly distemper, it is often bringing in the room of it worse and more dangerous disease, by breaking the mind; and then, in the place of a disorderly young fellow, you have a low-spirited moped creature: who, however with his unnatural sobriety he may please silly people, who commend tame inactive children, because they make no noise, nor give them any trouble; yet, at last, will probably prove as uncomfortable a thing to his friends, as he will be, all his life, an useless thing to himself and others.

§ 52.   Beating then, and all other sorts of slavish and corporal punishments, are not the discipline fit to be used in the education of those who would have wise, good, and ingenuous men; and therefore very rarely to be applied, and that only on great occasions, and cases of extremity. On the other side, to flatter children by rewards of things that are pleasant to them, is as carefully to be avoided. He that will give to his son apples, or sugar-plums, or what else of this kind he is most delighted with, to make him learn his book, does but authorise his love of pleasure, and cocker up that dangerous propensity, which he ought by all means to subdue and stifle in him. You can never hope to teach him to master it, whilst you compound for the check you give his inclination in one place, by the satisfaction you propose to it in another. To make a good, a wise, and a virtuous man, it is fit he should learn to cross his appetite, and deny his inclination to riches, finery, or pleasing his palate, &c. whenever his reason advises the contrary, and his duty requires it. But when you draw him to do any thing that is fit, by the offer of money; or reward the pains of learning his book, by the pleasure of a luscious morsel; when you promise him a lace-cravat, or a fine new suit, upon performance of some of his little tasks; what do you, by proposing these as rewards, but allow them to be the good things he should aim at, and thereby encourage his longing for them, and accustom him to place his happiness in them? Thus people, to prevail with children to be industrious about their grammar, dancing, or some other such matter, of no great moment to the happiness or usefulness of their lives, by misapplied rewards and punishments, sacrifice their virtue, invert the order of their education, and teach them luxury, pride, or covetousness, &c. For in this way, flattering those wrong inclinations, which they should restrain and suppress, they lay the foundations of those future vices, which cannot be avoided, but by curbing our desires, and accustoming them early to submit to reason. . . .

§ 54. But if you take away the rod on one hand, and these little encouragements, which they are taken with, on the other; how then (will you say) shall children be governed? Remove hope and fear, and there is an end of all discipline. I grant, that good and evil, reward and punishment, are the only motives to a rational creature; these are the spur and reins, whereby all mankind are set on work and guided, and therefore they are to be made use of to children too. For I advise their parents and governors always to carry this in their minds, that children are to be treated as rational creatures.

§ 56. The rewards and punishments then whereby we should keep children in order are quite of another kind; and of that force, that when we can get them once to work, the business, I think, is done, and the difficulty is over. Esteem and disgrace are, of all others, the most powerful incentives to the mind, when once it is brought to relish them. If you can once get into children a love of credit, and an apprehension of shame and disgrace, you have put into them the true principle, which will constantly work, and incline them to the right. . . .

§ 161. When he can write well, and quick, I think it may be convenient, not only to continue the exercise of his hand in writing, but also to improve the use of it farther in drawing, a thing very useful to a gentleman on several occasions, but especially if he travel, as that which helps a man often to express, in a few lines well put together, what a whole sheet of paper in writing would not be able to represent and make intelligible. How many buildings may a man see, how many machines and habits meet with, the ideas whereof would be easily retained and communicated by a little skill in drawing; which, being committed to words, are in danger to be lost, or at best but ill retained in the most exact descriptions? I do not mean that I would have your son a perfect painter; to be that to any tolerable degree, will require more time than a young gentleman can spare from his other improvements of greater moment; but so much insight into perspective, and skill in drawing, as will enable him to represent tolerably on paper any thing he sees, except faces, may, I think, be got in a little time, especially if he have a genius to it: but where that is wanting, unless it be in the things absolutely necessary, it is better to let him pass them by quietly, than to vex him about them to no purpose: and therefore in this, as in all other things not absolutely necessary, the rule holds, "Nihil invita Minerva."*

§ 162. As soon as he can speak English, it is time for him to learn some other language: this nobody doubts of, when French is proposed. And the reason is, because people are accustomed to the right way of teaching that language, which is by talking it into children in constant conversation, and not by grammatical rules. The Latin tongue would easily be taught the same way, if his tutor, being constantly with him, would talk nothing else to him, and make him answer still in the same language. But because French is a living language, and to be used more in speaking, that should be first learned, that the yet pliant organs of speech might be accustomed to a due formation of those sounds, and he get the habit of pronouncing French well, which is the harder to be done the longer it is delayed.

§ 163. When he can speak and read French well, which in this method is usually in a year or two, he should proceed to Latin, which it is a wonder parents, when they have had the experiment in French, should not think ought to be learned the same way, by talking and reading. Only care is to be taken, whilst he is learning these foreign languages, by speaking and reading nothing else with his tutor, that he do not forget to read English, which may be

---

* The full line, from Horace's *Ars poetica*, 385, reads: "*Tu nihil invita dices faciesve Minerva*" ("You will neither say nor do anything if Minerva is unwilling," i.e., if it goes against your natural inclinations) .—P. G.

preserved by his mother, or somebody else, hearing him read some chosen parts of the scripture or other English book, every day.

§ 164. Latin I look upon as absolutely necessary to a gentleman; and indeed custom, which prevails over every thing, has made it so much a part of education, that even those children are whipped to it, and made spend many hours of their precious time uneasily in Latin, who, after they are once gone from school, are never to have more to do with it, as long as they live. Can there be any thing more ridiculous, than that a father should waste his own money, and his son's time, in setting him to learn the Roman language, when, at the same time, he designs him for a trade, wherein he, having no use of Latin, fails not to forget that little which he brought from school, and which it is ten to one he abhors for the ill usage it procured him? Could it be believed, unless we had every where amongst us examples of it, that a child should be forced to learn the rudiments of a language, which he is never to use in the course of life that he is designed to, and neglect all the while the writing a good hand, and casting accounts, which are of great advantage in all conditions of life, and to most trades indispensably necessary? But though these qualifications, requisite to trade and commerce, and the business of the world, are seldom or never to be had at grammar-schools; yet thither not only gentlemen send their younger sons intended for trades, but even tradesmen and farmers fail not to send their children, though they have neither intention nor ability to make them scholars. If you ask them, why they do this? they think it as strange a question, as if you should ask them why they go to church? Custom serves for reason, and has, to those that take it for reason, so consecrated this method, that it is almost religiously observed by them; and they stick to it, as if their children had scarce an orthodox education, unless they learned Lilly's grammar.*

§ 165. But how necessary soever Latin be to some, and is thought to be to others, to whom it is of no manner of use or service, yet the ordinary way of learning it in a grammar-school, is that, which having had thoughts about, I cannot be forward to encourage. The reasons against it are so evident and cogent, that they have prevailed with some intelligent persons to quit the

---

* William Lily, or Lilye (c. 1468–1522), intimate of Thomas More and Erasmus, a fine Greek and Latin scholar, appointed by Colet the first high master of St. Paul's School in 1510. His *Brevissima institutio,* corrected by Erasmus, became a famous Latin grammar that continued to be used in Locke's time and after.— P. G.

ordinary road, not without success, though the method made use of was not exactly that which I imagine the easiest, and in short is this: to trouble the child with no grammar at all, but to have Latin, as English has been, without the perplexity of rules, talked into him; for, if you will consider it, Latin is no more unknown to a child, when he comes into the world, than English: and yet he learns English without master, rule, or grammar: and so might he Latin too, as Tully* did, if he had somebody always to talk to him in this language. And when we so often see a Frenchwoman teach an English girl to speak and read French perfectly, in a year or two, without any rule of grammar, or any thing else, but prattling to her; I cannot but wonder, how gentlemen have overseen this way for their sons, and thought them more dull or incapable than their daughters. . . .

FURTHER READING

J. W. Adamson, *Pioneers of Modern Education, 1600–1700* (1905) . Though old, still very useful.

Peter Gay, ed., John Locke, *Some Thoughts Concerning Education* (1964) . See Introduction for a brief evaluation.

Nina Reicyn, *La Pédagogie de John Locke* (1941) . A solid study.

* Marcus Tullius Cicero (106–43 B.C.) , familiarly called Tully by educated Englishmen through the eighteenth century, a mark of the high esteem in which Cicero was held.—P. G.

9 ❊ LOCKE

On the Reform of the Poor Laws

[From H. R. Fox Bourne, *The Life of John Locke,* 2 vols. (1876), II, 377–85.]

Locke's contributions to liberal political theory are as decisive as those to the theory of knowledge and of education. His celebrated two Treatises of Government, *though written before, were both published in 1690, and thus appeared as a defense of the Glorious Revolution of 1688. They could be so used, but Locke had originally written them to justify, not the expulsion of King James II, but rather James' exclusion from the English throne in the first place. The first* Treatise *is a detailed and devastating assault on the* Patriarcha *of Sir Robert Filmer, an extreme royalist tract that had been published posthumously in 1680 and created a considerable stir with its advocacy of absolute royal power entirely founded on the analogy of the authority a father must have over his children. Locke had little trouble demolishing Filmer's logic; in his second essay in political theory, the* Treatise of Civil Government, *he set up a positive theory of his own. Locke posited a state of nature that men give up for the advantages of civil society, but their voluntary submission to the overarching power of the state gives them certain rights of their own. There are circumstances when the authorities violate the social contract under which they govern, and forfeit the right to exact obedience. Locke was not an irresponsible revolutionary; just as he believed that the state must have enough power to govern in the first place, he believed that the provocation to assert one's original liberty must be great before rebellion becomes valid.*

Locke, then, was a liberal and a proponent of the right to rebellion. His theory of education, as we have seen, was equally advanced. But Locke must not be read as a modern democrat, let alone a revolutionary. Like other educated men of his day, he made a drastic distinction between gentlemen and poor. The problem that was to haunt the philosophes in the eighteenth century, how to integrate the "lower orders" into the scheme of general enlightenment, was not a problem for Locke: each social stratum had its proper place. This view, so characteristic of its time (and so important for us in demonstrating the problems the Enlightenment would have to face), is well expressed by a report that Locke wrote in 1697 in his capacity as a commissioner of trade and plantations. Nothing illustrates more vividly than these excerpts the distance separating the late seventeenth century from ours, and the certainties of the "pre-Enlightenment" from the problems of the Enlightenment.

The multiplying of the poor, and the increase of the tax for their maintenance, is so general an observation and complaint that it cannot be doubted of. . . .

If the causes of this evil be well looked into, we humbly conceive it will be found to have proceeded neither from scarcity of provisions nor from want of employment for the poor, since the goodness of God has blessed these times with plenty no less than the former, and a long peace during those reigns gave us as plentiful a trade as ever. The growth of the poor must therefore have some other cause, and it can be nothing else but the relaxation of discipline and corruption of manners; virtue and industry being as constant companions on the one side as vice and idleness are on the other.

The first step, therefore, towards the setting of the poor on work, we humbly conceive, ought to be a restraint of their debauchery by a strict execution of the laws provided against it, more particularly by the suppression of superfluous brandy shops and unnecessary alehouses, especially in country parishes not lying upon great roads.

Could all the able hands in England be brought to work, the greatest part of the burden that lies upon the industrious for maintaining the poor would immediately cease. For, upon a very moderate computation, it may be concluded that above one half of those who receive relief from the parishes are able to get their livelihood. And all of them who receive such relief from the parishes, we conceive, may be divided into these three sorts.

First, those who can do nothing at all towards their own support.

Secondly, those who, though they cannot maintain themselves wholly, yet are able to do something towards it.

Thirdly, those who are able to maintain themselves by their own labour. And these last may be again subdivided into two sorts; namely, either those who have numerous families of children whom they cannot or pretend they cannot support by their labour, or those who pretend they cannot get work and so live only by begging or worse.

For the suppression of this last sort of begging drones, who live unnecessarily upon other people's labour, there are already good and wholesome laws, sufficient for the purpose, if duly executed. We therefore humbly propose that the execution thereof may be at present revived by proclamation till other remedies can be provided; as also that order be taken every year, at the choosing of churchwardens and overseers of the poor, that the statutes of the 39th Eliz., cap. 4, and the 43rd Eliz., cap. 2* be read and considered, paragraph by paragraph, and the observation of them in all their parts pressed on those who are to be overseers; for we have reason to think that the greatest part of the overseers of the poor everywhere are wholly ignorant, and never so much as think that it is the greatest part, or so much as any part, of their duty to set people to work.

But for the more effectual restraining of idle vagabonds, we further humbly propose that a new law may be obtained, by which it be enacted,

That all men sound of limb and mind, above fourteen and under fifty years of age, begging in maritime counties out of their own parish without a pass, shall be seized on either by any officer of the parish where they so beg (which officers by virtue of their offices shall be authorised, and under a penalty required to do it), or by the inhabitants of the house themselves where they beg, and be by them or any of them brought before the next justice of the peace or guardian of the poor (to be chosen as hereafter mentioned) who in this case shall have the power of a justice of the peace, and, by such

* The former of these acts provided for the erection of houses of correction and the due punishment of vagabonds therein. The latter is the famous statute on which our poor laws are based, directing that there shall be overseers of the poor in every parish, empowered, conjointly with the justices of the peace, to levy poor's rates, set the able-bodied poor to work, provide for impotent paupers, apprentice out pauper children, and so forth.—H. R. F. B. (1876).

justice of the peace or guardian of the poor (after the due and usual correction in the case), be by a pass sent, not to the house of correction (since those houses are now in most counties complained of to be rather places of ease and preferment to the masters thereof than of correction and reformation to those who are sent thither), nor to their places of habitation (since such idle vagabonds usually name some remote part, whereby the county is put to great charge, and they usually make their escape from the negligent officers before they come thither and are at liberty for a new ramble), but, if it be in a maritime county as aforesaid, that they be sent to the next seaport town, there to be kept at hard labour, till some of his majesty's ships, coming in or near there, give an opportunity of putting them on board, where they shall serve three years, under strict discipline, at soldier's pay (subsistence money being deducted for their victuals on board), and be punished as deserters if they go on shore without leave, or, when sent on shore, if they either go further or stay longer than they have leave.

That all men begging in maritime counties without passes, that are maimed or above fifty years of age, and all of any age so begging without passes in inland counties nowhere bordering on the sea, shall be sent to the next house of correction, there to be kept at hard labour for three years. . . .

That whoever shall counterfeit a pass shall lose his ears for the forgery the first time that he is found guilty thereof, and the second time that he shall be transported to the plantations, as in case of felony.

That whatever female above fourteen years old shall be found begging out of her own parish without a pass (if she be an inhabitant of a parish within five miles' distance of that she is found begging in) shall be conducted home to her parish by the constable, tithing-man, overseer of the poor, churchwarden, or other sworn officer of the parish wherein she was found begging, who, by his place and office, shall be required to do it and to deliver her to the overseer of the poor of the parish to which she belongs, from whom he shall receive twelvepence for his pains, which twelvepence, if she be one that receives public relief, shall be deducted out of her parish allowance, or, if she be not relieved by the parish, shall be levied on her or her parents' or her master's goods.

That, whenever any such female above fourteen years old, within the same distance, commits the same fault a second time, and whenever the same or any such other female is found begging without a lawful pass, the first time, at a greater distance than five miles from the place of her abode, it shall be lawful for any justice of the peace or guardian of the poor, upon complaint made, to send her to the house of correction, there to be employed in hard work three months, and so much longer as shall be to the next quarter-sessions after the determination of the said three months, and that then, after due correction, she have a pass made her by the sessions to carry her home to the place of her abode.

That, if any boy or girl, under fourteen years of age, shall be found begging out of the parish where they dwell (if within five miles' distance of the said parish), they shall be sent to the next working school, there to be soundly whipped and kept at work till evening, so that they may be dismissed time enough to get to their place of abode that night. Or, if they live further than five miles off from the place where they are taken begging, that they be sent to the next house of correction, there to remain at work six weeks and so much longer as till the next sessions after the end of the said six weeks.

These idle vagabonds being thus suppressed, there will not, we suppose, in most country parishes, be many men who will have the pretence that they want work. However, in order to the taking away of that pretence, whenever it happens, we humbly propose that it may be further enacted,

That the guardian of the poor of the parish where any such pretence is made, shall, the next Sunday after complaint made to him, acquaint the parish that such a person complains he wants work, and shall then ask whether any one is willing to employ him at a lower rate than is usually given, which rate it shall then be in the power of the said guardian to set; for it is not to be supposed that any one should be refused to be employed by his neighbours whilst others are set to work, but for some defect in his ability or honesty, for which it is reasonable he should suffer, and he that cannot be set on work for twelvepence per diem, must be content with ninepence or tenpence rather than live idly. But, if nobody in the parish voluntarily accept such a person at the rate proposed by the guardians of the poor, that then it shall be in the power of the said guardian, with the rest of the parish, to make a list of days, according to the proportion of every one's tax in the parish to the poor, and that, according to such list, every inhabitant in the same parish shall be obliged, in their turn, to set such unemployed poor men of the same parish on work, at such under-rates as the guardians of the poor shall appoint; and, if any person refuse to set

the poor at work in his turn as thus directed, that such person shall
be bound to pay them their appointed wages, whether he employ
them or no.

That, if any poor man, otherwise unemployed, refuse to work
according to such order (if it be in a maritime county), he shall be
sent to the next port, and there put on board some of his majesty's
ships, to serve there three years as before proposed; and that what
pay shall accrue to him for his service there, above his diet and
clothes, be paid to the overseers of the poor of the parish to which
he belongs, for the maintenance of his wife and children, if he have
any, or else towards the relief of other poor of the same parish; but,
if it be not in a maritime county, that every poor man thus refusing
to work shall be sent to the house of correction. . . .

But the greatest part of the poor maintained by parish rates are
not absolutely unable nor wholly unwilling to do anything towards
the getting of their livelihoods; yet even these, either through want
of fit work provided for them, or their unskilfulness in working in
what might be a public advantage, do little that turns to any
account, but live idly upon the parish allowance or begging, if not
worse. Their labour, therefore, as far as they are able to work,
should be saved to the public, and what their earnings come short
of a full maintenance should be supplied out of the labour of
others, that is, out of the parish allowance.

These are of two sorts:—

1. Grown people, who, being decayed from their full strength,
could yet do something for their living, though, under pretence that
they cannot get work, they generally do nothing. In the same case
with these are most of the wives of day labourers, when they come to
have two or three or more children. The looking after their children gives them not liberty to go abroad to seek for work, and so,
having no work at home, in the broken intervals of their time they
earn nothing; but the aid of the parish is fain to come in to their
support, and their labour is wholly lost; which is so much loss to the
public.

Every one must have meat, drink, clothing, and firing. So much
goes out of the stock of the kingdom, whether they work or no.
Supposing then there be a hundred thousand poor in England, that
live upon the parish, that is, who are maintained by other people's
labour (for so is every one who lives upon alms without working),
if care were taken that every one of these, by some labour in the
woollen or other manufacture, should earn but a penny per diem

(which, one with another, they might well do and more), this would gain to England £130,000 per annum, which, in eight years, would make England above a million of pounds richer.

This, rightly considered, shows us what is the true and proper relief of the poor. It consists in finding work for them, and taking care they do not live like drones upon the labour of others. And in order to this end we find the laws made for the relief of the poor were intended; however, by an ignorance of their intention or a neglect of their due execution, they are turned only to the maintenance of people in idleness, without at all examining into the lives, abilities, or industry of those who seek for relief.

In order to the suppression of these idle beggars, the corporations in England have beadles authorised and paid to prevent the breach of the law in that particular; yet, nevertheless, the streets everywhere swarm with beggars, to the increase of idleness, poverty, and villany, and to the shame of Christianity. And, if it should be asked in any town in England, how many of these visible trespassers have been taken up and brought to punishment by those officers this last year, we have reason to think the number would be found to have been very small, because that of beggars swarming in the street is manifestly very great.

But the remedy of this disorder is so well provided by the laws now in force that we can impute the continuance and increase of it to nothing but a general neglect of their execution.

2. Besides the grown people above mentioned, the children of labouring people are an ordinary burden to the parish, and are usually maintained in idleness, so that their labour also is generally lost to the public till they are twelve or fourteen years old.

The most effectual remedy for this that we are able to conceive, and which we therefore humbly propose, is, that, in the forementioned new law to be enacted, it be further provided that working schools be set up in every parish, to which the children of all such as demand relief of the parish, above three and under fourteen years of age, whilst they live at home with their parents, and are not otherwise employed for their livelihood by the allowance of the overseers of the poor, shall be obliged to come.

By this means the mother will be eased of a great part of her trouble in looking after and providing for them at home, and so be at the more liberty to work; the children will be kept in much better order, be better provided for, and from infancy be inured to work, which is of no small consequence to the making of them sober and industrious all their lives after; and the parish will be either eased of this burden or at least of the misuse in the present management of it. For, a great number of children giving a poor man a title to an allowance from the parish, this allowance is given once a week or once a month to the father in money, which he not seldom spends on himself at the alehouse, whilst his children, for whose sake he had it, are left to suffer, or perish under the want of necessaries, unless the charity of neighbours relieve them.

We humbly conceive that a man and his wife in health may be able by their ordinary labour to maintain themselves and two children. More than two children at one time under the age of three years will seldom happen in one family. If therefore all the children above three years old be taken off from their hands those who have never so many, whilst they remain themselves in health, will not need any allowance for them.

We do not suppose that children of three years old will be able at that age to get their livelihoods at the working school, but we are sure that what is necessary for their relief will more effectually have that use if it be distributed to them in bread at that school than if it be given to their fathers in money. What they have at home from their parents is seldom more than bread and water, and that, many of them, very scantily too. If therefore care be taken that they have each of them their belly-full of bread daily at school, they will be in no danger of famishing, but, on the contrary, they will be healthier and stronger than those who are bred otherwise. Nor will this practice cost the overseers any trouble; for a baker may be agreed with to furnish and bring into the school-house every day the allowance of bread necessary for all the scholars that are there. And to this may be also added, without any trouble, in cold weather, if it be thought needful, a little warm water-gruel; for the same fire that warms the room may be made use of to boil a pot of it.

From this method the children will not only reap the forementioned advantages with far less charge to the parish than what is now done for them, but they will be also thereby the more obliged to come to school and apply themselves to work, because otherwise they will have no victuals, and also the benefit thereby both to themselves and the parish will daily increase; for, the earnings of their labour at school every day increasing, it may reasonably be concluded that, computing all the earnings of a child from three to fourteen years of age, the nourishment and teaching of such a child during that whole time will cost the parish nothing; whereas there is no child now which from its birth is maintained by the parish but, before the age of fourteen, costs the parish 50£ or 60£.

Another advantage also of bringing children thus to a working school is that by this means they may be obliged to come constantly to church every Sunday, along with their schoolmasters or dames, whereby they may be brought into some sense of religion; whereas ordinarily now, in their idle and loose way of breeding up, they are as utter strangers both to religion and morality as they are to industry.

In order therefore to the more effectual carrying on of this work to the advantage of this kingdom, we further humbly propose that these schools be generally for spinning or knitting, or some other part of the woollen manufacture, unless in countries [districts] where the place shall furnish some other materials fitter for the employment of such poor children; in which places the choice of those materials for their employment may be left to the prudence and direction of the guardians of the poor of that hundred. And that the teachers in these schools be paid out of the poor's rate, as can be agreed. . . .

FURTHER READING

John Dunn, *The Political Thought of John Locke: An Historical Account of the Argument of the 'Two Treatises of Government'* (1969). A controversial and interesting reading of Locke's intentions.

J. W. Gough, *John Locke's Political Philosophy* (1950). A collection of sensible essays.

C. B. Macpherson, *The Political Theory of Possessive Individualism: Hobbes to Locke* (1962). A Marxist interpretation, stimulating but hardly defensible.

Raymond Polin, *La Politique Morale de John Locke* (1960). A brilliant treatise.

IO ❧ BAYLE

Dictionnaire historique et critique

[From *The Dictionary Historical and Critical of
Mr. Peter Bayle*, 4 vols., 2nd ed. (1734–38),
III, 670–71.]

*One of the greatest teachers of the Enlightenment in manner as well
as matter was the eloquent seventeenth-century skeptic Pierre Bayle
(1647–1706). Born of a French Protestant family, Bayle briefly
embraced Roman Catholicism, but then returned to his original
Protestantism—though with a difference: in all his writings he
stressed not what men could know but what they could not know.
The themes of man's universal and indefeasible ignorance, paired
with their logical corollary, the need for forbearance and toleration,
dominate all of Bayle's work. The increasing pace of persecution of
French Huguenots in the later years of Louis XIV's reign drove
Bayle into exile in the Dutch Republic; there he continued the
immense scholarly productivity he had already displayed at home.*

*It is possible to read Bayle's philosophy as a type of humble
religiosity, fideism, which throws itself on the Divine mercy in
despair of ever finding certainty by purely human means. This
indeed is how Bayle has recently been read. But to the philosophes,
Bayle was above all a skeptic and the supreme adversary of superstition and fanaticism. They admired him almost as much as they
admired Newton, which is to say enormously. Bayle, Holbach said,
is that celebrated man "who teaches so well how to doubt."* The
philosophes read all of his writings, chiefly his* Pensées sur la comète
*(1682), which inveighs against the credulous terror widespread after
the appearance of Halley's comet of 1680, and his vast and sly
compendium, the* Historical and Critical Dictionary, *published in*

---

* Holbach, *Système de la nature*, 2 vols. (1770), II, 356n.

its first edition in 1697. Voltaire's Dictionnaire philosophique* *owes much to Bayle's bulky* Dictionary. *Hence it is not surprising that one pious journal, the* Bibliothèque germanique, *should say in some alarm in 1729: "The works of M. Bayle have unsettled a large number of readers and have cast doubt on some of the most widely accepted principles of morality and religion."† However we may estimate Bayle today, to the men of the Enlightenment he was the author, above all, of the article on Pyrrho, that ancient skeptic who held all convictions in suspension, and the great doubter who had revived for modern times Plutarch's remark that atheism is less damaging to the state than superstition—a "paradox," Gibbon wrote appreciatively, that "acquires a tenfold vigour when it is adorned with the colors of his wit, and pointed with the acuteness of his logic."‡*

The essay that follows is one of the shorter articles from Bayle's celebrated Dictionary, *presented in its entirety. It offers in brief compass some of Bayle's favorite tricks: his use of ponderous notes to disarm the reader with his learning, his placement of the most subversive of his information in footnotes, and his sly disavowal of convictions he wants to propagate.*

KNUZEN (Matthias) a native of the country of Holstein (a), arrived to such a degree of extravagancy, as publickly to maintain Atheism, and undertook great journies to gain proselytes. He was a restless man, who discovered his impieties first at Konigsberg in Prussia (b). He boasted, that he had a great number of persons of his opinion in the principal towns of Europe [A],

(a) Oldensworta Eiderstadiensis. *Moller. Isagoge ad Histor. Cherson. Cimbr. Part. III,* pag. 164.

(b) Tobias Pfannerus, *Systemata Theologiae gentilis,* pag. 35.

[A] *He boasted, that he had a great number of persons of his opinion in the principal towns of Europe.* These are his words. 'Nemo homo mihi vitio vertet, si una cum meis gregalibus, (quorum innumerus mihi numerus Lutetiae, Amstelodami, Lugduni, in Anglia, Hamburgi, Hasniae, nec non Holmiae, imo Romae & in contiguis locis adstipulatur)

* See below, selection 19.
† Quoted in Paul Hazard, *The European Mind: 1680–1715* (1963) , 114.
‡ *Autobiography,* ed. Dero A. Saunders (1961) , 89.

(1) Apud Micraelium
Syntagm. Histor.
Eccles. pag. 2291. Edit.
1699.

universa Biblio bellae fabellae loco habeam, qua belluae, id est, Christiani, rationem captivantes, & cum ratione insanientes delectantur (1) .— *No one will impute it to me as a crime, if, with my companions (an infinite number of whom, at Paris, Amsterdam, Leyden, in England, at Hamburgh, Copenhagen, Stockholm, and even at Rome, and the adjacent places, agree with me in opinion)* I look upon the whole Bible as a fine invented tale, *with which the beasts, that is the Christians, captivating their reason, and running reason-mad, are delighted.'* We must not imagine, that he used the stratagem of state-conspirators, who, to bring more people over to their party, always pretend they have a vast number of accomplices. It is more probable he spoke in this manner, because that he was a hair-brained fool.

(c) *See, below, citat.*
(4).

and even seven hundred in the single town of Iëna (c). His sect was called the Conscientiaries, because he said, there was no other God, religion, or lawful magistracy, than conscience, which teaches all men the three precepts of Justice, *to do no injury, to live honestly, and give every one his due.* He drew up a summary of his system, in a short letter, of which several copies were spread [B]. It is dated from Rome. You will find

(2) Haec epistola plus
millies descripta est.
Micrael ubi infra.

[B] *He drew up a summary of his system in a short letter, of which several copies were spread* (2). Micraelius's continuator has reduced the contents of that letter to six articles. 'I. Non esse Deum neque Diabolum. II. Magistratum nihil aestimandum, templa contemnenda, Sacerdotes rejiciendos. III. Loco Magistratus & loco Sacerdotum esse scientam & rationem cum conscientia conjunctam, quae doceat honeste vivere, neminem laedere, & suum cuique tribuere. IV. Conjugium à scortatione nihil differre. V. Unicam esse vitam: post hanc nec praemium nec poenam

(3) Micrael. Syntagm.
Hist. Eccles. pag. 2289.
Edit. 1699.

dari. VI. Scripturam sacram secum ipsam pugnare (3). — *I. That there is neither God, nor Devil. II. That the magistrates are to be looked upon as nothing, the churches are to be despised, and the priests rejected. III. That knowledge and reason, together with conscience, which teaches to live honestly, to hurt no body, and give every one his own, is in the room of magistrates and priests. IV. That there is no difference between marriage and whoring. V. That there is but one life: that after the present there is neither reward nor punishment. VI. That the Scripture contradicts itself.'* This system, besides its horrible impiety is also plainly extravagant; for one must be stark mad, to believe that mankind can subsist without magistrates. It is true, they would not be necessary, if all men would follow the dictates of conscience, which this impious man exhibits to us; but are they followed even in those countries, where the judges punish, with the greatest severity, the injustice done to our neighbour? I do not know but it may be said, that there is no impertinence, be it never so extravagant, but may teach us some truth or other. The follies of this German shew us, that the ideas of natural religion, the ideas of virtue, the impressions of reason, in a word, the light of conscience, may subsist in the mind of man, even after the ideas of the existence of God, and the firm belief of a life to come, are extinguished in it.

it entire in the last editions of Micraelius. He dispersed also some German writings (*d*). All this was confuted in the same tongue, by John Musaeus, a Lutheran professor [*C*]. This sect began about the year 1673.

[*C*] *He was confuted by John Musaeus, a Lutheran professor.* The author I have this from, observes, that Musaeus engaged in this work, to remove all suspicions that might be entertained to the disadvantage of the university of Iëna: for this wretched man had boasted of abundance of associates there (4). That book of Musaeus contains a great many ridiculous things, concerning the life of this spark; but, if you would have a solid apology for the scripture against the blasphemies of this man, you must have recourse to the second edition. And if you understand High-Dutch, consult, as Mr Mollerus advises (5), the book, which he names (6), and observe his reflexion. He says, that if people continue to make their enemies suspected of Atheism, as the author of this piece with a hasty zeal, and mixed with his passions, has done, they will afford matter enough to Mr Christian Thomasius, who is about an apology for those, who have been unjustly exposed to such accusations. The author of several Thoughts upon Comets has insinuated (7) the design of such a work, and given a curious idea of it. But let Mr Mollerus's words inform us of the malignity of such sort of accusers. 'Quo in opere optandum esset ut Theol. celeberrimus (*Jo. Mullerus Antistes Hamb.*) fuo in Antagonistas odio minus indulsisset, nec per insignem animi impotentiam, Schuppii τᾶ μακαρίτα Demegorias, piis omnibus commendatissimas, & Christ. Hoburgii, ad extremum Atheismo contrarium, superstitionem sc. & Enthusiasmum, proclivioris, scripta collo obtorto iis, quae Atheismum vel occultant, vel quadamtenus promovent, aggregasset. Certe, si zelo hujusmodi praecipiti, privatisque affectibus obnoxio, Theologi Atheomastiges sibi invisos in suspicionem impietatis Atheismo affinis pergent adducere, vereor ne calamo Christ. Thomasii ᾠαῤῥησιασιασικῷ, Gabr. Naudaei (qui magiae reis est patrocinatus) exemplo apologiam pro Atheismi falso insimulatis

(*d*) Mollerus, ubi supra, p. 165.

(4) Blasphemiis fuis. . . . in folo oppido Jenensi 700 cives atque studiosos falso jactabat adstipulari. *Mollerus, Isagoge ad Histor. Cherson. Cimbr. Part. III*, pag. 166.

(5) Ib. pag. 167.
(6) Atheismus devictus. *It was printed in the year 1672. The author calls himself Jo. Mullerus,* Antistes Hamburgensis.

(7) *In the preface to the Addition printed at Rotterdam,* 1694.

(8) Mollerus, ibid.

parturienti campus se pandat amplissimus innocentiam illorum, cum hominum cordatorum applausu, vindicandi (8) . — *In which work, it were to be wished, that the famous divine, John Mollerus, Antistes at Hamburgh, had less indulged his hatred towards his adversaries, and had not perversely, ranked among the writers, who conceal Atheism, or in some measure promote it, the* Demegoriae *of Schuppius, so acceptable to pious men, and the works of Christopher Hoburgius, who is more inclined to superstition and enthusiasm, the very reverse of Atheism. Certainly, if the divines, who write against Atheism go through such a rash and partial zeal, to charge with atheistical principles those whom they hate, I fear, lest, after the example of Gabriel Naudé, who defended those accused of Magic, the free pen of Christopher Thomasius may find ample occasion to justify, with the approbation of all sensible men, the innocence of those, who are falsely accused of Atheism.'*

A book was printed against Knuzen at Wittemberg in the year 1677 [*D*].

(9) *Intituled,* Introductio in Historiam Ecclesiasticam, pag. 879. *It was printed in* 1694, in 4*to*.

[*D*] *A book was printed against Knuzen at Wittemberg in 1677.* The title of it is, *Exercitationes Academicae II de Atheismo* Renato des Cartes & Matthiae Knuzen *oppositae. Autore* Valentino Greissingio Corona-Transsylvano *Elector. Saxon. alumno.* This I have from a book of Caspar Sagittarius (9) .

FURTHER READING

W. H. Barber, "Pierre Bayle: Faith and Reason," in Will Moore *et al.*, eds., *The French Mind: Studies in Honour of Gustave Rudler* (1952) , 109–25. Sees Bayle as essentially religious; a persuasive (though not wholly persuasive) essay.

Paul Dibon, ed., *Pierre Bayle: Le philosophe de Rotterdam* (1959). Contains important articles on many aspects of Bayle's thought.

Élisabeth Labrousse, *Pierre Bayle*, 2 vols.: *Du Pays de Foix à la cité d'Érasme* (1963), *Hétérodoxie et rigorisme* (1964). Splendidly scholarly biography that stresses Bayle's commitment to toleration.

Howard Robinson, *Bayle the Skeptic* (1931). Though now old, this interpretative biography holds up well as the most convincing statement of Bayle's essential unbelief.

II ❋ TILLOTSON

Of the Necessity of Good Works

[From Sermon CCVI, "Of the Necessity of
Good Works," in *The Works of Dr. John
Tillotson*, 10 vols. (1820), VIII, 558–61.]

*I insisted in the Introduction that the Enlightenment was at once
the name for a movement of philosophes and for a general cultural
atmosphere: the philosophes had many allies, most of them involuntary, to advance the work of rationalizing the world. Notable
among such allies were the English Latitudinarians, a group of
Anglican divines intent on proving the reasonableness of Christianity and thus making it acceptable to reasonable men. These
liberal theologians emphasized in their sermons man's excellent
chances for salvation and man's share in making that salvation
possible. The Latitudinarians cheerfully dispensed with most of the
usual baggage of piety; they made light of ritual and pushed the
question of miracles to one side. As the English poet Edward Young
summarized this easy Christianity, religion is essentially "the Proof
of Common Sense."*

*Most notable among the English Latitudinarians was John Tillot-
son (1630–1694) who in the last three years of his life held the
highest post the Anglican Church can bestow: the Archbishopric of
Canterbury. Many of the philosophes had their way to religious
unbelief eased by his optimistic, bland, rational sermons. From
Tillotson's claim that "the laws of God are reasonable" and command "nothing that is severe and against the grain of our nature"**
it was but one rapid step to deism—a step that many philosophes
took with ease. The passage that follows illustrates this kind of
tepid, pleasing, altogether unstrenuous religious thought.*

* "His commandments are not grievous," quoted in Norman Sykes, *Church
and State in England in the XVIIIth Century* (1934), 258–59.

I. If we consider the great end and design of religion in general, which is to make us happy, by possessing our minds with the belief of a God, and those other principles which have a necessary connexion with that belief; and by obliging us to the obedience and practice of his laws.

1. By possessing our minds with the belief of God, and of those other principles which have a necessary connexion with it. Such are the belief of the Divine perfections, of the infinite goodness, and wisdom, and power, and truth, and justice, and purity of the Divine nature; a firm persuasion of his providence, that he governs and administers the affairs of the world, and takes notice of the actions of men, and will call them to an account for them; of the immortality of our souls, and their endless duration after death, and consequently of the eternal rewards and punishments of another life. These are the great principles of natural religion, which mankind are in some measure possessed with, and persuaded of, without any external revelation from God; and these are necessary and fundamental to religion, as the apostle to the Hebrews declares: (Heb. xi. 6.) "Without faith it is impossible to please God;" that is, there can be no such thing as the practice of religion, without the belief of the principles of it; and what these are he tells us in the next words: "He that cometh to God, must believe that he is, and that he is a rewarder of them that diligently seek him."

But then we must not rest here, in the belief of a God and the principles of religion; for this faith is not required of us for itself, but in order to some farther end, which if it be not attained by us, the mere belief of the principles of religion is to no purpose, neither acceptable to God, nor useful and beneficial to ourselves. God would not have imprinted the notion of himself upon our nature, he would not have discovered himself to us, nor have required of us the belief of his being and providence, merely that we might know there is such a being as God in the world, who made us and governs us; but that this belief might have its proper influence upon us, to oblige us to the obedience of his laws, which are the proper causes and means of our happiness. It will not avail us at all, nor is it in the least acceptable to God, for men "to profess that they know him," when "in works they deny him, being abominable and disobedient, and to every good work reprobate," as the apostle describes some. (chap. i. 16) And therefore,

2. The great end and design of religion is, that our minds being possessed and prepared by the principles of religion, the belief of these should have its proper influence upon us, which is effectually to oblige us to the obedience and practice of God's laws. Now the laws which God hath given us to live by, as they are the rule and measure of our duty, by the performance whereof only we can hope to gain the favour of God, so they are the proper directions and means in order to our happiness; they teach us both the conditions of our happiness, and the proper qualification and disposition for it.

Obedience to the laws of God is the condition of our happiness, both temporal and eternal, both in this world and the other. The promises which God hath made of temporal felicity and blessings, are upon condition of our obedience to his laws; it is godliness only that hath the promise of this life as well as the other. (1 Tim. iv. 8) A truth so certain and evident, that the apostle thought fit to add that solemn seal to it which he prefaceth to the saying in the text, "This is a faithful saying." And though God be pleased, out of his excessive goodness, to bestow many temporal blessings and favours upon very bad men, that by this goodness of his he might lead them to repentance; yet God never made any promise of temporal blessings to wicked men; but, on the contrary, hath threatened them with great temporal evils and calamities; but all the promises, even of temporal good things, are made to the obeying of God's laws; "to them that keep his covenant, and remember his commandments to do them."

And this is not only the condition upon which the promises of temporal blessings are suspended, but generally, and for the most part, the natural cause and means of those blessings; for there is no moral duty enjoined by God, no virtue, the practice whereof he requires from us, which does not naturally tend to our temporal felicity in this world; as temperance and chastity to that invaluable blessing of health, and to the preservation of our estate, which is wasted by lewd and riotous living; humility and meekness to our quiet and safety; justice and integrity to our reputation and honour, one of the chief instruments of temporal prosperity and success. Kindness and charity, and a readiness to do good to all men as we have opportunity, are in their nature apt to recommend us exceedingly to the love and esteem of all men, and to their favourable regard and assistance, when we stand in need of it. And so, I might instance in all other virtues, the sincere practice whereof, though it be not in all cases certain and infallible, yet it is the best and wisest course that any man can take, to attain the greatest happiness which this world can afford, and to avoid the greatest miseries and calamities of it: as, on the contrary, there is no vice, no wicked practice, but is naturally productive of some great temporal mischief and inconvenience.

And then the practice of virtue and goodness, as it is the absolute and indispensable condition of our future happiness in another world, so is it the necessary and only proper qualification for it, and the certain and infallible means of attaining it.

FURTHER READING

Thomas Birch, ed., *Works of Tillotson*, 3 vols. (1752). Includes a biography.

Louis G. Locke, *Tillotson: A Study in Seventeenth Century Literature* (1954). Usefully concentrates on Tillotson's style.

Norman Sykes, *Church and State in England in the Eighteenth Century* (1934). Deservedly a classic.

————, *From Sheldon to Secker: Aspects of English Church History, 1660–1768* (1959). Another in the series of distinguished volumes Sykes wrote to illuminate the religious thought and institutions of the century.

II

Three Classics

While the essential ideas of the Enlightenment were adumbrated in England, the battleground on which these ideas were first tested was France. Even Rousseau, Genevan by birth, on whose mind Geneva retained its hold all his life, wrote most of his books in France and participated vigorously in the debates among French men of letters.

For this reason, some comments on France in the first half of the eighteenth century are in place here—the philosophes, after all, lived very much in the world. Cosmopolitan as they were, Montesquieu, Voltaire and the rest defined their thought in part by their affectionate study of the ancients, in part by their English reading and visits, but in largest part by experiencing the France of their day.

Louis XIV, that overwhelming, almost mythical figure who had dominated French domestic and diplomatic decisions for half a century, died in 1715. His successor, Louis XV, was a child of five, and a regency was inevitable. Equally inevitable was a reaction against the Sun King's unremitting efforts at governmental centralization. The Parlement of Paris, France's most powerful court, which Louis XIV had done much to reduce to obedience, cooperated with the dissolute Regent, Philippe of Orléans, to break the dead king's will and restore the authority of the French aristocracy. The old families, the "nobility of the sword," joined with more recent arrivals, the "nobility of the robe," to reassert their traditional share in the making (or, all too often, the sabotaging) of legislation. Much of French history in the first half of the eighteenth century—indeed, into its second half, right to the outbreak of the French Revolution—was a great contest between royal administrators and resistant nobility. The issue was not simply power, but power over money: since the privileged two orders, the Church and the nobility, escaped practically all imposts, the questions who had the authority to tax and who should bear the burden of taxation were of critical importance. One instructive incident showing the way the winds of power were blowing came in 1750, when Machault, the king's chancellor, imposed a five percent tax, the so-called vingtième, *on all orders. Louis XV at first supported the tax, but in 1751, under great pressure from the Church and the pious members of his own entourage, he deserted his minister and the offensive impost was dropped.*

France, with all its troubles, was a great power; boasting as it did more than twenty million inhabitants, a mighty army, and impressive natural resources, its interventions in Europe had to be taken with the utmost seriousness. Much like England, France under Louis XV first sought peace; the king's aged tutor, Cardinal Fleury, who was in effect Louis XV's first minister from 1726 practically to his death in 1743, managed to keep France out of most wars. Then, in 1741, much against Fleury's will, the French entered the War of the Austrian Succession on the side of Prussia, and the military conflicts of mid-century had begun.

There was much to satirize in a country like France—witness Montesquieu's celebrated early effort, The Persian Letters. *And there was, in contrast, much to admire abroad—witness Voltaire's* Philosophical Letters on the English. *The form these two books took shows the tension between some of France's leading intellectuals and the state: a cumbersome, complex, often irrational system of censorship prevented the expression of some opinions, but not of all. The rules of the game were clear and known to all: if criticism was voiced indirectly, suavely, and by someone with good connections, it might bring not prison but preferment. Rousseau scorned such compromises. But his career showed that the reward for total candor was isolation and, all too often, flight. In short, the philosophes' demands for freedom of speech and the press were deeply felt and deeply personal demands which, in the turbulent political life of eighteenth-century France, acquired general significance.*

FURTHER READING

Alfred Cobban, *A History of Modern France, 1715–1799,* Vol. I, 3rd edn. (1963).
    Compact, lucid, extremely informative.
Franklin L. Ford, *Robe and Sword: The Regrouping of the French Aristocracy
    after Louis XIV* (1953). An important analysis of the political coalescence of
    French nobles after 1715.
Robert Forster, *The Nobility of Toulouse in the Eighteenth Century: A Social*

and Economic Study (1960). A short but illuminating study of the French nobility in one urban center.

Pierre Goubert, *Louis XIV and Twenty Million Frenchmen* (tr. 1970). A valuable modern analysis of the political, economic, and social background out of which the France of the Enlightenment emerged.

John McManners, *French Ecclesiastical Society under the Ancien Régime: A Study of Angers in the Eighteenth Century* (1960). Though ostensibly narrow in scope, this classic study of a single cathedral town sheds much light on all of eighteenth-century France.

12 ❀ MONTESQUIEU

Lettres persanes

[From *The Persian Letters*, by Montesquieu,
translated by J. Robert Loy.*]

*If one is inclined to play the game of ranking writers, one might
advance the name of Montesquieu as the most influential writer of
the eighteenth century.* His essay in social satire, The Persian
Letters, *left its mark on French literature; his masterpiece,* The
Spirit of the Laws, *left its mark on all of Western civilization—on
French philosophes, on Scottish social scientists, on American
statesmen.*†

*Charles de Secondat, Baron de La Brède et de Montesquieu, was
born in 1689, of an old noble family with ties both to the nobility of
the sword and to that of the robe. Educated in the Oratorian* collège
*at Juilly, he, like the other philosophes, picked up a strong classical
education, and acquired his passion for classical philosophy, notably Stoicism, at school; some of his earliest literary efforts were a
eulogy on Cicero and a remarkable essay on the "religious politics"
of the ancient Romans: even as a young man he was interested in
the manner in which a political elite—here the Roman patriciate—
exploited the credulity of the lower orders for purposes of domination. "Antiquity," he noted, "enchants me."‡ This enchantment
lasted Montesquieu's lifetime.*

*Between 1705 and 1713, Montesquieu studied law, first at Bor-
deaux near his parental estate, then at Paris, where he underwent
his legal apprenticeship and made his first connections with social*

* Translation copyright © 1961 by Meridian Books, Inc. Reprinted by permission of the World Publishing Company.
† See below, selection 39, for excerpts and for biographical notes on his later
years.
‡ *Pensées*, in *Oeuvres complètes*, ed. André Masson, 3 vols. (1950–55), II, 37.

circles holding advanced, that is to say, irreligious, ideas. In 1716, Montesquieu inherited the judicial office of président à mortier *in the* parlement *(the sovereign court) of his region. In the French Old Regime, most offices, including high posts in the army and the judiciary, were private property; they could be bought and sold, and handed down in wills. Supporters of royal centralization condemned this "venality of office"—a survival from the early seventeenth century, the product of the French crown's desperate search for money. Supporters of the powers of the French aristocracy, on the other hand, welcomed this so-called venality as a safeguard against royal "despotism." Montesquieu, himself a beneficiary of this aristocratic system, supported it wholeheartedly and (as we shall see later) even gave it theoretical foundations in his* Spirit of the Laws.

But Montesquieu was something far better than a parasite on the system or an apologist for his caste. He did his legal duties to the best of his considerable capacities and his admittedly limited interests. For his real interest lay in observation, in travel, in writing. The Persian Letters, *published in 1721 and begun during his incumbency as* président à mortier *in Bordeaux, shows his real bent. The book made him famous, gave him entrée to the high society of Regency Paris, and, in 1728, a coveted seat in the Académie Française. It is a cross-cultural dialogue; Montesquieu imagines two Persians traveling in France and sending home their observations. The notion of criticizing domestic affairs by inventing the response of aliens was not a new one. But Montesquieu used a traditional form with new effect; he is more pointed, more interesting, and wittier, than his predecessors. The criticisms he expressed in* The Persian Letters *were casual: it moves lightly from subject to subject, it describes and denounces abuses with a certain amusement. The time for sustained analysis came later, with* The Spirit of the Laws. *Yet it will not do to take the social criticism of* The Persian Letters *too lightly; wit and humor are also weapons, and in a system in which serious criticism is barred they may be the best weapons at hand. Montesquieu's open detestation of cruelty and superstition and slavery were signs of, and weapons for, the Enlightenment.*

LETTER XXIX

Rica to Ibben in Smyrna

The Pope is the head of the Christians. He is an old idol worshiped out of habit. Formerly he was to be feared even by kings, for he deposed them as easily as our magnificent sultans depose the kings of Imirette and Georgia. But now he is no longer feared. He claims that he is the successor of one of the first Christians, who is called Saint Peter, and his is most certainly a rich succession, for he has immense treasures and a great country under his domination.

Bishops are lawyers subordinate to him, and they have, under his authority, two quite different functions. When they are assembled together they create, as does he, articles of faith. When they are acting individually they have scarcely any other function except to give dispensation from fulfilling the law. For you must know that the Christian religion is weighed down with an infinity of very difficult practices. And since it has been decided that it is less easy to fulfill these duties than to have bishops around who can dispense with them, this last alternative was chosen out of a sense of common good. In this way, if you don't wish to keep Ramadan, if you don't choose to be subjected to the formalities of marriage, if you wish to break your vows, if you would like to marry in contravention of the prohibitions of the law, even sometimes if you want to break a sworn oath—you go to the bishop or the Pope and you are given immediate dispensation.

Bishops do not create articles of faith by their own decision. There are countless doctors, most of them dervishes, who introduce among themselves thousands of new questions touching upon religion. They are allowed to dispute at great length, and the war goes on until a decision comes along to finish it.

And thus I can assure you that there never has been a kingdom where there are so many civil wars as in the Kingdom of Christ.

Those who propose some new proposition are called at first *heretics.* Each heresy has its own name, and this name becomes for those who are involved, something like a rallying cry. But no one has to be a heretic. One needs only split the difference in half and give some distinction to those who make accusations of heresy, and whatever the distinction—logical or not—it makes a man white as snow, and he may have himself called *orthodox.*

What I am telling you is valid for France and Germany, for I have heard it said that in Spain and Portugal there are certain dervishes who stand for no nonsense and will have a man burned as if he were straw. When people fall into the hands of those fellows, happy is he who has always prayed to God with little wooden beads in his hand, who has worn on his person two strips of cloth attached to two ribbons, or who has at some time been in a province called Galicia. Without that, the poor devil is in bad straits. Even should he swear like a pagan that he is orthodox, they might quite possibly disagree with him on his qualifications and burn him for a heretic. He could talk all he likes of distinctions to be made—there is no distinction, for he would be in ashes before they even considered listening to him.

Other judges assume that an accused man is innocent until proved guilty; these judges always assume him guilty. When in doubt, they have as their rule always to decide on the side of severity, apparently because they believe men to be bad. But then, from another point of view, they have such a good opinion of men that they never judge them capable of lying, for they receive the testimony of professed enemies, of women of evil repute, of those who ply an infamous profession. In their sentences they include a little compliment for those clad in the brimstone shirt by telling them that they are very vexed to see them so badly dressed, that they as judges are gentle people and abhor blood and are truly grieved to have condemned them. However, to console their grief, they confiscate all the property of these wretches to their own advantage.

Happy the land inhabited by the sons of the prophets! These sad spectacles are unknown there. The holy religion brought to that land by the angels is protected by its very truth; it needs none of these violent means to preserve itself.

From Paris, the 4th of the
Moon of Shalval, 1712

LETTER LX

Usbek to Ibben at Smyrna

You ask if there are any Jews in France. Know that wherever there is money, there are Jews. You ask me what they do. Exactly what they do in Persia: nothing can be so alike as an Asian Jew and a European Jew.

They make show among Christians, just as among us, of an invincible obstinacy in favor of their religion—an obstinacy that assumes the proportions of folly.

The Jewish religion is an old trunk that has produced two branches that have covered the earth; I mean Mohammedanism and Christianity. Or rather, it is a mother who has borne two daughters who have inflicted a thousand wounds upon her, for in matters of religion, those nearest to each other are the greatest enemies. But however bad the treatment she has received from them, she never ceases to glorify herself for having brought them into the world. She uses the two of them to embrace the whole world, while, on another plane, her venerable age embraces all time.

The Jews consider themselves, therefore, as the wellspring of all holiness and the origin of all religion. They look upon us, in contrast, as heretics who have changed the law, or rather as rebel Jews.

If the change had taken place gradually, they believe they would have been easily seduced. But as it took place suddenly and violently, and since they can mark the day and the hour of both births, they take offense at finding in us measured ages, and they hold firm to a religion that even the creation of the world did not antedate.

They have never known in Europe a calm similar to that they now enjoy. Christians are beginning to cast off that spirit of intolerance by which they were once animated. They found themselves in bad straits for having expelled the Jews from Spain, and in France they suffered for having harassed Christians whose belief differed a bit from that of the Prince. They have realized that the zeal for advancement of religion is different from the attachment one should have for it and that to love and observe one's religion, it is not necessary to hate and persecute those who do not observe it.

It would be desirable for our Mussulmans to think with as much common sense on that score as the Christians, and it would be desirable also for them to manage to make peace between Ali and abu-Bakr and to leave to God the problem of deciding on the relative merits of those holy prophets. I should like them to be honored by acts of veneration and respect, and not by vain show of preference, and I should like to see us deserve their favor whatever place God has assigned them, be it to the right or under the footstool of his throne.

From Paris, the 18th of the
Moon of Saphar, 1714

LETTER LXVIII

Rica to Usbek in ——

The other day I went to dinner at the home of a man of law who had several times invited me. After conversing with him on many subjects, I said to him: "Sir, your profession strikes me as being a very troublesome one."

"Not as much so as you might think," he replied. "The way we go about it, it is simple fun."

"But don't you always have your head jammed full with other people's troubles? Are you not always occupied with things that are not the slightest bit interesting?"

"You are right," he replied, "these things are not interesting to us at all, for we ourselves take not the slightest interest in them, and by that very reason our profession is not as tiring as you say."

When I saw that he was taking the matter so lightheartedly, I said: "Sir, I have never seen your office."

"I should think not, for I haven't any. When I took this practice, I needed money to pay for it. I sold my library, and the bookdealer left me, out of a tremendous number of volumes, with only my account book. Not that I miss them; we judges don't stuff ourselves with empty knowledge. What do we need with all those law books? Practically all the cases are hypothetical and do not conform to the general rule."

"But couldn't that be, sir, because you make them cease to conform to any general rule? For, after all, why should there exist laws among all the peoples of the world if they did not have a practical application? And how can you apply them if you don't know what they are?"

"If you knew the law court," replied my magistrate, "you would not be talking as you are. We possess living books, that is to say, lawyers. They work for us and are responsible for instructing us."

"And aren't they sometimes also responsible for deceiving you?" I rejoined. "You would do well to protect yourselves against their snares. They have arms with which they attack your justice. It would be a good thing for you to have some to defend it, a good thing not to go lightly dressed to battle people armed to the teeth."

From Paris, the 13th of the
Moon of Shahban, 1714

LETTER LXXV

Usbek to Rhedi in Venice

I must confess that I have not noticed in Christians that lively conviction of religion which obtains among the Mohammedans. There is much distance with them between profession of faith and belief, between belief and conviction, and between conviction and practice. Religion is less a matter of holiness than an excuse for dispute, open to everyone. Courtiers, warriors, even women, rise up against ecclesiastics and demand that the churchmen prove what they are resolved never to believe. It's not a question of their being determined by reason, nor is it a case of their having taken the trouble to examine the truth or falsehood of the religion they reject: these are rebels who have felt the yoke and shake it off before getting to know it. Thus they are no more certain of their disbelief than they are of their belief. They exist in an ebb and flow that carries them endlessly from one to the other. One of them told me one day: "I believe in the immortality of the soul by interval; my opinions are absolutely dependent on my physical constitution. Accordingly, as I possess more or less animal spirits, or as my stomach digests well or badly, as the air I breathe is fine or raw, as the food I eat is light or heavy, I am a Spinozist, a Socinian, a Catholic, a heathen, or a devout man. When the doctor is at my bedside, the confessor finds me much more cooperative. I know perfectly well how to keep religion from plaguing me when I feel well. But I allow it to console me when I am sick. When, in a given direction, I have nothing more to hope for, religion appears and wins me over with its promises. I am quite willing to give myself over to it and die on the side of hope."

A long time ago Christian princes freed all their slaves from servitude because, they said, Christianity makes all men equal. It is true that this act of religion was very useful to them: they thereby humbled the great lords, from whose power they retrieved the common masses. Subsequently, they made conquests in countries where they saw it was to their advantage to have slaves; they allowed the buying and selling of them, oblivious of the principle of their religion which had so touched them. How shall I put it? Truth in one era, falsehood in another. Why do we not do as the Christians! We are quite simple-minded to refuse business establishments and easy conquests in benign climates only because the water there is not sufficiently pure to allow us to wash according to the principles of the holy Koran!

I render thanks unto the all-powerful God, who sent Ali, his great prophet, that I profess a religion that comes first before all human concerns, and that is as pure as the heaven from which it descended.

From Paris, the 13th of the
Moon of Saphar, 1715

LETTER LXXVI

Usbek to his friend Ibben in Smyrna

European laws are merciless against those who take their own lives. They are made to die, so to speak, a second time. They are infamously dragged through streets; they are covered with ignominy; their possessions are confiscated.

It seems to me, Ibben, that such laws are quite unjust. When I am overwhelmed with grief, misfortune, scorn, why should they want to prevent me from putting an end to my troubles, and why cruelly deprive me of a remedy that lies in my own hands?

Why should they want me to go on working for a society of which I am no longer willing to be a part? Why should they insist, despite my feelings, that I hold to a convention that has been made without my consent? Society is founded on mutual benefit. But when it becomes a burden to me, who can keep me from renouncing it? Life was granted to me as a favor; therefore I can give it back when it is no longer one. The cause stops; the effect should therefore stop too.

Shall the prince desire that I be his subject when I receive no advantage from such subjection? Can my fellow citizens demand the unjust sharing of their utility and my despair? Can God, different from all other benefactors, wish to condemn me to accepting favors that overwhelm me?

I am obliged to follow the laws when I live under them. But when I no longer live under them, can they still bind me?

But, you will say, you are disturbing the order of providence. God has united your soul and your body and you are separating them. You are opposing his plan and you are resisting him.

What does all that mean? Am I disturbing the order of providence when I change the modifications of matter and square a ball which the primal laws of movement—that is to say, the laws of creation and conservation of matter—have made round? Certainly not, for I am only using a right given to me, and in this sense, I can disturb all of nature as much as I please without being told that I am obstructing providence.

When my soul is separated from my body, will there be less order and less arrangement in the universe? Do you believe that this new combination will be less perfect and less dependent on general laws? Do you think the world has lost something thereby? Or that the works of God will be less great, or, rather, less immense?

Do you believe that my body, having turned into an ear of grain, or a worm, or a piece of turf, will have turned into a work of nature less worthy of her? Do you think that my soul, cut off from everything earthly it once possessed, has become less sublime?

All these ideas, my dear Ibben, have no other source than our pride. We do not feel our insignificance, and come what may, we want to be of value in the universe, to figure in it, to be an important object in it. We imagine that the destruction of a being as perfect as ourselves would debase the whole of nature, and we cannot conceive that one man more or one man less in this world—what am I saying?—that all of mankind together, a hundred million earths like our own, are but a thin and tenuous atom that God perceives only because of the vastness of his knowledge.

From Paris, the 15th of the
Moon of Saphar, 1715

LETTER LXXXIV

Rica to ——

Yesterday I visited the Invalides. If I were a prince, I should like to have built that establishment every bit as much as to have won three battles. Everywhere in that building the hand of a great monarch is to be seen. I believe that it is the place most worthy of respect on the earth.

What a sight to see gathered together in the same place all these victims of their country, who draw breath only to defend it, and who, feeling the same spirit if not the same strength, complain only of their present inability to sacrifice themselves again for it.

What can be more admirable than to see these weakened warriors observe in their retirement a discipline as exacting as if they were forced to it by the presence of an enemy? What more admirable than to see them seek their final satisfaction in this image of war and to divide heart and mind between the duties of religion and the duties of warfare.

I should like to see the names of those who die for country preserved in temples and inscribed in registers that would become, as it were, the wellspring of glory and nobility.

From Paris, the 15th of the
Moon of Gemmadi I, 1715

LETTER LXXXV

Usbek to Mirza in Ispahan

You know, Mirza, that some of Shah Suleiman's ministers had formed the plan of forcing all Armenians in Persia to leave the realm or become Mohammedans, with the idea in mind that our empire would always be polluted as long as it kept the heathen in our midst.

Persian greatness would have come to an end if blind religious devotion had had its way on that occasion.

It is not known why the project failed: neither those who proposed it nor those who rejected it ever knew the train of events. Chance fulfilled the office of reason and policy, and saved the empire from a greater peril than it would have been exposed to by the loss of a battle and the capture of two cities.

By proscribing the Armenians, they were within an ace of destroying, in one single day, all the businessmen and almost all the artisans of the realm. I am sure that the great Shah Abbas would rather have had both arms cut off than have signed such an order, and that he would have considered sending his most industrious subjects to the Mogul and other kings of the Indies tantamount to giving them half of his states.

The persecutions made by our zealous Mohammedans at the expense of the Ghebers forced the latter to migrate en masse to the Indies, and thus deprived Persia of that people so diligent in husbandry that, by itself, it was in a position to conquer the sterility of our soil.

There remained only this second attempt for religious devotion to fall back on: that is, to destroy industry, in consequence of which the empire would have fallen apart of its own accord, and along with it, of necessity, the very religion that the zealots wanted to make so flourishing.

If I must reason straightforwardly, Mirza, I'm not sure that it wouldn't be a good thing for a state to have several religions.

It can be seen that those who live in religions that are only tolerated usually make themselves more helpful to their country than those living under the majority religion, and this because, shut off from official honors and able to distinguish themselves only by their opulence and wealth, they are motivated to acquire the latter by their hard work and to take over the most distasteful chores of society.

Moreover, since every religion contains some precepts useful to society, it is right that each should be observed with devotion. Now, what could be better calculated to animate such devotion than the multiplicity of religions?

Religions are rivals willing to forgive nothing. Their jealous pride comes down even to the individuals involved: each man is on his guard and is afraid of doing anything to dishonor his party or expose it to the scorn and unforgivable censure of the opposite party.

Thus, it has always been noted that introducing a new sect into a state was the surest way of correcting the excesses of an older one.

People can say what they will about it not being to the prince's best interest to have several religions in his state. If every sect in the whole world were to forgather there, such a turn would do him no harm, for there is not one of them that does not prescribe obedience and preach submission.

I admit that history books are filled with wars of religion. But let us pay closer attention: it is certainly not the multiplicity of religions that produced such wars, it is, rather, the spirit of intolerance which animated the one that believed itself in the majority.

It is the spirit of proselytization, which the Jews have caught from the Egyptians, and which has passed from them, like a common epidemic, to the Mohammedans and to the Christians.

It is, in fine, a spirit of intoxication, the progress of which can be counted only a total eclipse of human reason.

For, finally, were there no inhumanity involved in tyrannizing the conscience of others, even were there no ill effects germinating hundredfold therefrom, a man would still have to be mad to think of doing so. The man who wants to make me change my religion is doing so only because he would most certainly not change his own, even if someone tried to force him to. Thus, he finds it strange that I should not do something he would not do himself, even perhaps for the mastery of the whole world.

From Paris, the 26th of the
Moon of Gemmadi I, 1715

LETTER XCIV

Usbek to Rhedi in Venice

I have never heard people discuss public law without beginning by searching carefully for the origin of societies—which strikes me as ridiculous. If men never formed any societies, if they abandoned each other and fled each other's company, we should have to ask the reason for this and search out why they stand off from each other. But they are all mutually bound one to the other. A son is born in his father's proximity, and he stays there. There's your society and your reason for society.

International law is better known in Europe than in Asia. Nonetheless, it can be said that the passions of princes, the patience of peoples, and the fawning of writers have served to corrupt all its principles.

This law, such as it exists today, is a science that teaches princes just how far they can violate justice without jeopardizing their own interests. What an aim, Rhedi, to want to erect injustice into a system, to give the rules of the system, form its principles, and accordingly draw forth consequences—and all that in order to harden their consciences!

The unlimited power of our sublime sultans, which knows no other law than its own, produces no greater number of monsters than that unworthy art which hopes to bend to its will justice, rigidly inflexible though it may be.

One might say, Rhedi, that there exist two quite different justices: one that regulates individual affairs and that reigns in civil affairs, another that settles differences between nation and nation and that tyrannizes over public law—as if public law were not itself a form of civil law, not, in truth, of a particular country, but of the world.

On all this, I shall explain my views further in another letter.

From Paris, the 1st of the
Moon of Zilhage, 1716

LETTER XCV

Usbek to the same

Magistrates should administer justice between citizen and citizen. Each nation should administer justice between itself and another nation. In this second meting out of justice, no other principles can be used save those obtaining in the first.

Between nation and nation, a third party is rarely necessary as judge, for the terms of dispute are almost always clear and easy to conclude. The interests of the two nations are usually so different that one need only love justice to be able to find it. One can hardly be prejudiced for one's own cause.

This is not the case in conflicts arising between particular parties. Since they are living together in society, their interests are so mixed and confused, there are so many different kinds of interests, that a third party is necessary to disentangle what the selfish desires of the interested parties try to obscure.

There are only two kinds of just wars: those waged to repel an attacking enemy and those that result from coming to the assistance of an attacked ally.

There would be no justification for waging war over the personal quarrels of a prince unless the offense were so serious that it justified the death of the prince of the nation that committed it. Thus a prince cannot wage war because an honor due to him has been refused, or because some questionable procedure has been used with his ambassadors, or by reason of similar complaints—no more so than an individual can kill another who refuses him priority. The reason for this is, since a declaration of war should be an act of justice in which the punishment should always be in proportion to crime, one must always make sure that the person upon whom war is declared deserves to die, for to make war on someone is to want to punish him with death.

In international law, the most severe act of justice is war, for it can have as its effect the destruction of society.

Reparations constitute a second degree. Measuring the punishment by the crime is a law that courts have not been able to avoid carrying out.

A third act of justice is to deprive a prince of the advantages he can draw from us, ever mindful of measuring the punishment by the crime.

The fourth act of justice—which must be the most usual—is the renunciation of alliance with a people against whom justifiable complaints can be lodged. This punishment corresponds to the banishment that courts have established to isolate the guilty from a given society. Thus a prince from whose alliance we withdraw is isolated from our society and is no longer one of its constituent members.

No greater affront can be made to any prince than to refuse his alliance, and no greater honor can be paid him than to conclude such an alliance. Nothing among men can seem more glorious and even more useful to them than to see others constantly mindful of their preservation.

But if an alliance is to bind us, it must be a just one; thus a pact made between two nations in order to oppress a third is not legitimate and can be broken without committing a crime.

It is fitting neither to the honor nor the dignity of a prince to ally himself with a tyrant. It is said that an Egyptian monarch had the King of Samos apprised of his cruelty and tyranny and served notice on him to reform. Since the latter did nothing about it, he sent an emissary to say that he renounced his friendship and his alliance.

Conquest in itself gives no rights. When the conquered nation still exists, it forms a pledge of peace and of reparation for the wrong; if the nation is destroyed or scattered, it constitutes a monument to tyranny.

Peace treaties are so sacrosanct among men that they seem to be the voice of nature recovering her rights. They are legitimate when their conditions are such that both peoples can be preserved. Short of this, the nation that is to perish, deprived of its natural defense by the peace treaty, can seek that natural defense through war.

For nature, which has established varying degrees of strength and weakness among men, has also often equated weakness to strength by way of despair.

Here, my dear Rhedi, you have what I call public law. Here you have international law, or rather, the law of reason.

From Paris, the 4th of the
Moon of Zilhage, 1716

LETTER CXVII

Usbek to the same

The prohibition of divorce is not the sole cause of depopulation in Christian countries. The great number of eunuchs they keep is a no less considerable cause.

I am talking of the priests and dervishes, of both sexes, who vow themselves to eternal continence. With Christians, this is the virtue par excellence. And in this I cannot follow their reasoning, for I don't know what kind of a virtue is a virtue from which there results nothing.

I find that their learned doctors clearly contradict themselves when they say that marriage is sacred and that celibacy, which is the absolute opposite, is even more so. And this without mentioning that in the matter of precepts and fundamental dogmas the good is always the best.

The number of people professing celibacy is prodigious. In times past, fathers used to sentence their children to it from the cradle. Nowadays, they take vows themselves as early as the age of fourteen, which amounts to about the same thing.

This art or trade of continence has destroyed more men than pestilence and the bloodiest of wars. In every religious house there can be seen an eternal family in which nobody is born and which maintains itself at the expense of all the other families. These houses are always agape, like so many abysses where future races of men are buried.

This policy is quite different from that of the Romans, who established penal laws against those who refused to marry and chose to enjoy a freedom so contrary to the public utility.

I am speaking now only of Catholic countries. In the Protestant religion, everyone has the right to make children. This religion permits neither priests nor dervishes. If in its establishment, its founders, who brought everything back to primitive values, had not continually been accused of intemperance, there can be no doubt that, having made marriage a universal practice, they would have gone on to lighten the yoke still further and would thus have managed to remove the barrier that separates Nazarene and Moslem on this score.

However that may be, it is certain that religion gives Protestants an infinite advantage over Catholics.

I shall dare to put it thus: in the present state of Europe, it is impossible for the Catholic religion to last another five hundred years.

Prior to the humbling of Spanish power, the Catholics were much stronger than the Protestants. The latter have bit by bit managed to come to a position of equality. Protestants will continue to become richer and more powerful, and Catholics weaker.

Protestant countries should be and, in reality, are more populous than Catholic countries. From which it follows, first, that taxes are more considerable since they increase along with the number of those who pay, and second, that the soil is better cultivated, and finally, that commerce flourishes to a greater extent because there are more people to make a fortune and because with more needs there are more resources for fulfilling them. When the number of people is only sufficient to till the soil, commerce must perish, and when the number is only enough to maintain commerce, the cultivation of the soil lags. That is to say, both decline at the same time, for you cannot concentrate on one except at the expense of the other.

As for Catholic countries, not only is cultivation of crops abandoned, but even industry is pernicious. It consists solely in learning five or six words in some dead language. As soon as a man has got that stock under his belt, he need no longer worry about his fortune. In the cloister, he will find a peaceful life, which would have cost him sweat and tears in the world.

That's not all. The dervishes hold almost all the wealth of the state. They are a society of greedy people, who always take and never give in return. They accumulate revenue continuously, in order to acquire capital. All this great wealth falls, so to speak, into paralysis: no more circulation of money, no more commerce, no more arts, no more manufactures.

There is no Protestant prince who fails to raise more taxes on his subjects than the Pope raises on his, and yet these latter are poor, and the former live in abundance. Commerce brings everything to the first; monasticism universally brings death to the others.

From Paris, the 26th of the
Moon of Shahban, 1718

LETTER CXVIII

Usbek to the same

We have no more to say about Asia and Europe. Let us move on to Africa. We can, practically speaking, discuss only its coasts, for the interior is not known.

The Barbary coasts, where the Mohammedan religion is established, are no more populous than they were at the time of the Romans, for reasons that I have already given. As to the coasts of Guinea, they must be seriously stripped these past two hundred years, as the minor kings, or village chiefs, keep selling their subjects to European princes to be carried off to their colonies in America.

What is more unusual is that this America, which receives so many new inhabitants annually, is itself a desert land and does not profit by the continued losses of Africa. The slaves, transported into another climate, die by the thousands. The working of mines, in which aborigines or foreigners are always used, the malignant vapors that come from them, the quicksilver that must be used constantly—all this destroys irreparably.

Nothing could be quite as extravagant as to cause the death of countless men in order to dig gold and silver from the earth. These metals are absolutely useless in themselves and represent wealth only because they were chosen to be its symbol.

From Paris, the last of the
Moon of Shahban, 1718

LETTER CXXI

Usbek to the same

The normal effect of colonies is to weaken the countries from which they are drawn, without populating those to which they are sent.

Men should stay where they are. Some illnesses can arise from changing good air for bad; others are due precisely to the fact that there has been any change of it at all.

The air is laden, as are plants, with particles of the earth of each country. This works on us in such a way that our temperament is thereby established. When we are transported to another country, we become ill. Liquids are accustomed to a certain consistency, solids to a certain disposition, and both are accustomed to a certain degree of movement past which they cannot tolerate others; thus they resist a new bent.

When a given country is undersettled, it is the fault of some particular vice in the nature of the terrain or the climate. Thus, when men are torn away from propitious skies to be sent into such a country, just the opposite of what is hoped for gets accomplished.

The Romans knew all that through experience. They relegated all their criminals to Sardinia, and they had Jews transported there. They had to console themselves for their loss: a thing made very easy by the scorn they felt for these unfortunate people.

The great Shah Abbas, desirous of making it impossible for the Turks to maintain large armies on the frontier, transported almost all the Armenians out of their country and sent more than twenty thousand families of them into the province of Gilan, where almost all of them perished in a short time.

None of the shipments of people tried by Constantinople ever succeeded.

The prodigious number of Negroes we talked about have not filled up America.

Since the destruction of the Jews under Hadrian, Palestine remains without inhabitants.

It must therefore be admitted that great destructions are almost irreparable, because a people that declines to a certain degree will remain in that same condition. If, by chance, it is ever to become reestablished, it would take centuries.

But if, in a weakened condition, the very least of the circumstances I have mentioned comes into play, not only does the people not reestablish itself, but it fritters away each day and leans toward complete annihilation.

The expulsion of the Moors from Spain can still be felt now as on the first day; far from this great void being filled, it grows larger every day.

Since the devastation of America, the Spanish who took the place of its former inhabitants have not been able to replenish the population. On the contrary, by a fatality that I should do better to call divine justice, the destroyers are destroying themselves and consuming themselves from day to day.

Princes ought not plan upon peopling great countries by means of colonies. I do not say that they don't sometimes succeed. There are some climates so propitious that the species will always multiply there. Take, for example, those islands populated by sick people who had been abandoned by several vessels and who immediately recovered their health there.

But even should colonies succeed, instead of increasing the power of the mother country, they serve only to divide it—unless, of course, they be of minor size, like the colonies where people are sent to occupy some commercial position.

Like the Spanish, the Carthaginians had discovered America, or at least some large islands in which they set up a lucrative commercial enterprise. But when they noticed the number of their inhabitants declining, that wise republic forbade its subjects to continue such commerce and navigation.

Let me dare to say that instead of having Spaniards go to the Indies, we must have the Indians and half-castes come to Spain. That monarchy must have all its scattered people returned to it; if only the half of these great colonies were to be preserved, Spain would become the European power most to be feared.

One might compare an empire to a tree whose branches, too scattered, rob the trunk of all its sap and serve only to cast shadows.

Nothing could be better calculated to give princes a lesson against the madness of distant conquests than the example of the Spanish and Portuguese.

These two nations, having conquered immense kingdoms with amazing rapidity, were more astonished by their victories than were the conquered people by their defeat, and they pondered ways for consolidating the conquests. Each chose its own method of doing so.

The Spanish, despairing of ever holding their conquered nations by devotion, chose the expedient of destroying the natives and sending faithful citizens from Spain. A horrible plan was never more rapidly executed. The world saw a population as great as that of Europe disappear from the face of the earth upon the arrival of these barbarians, who appeared to have consciously discovered the Indies only so that they could disclose to mankind the last degree of cruelty.

By such barbarity, they kept the country under their domination. Judge by this case how deadly conquest can be, since its effects are such. For the frightful remedy was unique. How could they have held so many millions of men to obedience? How could they support a civil war from such a distance? What would have happened to the Spanish if they had given the natives time to recover from the admiration they felt upon the arrival of these new gods, and from the fear of their first thunderbolts?

As for the Portuguese, they decided on quite a different course; they made use of no cruelty. And so they were driven out of all the countries they had discovered. The Dutch were behind the revolt of these peoples and profited from it.

What prince would envy the lot of conquerors? Who could desire conquest at such a price? The one group was immediately driven out, and the other created deserts and made a desert of its own country to boot.

It is the destiny of heroes either to destroy themselves in the conquest of a country they suddenly lose or to subjugate nations they are forced of their own accord to destroy—just like that madman who consumed his means buying statues to throw into the sea, and mirrors to break as soon as they were purchased.

From Paris, the 18th of the
Moon of Ramadan, 1718

LETTER CXXII

Usbek to the same

Mildness of government contributes in a marvelous way to the propagation of the species. All republics are a constant proof of this, and more than all the others Switzerland and Holland, which is to say the worst countries in Europe if the nature of the terrain is taken into consideration. Yet they are the most populous.

Nothing will attract foreigners more than freedom and the abundance that always follows from it. The first is sought after for itself, and we are led by our needs to seek out the country where the other is found.

The human race multiplies in a country where abundance furnishes all the needs of children without in any way diminishing the subsistence of their fathers.

The very equality of citizens, which ordinarily produces equality of fortune, brings abundance and life into every organ of the body politic and extends such benefits generally.

The same cannot be said of countries subjected to arbitrary power: the prince, the courtiers, and a few individuals possess all the wealth, while the others moan in extreme poverty.

If a man is not well off and feels that he will produce children even poorer than himself, he will not marry; if he marries, he will be afraid of having too many children, who might finish off the paternal fortune and thus drop lower than their father's status.

I admit that the countryman or peasant, once married, will produce progeny indifferently whether he be poor or rich. Such a consideration does not touch him. He possesses a constant heritage to leave to his children—his grub ax—and nothing will prevent him from blindly following his natural instinct.

But of what use to a state is this great number of children wasting away in poverty? They practically all perish as soon as they are born. They never prosper: weak and debilitated, they die off singly in a thousand different ways, while they are carried off wholesale by the frequent epidemics that poverty and undernourishment always produce. Those who escape such ravages reach the age of manhood without the strength for it, and they waste away for the rest of their lives.

Men are like plants: they never grow well unless they are well cultivated. Among people living in poverty, the human race loses and even degenerates.

France can furnish an example of all of this. In past wars the fear of being enlisted in the army, which plagued every family, forced the children to marry, and that at too tender an age and in the midst of poverty. From all these marriages were born many children; to this day you can go looking for them in France all you like: poverty, famine, and sickness have caused them to disappear.

And if, under such a fortunate sky and in as orderly a kingdom as France, such remarks can be made, what do you think it must be like in other states?

From Paris, the 23rd of the
Moon of Ramadan, 1718

FURTHER READING

Geoffrey Atkinson, *The Extraordinary Voyage in French Literature, 1700–1720* (1922). Surveys the genre of which the *Persian Letters* is such a fine specimen.
Isaiah Berlin, *Montesquieu* (1955). A brilliant general appraisal.
Jean Ehrard, *L'Idée de la nature en France dans la première moitié du XVIIIe*

siècle (1963). A solid modern appraisal of the idea of nature; deeply relevant to Montesquieu's work.

Robert Shackleton, *Montesquieu: A Critical Biography* (1961). The authoritative Life.

See also below, "Further Reading" for section 39.

13 ❊ VOLTAIRE

Letters Concerning the English Nation

[From *Mr. de Voltaire, Letters Concerning the
English Nation* (1733), 27–45, 54–56, 65–92,
164–70. The style of the first edition has been
slightly modernized.]

*Voltaire, whom the eighteenth century saw as the archetypal phi-
losophe, was born François-Marie Arouet in 1694. The name Voltaire (or, as he liked to use it, de Voltaire) was his own creation.
But then so was his entire career—a triumph of wit harnessed to
serious moral, social, religious, and political preoccupations. The
son of a prosperous Parisian* notaire—*which meant something
rather more exalted than "notary"—Voltaire was educated at the
fashionable Jesuit Collège Louis-le-Grand; it was there that he
picked up his classical education, sharpened his formidable pen,
and made friendships that lasted his long lifetime. Once finished
with school, he entered the libertine circles of the Regency; in Paris
salons and at country houses, young François-Marie Arouet made
himself popular with his barbed wit and his facile verse. In 1717 he
was imprisoned in the Bastille for eleven months; he emerged with
his new name, and with his first tragedy,* Oedipe. *The public
accepted the first and hailed the second; in an age starved for good
plays and nostalgic about the great days of French drama under
Louis XIV,* Oedipe *appeared as a worthy successor to the plays of
Corneille, Racine, and Molière. This, as we have come to recognize,
was a misjudgment; but Voltaire all his life took inordinate pride
in his many tragedies and comedies, and made light of those
marvelous short stories—*Candide, Zadig, *and the others—on which
his literary reputation rests today.*

Intent as Voltaire was to secure literary fame, he was also from his *earliest years something of a political and religious rebel. The verses for which he was sent to the Bastille in 1717 were a lampoon on the Regent; his literary activity of the 1720s included poems that demonstrate his revulsion against Christianity and search for a deist—that is to say, naturalistic—religion. In early 1726 he was sent to the Bastille once again, and the indirect result of his imprisonment was his first great work of prose, the* Lettres philosophiques.*

The incident that brought him into prison for the second time is worth recounting as an instance of the arbitrariness under which Frenchmen labored in the Old Regime. Late in 1725, the Chevalier de Rohan, dissolute and insignificant, but a member of an ancient noble family and cousin to a cardinal, had made some disparaging remarks at Voltaire's expense, and Voltaire had talked back. In February 1726 Rohan lured Voltaire to come out from a dinner party and watched from his carriage while his lackeys beat up the offending bourgeois poet. Voltaire protested to his aristocratic friends, but, he discovered, they closed ranks against him, the upstart; he threatened to challenge Rohan to a duel, and the authorities, to avoid real trouble, had Voltaire—Voltaire, not the aggressor, Rohan—sent to the Bastille. There he stayed, fuming, and was released upon promising to leave Paris. England, in which he had long been interested, beckoned, and by May 1726 he saw it for himself for the first time. It left an impression that was never effaced; Voltaire became and remained an "Anglomaniac."

The reasons for his infatuation appear in the selections printed below; they are easy to understand. France's high society seemed to be open to talent—and Voltaire's talent was admitted by all, even his enemies, to be formidable—and yet, upon the slightest challenge, it proved itself to be a caste after all. England was different; living as he did in England for more than two years, Voltaire was driven to make comparisons, and the comparisons were all invidious ones—invidious, that is, to France. Voltaire's letters to his friends, many of them in his charming, newfound English, are an anthology*

---

* The publishing history of the book is somewhat complex. It was first brought out in England, in English, in 1733; that version, though substantially complete, lacks the long final letter, the twenty-fifth, which is not on England at all, but rather a debate with Pascal, the "sublime misanthrope," against whose profoundly pessimistic appraisal of human nature Voltaire pitted a rather less grim and in any case wholly secular appraisal. The English title is the title heading of this selection; the title under which the book is best known is *Lettres philosophiques*.

of his discovery. "This is a country where all the arts are honored and rewarded," he wrote to his intimate, Thieriot, in August 1726, "where there are differences in rank, but only those based on merit. This is a country where one thinks freely and nobly without being held back by any servile fear."* And a little more than two months later he invited Thieriot to see for himself, and to visit "a nation fond of their liberty, learned, witty, despising life and death, a nation of philosophers."†

Voltaire's animus, it is clear, had deep personal roots; it is as a man of letters, a self-reliant bourgeois despised and insulted at home, that he learns to love England. But this personal animus had general historical significance: experiencing greater freedom as an actuality rather than as a fantasy, the Continental philosophes could make Anglomania into a potent force for political criticism, if not for reform.

After a little over two years, Voltaire returned, his religious and political convictions confirmed and expanded by his instructive visit. The great French scholar Gustave Lanson said half a century ago that "Voltaire left France a poet, he returned to it a sage." But this claim undervalues the work that Voltaire had already done for himself before 1726. In any event, the English visit gave him much new ammunition. The Letters Concerning the English Nation, *published clandestinely in its complete French version in 1734, is the precipitate. Here is England, a commercial nation, rich and free, and free because it is rich; the celebrated passage on the stock exchange‡ is a brilliant extended metaphor for what Voltaire had learned, and for the civilization he thought desirable. But this was by no means the only lesson that England had for Voltaire. Here was a "nation of philosophers," and Voltaire took care to popularize the new philosophy (which prominently included the Newtonian sciences) among his compatriots. That is why the French title,* Lettres philosophiques, *is really accurate. The book was condemned (mainly for its passages on* Pascal) *and gave Voltaire new notoriety. To be burned, as these* Letters *were, publicly by the common hangman in the courtyard of the Palais de Justice in Paris, was to receive advertisement invaluable for an author in search of a public. But Voltaire, with all his boasts that his "fortune grew*

* Aug. 12, 1726, *Voltaire's Correspondence,* ed. Theodore Besterman, 107 vols. (1953–65), II, 31.

† In English, *ibid.,* 37.

‡ See below, pages 150–151.

always bolder when they indeavor'd at submitting it," had pru-
dently left Paris before the public execution of his tract. He was at
Cirey, at the château of a new mistress, the brilliant bluestocking
Madame du Châtelet. At her château, and with her collaboration,
Voltaire was to prepare the historical works and religious polemics
that dominated his later career.*

LETTER V

On the Church of England

England is properly the country of sectarists. *Multae sunt man-
siones in domo patris mei* (In my father's house are many mansions). An Englishman, as one to whom liberty is natural, may go to
heaven his own way.

Nevertheless, though everyone is permitted to serve God in whatever mode of fashion he thinks proper, yet their true religion, that
in which a man makes his fortune, is the sect of Episcoparians or
Churchmen, called the Church of England, or simply the Church,
by way of eminence. No person can possess an employment either in
England or Ireland unless he be ranked among the faithful, that is,
professes himself a member of the Church of England. This reason
(which carries mathematical evidence with it) has converted such
numbers of Dissenters of all persuasions, that not a twentieth part
of the nation is out of the pale of the established church. The
English clergy have retained a great number of the Romish ceremonies, and especially that of receiving, with a most scrupulous
attention, their tithes. They also have the pious ambition to aim at
superiority.

Moreover, they inspire very religiously their flock with a holy zeal
against Dissenters of all denominations. This zeal was pretty violent
under the Tories, in the four last years of Queen Anne, but was
productive of no greater mischief than the breaking the windows of
some meeting-houses, and the demolishing of a few of them. For
religious rage ceased in England with the Civil Wars; and was no

* Voltaire to Thieriot, January 1735; in English, *Correspondence*, IV, 12–13.

more under Queen Anne than the hollow noise of a sea whose billows still heaved, though so long after the storm, when the Whigs and Tories laid waste their native country, in the same manner as the Guelphs and Gibelins formerly did theirs. It was absolutely necessary for both parties to call in religion on this occasion; the Tories declared for episcopacy, and the Whigs, as some imagined, were for abolishing it; however, after these had got the upper hand, they contented themselves with only abridging its power.

At the time when the Earl of Oxford and the Lord Bolingbroke used to drink healths to the Tories, the Church of England considered those noblemen as the defenders of its holy privileges. The lower house of Convocation (a kind of House of Commons), composed wholly of the clergy, was in some credit at that time; at least the members of it had the liberty to meet, to dispute on ecclesiastical matters, to sentence impious books from time to time to the flames, that is, books written against themselves. The Ministry, which is now composed of Whigs, does not so much as allow those gentlemen to assemble, so that they are at this time reduced (in the obscurity of their respective parishes) to the melancholy occupation of praying for the prosperity of the government whose tranquillity they would willingly disturb. With regard to the bishops, who are twenty-six in all, they still have seats in the House of Lords in spite of the Whigs, because the ancient abuse of considering them as barons subsists to this day. There is a clause, however, in the oath which the government requires from these gentlemen, that puts their Christian patience to a very great trial, *viz.* that they shall be of the Church of England as by law established. There are few bishops, deans, or other dignitaries but imagine they are so *jure divino;* it is consequently a great mortification to them to be obliged to confess that they owe their dignity to a pitiful law enacted by a set of profane laymen. A learned monk (Father Courayer) wrote a book lately to prove the validity and succession of English ordinations. This book was forbid in France; but do you believe that the English Ministry were pleased with it? Far from it. Those damned Whigs don't value a straw whether the episcopal succession among them has been interrupted or not, or whether Bishop Parker was consecrated (as it is pretended) in a tavern, or a church; for these Whigs are much better pleased that the bishops should derive their authority from the Parliament, than from the Apostles. The Lord B—— observed that this notion of divine right would only make so many tyrants in lawn-sleeves, but that the laws made so many citizens.

With regard to the morals of the English clergy, they are more regular than those of France, and for this reason. All the clergy (a very few excepted) are educated in the universities of Oxford or Cambridge, far from the depravity and corruption which reign in the capital. They are not called to dignities till very late, in an age when men are sensible of no other passion but avarice, that is, when their ambition craves a supply. Employments are here bestowed, both in the church and the army, as a reward for long services; and we never see youngsters made bishops or colonels immediately upon their laying aside the academical gown; and, besides, most of the clergy are married. The stiff and awkward air contracted by them at the university, and the little familiarity the men of this country have with the ladies, commonly oblige a bishop to confine himself to and rest contented with his own. Clergymen sometimes take a glass at the tavern, custom giving them a sanction on this occasion; and if they fuddle themselves it is in a very serious manner, and without giving the least scandal.

That sable mixed being (not to be defined) who is neither of the clergy nor of the laity, in a word, the thing called *abbé* in France, is a species quite unknown in England. All the clergy here are very much upon the reserve, and most of them pedants. When these are told that in France, young fellows famous for their dissoluteness and raised to the highest dignities of the church by female intrigues, address the fair publicly in an amorous way, amuse themselves in writing tender love songs, entertain their friends very splendidly every night at their own houses, and, after the banquet is ended, withdraw to invoke the assistance of the Holy Ghost, and call themselves boldly the successors of the Apostles, they bless God for their being Protestants. But these are shameless heretics who deserve to be blown hence through the flames to Old Nick, as Rabelais says, and for this reason I don't trouble myself about them.

LETTER VI

On the Presbyterians

The Church of England is confined almost to the kingdom whence it received its name, and to Ireland, for Presbyterianism is the established religion in Scotland. This Presbyterianism is directly the same with Calvinism as it was established in France and is now professed at Geneva. As the priests of this sect receive but very inconsiderable stipends from their churches, and consequently cannot emulate the splendid luxury of bishops, they exclaim very naturally against honours which they can never attain to. Figure to yourself the haughty Diogenes, trampling under foot the pride of Plato. The Scotch Presbyterians are not very unlike that proud though tattered reasoner. Diogenes did not use Alexander half so impertinently as these treated King Charles the Second; for when they took up arms in his cause, in opposition to Oliver, who had deceived them, they forced that poor monarch to undergo the hearing of three or four sermons every day; would not suffer him to play, reduced him to a state of penitence and mortification; so that Charles soon grew sick of these pedants, and accordingly eloped from them with as much joy as a youth does from school.

A Church of England minister appears as another Cato in presence of a juvenile, sprightly French graduate, who bawls for a whole morning together in the divinity schools, and hums a song in chorus with ladies in the evening: But this Cato is a very spark when before a Scotch Presbyterian. The latter affects a serious gait, puts on a sour look, wears a vastly broad-brimmed hat, and a long cloak over a very short coat; preaches through the nose, and gives the name of the whore of Babylon to all churches where the ministers are so fortunate as to enjoy an annual revenue of five or six thousand pounds, and where the people are weak enough to suffer this and to give them the titles of my lord, your lordship, or your eminence.

These gentlemen, who have also some churches in England, introduced there the mode of grave and severe exhortations. To them is owing the sanctification of Sunday in the three kingdoms. People are there forbid to work or take any recreation on that day, in which the severity is twice as great as that of the Romish church. No operas, plays or concerts are allowed in London on Sundays; and even cards are so expressly forbid, that none but persons of quality and those we call the genteel play on that day; the rest of the nation go either to church, to the tavern, or to see their mistresses.

Though the Episcopal and Presbyterian sects are the two prevailing ones in Great Britain, yet all others are very welcome to come and settle in it, and live very sociably together, though most of their preachers hate one another almost as cordially as a Jansenist damns a Jesuit.

Take a view of the Royal Exchange in London, a place more venerable than many courts of justice, where the representatives of all nations meet for the benefit of mankind. There the Jew, the Mahometan, and the Christian transact together as though they all professed the same religion, and give the name of Infidel to none but bankrupts. There the Presbyterian confides in the Anabaptist, and the Churchman depends on the Quaker's word. At the breaking up of this pacific and free assembly, some withdraw to the synagogue, and others to take a glass. This man goes and is baptized in a great tub, in the name of the Father, Son, and Holy Ghost: That man has his son's foreskin cut off, whilst a set of Hebrew words (quite unintelligible to him) are mumbled over his child. Others retire to their churches, and there wait for the inspiration of heaven with their hats on, and all are satisfied.

If one religion only were allowed in England, the government would very possibly become arbitrary; if there were but two, the people would cut one another's throats; but as there are such a multitude, they all live happy and in peace.

LETTER VII

On the Socinians, or Arians, or Antitrinitarians

There is a little sect here composed of clergymen, and of a few very learned persons among the laity, who, though they don't call themselves Arians or Socinians, do yet dissent entirely from Saint Athanasius, with regard to their notions of the Trinity, and declare very frankly that the Father is greater than the Son.

Do you remember what is related of a certain orthodox bishop, who in order to convince an emperor of the reality of consubstantiation, put his hand under the chin of the monarch's son, and took him by the nose in presence of his sacred majesty? The emperor was going to order his attendants to throw the bishop out of the window, when the good old man gave him this convincing reason: "Since your majesty," says he, "is angry when your son has not due respect shown him, what punishment do you think will God the father inflict on those who refuse his son Jesus the titles due to him?" The persons I just now mentioned declare that the holy bishop took a very strong step; that his argument was inconclusive, and that the emperor should have answered him thus: "Know that there are two ways by which men may be wanting in respect to me; first, in not doing honour sufficient to my son; and secondly, in paying him the same honour as to me."

Be this as it will, the principles of Arius began to revive, not only in England but in Holland and Poland. The celebrated Sir Isaac Newton honoured this opinion so far as to countenance it. This philosopher thought that the Unitarians argued more mathematically than we do. But the most sanguine stickler for Arianism is the illustrious Dr. Clarke. This man is rigidly virtuous, and of a mild disposition; is more fond of his tenets than desirous of propagating them; and absorbed so entirely in problems and calculations, that he is a mere reasoning machine.

It is he who wrote a book which is much esteemed and little understood, on the existence of God; and another more intelligible, but pretty much condemned, on the truth of the Christian religion.

He never engaged in scholastic disputes, which our friend calls venerable trifles. He only published a work containing all the testimonies of the primitive ages, for and against the Unitarians, and leaves to the reader the counting of the voices, and the liberty of forming a judgment. This book won the doctor a great number of partisans, and lost him the See of Canterbury: But in my humble opinion, he was out in his calculation, and had better have been Primate of all England than merely an Arian parson.

You see that opinions are subject to revolutions as well as empires. Arianism, after having triumphed during three centuries, and then having been forgot twelve, rises at last out of its own ashes; but it has chosen a very improper season to make its appearance in, the present age being quite cloyed with disputes and sects. The members of this sect are, besides, too few to be indulged the liberty of holding public assemblies, which, however, they will doubtless be permitted to do in case they spread considerably. But people are now so very cold with respect to all things of this kind, that there is little probability any new religion, or old one that may be revived, will meet with favour. Is it not whimsical enough that Luther, Calvin and Zwinglius, all of them wretched authors, should have founded sects which are now spread over a great part of Europe; that Mahomet, though so ignorant, should have given a religion to Asia and Africa; and that Sir Isaac Newton, Dr. Clarke, Mr. Locke, Mr. Le Clerc, etc., the greatest philosophers as well as the ablest writers of their ages, should scarce have been able to raise a little flock, which even decreases daily?

This it is to be born at a proper period of time. Were Cardinal de Retz to return again into the world, neither his eloquence nor his intrigues would draw together ten women in Paris.

Were Oliver Cromwell, he who beheaded his sovereign and seized upon the kingly dignity, to rise from the dead, he would be a wealthy city trader, and no more.

LETTER VIII

On the Parliament

The Members of the English Parliament are fond of comparing themselves to the old Romans.

Not long since, Mr. Shippen opened a speech in the House of Commons with these words: "The majesty of the people of England would be wounded." The singularity of the expression occasioned a loud laugh; but this gentleman, so far from being disconcerted, repeated the same words with a resolute tone of voice, and the laugh ceased. In my opinion, the majesty of the people of England has nothing in common with that of the people of Rome, much less is there any affinity between their governments. There is in London a senate, some of the members whereof are accused (doubtless very unjustly) of selling their voices on certain occasions, as was done in Rome; this is the only resemblance. Besides, the two nations appear to me quite opposite in character with regard both to good and evil. The Romans never knew the dreadful folly of religious wars, an abomination reserved for devout preachers of patience and humility. Marius and Sylla, Caesar and Pompey, Anthony and Augustus, did not draw their swords and set the world in a blaze merely to determine whether the Flamen should wear his shirt over his robe, or his robe over his shirt; or whether the sacred chickens should eat and drink, or eat only, in order to take the augury. The English have hanged one another by law, and cut one another to pieces in pitched battles, for quarrels of as trifling a nature. The sects of the Episcoparians and Presbyterians quite distracted these very serious heads for a time. But I fancy they'll hardly ever be so silly again, they seeming to be grown wiser at their own expence; and I don't perceive the least inclination in them to murder one another merely about syllogisms, as some zealots among them once did.

But here follows a more essential difference between Rome and England, which gives the advantage entirely to the latter, *viz.* that the civil wars of Rome ended in slavery, and those of the English in liberty. The English are the only people upon earth who have been able to prescribe limits to the power of kings by resisting them; and who, by a series of struggles, have at last established that wise government where the prince is all powerful to do good, and at the same time is restrained from committing evil; where the nobles are great without insolence, though there are no vassals; and where the people share in the government without confusion.

The House of Lords and that of the Commons divide the legislative power under the King, but the Romans had no such balance. The Patricians and Plebeians in Rome were perpetually at variance, and there was no intermediate power to reconcile them. The Roman Senate, who were so unjustly, so criminally proud, as not to suffer the Plebeians to share with them in anything, could find no other artifice to keep the latter out of the Administration than by employing them in foreign wars. They considered the Plebeians as a wild beast, whom it behooved them to let loose upon their neighbours, for fear they should devour their masters. Thus the greatest defect in the government of the Romans raised them to be conquerors. By being unhappy at home, they triumphed over and possessed themselves of the world, till at last their divisions sank them to slavery.

The government of England will never rise to so exalted a pitch of glory, nor will its end be so fatal. The English are not fired with the splendid folly of making conquests, but would only prevent their neighbours from conquering. They are not only jealous of their own liberty, but even of that of other nations. The English were exasperated against Louis the Fourteenth for no other reason but because he was ambitious; and declared war against him merely out of levity, not from any interested motives.

The English have doubtless purchased their liberties at a very high price, and waded through seas of blood to drown the idol of arbitrary power. Other nations have been involved in as great calamities, and have shed as much blood; but then the blood they spilt in defence of their liberties only enslaved them the more.

That which rises to a revolution in England is no more than a sedition in other countries. A city in Spain, in Barbary, or in Turkey takes up arms in defence of its privileges, when immediately it is stormed by mercenary troops, it is punished by executioners, and the rest of the nation kiss the chains they are loaded with. The French are of the opinion that the government of this island is more tempestuous than the sea which surrounds it, which indeed is true; but then it is never so but when the King raises the storm, when he attempts to seize the ship of which he is only the chief pilot. The civil wars of France lasted longer; were more cruel, and productive of greater evils than those of England: But none of these civil wars had a wise and prudent liberty for their object.

In the detestable reigns of Charles the Ninth and Henry the Third, the whole affair was only whether the people should be slaves to the Guises. With regard to the last war of Paris, it deserves only to be hooted at. Methinks I see a crowd of schoolboys rising up in arms against their master, and afterwards whipped for it. Cardinal de Retz, who was witty and brave, but to no purpose, rebellious without a cause, factious without design, and head of a defenceless party, caballed for caballing sake, and seemed to foment the civil war merely out of diversion. The parliament did not know what he intended, nor what he did not intend. He levied troops by act of parliament, and the next moment cashiered them. He threatened, he begged pardon; he set a price upon Cardinal Mazarin's head, and afterwards congratulated him in a public manner. Our civil wars under Charles the Sixth were bloody and cruel, those of the League execrable, and that of the Frondeurs ridiculous.

That for which the French chiefly reproach the English nation is the murder of King Charles the First, whom his subjects treated exactly as he would have treated them had his reign been prosperous. After all, consider, on one side, Charles the First defeated in a pitched battle, imprisoned, tried, sentenced to die in Westminster Hall, and then beheaded; and on the other, the Emperor Henry the Seventh, poisoned by his chaplain at his receiving the sacrament; Henry the Third stabbed by a monk; thirty assassinations projected against Henry the Fourth; several of them put in execution, and the last bereaving that great monarch of his life. Weigh, I say, all these wicked attempts, and then judge.

LETTER X

On Trade

As trade enriched the citizens in England, so it contributed to their freedom, and this freedom on the other side extended their commerce, whence arose the grandeur of the state. Trade raised by insensible degrees the naval power, which gives the English a superiority over the Seas, and they are now masters of very near two hundred ships of war. Posterity will very possibly be surprised to hear that an island whose only produce is a little lead, tin, fuller's earth, and coarse wood, should become so powerful by its commerce as to be able to send, in 1723, three fleets at the same time to three different and far distanced parts of the globe: one before Gibraltar, conquered and still possessed by the English; a second to Porto Bello, to dispossess the King of Spain of the treasures of the West Indies; and a third into the Baltic, to prevent the Northern Powers from coming to an engagement.

At the time when Louis XIV made all Italy tremble, and his armies, which had already possessed themselves of Savoy and Piedmont, were upon the point of taking Turin, Prince Eugene was obliged to march from the middle of Germany in order to succour Savoy. Having no money, without which cities cannot be either taken or defended, he addressed himself to some English merchants. These, at an hour and a half's warning, lent him five millions, whereby he was enabled to deliver Turin and to beat the French; after which he wrote the following short letter to the persons who had disbursed him the abovementioned sums: "Gentlemen, I have received your money, and flatter myself that I have laid it out to your satisfaction." Such a circumstance as this raises a just pride in an English merchant, and makes him presume (not without some reason) to compare himself to a Roman citizen; and indeed a peer's brother does not think traffic beneath him. When the Lord Townshend was Minister of State, a brother of his was content to be a city merchant; and at the time that the Earl of Oxford governed Great Britain, his younger brother was no more than a factor in Aleppo, where he chose to live, and where he died. This custom, which begins, however, to be laid aside, appears monstrous to Germans, vainly puffed up with their extraction. These think it morally impossible that the son of an English peer should be no more than a rich and powerful citizen, for all are princes in Germany. There have been thirty highnesses of the same name, all whose patrimony consisted only in their escutcheons and their pride.

In France the title of marquis is given *gratis* to any one who will accept of it; and whosoever arrives at Paris from the midst of the most remote provinces with money in his purse and a name terminating in *ac* or *ille,* may strut about, and cry, "Such a man as I! A man of my rank and figure!" And may look down upon a trader with sovereign contempt; whilst the trader, on the other side, by thus often hearing his profession treated so disdainfully, is fool enough to blush at it. However, I cannot say which is most useful to a nation: a lord, powdered in the tip of the mode, who knows exactly at what o'clock the King rises and goes to bed, and who gives himself airs of grandeur and state, at the same time that he is acting the slave in the antechamber of a Prime Minister; or a merchant, who enriches his country, dispatches orders from his counting-house to Surat and Grand Cairo, and contributes to the felicity of the world.

LETTER XII

On the Lord Bacon

Not long since, the trite and frivolous question following was debated in a very polite and learned company, *viz.* who was the greatest man, Caesar, Alexander, Tamerlane, Cromwell, etc.

Somebody answered that Sir Isaac Newton excelled them all. The gentleman's assertion was very just; for if true greatness consists in having received from Heaven a mighty genius, and in having employed it to enlighten our own minds and that of others, a man like Sir Isaac Newton, whose equal is hardly found in a thousand years, is the truly great man. And those politicians and conquerors (and all ages produce some) were generally so many illustrious wicked men. That man claims our respect who commands over the minds of the rest of the world by the force of truth, not those who enslave their fellow creatures; he who is acquainted with the universe, not they who deface it.

Since therefore you desire me to give you an account of the famous personages which England has given birth to, I shall begin with Lord Bacon, Mr. Locke, Sir Isaac Newton, etc. Afterwards the warriors and ministers of state shall come in their order.

I must begin with the celebrated Viscount Verulam, known in Europe by the Name of Bacon, which was that of his family. His father had been Lord Keeper, and himself was a great many years Lord Chancellor under King James the First. Nevertheless, amidst the intrigues of a court, and the affairs of his exalted employment, which alone were enough to engross his whole time, he yet found so much leisure for study as to make himself a great philosopher, a good historian, and an elegant writer; and a still more surprising circumstance is that he lived in an age in which the art of writing justly and elegantly was little known, much less true philosophy. Lord Bacon, as is the fate of man, was more esteemed after his death than in his lifetime. His enemies were in the British court, and his admirers were foreigners.

When the Marquis d'Effiat attended in England upon the Princess Henrietta Maria, daughter to Henry the Fourth, whom King Charles the First had married, that Minister went and visited the Lord Bacon, who, being at that time sick in his bed, received him with the curtains shut close. "You resemble the angels," says the Marquis to him; "we hear those beings spoken of perpetually, and we believe them superior to men, but are never allowed the consolation to see them."

You know that this great man was accused of a crime very unbecoming a philosopher, I mean bribery and extortion. You know that he was sentenced by the House of Lords to pay a fine of about four hundred thousand French livres; to lose his peerage and his dignity of Chancellor. But in the present age, the English revere his memory to such a degree that they will scarce allow him to have been guilty. In case you should ask what are my thoughts on this head, I shall answer you in the words which I heard the Lord Bolingbroke use on another occasion. Several gentlemen were speaking, in his company, of the avarice with which the late Duke of Marlborough had been charged; some examples whereof being given, the Lord Bolingbroke was appealed to (who, having been in the opposite party, might perhaps, without the imputation of indecency, have been allowed to clear up that Matter). "He was so great a man," replied his Lordship, "that I have forgot his vices."

I shall therefore confine my self to those things which so justly gained Lord Bacon the esteem of all Europe.

The most singular, and the best of all his pieces, is that which, at this time, is the most useless and the least read, I mean his *Novum Scientiarum Organum*. This is the scaffold with which the new philosophy was raised; and when the edifice was built, part of it at least, the Scaffold, was no longer of Service.

The Lord Bacon was not yet acquainted with nature, but then he knew, and pointed out, the several paths that lead to it. He had despised in his younger years the thing called philosophy in the universities, and did all that lay in his power to prevent those societies of men, instituted to improve human reason, from depraving it by their quiddities, their horrors of the vacuum, their substantial forms, and all those impertinent terms which not only ignorance had rendered venerable, but which had been sacred by their being ridiculously blended with religion.

He is the father of experimental philosophy. It must indeed be confessed that very surprising secrets had been found out before his time. The sea-compass, printing, engraving on copper plates, oil-painting, looking-glasses; the art of restoring, in some measure, old men to their sight by spectacles; gunpowder, etc., had been discovered. A New World had been sought for, found, and conquered. Would not one suppose that these sublime discoveries had been made by the greatest philosophers, and in ages much more enlightened than the present? But it was far otherwise; all these great changes happened in the most stupid and barbarous times. Chance only gave birth to most of those inventions; and it is very probable that what is called chance contributed very much to the discovery of America; at least it has been always thought that Christopher Columbus undertook his voyage merely on the relation of a captain of a ship which a storm had driven as far westward as the Caribee Islands. Be this as it will, Men had sailed round the world, and could destroy cities by an artificial thunder more dreadful than the real one. But then they were not acquainted with the circulation of the blood, the weight of the air, the laws of motion, light, the number of our planets, etc. And a man who maintained a thesis on Aristotle's categories, on the universals *a parte rei*, or such like nonsense, was looked upon as a prodigy.

The most astonishing, the most useful Inventions, are not those which reflect the greatest honour on the human mind. It is to a mechanical instinct, which is found in many men, and not to true philosophy, that most arts owe their origin.

The discovery of fire, the art of making bread, of melting and preparing metals, of building houses, and the invention of the shuttle, are infinitely more beneficial to mankind than printing or the sea-compass; and yet these arts were invented by uncultivated, savage men.

What a prodigious use the Greeks and Romans made afterwards of Mechanics! Nevertheless, they believed that there were crystal heavens; that the stars were small lamps which sometimes fell into the sea; and one of their greatest philosophers, after long researches, found that the stars were so many flints which had been detached from the earth.

In a word, no one, before the Lord Bacon, was acquainted with experimental philosophy, nor with the several physical experiments which have been made since his time. Scarce one of them but is hinted at in his work, and he himself had made several. He made a kind of pneumatic engine by which he guessed the elasticity of the air. He approached, on all sides as it were, to the discovery of its weight, and had very near attained it, but some time after *Toricelli* seized upon this truth. In a little time experimental philosophy began to be cultivated on a sudden in most parts of Europe. It was a hidden treasure which the Lord Bacon had some notion of, and which all the philosophers, encouraged by his promises, endeavoured to dig up.

But that which surprised me most was to read in his work, in express terms, the new attraction, the invention of which is ascribed to Sir Isaac Newton.

We must search, says Lord Bacon, whether there may not be a kind of magnetic power which operates between the earth and heavy bodies, between the moon and the ocean, between the Planets, etc. In another place he says heavy bodies either must be carried towards the center of the earth or must be reciprocally attracted by it; and in the latter case it is evident that the nearer bodies, in their falling, draw towards the earth, the stronger they will attract one another. We must, says he, make an experiment to see whether the same clock will go faster on the top of a mountain or at the bottom of a mine; whether the strength of the weights decreases on the mountain and increases in the mine. It is probable that the earth has a true attractive power.

This forerunner in philosophy was also an elegant writer, an historian and a wit.

His moral essays are greatly esteemed, but they were drawn up in the view of instructing rather than of pleasing; and as they are not a satire upon mankind, like La Rochefoucauld's *Maxims,* nor written upon a sceptical plan, like Montaigne's *Essays,* they are not so much read as those two ingenious authors.

His *History of Henry the Seventh* was looked upon as a masterpiece, but how is it possible that some persons can presume to compare so little a work with the *History* of our illustrious Thuanus?*

Speaking about the famous impostor Perkin, son to a converted Jew, who assumed boldly the name and title of Richard the Fourth, King of England, at the instigation of the Duchess of Burgundy, and who disputed the crown with Henry the Seventh, the Lord Bacon writes as follows:

"At this time the King began again to be haunted with sprites, by the magick and curious arts of the Lady Margaret; who raised up the Ghost of Richard Duke of York, second Son to King Edward the Fourth, to walk and vex the King. . . .

"After such time as she [Margaret of Burgundy] thought he

---

* Jacques-Auguste de Thou (1553–1617), author of *Historia sui temporis.*—P.G.

[Perkin Warbeck] was perfect in his lesson, she began to cast with her self from what coast this Blazing-Starre should first appear, and at what time it must be upon the horizon of Ireland; for there had the like meteor strong influence before."

Methinks our sagacious Thuanus does not give into such fustian, which formerly was looked upon as sublime, but in this age is justly called nonsense.

LETTER XIII

On Mr. Locke

Perhaps no man ever had a more judicious or more methodical genius or was a more acute logician than Mr. Locke, and yet he was not deeply skilled in the mathematics. This great man could never subject himself to the tedious fatigue of calculations, nor to the dry pursuit of mathematical truths, which do not at first present any sensible objects to the mind; and no one has given better proofs than he that it is possible for a man to have a geometrical head without the assistance of geometry. Before his time, several great philosophers had declared, in the most positive terms, what the soul of man is; but as these absolutely knew nothing about it, they might very well be allowed to differ entirely in opinion from one another.

In Greece, the infant seat of arts and of errors, and where the grandeur as well as the folly of the human mind went such prodigious lengths, the people used to reason about the soul in the very same manner as we do.

The divine Anaxagoras, in whose honor an altar was erected, for his having taught mankind that the sun was greater than Peloponnesus, that snow was black, and that the heavens were of stone, affirmed that the soul was an aerial spirit, but at the same time immortal. Diogenes (not he who was a cynical philosopher after having coined base money) declared that the soul was a portion of the substance of God; an idea which we must confess was very sublime. Epicurus maintained that it was composed of parts in the same manner as the body.

Aristotle, who has been explained a thousand ways, because he is unintelligible, was of the opinion, according to some of his disciples, that the understanding in all men is one and the same substance.

The divine Plato, master of the divine Aristotle, and the divine

Socrates, master of the divine Plato, used to say that the soul was corporeal and eternal. No doubt but the demon of *Socrates* had instructed him in the nature of it. Some people, indeed, pretend that a man who boasted his being attended by a familiar genius must infallibly be either a knave or a madman, but this kind of people are seldom satisfied with anything but reason.

With regard to the Fathers of the Church, several in the primitive ages believed that the soul was human, and the angels and God corporeal. Men naturally improve upon every system. Saint Bernard, as Father Mabillon confesses, taught that the soul after death does not see God in the celestial regions, but converses with Christ's human nature only. However, he was not believed this time on his bare word; the adventure of the Crusade having a little sunk the credit of his oracles. Afterwards a thousand Schoolmen arose, such as the Irrefragable Doctor [Alexander of Hales] the Subtile Doctor [Duns Scotus], the Angelic Doctor [Saint Thomas Aquinas], the Seraphic Doctor [Saint Bonaventure], and the Cherubic Doctor, who were all sure that they had a very clear and distinct idea of the soul, and yet wrote in such a manner that one would conclude they were resolved no one should understand a word in their writings. Our Descartes, born not to discover the errors of antiquity, but to substitute his own in the room of them, and hurried away by the systematic spirit which throws a cloud over the minds of the greatest men, thought he had demonstrated that the soul is the same thing as thought, in the same manner as matter, in his opinion, is the same as extension. He asserted that man thinks eternally, and that the soul, at its coming into the body, is informed with the whole series of metaphysical notions; knowing God, infinite space, possessing all abstract ideas; in a word, completely endued with the most sublime lights, which it unhappily forgets at its issuing from the womb.

Father Malebranche, in his sublime illusions, not only admitted innate ideas, but did not doubt of our living wholly in God, and that God is, as it were, our soul.

Such a multitude of reasoners having written the romance of the soul, a sage at last arose who gave, with an air of the greatest modesty, the history of it. Mr. Locke has displayed the human soul in the same manner as an excellent anatomist explains the springs of the human body. He everywhere takes the light of physics for his Guide. He sometimes presumes to speak affirmatively, but then he presumes also to doubt. Instead of concluding at once what we know not, he examines gradually what we would know. He takes an infant at the instant of his Birth; he traces, step by step, the progress of his understanding; examines what things he has in common with beasts, and what he possesses above them. Above all he consults himself; the being conscious that he himself thinks.

I shall leave, says he, to those who know more of this matter than myself, the examining whether the soul exists before or after the organization of our bodies. But I confess that it is my lot to be animated with one of those heavy souls which do not think always; and I am even so unhappy as not to conceive that it is more necessary the soul should think perpetually than that bodies should be for ever in motion.

With regard to myself, I shall boast that I have the honour to be as stupid in this particular as Mr. Locke. No one shall ever make me believe that I think always; and I am as little inclined as he could be to fancy that some weeks after I was conceived I was a very learned soul, knowing at that time a thousand things which I forgot at my birth, and possessing when in the womb (though to no manner of purpose) knowledge which I lost the instant I had occasion for it, and which I have never since been able to recover perfectly.

Mr. Locke, after having destroyed innate ideas; after having fully renounced the vanity of believing that we think always; after having laid down, from the most solid principles, that ideas enter the mind through the senses; having examined our simple and complex ideas; having traced the human mind through its several operations; having showed that all the languages in the world are imperfect, and the great abuse that is made of words every moment; he at last comes to consider the extent or rather the narrow limits of human knowledge. It was in this chapter he presumed to advance, but very modestly, the following words: "We shall, perhaps, never be capable of knowing, whether a Being, purely material, thinks or not." This sage assertion was, by more divines than one, looked upon as a scandalous declaration that the soul is material and mortal. Some Englishmen, devout after their way, sounded an alarm. The superstitious are the same in society as cowards in an army; they themselves are seized with a panic fear, and communicate it to others. It was loudly exclaimed that Mr. Locke intended to destroy religion; nevertheless, religion had nothing to do in the affair, it being a question purely philosophical, altogether independent of faith and revelation. Mr. Locke's opponents needed but to examine, calmly and impartially, whether the declaring that matter can think implies a contradiction, and whether God is able to communicate thought to matter. But divines are too apt to begin their declarations with saying that God is offended when people differ from them in opinion; in which they too much resemble the bad poets who used to declare publicly that Boileau spoke irreverently of Louis XIV because he ridiculed their stupid productions. Bishop Stillingfleet got the reputation of a calm and unprejudiced divine because he did not expressly make use of injurious terms in his dispute with Mr. Locke. That divine entered the lists against him, but was defeated; for he argued as a Schoolman, and Locke as a philosopher, who was perfectly acquainted with the strong as well as the weak side of the human mind, and who fought with weapons whose temper he knew. If I might presume to give my opinion on so delicate a subject after Mr. Locke, I would say that men have long disputed on the nature and the immortality of the soul. With regard to its immortality, it is impossible to give a demonstration of it, since its nature is still the subject of controversy; which, however, must be thoroughly understood before a person can be able to determine whether it be immortal or not. Human reason is so little able, merely by its own strength, to demonstrate the immortality of the soul, that it was absolutely necessary religion should reveal it to us. It is of advantage to society in general that mankind should believe the soul to be immortal; faith commands us to do this; nothing more is required, and the matter is cleared up at once. But it is otherwise with respect to its nature; it is of little importance to religion, which only requires the soul to be virtuous, what substance it may be made of. It is a clock which is given us to regulate, but the artist has not told us of what materials the spring of this clock is composed.

I am a body and, I think, that's all I know of the matter. Shall I ascribe to an unknown cause what I can so easily impute to the only second cause I am acquainted with? Here all the School philosophers interrupt me with their arguments and declare that there is only extension and solidity in bodies, and that there they can have nothing but motion and figure. Now, motion, figure, extension and solidity cannot form a thought, and consequently the soul cannot be matter. All this, so often repeated, mighty series of reasoning, amounts to no more than this: I am absolutely ignorant what matter is; I guess but imperfectly some properties of it; now, I absolutely cannot tell whether these properties may be joined to thought. As I therefore know nothing, I maintain positively that matter cannot think. In this manner do the Schools reason.

Mr. Locke addressed these gentlemen in the candid, sincere manner following: At least confess yourselves to be as ignorant as I. Neither your imaginations nor mine are able to comprehend in what manner a body is susceptible of ideas; and do you conceive better in what manner a substance, of what kind soever, is susceptible of them? As you cannot comprehend either matter or spirit, why will you presume to assert anything?

The superstitious man comes afterwards, and declares that all those must be burnt for the good of their souls who so much as suspect that it is possible for the body to think without any foreign assistance. But what would these people say should they themselves be proved irreligious? And, indeed, what man can presume to assert, without being guilty at the same time of the greatest impiety, that it is impossible for the Creator to form matter with thought and sensation? Consider only, I beg you, what a dilemma you bring yourselves into, you who confine in this manner the power of the Creator. Beasts have the same organs, the same sensations, the same perceptions as we; they have memory, and combine certain ideas. In case it was not in the power of God to animate matter and inform it with sensation, the consequence would be either that beasts are mere machines or that they have a spiritual soul.

Methinks it is clearly evident that beasts cannot be mere machines, which I prove thus: God has given them the very same organs of sensation as to us: If therefore they have no sensation, God has created a useless thing; now, according to your own confession, God does nothing in vain; he therefore did not create so many organs of sensation merely for them to be uninformed with this faculty; consequently beasts are not mere machines. Beasts, according to your assertion, cannot be animated with a spiritual soul; you will therefore, in spight of yourself, be reduced to this only assertion, *viz.* that God has endued the organs of beasts, who are mere matter, with the faculties of sensation and perception, which you call instinct in them. But why may not God, if he pleases, communicate to our more delicate organs that faculty of feeling, perceiving and thinking which we call human reason? To whatever side you turn, you are forced to acknowledge your own ignorance and the boundless power of the Creator. Exclaim therefore no more against the sage, the modest philosophy of Mr. Locke, which, so far from interfering with religion, would be of use to demonstrate the truth of it, in case Religion wanted any such support. For what philosophy can be of a more religious nature than that which, affirming nothing but what it conceives clearly, and conscious of its own weakness, declares that we must always have recourse to God in our examining of the first principles.

Besides, we must not be apprehensive that any philosophical opinion will ever prejudice the religion of a country. Though our demonstrations clash directly with our mysteries, that's nothing to the purpose, for the latter are not less revered upon that account by our Christian philosophers, who know very well that the objects of reason and those of faith are of a very different nature. Philosophers will never form a religious sect, the reason of which is, their writings are not calculated for the vulgar, and they themselves are free from enthusiasm. If we divide mankind into twenty parts, it will be found that nineteen of these consist of persons employed in manual labour, who will never know that such a man as Mr. Locke existed. In the remaining twentieth part how few are readers? And among such as are so, twenty amuse themselves with romances to one who studies philosophy. The thinking part of mankind are confined to a very small number, and these will never disturb the peace and tranquillity of the world.

Neither Montaigne, Locke, Bayle, Spinoza, Hobbes, Lord Shaftesbury, Collins nor Toland lighted up the firebrand of discord in their countries; this has generally been the work of divines, who, being at first puffed up with the ambition of becoming chiefs of a sect, soon grew very desirous of being at the head of a party. But what do I say? All the works of the modern philosophers put together will never make so much noise as even the dispute which arose among the Franciscans merely about the fashion of their sleeves and of their cowls.

LETTER XIV

On Descartes and Sir Isaac Newton

A Frenchman who arrives in London will find philosophy, like everything else, very much changed there. He had left the world a *plenum,* and he now finds it a *vacuum*. At Paris the universe is seen composed of vortices of subtile matter; but nothing like it is seen in London. In France it is the pressure of the moon that causes the tides; but in England it is the sea that gravitates towards the moon; so that when you think that the moon should make it flood with us, those gentlemen fancy it should be ebb, which, very unluckily, cannot be proved. For to be able to do this it is necessary the moon and the tides should have been enquired into at the very instant of the Creation.

You'll observe farther that the sun, which in France is said to have nothing to do in the affair, comes in here for very near a quarter of its assistance. According to your Cartesians, everything is performed by an impulsion, of which we have very little notion; and according to Sir Isaac Newton, it is by an attraction, the cause of which is as much unknown to us. At Paris you imagine that the earth is shaped like a melon, or of an oblique figure; at London it has an oblate one. A Cartesian declares that light exists in the air; but a Newtonian asserts that it comes from the sun in six minutes and a half. The several operations of your chemistry are performed by acids, alkalies and subtile matter; but attraction prevails even in chymistry among the English.

The very essence of things is totally changed. You neither are agreed upon the definition of the soul nor on that of matter. Descartes, as I observed in my last, maintains that the soul is the same thing with thought, and Mr. Locke has given a pretty good proof of the contrary.

Descartes asserts farther, that extension alone constitutes matter, but Sir Isaac adds solidity to it.

How furiously contradictory are these opinions!

> *Non nostrum inter vos tantas componere lites.*
> VIRGIL, Eclog. III.
> 'Tis not for us to end such great Disputes.

This famous Newton, this destroyer of the Cartesian system, died in March Anno 1727. His countrymen honoured him in his lifetime, and interred him as though he had been a king who had made his people happy.

The English read with the highest satisfaction, and translated into their tongue, the elogium of Sir Isaac Newton which Mr. de Fontenelle spoke in the Academy of Sciences. Mr. de Fontenelle presides as judge over philosophers; and the English expected his decision as a solemn declaration of the superiority of the English philosophy over that of the French. But when it was found that this gentleman had compared Descartes to Sir Isaac, the whole Royal Society in London rose up in arms. So far from acquiescing with Mr. de Fontenelle's judgment, they criticized his discourse. And even several (who, however, were not the ablest philosophers in that body) were offended at the comparison, and for no other reason but because Descartes was a Frenchman.

It must be confessed that these two great men differed very much in conduct, in fortune, and in philosophy.

Nature had indulged Descartes a shining and strong imagination, whence he became a very singular person both in private life and in his manner of reasoning. This imagination could not conceal itself even in his philosophical works, which are everywhere adorned with very shining, ingenious metaphors and figures. Nature had almost made him a poet; and indeed he wrote a piece of poetry for the entertainment of Christina, Queen of Sweden, which, however, was suppressed in honour to his memory.

He embraced a military life for some time, and afterwards becoming a complete philosopher, he did not think the passion of love derogatory to his character. He had by his mistress a daughter called *Froncine,* who died young and was very much regretted by him. Thus he experienced every passion incident to mankind.

He was a long time of the opinion that it would be necessary for him to fly from the society of his fellow creatures, and especially from his native country, in order to enjoy the happiness of cultivating his philosophical studies in full liberty.

Descartes was very right, for his contemporaries were not knowing enough to improve and enlighten his understanding, and were capable of little else than of giving him uneasiness.

He left France purely to go in search of truth, which was then persecuted by the wretched philosophy of the Schools. However, he found that reason was as much disguised and depraved in the universities of Holland, into which he withdrew, as in his own country. For at the time that the French condemned the only propositions of his philosophy which were true, he was persecuted by the pretended philosophers of Holland, who understood him no better, and who, having a nearer view of his glory, hated his person the more, so that he was obliged to leave Utrecht. Descartes was injuriously accused of being an atheist, the last refuge of religious scandal; and he who had employed all the sagacity and penetration of his genius in searching for new proofs of the existence of a God was suspected to believe there was no such Being.

Such a persecution from all sides must necessarily suppose a most exalted merit as well as a very distinguished reputation, and indeed he possessed both. Reason at that time darted a ray upon the world through the gloom of the Schools and the prejudices of popular superstition. At last his name spread so universally that the French were desirous of bringing him back into his native country by rewards, and accordingly offered him an annual pension of a thousand crowns. Upon these hopes Descartes returned to France, paid the fees of his patent, which was sold at that time, but no pension was settled upon him. Thus disappointed, he returned to his solitude in North Holland, where he again pursued the study of philosophy, whilst the great Galileo, at fourscore years of age, was groaning in the prisons of the Inquisition, only for having demonstrated the earth's motion.

At last Descartes was snatched from the world in the flower of his age at Stockholm. His death was owing to a bad regimen, and he expired in the midst of some *literati* who were his enemies, and under the hands of a physician to whom he was odious.

The progress of Sir Isaac Newton's life was quite different. He lived happy and very much honoured in his native country, to the age of fourscore and five years.

It was his peculiar felicity not only to be born in a country of liberty, but in an age when all Scholastic impertinencies were banished from the world. Reason alone was cultivated, and mankind could only be his pupil, not his enemy.

One very singular difference in the lives of these two great men is that Sir Isaac, during the long course of years he enjoyed, was never sensible to any passion, was not subject to the common frailties of mankind, nor ever had any commerce with women; a circumstance which was assured me by the physician and surgeon who attended him in his last moments.

We may admire Sir Isaac Newton on this occasion, but then we must not censure Descartes.

The opinion that generally prevails in *England* with regard to these two philosophers is that the latter was a dreamer and the former a sage.

Very few people in England read Descartes, whose works indeed are now useless. On the other side, but a small number peruse those of Sir Isaac, because to do this the student must be deeply skilled in the mathematics, otherwise those works will be unintelligible to him. But notwithstanding this, these great men are the subject of everyone's discourse. Sir Isaac Newton is allowed every advantage, whilst Descartes is not indulged a single one. According to some, it is to the former that we owe the discovery of a vacuum, that the air is a heavy body, and the invention of telescopes. In a word, Sir Isaac Newton is here as the Hercules of fabulous story, to whom the ignorant ascribed all the feats of ancient heroes.

In a critique that was made in London on Mr. de Fontenelle's discourse, the writer presumed to assert that Descartes was not a great geometrician. Those who make such a declaration may justly be reproached with flying in their master's face. Descartes extended the limits of geometry as far beyond the place where he found them as Sir Isaac did after him. The former first taught the method of expressing curves by equations. This geometry, which, thanks to him for it, is now grown common, was so abstruse in his time that not so much as one professor would undertake to explain it; and Schotten in Holland, and Format in France, were the only men who understood it.

He applied this geometrical and inventive genius to dioptrics, which, when treated of by him, became a new art. And if he was mistaken in some things, the reason of that is, a man who discovers a new tract of land cannot at once know all the properties of the soil. Those who come after him, and make these Lands fruitful, are at least obliged to him for the discovery. I will not deny but that there are innumerable errors in the rest of Descartes's works.

Geometry was a guide he himself had in some measure fashioned, which would have conducted him safely through the several paths of natural philosophy. Nevertheless he at last abandoned this guide, and gave entirely into the humour of forming hypotheses; and then philosophy was no more than an ingenious romance, fit only to amuse the ignorant. He was mistaken in the nature of the soul, in the proofs of the existence of a God, in matter, in the laws of motion, and in the nature of light. He admitted innate ideas, he invented new elements, he created a world; he made Man according to his own fancy; and it is justly said that the Man of Descartes is in fact that of Descartes only, very different from the real one.

He pushed his metaphysical errors so far as to declare that two and two make four for no other reason but because God would have it so. However, it will not be making him too great a compliment if we affirm that he was valuable even in his mistakes. He deceived himself, but then it was at least in a methodical way. He destroyed all the absurd chimaeras with which youth had been infatuated for two thousand years. He taught his contemporaries how to reason, and enabled them to employ his own weapons against himself. If Descartes did not pay in good money, he however did great service in crying down that of a base alloy.

I indeed believe that very few will presume to compare his philosophy in any respect with that of Sir Isaac Newton. The former is an essay, the latter a masterpiece. But then the man who first brought us to the path of truth was perhaps as great a genius as he who afterwards conducted us through it.

Descartes gave sight to the blind. These saw the errors of antiquity and of the sciences. The path he struck out is since become boundless. Rohault's little work was during some years a complete system of physics; but now all the transactions of the several academies in Europe put together do not form so much as the beginning of a system. In fathoming this abyss no bottom has been found. We are now to examine what discoveries Sir Isaac Newton has made in it.

LETTER XXIII

On the Regard That Ought to Be Shown to Men of Letters

Neither the English nor any other people have foundations established in favour of the polite arts like those in France. There are universities in most countries, but it is in France only that we meet with so beneficial an encouragement for astronomy and all parts of the mathematics, for physics, for researches into antiquity, for painting, sculpture and architecture. Louis XIV has immortalized his name by these several foundations, and this immortality did not cost him two hundred thousand livres a year.

I must confess that one of the things I very much wonder at is that as the Parliament of Great Britain have promised a reward of twenty thousand pounds sterling to any person who may discover the longitude, they should never have once thought to imitate Louis XIV in his munificence with regard to the arts and sciences.

Merit indeed meets in England with rewards of another kind, which redound more to the honour of the nation. The English have so great a veneration for exalted talents that a man of merit in their country is always sure of making his fortune. Mr. Addison in France would have been elected a member of one of the academies, and, by the credit of some women, might have obtained a yearly pension of twelve hundred livres; or else might have been imprisoned in the Bastille, upon pretence that certain strokes in his tragedy of *Cato* had been discovered which glanced at the porter of some man in power. Mr. Addison was raised to the Post of Secretary of State in England. Sir Isaac Newton was made Warden of the Royal Mint. Mr. Congreve had a considerable employment. Mr. Prior was Plenipotentiary. Dr. Swift is Dean of St. Patrick in Dublin, and is more revered in Ireland than the Primate himself. The religion which Mr. Pope professes excludes him indeed from preferments of every kind, but then it did not prevent his gaining two hundred thousand livres by his excellent translation of Homer. I myself saw a long time in France the author of *Rhadamistus* [Crébillon] ready to perish for Hunger; and the son of one of the greatest men our Country ever gave birth to [Racine], and who was beginning to run the noble career which his father had set him, would have been reduced to the extremes of misery had he not been patronized by Monsieur Fagon.

But the circumstance which mostly encourages the arts in England is the great veneration which is paid them. The picture of the Prime Minister hangs over the chimney of his own closet, but I have seen that of Mr. Pope in twenty noblemen's houses. Sir Isaac Newton was revered in his lifetime, and had a due respect paid to him after his death, the greatest men in the nation disputing who should have the honour of holding up his pall. Go into Westminster Abbey and you'll find that what raises the admiration of the spectator is not the mausoleums of the English Kings, but the monuments which the gratitude of the nation has erected to perpetuate the memory of those illustrious men who contributed to its glory. We view their statues in that Abbey in the same manner as those of Sophocles, Plato and other immortal personages were viewed in Athens; and I am persuaded that the bare sight of those glorious monuments has fired more than one breast, and been the occasion of their becoming great men.

The English have even been reproached with paying too extravagant honours to mere merit, and censured for interring the celebrated actress Mrs. Oldfield in Westminster Abbey, with almost the same pomp as Sir Isaac Newton. Some pretend that the English had paid her these great funeral honours purposely to make us more strongly sensible of the barbarity and injustice which they object to us for having buried Mademoiselle Lecouvreur ignominiously in the fields.

But be assured from me that the English were prompted by no other principle, in burying Mrs. Oldfield in Westminster Abbey, than their good sense. They are far from being so ridiculous as to brand with infamy an art which has immortalized an Euripides and a Sophocles; or to exclude from the body of their citizens a set of people whose business is to set off with the utmost grace of speech and action those pieces which the nation is proud of.

Under the reign of Charles I, and in the beginning of the Civil

Wars raised by a number of rigid fanatics, who at last were the victims to it, a great many pieces were published against theatrical and other shows, which were attacked with the greater virulence because that monarch and his Queen, daughter to Henry IV of France, were passionately fond of them.

One Mr. Prynne, a man of most furiously scrupulous principles, who would have thought himself damned had he worn a cassock instead of a short cloak, and have been glad to see one half of mankind cut the other to pieces for the glory of God and the *Propaganda Fide,* took it into his head to write a most wretched satire against some pretty good comedies which were exhibited very innocently every night before their Majesties. He quoted the authority of the rabbis, and some passages from Saint Bonaventure, to prove that the *Oedipus* of Sophocles was the work of the Evil Spirit; that Terence was excommunicated *ipso facto;* and added that doubtless Brutus, who was a very severe Jansenist, assassinated Julius Cæsar for no other reason but because he, who was *Pontifex Maximus,* presumed to write a tragedy the subject of which was Oedipus. Lastly, he declared that all who frequented the theatre were excommunicated, as they thereby renounced their baptism. This was casting the highest insult on the King and all the Royal Family; and as the English loved their Prince at that time, they could not bear to hear a writer talk of excommunicating him, though they themselves afterwards cut his head off. Prynne was summoned to appear before the Star Chamber; his wonderful book, from which Father Le Brun stole his, was sentenced to be burnt by the common hangman, and himself to lose his ears. His trial is now extant.

The Italians are far from attempting to cast a blemish on the opera, or to excommunicate Signor Senesino or Signora Cuzzoni. With regard to myself, I could presume to wish that the magistrates would suppress I know not what contemptible pieces written against the stage. For when the English and Italians hear that we brand with the greatest mark of infamy an art in which we excel; that we excommunicate persons who receive salaries from the King; that we condemn as impious a spectacle exhibited in convents and monasteries; that we dishonour sports in which Louis XIV and Louis XV performed as actors; that we give the title of the Devil's works to pieces which are received by magistrates of the most severe character, and represented before a virtuous Queen; when, I say, foreigners are told of this insolent authority, and this Gothic rusticity which some presume to call Christian severity, what an idea must they entertain of our nation? And how will it be possible for them to conceive, either that our laws give a sanction to an art which is declared infamous, or that some persons dare to stamp with infamy an art which receives a sanction from the laws, is rewarded by kings, cultivated and encouraged by the greatest men, and admired by whole nations? And that Father Le Brun's impertinent libel against the stage is seen in a bookseller's shop, standing the very next to the immortal labours of Racine, of Corneille, of Molière, etc.

FURTHER READING

Theodore Besterman, *Voltaire* (1969). While dependable on dates and other facts, this extensive biography by the editor of Voltaire's correspondence is feeble on what, after all, matters most: Voltaire's ideas.

Peter Gay, *Voltaire's Politics: The Poet as Realist* (1959). An attempt to portray Voltaire as a tough-minded observer; Chapter I concentrates on the *Letters Concerning the English Nation.*

Gustave Lanson, *Voltaire* (tr. 1966). This old biographical essay of 1906 retains a great deal of vitality.

Norman L. Torrey, *The Spirit of Voltaire* (1938). An interesting interpretative essay, not strong on politics.

Ira O. Wade, *Voltaire and Madame du Châtelet* (1941). Significantly revises earlier biographies (including Lanson), on Voltaire's middle years from the early 1730s to the late 1740s, and shows them to have been years of hard work.

See also below, "Further Reading" for selection 19.

14 ❈ ROUSSEAU

Discours sur l'origine de l'inégalité

[From the book *The Social Contract and Discourses and Other Essays by Jean Jacques Rousseau*, translated and with an introduction by G. D. H. Cole (1950), 176–81, 189–95, 196–99, 204–5, 208–10, 234–38.*]

Jean-Jacques Rousseau was the maverick of the Enlightenment. The other philosophes had as much trouble classifying him as later scholars would placing him in the right pigeonhole. With his unashamed if often inaccurate self-revelations, with his pleasure in sentiment, with his love for the simple virtues and the out-of-doors, coupled with his repudiation of his old associates, it has been tempting to separate Rousseau from the philosophes and treat him as a precursor of some later age—a kind of Romantic cuckoo in the Enlightened nest. It is of course true that his voluminous and disparate writings have been read in many ways and used for many purposes. It is true, too, that his cultural criticism was more unsparing and his political theory more far-reaching than the criticism and the theory of the other philosophes. But at heart Rousseau belongs to the Enlightenment. He was, like many of the other philosophes, a deist; he believed, like all of them, in searching for ways in which man might become autonomous; he was, more than most of the other philosophes, an educator. By conviction as well as by temperament, Rousseau stands alone. But he stands within a larger camp, with more ties to his fellows than he and his fellows were ready to acknowledge.

Rousseau was born in 1712 in the small republic of Geneva, and

* Everyman's Library edition, published by E. P. Dutton & Company, Inc., and J. M. Dent & Sons, Ltd., and used with their permission.

remained "citizen of Geneva" in his mind, if not by residence. His mother died after giving birth to him, and his father, a capable but shiftless watchmaker, abandoned him to an odd succession of foster homes, where he learned more about the seamy side of life than was good for him. In 1728 he set out on his wanderings, and for some years he was a Roman Catholic. In 1731 he moved in with Madame de Warens, who was a dozen years older than he, and with whom he lived in her house in Annecy off and on for over ten years, first as her young friend, then as her lover. Living the life almost of a recluse, Rousseau found ample time to educate himself. Finally, in 1742, supplanted in "Maman's" bed—Rousseau always called Madame de Warens "Maman"—he went to Paris. There he fell in with the philosophes and made something of an impression on fashionable society as a rather rustic but doubtless promising thinker.

One of his closest early friends was Denis Diderot, who, in 1747, undertook to edit an ambitious new encyclopedia.* But in 1749 Diderot was imprisoned in the Fortress of Vincennes for writing a subversive philosophical tract; Vincennes is near Paris, and as Rousseau walked toward the fortress to visit his friend, his eye fell on an announcement of the Academy of Dijon, advertising a prize contest on the question "Has the progress of the arts and sciences corrupted or improved human conduct?" What follows remains in dispute. Rousseau claims to have had an instant, overwhelming, near-religious vision of the right answer: God has made man good, but man has wasted his divine gifts and constructed an evil society. Stunned (he later reported), Rousseau found himself sitting under a tree, bathed in tears, and with a philosophy of culture ready in his mind. Diderot later disputed this dramatic account of how Rousseau discovered his true thought: everyone will take an affirmative stance, Diderot remembers he told Rousseau; take the negative one instead.

Whatever the real history of Rousseau's first work, he submitted a short discourse highly critical of man's cultural achievement, and won the prize. This made him famous and highly controversial. Rousseau's second discourse, submitted once again to Dijon in 1754, is far longer than the first; it was less successful with the prize committee, but far more successful intellectually. The Discourse on the Origin of Inequality *retains the critical posture of the first discourse, but it is far more discriminating in its condemnation of*

---

* For Diderot and the *Encyclopédie*, see below, pages 287–292.

civilization, and far more inventive in its exuberant detail. In this second discourse, Rousseau made distinctions among types of inequality and speculated on the moral effect of the origins of property.

His two discourses do not stand alone in Rousseau's work; they are, like other writings of the *1750s*, the essence of Rousseau's critical phase. His second phase of the early *1760s*, when he published that great trio La Nouvelle Héloïse, Émile, *and the* Contrat social,* depends on the work of demolition he had done in the *1750s*.

The Discourse on the Origin of Inequality, *published in 1755, was a profoundly innovative and upsetting essay, but Rousseau's friendship with Diderot and his long-standing admiration for Voltaire remained for the time being unimpaired. In 1754 he had decided to return to Geneva, and to resume his Protestant faith; the dedication of his second discourse celebrates his return. The great years of constructive achievement and the dark years of paranoia were still in the future.*†

DEDICATION TO THE REPUBLIC OF GENEVA

Most Honorable, Magnificent and Sovereign Lords, convinced that only a virtuous citizen can confer on his country honors which it can accept, I have been for thirty years past working to make myself worthy to offer you some public homage; and, this fortunate opportunity supplementing in some degree the insufficiency of my efforts, I have thought myself entitled to follow in embracing it the dictates of the zeal which inspires me, rather than the right which should have been my authorization. Having had the happiness to be born among you, how could I reflect on the equality which nature has ordained between men, and the inequality which they have introduced, without reflecting on the profound wisdom by which both are in this State happily combined and made to coincide, in the manner that is most in conformity with natural law, and most favorable to society, to the maintenance of public order and to the happiness of individuals? In my researches after the best rules common sense can lay down for the constitution of a govern-

* See below, pages 303ff., 321f.
† See below, page 321f.

ment, I have been so struck at finding them all in actuality in your own, that even had I not been born within your walls I should have thought it indispensable for me to offer this picture of human society to that people, which of all others seems to be possessed of its greatest advantages, and to have best guarded against its abuses.

If I had had to make choice of the place of my birth, I should have preferred a society which had an extent proportionate to the limits of the human faculties; that is, to the possibility of being well governed: in which every person being equal to his occupation, no one should be obliged to commit to others the functions with which he was entrusted: a State, in which all the individuals being well known to one another, neither the secret machinations of vice, nor the modesty of virtue should be able to escape the notice and judgment of the public; and in which the pleasant custom of seeing and knowing one another should make the love of country rather a love of the citizens than of its soil.

I should have wished to be born in a country in which the interest of the Sovereign and that of the people must be single and identical; to the end that all the movements of the machine might tend always to the general happiness. And as this could not be the case, unless the Sovereign and the people were one and the same person, it follows that I should have wished to be born under a democratic government, wisely tempered.

I should have wished to live and die free: that is, so far subject to the laws that neither I nor anybody else should be able to cast off their honorable yoke: the easy and salutary yoke which the haughtiest necks bear with the greater docility, as they are made to bear no other.

I should have wished then that no one within the State should be able to say he was above the law; and that no one without should be able to dictate so that the State should be obliged to recognize his authority. For, be the constitution of a government what it may, if there be within its jurisdiction a single man who is not subject to the law, all the rest are necessarily at his discretion. And if there be a national ruler within, and a foreign ruler without, however they may divide their authority, it is impossible that both should be duly obeyed, or that the State should be well governed.

I should not have chosen to live in a republic of recent institution, however excellent its laws; for fear the government, being perhaps otherwise framed than the circumstances of the moment might require, might disagree with the new citizens, or they with it, and the State run the risk of overthrow and destruction almost as soon as it came into being. For it is with liberty as it is with those solid and succulent foods, or with those generous wines which are well adapted to nourish and fortify robust constitutions that are used to them, but ruin and intoxicate weak and delicate constitutions to which they are not suited. Peoples once accustomed to masters are not in a condition to do without them. If they attempt to shake off the yoke they still more estrange themselves from freedom, as, by mistaking for it an unbridled license to which it is diametrically opposed, they nearly always manage, by their revolutions, to hand themselves over to seducers, who only make their chains heavier than before. The Roman people itself, a model for all free peoples, was wholly incapable of governing itself when it escaped from the oppression of the Tarquins. Debased by slavery, and the ignominious tasks which had been imposed upon it, it was first no better than a stupid mob, which it was necessary to control and govern with the greatest wisdom; in order that, being accustomed by degrees to breathe the health-giving air of liberty, minds which had been enervated or rather brutalized under tyranny, might gradually acquire that severity of morals and spirit of fortitude which made it at length the people of all most worthy of respect. I should, then, have sought out for my country some peaceful and happy Republic, of an antiquity that lost itself, as it were, in the night of time: which had experienced only such shocks as served to manifest and strengthen the courage and patriotism of its subjects; and whose citizens, long accustomed to a wise independence, were not only free, but worthy to be so.

I should have wished to choose myself a country, diverted, by a fortunate impotence, from the brutal love of conquest, and secured, by a still more fortunate situation, from the fear of becoming itself the conquest of other States: a free city situated between several nations, none of which should have any interest in attacking it, while each had an interest in preventing it from being attacked by the others; in short, a Republic which should have nothing to tempt the ambition of its neighbors, but might reasonably depend on their assistance in case of need. It follows that a republican State so happily situated could have nothing to fear but from itself; and that, if its members trained themselves to the use of arms, it would be rather to keep alive that military ardor and courageous spirit which are so proper among freemen, and tend to keep up their taste for liberty, than from the necessity of providing for their defense.

I should have sought a country, in which the right of legislation was vested in all the citizens; for who can judge better than they of the conditions under which they had best dwell together in the same society? Not that I should have approved of *plebiscita,* like those among the Romans; in which the rulers in the State, and those most interested in its preservation, were excluded from the deliberations on which in many cases its security depended; and in which, by the most absurd inconsistency, the magistrates were deprived of rights which the meanest citizens enjoyed.

On the contrary, I should have desired that, in order to prevent self-interested and ill-conceived projects, and all such dangerous innovations as finally ruined the Athenians, each man should not be at liberty to propose new laws at pleasure; but that this right should belong exclusively to the magistrates; and that even they should use it with so much caution, the people, on its side, be so reserved in giving its consent to such laws, and the promulgation of them be attended with so much solemnity, that before the constitution could be upset by them, there might be time enough for all to be convinced, that it is above all the great antiquity of the laws which makes them sacred and venerable, that men soon learn to despise laws which they see daily altered, and that States, by accustoming themselves to neglect their ancient customs under the pretext of improvement, often introduce greater evils than those they endeavor to remove.

I should have particularly avoided, as necessarily ill-governed, a Republic in which the people, imagining themselves in a position to do without magistrates, or at least to leave them with only a precarious authority, should imprudently have kept for themselves the administration of civil affairs and the execution of their own laws. Such must have been the rude constitution of primitive governments, directly emerging from a state of nature; and this was another of the vices that contributed to the downfall of the Republic of Athens.

But I should have chosen a community in which the individuals, content with sanctioning their laws, and deciding the most important public affairs in general assembly and on the motion of the rulers, had established honored tribunals, carefully distinguished the several departments, and elected year by year some of the most capable and upright of their fellow-citizens to administer justice and govern the State; a community, in short, in which, the virtue of the magistrates thus bearing witness to the wisdom of the people, each class reciprocally did the other honor. If in such a case any fatal misunderstandings arose to disturb the public peace, even these intervals of blindness and error would bear the marks of moderation, mutual esteem, and a common respect for the laws; which are sure signs and pledges of a reconciliation as lasting as sincere. Such are the advantages, most honorable, magnificent, and sovereign lords, which I should have sought in the country in which I should have chosen to be born. And if providence had added to all these a delightful situation, a temperate climate, a fertile soil, and the most beautiful countryside under Heaven, I should have desired only, to complete my felicity, the peaceful enjoyment of all these blessings in the bosom of this happy country; to live at peace in the sweet society of my fellow-citizens, and practicing toward them, from their own example, the duties of friendship, humanity, and every other virtue, to leave behind me the honorable memory of a good man, and an upright and virtuous patriot,

PREFACE

Of all human sciences the most useful and most imperfect appears to me to be that of mankind: and I will venture to say, the single inscription on the Temple of Delphi contained a precept more difficult and more important than is to be found in all the huge volumes that moralists have ever written. I consider the subject of the following discourse as one of the most interesting questions philosophy can propose, and, unhappily for us, one of the most thorny that philosophers can have to solve. For how shall we know the source of inequality between men, if we do not begin by knowing mankind? And how shall man hope to see himself as nature made him, across all the changes which the succession of place and time must have produced in his original constitution? How can he distinguish what is fundamental in his nature from the changes and additions which his circumstances and the advances he has made have introduced to modify his primitive condition? Like the statue of Glaucus, which was so disfigured by time, seas, and tempests, that it looked more like a wild beast than a god, the human soul, altered in society by a thousand causes perpetually recurring, by the acquisition of a multitude of truths and errors, by the changes happening to the constitution of the body, and by the continual jarring of the passions, has, so to speak, changed in appearance, so as to be hardly recognizable. Instead of a being, acting constantly from fixed and invariable principles, instead of that celestial and majestic simplicity, impressed on it by its divine Author, we find it only the frightful contrast of passion mistaking itself for reason, and of understanding grown delirious.

It is still more cruel that, as every advance made by the human species removes it still farther from its primitive state, the more discoveries we make, the more we deprive ourselves of the means of making the most important of all. Thus it is, in one sense, by our very study of man, that the knowledge of him is put out of our power.

It is easy to perceive that it is in these successive changes in the constitution of man that we must look for the origin of those differences which now distinguish men, who, it is allowed, are as equal among themselves as were the animals of every kind, before physical causes had introduced those varieties which are now observable among some of them.

It is, in fact, not to be conceived that these primary changes, however they may have arisen, could have altered, all at once and in the same manner, every individual of the species. It is natural to think that, while the condition of some of them grew better or worse, and they were acquiring various good or bad qualities not inherent in their nature, there were others who continued a longer time in their original condition. Such was doubtless the first source of the inequality of mankind, which it is much easier to point out thus in general terms, than to assign with precision to its actual causes.

Let not my readers therefore imagine that I flatter myself with having seen what it appears to me so difficult to discover. I have here entered upon certain arguments, and risked some conjectures, less in the hope of solving the difficulty, than with a view of throwing some light upon it, and reducing the question to its proper form. Others may easily proceed farther on the same road, and yet no one find it very easy to get to the end. For it is by no means a light undertaking to distinguish properly between what is original and what is artificial in the actual nature of man, or to form a true idea of a state which no longer exists, perhaps never did exist, and probably never will exist; and of which it is, nevertheless necessary to have true ideas, in order to form a proper judgment of our present state. It requires, indeed, more philosophy than can be imagined to enable any one to determine exactly what precautions

he ought to take, in order to make solid observations on this subject; and it appears to me that a good solution of the following
problem would be not unworthy of the Aristotles and Plinys of the
present age. *What experiments would have to be made, to discover
the natural man? And how are those experiments to be made in a
state of society?*

So far am I from undertaking to solve this problem, that I think I
have sufficiently considered the subject, to venture to declare beforehand that our greatest philosophers would not be too good to
direct such experiments, and our most powerful sovereigns to make
them. Such a combination we have very little reason to expect,
especially attended with the perseverance, or rather succession of
intelligence and goodwill, necessary on both sides to success.

These investigations, which are so difficult to make, and have
been hitherto so little thought of, are, nevertheless, the only means
that remain of obviating a multitude of difficulties which deprive us
of the knowledge of the real foundations of human society. It is this
ignorance of the nature of man which casts so much uncertainty
and obscurity on the true definition of natural right: for, the idea
of right, says Burlamaqui, and more particularly that of natural
right, are ideas manifestly relative to the nature of man. It is, then,
from this very nature itself, he goes on, from the constitution and
state of man, that we must deduce the first principles of this science.

We cannot see without surprise and disgust how little agreement
there is between the different authors who have treated this great
subject. Among the more important writers there are scarcely two of
the same mind about it. Not to speak of the ancient philosophers,
who seem to have done their best purposely to contradict one
another on the most fundamental principles, the Roman jurists
subjected man and the other animals indiscriminately to the same
natural law, because they considered, under that name, rather the
law which nature imposes on herself than that which she prescribes
to others; or rather because of the particular acceptation of the term
"law" among those jurists; who seem on this occasion to have
understood nothing more by it than the general relations established by nature between all animated beings, for their common
preservation. The moderns, understanding by the term "law"
merely a rule prescribed to a moral being, that is to say intelligent,
free, and considered in his relations to other beings, consequently
confine the jurisdiction of natural law to man, as the only animal
endowed with reason. But, defining this law, each after his own

fashion, they have established it on such metaphysical principles, that there are very few persons among us capable of comprehending them, much less of discovering them for themselves. So that the definitions of these learned men, all differing in everything else, agree only in this, that it is impossible to comprehend the law of nature and consequently to obey it, without being a very subtle casuist and a profound metaphysician. All which is as much as to say that mankind must have employed, in the establishment of society, a capacity which is acquired only with great difficulty, and by very few persons, even in a state of society.

Knowing so little of nature, and agreeing so ill about the meaning of the word "law," it would be difficult for us to fix on a good definition of natural law. Thus all the definitions we meet with in books, setting aside their defect in point of uniformity, have yet another fault, in that they are derived from many kinds of knowledge, which men do not possess naturally, and from advantages of which they can have no idea until they have already departed from that state. Modern writers begin by inquiring what rules it would be expedient for men to agree on for their common interest, and then give the name of natural law to a collection of these rules, without any other proof than the good that would result from their being universally practiced. This is undoubtedly a simple way of making definitions, and of explaining the nature of things by almost arbitrary conveniences.

But as long as we are ignorant of the natural man, it is in vain for us to attempt to determine either the law originally prescribed to him or that which is best adapted to his constitution. All we can know with any certainty respecting this law is that, if it is to be a law, not only the wills of those it obliges must be sensible of their submission to it; but also, to be natural, it must come directly from the voice of nature.

Throwing aside, therefore, all those scientific books which teach us only to see men such as they have made themselves, and contemplating the first and most simple operations of the human soul, I think I can perceive in it two principles prior to reason, one of them deeply interesting us in our own welfare and preservation, and the other exciting a natural repugnance at seeing any other sensible being, and particularly any of our own species, suffer pain or death. It is from the agreement and combination which the understanding is in a position to establish between these two principles, without its being necessary to introduce that of sociability, that all the rules of natural right appear to me to be derived—rules which our reason is afterward obliged to establish on other foundations, when by its successive developments it has been led to suppress nature itself.

In proceeding thus, we shall not be obliged to make man a philosopher before he is a man. His duties toward others are not dictated to him only by the later lessons of wisdom; and, so long as he does not resist the internal impulse of compassion, he will never hurt any other man, nor even any sentient being, except on those lawful occasions on which his own preservation is concerned and he is obliged to give himself the preference. By this method also we put an end to the time-honored disputes concerning the participation of animals in natural law: for it is clear that, being destitute of intelligence and liberty, they cannot recognize that law; as they partake, however, in some measure of our nature, in consequence of the sensibility with which they are endowed, they ought to partake of natural right; so that mankind is subjected to a kind of obligation even toward the brutes. It appears, in fact, that if I am bound to do no injury to my fellow-creatures, this is less because they are rational than because they are sentient beings: and this quality, being common both to men and beasts, ought to entitle the latter at least to the privilege of not being wantonly ill-treated by the former.

The very study of the original man, of his real wants, and the fundamental principles of his duty, is, besides, the only proper method we can adopt to obviate all the difficulties which the origin of moral inequality presents, on the true foundations of the body politic, on the reciprocal rights of its members, and on many other similar topics equally important and obscure.

If we look at human society with a calm and disinterested eye, it seems, at first, to show us only the violence of the powerful and the oppression of the weak. The mind is shocked at the cruelty of the one, or is induced to lament the blindness of the other; and as nothing is less permanent in life than those external relations, which are more frequently produced by accident than wisdom, and which are called weakness or power, riches or poverty, all human institutions seem at first glance to be founded merely on banks of shifting sand. It is only by taking a closer look, and removing the dust and sand that surround the edifice, that we perceive the immovable basis on which it is raised, and learn to respect its foundations. Now, without a serious study of man, his natural faculties and their successive development, we shall never be able to make these necessary distinctions, or to separate, in the actual constitution of things, that which is the effect of the divine will from the innovations attempted by human art. The political and moral investigations, therefore, to which the important question before us leads, are in every respect useful; while the hypothetical history of governments affords a lesson equally instructive to mankind.

A Dissertation on the Origin and Foundation of the Inequality of Mankind

It is of man that I have to speak; and the question I am investigating shows me that it is to men that I must address myself: for questions of this sort are not asked by those who are afraid to honor truth. I shall, then, confidently uphold the cause of humanity before the wise men who invite me to do so, and shall not be dissatisfied if I acquit myself in a manner worthy of my subject and of my judges.

I conceive that there are two kinds of inequality among the human species: one, which I call natural or physical, because it is established by nature, and consists in a difference of age, health, bodily strength, and the qualities of the mind or of the soul; and another, which may be called moral or political inequality, because it depends on a kind of convention, and is established, or at least authorized, by the consent of men. This latter consists of the different privileges which some men enjoy to the prejudice of others; such as that of being more rich, more honored, more powerful, or even in a position to exact obedience.

It is useless to ask what is the source of natural inequality, because that question is answered by the simple definition of the word. Again, it is still more useless to inquire whether there is any essential connection between the two inequalities; for this would be only asking, in other words, whether those who command are necessarily better than those who obey, and if strength of body or of mind, wisdom, or virtue are always found in particular individuals, in proportion to their power or wealth: a question fit perhaps to be discussed by slaves in the hearing of their masters, but highly unbecoming to reasonable and free men in search of the truth.

The subject of the present discourse, therefore, is more precisely this: to mark, in the progress of things, the moment at which right took the place of violence and nature became subject to law, and to explain by what sequence of miracles the strong came to submit to serve the weak, and the people to purchase imaginary repose at the expense of real felicity.

The philosophers, who have inquired into the foundations of society, have all felt the necessity of going back to a state of nature; but not one of them has got there. Some of them have not hesitated to ascribe to man, in such a state, the idea of just and unjust, without troubling themselves to show that he must be possessed of such an idea, or that it could be of any use to him. Others have spoken of the natural right of every man to keep what belongs to him, without explaining what they meant by "belongs." Others again, beginning by giving the strong authority over the weak, proceeded directly to the birth of government, without regard to the time that must have elapsed before the meaning of the words "authority" and "government" could have existed among men. Every one of them, in short, constantly dwelling on wants, avidity, oppression, desires, and pride, has transferred to the state of nature ideas which were acquired in society; so that, in speaking of the savage, they described the social man. It has not even entered into the heads of most of our writers to doubt whether the state of nature ever existed; but it is clear from the Holy Scriptures that the first man, having received his understanding and commandments immediately from God, was not himself in such a state; and that, if we give such credit to the writings of Moses as every Christian philosopher ought to give, we must deny that, even before the deluge, men were ever in the pure state of nature; unless, indeed, they fell back into it from some very extraordinary circumstance: a paradox which it would be very embarrassing to defend, and quite impossible to prove.

Let us begin, then, by laying facts aside, as they do not affect the question. The investigations we may enter into, in treating this subject, must not be considered as historical truths, but only as mere conditional and hypothetical reasonings, rather calculated to explain the nature of things than to ascertain their actual origin; just like the hypotheses which our physicists daily form respecting the formation of the world. Religion commands us to believe that God Himself having taken men out of a state of nature immediately after the creation, they are unequal only because it is His will they should be so: but it does not forbid us to form conjectures based solely on the nature of man, and the beings around him, concerning what might have become of the human race if it had been left to itself. This, then, is the question asked me, and that which I propose to discuss in the following discourse. As my subject interests mankind in general, I shall endeavor to make use of a style adapted to all nations, or rather, forgetting time and place, to attend only to men to whom I am speaking. I shall suppose myself in the Lyceum of Athens, repeating the lessons of my masters, with Plato and Xenocrates for judges, and the whole human race for audience.

O man, of whatever country you are, and whatever your opinions may be, behold your history, such as I have thought to read it, not in books written by your fellow-creatures, who are liars, but in nature, which never lies. All that comes from her will be true; nor will you meet with anything false, unless I have involuntarily put in something of my own. The times of which I am going to speak are very remote: how much are you changed from what you once were! It is, so to speak, the life of your species which I am going to write, after the qualities which you have received, which your education and habits may have depraved, but cannot have entirely destroyed. There is, I feel, an age at which the individual man would wish to stop: you are about to inquire about the age at which you would have liked your whole species to stand still. Discontented with your present state, for reasons which threaten your unfortunate descendants with still greater discontent, you will perhaps wish it were in your power to go back; and this feeling should be a panegyric on your first ancestors, a criticism of your contemporaries, and a terror to the unfortunates who will come after you.

THE FIRST PART

. . . With respect to sickness, I shall not repeat the vain and false declamations which most healthy people pronounce against medicine; but I shall ask if any solid observations have been made from which it may be justly concluded that, in the countries where the art of medicine is most neglected, the mean duration of man's life is less than in those where it is most cultivated. How indeed can this be the case, if we bring on ourselves more diseases than medicine can furnish remedies? The great inequality in manner of living, the extreme idleness of some, and the excessive labor of others, the easiness of exciting and gratifying our sensual appetites, the too exquisite foods of the wealthy which overheat and fill them with indigestion, and, on the other hand, the unwholesome food of the poor, often, bad as it is, insufficient for their needs, which induces them, when opportunity offers, to eat voraciously and overcharge their stomachs; all these, together with sitting up late, and excesses of every kind, immoderate transports of every passion, fatigue, mental exhaustion, the innumerable pains and anxieties inseparable from every condition of life, by which the mind of man is incessantly tormented; these are too fatal proofs that the greater part of our ills are of our own making, and that we might have avoided them nearly all by adhering to that simple, uniform, and solitary manner of life which nature prescribed. If she destined man to be healthy, I venture to declare that a state of reflection is a state contrary to nature, and that a thinking man is a depraved animal. When we think of the good constitution of the savages, at least of those whom we have not ruined with our spirituous liquors, and reflect that they are troubled with hardly any disorders, save wounds and old age, we are tempted to believe that, in following the history of civil society, we shall be telling also that of human sickness. Such, at least, was the opinion of Plato, who inferred from certain remedies prescribed, or approved, by Podalirius and Machaon at the siege of Troy, that several sicknesses which these remedies gave rise to in his time were not then known to mankind: and Celsus tells us that diet, which is now so necessary, was first invented by Hippocrates.

Being subject therefore to so few causes of sickness, man, in the state of nature, can have no need of remedies, and still less of physicians: nor is the human race in this respect worse off than other animals, and it is easy to learn from hunters whether they meet with many infirm animals in the course of the chase. It is certain they frequently meet with such as carry the marks of having been considerably wounded, with many that have had bones or even limbs broken, yet have been healed without any other surgical assistance than that of time, or any other regimen than that of their ordinary life. At the same time their cures seem not to have been less perfect for their not having been tortured by incisions, poisoned with drugs, or wasted by fasting. In short, however useful medicine, properly administered, may be among us, it is certain that, if the savage, when he is sick and left to himself, has nothing to hope but from nature, he has, on the other hand, nothing to fear but from his disease; which renders his situation often preferable to our own. . . .

Every animal has ideas, since it has senses; it even combines those ideas in a certain degree; and it is only in degree that man differs, in this respect, from the brute. Some philosophers have even maintained that there is a greater difference between one man and another than between some men and some beasts. It is not, therefore, so much the understanding that constitutes the specific difference between the man and the brute, as the human quality of free agency. Nature lays her commands on every animal, and the brute obeys her voice. Man receives the same impulsion, but at the same time knows himself at liberty to acquiesce or resist: and it is particularly in his consciousness of this liberty that the spirituality of his soul is displayed. For physics may explain, in some measure, the mechanism of the senses and the formation of ideas; but in the power of willing, or rather of choosing, and in the feeling of this power, nothing is to be found but acts which are purely spiritual and wholly inexplicable by the laws of mechanism.

However, even if the difficulties attending all these questions should still leave room for difference in this respect between men and brutes, there is another very specific quality which distinguishes them, and which will admit of no dispute. This is the faculty of self-improvement, which, by the help of circumstances, gradually develops all the rest of our faculties, and is inherent in the species as in the individual: whereas a brute is, at the end of a few months, all he will ever be during his whole life, and his species, at the end of a thousand years, exactly what it was the first year of that thousand. Why is man alone liable to grow into a dotard? Is it not because he returns, in this, to his primitive state; and that, while the brute, which has acquired nothing and has therefore nothing to lose, still retains the force of instinct, man, who loses, by age or accident, all that his *perfectibility* had enabled him to gain, falls by this means lower than the brutes themselves? It would be melancholy were we forced to admit that this distinctive and almost unlimited faculty is the source of all human misfortunes; that it is this which, in time, draws man out of his original state, in which he would have spent his days insensibly in peace and innocence; that it is this faculty which, successively producing in different ages his discoveries and his errors, his vices and his virtues, makes him at length a tyrant both over himself and over nature. It would be shocking to be obliged to regard as a benefactor the man who first suggested to the Oroonoko Indians the use of the boards they apply to the temples of their children, which secure to them some part at least of their imbecility and original happiness.

Savage man, left by nature solely to the direction of instinct, or rather indemnified for what he may lack by faculties capable at first of supplying its place, and afterward of raising him much above it, must accordingly begin with purely animal functions: thus seeing and feeling must be his first condition, which would be common to him and all other animals. To will, and not to will, to desire and to fear, must be the first, and almost the only operations of his soul, till new circumstances occasion new developments of his faculties.

Whatever moralists may hold, the human understanding is greatly indebted to the passions, which, it is universally allowed, are also much indebted to the understanding. It is by the activity of the passions that our reason is improved; for we desire knowledge only because we wish to enjoy; and it is impossible to conceive any reason why a person who has neither fears nor desires should give himself the trouble of reasoning. The passions, again, originate in our wants, and their progress depends on that of our knowledge; for we cannot desire or fear anything except from the idea we have of it, or from the simple impulse of nature. Now, savage man, being destitute of every species of intelligence, can have no passions save those of the latter kind: his desires never go beyond his physical wants. The only goods he recognizes in the universe are food, a female, and sleep: the only evils he fears are pain and hunger. . . .

THE SECOND PART

The first man who, having enclosed a piece of ground, bethought himself of saying "This is mine," and found people simple enough to believe him, was the real founder of civil society. From how many crimes, wars, and murders, from how many horrors and misfortunes might not anyone have saved mankind, by pulling up the stakes, or filling up the ditch, and crying to his fellows: "Beware of listening to this impostor; you are undone if you once forget that the fruits of the earth belong to us all, and the earth itself to nobody." But there is great probability that things had then already come to such a pitch that they could no longer continue as they were; for the idea of property depends on many prior ideas, which could only be acquired successively, and cannot have been formed all at once in the human mind. Mankind must have made very considerable progress, and acquired considerable knowledge and industry which they must also have transmitted and increased from age to age, before they arrived at this last point of the state of nature. Let us, then, go farther back, and endeavor to unify under a single point of view that slow succession of events and discoveries in the most natural order.

Man's first feeling was that of his own existence, and his first care that of self-preservation. The produce of the earth furnished him with all he needed, and instinct told him how to use it. Hunger and other appetites made him at various times experience various modes of existence; and among these was one which urged him to propagate his species—a blind propensity that, having nothing to do with the heart, produced a merely animal act. The want once gratified, the two sexes knew each other no more; and even the offspring was nothing to its mother, as soon as it could do without her.

Such was the condition of infant man: the life of an animal limited at first to mere sensations, and hardly profiting by the gifts nature bestowed on him, much less capable of entertaining a thought of forcing anything from her. But difficulties soon presented themselves, and it became necessary to learn how to surmount them: the height of the trees, which prevented him from gathering their fruits, the competition of other animals desirous of the same fruits, and the ferocity of those who needed them for their own preservation, all obliged him to apply himself to bodily exercises. He had to be active, swift of foot, and vigorous in fight. Natural weapons, stones, and sticks, were easily found: he learned to surmount the obstacles of nature, to contend in case of necessity with other animals, and to dispute for the means of subsistence even with other men, or to indemnify himself for what he was forced to give up to a stronger.

In proportion as the human race grew more numerous, men's cares increased. The difference of soils, climates, and seasons must have introduced some differences into their manner of living. Barren years, long and sharp winters, scorching summers which parched the fruits of the earth, must have demanded a new industry. On the seashore and the banks of rivers, they invented the hook and line, and became fishermen and eaters of fish. In the forests they made bows and arrows, and became huntsmen and warriors. In cold countries they clothed themselves with the skins of the beasts they had slain. The lightning, a volcano, or some lucky chance acquainted them with fire, a new resource against the rigors of winter: they next learned how to preserve this element, then how to reproduce it, and finally how to prepare with it the flesh of animals which before they had eaten raw.

This repeated relevance of various beings to himself, and one to another, would naturally give rise in the human mind to the perceptions of certain relations between them. Thus the relations which we denote by the terms *great, small, strong, weak, swift, slow, fearful, bold,* and the like, almost insensibly compared at need, must have at length produced in him a kind of reflection, or rather a mechanical prudence, which would indicate to him the precautions most necessary to his security.

The new intelligence which resulted from this development increased his superiority over other animals, by making him sensible of it. He would now endeavor, therefore, to ensnare them, would play them a thousand tricks and, though many of them might surpass him in swiftness or in strength, would in time become the master of some and the scourge of others. Thus, the first time he looked into himself he felt the first emotion of pride; and, at a time when he scarce knew how to distinguish the different orders of beings, by looking upon his species as of the highest order he prepared the way for assuming preeminence as an individual.

Other men, it is true, were not then to him what they now are to us, and he had no greater intercourse with them than with other animals; yet they were not neglected in his observations. The conformities which he would in time discover between them, and between himself and his female, led him to judge of others which were not then perceptible; and finding that they all behaved as he himself would have done in like circumstances, he naturally inferred that their manner of thinking and acting was altogether in conformity with his own. This important truth, once deeply impressed on his mind, must have induced him, from an intuitive feeling more certain and much more rapid than any kind of reasoning, to pursue the rules of conduct which he had best observe toward them for his own security and advantage.

Taught by experience that the love of well-being is the sole motive of human actions, he found himself in a position to distinguish the few cases in which mutual interest might justify him in relying upon the assistance of his fellows; and also the still fewer cases in which a conflict of interests might give cause to suspect them. In the former case, he joined in the same herd with them, or at most in some kind of loose association, that laid no restraint on its members, and lasted no longer than the transitory occasion that formed it. In the latter case, everyone sought his own private advantage, either by open force, if he thought himself strong enough, or by address and cunning, if he felt himself the weaker.

In this manner, men may have insensibly acquired some gross

ideas of mutual undertakings, and of the advantages of fulfilling them: that is, just so far as their present and apparent interest was concerned; for they were perfect strangers to foresight, and were so far from troubling themselves about the distant future that they hardly thought of the morrow. If a deer was to be taken, everyone saw that, in order to succeed, he must abide faithfully by his post; but if a hare happened to come within the reach of any one of them, it is not to be doubted that he pursued it without scruple and, having seized his prey, cared very little if by so doing he caused his companions to miss theirs.

It is easy to understand that such intercourse would not require a language much more refined than that of rooks or monkeys, who associate together for much the same purpose. Inarticulate cries, plenty of gestures, and some imitative sounds must have been for a long time the universal language; and by the addition, in every country, of some conventional articulate sounds (of which, as I have already intimated, the first institution is not too easy to explain) particular languages were produced; but these were rude and imperfect, and nearly such as are now to be found among some savage nations.

Hurried on by the rapidity of time, by the abundance of things I have to say, and by the almost insensible progress of things in their beginnings, I pass over in an instant a multitude of ages; for the slower the events were in their succession, the more rapidly may they be described.

These first advances enabled men to make others with greater rapidity. In proportion as they grew enlightened, they grew industrious. They ceased to fall asleep under the first tree or in the first cave that afforded them shelter; they invented several kinds of implements of hard and sharp stones, which they used to dig up the earth, and to cut wood; they then made huts out of branches, and afterward learned to plaster them over with mud and clay. This was the epoch of a first revolution, which established and distinguished families, and introduced a kind of property, in itself the source of a thousand quarrels and conflicts. As, however, the strongest were probably the first to build themselves huts which they felt themselves able to defend, it may be concluded that the weak found it much easier and safer to imitate than to attempt to dislodge them; and of those who were once provided with huts, none could have any inducement to appropriate that of his neighbor; not indeed so much because it did not belong to him, as because it could be of no use, and he could not make himself master of it without exposing himself to a desperate battle with the family which occupied it.

The first expansion of the human heart were the effects of a novel situation which united husbands and wives, fathers and children, under one roof. The habit of living together soon gave rise to the finest feelings known to humanity, conjugal love and paternal affection. Every family became a little society, the more united because liberty and reciprocal attachment were the only bonds of its union. The sexes, whose manner of life had been hitherto the same, began now to adopt different ways of living. The women became more sedentary, and accustomed themselves to mind the hut and their children, while the men went abroad in search of their common subsistence. From living a softer life, both sexes also began to lose something of their strength and ferocity; but, if individuals became to some extent less able to encounter wild beasts separately, they found it, on the other hand, easier to assemble and resist in common.

FURTHER READING

Ernst Cassirer, *The Question of Jean-Jacques Rousseau* (tr. 1954). A brilliant essay unifying Rousseau's life and writings.

Peter Gay, "Reading about Rousseau," *The Party of Humanity: Essays in the French Enlightenment* (1964), 211–61. Critically surveys the voluminous literature on Rousseau, and suggests approaches to a biography. (Should be supplemented with *The Enlightenment: An Interpretation*, Vol. II, *The Science of Freedom* [1969], 529–52, 694–700, which advances the suggestion and brings the bibliography up to date.)

Jean Guéhenno, *Jean Jacques Rousseau*, 2 vols. (tr. 1966). A detailed and intelligent biography deliberately eschewing the advantages of hindsight.

Jean Starobinski, *Jean-Jacques Rousseau: La Transparence et l'obstacle* (1957). A sensitive psychological (though not psychoanalytical) study that unifies the totality of Rousseau's experience.

See also below, "Further Reading" for selections 26 and 27.

III

The Critique of "Superstition" and "Fanaticism"

*Deeply as the issue of religion divided the philosophes from their
Christian culture, they could count on allies even there. But most of
the alliances were unwitting. While the work of the Humanists and
of the erudite scholars of the seventeenth century had tended to
widen the intellectual and raise the religious horizons of European
civilization, practically all of them had been loyal, even pious
Christians. There was, as yet, no conflict between science and religion. Indeed, the periodic renewals of religious fervor—Pietism in
late-seventeenth-century Germany and Methodism in mid-
eighteenth-century England—emphasized a faith of the heart, a
turning away from Scholastic obsessions with finicky details of
textual interpretation, and a return to a religious inwardness inaccessible to rational proofs or disproofs.*

*At the same time, the late seventeenth and early eighteenth
centuries witnessed the rise of a reasonable religiosity in Protestant
and Catholic countries alike, and this new religiosity, though
clearly distinct from unbelief, yet advanced its cause. John Locke,
in his little book* The Reasonableness of Christianity *(1695), reduced the number of tenets a believing Christian must hold and
still remain a Christian to precisely one: the belief that Christ is the
Messiah. This seemed a long march toward deism, though the
philosophes made it clear that they did not think it identical with
Enlightenment. "Mr. Lock's reasonableness of Christian relligion is
really a new relligion," Voltaire wrote into one of his English notebooks.* And the philosophes were too busy assailing the old religion to wish to found a new one.*

*Still, this kind of Latitudinarianism prepared the minds of many
for the hardier fare of the philosophes. In England, bland Anglican
theologians—we have had a glimpse of them earlier, with a sermon
by Archbishop Tillotson—reduced the strenuousness of religious
obligation; in France, modern Jesuits did the same; in the German*

---

* *Voltaire's Notebooks,* ed. Theodore Besterman, 2 vols., continuously paginated
(1952) , 45.

states, a group of scholarly pastors known as the Neologians preached a rational religion almost indistinguishable from mere philosophy. "All revealed religion," as the German philosophe Lessing wrote in some disgust, "is nothing but a reconfirmation of the religion of reason. Either it has no mysteries or, if it does, it is indifferent whether the Christian combines them with one idea or another, or with none at all."*

The chief targets of these modern, rationalist theologians were obscurantism, fanaticism, and superstition. There was in all their work an open social bias: the poor, the illiterate—the "mob," in a word—needed the kind of consolation that superstitious beliefs could bring, the kind of reassurance available in the telling of ridiculous stories about saints or miracles, the kind of vulgar pleasure that could be extracted from colorful services, and the far from harmless release that came with outbursts of emotionalism. The writings of a Swift or a Voltaire on these matters are indistinguishable from each other.

Yet while the attacks of reasonable Christians and irreligious philosophes sounded alike, they were not the same. That is why I have placed cautionary quotation marks around the words "superstition" and "fanaticism" in the title of this section. It was splendid protective mimicry for, say, an atheist like Holbach or an extreme deist like Voltaire to pretend to be "merely" opposing superstitious beliefs and fanatical outbursts, in the name of "true" religion. Once we examine the philosophes' writings on these matters we find that their definition of superstition practically coincides with their definition of religion. The philosophes thus used their Christian allies in two ways: they exploited Christian scholarship for irreligious purposes, and they stood in the protective shadow of rationalist Christian writers to prepare their assault on all religion relatively unobserved and with an air of innocence. The selections that follow illustrate these techniques in a variety of ways; they also briefly demonstrate the general cultural atmosphere in which both the authentic and the exploitative fight against the "excrescences of religion" were carried on in the Age of the Enlightenment.

---

* "Gegensätze des Herausgebers," in Lessing, *Sämmtliche Schriften*, ed. Karl Lachmann and Franz Muncker, 23 vols. (1886–1924), XII, 431.

FURTHER READING

Arthur O. Lovejoy, "The Parallel of Deism and Classicism," in *Essays in the History of Ideas* (1948). Though not wholly convincing, an important attempt to "place" deism.

G. R. Cragg, *The Church and the Age of Reason (1648–1789)* (1960). A popular, brief, but judicious account of the established institution against which the philosophes mounted their attack.

R. R. Palmer, *Catholics and Unbelievers in Eighteenth Century France* (1939). The best study of the "other side"—Roman Catholic thought in France in the Age of the Enlightenment.

Leslie Stephen, *A History of English Thought in the Eighteenth Century*, 2 vols. (1876; 3rd edn., 1902). Vigorous, detailed study of English thought from deism and skepticism on the left to conservatism on the right. Responsible for the old division between constructive and critical deism, it needs revision at many points but remains eminently worth reading.

Roland N. Stromberg, *Religious Liberalism in Eighteenth-Century England* (1954). Full and fair-minded, this may be read in conjunction with Stephen's older work.

Ira O. Wade, *The Clandestine Organization and Diffusion of Philosophic Ideas in France from 1700 to 1750* (1938). Technical and illuminating discussion of writings that could circulate only in manuscript.

15 ❧ SWIFT

A Discourse Concerning the Mechanical Operation of the Spirit

[From "A Discourse Concerning the Mechanical
Operation of the Spirit," in Jonathan Swift,
The Prose Works, 12 vols. (1897–1908), I, 190–
210. Complete section. The fragmentary appearance of the essay is a deliberate mystifica-
tion on Swift's part.]

*Jonathan Swift, one of the great satirists in the English language,
was born in Dublin in 1667, spent much of his life there, and died
there in 1745. An Anglican priest from the early 1690s, he became
dean of St. Patrick's in his native city in 1713, and expended much
energy seeking to better the lot of the Irish clergy. But as a literate
and an articulate and prolific political pamphleteer, he also spent
some important years in London, where he knew the Whig jour-
nalists and political figures like Joseph Addison and Richard Steele,
and was closely associated with the leading literary lights of the age,
notably Alexander Pope and John Gay. His most famous book, of
course, is the* Gulliver's Travels *of 1726, but for all its celebrity its
precise significance (especially the target of the mordant fourth
book detailing Gulliver's adventures in the world of rational horses,
the Houyhnhnms, and degraded men, the Yahoos) remains a
matter of debate. In fact, Swift's private religious views have been
subjected to minute scrutiny and much discussion. It is perhaps
safest to accept the most obvious interpretation: that he was a sound
Anglican who detested superficiality, irrationality, and humbug in
religion as everywhere else. His biting, often scatological satire,* The
Mechanical Operation of the Spirit, *is characteristic of his satirical
procedure. Its analysis of religious enthusiasm as a physiological*

phenomenon is brilliant and devastating. Voltaire would have been proud to have written it; in any event, that Swift should have written it made Voltaire's work easier.

You will read it very gravely remarked in the books of those illustrious and right eloquent penmen, the modern travellers, that the fundamental difference in point of religion between the wild Indians and us, lies in this—that we worship God, and they worship the devil. But there are certain critics who will by no means admit of this distinction, rather believing that all nations whatsoever adore the true God, because they seem to intend their devotions to some invisible power of greatest goodness and ability to help them; which perhaps will take in the brightest attributes ascribed to the Divinity. Others again inform us that those idolators adore two principles—the principle of good, and that of evil; which indeed I am apt to look upon as the most universal notion that mankind, by the mere light of nature, ever entertained of things invisible. How this idea has been managed by the Indians and us, and with what advantage to the understandings of either, may well deserve to be examined. To me the difference appears little more than this, that they are put oftener upon their knees by their fears, and we by our desires; that the former set them a praying, and us a cursing. What I applaud them for is, their discretion in limiting their devotions and their deities to their several districts, nor ever suffering the liturgy of the white God to cross or to interfere with that of the black. Not so with us, who, pretending by the lines and measures of our reason to extend the dominion of one invisible power, and contract that of the other, have discovered a gross ignorance in the natures of good and evil, and most horribly confounded the frontiers of both. After men have lifted up the throne of their divinity to the *coelum empyraeum,* adorned with all such qualities and accomplishments as themselves seem most to value and possess— after they have sunk their principle of evil to the lowest centre, bound him with chains, loaded him with curses, furnished him with viler dispositions than any rake-hell of the town, accoutred him with tail, and horns, and huge claws, and saucer eyes—I laugh aloud to see these reasoners at the same time engaged in wise dispute, about certain walks and purlieus, whether they are in the verge of God or the devil; seriously debating whether such and such influences come into men's minds from above or below; whether certain passions and affections are guided by the evil spirit or the good:

> Dum fas atque nefas exiguo fine libidinum
> Discernunt avidi.

Thus do men establish a fellowship of Christ with Belial, and such is the analogy they make between cloven tongues and cloven feet. Of the like nature is the disquisition before us: it has continued these hundred years an even debate whether the deportment and the cant of our English enthusiastic preachers were possession or inspiration; and a world of argument has been drained on either side, perhaps to little purpose. For I think it is in life as in tragedy, where it is held a conviction of great defect, both in order and invention, to interpose the assistance of preternatural power without an absolute and last necessity. However, it is a sketch of human vanity for every individual to imagine the whole universe is interested in his meanest concern. If he has got cleanly over a kennel, some angel unseen descended on purpose to help him by the hand; if he has knocked his head against a post, it was the devil for his sins let loose from hell on purpose to buffet him. Who that sees a little paltry mortal, droning, and dreaming, and drivelling to a multitude, can think it agreeable to common good sense that either heaven or hell should be put to the trouble of influence or inspection upon what he is about? Therefore I am resolved immediately to weed this error out of mankind, by making it clear that this mystery of vending spiritual gifts is nothing but a trade, acquired by as much instruction, and mastered by equal practice and application, as others are. This will best appear by describing and deducting the whole process of the operation, as variously as it hath fallen under my knowledge or experience.

. . . .

[*Here the whole scheme of spiritual mechanism was deduced and explained, with an appearance of great reading and observation; but it was thought neither safe nor convenient to print it.*]

. . . .

Here it may not be amiss to add a few words upon the laudable practice of wearing quilted caps; which is not a matter of mere custom, humour, or fashion, as some would pretend, but an institution of great sagacity and use: these, when moistened with sweat, stop all perspiration; and, by reverberating the heat, prevent the spirit from evaporating any way but at the mouth; even as a skilful housewife that covers her still with a wet clout for the same reason, and finds the same effect. For it is the opinion of choice *virtuosi* that the brain is only a crowd of little animals, but with teeth and claws extremely sharp, and therefore cling together in the contexture we behold, like the picture of Hobbes' *Leviathan,* or like bees in perpendicular swarm upon a tree, or like a carrion corrupted into vermin, still preserving the shape and figure of the mother animal: that all invention is formed by the morsure of two or more of these animals upon certain capillary nerves which proceed from thence, whereof three branches spread into the tongue, and two into the right hand. They hold also that these animals are of a constitution extremely cold; that their food is the air we attract, their excrement phlegm; and that what we vulgarly call rheums, and colds, and distillations, is nothing else but an epidemical looseness, to which that little commonwealth is very subject from the climate it lies under. Further, that nothing less than a violent heat can disentangle these creatures from their hamated station of life, or give them vigour and humour to imprint the marks of their little teeth. That if the morsure be hexagonal it produces poetry; the circular gives eloquence: if the bite hath been conical, the person whose nerve is so affected shall be disposed to write upon politics; and so of the rest.

I shall now discourse briefly by what kind of practices the voice is best governed toward the composition and improvement of the spirit; for, without a competent skill in tuning and toning each word, and syllable, and letter, to their due cadence, the whole operation is incomplete, misses entirely of its effect on the hearers, and puts the workman himself to continual pains for new supplies, without success. For it is to be understood that, in the language of the spirit, cant and droning supply the place of sense and reason in the language of men: because, in spiritual harangues, the disposition of the words according to the art of grammar has not the least use, but the skill and influence wholly lie in the choice and cadence of the syllables; even as a discreet composer, who, in setting a song, changes the words and order so often, that he is forced to make it nonsense before he can make it music. For this reason it has been held by some that the art of canting is ever in greatest perfection when managed by ignorance; which is thought to be enigmatically meant by Plutarch, when he tells us that the best musical instruments were made from the bones of an ass. And the profounder critics upon that passage are of opinion, the word, in its genuine signification, means no other than a jaw-bone; though some rather think it to have been the *os sacrum;* but in so nice a case I shall not take upon me to decide; the curious are at liberty to pick from it whatever they please.

The first ingredient toward the art of canting is, a competent share of inward light; that is to say, a large memory, plentifully fraught with theological polysyllables and mysterious texts from holy writ, applied and digested by those methods and mechanical operations already related: the bearers of this light resembling lanterns compact of leaves from old Geneva bibles; which invention, Sir Humphrey Edwin, during his mayoralty, of happy memory highly approved and advanced; affirming the Scripture to be now fulfilled, where it says, Thy word is a lantern to my feet, and a light to my paths.

Now, the art of canting consists in skilfully adapting the voice to whatever words the spirit delivers, that each may strike the ears of the audience with its most significant cadence. The force or energy of this eloquence is not to be found, as among ancient orators, in the disposition of words to a sentence, or the turning of long periods; but, agreeably to the modern refinements in music, is taken up wholly in dwelling and dilating upon syllables and letters. Thus, it is frequent for a single vowel to draw sighs from a multitude, and for a whole assembly of saints to sob to the music of one solitary liquid. But these are trifles, when even sounds inarticulate are observed to produce as forcible effects. A master workman shall blow his nose so powerfully as to pierce the hearts of his people, who were disposed to receive the excrements of his brain with the same reverence as the issue of it. Hawking, spitting, and belching, the defects of other men's rhetoric are the flowers, and figures, and ornaments of his. For the spirit being the same in all, it is of no import through what vehicle it is conveyed.

It is a point of too much difficulty to draw the principles of this famous art within the compass of certain adequate rules. However, perhaps I may one day oblige the world with my critical essay upon the art of canting; philosophically, physically, and musically considered.

But, among all improvements of the spirit, wherein the voice has borne a part, there is none to be compared with that of conveying the sound through the nose, which, under the denomination of snuffling, has passed with so great applause in the world. The originals of this institution are very dark: but, having been initiated into the mystery of it, and leave being given me to publish it to the world, I shall deliver as direct a relation as I can.

This art, like many other famous inventions, owed its birth, or at least improvement and perfection, to an effect of chance; but was established upon solid reasons, and has flourished in this island ever since with great lustre. All agree that it first appeared upon the decay and discouragement of bagpipes, which, having long suffered under the mortal hatred of the brethren, tottered for a time, and at last fell with monarchy. The story is thus related.

As yet snuffling was not, when the following adventure happened to a Banbury saint. Upon a certain day, while he was far engaged among the tabernacles of the wicked, he felt the outward man put into odd commotions, and strangely pricked forward by the inward; an effect very usual among the modern inspired. For some think that the spirit is apt to feed on the flesh, like hungry wines upon raw beef. Others rather believe there is a perpetual game at leap-frog between both; and sometimes the flesh is uppermost, and sometimes the spirit; adding that the former, while it is in the state of a rider, wears huge Rippon spurs; and, when it comes to the turn of being bearer, is wonderfully headstrong and hard-mouthed. However it came about, the saint felt his vessel full extended in every part (a very natural effect of strong inspiration) ; and the place and time falling out so unluckily that he could not have the convenience of evacuating upwards, by repetition, prayer, or lecture, he was forced to open an inferior vent. In short, he wrestled with the flesh so long, that he at length subdued it, coming off with honourable wounds all before. The surgeon had now cured the parts primarily affected; but the disease, driven from its post, flew up into his head; and, as a skilful general, valiantly attacked in his trenches, and beaten from the field, by flying marches withdraws to the capital city, breaking down the bridges to prevent pursuit; so the disease, repelled from its first station, fled before the rod of Hermes to the upper region, there fortifying itself; but, finding the foe making attacks at the nose, broke down the bridge and retired to the head-quarters. Now, the naturalists observe that there is in human noses an idiosyncrasy, by virtue of which, the more the passage is obstructed, the more our speech delights to go through, as the music of a flageolet is made by the stops. By this method the twang of the nose becomes perfectly to resemble the snuffle of a bagpipe, and is found to be equally attractive of British ears; whereof the saint had sudden experience, by practising his new faculty with wonderful success, in the operation of the spirit; for, in a short time, no doctrine passed for sound and orthodox unless it were delivered through the nose. Straight every pastor copied after this original; and those who could not otherwise arrive to a perfection, spirited by a noble zeal, made use of the same experiment to acquire it; so that, I think, it may be truly affirmed the saints owe their empire to the snuffling of one animal, as Darius did his to the neighing of another; and both stratagems were performed by the same art; for we read how the Persian beast acquired his faculty by covering a mare the day before [Herodotus].

I should now have done, if I were not convinced that whatever I have yet advanced upon this subject is liable to great exception. For, allowing all I have said to be true, it may still be justly objected that there is in the commonwealth of artificial enthusiasm some real foundation for art to work upon, in the temper and complexion of individuals, which other mortals seem to want. Observe but the gesture, the motion, and the countenance of some choice professors, though in their most familiar actions, you will find them of a different race from the rest of human creatures. Remark your commonest pretender to a light within, how dark, and dirty, and gloomy he is without; as lanterns, which, the more light they bear in their bodies, cast out so much the more soot, and smoke, and fuliginous matter to adhere to the sides. Listen but to their ordinary talk, and look on the mouth that delivers it, you will imagine you are hearing some ancient oracle, and your understanding will be equally informed. Upon these, and the like reasons, certain objectors pretend to put it beyond all doubt that there must be a sort of preternatural spirit possessing the heads of the modern saints; and some will have it to be the heat of zeal working upon the dregs of ignorance, as other spirits are produced from lees by the force of fire. Some again think, that when our earthly tabernacles are disordered and desolate, shaken and out of repair, the spirit delights to dwell within them; as houses are said to be haunted when they are forsaken and gone to decay.

To set this matter in as fair a light as possible, I shall here very briefly deduce the history of fanaticism from the most early ages to the present. And if we are able to fix upon any one material or fundamental point, wherein the chief professors have universally agreed, I think we may reasonably lay hold on that, and assign it for the great seed or principle of the spirit.

The most early traces we meet with of fanatics in ancient story are among the Egyptians, who instituted those rites known in Greece by the names of Orgia, Panegyres and Dionysia; whether introduced there by Orpheus or Melampus we shall not dispute at present, nor in all likelihood at any time for the future [Diod. Sic., l. i. Plut, de Iside et Osiride]. These feasts were celebrated to the honour of Osiris, whom the Grecians called Dionysius, and is the same with Bacchus: which has betrayed some superficial readers to imagine that the whole business was nothing more than a set of roaring, scouring companions, overcharged with wine; but this is a scandalous mistake, foisted on the world by a sort of modern authors, who have too literal an understanding; and, because antiquity is to be traced backwards, do therefore, like Jews, begin their books at the wrong end, as if learning were a sort of conjuring. These are the men who pretend to understand a book by scouring through the index; as if a traveller should go about to describe a palace, when he had seen nothing but the privy; or like certain fortune-tellers in Northern America, who have a way of reading a man's destiny by peeping into his breech. For, at the time of instituting these mysteries, there was not one vine in all Egypt [Herodotus, l. ii.], the natives drinking nothing but ale; which liquor seems to have been far more ancient than wine, and has the honour of owing its invention and progress, not only to the Egyptian Osiris [Diod. Sic., l. i. and iii.], but to the Grecian Bacchus; who, in their famous expedition, carried the receipt of it along with them, and gave it to the nations they visited or subdued. Besides, Bacchus himself was very seldom or never drunk; for it is recorded of him that he was the first inventor of the mitre [Id., l. iv.], which he wore continually on his head (as the whole company of bacchanals did), to prevent vapours and the headache after hard drinking. And for this reason, say some, the scarlet whore, when she makes the kings of the earth drunk with her cup of abomination, is always sober herself, though she never balks the glass in her turn, being, it seems, kept upon her legs by the virtue of her triple mitre. Now these feasts were instituted in imitation of the famous expedition Osiris made through the world, and of the company that attended him, whereof the bacchanalian ceremonies were so many types and symbols. From which account [Diod. Sic., l. i. and iii.] it is manifest that the fanatic rites of these bacchanals cannot be imputed to intoxications by wine, but must needs have had a deeper foundation. What this was, we may gather large hints from certain circumstances in the course of their mysteries. For, in the first place, there was, in their processions, an entire mixture and confusion of sexes; they affected to ramble about hills and deserts; their garlands were of ivy and vine, emblems of cleaving and clinging; or of fir, the parent of turpentine. It is added that they imitated satyrs, were attended by goats, and rode upon asses, all companions of great skill and practice in affairs of gallantry. They bore for their ensigns certain curious figures, perched upon long poles, made into the shape and size of the *virga genitalis,* with its appurtenances; which were so many shadows and emblems of the whole mystery, as well as trophies set up by the female conquerors. Lastly, in a certain town of Attica, the whole solemnity, stripped of all its types [Dionysia Brauronia], was performed *in puris naturalibus,* the votaries not flying in coveys, but sorted into couples. The same may be further conjectured from the death of Orpheus, one of the institutors of these mysteries, who was torn in pieces by women, because he refused to communicate his orgies to them [*Vide* Photium in excerptis è Conone]; which others explained by telling us he had castrated himself upon grief for the loss of his wife.

Omitting many others of less note, the next fanatics we meet with of any eminence were the numerous sects of heretics appearing in the five first centuries of the Christian era, from Simon Magus and his followers to those of Eutyches. I have collected their systems from infinite reading, and, comparing them with those of their successors in the several ages since, I find there are certain bounds set even to the irregularity of human thought, and those a great deal narrower than is commonly apprehended. For, as they all frequently interfere even in their wildest ravings, so there is one fundamental point wherein they are sure to meet, as lines in a centre, and that is, the community of women. Great were their solicitudes in this matter, and they never failed of certain articles, in their schemes of worship, on purpose to establish it.

The last fanatics of note were those which started up in Germany a little after the reformation of Luther, springing as mushrooms do at the end of a harvest; such were John of Leyden, David George, Adam Neuster, and many others, whose visions and revelations always terminated in leading about half a dozen sisters a-piece, and making that practice a fundamental part of their system. For human life is a continual navigation, and if we expect our vessels to pass with safety through the waves and tempests of this fluctuating world, it is necessary to make a good provision of the flesh, as seamen lay in store of beef for a long voyage.

Now, from this brief survey of some principal sects among the fanatics in all ages (having omitted the Mahometans and others, who might also help to confirm the argument I am about) , to which I might add several among ourselves, such as the family of love, sweet singers of Israel, and the like; and, from reflecting upon that fundamental point in their doctrines about women wherein they have so unanimously agreed, I am apt to imagine that the seed or principle which has ever put men upon visions in things invisible is of a corporeal nature; for the profounder chemists inform us that the strongest spirits may be extracted from human flesh. Besides, the spinal marrow, being nothing else but a continuation of the brain, must needs create a very free communication between the superior faculties and those below; and thus the thorn in the flesh serves for a spur to the spirit. I think it is agreed among physicians that nothing affects the head so much as a tentiginous humour, repelled and elated to the upper region, found, by daily practice, to run frequently up into madness. A very eminent member of the faculty assured me that when the Quakers first appeared he seldom was without some female patients among them for the *furor*—; persons of a visionary devotion, either men or women, are, in their complexion, of all others, the most amorous; for zeal is frequently kindled from the same spark with other fires, and, from inflaming brotherly love, will proceed to raise that of a gallant. If we inspect into the usual process of modern courtship, we shall find it to consist in a devout turn of the eyes, called ogling; an artificial form of canting and whining by rote, every interval for want of other matter, made up with a shrug or a hum, a sigh or a groan; the style compact of insignificant words, incoherences, and repetition. These I take to be the most accomplished rules of address to a mistress; and where are these performed with more dexterity than by the saints? Nay, to bring this argument yet closer, I have been informed by certain sanguine brethren of the first class, that, in the height and orgasmus of their spiritual exercise, it has been frequent with them . . . ; immediately after which, they found the spirit to relax and flag of a sudden with the nerves, and they were forced to hasten to a conclusion. This may be further strengthened by observing, with wonder, how unaccountably all females are attracted by visionary or enthusiastic preachers, though ever so contemptible in their outward mien; which is usually supposed to be done upon considerations purely spiritual, without any carnal regards at all. But I have reason to think the sex has certain characteristics, by which they form a truer judgment of human abilities and performings than we ourselves can possibly do of each other. Let that be as it will, thus much is certain, that, however spiritual intrigues begin, they generally conclude like all others; they may branch upward toward heaven, but the root is in the earth. Too intense a contemplation is not the business of flesh and blood; it must, by the necessary course of things, in a little time let go its hold, and fall into matter. Lovers for the sake of celestial converse are but another sort of Platonics, who pretend to see stars and heaven in ladies' eyes, and to look or think no lower; but the same pit is provided for both; and they seem a perfect moral to the story of that philosopher, who, while his thoughts and eyes were fixed upon the constellations, found himself seduced by his lower parts into a ditch.

I had somewhat more to say upon this part of the subject; but the post is just going, which forces me in great haste to conclude,

Sir, yours, etc.

Pray burn this letter as soon as it comes to your hands.

FURTHER READING

Herbert Davis, *The Satire of Jonathan Swift* (1947). A dependable appraisal by a leading specialist.

Irving Ehrenpreis, *Swift: The Man, His Work, and the Age,* 2 vols. so far (1962, 1967). Promises to become the standard biography.

Louis A. Landa, *Swift and the Church of Ireland* (1954). An authoritative study of Swift's relation to the Church of his country.

Ricardo Quintana, *The Mind and Art of Jonathan Swift,* 2nd edn. (1953). An illuminating general analysis.

Edward W. Rosenheim, Jr., *Swift and the Satirist's Art* (1963). Interesting as a study of Swift's greatest gift.

16 ❧ POPE

An Essay on Man

[From *An Essay on Man*, Epistle I, in *The Works of Alexander Pope*, 10 vols. (1871), II, 347–71; notes omitted.]

During much of the nineteenth century, the reputation of Alexander Pope was in eclipse; his rhymed couplets and elegant diction placed him under suspicion of superficiality. It is only in recent decades that the profundity of his wit has been appreciated once more; in a sense, the modern reputation of Pope has returned to the reputation he enjoyed in his own time, not merely in England, but among educated persons—including, of course, the philosophes—on the Continent.

Born in 1688 in London, Pope faced and mastered some formidable social, religious, and personal handicaps in his life: he was the son of a linen draper, a Roman Catholic, and a frail child. Unable, as a Catholic, to attend the university or participate in politics, Pope made his mark as a wit, and was soon at the center of the liveliest literary circle in the English capital. He wrote a great deal of poetry, notably his Essay on Criticism *(1711), his mock-heroic* Rape of the Lock *(larger version, 1714), his celebrated and profitable translations from Homer—the* Iliad *appeared between 1715 and 1720, the* Odyssey *between 1725 and 1726—and his equally celebrated assault on foolishness, the* Dunciad *(final version, 1743). The* Essay on Man, *of which the first epistle is here reprinted in full, is an ambitious attempt to translate fashionable philosophizing into pleasing verse. It appeared in four epistles between 1732 and 1734.*

The doctrines of Pope's Essay on Man *are of considerable interest to the student of the Enlightenment. The poem sounds like sheer deism, with its vision of a reasonable god who has placed man in his proper place on the great chain of being, and who exacts only acceptance of his decrees. This is how the philosophes read him: as something of a deist. What is perhaps even more interesting is that Pope was constrained to deny this interpretation, and to make cruel fun of the deists in his* Dunciad. *This is significant, showing how easily intelligent and well-informed observers could confuse liberal Christianity with non-Christian philosophizing.*

Pope was of interest to the Enlightenment in still another way. He was among the first writers to claim and defend his independence as a man of letters. In selling his translations of Homer by subscription (and realizing £9,000), and in pointedly dedicating his Iliad *to Congreve, a fellow man of letters rather than a nobleman, Pope set a model of self-respect that was not lost on other philosophes, especially Voltaire, who knew and admired Pope's work well enough to imitate it in an* Épître en vers sur l'homme *of his own.*

Awake, my St. John! leave all meaner things
To low ambition, and the pride of kings.
Let us, since life can little more supply
Than just to look about us and to die,
Expatiate free o'er all this scene of man,
→ A mighty maze! but not without a plan,   *orderly*
A wild, where weeds and flow'rs promiscuous shoot;
Or garden tempting with forbidden fruit.
Together let us beat this ample field,
Try what the open, what the covert yield;
The latent tracts, the giddy heights, explore,
Of all who blindly creep, or sightless soar;
Eye nature's walks, shoot folly as it flies,
And catch the manners living as they rise;
Laugh where we must, be candid where we can;
But vindicate the ways of God to man.
    I. Say first, of God above or man below,
What can we reason but from what we know?
Of man, what see we but his station here,

From which to reason, or to which refer?
Through worlds unnumbered though the God be known,
'Tis ours to trace him only in our own.
He, who through vast immensity can pierce,
See worlds on worlds compose one universe,
Observe how system into system runs,
What other planets circle other suns,
What varied being peoples ev'ry star,
May tell why heav'n has made us as we are.
But of this frame, the bearings and the ties,
The strong connections, nice dependencies,
Gradations just, has thy pervading soul
Looked through, or can a part contain the whole?
  Is the great chain that draws all to agree,
And drawn supports, upheld by God or thee?
  II. Presumptuous man! the reason wouldst thou find,
Why formed so weak, so little, and so blind?
First, if thou canst, the harder reason guess,
Why formed no weaker, blinder, and no less?
Ask of thy mother earth, why oaks are made
Taller or stronger than the weeds they shade!
Or ask of yonder argent fields above
Why Jove's satellites are less than Jove!
  Of systems possible, if 'tis confessed
That wisdom infinite must form the best,
Where all must full or not coherent be,
And all that rises rise in due degree,
Then, in the scale of reas'ning life, 'tis plain,
There must be, somewhere, such a rank as man:
And all the question (wrangle e'er so long)
Is only this, if God has placed him wrong.
  Respecting man, whatever wrong we call,
May, must be right, as relative to all.
In human works, though laboured on with pain,
A thousand movements scarce one purpose gain;
In God's, one single can its end produce;
Yet serves to second too some other use.
So man, who here seems principal alone,
Perhaps acts second to some sphere unknown,
Touches some wheel, or verges to some goal;

'Tis but a part we see, and not a whole.
    When the proud steed shall know why man restrains
His fiery course, or drives him o'er the plains;
When the dull ox, why now he breaks the clod,
Is now a victim, and now Egypt's god;
Then shall man's pride and dulness comprehend
His actions', passions', being's, use and end;
Why doing, suff'ring, checked, impelled; and why
This hour a slave, the next a deity.
    Then say not man's imperfect, heav'n in fault;
Say rather man's as perfect as he ought:
His knowledge measured to his state and place,
His time a moment, and a point his space.
If to be perfect in a certain sphere,
What matter, soon or late, or here or there?
The bless'd to-day is as completely so,
As who began a thousand years ago.
    III. Heav'n from all creatures hides the book of fate,
All but the page prescribed, their present state;
From brutes what men, from men what spirits know;
Or who could suffer being here below?
The lamb thy riot dooms to bleed to-day,
Had he thy reason, would he skip and play?
Pleased to the last he crops the flow'ry food,
And licks the hand just raised to shed his blood.
O blindness to the future! kindly giv'n,
That each may fill the circle marked by heav'n:
Who sees with equal eye, as God of all,
A hero perish, or a sparrow fall,
Atoms or systems into ruin hurled,
And now a bubble burst, and now a world.
    Hope humbly then; with trembling pinions soar;
Wait the great teacher death, and God adore.
What future bliss he gives not thee to know,
But gives that hope to be thy blessing now.
Hope springs eternal in the human breast;
Man never is, but always to be blessed.
The soul, uneasy, and confined from home,
Rests and expatiates in a life to come.
    Lo, the poor Indian! whose untutored mind

Sees God in clouds, or hears him in the wind;
His soul proud science never taught to stray
Far as the solar walk or milky way;
Yet simple nature to his hope has giv'n,
Behind the cloud-topped hill, an humbler heav'n;
Some safer world in depth of woods embraced,
Some happier island in the wat'ry waste,
Where slaves once more their native land behold,
No fiends torment, no christians thirst for gold.
To be, contents his natural desire;
He asks no angel's wing, no seraph's fire;
But thinks, admitted to that equal sky,
His faithful dog shall bear him company.
    IV. Go, wiser thou! and in thy scale of sense,
Weigh thy opinion against Providence;
Call imperfection what thou fanci'st such,
Say, Here he gives too little, there too much!
Destroy all creatures for thy sport or gust,
Yet cry, If man's unhappy, God's unjust;
If man alone ingross not heav'n's high care,
Alone made perfect here, immortal there:
Snatch from his hand the balance and the rod,
Re-judge his justice, be the god of God.
In pride, in reas'ning pride, our error lies;
All quit their sphere and rush into the skies!
Pride still is aiming at the bless'd abodes,
Men would be angels, angels would be gods.
Aspiring to be gods if angels fell,
Aspiring to be angels men rebel:
And who but wishes to invert the laws
Of order, sins against th' Eternal Cause.
    V. Ask for what end the heav'nly bodies shine,
Earth for whose use, Pride answers, " 'Tis for mine!
For me kind nature wakes her genial pow'r,
Suckles each herb, and spreads out every flow'r;
Annual for me, the grape, the rose renew
The juice nectareous, and the balmy dew;
For me the mine a thousand treasures brings;
For me health gushes from a thousand springs;
Seas roll to waft me, suns to light me rise;

My footstool earth, my canopy the skies!"
    But errs not nature from this gracious end,
From burning suns when livid deaths descend,
When earthquakes swallow, or when tempests sweep
Towns to one grave, whole nations to the deep?
"No," 'tis replied, "the first Almighty Cause
Acts not by partial but by gen'ral laws:
Th' exceptions few; some change since all began;
And what created perfect?"—Why then man?
If the great end be human happiness,
Then nature deviates; and can man do less?
As much that end a constant course requires
Of show'rs and sunshine, as of man's desires:
As much eternal springs and cloudless skies,
As men for ever temp'rate, calm, and wise.
If plagues or earthquakes break not heaven's design,
Why then a Borgia or a Catiline?
Who knows but He, whose hand the lightning forms,
Who heaves old ocean, and who wings the storms;
Pours fierce ambition in a Cæsar's mind,
Or turns young Ammon loose to scourge mankind?
From pride, from pride our very reas'ning springs;
Account for moral, as for nat'ral things:
Why charge we heav'n in those, in these acquit?
In both to reason right is to submit.
    Better for us, perhaps, it might appear,
Were there all harmony, all virtue here;
That never air or ocean felt the wind;
That never passion discomposed the mind.
But all subsists by elemental strife;
And passions are the elements of life.
The gen'ral order, since the whole began,
Is kept in nature, and is kept in man.
    VI. What would this Man? now upward will he soar,
And little less than angel, would be more!
Now looking downwards, just as grieved appears
To want the strength of bulls, the fur of bears.
Made for his use, all creatures if he call,
Say what their use, had he the pow'rs of all:
Nature to these without profusion kind,
The proper organs, proper pow'rs assigned;

Each seeming want compensated of course,
Here with degrees of swiftness, there of force:
All in exact proportion to the state;
Nothing to add, and nothing to abate.
Each beast, each insect, happy in its own:
Is Heav'n unkind to man, and man alone?
Shall he alone, whom rational we call,
Be pleased with nothing, if not blessed with all?
   The bliss of man (could pride that blessing find)
Is not to act or think beyond mankind;
No pow'rs of body or of soul to share,
But what his nature and his state can bear.
Why has not man a microscopic eye?
For this plain reason, man is not a fly.
Say what the use, were finer optics giv'n,
T' inspect a mite, not comprehend the heav'n?
Or touch, if tremblingly alive all o'er,
To smart and agonize at ev'ry pore?
Or quick effluvia darting through the brain,
Die of a rose in aromatic pain?
If nature thundered in his op'ning ears,
And stunned him with the music of the spheres,
How would he wish that heav'n had left him still
The whisp'ring zephyr, and the purling rill?
Who finds not Providence all good and wise,
Alike in what it gives, and what denies?
   VII. Far as creation's ample range extends,
The scale of sensual, mental pow'rs ascends:
Mark how it mounts to man's imperial race,
From the green myriads in the peopled grass;
What modes of sight betwixt each wide extreme,
The mole's dim curtain, and the lynx's beam:
Of smell, the headlong lioness between,
And hound sagacious on the tainted green:
Of hearing, from the life that fills the flood,
To that which warbles through the vernal wood!
The spider's touch how exquisitely fine!
Feels at each thread, and lives along the line:
In the nice bee, what sense so subtly true
From pois'nous herbs extracts the healing dew?
How instinct varies in the grov'ling swine,

Compared, half-reas'ning elephant, with thine!
'Twixt that and reason, what a nice barrier!
For ever sep'rate, yet for ever near!
Remembrance and reflection how allied;
What thin partitions sense from thought divide;
And middle natures, how they long to join,
Yet never pass th' insuperable line!
Without this just gradation could they be
Subjected, these to those, or all to thee?
The pow'rs of all subdued by thee alone,
Is not thy reason all these pow'rs in one?
    VIII. See, through this air, this ocean, and this earth,
All matter quick, and bursting into birth.
Above, how high progressive life may go!
Around, how wide! how deep extend below!
Vast chain of being! which from God began,
Natures ethereal, human, angel, man,
Beast, bird, fish, insect, what no eye can see,
No glass can reach; from infinite to thee,
From thee to nothing. On superior pow'rs
Were we to press, inferior might on ours:
Or in the full creation leave a void,
Where, one step broken, the great scale's destroyed:
From nature's chain whatever link you strike,
Tenth or ten thousandth, breaks the chain alike.
    And if each system in gradation roll
Alike essential to th' amazing whole,
The least confusion but in one, not all
That system only, but the whole must fall.
Let earth unbalanced from her orbit fly,
Planets and suns run lawless through the sky;
Let ruling angels from their spheres be hurled,
Being on being wrecked, and world on world;
Heav'n's whole foundations to their centre nod
And nature tremble to the throne of God!
All this dread order break—for whom? for thee?
Vile worm!—O madness! pride! impiety!
    IX. What if the foot, ordained the dust to tread,
Or hand, to toil, aspired to be the head?
What if the head, the eye, or ear repined
To serve mere engines to the ruling mind?

Just as absurd for any part to claim
To be another, in this gen'ral frame:
Just as absurd, to mourn the tasks or pains
The great directing Mind of all ordains.

   All are but parts of one stupendous whole
Whose body nature is, and God the soul;
That, changed through all, and yet in all the same,
Great in the earth, as in th' ethereal frame,
Warms in the sun, refreshes in the breeze,
Glows in the stars, and blossoms in the trees,
Lives thro' all life, extends through all extent,
Spreads undivided, operates unspent;
Breathes in our soul, informs our mortal part,
As full, as perfect in a hair as heart;
As full, as perfect in vile man that mourns,
As the rapt seraph that adores and burns:
To him no high, no low, no great, no small;
He fills, he bounds, connects, and equals all.

   X. Cease then, nor order imperfection name:
Our proper bliss depends on what we blame.
Know thy own point: this kind, this due degree
Of blindness, weakness, heav'n bestows on thee.
Submit: in this, or any other sphere,
Secure to be as blessed as thou canst bear;
Safe in the hand of one disposing Pow'r,
Or in the natal, or the mortal hour.
All nature is but art unknown to thee,
All chance, direction which thou canst not see;
All discord, harmony not understood;
All partial evil, universal good;
And, spite of pride, in erring reason's spite,
One truth is clear, Whatever is, is right.

FURTHER READING

Reuben Arthur Brower, *Alexander Pope: The Poetry of Allusion* (1959). A splendidly lucid and informative account of Pope's use of classical sources.

Maynard Mack, ed., *An Essay on Man*, Twickenham edn. (1950), Vol. III.

The best critical edition of Pope's most controversial poem, with a fine introduction that places Pope in the religious world of his time.

James Sutherland, *A Preface to Eighteenth Century Poetry* (1948). An elegant essay on poetry and society, in which Pope plays a leading role.

Geoffrey Tillotson, *On the Poetry of Pope*, 2nd edn. (1950). Short and elegant; very valuable.

17 ❉ REIMARUS

Third Fragment: Passage of the Israelites Through the Red Sea

[From *Deism: An Anthology,* by Peter Gay,
pp. 160–163, translated by Peter Gay.*]

Deism—a religion without "superstition"—was the religion of many philosophes, especially of those in the first and second generation. While, in mid-eighteenth-century, deist tenets were successfully challenged and deist propaganda waned, deism remained for many the most sensible, indeed the only sensible, religion. Perhaps its best definition comes from one of its most relentless adversaries, Jonathan Edwards. "The Deists," he wrote, "wholly cast off the Christian religion, and are professed infidels." Unlike various heretics who accept Christianity but reject this or that among its doctrines, the deists "deny the whole Christian religion." While "they own the being of God," they "deny that Christ was the son of God, and say he was a mere cheat; and so they say all the prophets and apostles were: and they deny the whole Scripture. They deny that any of it is the word of God. They deny any revealed religion, or any word of God at all; and say that God has given mankind no other light to walk by but their own reason."†

As Jonathan Edwards' unsympathetic but accurate definition makes clear, deist doctrine contains both negative and positive elements; the deists at once attacked what they considered the wicked nonsense that priests had spread across the world for centuries, and defended what they considered to be the only true religion. For

---

† *History of the Works of Redemption,* in *The Works of President Edwards,* 4 vols. (1857), I, 467.

many years, in fact, students of the movement distinguished between critical and constructive deists. But while the stress on criticism or construction differed from polemicist to polemicist, all deists were essentially both critical and constructive. The two activities were different aspects of a single enterprise: like the philosophes, the deists destroyed that they might build.

Perhaps the first thinker to whom the label "deist" is properly applied is Lord Herbert of Cherbury (1583–1648), whose De veritate *(1624) and* Autobiography *(published only in 1886) contain the doctrine in detail. Like other sincere religious men, Herbert was appalled by the continuing dissensions among theologians, and sought to establish the doctrines on which all serious seekers could agree. He proposed that there were five of these—"five Common Notions"—which make up the true religion: there is a supreme God, He ought to be worshiped, the most important part of religious practice is to conform piety with virtue, vice and crime must be expiated by repentance, and there is reward and punishment after this life.*

The absence of ritual and of miracles could scarcely commend so reasonable a faith to the seventeenth century, and deism or philosophical systems sympathetic to it were held by a small minority of heretics and eccentrics. Thomas Hobbes (1588–1679) and Baruch Spinoza (1632–1677) were among the most notorious of these outsiders in the seventeenth century, and among the most respected models for the philosophes. In his time, Hobbes was decried as a materialist, and Spinoza as an atheist; it was not until late in the eighteenth century that the true complexity of their ideas became plain to careful readers. But what mattered to the burgeoning deist movement was that both Hobbes and Spinoza took a critical view of Scriptures and of religious experience; Hobbes coolly examined visions and religious inspiration and showed most of them to be mere fancies; Spinoza pointed to contradictions within the Bible and urged that the Good Book be read like any other. While the seventeenth century moved, as we have seen, toward a reasonable religion, few thinkers followed Herbert of Cherbury into outright rationalist religiosity. Charles Blount (1654–1693), a minor English controversialist, was a rare figure; he expanded Herbert's five essential points to seven, and added a weapon to the deist arsenal that the philosophes would later use with considerable effectiveness: as a good scholar, Blount used the writings of classical pagans to combat the doctrines of modern Christians.

If one is inclined to give the movement a specific birth date, that

date would be 1696. In that year, John Toland (1670–1722) published *his* Christianity Not Mysterious, *in which he had greatly
reduced the traditional creed of Christendom and shown his shorn
Christianity to be reasonable. Toland, claiming (much to Locke's
annoyance) to be a disciple of Locke's, now took the single but
portentous step of arguing that the true religion cannot be mysterious, so that a single "mysterious"—that is, supernatural—doctrine,
no matter how reasonably a Locke might defend it, is unreasonable
and thus unacceptable.*

   *Toland was a gifted and prolific publicist; so was Matthew
Tindal (1656–1733), another leading English deist. But among the
other prominent deists in England only Anthony Collins (1676–
1729) could lay claim to real philosophical competence. The other
deists were by and large distinctly minor figures, men of one passion
and cranky to a degree; they are remembered mainly by specialists.
The truth was that those who wanted reason in theology but had no
use for the dogmatic quality of deism—wits like Alexander Pope
and deft metaphysicians like David Hume—could outtalk, out-
write, and outthink the deists at every turn.*

   *Yet, though the deist cause gradually collapsed from lack of
support, deist ideas retained their hold on much of the Enlightenment. Voltaire was a lifelong deist, so were Rousseau and Thomas
Paine. Both the abuse that the deists heaped on priestcraft and the
worship they lavished on a remote and rational God retained their
appeal. And so, even after the deist debate had died down in
England, the country of its origin, it continued on the Continent.*

   *One of the most interesting yet one of the least known of the
Continental deists was the German scholar Hermann Samuel
Reimarus (1694–1768). A teacher in Hamburg with no public
notoriety at all, Reimarus had battled his way out of Christianity
and into the religion of reason by himself, in prolonged and
agonized private combat. When he died, he left behind a large
manuscript, an* Apology or Defense for the Reasonable Worshipers of
God, *the* Apologie oder Schutzschrift für die vernünftigen Verehrer
Gottes. *It was discovered by Lessing and published by him in a
series of fragments between 1774 and 1778, until he was prevented
from publishing more. What these fragments assert is, in short, that
the true teaching of Jesus is simple and pure, and has been corrupted by self-seeking priests; it is a dire error to denounce reason,
since reason offers man the only hope for discovering the true religion; religion is a natural order as moral as it is free from miracles.
The only way to cut through to these truths is to unmask the lies*

that cover them. Hence Reimarus' detailed, even nagging, examination of passages in the Bible for nonsensical tales and internal contradictions, of which the fragment that follows is a good specimen.

If we look at . . . the miracle of the passage through the Red Sea, its inner contradiction, its impossibility, is quite palpable. Six hundred thousand Israelites of military age leave Egypt, armed, and in battle order. They have with them their wives and their children and a good deal of rabble that had joined them. Now, we must count for each man of military age, four others at least: partly women, partly children, partly the aged, partly servants. The number of the emigrants, therefore, in proportion to those of military age, must be at least 3,000,000 souls. They take with them all their sheep and oxen, that is to say a large number of cattle. If we count only 300,000 heads of households, and give each of them one cow or ox and two sheep, that would add up to 300,000 oxen and cows, and 600,000 sheep and goats. In addition, we must count on at least 1,000 wagon loads of hay or fodder; to say nothing of the many other wagons containing the golden and silver vessels which they had purloined, and piles of baggage and tents needed for such an enormous army—even if we count only 5,000 wagons, which is one wagon to sixty persons. At last they arrived at the Red Sea, and put down their camp near its shore. Pharaoh followed them, with 600 selected wagons and all the wagons left in Egypt, in addition to all the cavalry and infantry, and, as it was nightfall, he settled down not far from them. Josephus estimates this army at 50,000 cavalrymen and 200,000 infantry. It cannot have been small, for it was planning to confront an army of 600,000. But let us only count half of this—namely 25,000 cavalrymen, and 100,000 infantry, plus the wagons. During the night, the column of cloud and fire places itself between the Israelites and the Egyptians; God then sends a strong easterly wind which through the whole night pushes away the sea and makes the ground dry. Then the Israelites enter, dry of foot, and the Egyptians follow them, so that the former have crossed while the latter are in the middle of the sea. In the watch of the morning, God looks down upon the army of the Egyptians, allows the water to return so that it is restored to its full flood, and thus all the Egyptians drown, and not a one remains. It is this that the Biblical narrative partly tells us explicitly, partly compels us to infer.

I shall here set aside all other circumstances, and consider only the fantastic march in comparison to the short time, to the mass of men and beasts, to the inconvenient road and the dark night. As the easterly wind had been blowing all night to dry the sea, it cannot have been dry before midnight. Now, in the watch of the morning—that is, after three in the morning—the Egyptians are already in the middle of the sea, with horse and baggage. Then, toward morning, the water returns; the Egyptians flee back, but run into the water and drown. It follows that in the time between midnight and three or four in the morning, not merely all Israelites had marched through the sea to the other shore, but also all the Egyptians had marched to the middle of the sea. Whoever has, I will not even say, marched with an army, but even read or heard of one, can easily understand that such a quick flight is a complete impossibility, especially considering the quantity of men and beasts, and all the attendant circumstances. The men add up to 3,100,000; then the Israelites have 6,000 wagons with fodder and baggage, drawn by the above-mentioned oxen. The Egyptians had a large number of military wagons, equipped with two, four, or perhaps more horses—at least, with the cavalry, 100,000 horses. Add the cattle of the Israelites: 300,000 oxen and cows, and 600,000 sheep. When such an enormous number of men and cattle sets up a camp, it would need a space of many square miles; we learn this not merely from our contemporary experience, but from the ancient manner of camping. The camp of the Hebrews, as we can see from the meeting tent and the cities of the Levites, was square. And it is logical that an army waiting for a hostile assault would not spread itself out lengthwise and thus weaken itself, but would be kept together. A square would therefore be most convenient; and, indeed, the Romans and other nations liked square camps. Now, even if we put ten persons in each tent, the number of 3,000,000 persons gives us 300,000 tents. And they would be put into a square, but taking into the center the baggage, the wagons, and the cattle, for their protection. Now, if we consider the enormous space required by 300,000 oxen, 600,000 sheep, and thousands of baggage wagons, and how far 300,000 tents would have to extend around them, then we say very little if we claim that no matter how cleverly it was all arranged, the whole must cover more than two German square miles. Now, since there would have to be a great distance between the army of the Israelites and the Egyptians, it is further obvious that we are not exaggerating when we say that the nearest Egyptian would have to be at least a mile from the Israelites—that is to say, three miles from the sea. The sea itself, if we measure it in accord with the narrative, must have been at least a German mile wide, considering that Pharaoh's whole army, with so many horses and wagons, found, all at once, room and its grave in it. So that the nearest Egyptians must have been at least four German miles from the place in which they drowned, and the last of the Israelites too must have been about four German miles from that spot in the Red Sea.

Now, one might think that it is not really impossible to march four miles in four hours. However, if one is used to visualizing matters with all their circumstances with any clarity, and especially if one knows the habits of Orientals and the bottom of the sea, then one will have no trouble recognizing that such a march—four German miles long, in four hours, across the bottom of the sea permitting passage to only a few at a time—would be an absolute impossibility [etc., etc.].

FURTHER READING

Karl Aner, *Die Theologie der Lessingzeit* (1929). An impressive analysis of German theological thought in the days of Reimarus and Lessing.

Peter Gay, *Deism, An Anthology* (1968). A collection of Deist texts from England, the Continent, and America, with a critical introduction.

David Friedrich Strauss, *Hermann Samuel Reimarus und seine Schutzschrift für die vernünftigen Verehrer Gottes* (1862). Still the most detailed analysis of Reimarus.

18 ❧ HUME

The History of England

[From David Hume, *The History of England*,
5 vols. (1864 edn.), I, 363–64, 533–34, 541–42.]

*The Scottish philosophe and philosopher David Hume, of whom
several representative selections appear in this anthology, was one
of the most remarkable members of the enlightened family. Witty,
amiable, and versatile, he made signal contributions to the theory
of knowledge, to aesthetic and political thought, and to a variety of
social sciences including political science, economics, and demography. With Kant, he ranks as the most profound thinker of the
age. Born in 1711, Hume was educated at Edinburgh; after a
crisis in adolescence, he abandoned Christianity and developed a
moderate skepticism critical of all dogmas, including those of his
intellectual brethren, the deists and atheists. The point of his
philosophical teaching was that it is more dignified to live with
uncertainty than with false certainty. His first and greatest work,
the* Treatise of Human Nature, *published in 1739 and 1740, was
not a success; undismayed, Hume recast his ideas into somewhat
more popular form. The* Enquiry Concerning Human Understanding *came out in 1748, the* Enquiry Concerning the Principles of
Morals *in 1751. By the 1750s, too, Hume had published a considerable number of essays on a wide variety of subjects* and was
engaged in an enterprise that markedly increased his growing reputation, the many-volumed* History of England. *Hume wrote and
published that history backward, as it were, beginning with the
most recent dynasty, the Stuarts, moving back to its predecessors,
the Tudors, and completing his ambitious enterprise in 1762 with
early and medieval Britain.*

* See below, pages 441ff., 525ff., 535ff.

Hume's later career, and the place of historical writing in the Enlightenment, will receive our attention below. So will the philosophes' attitude toward the Jews.* Suffice it here to remark that the philosophes' histories, though they were authentic, often pioneering works of history, also served Enlightenment propaganda. Hume, like Gibbon,† did not hesitate to belabor priests, decry ignorance, and hail the appearance of reason and humanity in works devoted to a scholarly elucidation of the past. Thus it is appropriate to offer here an instance from historical writings in evidence of the philosophes' campaign against superstition and fanaticism—in this case attacking pious Christians by defending an unpopular people.

The king [Richard I], impelled more by the love of military glory than by superstition, acted, from the beginning of his reign, as if the sole purpose of his government had been the relief of the Holy Land, and the recovery of Jerusalem from the Saracens. This zeal against infidels, being communicated to his subjects, broke out in London on the day of his coronation, and made them find a crusade less dangerous and attended with more immediate profit. The prejudices of the age had made the lending of money on interest pass by the invidious name of usury: yet the necessity of the practice had still continued it, and the greater part of that kind of dealing fell every where into the hands of the Jews, who, being already infamous on account of their religion, had no honour to lose, and were apt to exercise a profession, odious in itself, by every kind of rigour, and even sometimes by rapine and extortion. The industry and frugality of this people had put them in possession of all the ready money which the idleness and profusion common to the English with other European nations, enabled them to lend at exorbitant and unequal interest. The monkish writers represent it as a great stain on the wise and equitable government of Henry [II], that he had carefully protected this infidel race from all injuries and insults; but the zeal of Richard afforded the populace a pretence for venting their animosity against them. The king had

* See below, pages 263, 618ff., 746ff.
† See below, pages 257ff.

issued an edict, prohibiting their appearance at his coronation; but some of them, bringing him large presents from their nation, presumed, in confidence of that merit, to approach the hall in which he dined: being discovered, they were exposed to the insults of the bystanders; they took to flight; the people pursued them; the rumour was spread that the king had issued orders to massacre all the Jews; a command so agreeable was executed in an instant on such as fell into the hands of the populace; those who had kept at home were exposed to equal danger; the people, moved by rapacity and zeal, broke into their houses which they plundered, after having murdered the owners: where the Jews barricadoed their doors, and defended themselves with vigour, the rabble set fire to their houses and made way through the flames to exercise the pillage and violence; the usual licentiousness of London, which the sovereign power with difficulty restrained, broke out with fury, and continued these outrages; the houses of the richest citizens, though Christians, were next attacked and plundered; and weariness and satiety at last put an end to the disorder: yet when the king empowered Glanville, the justiciary, to inquire into the authors of these crimes, the guilt was found to involve so many of the most considerable citizens, that it was deemed more prudent to drop the prosecution; and very few suffered the punishment due to this enormity. But the disorder stopped not at London. The inhabitants of the other cities of England, hearing of this slaughter of the Jews, imitated the example: in York five hundred of that nation who had retired into the castle for safety, and found themselves unable to defend the place, murdered their own wives and children, threw the dead bodies over the walls upon the populace, and then setting fire to the houses, perished in the flames. The gentry of the neighborhood, who were all indebted to the Jews, ran to the cathedral, where their bonds were kept, and made a solemn bonfire of the papers before the altar. The compiler of the Annals of Waverley, in relating these events, blesses the Almighty for thus delivering over this impious race to destruction. . . .

Interest had in that age amounted to an enormous height, as might be expected from the barbarism of the times and men's ignorance of commerce. Instances occur of fifty per cent. paid for money. There is an edict of Philip Augustus near this period, limiting the Jews in France to forty-eight per cent. Such profits tempted the Jews to remain in the kingdom, notwithstanding the grievous oppressions to which, from the prevalent bigotry and rapine of the age, they were continually exposed. It is easy to imagine how precarious their state must have been under an indigent prince, somewhat restrained in his tyranny over his native subjects, but who possessed an unlimited authority over the Jews, the sole proprietors of money in the kingdom, and hated, on account of their riches, their religion, and their usury: yet will our ideas scarcely come up to the extortions which, in fact, we find to have been practised upon them. In the year 1241, twenty thousand marks were exacted from them: two years after money was again extorted; and one Jew alone, Aaron of York, was obliged to pay above four thousand marks. In 1250, Henry [III] renewed his oppressions; and the same Aaron was condemned to pay him thirty thousand marks upon an accusation of forgery: the high penalty imposed upon him, and which, it seems, he was thought able to pay, is rather a presumption of his innocence than of his guilt. In 1255, the king demanded eight thousand marks from the Jews, and threatened to hang them if they refused compliance. They now lost all patience, and desired leave to retire with their effects out of the kingdom. But the king replied: "How can I remedy the oppressions you complain of? I am myself a beggar. I am spoiled, I am stripped of all my revenues: I owe above two hundred thousand marks; and if I had said three hundred thousand, I should not exceed the truth: I am obliged to pay my son, Prince Edward, fifteen thousand marks a year: I have not a farthing; and I must have money, from any hand, from any quarter, or by any means." He then delivered over the Jews to the Earl of Cornwall, that those whom the one brother had flayed, the other might embowel, to make use of the words of the historian. King John, his father, once demanded ten thousand marks from a Jew of Bristol; and on his refusal, ordered one of his teeth to be drawn every day till he should comply. The Jew lost seven teeth, and then paid the sum required of him. One talliage laid upon the Jews in 1243 amounted to sixty thousand marks; a sum equal to the whole yearly revenue of the crown.

To give a better pretence for extortions, the improbable and absurd accusation, which has been at different times advanced against that nation, was revived in England, that they had crucified a child in derision of the sufferings of Christ. Eighteen of them were hanged at once for this crime: though it is nowise credible, that even the antipathy borne them by the Christians, and the oppressions under which they laboured, would ever have pushed them to be guilty of that dangerous enormity. But it is natural to imagine, that a race, exposed to such insults and indignities, both from king and people, and who had so uncertain an enjoyment of their riches, would carry usury to the utmost extremity, and by their great profits make themselves some compensation for their continual perils.

Though these acts of violence against the Jews proceeded much from bigotry, they were still more derived from avidity and rapine. So far from desiring in that age to convert them, it was enacted by law in France, that if any Jew embraced Christianity, he forfeited all his goods, without exception, to the king, or his superior lord. These plunderers were careful, lest the profits, accruing from their dominion over that unhappy race, should be diminished by their conversion. . . .

Among the various disorders to which the kingdom was subject, no one was more universally complained of than the adulteration of the coin; and as this crime required more art than the English of that age, who chiefly employed force and violence in their iniquities, were possessed of, the imputation fell upon the Jews. Edward [I] also seems to have indulged a strong prepossession against that nation; and this ill-judged zeal for Christianity being natually augmented by an expedition to the Holy Land, he let loose the whole rigour of his justice against that unhappy people. Two hundred and eighty of them were hanged at once for this crime in London alone, besides those who suffered in other parts of the kingdom. The houses and lands (for the Jews had of late ventured to make purchases of that kind), as well as the goods of great multitudes, were sold and confiscated; and the king, lest it should be suspected that the riches of the sufferers were the chief part of their guilt, ordered a moiety of the money raised by these confiscations to be set apart and bestowed upon such as were willing to be converted to Christianity. But resentment was more prevalent with them than any temptation from their poverty; and very few of them could be induced, by interest, to embrace the religion of their persecutors. The miseries of this people did not here terminate. Though the arbitrary talliages and exactions levied upon them had yielded a constant and considerable revenue to the crown, Edward, prompted by his zeal and his rapacity, resolved some time after to purge the kingdom entirely of that hated race, and to seize to himself at once their whole property as the reward of his labour. He left them only money sufficient to bear their charges into foreign countries, where new persecutions and extortions awaited them: but the inhabitants of the cinque-ports, imitating the bigotry and avidity of their sovereign, despoiled most of them of this small pittance, and even threw many of them into the sea: a crime for which the king, who was determined to be the sole plunderer in his dominions, inflicted a capital punishment upon them. No less than fifteen thousand Jews were at this time robbed of their effects, and banished the kingdom: very few of that nation have since lived in England: and as it is impossible for a nation to subsist without lenders of money, and none will lend without a compensation, the practice of usury, as it was then called, was thenceforth exercised by the English themselves upon their fellow citizens, or by Lombards and other foreigners. It is very much to be questioned, whether the dealings of these new usurers were equally open and unexceptionable with those of the old. By a law of Richard it was enacted, that three copies should be made of every bond given to a Jew; one to be put into the hands of a public magistrate, another into those of a man of credit, and a third to remain with the Jew himself. But as the canon law, seconded by the municipal, permitted no Christian to take interest, all transactions of this kind, must, after the banishment of the Jews, have become more secret and clandestine; and the lender, of consequence, be paid both for the use of his money, and for the infamy and danger which he incurred by lending it.

FURTHER READING

Ralph Church, *Hume's Theory of the Understanding* (1935). A technical analysis.

E. C. Mossner, *The Life of David Hume* (1954). The standard biography; very full, but unhelpful with what really mattered about Hume—his ideas.

John Passmore, *Hume's Intentions* (1952). An interesting and convincing essay stressing the constructive side of Hume's thought.

Norman Kemp Smith, *The Philosophy of David Hume: A Critical Study of Its Origins and Central Doctrines* (1941). Technical, exhaustive, indispensable.

———, ed., *Hume's Dialogues Concerning Natural Religion* (2nd edn., 1947). Contains the authoritative text of Hume's most attractive work (a devastating analysis of deist pretensions to certainty in religion) and a brilliant lengthy analytical introduction.

See also below, "Further Reading" for selections 21, 34, and 38.

19 ❧ VOLTAIRE

Dictionnaire philosophique

[From Voltaire, *Philosophical Dictionary*, translated by Peter Gay (1962), 79–80, 83–86, 93–95, 267–69, 279–83, 301–7, 328–32.*]

Among the innumerable polemics the philosophes poured out in the eighteenth century to pillory the stupidity of religious men, the absurdity of religious doctrine, the viciousness of priests and the cruelties inspired by dogma, Voltaire's Dictionnaire philosophique *is the most famous. It was first published in 1764, but Voltaire had begun to write some of its articles much earlier, around 1752, and to think about it even before that.*

In the early 1730s, as we have seen,† Voltaire, already a famous playwright and notorious wit, began his intimate association with a formidable bluestocking, Madame du Châtelet. His mistress— though she was not his alone—was a better linguist than Voltaire, and a better mathematician. In her company, and with her help, Voltaire studied Newton and published, in 1738, one of the best popularizations of the new physics in the eighteenth century, the Éléments de la philosophie de Newton. *At her château at Cirey, Voltaire began to write some of the great histories to be published later, in the 1750s. But most important, he and Madame du Châtelet studied the Bible, deist propaganda, and pious works of apologetics. By the 1740s, Voltaire's command of religious scholarship was impressive. Then, in 1749, his mistress died in giving birth to a child that neither her husband nor her official lover had fathered. Disconsolate, Voltaire finally yielded to the importunate invitations of Frederick II, and moved to the court of Prussia.*

The visit was not a success; while it was in Frederick's aggres-

---

* Reprinted with the permission of the publishers, Basic Books, Inc.
† See above, pages 144–147.

sively impious ambiance that Voltaire wrote the first articles of his Philosophical Dictionary, *by the winter of 1752 he had quarreled with his imperious royal patron and left Prussia forever. For some years he wandered about, a privileged and restless guest, until in 1755–56 he discovered the region where he wanted to spend the rest of his life. He settled down first on Genevan territory, in his villa Les Délices, and then moved some miles away onto French soil, to Ferney. In this environment, he grew old and even more famous, entertained philosophes at his hospitable table, intervened in political and legal issues all across Europe, wrote his now immortal tales, and kept adding articles to his one-man encyclopedia, the* Philosophical Dictionary. *When it appeared in 1764, it was still relatively small; it was announced as "portable." But its immense success prompted Voltaire, more passionate than ever in humane and anticlerical causes, to reissue and expand the book. The largest edition, from which our selections are taken, appeared in 1769, but Voltaire did not cease writing this kind of informal propaganda; though he was by then in his middle seventies, his energy did not wane, and another compendium, the* Questions sur l'Encyclopédie, *began to appear after 1770. Indeed, it was not until the year of his death, 1778, when Voltaire came back to his native Paris, that his polemical activity in behalf of humanity ceased.*

The Dictionnaire philosophique *follows only one formal requirement: it is alphabetical. In scores of articles, Voltaire writes on politics and throws in a little gossip. But his chief target is always supernatural religion and its profiteers—churches of all kinds. Voltaire did not address his target directly; he liked to pose as an outraged true believer, he denounced at length beliefs he himself held, and he adopted a variety of other poses. They were transparent poses, so that the reader would never be deceived into getting the wrong impression. But his playfulness allowed Voltaire to be both continuously interesting and immensely daring.*

ANTITRINITAIRES · UNITARIANS

To reveal their sentiments, it is enough to say:

That they maintain that nothing is more contrary to reason than what is taught among Christians about the trinity of persons in a single divine essence, of whom the second is begotten by the first, and the third proceeds from the other two.

That this unintelligible doctrine is not found anywhere in Scripture.

That no passage can be produced authorizing it, or to which we cannot give a sense clearer, more natural, or more consistent with usual notions and first and immutable truths, without departing from the spirit of the text in any way.

That to maintain, as their adversaries do, that there are several distinct *persons* in the divine essence, and that the Eternal is not the only true God, but that the Son and the Holy Spirit must be joined to him, is to introduce into the Church of Jesus Christ the crudest and most dangerous error, since it openly promotes polytheism.

That it implies a contradiction to say that there is but one God and that nevertheless there are three *persons,* each of which is truly God.

That this distinction of one in essence and three in person was never in Scripture.

That it is manifestly false, since it is certain that there are no fewer *essences* than *persons,* nor *persons* than *essences.*

That the three persons of the Trinity are either three different substances or accidents of the divine essence, or that essence itself without division.

That in the first case, you have three Gods.

That in the second case, you have God composed of accidents, you worship accidents, and metamorphose accidents into persons.

That in the third case, you needlessly and groundlessly divide an indivisible subject, and distinguish into *three* that which is not distinguished within itself.

That if you say that the three *personalities* are neither different substances in the divine essence nor accidents of that essence, you will have trouble persuading yourself that they are anything at all.

That it must not be believed that the most rigid and decided *Trinitarians* have themselves any clear idea of the way in which the three *hypostases* subsist in God without dividing his substance, and consequently without multiplying it.

That after he advanced a thousand arguments on this subject, as false as they are obscure, Saint Augustine himself was forced to concede that nothing intelligible could be said about the matter.

Then they repeat a passage by this Father, which is indeed very odd: "When it is asked," he says, "what are *the three,* the language of man fails, and there are no terms to express them; however, people have said *three persons,* not in order to say anything, but because we must speak and not remain silent." *Dictum est tamen tres personae, non ut aliquid diceretur, sed ne taceretur.* (*De Trinit.,* Book V, Chap. 9.)

That modern theologians have not cleared up this matter any better.

That when they are asked what they understand by this word *person,* they explain it only by saying that it is a certain incomprehensible distinction which causes us to distinguish a Father, a Son, and a Holy Spirit in a nature single in number.

That the explanation they give of the terms *begetting* and *proceeding* is no more satisfactory, since it comes down to saying that these terms indicate certain incomprehensible relationships among the three persons of the Trinity.

That hence we may gather that at this point the controversy between the anti-Trinitarians and the orthodox is over whether there are in God three distinctions of which we have no idea, and among which there are certain relations of which we have no more idea.

They conclude from all this that it would be wiser to stick to the authority of the Apostles, who never spoke of the Trinity, and to banish from religion forever all terms which are not in the Scriptures, such as *Trinity, person, essence, hypostatic and personal union, incarnation, generation, proceeding,* and many others like them, which are absolutely meaningless, since they are not represented in nature by a real being, and can excite in the understanding nothing but false, vague, obscure, and undefinable notions.

(*Taken from the article* UNITAIRES *of the* Encyclopédie, *which article is by the Abbé de Bragelogue.*)

To this article let me add what dom Calmet says in his dissertation on the following passage from the Epistle of John the Evangelist: "There are three that bear witness on the earth, the spirit, the water, and the blood; and these three are one. There are three that bear witness in heaven, the Father, the Word, and the Spirit, and these three are one." Dom Calmet acknowledges that these two passages are not in any ancient Bible; indeed, it would be very strange if Saint John had spoken of the Trinity in a letter and said not a single word about it in his Gospel. We find no trace of this dogma either in the canonical or in the apocryphal Gospels. All these reasons and many others might excuse the anti-Trinitarians, if the councils had not decided against them. But since the heretics make light of councils, we no longer know what to do to confound them.

ARIUS

Here is an incomprehensible question that has aroused curiosity, sophistic subtlety, bitterness, the spirit of cabal, the passion for domination, the rage to persecute, blind and bloody fanaticism, and barbarous credulity for more than sixteen hundred years, and has produced more horrors than the ambitions of princes, which surely have produced a great deal. Is Jesus Word? If he is Word, did he emanate from God in time or before time? If he emanated from God, is he coeternal and consubstantial with him, or is he of a similar substance? Is he distinct from him, or is he not? Is he made or begotten? Can he beget in his turn? Has he paternity or productive virtue without paternity? Is the Holy Spirit made, or begotten, or produced, or does he proceed from the Father, or proceed from the Son, or proceed from the two of them? Can he beget, can he produce? Is his hypostasis consubstantial with the hypostasis of the Father and the Son? And how is it that, having precisely the same nature, the same essence, as the Father and the Son, he cannot do the same things as these two persons who are himself?

Certainly I don't understand any of this; nobody has ever understood any of this, and this is why people have cut one another's throats!

Among the Christians before the time of Arius and Athanasius, they subtilized, they quibbled, they hated and they excommunicated one another because of some of these dogmas inaccessible to the human mind. The Egyptian Greeks were clever people; they split a hair in four, but this time they split it only in three. Alexandros, bishop of Alexandria, took it into his head to preach that since God is necessarily individual, single, a monad in the strictest sense of the word, this monad is triune.

The priest Arios or Arious, whom we call Arius, was quite shocked by Alexandros' monad; he explained the matter differently: he quibbled partly like the priest Sabellius, who had quibbled like the Phrygian Praxeas, a great quibbler. Alexandros quickly assembled a small council of persons who agreed with him, and excommunicated his priest. Eusebius, bishop of Nicomedia, took the side of Arios: the whole Church was in flames.

The Emperor Constantine was a scoundrel, I confess it; a parricide who smothered his wife in a bath, butchered his son, assassinated his father-in-law, his brother-in-law, and his nephew, I don't deny it; a man bloated with pride and immersed in pleasures, I concede it; a detestable tyrant, like his children, *transeat;* but he had good sense. One does not get an empire, one does not subdue all one's rivals, without reasoning closely.

When he saw civil war kindled in scholastic brains, he dispatched the celebrated Bishop Hosius with dissuading letters to the two belligerent parties. "You are great madmen," he tells them in so many words in this letter, "to quarrel about things you don't understand. It is unworthy of the gravity of your ministries to make so much noise about such a trifling matter."

By "such a trifling matter" Constantine did not mean that which concerns the Divinity, but the incomprehensible manner in which they were straining to explain the nature of the Divinity. The Arabian patriarch who wrote the *History of the Church of Alexandria* has Hosius say, when he presents the emperor's letter:

"My brethren, Christianity is scarcely beginning to enjoy peace, and you wish to plunge it into eternal discord. The emperor is only too right to tell you that you are *quarreling about a very trifling matter.* Surely, if the object of the dispute were essential, Jesus Christ, whom we all acknowledge as our legislator, would have mentioned it; God would not have sent his son to earth in order not to teach us our catechism. Whatever he has not expressly told us is the work of men, and their destiny is to err. Jesus has commanded you to love one another, and you start out by disobeying him in hating one another, stirring up discord in the empire. Pride alone gives birth to disputes, and Jesus, your master, has commanded you to be humble. Not one of you can know whether Jesus is made or begotten. And what does his nature matter to you, provided yours is to be just and reasonable? What has a frivolous science of words in common with the morality that should guide your actions? You encumber doctrine with mysteries—you, who were made only to strengthen religion by virtue. Do you want the Christian religion to be nothing but a mass of sophistries? Is it for this that Christ came? Cease arguing; worship, edify, humble yourselves, feed the poor, make up family quarrels, instead of shocking the whole empire with your dissensions."

Hosius spoke to obstinate men. They assembled the Council of

Nicaea, and a civil war rent the Roman Empire. This war led to others, and there has been mutual persecution through the centuries, down to our own time.

FANATISME · FANATICISM

Fanaticism is to superstition what delirium is to fever and rage to anger. The man visited by ecstasies and visions, who takes dreams for realities and his fancies for prophecies, is an enthusiast; the man who supports his madness with murder is a fanatic. Jean Diaz, in retreat at Nuremberg, was firmly convinced that the Pope was the Antichrist of the Apocalypse, and that he bore the sign of the beast; he was merely an enthusiast; his brother, Bartholomew Diaz, who came from Rome to assassinate his brother out of piety, and who did in fact kill him for the love of God, was one of the most abominable fanatics ever raised up by superstition.

Polyeucte, who goes to the temple on a solemn holiday to knock over and smash the statues and ornaments, is a less dreadful but no less ridiculous fanatic than Diaz. The assassins of the Duke François de Guise, of William, Prince of Orange, of King Henri III, of King Henri IV, and of so many others, were fanatics sick with the same mania as Diaz'.

The most detestable example of fanaticism was that of the burghers of Paris who on St. Bartholomew's Night went about assassinating and butchering all their fellow citizens who did not go to mass, throwing them out of windows, cutting them in pieces.

There are coldblooded fanatics: such as judges who condemn to death those who have committed no other crime than failing to think like them; and these judges are all the more guilty, all the more deserving of the execration of mankind, since, unlike Clément, Châtel, Ravaillac, Damiens, they were not suffering from an attack of insanity; surely they should have been able to listen to reason.

Once fanaticism has corrupted a mind, the malady is almost incurable. I have seen convulsionaries who, speaking of the miracles of Saint Pâris, gradually grew impassioned despite themselves: their eyes got inflamed, their limbs trembled, madness disfigured their faces, and they would have killed anyone who contradicted them.

The only remedy for this epidemic malady is the philosophical spirit which, spread gradually, at last tames men's habits and prevents the disease from starting; for, once the disease has made any progress, one must flee and wait for the air to clear itself. Laws and religion are not strong enough against the spiritual pest; religion, far from being healthy food for infected brains, turns to poison in them. These miserable men have forever in their minds the example of Ehud, who assassinated King Eglon; of Judith, who cut off Holofernes' head while she was sleeping with him; of Samuel, who chopped King Agag in pieces. They cannot see that these examples which were respectable in antiquity are abominable in the present; they borrow their frenzies from the very religion that condemns them.

Even the law is impotent against these attacks of rage; it is like reading a court decree to a raving maniac. These fellows are certain that the holy spirit with which they are filled is above the law, that their enthusiasm is the only law they must obey.

What can we say to a man who tells you that he would rather obey God than men, and that therefore he is sure to go to heaven for butchering you?

Ordinarily fanatics are guided by rascals, who put the dagger into their hands; these latter resemble that Old Man of the Mountain who is supposed to have made imbeciles taste the joys of Paradise and who promised them an eternity of the pleasures of which he had given them a foretaste, on condition that they assassinated all those he would name to them. There is only one religion in the world that has never been sullied by fanaticism, that of the Chinese men of letters. The schools of philosophers were not only free from this pest, they were its remedy; for the effect of philosophy is to make the soul tranquil, and fanaticism is incompatible with tranquility. If our holy religion has so often been corrupted by this infernal delirium, it is the madness of men which is at fault.

> *Ainsi du plumage qu'il eut*
> *Icare pervertit l'usage;*
> *Il le reçut pour son salut,*
> *Il s'en servit pour son dommage.*

> Thus Icarus abused
> His newly acquired plumage:
> He got it for his flight,
> He used it to his damage.
> —Bertaut, Bishop of Séez

FRAUDE · FRAUD

Should Pious Frauds Be Practiced on the Common People?

One day the fakir Bambabef met one of the disciples of Confutzee, whom we call Confucius, and that disciple's name was Ouang. Bambabef maintained that the people needed to be deceived, and Ouang maintained that we should never deceive anyone; and here's the abstract of their debate.

BAMBABEF. We must imitate the supreme Being, who does not show us things as they are; he makes us see the sun as having a diameter of two or three feet, although that star is a million times larger than the earth; he makes us see the moon and the stars as being attached to the same blue ground, while they are at different distances. He wishes us to see a square tower as being round from a distance; he wishes us to feel fire as hot, although it is neither hot nor cold; in short, he surrounds us with errors that suit our nature.

OUANG. What you call error isn't one at all. The real sun, placed millions and millions of lis* from our globe, is not the one we see. We really perceive, and we can only perceive, the sun that is painted on our retina, at a fixed angle. We were not given our eyes to know sizes and distances; other aids and other methods are needed to know them.

Bambabef appeared quite astonished at this remark. Ouang, who was extremely patient, explained the theory of optics to him; and Bambabef, who had a good brain, yielded to the demonstration that Confucius' disciple gave him; then he resumed the debate.

BAMBABEF. If God does not deceive us through the agency of our senses, as I had thought, at least admit that doctors always deceive children for their own good: they tell them they are giving them sugar when they are really giving them rhubarb. Hence, as a fakir, I may deceive the common people, who are as ignorant as children.

OUANG. I have two sons, and I have never deceived them; I told them when they were sick: "Here is a very bitter medicine, you must have the courage to take it; it would harm you if it were sweet." I have never allowed their governesses and their tutors to scare them with ghosts, spirits, goblins, witches; in this way I have made courageous and sensible young citizens of them.

BAMBABEF. When the common people are born, they are not as fortunate as your family.

* A li is 124 feet.

OUANG. All men resemble one another; they are born with the same dispositions. It is the fakirs who corrupt the nature of men.

BAMBABEF. We teach them errors, I confess; but it is for their own good. We make them believe that if they don't buy our blessed nails, if they don't expiate their sins by giving us money, they will turn into post-horses, dogs, or lizards in another life; that intimidates them, and they become decent people.

OUANG. Don't you see that you are perverting these poor people? Far many more of them are rational than you might believe; they laugh at your miracles, at your superstitions; they know perfectly well that they will not be changed into lizards or post-horses. What happens? They have enough good sense to see that you preach an insolent religion to them, but they don't have enough sense to raise themselves to a pure religion, free from superstitions, such as our own. Their passions lead them to believe that there is no religion, since the only religion they are taught is ridiculous; you make yourself guilty of all the vices into which they plunge.

BAMBABEF. Not at all, for we teach them only good morals.

OUANG. You'd be stoned by the people if you taught them impure morals. Men are so made that, though they would enjoy doing evil, they don't want it preached to them. But a wise morality should not be mixed up with absurd fables, because with your impostures, which you could dispense with, you weaken the very morality you are obliged to teach.

BAMBABEF. Really! Do you think that one can teach the common people the truth without sustaining it with fables?

OUANG. I believe it firmly. Our men of letters are of the same stuff as our tailors, our weavers, and our day laborers. They worship a God who creates, rewards, and avenges. They sully their cult neither by absurd systems nor by extravagant ceremonies; and there are far fewer crimes among the men of letters than among the common people. Why not deign to instruct our workers as we instruct our men of letters?

BAMBABEF. You'd be doing something very foolish; you might as well ask them to have the same politeness, or to be lawyers: that's neither possible nor desirable. There must be white bread for the master and brown bread for his servants.

OUANG. I admit that all men should not have the same education; but there are things that all men need. Everyone needs to be just, and the surest method of instilling justice into all men is to instill them with a religion free from superstition.

BAMBABEF. That's a fine project, but it's impracticable. Do you think that it is enough for men to believe in a God who punishes and rewards? You said to me that it often happens that the shrewdest among the common people rebel against my fables; they will rebel just as much against your truth. They will say: "Who will guarantee that God punishes and rewards? Where is the proof? What authority do you have? What miracle have you performed that I should believe you?" They will laugh at you much more than at me.

OUANG. That is where you are wrong. You imagine that men will shake off the yoke of an idea that is honest, probable, useful to everybody, an idea about which human reason is in agreement, just because they reject things that are dishonest, absurd, useless, dangerous, which make good sense shudder. The common people are strongly inclined to believe their magistrates: when their magistrates simply suggest to them a reasonable belief, they happily embrace it. They need no prodigies to believe in a just God, who reads the hearts of men; that idea is too natural to be opposed. It is not necessary to say precisely how God will punish and reward; it is enough to believe in his justice. I assure you that I have seen whole towns which had practically no other dogmas, and they were the ones in which I saw the most virtue.

BAMBABEF. Watch out; in those towns you'll find philosophers who will deny both punishments and rewards.

OUANG. You must concede that those philosophers will deny your inventions far more vehemently; so you won't gain anything by that. If there should be philosophers who don't accept my principles, they will be no less virtuous for that; they will cultivate virtue, which should be embraced out of love and not fear. But, further, I maintain that no philosopher will ever be sure that Providence does not reserve punishments for evil men and rewards for good; for if they ask me who told me that God punishes, I shall ask them who told them that God doesn't punish. In a word, I maintain that the philosophers, far from contradicting me, will help me. Would you like to be a philosopher?

BAMBABEF. Gladly; but don't tell the fakirs that.

GUERRE · WAR

Famine, plague, and war are the three most precious ingredients of this vile world.

Under the classification of famine we may include all the unhealthy nourishment we are compelled to resort to in times of scarcity, abridging our life in the hope of sustaining it. In plague we include all the contagious illnesses, which number two to three thousand. These two gifts come to us from Providence.

But war, which unites all these gifts, comes to us from the imagination of three or four hundred people scattered over the surface of the globe under the name of princes or ministers; and it is perhaps for this reason that in dedications to some books they are called the living images of divinity.

The most determined courtier will easily agree that war always brings plague and famine in its train, if he has seen even a little of the hospitals of the German armies, and passed through some villages in which some great exploit of war had taken place.

Surely the art that desolates the countryside, destroys habitations, and, in an average year, leads to the death of forty thousand out of a hundred thousand men, is a very fine art. At first it was cultivated by nations who mobilized for their common good; for instance, the Diet of the Greeks declared to the Diet of Phrygia and neighboring nations that it intended to arrive on a thousand fishing boats in order to exterminate them if it could. The Roman people in assembly decided that it was to its interest to fight before harvest time against the people of Veii, or the Volscians. And some years later all the Romans, angry at all the Carthaginians, fought them for a long time on land and on sea. It's not this way today.

A genealogist proves to a prince that he is the direct descendant of a count whose parents had made a family compact, three or four hundred years ago, with a house that has disappeared even from memory. This house had farfetched claims to a province whose last proprietor died of apoplexy: the prince and his council conclude without difficulty that the province belongs to him by divine right. The province, which is several hundred miles away, protests in vain that it does not know him, that it has no desire to be governed by him, that one must at least have a people's consent before one gives it laws: these speeches don't even reach the ears of the prince, whose right is incontestable. At once he assembles a large number of men who have nothing to lose; he dresses them in coarse blue cloth at a hundred and ten sous the ell, edges their hats with coarse white yarn, makes them turn right and left, and marches to glory.

The other princes who hear of this escapade take part in it, each according to his strength, and cover a small space of land with more mercenary murderers than Genghis Khan, Tamerlane, or Bajazet ever had in their train.

Distant nations hear that there is going to be some fighting, and that they can make five or six sous a day if they want to join in: right away they divide themselves into two groups, like reapers, and sell their services to anyone ready to employ them.

These multitudes become infuriated with each other, not only without having any business in the proceedings, but even without knowing what is at stake.

At once there are five or six belligerent powers, sometimes three against three, sometimes two against four, sometimes one against five, all detesting one another equally, uniting and fighting with each other in turn; all in agreement on a single point, to do as much harm as possible.

The marvelous part of this infernal enterprise is that every murderer's chief has his flags blessed, and solemnly invokes the Lord before he goes out to exterminate his neighbors. If a chief has had the good fortune to butcher only two or three thousand men, he does not thank God for it; but when he has had ten thousand exterminated by fire and sword, and when, his grace abounding, some town has been destroyed from top to bottom, then they sing a long song in four parts, composed in a language unknown to all who did the fighting, and which besides is crammed with solecisms. The same song serves for marriages and births, as well as for murders: which is unforgivable, above all in the nation best known for new songs.

A thousand times natural religion has prevented citizens from committing crimes. A well-disposed soul is unwilling to commit them; a tender soul is afraid of them—a just and avenging God appears before it. But artificial religion encourages all the cruelties which are committed in company—conspiracies, seditions, pillagings, ambushes, taking towns by surprise, plundering, murders. Everyone marches gaily off to crime under the banner of his saint.

Everywhere a certain number of orators are paid to celebrate these murderous days; some are dressed in a long black jerkin, encumbered by a cropped cloak; others have a shirt over a gown; some wear two pendants of motley cloth over their shirt. All talk for a long time; they point to what was done of old in Palestine, applying it to a battle in Veteravia.

The rest of the year, these fellows declaim against vices. They prove in three propositions and by antitheses that ladies who spread a little rouge on their blooming cheeks will be the eternal objects of the eternal vengeance of the Eternal; that *Polyeucte* and *Athalie* are works of the Devil; that a man who has two hundred écus'

worth of fresh-water fish served at his table during Lent will infallibly be saved, while a poor man who eats two and a half sous'
worth of mutton will forever go to all the devils.

Of five or six thousand declamations of this kind, there are at
most three or four, composed by a Gaul named Massillon, which an
honest man can read without disgust; but among all these speeches
you will hardly find two in which the orator dares to stand up
against war, this scourge and crime which includes all other
scourges and crimes. These miserable orators ceaselessly speak
against love, which is the sole consolation of mankind and the sole
means of restoring it; they say nothing about our abominable efforts
to destroy mankind.

O Bourdaloue, you have delivered a very poor sermon on im-
purity! But not one on these murders, so widely varied, on these
rapes, these pillagings, this universal mania which desolates the
world. All the vices of all ages and all places put together can never
equal the evils produced by a single campaign.

Miserable physicians of souls, you shout for an hour and a
quarter about some pinpricks, and you say nothing about the
malady that tears us in a thousand pieces! Moral philosophers, burn
all your books. As long as thousands of our brothers are honestly
butchered for the caprice of some men, the part of mankind consecrated to heroism will be the most horrible thing in all nature.

What becomes of humanity, modesty, temperance, gentleness,
wisdom, piety; and what do I care about them while half a pound
of lead, shot from six hundred feet away, shatters my body, and
while I die at the age of twenty in inexpressible torments in the
midst of five or six thousand dying men; while my eyes, opening for
the last time, see the town in which I was born destroyed by iron
and fire, and while the last sounds in my ears are the cries of women
and children expiring under the ruins—all for the alleged interest
of a man whom we don't know?

What is worse is that war is an inevitable scourge. If we look at it
closely, we see that all men have worshiped the god Mars: Sabaoth,
among the Jews, signifies the god of arms; but Minerva, in Homer,
calls Mars a savage, insane, infernal god.

HISTOIRE DES ROIS JUIFS ET PARALIPOMÈNES
HISTORY OF JEWISH KINGS AND CHRONICLES

All nations have written down their history as soon as they could write. The Jews have also written theirs. Before they had kings, they lived under a theocracy; they were supposedly governed by God himself.

When the Jews desired a king like other neighboring nations, the prophet Samuel, strongly intent on not having a king, announced to them in God's name that they were rejecting God himself; thus, among the Jews theocracy ended when monarchy began.

Therefore we may say without blaspheming that the history of the Jewish kings has been written like that of other nations, and that God himself didn't take the trouble to dictate the history of a people he no longer governed.

We advance this opinion only with the most extreme diffidence. What might confirm it is that the Chronicles very often contradict the Book of Kings in chronology and in facts, just as our profane historians sometimes contradict one another. Moreover, if God had always written the history of the Jews, we would then have to believe that he is still writing it, for the Jews are still his cherished people. One day they will be converted, and then apparently they will have as much right to regard the history of their dispersion as sacred as they have the right to say that God wrote the history of their kings.

We might add a reflection: since God was their only king for a very long time, and then was their historian, we should have the profoundest respect for all Jews. There isn't a single Jewish peddler who isn't infinitely superior to Caesar and Alexander. Why not prostrate ourselves before a peddler who can prove to you that his history was written by Divinity itself, while Greek and Roman history was transmitted to us by mere profane men?

While the style of the Book of Kings and of Chronicles is divine, still the actions reported in these histories are perhaps not so divine. David assassinates Uriah; Ishbosheth and Mephibosheth are assassinated; Absalom assassinates Amnon; Joab assassinates Absalom; Solomon assassinates Adonijah, his brother; Baasha assassinates Nadab; Zimri assassinates Elah; Omri assassinates Zimri; Ahab assassinates Naboth; Jehu assassinates Ahab and Joram; the inhabitants of Jerusalem assassinate Amaziah, son of Joash; Shallum, son of Jabesh, assassinates Zachariah, son of Jeroboam; Menahem assassinates Shallum, son of Jabesh; Pekah, son of Remaliah, assassinates Pekahiah, son of Menahem; Hoshea, son of Elah, assassinates Pekah, son of Remaliah. I pass over in silence many other minor assassinations. It must be admitted that if the Holy Spirit wrote this history, he didn't choose a very edifying subject.

INQUISITION

As you know, the Inquisition is an admirable and wholly Christian invention to make the pope and the monks more powerful and turn a whole kingdom into hypocrites.

Saint Dominick is generally considered the first to whom we owe this sacred institution. In fact, we still have a patent granted by this great saint, which is in these very words: "I, Brother Dominick, reconcile to the Church one Roger, bearer of these presents, on condition that he will let himself be whipped by a priest, on three consecutive Sundays, from the town gate to the church door, that he will abstain from meat all his life, that he will fast for three Lents a year, that he will never drink wine, that he will wear the *san-benito* with crosses, that he will recite the breviary every day, say ten Paters during the day and twenty at midnight, that he will henceforth keep chaste, and present himself to the parish curate every month, etc., all this on pain of being treated like a heretic, perjurer, and impenitent."

Although Dominick was the true founder of the Inquisition, Louis de Paramo, one of the most respectable writers and most brilliant luminaries of the Holy Office, nevertheless reports in the second chapter of his second book that God was the first founder of the Holy Office, and that he exercised the power of the preaching brethren against Adam. At first, Adam is summoned before the tribunal: *"Adam, ubi es?"* And in fact, he adds, the lack of a summons would have rendered God's proceeding void.

The clothing of skin God made for Adam and Eve was the model for the *san-benito* which the Holy Office makes the heretics wear. It is true that with this argument one can prove that God was the first tailor; but it is no less obvious that he was the first Inquisitor.

Adam was deprived of all the immovable property he possessed in the great terrestrial Paradise: hence the confiscations of the properties of all those condemned by the Holy Office.

Louis de Paramo observes that the inhabitants of Sodom were

burned as heretics, because sodomy is expressly a heresy. From this he moves on to the history of the Jews; there he finds the Holy Office everywhere.

Jesus Christ is the first Inquisitor of the new law; the popes were Inquisitors by divine right; and finally they communicated their power to Saint Dominick.

Then he enumerates all those whom the Inquisition has put to death; he finds far more than a hundred thousand of them.

His book was printed in Madrid in 1598 and had the approval of the scholars, the praises of the bishops, and the permission of the king. Today we can't imagine such horrors, at once so extravagant and so abominable; but then nothing seemed more natural and more edifying. All men resemble Louis de Paramo when they are fanatics.

This Paramo was a plain man, very exact in his dates, who omitted no interesting fact and scrupulously calculated the number of human victims immolated by the Holy Office throughout the world.

With the greatest naïveté he recounts the establishment of the Inquisition in Portugal, and he is perfectly in agreement with four other historians who all sound like him. This is their unanimous report:

Long before, at the beginning of the fifteenth century, Pope Boniface IX had delegated the preaching brethren to go from town to town in Portugal, to burn heretics, Moslems, and Jews; but they were itinerants, and the kings themselves several times complained about the annoyance they caused. Pope Clement VII wished to give them a settled establishment in Portugal, as they had in Aragon and Castile. There were difficulties between the courts of Rome and Lisbon; tempers got strained; the Inquisition suffered from this and was not completely established.

In 1539 a papal legate appeared at Lisbon; he had come, he said, to establish the Holy Inquisition on unshakable foundations. He brought King John III letters from Pope Paul III. He had other letters from Rome for the principal officials of the court; his patent as legate was duly sealed and signed: he showed the most ample authority to create a Grand Inquisitor and all the judges of the Holy Office. He was an impostor named Saavedra, who could forge every kind of handwriting and fabricate and affix false seals and false stamps. He had learned this trade in Rome and perfected it in Seville, where he arrived with two other rascals. His train was magnificent; it was composed of more than a hundred and twenty domestics. To subsidize this enormous expenditure, he and his confidants borrowed immense sums at Seville in the name of the apostolic chamber of Rome; everything had been planned with the most dazzling artifice.

At first the king of Portugal was astonished at the Pope's sending him a legate *a latere* without notifying him in advance. The legate replied proudly that in a matter of such urgency as the solid establishment of the Inquisition, His Holiness could brook no delays, and that the king should be honored that the first courier to bring him the news should be a legate of the Holy Father. The king dared not reply. Thereafter, the legate established a Grand Inquisitor, sent around everywhere to collect the tithe; and before the court could receive an answer from Rome, he had already had two hundred people burned and collected more than two hundred thousand écus.

However, at Seville, the legate had borrowed a very considerable sum on forged bills from the Marquis of Villanova, a Spanish nobleman, who now thought it best to repay himself with his own hands instead of going to Lisbon to get involved with the impostor. Villanova marched with fifty armed men to the frontiers of Spain, near which the legate was at that time making his circuit, kidnapped him, and brought him to Madrid.

The imposture was soon discovered in Lisbon, and the council of Madrid condemned Saavedra to a flogging and ten years in the galleys; but what is remarkable is that afterward Pope Paul IV confirmed everything the impostor had done; he rectified, with the plenitude of his divine power, all the little irregularities of procedure, and made sacred what had been purely human.

> *Qu'importe de quel bras Dieu daigne se servir?*
> What does it matter what arm God deigns to employ?

This is how the Inquisition established itself in Lisbon, and the whole kingdom marveled at Providence.

Still, all the procedures of this tribunal are familiar; it is well known how it opposes the false equity and blind reason of all the other tribunals of the universe. It imprisons people on the mere denunciation of the most sordid persons; a son can denounce his father, a wife her husband; one can never confront one's accusers; property is confiscated for the benefit of the judges: that at least is how the Inquisition has behaved up to our time. There is something divine in it, for it passes reason how men should have borne this yoke patiently. . . .

And now at last Count Aranda has been blessed by all of Europe for paring the nails and filing the teeth of the monster; but it still breathes.

AMOUR-PROPRE · EGOTISM

A beggar of the vicinity of Madrid grandly asked for alms; a passerby said to him: "Aren't you ashamed to carry on this sordid trade, when you could work?" "Sir," replied the mendicant, "I asked you for money, not for advice"; and turned his back on him, preserving all his Castilian dignity. This gentleman was a proud beggar; very little was needed to wound his vanity. He asked for alms out of self-love and couldn't bear the reprimand he got from another self-love.

A missionary traveling in India met a fakir loaded with chains, naked as a monkey, lying on his stomach, and having himself lashed for the sins of his compatriots, who gave him a few pennies. "What self-renunciation!" said one of the spectators. "Self-renunciation!" replied the fakir. "Let me inform you that I only have myself lashed in this world to pay you back in the next, when you will be the horse and I shall be the rider."

Those who say that love of ourselves is the basis of all our feelings and all our actions are therefore quite right about India, Spain, and all the habitable world; and just as people don't write to prove to men that they have a face, there is no need to prove to them that they are egotistical. This egotism is the instrument of our preservation; it resembles the instrument for the perpetuation of the species: we need it, we cherish it, it gives us pleasure, and we must hide it.

FURTHER READING

Peter Gay, "The Philosophe in His Dictionary," *The Party of Humanity* (1964). A lengthy introduction to Voltaire's devices, and an attempt to place the book in Voltaire's life and Voltaire's century.

René Pomeau, *La Religion de Voltaire* (1956). An exhaustively detailed, wholly dependable survey of Voltaire's religious convictions, chronologically arranged.

Norman L. Torrey, *Voltaire and the English Deists* (1930). Useful analysis of Voltaire's reading among English Deists who gave him many ideas, even turns of phrase.

20 ✸ GIBBON

The Decline and Fall
of the Roman Empire

[From Edward Gibbon, *The History of the Decline and Fall of the Roman Empire,* ed. J. B. Bury, 7 vols. (1896–1902), II, 29–32, 35–36, 56. Footnotes omitted.]

All the philosophes read the classics with healthy appetite, but none of them was more voracious a consumer of the ancients than the historian Edward Gibbon. Born in 1737, he was kept from formal schooling as a boy through his delicate health; nor did his stay at Magdalen College, Oxford, serve to teach him anything. The fellows struck him as idle, pedantic, and ignorant; all that happened to him at the university was that he converted to Roman Catholicism. In 1753, his father, alarmed and outraged, packed him off to Lausanne, to be subjected to good Calvinist antidotes, and by 1755 Gibbon was back home. "I am now good protestant," he wrote to his aunt, and "extremely glad of it."* Actually, Catholicism's loss was not Protestantism's gain: Gibbon had become, and remained all his life, a thoroughgoing skeptic.

Remembering that critical year, 1755, later in his witty autobiography, Gibbon recalled less his return to Protestantism than his hunger for the classics. In "the last eight months of the year 1755," a "period of the most extraordinary diligence and rapid progress," Gibbon devoured Cicero, reading "with application and pleasure all the epistles, all the orations, and the most important treatises of rhetoric and philosophy." He found Cicero's language beautiful,

---

* Gibbon to Catherine Porten, February 1755, in Edward Gibbon, *Letters,* ed. J. E. Norton, 3 vols. (1956), I, 3.

his spirit free, and his writings, like his conduct, exemplary. Then *"after finishing this great author, a library of eloquence and reason, I formed a more extensive plan of reviewing the Latin classics under the four divisions of (1) historians, (2) poets, (3) orators, and (4) philosophers, in a chronological series from the days of Plautus and Sallust to the decline of the language and empire of Rome; and this plan, in the last twenty-seven months of my residence at Lausanne, (January 1756–April 1758) I nearly accomplished."* He insisted that while he had read rapidly, he had been thorough: *"I indulged myself in a second and even a third perusal of Terence, Virgil, Horace, Tacitus, etc., and studied to imbibe the sense and spirit most congenial to my own."* The selection that follows suggests what that congenial sense and spirit was: an amused contempt for fanaticism and superstition, coupled with a superb failure to understand the religious mind.

Whatever the consequences, Gibbon continued to read passionately. Whenever he talked of reading the ancients, his metaphors are those of eating. Serving with the militia, he was kept from his favorite activity, but once he was free again, he resumed his gluttonous activity: *"After this long fast, the longest which I have ever known, I once more tasted at Dover the pleasures of reading and thinking; and the hungry appetite with which I opened a volume of Tully's [i.e., Cicero's] philosophical works is still present to my memory."**

He dabbled in literature, contemplated a variety of literary enterprises, but then, in 1764, on a visit to Italy, he found his vocation. *"My temper,"* he later wrote, *"is not very susceptible of enthusiasm, and the enthusiasm which I do not feel I have ever scorned to affect. But at the distance of twenty-five years I can neither forget nor express the strong emotions which agitated my mind as I first approached and entered the Eternal City."* After several days of antiquarian intoxication, the great moment came: *"It was at Rome, on the 15th of October 1764, as I sat musing amid the ruins of the Capitol, while the barefooted friars were singing vespers in the temple of Jupiter, that the idea of writing the decline and fall of the city first started to my mind."*†

The irony of that scene—the barefoot monks in possession of the pagan temple—provided him with his life's work. While he served in the House of Commons from 1774 to 1783, his mind was mainly

---

* *Autobiography,* ed. Dero A. Saunders (1961), 98–100, 135.
† *Ibid.,* 152, 154.

on his history, and he even put his public service to account in his analysis of Roman imperial politics. The first volume of the Decline and Fall of the Roman Empire *appeared in 1776, the last in 1788; when Gibbon died in 1794, he knew himself to be a famous man and a great historian. Some of the implications of his historical work will occupy our attention below,* the selection reprinted here, from the notorious fifteenth chapter, illustrates what the earlier selection from Hume's* History of England *also illustrated: the polemical uses to which the philosophes put even their historical writings. Gibbon always claimed, with injured innocence, that he was merely writing the history of the origins of a human institution, the Church, without in any sense assailing the divine doctrines it taught. But no one was deceived—and Gibbon would have been disappointed if anyone had been.*

The miracles of the primitive church, after obtaining the sanction of ages, have been lately attacked in a very free and ingenious inquiry; which, though it has met with the most favourable reception from the Public, appears to have excited a general scandal among the divines of our own as well as of the other Protestant churches of Europe. Our different sentiments on this subject will be much less influenced by any particular arguments than by our habits of study and reflection; and, above all, by the degree of the evidence which we have accustomed ourselves to require for the proof of a miraculous event. The duty of an historian does not call upon him to interpose his private judgment in this nice and important controversy; but he ought not to dissemble the difficulty of adopting such a theory as may reconcile the interest of religion with that of reason, of making a proper application of that theory, and of defining with precision the limits of that happy period, exempt from error and from deceit, to which we might be disposed to extend the gift of supernatural powers. From the first of the fathers to the last of the popes, a succession of bishops, of saints, of martyrs, and of miracles is continued without interruption, and the progress of superstition was so gradual and almost imperceptible that we know not in what particular link we should break the chain of

* See below, page 618.

tradition. Every age bears testimony to the wonderful events by which it was distinguished, and its testimony appears no less weighty and respectable than that of the preceding generation, till we are insensibly led on to accuse our own inconsistency, if in the eighth or in the twelfth century we deny to the venerable Bede, or to the holy Bernard, the same degree of confidence which, in the second century, we had so liberally granted to Justin or to Irenæus. If the truth of any of those miracles is appreciated by their apparent use and propriety, every age had unbelievers to convince, heretics to confute, and idolatrous nations to convert; and sufficient motives might always be produced to justify the interposition of Heaven. And yet, since every friend to revelation is persuaded of the reality, and every reasonable man is convinced of the cessation, of miraculous powers, it is evident that there must have been *some period* in which they were either suddenly or gradually withdrawn from the Christian church. Whatever æra is chosen for that purpose, the death of the apostles, the conversion of the Roman empire, or the extinction of the Arian heresy, the insensibility of the Christians who lived at that time will equally afford a just matter of surprise. They still supported their pretensions after they had lost their power. Credulity performed the office of faith; fanaticism was permitted to assume the language of inspiration, and the effects of accident or contrivance were ascribed to supernatural causes. The recent experience of genuine miracles should have instructed the Christian world in the ways of Providence, and habituated their eye (if we may use a very inadequate expression) to the style of the divine artist. Should the most skilful painter of modern Italy presume to decorate his feeble imitations with the name of Raphael or of Correggio, the insolent fraud would be soon discovered and indignantly rejected.

Whatever opinion may be entertained of the miracles of the primitive church since the time of the apostles, this unresisting softness of temper, so conspicuous among the believers of the second and third centuries, proved of some accidental benefit to the cause of truth and religion. In modern times, a latent, and even involuntary, scepticism adheres to the most pious dispositions. Their admission of supernatural truths is much less an active consent than a cold and passive acquiescence. Accustomed long since to observe and to respect the invariable order of Nature, our reason, or at least our imagination, is not sufficiently prepared to sustain the visible action of the Deity. But, in the first ages of Christianity, the situation of mankind was extremely different. The most curious, or the most credulous, among the Pagans were often persuaded to enter into a society which asserted an actual claim of miraculous powers. The primitive Christians perpetually trod on mystic ground, and their minds were exercised by the habits of believing the most extraordinary events. They felt, or they fancied, that on every side they were incessantly assaulted by dæmons, comforted by visions, instructed by prophecy, and surprisingly delivered from danger, sickness, and from death itself, by the supplications of the church. The real or imaginary prodigies, of which they so frequently conceived themselves to be the objects, the instruments, or the spectators, very happily disposed them to adopt, with the same ease, but with far greater justice, the authentic wonders of the evangelic history; and thus miracles that exceeded not the measure of their own experience inspired them with the most lively assurance of mysteries which were acknowledged to surpass the limits of their understanding. It is this deep impression of supernatural truths which has been so much celebrated under the name of faith; a state of mind described as the surest pledge of the divine favour and of future felicity, and recommended as the first or perhaps the only merit of a Christian. According to the more rigid doctors, the moral virtues, which may be equally practised by infidels, are destitute of any value or efficacy in the work of our justification.

But the primitive Christian demonstrated his faith by his virtues; and it was very justly supposed that the divine persuasion, which enlightened or subdued the understanding, must, at the same time, purify the heart, and direct the actions, of the believer. The first apologists of Christianity who justify the innocence of their brethren, and the writers of a later period who celebrate the sanctity of their ancestors, display, in the most lively colours, the reformation of manners which was introduced into the world by the preaching of the gospel. As it is my intention to remark only such human causes as were permitted to second the influence of revelation, I shall slightly mention two motives which might naturally render the lives of the primitive Christians much purer and more austere than those of their Pagan contemporaries, or their degenerate successors; repentance for their past sins, and the laudable desire of supporting the reputation of the society in which they were engaged.

The acquisition of knowledge, the exercise of our reason or fancy, and the cheerful flow of unguarded conversation, may employ the leisure of a liberal mind. Such amusements, however, were rejected with abhorrence, or admitted with the utmost caution, by the severity of the fathers, who despised all knowledge that was not useful to salvation, and who considered all levity of discourse as a criminal abuse of the gift of speech. In our present state of existence, the body is so inseparably connected with the soul that it seems to be our interest to taste, with innocence and moderation, the enjoyments of which that faithful companion is susceptible. Very different was the reasoning of our devout predecessors; vainly aspiring to imitate the perfection of angels, they disdained, or they affected to disdain, every earthly and corporeal delight. Some of our senses indeed are necessary for our preservation, others for our subsistence, and others again for our information, and thus far it was impossible to reject the use of them. The first sensation of pleasure was marked as the first moment of their abuse. The unfeeling candidate for Heaven was instructed, not only to resist the grosser allurements of the taste or smell, but even to shut his ears against the profane harmony of sounds, and to view with indifference the most finished productions of human art. Gay apparel, magnificent houses, and elegant furniture were supposed to unite the double guilt of pride and of sensuality: a simple and mortified appearance was more suitable to the Christian who was certain of his sins and doubtful of his salvation. In their censures of luxury, the fathers are extremely minute and circumstantial; and among the various articles which excite their pious indignation, we may enumerate false hair, garments of any colour except white, instruments of music, vases of gold or silver, downy pillows (as Jacob reposed his head on a stone), white bread, foreign wines, public salutations, the use of warm baths, and the practice of shaving the beard, which, according to the expression of Tertullian, is a lie against our own faces, and an impious attempt to improve the works of the Creator. When Christianity was introduced among the rich and the polite, the observation of these singular laws was left, as it would be at present, to the few who were ambitious of superior sanctity. But it is always easy, as well as agreeable, for the inferior ranks of mankind to claim a merit from the contempt of that pomp and pleasure, which fortune has placed beyond their reach. The virtue of the primitive Christians, like that of the first Romans, was very frequently guarded by poverty and ignorance.

The chaste severity of the fathers, in whatever related to the commerce of the two sexes, flowed from the same principle; their abhorrence of every enjoyment which might gratify the sensual, and degrade the spiritual, nature of man. It was their favourite opinion that, if Adam had preserved his obedience to the Creator, he would have lived for ever in a state of virgin purity, and that some harmless mode of vegetation might have peopled paradise with a race of innocent and immortal beings. The use of marriage was permitted only to his fallen posterity, as a necessary expedient to continue the human species, and as a restraint, however imperfect, on the natural licentiousness of desire. The hesitation of the orthodox casuists on this interesting subject betrays the perplexity of men, unwilling to approve an institution which they were compelled to tolerate. The enumeration of the very whimsical laws, which they most circumstantially imposed on the marriage-bed, would force a smile from the young, and a blush from the fair. It was their unanimous sentiment that a first marriage was adequate to all the purposes of nature and of society. The sensual connexion was refined into a resemblance of the mystic union of Christ with his church, and was pronounced to be indissoluble either by divorce or by death.

. . . The decline of ancient prejudice exposed a very numerous portion of human kind to the danger of a painful and comfortless situation. A state of scepticism and suspense may amuse a few inquisitive minds. But the practice of superstition is so congenial to the multitude that, if they are forcibly awakened, they still regret the loss of their pleasing vision. Their love of the marvellous and supernatural, their curiosity with regard to future events, and their strong propensity to extend their hopes and fears beyond the limits of the visible world, were the principal causes which favoured the establishment of Polytheism. So urgent on the vulgar is the necessity of believing that the fall of any system of mythology will most probably be succeeded by the introduction of some other mode of superstition. Some deities of a more recent and fashionable cast might soon have occupied the deserted temples of Jupiter and Apollo, if, in the decisive moment, the wisdom of Providence had not interposed a genuine revelation, fitted to inspire the most rational esteem and conviction, whilst, at the same time, it was adorned with all that could attract the curiosity, the wonder, and the veneration of the people. In their actual disposition, as many were almost disengaged from their artificial prejudices, but equally susceptible and desirous of a devout attachment; an object much less deserving would have been sufficient to fill the vacant place in their hearts, and to gratify the uncertain eagerness of their passions. Those who are inclined to pursue this reflection, instead of viewing with astonishment the rapid progress of Christianity, will perhaps be surprised that its success was not still more rapid and still more universal.

FURTHER READING

Harold L. Bond, *The Literary Art of Edward Gibbon* (1960). An intelligent
    discussion of Gibbon's techniques.
Shelby T. McCloy, *Gibbon's Antagonism to Christianity and the Discussions That
    It Has Provoked* (1933). Addresses itself to the subject of this selection.
See also below, "Further Reading" for selection 45.

21 ❧ BOSWELL

Conversation with Hume

[From *Boswell in Extremes, 1776–1778,* edited
by Charles C. McC. Weis and Frederick A.
Pottle, 11–15.*]

In the 1760s, David Hume, corpulent and cheerful, traveled in Europe, continued to tinker with his favorite polemic, the Dialogues Concerning Natural Religion, *and revised his successful history of England. Then, in 1772, he began to lose weight, and his health began to alarm his friends. By 1775 he was thin and frail, though not in pain; he knew that his death was not far off. But Hume died as he had lived, courteously and courageously. He comforted his friends, he hailed their writings—in the spring of his last year, 1776, he had occasion to applaud two masterpieces, his friend Adam Smith's* Wealth of Nations† *and his acquaintance Gibbon's first volume of the* Decline and Fall—*and he amused himself by reading his old pagan favorites, Lucretius and Lucian, neither of whom had entertained the slightest belief in immortality.*

Then, on July 7, 1776, only seven weeks before his death, Hume received the visit of James Boswell (1740–95). Typical of the journalist in his intrusive tastelessness, Boswell questioned Hume on the most delicate matters, only to find himself bested at every turn. The confrontation is more than an amusing anecdote; it is the great confrontation of the eighteenth century: Christian against pagan. In August, Hume died at Edinburgh, "the death of a philosopher."‡

---

* Copyright © 1970 by Yale University. Used with the permission of McGraw-Hill Book Company and William Heinemann, Ltd.

† See below, page 571.

‡ Gibbon, *Autobiography,* ed. Dero A. Saunders (1961), 177.

An Account of My Last Interview
with David Hume, Esq.

BY JAMES BOSWELL

[Partly recorded in my Journal, partly enlarged from my memory, 3 March 1777.]

On Sunday forenoon the 7 of July 1776, being too late for church, I went to see Mr. David Hume, who was returned from London and Bath, just a-dying. I found him alone, in a reclining posture in his drawing-room. He was lean, ghastly, and quite of an earthy appearance. He was dressed in a suit of grey cloth with white metal buttons, and a kind of scratch wig. He was quite different from the plump figure which he used to present. He had before him Dr. Campbell's *Philosophy of Rhetoric.* He seemed to be placid and even cheerful. He said he was just approaching to his end. I think these were his words. I know not how I contrived to get the subject of immortality introduced. He said he never had entertained any belief in religion since he began to read Locke and Clarke. I asked him if he was not religious when he was young. He said he was, and he used to read *The Whole Duty of Man;* that he made an abstract from the catalogue of vices at the end of it, and examined himself by this, leaving out murder and theft and such vices as he had no chance of committing, having no inclination to commit them. This, he said, was strange work; for instance, to try if, notwithstanding his excelling his schoolfellows, he had no pride or vanity. He smiled in ridicule of this as absurd and contrary to fixed principles and necessary consequences, not adverting that religious discipline does not mean to extinguish, but to moderate, the passions; and certainly an excess of pride or vanity is dangerous and generally hurtful. He then said flatly that the morality of every religion was bad, and, I really thought, was not jocular when he said that when he heard a man was religious, he concluded he was a rascal, though he had known some instances of very good men being religious. This was just an extravagant reverse of the common remark as to infidels.

I had a strong curiosity to be satisfied if he persisted in disbelieving a future state even when he had death before his eyes. I was persuaded from what he now said, and from his manner of saying it, that he did persist. I asked him if it was not possible that there might be a future state. He answered it was possible that a piece of coal put upon the fire would not burn; and he added that it was a most unreasonable fancy that we should exist for ever. That immortality, if it were at all, must be general; that a great proportion of the human race has hardly any intellectual qualities; that a great proportion dies in infancy before being possessed of reason; yet all these must be immortal; that a porter who gets drunk by ten o'clock with gin must be immortal; that the trash of every age must be preserved, and that new universes must be created to contain such infinite numbers. This appeared to me an unphilosophical objection, and I said, "Mr. Hume, you know spirit does not take up space."

I may illustrate what he last said by mentioning that in a former conversation with me on this subject he used pretty much the same mode of reasoning, and urged that Wilkes and his mob must be immortal. One night last May as I was coming up King Street, Westminster, I met Wilkes, who carried me into Parliament Street to see a curious procession pass: the funeral of a lamplighter attended by some hundreds of his fraternity with torches. Wilkes, who either is, or affects to be, an infidel, was rattling away, "I think there's an end of that fellow. I think he won't rise again." I very calmly said to him, "You bring into my mind the strongest argument that ever I heard against a future state"; and then told him David Hume's objection that Wilkes and his mob must be immortal. It seemed to make a proper impression, for he grinned abashment, as a Negro grows whiter when he blushes. But to return to my last interview with Mr. Hume.

I asked him if the thought of annihilation never gave him any uneasiness. He said not the least; no more than the thought that he had not been, as Lucretius observes. "Well," said I, "Mr. Hume, I hope to triumph over you when I meet you in a future state; and remember you are not to pretend that you was joking with all this infidelity." "No, no," said he. "But I shall have been so long there before you come that it will be nothing new." In this style of good humour and levity did I conduct the conversation. Perhaps it was wrong on so awful a subject. But as nobody was present, I thought it could have no bad effect. I however felt a degree of horror, mixed with a sort of wild, strange, hurrying recollection of my excellent mother's pious instructions, of Dr. Johnson's noble lessons, and of my religious sentiments and affections during the course of my life. I was like a man in sudden danger eagerly seeking his defensive arms; and I could not but be assailed by momentary doubts while I had actually before me a man of such strong abilities and extensive inquiry dying in the persuasion of being annihilated. But I maintained my faith. I told him that I believed the Christian religion as I believed history. Said he: "You do not believe it as you believe the [Glorious] Revolution." "Yes," said I; "but the difference is that I am not so much interested in the truth of the Revolution; otherwise I should have anxious doubts concerning it. A man who is in love has doubts of the affection of his mistress, without cause." I mentioned Soame Jenyns's little book in defence of Christianity, which was just published but which I had not yet read. Mr. Hume said, "I am told there is nothing of his usual spirit in it."

He had once said to me, on a forenoon while the sun was shining bright, that he did not wish to be immortal. This was a most wonderful thought. The reason he gave was that he was very well in this state of being, and that the chances were very much against his being so well in another state; and he would rather not be more than be worse. I answered that it was reasonable to hope he would be better; that there would be a progressive improvement. I tried him at this interview with that topic, saying that a future state was surely a pleasing idea. He said no, for that it was always seen through a gloomy medium; there was always a Phlegethon or a hell. "But," said I, "would it not be agreeable to have hopes of seeing our friends again?" and I mentioned three men lately deceased, for whom I knew he had a high value: Ambassador Keith, Lord Alemoor, and Baron Mure. He owned it would be agreeable, but added that none of them entertained such a notion. I believe he said, such a foolish, or such an absurd, notion; for he was indecently and impolitely positive in incredulity. "Yes," said I, "Lord Alemoor was a believer." David acknowledged that *he* had *some* belief.

I somehow or other brought Dr. Johnson's name into our conversation. I had often heard him speak of that great man in a very illiberal manner. He said upon this occasion, "Johnson should be pleased with my *History*." Nettled by Hume's frequent attacks upon my revered friend in former conversations, I told him now that Dr. Johnson did not allow him much credit; for he said, "Sir, the fellow is a Tory by chance." I am sorry that I mentioned this at such a time. I was off my guard; for the truth is that Mr. Hume's pleasantry was such that there was no solemnity in the scene; and death for the time did not seem dismal. It surprised me to find him talking of different matters with a tranquillity of mind and a clearness of head which few men possess at any time. Two particulars I remember: Smith's *Wealth of Nations,* which he commended much, and Monboddo's *Origin of Language,* which he treated contemptuously. I said, "If I were you, I should regret annihilation. Had I written such an admirable history, I should be sorry to leave it." He said, "I shall leave that history, of which you are pleased to speak so favourably, as perfect as I can." He said, too, that all the great abilities with which men had ever been endowed were relative to this world. He said he became a greater friend to the Stuart family as he advanced in studying for his history; and he hoped he had vindicated the two first of them so effectually that they would never again be attacked.

Mr. Lauder, his surgeon, came in for a little, and Mr. Mure, the Baron's son, for another small interval. He was, as far as I could judge, quite easy with both. He said he had no pain, but was wasting away. I left him with impressions which disturbed me for some time.

FURTHER READING

Peter Gay, *The Enlightenment: An Interpretation,* Vol. I, *The Rise of Modern Paganism* (1966), 355–57. A short analysis of the encounter between Boswell and Hume.

Frederick A. Pottle, *The Literary Career of James Boswell, Esq.* (1929). Excellent study; to be superseded only by Pottle's definitive biography of Boswell, now in progress.

D. A. Stauffer, *The Art of Biography in Eighteenth-Century England* (1941). A fine survey.

22 ❀ JEFFERSON

Letter to Dr. Benjamin Rush

[From *The Writings of Thomas Jefferson,*
edited by Andrew A. Lipscomb, 20 vols.
(1903–4), X, 379–85.]

*The selection that follows—a letter that Thomas Jefferson wrote
while he was President of the United States—illuminates the enormous complexities of that movement and style of thought we call
the Enlightenment. Jefferson, born in 1743 in Virginia, was much
like his European counterparts: he imbibed Latin learning at
school, and emerged a worshiper of Cicero. He admired Cicero's self-
reliance, his contempt for the fear of death, and his freedom from
superstition. As a young man, Jefferson thought the Christian system doubtful and a pagan philosophy of life eminently satisfactory.
In his later years he returned to Christianity, but it was always a
liberal Protestantism. And, as every student of American history
knows, his interest in religious toleration and freedom of speech
never waned.*

Washington, April 21, 1803.

Dear Sir,—In some of the delightful conversations with you, in the
evenings of 1798–99, and which served as an anodyne to the afflictions of the crisis through which our country was then laboring, the
Christian religion was sometimes our topic; and I then promised
you, that one day or other, I would give you my views of it. They
are the result of a life of inquiry and reflection, and very different
from that anti-Christian system imputed to me by those who know

nothing of my opinions. To the corruptions of Christianity I am, indeed, opposed; but not to the genuine precepts of Jesus himself. I am a Christian, in the only sense in which he wished any one to be; sincerely attached to his doctrines, in preference to all others; ascribing to himself every *human* excellence; and believing he never claimed any other. At the short interval since these conversations, when I could justifiably abstract my mind from public affairs, the subject has been under my contemplation. But the more I considered it, the more it expanded beyond the measure of either my time or information. In the moment of my late departure from Monticello, I received from Dr. Priestley, his little treatise of "Socrates and Jesus Compared." This being a section of the general view I had taken of the field, it became a subject of reflection while on the road, and unoccupied otherwise. The result was, to arrange in my mind a syllabus, or outline of such an estimate of the comparative merits of Christianity, as I wished to see executed by some one of more leisure and information for the task, than myself. This I now send you, as the only discharge of my promise I can probably ever execute. And in confiding it to you, I know it will not be exposed to the malignant perversions of those who make every word from me a text for new misrepresentations and calumnies. I am moreover averse to the communication of my religious tenets to the public; because it would countenance the presumption of those who have endeavored to draw them before that tribunal, and to seduce public opinion to erect itself into that inquisition over the rights of conscience, which the laws have so justly proscribed. It behooves every man who values liberty of conscience for himself, to resist invasions of it in the case of others; or their case may, by change of circumstances, become his own. It behooves him, too, in his own case, to give no example of concession, betraying the common right of independent opinion, by answering questions of faith, which the laws have left between God and himself. Accept my affectionate salutations.

Syllabus of an Estimate of the Merit of the Doctrines of Jesus, compared with those of others.

In a comparative view of the Ethics of the enlightened nations of antiquity, of the Jews and of Jesus, no notice should be taken of the corruptions of reason among the ancients, to wit, the idolatry and superstition of the vulgar, nor of the corruptions of Christianity by the learned among its professors.

Let a just view be taken of the moral principles inculcated by the most esteemed of the sects of ancient philosophy, or of their individuals; particularly Pythagoras, Socrates, Epicurus, Cicero, Epictetus, Seneca, Antoninus.

I. Philosophers. 1. Their precepts related chiefly to ourselves, and the government of those passions which, unrestrained, would disturb our tranquillity of mind.* In this branch of philosophy they were really great.

2. In developing our duties to others, they were short and defective. They embraced, indeed, the circles of kindred and friends, and inculcated patriotism, or the love of our country in the aggregate, as a primary obligation: towards our neighbors and countrymen they taught justice, but scarcely viewed them as within the circle of benevolence. Still less have they inculcated peace, charity and love to our fellow men, or embraced with benevolence the whole family of mankind.

II. Jews. 1. Their system was Deism; that is, the belief in one only God. But their ideas of him and of his attributes were degrading and injurious.

2. Their Ethics were not only imperfect, but often irreconcilable with the sound dictates of reason and morality, as they respect intercourse with those around us; and repulsive and anti-social, as respecting other nations. They needed reformation, therefore, in an eminent degree.

III. Jesus. In this state of things among the Jews, Jesus appeared. His parentage was obscure; his condition poor; his education null; his natural endowments great; his life correct and innocent: he was meek, benevolent, patient, firm, disinterested, and of the sublimest eloquence.

The disadvantages under which his doctrines appear are remarkable.

1. Like Socrates and Epictetus, he wrote nothing himself.

2. But he had not, like them, a Xenophon or an Arrian to write

---

* To explain, I will exhibit the heads of Seneca's and Cicero's philosophical works, the most extensive of any we have received from the ancients. Of ten heads in Seneca, seven relate to ourselves, viz. *de ira, consolatio, de tranquilitate, de constantia sapientis, de otio sapientis, de vita beata, de brevitate vitae;* two relate to others, *de clementia, de beneficiis;* and one relates to the government of the world, *de providentia.* Of eleven tracts of Cicero, five respect ourselves, viz. *de finibus, Tusculana, academica, paradoxa, de Senectute;* one, *de officiis,* relates partly to ourselves, partly to others; one, *de amicitia,* relates to others; and four are on different subjects, to wit, *de natura deorum, de divinatione, de fato,* and *somnium Scipionis.*

for him. I name not Plato, who only used the name of Socrates to cover the whimsies of his own brain. On the contrary, all the learned of his country, entrenched in its power and riches, were opposed to him, lest his labors should undermine their advantages; and the committing to writing his life and doctrines fell on unlettered and ignorant men; who wrote, too, from memory, and not till long after the transactions had passed.

3. According to the ordinary fate of those who attempt to enlighten and reform mankind, he fell an early victim to the jealousy and combination of the altar and the throne, at about thirty-three years of age, his reason having not yet attained the *maximum* of its energy, nor the course of his preaching, which was but of three years at most, presented occasions for developing a complete system of morals.

4. Hence the doctrines which he really delivered were defective as a whole, and fragments only of what he did deliver have come to us mutilated, misstated, and often unintelligible.

5. They have been still more disfigured by the corruptions of schismatizing followers, who have found an interest in sophisticating and perverting the simple doctrines he taught, by engrafting on them the mysticisms of a Grecian sophist, frittering them into subtleties, and obscuring them with jargon, until they have caused good men to reject the whole in disgust, and to view Jesus himself as an impostor.

Notwithstanding these disadvantages, a system of morals is presented to us, which, if filled up in the style and spirit of the rich fragments he left us, would be the most perfect and sublime that has ever been taught by man.

The question of his being a member of the Godhead, or in direct communication with it, claimed for him by some of his followers, and denied by others, is foreign to the present view, which is merely an estimate of the intrinsic merits of his doctrines.

1. He corrected the Deism of the Jews, confirming them in their belief of one only God, and giving them juster notions of his attributes and government.

2. His moral doctrines, relating to kindred and friends, were more pure and perfect than those of the most correct of the philosophers, and greatly more so than those of the Jews; and they went far beyond both in inculcating universal philanthropy, not only to kindred and friends, to neighbors and countrymen, but to all mankind, gathering all into one family, under the bonds of love, charity, peace, common wants and common aids. A development of

this head will evince the peculiar superiority of the system of Jesus over all others.

3. The precepts of philosophy, and of the Hebrew code, laid hold of actions only. He pushed his scrutinies into the heart of man; erected his tribunal in the region of his thoughts, and purified the waters at the fountain head.

4. He taught, emphatically, the doctrines of a future state, which was either doubted, or disbelieved by the Jews; and wielded it with efficacy, as an important incentive, supplementary to the other motives to moral conduct.

FURTHER READING

Gilbert Chinard, ed., *The Literary Bible of Thomas Jefferson: His Commonplace Book of Philosophers and Poets* (1928). An instructive publication of Jefferson's private views.

Richard Hofstadter, *The American Political Tradition* (1948), Chapters I and II. Brilliant essays on the Founding Fathers.

Adrienne Koch, ed., *The American Enlightenment* (1965). Useful, extensive anthology, complete with introductions.

Dumas Malone, *Jefferson and His Time*, 4 vols. so far (1948ff.). *The* biography, though very admiring.

Merrill L. Peterson, *Thomas Jefferson and the New Nation: A Biography* (1970). An excellent interpretative account.

23 ❀ ADDISON

The Spectator

[From *The Spectator*, edited by George A.
Aitken, 8 vols. (1898), I, 37–42, 52–56, 118–19,
121–23, 358–60, 362.]

*This selection is a reminder of my general argument that the
Enlightenment was wider than the little band of philosophes; that
the eighteenth century was, in general, an age interested in human-
izing itself and in enhancing the empire of reason—which meant,
for most, a reasonable piety, and a celebration of the unheroic
commercial virtues. One vehicle for this enterprise was the didactic
periodical literature that began to flourish across civilized Europe
early in the Age of the Enlightenment. Daniel Defoe (?1660–1731),
whom everyone remembers as the author of* Robinson Crusoe, *may
claim to be the first author-editor of such a periodical; in 1704, he
began a* Review *which ran almost for a decade and advertised itself
as "a weekly history of Nonsense, Impertinence, Vice, and Debauchery." It was, in other words, a moral—that is to say, moraliz-
ing—weekly. Others followed, in England, in France, in the
German states. Clearly the most important of these, and the model
for all the others, were the two periodicals started by Joseph
Addison (1672–1719) and Richard Steele (1672–1729). The editors
were at once men of letters and statesmen, a combination that
foreign visitors like Voltaire found so admirable. The* Tatler *and
The Spectator *had only a short life span; between them they lasted
from 1709 to 1714. But they were bought by thousands and read by
thousands more, and those who did not read the issues as they
appeared read them later, in one of the many editions of bound
volumes in which the two editors and their distinguished con-
tributors—who included Jonathan Swift among others—spread
their message of decency, humor, reasonableness. One reason why*

they could spread it so successfully was that they strove to embody their teachings in their style, and made every effort to be easy to read. Blandness, they seemed to say, conquers all. "I shall spare no pains," Addison declared in the celebrated tenth number of The Spectator, *"to make their instruction agreeable, and their diversion useful, for which reasons I shall endeavour to enliven morality with wit, and to temper wit with morality . . ." In this sense, Addison and Steele became, in their own estimation, the Socrates of the modern world. Socrates, they noted, had brought philosophy down from heaven to dwell among men; they brought philosophy "out of closets and libraries, schools and colleges, to dwell in clubs and assemblies, at tea-tables and in coffee-houses." It is one of the most characteristic features of the Age of the Enlightenment—at once pleasing and problematic—that it thought problems not beyond solution, and best presented in the easy tones of the club.*

No. 7. *Thursday, March 8, 1711*

Somnia, terrores magicos, miracula, sagas,
Nocturnos lemures, portentaque Thessala rides?
—Hor., 2 *Ep.* ii. 208.

Going yesterday to dine with an old acquaintance, I had the misfortune to find his whole family very much dejected. Upon asking him the occasion of it, he told me that his wife had dreamt a very strange dream the night before, which they were afraid portended some misfortune to themselves or to their children. At her coming into the room I observed a settled melancholy in her countenance, which I should have been troubled for, had I not heard from whence it proceeded. We were no sooner sat down but, after having looked upon me a little while, "My dear," says she, turning to her husband, "you may now see the stranger that was in the candle last night." Soon after this, as they began to talk of family affairs, a little boy at the lower end of the table told her that he was to go into join-hand on Thursday. "Thursday?" says she; "no, child, if it please God, you shall not begin upon Childermas Day.* Tell your writing-master that Friday will be soon enough." I

* The Feast of the Holy Innocents (Dec. 28) .—G.A.A.

was reflecting with myself on the oddness of her fancy, and wondering that anybody would establish it as a rule to lose a day in every week. In the midst of these my musings she desired me to reach her a little salt upon the point of my knife, which I did in such a trepidation and hurry of obedience that I let it drop by the way, at which she immediately startled and said it fell towards her. Upon this I looked very blank, and, observing the concern of the whole table, began to consider myself, with some confusion, as a person that had brought a disaster upon the family. The lady, however, recovering herself after a little space, said to her husband with a sigh, "My dear, misfortunes never come single." My friend, I found, acted but an underpart at his table, and being a man of more good-nature than understanding, thinks himself obliged to fall in with all the passions and humours of his yoke-fellow: "Do not you remember, child," says she, "that the pigeon-house fell the very afternoon that our careless wench spilt the salt upon the table?" "Yes," says he, "my dear, and the next post brought us an account of the battle of Almanza."* The reader may guess at the figure I made after having done all this mischief. I despatched my dinner as soon as I could with my usual taciturnity, when, to my utter confusion, the lady seeing me quitting my knife and fork and laying them across one another upon my plate, desired me that I would humour her so far as to take them out of that figure and place them side by side. What the absurdity was which I had committed I did not know, but I suppose there was some traditionary superstition in it; and therefore, in obedience to the lady of the house, I disposed of my knife and fork in two parallel lines, which is the figure I shall always lay them in for the future, though I do not know any reason for it.

It is not difficult for a man to see that a person has conceived an aversion to him. For my own part, I quickly found by the lady's looks that she regarded me as a very odd kind of fellow, with an unfortunate aspect; for which reason I took my leave immediately after dinner and withdrew to my own lodgings. Upon my return home I fell into a profound contemplation on the evils that attend these superstitious follies of mankind; how they subject us to imaginary afflictions and additional sorrows that do not properly come within our lot. As if the natural calamities of life were not sufficient for it, we turn the most indifferent circumstances into

* At the battle of Almanza (April 25, 1707) the English and their allies, led by Lord Galway, were defeated by the French and Spaniards, under the Duke of Berwick, son of James II.—G.A.A.

misfortunes, and suffer as much from trifling accidents as from real evils. I have known the shooting of a star spoil a night's rest; and have seen a man in love grow pale and lose his appetite upon the plucking of a merry-thought. A screech-owl at midnight has alarmed a family more than a band of robbers; nay, the voice of a cricket hath struck more terror than the roaring of a lion. There is nothing so inconsiderable, which may not appear dreadful to an imagination that is filled with omens and prognostics. A rusty nail or a crooked pin shoot up into prodigies. . . .

I know but one way of fortifying my soul against these gloomy presages and terrors of mind, and that is, by securing to myself the friendship and protection of that Being who disposes of events, and governs futurity. He sees, at one view, the whole thread of my existence, not only that part of it which I have already passed through, but that which runs forward into all the depths of eternity. When I lay me down to sleep, I recommend myself to His care; when I awake, I give myself up to His direction. Amidst all the evils that threaten me, I will look up to Him for help, and question not but He will either avert them, or turn them to my advantage. Though I know neither the time nor the manner of the death I am to die, I am not at all solicitous about it; because I am sure that He knows them both, and that He will not fail to comfort and support me under them.

No. 10. *Monday, March 12, 1711*

> *Non aliter quam qui adverso vix flumine lembum*
> *Remigiis subigit: si brachia forte remisit,*
> *Atque illum in praeceps prono rapit alveus amni.*
> —Virg., *Georg.* i. 201.

It is with much satisfaction that I hear this great city inquiring day by day after these my papers, and receiving my morning lectures with a becoming seriousness and attention. My publisher tells me that there are already three thousand of them distributed every day, so that if I allow twenty readers to every paper, which I look upon as a modest computation, I may reckon about threescore thousand disciples in London and Westminster, who, I hope, will take care to distinguish themselves from the thoughtless herd of their ignorant and unattentive brethren. Since I have raised to myself so great an audience, I shall spare no pains to make their instruction agreeable, and their diversion useful, for which reasons

I shall endeavour to enliven morality with wit, and to temper wit with morality, that my readers may, if possible, both ways find their account in the speculation of the day. And to the end that their virtue and discretion may not be short, transient, intermitting starts of thought, I have resolved to refresh their memories from day to day, till I have recovered them out of that desperate state of vice and folly into which the age is fallen. The mind that lies fallow but a single day sprouts up in follies that are only to be killed by a constant and assiduous culture. It was said of Socrates that he brought philosophy down from heaven to inhabit among men; and I shall be ambitious to have it said of me that I have brought philosophy out of closets and libraries, schools and colleges, to dwell in clubs and assemblies, at tea-tables and in coffee-houses.

I would therefore in a very particular manner recommend these my speculations to all well-regulated families that set apart an hour in every morning for tea and bread and butter, and would earnestly advise them for their good to order this paper to be punctually served up, and to be looked upon as a part of the tea equipage. . . .

In the next place, I would recommend this paper to the daily perusal of those gentlemen whom I cannot but consider as my good brothers and allies; I mean the fraternity of spectators who live in the world without having anything to do in it, and either by the affluence of their fortunes or laziness of their dispositions, have no other business with the rest of mankind but to look upon them. . . .

There is another set of men that I must likewise lay a claim to, whom I have lately called the blanks of society, as being altogether unfurnished with ideas till the business and conversation of the day has supplied them. . . .

But there are none to whom this paper will be more useful than to the female world. I have often thought there has not been sufficient pains taken in finding out proper employments and diversions for the fair ones. Their amusements seem contrived for them rather as they are women than as they are reasonable creatures, and are more adapted to the sex than to the species. The toilet is their great scene of business, and the right adjusting of their hair the principal employment of their lives. The sorting of a suit of ribbons is reckoned a very good morning's work; and if they make an excursion to a mercer's or a toy-shop, so great a fatigue makes them unfit for anything else all the day after. Their more serious occupations are sewing and embroidery, and their greatest drudgery the preparation of jellies and sweetmeats. This, I say, is the state of ordinary women; though I know there are multitudes of those of a more elevated life and conversation, that move in an exalted sphere of knowledge and virtue, that join all the beauties of the mind to the ornaments of dress, and inspire a kind of awe and respect, as well as love, into their male beholders. I hope to increase the number of these by publishing this daily paper, which I shall always endeavour to make an innocent if not an improving entertainment, and by that means at least divert the minds of my female readers from greater trifles. At the same time, as I would fain give some finishing touches to those which are already the most beautiful pieces in human nature, I shall endeavour to point out all those imperfections that are the blemishes, as well as those virtues which are the embellishments of the sex. In the meanwhile I hope these my gentle readers, who have so much time on their hands, will not grudge throwing away a quarter of an hour in a day on this paper, since they may do it without any hindrance to business. . . .

No. 23. *Tuesday, March 27, 1711*

> *Saevit atrox Volscens, nec teli conspicit usquam*
> *Auctorem, nec quo se ardens immittere possit.*
> —Virg., *Aen.* ix. 420.

There is nothing that more betrays a base ungenerous spirit, than the giving of secret stabs to a man's reputation. Lampoons and satires, that are written with wit and spirit, are like poisoned darts, which not only inflict a wound, but make it incurable. For this reason, I am very much troubled when I see the talents of humour and ridicule in the possession of an ill-natured man. There cannot be a greater gratification to a barbarous and inhuman wit, than to stir up sorrow in the heart of a private person, to raise uneasiness among near relations, and to expose whole families to derision, at the same time that he remains unseen and undiscovered. If, besides the accomplishments of being witty and ill-natured, a man is vicious into the bargain, he is one of the most mischievous creatures that can enter into a civil society. His satire will then chiefly fall upon those who ought to be the most exempt from it. Virtue, merit, and everything that is praiseworthy, will be made the subject of ridicule and buffoonery. It is impossible to enumerate the evils which arise from these arrows that fly in the dark, and I know no other excuse that is or can be made for them, than that the wounds they give are only imaginary, and produce nothing more than a secret shame or sorrow in the mind of the suffering person. It must indeed be confessed that a lampoon or a satire do not carry in them robbery or murder; but at the same time, how many are there that would not rather lose a considerable sum of money, or even life itself, than be set up as a mark of infamy and derision? And in this case a man should consider, that an injury is not to be measured by the notions of him that gives, but of him that receives it.

Those who can put the best countenance upon the outrages of this nature which are offered them, are not without their secret anguish. I have often observed a passage in Socrates's behaviour at his death, in a light wherein none of the critics have considered it. That excellent man, entertaining his friends, a little before he drank the bowl of poison, with a discourse on the immortality of the soul, at his entering upon it says, that he does not believe any the most comic genius can censure him for talking upon such a subject at such a time. This passage, I think, evidently glances upon Aristophanes, who wrote a comedy on purpose to ridicule the discourses of that divine philosopher. It has been observed by many writers, that Socrates was so little moved at this piece of buffoonery, that he was several times present at its being acted upon the stage, and never expressed the least resentment of it. But with submission, I think the remark I have here made shows us that this unworthy treatment made an impression upon his mind, though he had been too wise to discover it. . . .

. . . For my own part, I would never trust a man that I thought was capable of giving these secret wounds; and cannot but think that he would hurt the person, whose reputation he thus assaults, in his body or in his fortune, could he do it with the same security. There is indeed something very barbarous and inhuman in the ordinary scribblers of lampoons. An innocent young lady shall be exposed, for an unhappy feature; a father of a family turned to ridicule, for some domestic calamity; a wife be made uneasy all her life, for a misinterpreted word or action. Nay, a good, a temperate, and a just man shall be put out of countenance by the representation of those qualities that should do him honour. So pernicious a thing is wit, when it is not tempered with virtue and humanity.

I have indeed heard of heedless inconsiderate writers, that, without any malice, have sacrificed the reputation of their friends and acquaintance to a certain levity of temper and a silly ambition of distinguishing themselves by a spirit of raillery and satire: as if it were not infinitely more honourable to be a good-natured man than a wit. Where there is this little petulant humour in an author, he is often very mischievous without designing to be so. For which reason I always lay it down as a rule, that an indiscreet man is more hurtful than an ill-natured one; for as the former will only attack his enemies, and those he wishes ill to, the other injures indifferently both friends and foes. I cannot forbear on this occasion transscribing a fable out of Sir Roger l'Estrange, which accidentally lies before me. "A company of waggish boys were watching of frogs at the side of a pond, and still as any of them put up their heads they'd be pelting them down again with stones. 'Children,' says one of the frogs, 'you never consider that though this may be play to you, 'tis death to us.' ". . .

No. 69. Saturday, May 19, 1711

> *Hic segetes, illic veniunt felicius uvae:*
> *Arborei faetus alibi, atque injussa virescunt*
> *Gramina. Nonne vides, croceos ut Tmolus odores,*
> *India mittit ebur, molles sua thura Sabaei?*
> *At Chalybes nudi ferrum, virosaque Pontus.*
> *Castorea, Eliadum palmas Epirus equarum?*
> *Continuo has leges aeternaque faedera certis*
> *Imposuit natura locis. . . .*
>
> —Vir., *Georg.* i. 54.

There is no place in the town which I so much love to frequent as the Royal Exchange. It gives me a secret satisfaction, and, in some measure, gratifies my vanity, as I am an Englishman, to see so rich an assembly of countrymen and foreigners consulting together upon the private business of mankind, and making this metropolis a kind of emporium for the whole earth. I must confess I look upon High 'Change to be a great council, in which all considerable nations have their representatives. Factors in the trading world are what ambassadors are in the politic world; they negotiate affairs, conclude treaties, and maintain a good correspondence between those wealthy societies of men that are divided from one another by seas and oceans, or live on the different extremities of a continent. I have often been pleased to hear disputes adjusted between an inhabitant of Japan and an alderman of London, or to see a subject of the Great Mogul entering into a league with one of the Czar of Muscovy. I am infinitely delighted in mixing with these several ministers of commerce, as they are distinguished by their different walks and different languages: sometimes I am jostled among a body of Armenians; sometimes I am lost in a crowd of Jews; and sometimes make one in a group of Dutchmen. I am a Dane, Swede, or Frenchman at different times, or rather fancy myself like the old philosopher,* who, upon being asked what countryman he was, replied that he was a citizen of the world.

Though I very frequently visit this busy multitude of people, I am known to nobody there but my friend Sir Andrew, who often smiles upon me as he sees me bustling in the crowd, but at the same time connives at my presence without taking any further notice of me. There is indeed a merchant of Egypt who just knows me by sight, having formerly remitted me some money to Grand Cairo; but as I am not versed in the modern Coptic, our conferences go no further than a bow and a grimace.

This grand scene of business gives me an infinite variety of solid and substantial entertainments. As I am a great lover of mankind, my heart naturally overflows with pleasure at the sight of a prosperous and happy multitude, insomuch that at many public solemnities I cannot forbear expressing my joy with tears that have stolen down my cheeks. For this reason I am wonderfully delighted to see such a body of men thriving in their own private fortunes, and at the same time promoting the public stock; or in other words, raising estates for their own families, by bringing into their country whatever is wanting, and carrying out of it whatever is superfluous.

Nature seems to have taken a particular care to disseminate her blessings among the different regions of the world, with an eye to this mutual intercourse and traffic among mankind, that the natives of the several parts of the globe might have a kind of dependence upon one another, and be united together by their common interest. Almost every degree produces something peculiar to it. The food often grows in one country, and the sauce in another. The fruits of Portugal are corrected by the products of Barbados; the infusion of a China plant sweetened with the pith of an Indian cane; the Philippic Islands give a flavour to our European bowls. The single dress of a woman of quality is often the product of a hundred climates. The muff and the fan come together from the different ends of the earth. The scarf is sent from the torrid zone, and the tippet from beneath the pole. The brocade petticoat rises out of the mines of Peru, and the diamond necklace out of the bowels of Indostan. . . .

For these reasons there are not more useful members in a com-

* Diogenes.

monwealth than merchants. They knit mankind together in a mutual intercourse of good offices, distribute the gifts of nature, find work for the poor, add wealth to the rich, and magnificence to the great. Our English merchant converts the tin of his own country into gold, and exchanges his wool for rubies. The Mahomedans are clothed in our British manufacture, and the inhabitants of the frozen zone warmed with the fleeces of our sheep.

FURTHER READING

Donald F. Bond, ed., *The Spectator,* 5 vols. (1965). A splendid, indeed definitive, edition.

Peter Gay, "The Spectator as Actor: Addison in Perspective," *Encounter,* Vol. XXIX, No. 6 (December 1967), 27–32. An attempt to put the moral weeklies in their cultural context.

Peter Smithers, *The Life of Joseph Addison* (1954). A full and informative biography.

IV

Changing the General Way of Thinking

In the fall of 1747, after a year of negotiating with someone else, a consortium of Parisian publishers asked Denis Diderot, a young man of letters, and his friend, the mathematician Jean le Rond d'Alembert, to edit an encyclopedia for them. On the face of it, this was an innocuous commercial venture; in the hands of these two energetic philosophes to whom the publishers entrusted the task of establishing a table of contents, finding collaborators, and writing many of the articles themselves, it became a critical moment in the history of the Enlightenment. Contemporaries thought the Encyclopédie, *which began to appear in 1751, a portentous event; historians have agreed with them. When Diderot's* Prospectus *appeared in the late fall of 1750, it announced an extraordinarily ambitious plan of embracing and preserving all knowledge. This theme was echoed and underscored in the long and brilliant* Preliminary Discourse *that d'Alembert prefixed to the first volume of the* Encyclopédie *in 1751. And like their contemporaries and their historians, the editors too knew they were about to launch something of vital interest to their civilization. "I can assure you," wrote d'Alembert to a friend in December 1752 about his* Preliminary Discourse, *"that while writing this work, I had posterity before my eyes at every line."** Diderot, who carried the main burden of publishing this vast engine of progress, put it in a memorable phrase in his article "Encyclopedia" when he told his readers that he considered the task of an encyclopedia to be "to change the general way of thinking."*

As we shall see, the road of the multivolume Encyclopédie *proved a troubled one,† but there can be little question that it contributed to changing the general way of thinking—which is a lapidary and immensely useful way of describing the self-imposed task of the philosophes. The point was not simply to pillory this abuse or to*

* D'Alembert to Madame du Deffand, Dec. 22, 1752, quoted by Richard N. Schwab in his introduction to d'Alembert, *Preliminary Discourse to the Encyclopedia of Diderot* (1963), ix.

† See below, pages 287ff., 293ff.

ridicule that superstition, but to assault the Christian scheme of things—its philosophical presuppositions, its religious worship, its science, its view of community, its morals—as a whole. To begin with, as I have said before, this meant an insistence on the right to criticize everything without reserve. "All things must be examined, debated, investigated without exception and without regard for anyone's feelings," Diderot said, in his emphatic way, in his article "Encyclopedia"; and he added, "We must ride roughshod over all these ancient puerilities, overturn the barriers that reason never erected, give back to the arts and sciences the liberty that is so precious to them." It was only after this that rational and free men could construct a new, more acceptable philosophy and society.

The selections that follow give some idea of the spectrum of subjects across which the men of the Enlightenment ranged, and some of the devices they used to change the general way of thinking. They illustrate, if in fragmentary fashion, that the Enlightenment was not content with tinkering; everything had to be examined, everything improved. That is why that very embodiment of comprehensiveness, an encyclopedia, is an apt symbol for the Enlightenment.

FURTHER READING

Pierre Grosclaude, *Un Audacieux Message: L'Encyclopédie* (1951). A comprehensive treatment of the work designed to "change the general way of thinking."

Norman Hampson, *A Cultural History of the Enlightenment* (1969). Sound, well-written, popular survey of the leading ideas of the age.

Frank E. Manuel, *The Eighteenth Century Confronts the Gods* (1959). Interesting analysis of the way in which eighteenth-century scholars treated the origins of religion.

Daniel Mornet, *Les Origines intellectuelles de la Révolution française* (1933). Though somewhat dated in its interpretations and manner of asking questions, still a most useful compendium of information of what advanced French circles were reading in this changing time.

24 ❃ DIDEROT

"Encyclopedia"

[From Denis Diderot, *The Encyclopedia, Selections,* edited and translated by Stephen Gendzier (1967), 92–95.*]

Denis Diderot is one of the most difficult among the philosophes to capture: versatile, volatile, erotic, experimental, profoundly original, he belongs to no single category, and puzzled everyone who knew him. He puzzled even himself. He was an inventive writer of short stories, dialogues and novels, a pioneering critic of the arts and a close student of literature, an ambitious if mediocre playwright and a brilliant observer of acting, a diligent and patient editor and a bold speculator in what we might call the metaphysics of biology. Born in 1713 at Langres, the son of a provincial craftsman, he drifted to Paris as a young man, made a precarious living as a translator from the English, met other philosophes; then, in 1747, he became editor of the Encyclopédie. *By that time he already had something of a reputation for originality and daring; in 1749, in fact, he was imprisoned in the fortress of Vincennes outside Paris for his impious* Pensées philosophiques, *and was freed only after the intervention of his publishers.*

Life outside prison was more exciting than inside:† the appearance of the first volume of the Encyclopédie *in 1751 brought attacks from the Jesuits, and after the publication of the second volume, in the following year, the work was officially suppressed for presumably containing subversive ideas. Friends in the highest circles, including Madame de Pompadour, the king's mistress, smoothed things over, and in 1753 the third volume was free to appear. Its several thousand subscribers, and its censors and critics, found the* Encyclopédie

---

* Reprinted by permission of Harper & Row.
† For Diderot's later life, see below, pages 391–392, 464–465.

*hard to judge. It contained numerous articles of irreproachable
probity; the pieces on the arts and crafts, and the articles of general
information on history, philosophy, and geography, seemed both
informative and innocent. But the enterprise contained overtones—
or, perhaps better, undertones—suggesting to pious and alert
readers that the* Encyclopédie *was an agent of disbelief; it seemed
eager to see the world through secular eyes.*

*Yet, between 1754 and 1756, amid increasing suspicions and
continuing sniping, Volumes Four to Six appeared. Diderot's article
"Encyclopedia"—Diderot wrote much of the work himself—appeared in the fifth volume, in 1755. It sums up the faith of the
Encyclopedists in cooperation among learned men, in freedom of
thought and expression, and in the possibility of progress through
knowledge.*

ENCYCLOPEDIA, f. n. (*Philosophy*). This word means the
interrelation of all knowledge; it is made up of the Greek prefix *en,*
in, and the nouns *kyklos,* circle, and *paideia,* instruction, science,
knowledge. In truth, the aim of an *encyclopedia* is to collect all the
knowledge scattered over the face of the earth, to present its general
outlines and structure to the men with whom we live, and to transmit this to those who will come after us, so that the work of past
centuries may be useful to the following centuries, that our children, by becoming more educated, may at the same time become
more virtuous and happier, and that we may not die without
having deserved well of the human race. . . .

We have seen that our *Encyclopedia* could only have been the
endeavor of a philosophical century; that this age has dawned, and
that fame, while raising to immortality the names of those who will
perfect man's knowledge in the future, will perhaps not disdain to
remember our own names. We have been heartened by the ever so
consoling and agreeable idea that people may speak to one another
about us, too, when we shall no longer be alive; we have been
encouraged by hearing from the mouths of a few of our contemporaries a certain voluptuous murmur that suggests what may be said
of us by those happy and educated men in whose interests we have
sacrificed ourselves, whom we esteem and whom we love, even
though they have not yet been born. We have felt within ourselves

the development of those seeds of emulation which have moved us to renounce the better part of ourselves to accomplish our task, and which have ravished away into the void the few moments of our existence of which we are genuinely proud. Indeed, man reveals himself to his contemporaries and is seen by them for what he is: a peculiar mixture of sublime attributes and shameful weaknesses. But our weaknesses follow our mortal remains into the tomb and disappear with them; the same earth covers them both, and there remains only the total result of our attributes immortalized in the monuments we raise to ourselves or in the memorials that we owe to public respect and gratitude—honors which a proper awareness of our own deserts enables us to enjoy in anticipation, an enjoyment that is as pure, as great, and as real as any other pleasure and in which there is nothing imaginary except, perhaps, the titles on which we base our pretensions. Our own claims are deposited in the pages of this work, and posterity will judge them.

I have said that it could only belong to a philosophical age to attempt an *encyclopedia;* and I have said this because such a work constantly demands more intellectual daring than is commonly found in ages of pusillanimous taste. All things must be examined, debated, investigated without exception and without regard for anyone's feelings. . . . We must ride roughshod over all these ancient puerilities, overturn the barriers that reason never erected, give back to the arts and sciences the liberty that is so precious to them. . . . We have for quite some time needed a reasoning age when men would no longer seek the rules in classical authors but in nature, when men would be conscious of what is false and true about so many arbitrary treatises on aesthetics: and I take the term *treatise on aesthetics* in its most general meaning, that of a system of given rules to which it is claimed that one must conform in any genre whatsoever in order to succeed. . . .

It would be desirable for the government to authorize people to go into the factories and shops, to see the craftsmen at their work, to question them, to draw the tools, the machines, and even the premises.

There are special circumstances when craftsmen are so secretive about their techniques that the shortest way of learning about them would be to apprentice oneself to a master or to have some trustworthy person do this. There would be few secrets that one would fail to bring to light by this method, and all these secrets would have to be divulged without any exception.

I know that this feeling is not shared by everyone. These are narrow minds, deformed souls, who are indifferent to the fate of the human race and who are so enclosed in their little group that they see nothing beyond its special interest. These men insist on being called good citizens, and I consent to this, provided that they permit me to call them *bad men.* To listen to them talk, one would say that a successful *encyclopedia,* that a general history of the mechanical arts, should only take the form of an enormous manuscript that would be carefully locked up in the king's library, inaccessible to all other eyes but his, an official document of the state, not meant to be consulted by the people. What is the good of divulging the knowledge a nation possesses, its private transactions, its inventions, its industrial processes, its resources, its trade secrets, its enlightenment, its arts, and all its wisdom? Are not these the things to which it owes a part of its superiority over the rival nations that surround it? This is what they say; and this is what they might add: would it not be desirable if, instead of enlightening the foreigner, we could spread darkness over him or even plunge all the rest of the world into barbarism so that we could dominate more securely over everyone? These people do not realize that they occupy only a single point on our globe and that they will endure only a moment in its existence. To this point and to this moment they would sacrifice the happiness of future ages and that of the entire human race.

They know as well as anyone that the average duration of empires is not more than two thousand years and that in less time, perhaps, the name *Frenchman,* a name that will endure forever in history, will be sought after in vain over the surface of the earth. These considerations do not broaden their point of view; for it seems that the word *humanity* is for them a word without meaning. All the same, they should be consistent! For they also fulminate against the impenetrability of the Egyptian sanctuaries; they deplore the loss of the knowledge of the ancients; they accuse the writers of the past for having been silent or negligent in writing so badly on an infinite number of important subjects; and these illogical critics do not see that they demand of the writers of earlier ages something they call a crime when it is committed by a contemporary, that they are blaming others for having done what they think it honorable to do.

These *good citizens* are the most dangerous enemies that we have had. In general we have tried to profit from just criticism without defending ourselves, while we have simply ignored all unfounded attacks. Is it not a rather pleasant prospect for those who have persisted stubbornly in blackening paper with their censure of us

that if ten years from now the *Encyclopedia* has retained the reputation it enjoys today, no one will read or even remember their
opinions; and if by chance our work is forgotten, their abusive
remarks will fall into total oblivion!

I have heard it said that M. de Fontenelle's rooms were not large
enough to hold all the works that had been published against him.
Who knows the title of a single one of them? Montesquieu's *Spirit
of Laws* and Buffon's *Natural History* have only just appeared, and
the harsh criticism against them has been entirely forgotten. We
have already remarked that among those who have set themselves
up as censors of the *Encyclopedia* there is hardly a single one who
had enough talent to enrich it by even one good article. I do not
think I would be exaggerating if I should add that it is a work the
greater part of which is about subjects that these people have yet to
study. It has been composed with a philosophical spirit, and in this
respect most of those who pass adverse judgment on us fall far short
of the level of their own century. I call their works in evidence. It is
for this reason that they will not endure and that we venture to say
that our *Encyclopedia* will be more widely read and more highly
appreciated in a few years' time than it is today. It would not be
difficult to cite other authors who have had, and will have, a similar
fate. Some (as we have already said) were once praised to the skies
because they wrote for the multitude, followed the prevailing ideas,
and accommodated their standards to those of the average reader,
but they have lost their reputations in proportion as the human
mind has made progress, and they have finally been forgotten
altogether. Others, by contrast, too daring for the times in which
their works appeared, have been little read, hardly understood, not
appreciated, and have long remained in obscurity, until the day
when the age they had outstripped had passed away and another
century, to which they really belonged in spirit, overtook them at
last and finally gave them the justice their merits deserved.

FURTHER READING

Douglas H. Gordon and Norman L. Torrey, *The Censoring of Diderot's Encyclopédie and the Re-established Text* (1947). A brief, informative monograph, showing the extent of official interference and publisher's self-censorship.

Jacques Proust, *Diderot et l'Encyclopédie* (1962). An excellent analysis of the man and the work he superintended.

Jean Thomas, *L'Humanisme de Diderot*, 2nd edn. (1938). Amid a wide literature, a sensible appraisal well worth reading.

Arthur M. Wilson, *Diderot*, 2 vols. in one (1972). The standard biography, severely chronological and wholly dependable.

25 ❧ D'ALEMBERT

"Geneva"

[From Jean le Rond d'Alembert, "Geneva," in
Encyclopedia: Selections, by Diderot,
d'Alembert and A Society of Men of Letters,
translated by Nelly S. Hoyt and Thomas
Cassirer, 124–39.*]

*When Jean le Rond d'Alembert wrote the article on Geneva for the
seventh volume of the* Encyclopédie, *its future seemed uncertain. In
August 1756, d'Alembert had visited Voltaire at his recently acquired Genevan estate, Les Délices, where he met local notables,
including prominent pastors, and listened quietly as they talked
freely. When the upshot of his listening appeared in 1757, the atmosphere surrounding the* Encyclopédie, *already laden with recrimi-
nations, had thickened. In that year, a madman named Damiens
had tried to kill King Louis XV, and the government responded by
passing ferocious repressive legislation against the voicing of views
that might bring about a repetition of the incident. There was little
intention of enforcing the provisions of the law, but advanced
thinkers grew more cautious, and talked more circumspectly, than
before.*

*That is, all but d'Alembert. A brilliant and sociable scientist, he
was noted neither for his tact nor for his discretion. Born in 1717 as
an illegitimate child and abandoned on the steps of the Church of
Jean-le-Rond in Paris—hence his name—he had made an early
reputation for himself with his remarkable* Treatise on Dynamics
*(1743). He was among that small band of French physicists and
mathematicians who pushed Newtonian mechanics to new levels of*

comprehensiveness and clarity. But d'Alembert also made his mark in society, and his freethinking views commended him to the other philosophes in Paris. For some years he diligently collaborated with his friend Diderot; but then, in 1758, the storm broke, partly because of his article, partly because Helvétius had published a scandalous hedonist treatise, De l'Esprit, *which, though Helvétius was not an Encyclopedist, was widely blamed on the "encyclopedist spirit." Prudent for once, d'Alembert withdrew from the* Encyclo-pédie, *to let Diderot carry on alone.*

For the modern reader, "Geneva" seems scarcely offensive. But to contemporaries, d'Alembert's approval of Genevan pastors who are practically deists was outrageous. If true, it was an indiscreet way of praising one's social acquaintances; if untrue, it was a slander on men of God; in either case, it was an invitation to desert the True Faith. We should note one other point: in the course of the article, d'Alembert criticizes the Genevans for prohibiting theaters in their republic. This point was taken up by Jean-Jacques Rousseau, "citizen of Geneva," in his Lettre à M. d'Alembert sur les spectacles, *in which Rousseau vehemently defended the policy of his native city.*

This city is situated on two hills, at the foot of the lake which today is named after the city but formerly was called Lake Leman. It is very pleasantly situated. On one side one sees the lake, on the other the Rhone, and all around the smiling countryside. Along the lake there are hills dotted with country houses, while a few miles away rise the Alpine peaks, which are always covered with ice and look as if they were made of silver when on a fine day the sun shines on them. As a rich and busy trading center, Geneva owes its prominence to the harbor, with its jetties, its boats, its markets, etc., as well as to its location between France, Italy, and Germany. The city has several fine buildings and attractive promenades. The streets are lighted at night, and on the banks of the Rhone a very simple pumping machine has been installed that provides water even for the highest quarters, located a hundred feet above. The lake is approximately eighteen leagues long and four to five across at its widest point. It is a kind of little sea with storms and other remarkable phenomena. . . .

Between the two doors of Geneva's city hall one can still see a

Latin inscription commemorating the abolition of the Catholic religion. In it the pope is called "Antichrist." This name, which the Genevans' fanatic love of liberty and innovation gave him in a century that was still half barbarous, today seems scarcely worthy of a city so imbued with the philosophic spirit. We venture to suggest that the Genevans replace this insulting and vulgar monument with an inscription that is truer, nobler, and simpler. For Catholics the pope is the head of the true Church, for reasonable and moderate Protestants he is a sovereign whom they respect as a prince without obeying him, but in a century such as ours there is no one for whom he is still the Antichrist. . . .

The Genevans, wishing to bring fame to their city, called in Calvin. He enjoyed a great and well-deserved reputation because he was a man of letters of the first rank, who wrote Latin as well as a dead language can be written, and French with a purity of style that was exceptional for his time. This purity, which our grammarians still admire today, renders his writings far superior to almost all others written in his century, just as today the works of the Messieurs of Port-Royal still seem far superior to the barbarous rantings of their adversaries and contemporaries. Calvin was both an excellent jurist and as enlightened a theologian as a heretic can be, and together with the magistrates he drew up a compendium of civil and ecclesiastical laws that was approved in 1543 by the people and has become the basic code of the republic. The excess of ecclesiastical property, which before the Reformation fed the luxury of the bishops and their subordinates, was now used to found a hospital, a college, and an academy; but the wars in which Geneva had to engage for almost sixty years prevented the arts and commerce from flourishing as much as the sciences. In 1602 the failure of the attempt by the duke of Savoy to scale the walls brought peace to the republic. The Genevans repulsed their enemies who had attacked by surprise, and they hanged thirteen of the leading enemy generals in order to give the duke of Savoy a distaste for such undertakings. They thought they were justified in treating men who attacked their city without a declaration of war as if they were highwaymen. The strange new policy of waging war without having declared it was not yet known in Europe; and even if it had then been followed by the great states, it would still be true that it is too much against the interest of small states ever to gain favor among them. . . .

It is very remarkable that a city which scarcely counts 24,000 souls and has a fragmented territory containing fewer than thirty villages is nevertheless a sovereign state and one of the most prosperous cities of Europe. Geneva is rich because of its liberty and its commerce and often sees everything around it in flames without being in any way affected. The events that disturb Europe are only a spectacle for this city from which it profits without taking any part. Because it is linked to France by treaties and commerce and to England by commerce and religion, it maintains an impartial opinion on the rights and wrongs of the wars which those two powerful nations wage against each other, and at the same time it is too prudent to take any part in these wars. Geneva judges all the sovereigns of Europe without flattery, insult, or fear.

The city is well fortified, especially on the side facing the prince it fears the most, the king of Sardinia. The side bordering France has been left almost completely open and undefended. Military service, however, is performed as in a fortress city. The arsenals and military storehouses are well stocked and every citizen is a soldier, as in Switzerland or in ancient Rome. Genevans are permitted to serve in foreign armies, but the state does not supply any power with bodies of troops and no recruiting is allowed on its territory.

While the city is wealthy, the state is poor because of the people's aversion to all new taxes, even the least burdensome. The revenue of the state comes to less than five hundred thousand livres in French money, but the admirable economy with which this is administered makes it quite sufficient for all the needs of the city and even produces reserves for emergencies.

There are four classes of inhabitants in Geneva. The *citizens* [are those] who are the sons of bourgeois and were born in the city; they alone can become magistrates. The *bourgeois* [are those] who are the sons of bourgeois or of citizens but were born in a foreign country, or who are foreigners to whom the magistracy has granted the rights of a bourgeois, which it has the power to do; these can be members of the General Council and even of the Grand Conseil, called the "Council of the Two Hundred." The *residents* are foreigners who have the permission of the magistrate to reside in the city but do not exercise any function. Lastly, the *natives* are the children of residents; they have some privileges which their fathers did not possess, but they are excluded from the government.

The government is headed by four *syndics,* who can hold this position for only one year and must wait at least four years before holding it again. They are aided by the Petit Conseil, composed of twenty counselors, a treasurer, and two secretaries of state, and by another body called the Corps de la Justice. These two bodies deal with the daily business that demands immediate action, whether criminal or civil.

The Grand Conseil is composed of two hundred and fifty citizens or bourgeois. It judges major civil suits, it grants pardons, coins money, elects the members of the Petit Conseil and decides what matters should be brought before the General Council. This General Council comprises all citizens and bourgeois, with the exception of those under twenty-five years of age, and of those who are bankrupt or have incurred censure of some sort. This assembly holds the legislative power; it has the right of decision over war and peace, the right to form alliances, levy taxes, and elect the principal magistrates. The election is conducted with orderly decorum in the cathedral, even though there are about 1,500 electors.

This fact shows us that the government of Geneva has all the advantages and none of the drawbacks of democracy: everything is under the direction of the syndics, everything is originally discussed in the Petit Conseil, which also has the ultimate executive responsibility. . . .

Criminal justice is dispensed scrupulously rather than harshly. Torture, which has already been abolished in several states and should be abolished everywhere because it is useless cruelty, is forbidden in Geneva. It is administered only to criminals who are already condemned to death, in order to discover their accomplices, if that is necessary. The accused has the right to ask for a transcript of the proceedings and to be assisted by his relatives and a lawyer who defends his case before the judges in open court. Criminal sentences are rendered by the syndics in the public square with great ceremony. . . .

No theater is permitted in Geneva. There is no objection to plays in themselves, but it is feared that troupes of actors would spread the taste for adornment, dissipation, and loose morals among the youth. Would not, however, a series of laws, strictly applied, on the conduct of the actors counteract this undesirable effect? In this way Geneva would possess both theater and good morals and would enjoy the advantages of both. Theatrical performances would educate the taste of the citizens and endow them with a delicacy of tact and a subtlety of feeling which it is very difficult to acquire otherwise. Literature would profit, while morals would not decline, and Geneva would add to the wisdom of Sparta the civility of Athens. There is another consideration, worthy of a republic that is so wise and enlightened, which might induce it to allow a theater. One of the principal causes of the loose morals for which we reproach actors is undoubtedly the barbarous prejudice against the acting profession. These men who are so indispensable to the progress and the vitality of the arts have been forced to live in a state of degradation. They seek in pleasures compensations for the esteem their estate cannot bring them. An actor whose morals are good should be doubly respected, but he is given scarcely any credit for his morality. The tax farmer who is an affront to the penury of the nation from which he draws his wealth, the courtier who fawns and does not pay his debts, those are the types of men we honor most highly. It would be better if actors were not only tolerated in Geneva but were first restrained by wise regulations, then protected, and even granted respect as soon as they were worthy of it. In short, if they were treated exactly like other citizens, the city would soon enjoy the advantage of having a company of honorable actors, something that we believe to be so rare and yet is rare only by our own fault. I might add that such a company would soon be the best in Europe. Many people would hasten to Geneva who have great inclination and talent for the theater but who at present fear they would be dishonored by acting. There they would cultivate a talent that is so pleasing and so unusual, not only without shame but even in an atmosphere of respect. While many Frenchmen now find a stay in Geneva depressing because they are deprived of seeing plays, the city, which is already the abode of philosophy and liberty, would then also be the abode of respectable pleasure. Foreigners would no longer be surprised that in a city where regular performances of decent plays are forbidden, vulgar and stupid farces, as offensive to good taste as to good morals, may be presented. This is not all. Little by little the example of the Genevan actors, their steady conduct, and the esteem it would bring them would serve as a model to the actors of other nations and as a lesson to those who until now have treated them so inconsistently and even harshly. We would no longer see them being on the one hand pensioners of the government and on the other the objects of anathema. Our priests would lose the habit of excommunicating them and our bourgeois of viewing them with disdain. Then a small republic could claim the glory of having reformed Europe in this respect, and this is perhaps more important than one thinks. . . .

After England, Geneva was the first to practice smallpox inoculation, which is so difficult to introduce in France and which nevertheless will be introduced, although a number of our doctors still fight it, as their predecessors fought the circulation of the blood, emetic, and so many other incontrovertible truths and useful practices.

All the sciences and almost all the arts have been so well culti-vated in Geneva that one would be surprised to see the list of scholars and artists of all kinds produced by the city during the last two centuries. Sometimes it has even had the good fortune to have famous foreigners choose to live in Geneva because of its pleasant location and the freedom enjoyed by its inhabitants. M. de Voltaire, who took up residence in Geneva three years ago, is now accorded the same tokens of esteem and respect by these republicans which he formerly received from several monarchs. . . .

We must still speak of religion in Geneva. This is the section of the article that is perhaps of greatest interest to philosophers. We are now going to take up this subject, but we beg our readers to remember that we are writing only as historians, not as partisans. Our theological articles are intended to serve as antidote to the present article, and, besides, to recount is not to approve. We refer our readers to the words "Eucharist," "Hell," "Faith," "Chris-tianity," etc., to caution them beforehand against what we are going to say.

The ecclesiastical constitution of Geneva is purely presbyterian. There are no bishops, not to speak of canons. Not that there is objection to the institution of episcopacy, but the Genevans do not grant it any divine right and are of the opinion that a small repub-lic is better served by ministers who are not as rich and influential as the bishops.

The ministers are either pastors, like our parish priests, or postulants, like those of our priests who do not have a living. The minister's income does not exceed 1,200 livres, and there are no perquisites. The state provides the income, since the church owns nothing. No one is accepted into the ministry before the age of twenty-four and only after examinations that are very strict in respect to knowledge and to morality. One would wish that most of our Catholic churches would follow this example. . . .

The clergy of Geneva have exemplary morals. The ministers live in great concord. One does not see them, as in other countries, quarrel bitterly among themselves about unintelligible subjects, persecute each other, and accuse each other in unseemly fashion before the magistrates. Yet they are far from all thinking alike on the articles that elsewhere are considered the most essential to reli-gion. Several no longer believe in the divinity of Jesus Christ, which

Calvin, their leader, defended with such zeal that he had Servetus burned at the stake. When anyone speaks to them about this execution, which mars the charity and moderation of their patriarch, they do not attempt to justify him. They admit that Calvin's action was very reprehensible, and they confine themselves (if it is a Catholic who speaks with them) to contrasting the execution of Servetus with that dreadful Saint Bartholomew's Day which every good Frenchman would wish to erase from our history with his own blood. They also compare it to the execution of John Hus, which even the Catholics, they remind their interlocutor, no longer attempt to justify; it was an action that equally violated humanity and good faith and should cover the memory of the Emperor Sigismund with opprobrium for all time.

"It is no small sign of the progress of human reason," writes M. de Voltaire, "that it was possible to publish in Geneva, with public approval, the statement [in the *Essai sur l'histoire universelle* by the same author] that Calvin had a cruel soul as well as an enlightened mind. The murder of Servetus today seems abominable." We believe that the praise which this noble freedom of thought and of writing deserves should be addressed equally to the author, to his century, and to Geneva. How many countries are there where philosophy has made just as much progress but where truth is still captive, where reason does not dare raise her voice to thunder against abuses she condemns in silence, where we find only too many pusillanimous writers, called "wise men," still respecting prejudices they could combat with complete propriety and safety!

Hell, one of the principal tenets of our faith, is no longer given such importance by several ministers in Geneva. According to them it would be an insult to the Divinity if we imagined that this Being full of goodness and justice were capable of punishing our offenses with eternal torments. They explain as best they can the passages in the Bible which are explicitly contrary to their opinion and assert that in the Holy Scriptures one must never take anything literally if it seems to go against humanity and reason. They believe that there is punishment in the afterlife, but that it is only temporary. Thus purgatory, once one of the principal causes of the separation of the Protestants from the Roman Catholic Church, is today the only punishment after death that many of the former will accept. Here is another item to add to the history of human contradictions.

In short, many of the ministers of Geneva have no other religion than a perfect Socinianism; they reject everything called "mystery" and imagine that the first principle of a true religion is not to propose any belief that conflicts with reason. When they are pressed on the question of the "necessity" of revelation, a dogma that is so basic to Christianity, many substitute the term "utility," which seems more agreeable to them. If they are not orthodox in this, at least they are true to their principles. See "Socinianism."

A clergy holding these opinions must needs be tolerant and is tolerant enough to be viewed with disfavor by the ministers of the other reformed churches. One might add further, without any intention of approving the religion of Geneva, that there are few countries where the theologians and the clergymen are more opposed to superstition. As a result, because intolerance and superstition serve only to increase the number of unbelievers, one hears less complaint in Geneva than elsewhere about the spread of unbelief, and this should not surprise us. Here religion consists almost entirely in the adoration of a single God, at least among all classes other than the common people. Respect for Jesus Christ and for the Scriptures is perhaps all that distinguishes the Christianity of Geneva from pure deism.

The clergymen of Geneva are not merely tolerant: they remain entirely within their province and are the first to set an example for the citizens by submitting to the laws. The Consistory, charged with watching over morals, inflicts only spiritual punishment. The great quarrel between the priesthood and the Empire, which in the age of ignorance imperiled the crown of many an emperor, and which—we know this only too well—causes troublesome disturbances in more enlightened times, is unknown in Geneva, where the clergy does nothing without the approval of the magistrates.

Worship is very simple in Geneva. The churches contain no images, no lights or ornaments. However, a portal in very good taste has just been added to the cathedral; little by little the interior of the churches will perhaps be embellished. Indeed, what objection could there be to having paintings and statues? If one wishes, the common people could be told not to worship them and to look on them only as monuments destined to recount in a striking and pleasing manner the principal events of religion. This would be to the advantage of the arts, yet would bring no profit to superstition. The reader surely realizes that we are speaking here according to the principles of the ministers of Geneva, and not those of the Catholic Church.

The divine service includes both sermons and singing. The sermons are almost entirely concerned with morality and are all the better for that. The singing is in rather bad taste, and the French verses that are sung are in even worse taste. It is to be hoped that Geneva will become reformed on these two points. An organ has just been placed in the cathedral and perhaps God will now be praised in better language and in better music. We must admit, however, that the Supreme Being is honored in Geneva with a seemliness and calm that is not noticeable in our churches.

Perhaps we will not devote articles of such length to the greatest monarchies, but in the eyes of the philosopher the Republic of the Bees is no less interesting than the history of great empires. It may be that the model of a perfect political administration can be found only in small states. If religion does not allow us to believe that the Genevans have successfully worked for their happiness in the next world, reason forces us to believe that they are perhaps as happy as one can be in this world:

> *O fortunatos nimium, sua si bona norint!*
> Oh, how very happy they are if they know their blessing!
> —Virgil, *Georgics*, II, 458

FURTHER READING

Ronald Grimsley, *Jean d'Alembert, 1717–83* (1963). The best biography in English.

Maurice Muller, *Essai sur la philosophie de Jean d'Alembert* (1926). Just that: an essay.

John N. Pappas, *Voltaire and d'Alembert* (1962). A brief consideration of their relationship.

Marta Rezler, *The Voltaire–d'Alembert Correspondence* (1962). (This is Vol. XX of *Studies on Voltaire and the Eighteenth Century*, ed. Theodore Bester-man.) A scholarly survey.

26 ❧ ROUSSEAU

Émile

[From the book *Émile: or, Education, by Jean-
Jacques Rousseau,* Translated by Barbara
Foxley (1911), 5–6, 70–73, 84–85, 131–33,
146–50, 156–59.*]

With Émile *(published in 1762), and with its intimate companions, the* Contrat social *(published the same year) and the epis-
tolary and didactic novel* La Nouvelle Héloise *(published the year
before), Rousseau moved into his constructive phase. In the early
writings he had told the civilized world what was wrong with its
civilization,† now he was ready to outline a civilization worth living
in.*

Émile *stands in the great tradition of treatises on education that
goes back to Plato. In the body of* Émile, *Rousseau self-consciously
drew on that tradition, and made himself its heir as well as its critic.
The centrality of its place in Rousseau's thought is evident almost
at first glance. Adults are children first, and (Rousseau knew this
long before Wordsworth said it) the child is father to the man.
Hence, what we do to the child we do in the long run to civilization. Thus, if civiliation is hopelessly corrupted, its education can
only serve hopelessly to corrupt its future rulers. Hence Rousseau
decided to perform a kind of thought experiment: to take the child
away from all possible formative influences—including his family—
and give him a chance to grow up in accord with nature. Locke (as
I showed before‡) had seen much of this; Rousseau took the principle of "negative education" to its logical—and sometimes illogi-*

---

* Everyman's Library edition, published by E. P. Dutton & Company, Inc., and
J. M. Dent & Sons, Ltd., and used with their permission.
† See above, pages 175–195.
‡ See above, pages 71, 89–98.

*cal—conclusion. The result was what we may justly call the most
influential educational tract ever written. Modern pedagogic principles of learning by doing, of stressing the "useful" over the
"decorative," and of inciting the child's desire to learn to form a
sincere and well-integrated being first find their full expression in
Émile.*

BOOK I

God makes all things good; man meddles with them and they
become evil. He forces one soil to yield the products of another, one
tree to bear another's fruit. He confuses and confounds time, place,
and natural conditions. He mutilates his dog, his horse, and his
slave. He destroys and defaces all things; he loves all that is deformed and monstrous; he will have nothing as nature made it, not
even man himself, who must learn his paces like a saddle-horse, and
be shaped to his master's taste like the trees in his garden.

Yet things would be worse without this education, and mankind
cannot be made by halves. Under existing conditions a man left to
himself from birth would be more of a monster than the rest.
Prejudice, authority, necessity, example, all the social conditions
into which we are plunged, would stifle nature in him and put
nothing in her place. She would be like a sapling chance sown in
the midst of the highway, bent hither and thither and soon crushed
by the passers-by.

Tender, anxious mother, I appeal to you. You can remove this
young tree from the highway and shield it from the crushing force
of social conventions. Tend and water it ere it dies. One day its
fruit will reward your care. From the outset raise a wall round your
child's soul; another may sketch the plan, you alone should carry it
into execution.

Plants are fashioned by cultivation, man by education. If a man
were born tall and strong, his size and strength would be of no good
to him till he had learned to use them; they would even harm him
by preventing others from coming to his aid; left to himself he
would die of want before he knew his needs. We lament the help-

lessness of infancy; we fail to perceive that the race would have perished had not man begun by being a child.

We are born weak, we need strength; helpless, we need aid; foolish, we need reason. All that we lack at birth, all that we need when we come to man's estate, is the gift of education.

This education comes to us from nature, from men, or from things. This inner growth of our organs and faculties is the education of nature, the use we learn to make of this growth is the education of men, what we gain by our experience of our surroundings is the education of things.

Thus we are each taught by three masters. If their teaching conflicts, the scholar is ill-educated and will never be at peace with himself; if their teaching agrees, he goes straight to his goal, he lives at peace with himself, he is well educated.

Now, of these three factors in education nature is wholly beyond our control, things are only partly in our power; the education of men is the only one controlled by us; and even here our power is largely illusory, for who can hope to direct every word and deed of all with whom the child has to do?

Viewed as an art, the success of education is almost impossible, since the essential conditions of success are beyond our control. Our efforts may bring us within sight of the goal, but fortune must favor us if we are to reach it.

What is this goal? As we have just shown, it is the goal of nature. . . .

The finest thoughts may spring from a child's brain, or rather the best words may drop from his lips, just as diamonds of great worth may fall into his hands, while neither the thoughts nor the diamonds are his own: at that age neither can be really his. The child's sayings do not mean to him what they mean to us, the ideas he attaches to them are different. His ideas, if indeed he has any ideas at all, have neither order nor connection; there is nothing sure, nothing certain, in his thoughts. Examine your so-called prodigy. Now and again you will discover in him extreme activity of mind and extraordinary clearness of thought. More often this same mind will seem slack and spiritless, as if wrapped in mist. Sometimes he goes before you, sometimes he will not stir. One moment you would call him a genius, another a fool. You would be mistaken in both; he is a child, an eaglet who soars aloft for a moment, only to drop back into the nest.

Treat him, therefore, according to his age, in spite of appearances, and beware of exhausting his strength by over-much exercise. If the young brain grows warm and begins to bubble, let it work freely, but do not heat it any further, lest it lose its goodness, and when the first gases have been given off, collect and compress the rest so that in after years they may turn to life-giving heat and real energy. If not, your time and your pains will be wasted, you will destroy your own work, and after foolishly intoxicating yourself with these heady fumes, you will have nothing left but an insipid and worthless wine.

Silly children grow into ordinary men. I know no generalization more certain than this. It is the most difficult thing in the world to distinguish between genuine stupidity and that apparent and deceitful stupidity which is the sign of a strong character. At first sight it seems strange that the two extremes should have the same outward signs; and yet it may well be so, for at an age when man has as yet no true ideas, the whole difference between the genius and the rest consists in this: the latter only take in false ideas, while the former, finding nothing but false ideas, receives no ideas at all. In this he resembles the fool; the one is fit for nothing, the other finds nothing fit for him. The only way of distinguishing between them depends upon chance, which may offer the genius some idea which he can understand, while the fool is always the same. As a child, the young Cato was taken for an idiot by his parents; he was obstinate and silent, and that was all they perceived in him; it was only in Sulla's antechamber that his uncle discovered what was in him. Had he never found his way there, he might have passed for a fool till he reached the age of reason. Had Caesar never lived, perhaps this same Cato, who discerned his fatal genius and foretold his great schemes, would have passed for a dreamer all his days. Those who judge children hastily are apt to be mistaken; they are often more childish than the child himself. I knew a middle-aged man,* whose friendship I esteemed an honor, who was reckoned a fool by his family. All at once he made his name as a philosopher, and I have no doubt posterity will give him a high place among the greatest thinkers and the profoundest metaphysicians of his day.

Hold childhood in reverence, and do not be in any hurry to judge it for good or ill. Leave exceptional cases to show themselves, let their qualities be tested and confirmed, before special methods are adopted. Give nature time to work before you take over her business, lest you interfere with her dealings. You assert that you

* The Abbé de Condillac.—B.F.

know the value of time and are afraid to waste it. You fail to perceive that it is a greater waste of time to use it ill than to do nothing, and that a child ill-taught is further from virtue than a child who has learned nothing at all. You are afraid to see him spending his early years doing nothing. What! is it nothing to be happy, nothing to run and jump all day? He will never be so busy again all his life long. Plato, in his *Republic,* which is considered so stern, teaches the children only through festivals, games, songs, and amusements. It seems as if he had accomplished his purpose when he had taught them to be happy; and Seneca, speaking of the Roman lads in olden days, says, "They were always on their feet, they were never taught anything which kept them sitting." Were they any the worse for it in manhood? Do not be afraid, therefore, of this so-called idleness. What would you think of a man who refused to sleep lest he should waste part of his life? You would say, "He is mad; he is not enjoying his life, he is robbing himself of part of it; to avoid sleep he is hastening his death." Remember that these two cases are alike, and that childhood is the sleep of reason.

The apparent ease with which children learn is their ruin. You fail to see that this very facility proves that they are not learning. Their shining, polished brain reflects, as in a mirror, the things you show them, but nothing sinks in. The child remembers the words, and the ideas are reflected back; his hearers understand them, but to him they are meaningless.

Although memory and reason are wholly different faculties, the one does not really develop apart from the other. Before the age of reason the child receives images, not ideas; and there is this difference between them: images are merely the pictures of external objects, while ideas are notions about those objects determined by their relations. An image when it is recalled may exist by itself in the mind, but every idea implies other ideas. When we image we merely perceive, when we reason we compare. Our sensations are merely passive, our notions or ideas spring from an active principle which judges. The proof of this will be given later.

I maintain, therefore, that as children are incapable of judging, they have no true memory. They retain sounds, form, sensation, but rarely ideas, and still more rarely relations. You tell me they acquire some rudiments of geometry, and you think you prove your case; not so, it is mine you prove; you show that far from being able to reason themselves, children are unable to retain the reasoning of others; for if you follow the method of these little geometricians you will see they retain only the exact impression of the figure and the terms of the demonstration. They cannot meet the slightest new objection; if the figure is reversed they can do nothing. All their knowledge is on the sensation level, nothing has penetrated to their understanding. Their memory is little better than their other powers, for they always have to learn over again, when they are grown up, what they learned as children.

I am far from thinking, however, that children have no sort of reason.* On the contrary, I think they reason very well with regard to things that affect their actual and sensible well-being. But people are mistaken as to the extent of their information, and they attribute to them knowledge they do not possess, and make them reason about things they cannot understand. Another mistake is to try to turn their attention to matters which do not concern them in the least, such as their future interest, their happiness when they are grown up, the opinion people will have of them when they are men—terms which are absolutely meaningless when addressed to creatures who are entirely without foresight. But all the forced studies of these poor little wretches are directed toward matters utterly remote from their minds. You may judge how much attention they can give to them.

The pedagogues, who make a great display of the teaching they give their pupils, are paid to say just the opposite; yet their actions show that they think just as I do. For what do they teach? Words! words! words! Among the various sciences they boast of teaching their scholars, they take good care never to choose those which might be really useful to them, for then they would be compelled to deal with things and would fail utterly; the sciences they choose are those we seem to know when we know their technical terms— heraldry, geography, chronology, languages, etc., studies so remote

---

* I have noticed again and again that it is impossible in writing a lengthy work to use the same words always in the same sense. There is no language rich enough to supply terms and expressions sufficient for the modifications of our ideas. The method of defining every term and constantly substituting the definition for the term defined looks well, but it is impracticable. For how can we escape from our vicious circle? Definitions would be all very well if we did not use words in the making of them. In spite of this I am convinced that even in our poor language we can make our meaning clear, not by always using words in the same sense, but by taking care that every time we use a word the sense in which we use it is sufficiently indicated by the sense of the context, so that each sentence in which the word occurs acts as a sort of definition. Sometimes I say children are incapable of reasoning. Sometimes I say they reason cleverly. I must admit that my words are often contradictory, but I do not think there is any contradiction in my ideas.

from man, and even more remote from the child, that it is a wonder if he can ever make any use of any part of them.

You will be surprised to find that I reckon the study of languages among the useless lumber of education; but you must remember that I am speaking of the studies of the earliest years, and whatever you may say, I do not believe any child under twelve or fifteen ever really acquired two languages. . . .

When education is most carefully attended to, the teacher issues his orders and thinks himself master, but it is the child who is really master. He uses the tasks you set him to obtain what he wants from you, and he can always make you pay for an hour's industry by a week's complaisance. You must always be making bargains with him. These bargains, suggested in your fashion, but carried out in his, always follow the direction of his own fancies, especially when you are foolish enough to make the condition some advantage he is almost sure to obtain whether he fulfills his part of the bargain or not. The child is usually much quicker to read the master's thoughts than the master to read the child's feelings. And that is as it should be, for all the sagacity which the child would have devoted to self-preservation had he been left to himself is now devoted to the rescue of his native freedom from the chains of his tyrant; while the latter, who has no such pressing need to understand the child, sometimes finds that it pays him better to leave him in idleness or vanity.

Take the opposite course with your pupil: let him always think he is master while you are really master. There is no subjection so complete as that which preserves the forms of freedom; it is thus that the will itself is taken captive. Is not this poor child, without knowledge, strength, or wisdom, entirely at your mercy? Are you not master of his whole environment so far as it affects him? Cannot you make of him what you please? His work and play, his pleasure and pain, are they not, unknown to him, under your control? No doubt he ought only to do what he wants, but he ought to want to do nothing but what you want him to do. He should never take a step you have not foreseen, nor utter a word you could not foretell.

Then he can devote himself to the bodily exercises adapted to his age without brutalizing his mind; instead of developing his cunning to evade an unwelcome control, you will then find him entirely occupied in getting the best he can out of his environment with a view to his present welfare, and you will be surprised by the subtlety of the means he devises to get for himself such things as he can obtain, and to really enjoy things without the aid of other people's ideas. You leave him master of his own wishes, but you do not multiply his caprices. When he does only what he wants, he will soon do only what he ought, and although his body is constantly in motion so far as his sensible and present interests are concerned, you will find him developing all the reason of which he is capable, far better and in a manner much better fitted for him than in purely theoretical studies.

Thus when he does not find you continually thwarting him, when he no longer distrusts you, no longer has anything to conceal from you, he will neither tell you lies nor deceive you; he will show himself fearlessly as he really is, and you can study him at your ease, and surround him with all the lessons you would have him learn, without awaking his suspicions.

Neither will he keep a curious and jealous eye on your own conduct, nor take a secret delight in catching you at fault. It is a great thing to avoid this. One of the child's first objects is, as I have said, to find the weak spots in its rulers. Though this leads to spitefulness, it does not arise from it, but from the desire to evade a disagreeable control. Overburdened by the yoke laid upon him, he tries to shake it off, and the faults he finds in his master give him a good opportunity for this. Still the habit of spying out faults and delighting in them grows upon people. Clearly we have stopped another of the springs of vice in Emile's heart. Having nothing to gain from my faults, he will not be on the watch for them, nor will he be tempted to look out for the faults of others. . . .

Let us transform our sensations into ideas, but do not let us jump all at once from the objects of sense to objects of thought. The latter are attained by means of the former. Let the senses be the only guide for the first workings of reason. No book but the world, no teaching but that of fact. The child who reads ceases to think, he only reads. He is acquiring words, not knowledge.

Teach your scholar to observe the phenomena of nature; you will soon rouse his curiosity, but if you would have it grow, do not be in too great a hurry to satisfy this curiosity. Put the problems before him and let him solve them himself. Let him know nothing because you have told him, but because he has learned it for himself. Let him not be taught science, let him discover it. If ever you substitute authority for reason, he will cease to reason; he will be a mere plaything of other people's thoughts.

You wish to teach this child geography and you provide him with globes, spheres, and maps. What elaborate preparations! What is the use of all these symbols? Why not begin by showing him the real thing so that he may at least know what you are talking about?

One fine evening we are walking in a suitable place where the wide horizon gives us a full view of the setting sun, and we note the objects which mark the place where it sets. Next morning we return to the same place for a breath of fresh air before sunrise. We see the rays of light which announce the sun's approach; the glow increases, the east seems afire, and long before the sun appears the light leads us to expect its return. Every moment you expect to see it. There it is at last! A shining point appears like a flash of lightning and soon fills the whole space; the veil of darkness rolls away, man perceives his dwelling place in fresh beauty. During the night the grass has assumed a fresher green; in the light of early dawn, and gilded by the first rays of the sun, it seems covered with a shining network of dew reflecting the light and color. The birds raise their chorus of praise to greet the Father of life, not one of them is mute; their gentle warbling is softer than by day, it expresses the languor of a peaceful waking. All these produce an impression of freshness which seems to reach the very soul. It is a brief hour of enchantment which no man can resist; a sight so grand, so fair, so delicious, that none can behold it unmoved.

Fired with this enthusiasm, the master wishes to impart it to the child. He expects to rouse his emotion by drawing attention to his own. Mere folly! The splendor of nature lives in man's heart; to be seen, it must be felt. The child sees the objects themselves, but does not perceive their relations, and cannot hear their harmony. It needs knowledge he has not yet acquired, feelings he has not yet experienced, to receive the complex impression which results from all these separate sensations. If he has not wandered over arid plains, if his feet have not been scorched by the burning sands of the desert, if he has not breathed the hot and oppressive air reflected from the glowing rocks, how shall he delight in the fresh air of a fine morning? The scent of flowers, the beauty of foliage, the moistness of the dew, the soft turf beneath his feet, how shall all these delight his senses? How shall the song of the birds arouse voluptuous emotion if love and pleasure are still unknown to him? How shall he behold with rapture the birth of this fair day if his imagination cannot paint the joys it may bring in its track? How can he feel the beauty of nature while the hand that formed it is unknown?

Never tell the child what he cannot understand: no descriptions, no eloquence, no figures of speech, no poetry. The time has not come for feeling or taste. Continue to be clear and cold; the time will come only too soon when you must adopt another tone.

Brought up in the spirit of our maxims, accustomed to make his own tools and not to appeal to others until he has tried and failed, he will examine everything he sees carefully and in silence. He thinks rather than questions. Be content, therefore, to show him things at a fit season; then, when you see that his curiosity is thoroughly aroused, put some brief question which will set him trying to discover the answer.

On the present occasion when you and he have carefully observed the rising sun, when you have called his attention to the mountains and other objects visible from the same spot, after he has chattered freely about them, keep quiet for a few minutes as if lost in thought and then say, "I think the sun set over there last night; it rose here this morning. How can that be?" Say no more; if he asks questions, do not answer them; talk of something else. Let him alone, and be sure he will think about it.

To train a child to be really attentive so that he may be really impressed by any truth of experience, he must spend anxious days before he discovers that truth. If he does not learn enough in this way, there is another way of drawing his attention to the matter. Turn the question about. If he does not know how the sun gets from the place where it sets to where it rises, he knows at least how it travels from sunrise to sunset, his eyes teach him that. Use the second question to throw light on the first; either your pupil is a regular dunce or the analogy is too clear to be missed. This is his first lesson in cosmography.

As we always advance slowly from one sensible idea to another, and as we give time enough to each for him to become really familiar with it before we go on to another, and lastly as we never force our scholar's attention, we are still a long way from a knowledge of the course of the sun or the shape of the earth; but as all the apparent movements of the celestial bodies depend on the same principle, and the first observation leads on to all the rest, less effort is needed, though more time, to proceed from the diurnal revolution to the calculation of eclipses, than to get a thorough understanding of day and night.

Since the sun revolves around the earth it describes a circle, and every circle must have a center; that we know already. This center is invisible, it is in the middle of the earth, but we can mark out two opposite points on the earth's surface which correspond to it. A skewer passed through the three points and prolonged to the sky at either end would represent the earth's axis and the sun's daily course. A round teetotum revolving on its point represents the sky turning on its axis, the two points of the teetotum are the two poles; the child will be delighted to find one of them, and I show him the tail of the Little Bear. Here is another game for the dark. Little by little we get to know the stars, and from this comes a wish to know the planets and observe the constellations.

We saw the sun rise at midsummer, we shall see it rise at Christmas or some other fine winter's day; for you know we are no lie-a-beds and we enjoy the cold. I take care to make this second observation in the same place as the first, and if skillfully led up to, one or other will certainly exclaim, "What a funny thing! The sun is not rising in the same place; here are our landmarks, but it is rising over there. So there is the summer east and the winter east, etc." Young teacher, you are on the right track. These examples should show you how to teach the sphere without any difficulty, taking the earth for the earth and the sun for the sun.

As a general rule—never substitute the symbol for the thing signified, unless it is impossible to show the thing itself; for the child's attention is so taken up with the symbol that he will forget what it signifies. . . .

Never show a child what he cannot see. Since mankind is almost unknown to him, and since you cannot make a man of him, bring the man down to the level of the child. While you are thinking what will be useful to him when he is older, talk to him of what he knows he can use now. Moreover, as soon as he begins to reason let there be no comparison with other children, no rivalry, no competition, not even in running races. I would far rather he did not learn anything than have him learn it through jealousy or self-conceit. Year by year I shall just note the progress he has made, I shall compare the results with those of the following year, I shall say, "You have grown so much; that is the ditch you jumped, the weight you carried, the distance you flung a pebble, the race you ran without stopping to take breath, etc.; let us see what you can do now."

In this way he is stimulated to further effort without jealousy. He wants to excel himself as he ought to do; I see no reason why he should not emulate his own performances.

I hate books; they only teach us to talk about things we know nothing about. Hermes, they say, engraved the elements of science on pillars lest a deluge should destroy them. Had he imprinted them on men's hearts they would have been preserved by tradition. Well-trained minds are the pillars on which human knowledge is most deeply engraved.

Is there no way of correlating so many lessons scattered through so many books, no way of focusing them on some common objects, easy to see, interesting to follow, and stimulating even to a child? Could we but discover a state in which all man's needs appear in such a way as to appeal to the child's mind, a state in which the ways of providing for these needs are as easily developed, the simple and stirring portrayal of this state should form the earliest training of the child's imagination.

Eager philosopher, I see your own imagination at work. Spare yourself the trouble; this state is already known, it is described, with due respect to you, far better than you could describe it, at least with greater truth and simplicity. Since we must have books, there is one book which, to my thinking, supplies the best treatise on an education according to nature. This is the first book Emile will read; for a long time it will form his whole library, and it will always retain an honored place. It will be the text to which all our talks about natural science are but the commentary. It will serve to test our progress toward a right judgment, and it will always be read with delight, so long as our taste is unspoiled. What is this wonderful book? Is it Aristotle? Pliny? Buffon? No; it is *Robinson Crusoe*.

Robinson Crusoe on his island, deprived of the help of his fellow men, without the means of carrying on the various arts, yet finding food, preserving his life, and procuring a certain amount of comfort: this is the thing to interest people of all ages, and it can be made attractive to children in all sorts of ways. We shall thus make a reality of that desert island which formerly served as an illustration. The condition, I confess, is not that of a social being, nor is it in all probability Emile's own condition, but he should use it as a standard of comparison for all other conditions. The surest way to raise him above prejudice and to base his judgments on the true relations of things, is to put him in the place of a solitary man, and to judge all things as they would be judged by such a man in relation to their own utility.

This novel, stripped of irrelevant matter, begins with Robinson's shipwreck on his island, and ends with the coming of the ship which bears him from it, and it will furnish Emile with material, both for work and play, during the whole period we are considering. His head should be full of it, he should always be busy with his castle,

his goats, his plantations. Let him learn in detail, not from books
but from things, all that is necessary in such a case. Let him think
he is Robinson himself; let him see himself clad in skins, wearing a
tall cap, a great cutlass, all the grotesque getup of Robinson Crusoe,
even to the umbrella which he will scarcely need. He should anxiously consider what steps to take; will this or that be wanting. He
should examine his hero's conduct: has he omitted nothing; is there
nothing he could have done better? He should carefully note his
mistakes, so as not to fall into them himself in similar circumstances, for you may be sure he will plan out just such a settlement
for himself. This is the genuine castle in the air of this happy age,
when the child knows no other happiness but food and freedom.

What a motive will this infatuation supply in the hands of a
skillful teacher who has aroused it for the purpose of using it. The
child who wants to build a storehouse on his desert island will be
more eager to learn than the master to teach. He will want to know
all sorts of useful things and nothing else; you will need the curb as
well as the spur. Make haste, therefore, to establish him on his
island while this is all he needs to make him happy; for the day is at
hand when, if he must still live on his island, he will not be content
to live alone, when even the companionship of Man Friday, who is
almost disregarded now, will not long suffice.

The exercise of the natural arts, which may be carried on by one
man alone, leads on to the industrial arts which call for the co-
operation of many hands. The former may be carried on by hermits,
by savages, but the others can arise only in a society, and they make
society necessary. So long as only bodily needs are recognized, man
is self-sufficing; with superfluity comes the need for division and
distribution of labor, for though one man working alone can earn a
man's living, one hundred men working together can earn the
living of two hundred. As soon as some men are idle, others must
work to make up for their idleness.

Your main object should be to keep out of your scholar's way all
idea of such social relations as he cannot understand, but when the
development of knowledge compels you to show him the mutual
dependence of mankind, instead of showing him its moral side, turn
all his attention at first toward industry and the mechanical arts
which make men useful to one another. While you take him from
one workshop to another, let him try his hand at every trade you
show him, and do not let him leave it till he has thoroughly
learned why everything is done, or at least everything that has
attracted his attention. With this aim you should take a share in his

work and set him an example. Be yourself the apprentice that he may become a master; you may expect him to learn more in one hour's work than he would retain after a whole day's explanation.

The value set by the general public on the various arts is in inverse ratio to their real utility. They are even valued directly according to their uselessness. This might be expected. The most useful arts are the worst paid, for the number of workmen is regulated by the demand, and the work which everybody requires must necessarily be paid at a rate which puts it within the reach of the poor. On the other hand, those great people who are called artists, not artisans, who labor only for the rich and idle, put a fancy price on their trifles; and as the real value of this vain labor is purely imaginary, the price itself adds to their market value, and they are valued according to their costliness. The rich think so much of these things, not because they are useful, but because they are beyond the reach of the poor. *Nolo habere bona, nisi quibus populus inviderit.*

What will become of your pupils if you let them acquire this foolish prejudice, if you share it yourself? If, for instance, they see you show more politeness in a jeweler's shop than in a locksmith's. What idea will they form of the true worth of the arts and the real value of things when they see, on the one hand, a fancy price and, on the other, the price of real utility, and that the more a thing costs the less it is worth? As soon as you let them get hold of these ideas, you may give up all attempt at further education; in spite of you they will be like all the other scholars—you have wasted fourteen years.

Emile, bent on furnishing his island, will look at things from another point of view. . . .

"My son will have to take the world as he finds it, he will not live among the wise but among fools; he must therefore be acquainted with their follies, since they must be led by this means. A real knowledge of things may be a good thing in itself, but the knowledge of men and their opinions is better, for in human society man is the chief tool of man, and the wisest man is he who best knows the use of this tool. What is the good of teaching children an imaginary system, just the opposite of the established order of things, among which they will have to live? First teach them wisdom, then show them the follies of mankind."

These are the specious maxims by which fathers, who mistake them for prudence, strive to make their children the slaves of the prejudices in which they are educated, and the puppets of the senseless crowd which they hope to make subservient to their passions. How much must be known before we attain to a knowledge of man. This is the final study of the philosopher, and you expect to make it the first lesson of the child! Before teaching him our sentiments, first teach him to judge of their worth. Do you perceive folly when you mistake it for wisdom? To be wise we must discern between good and evil. How can your child know men when he can neither judge of their judgments nor unravel their mistakes? It is a misfortune to know what they think, without knowing whether their thoughts are true or false. First teach him things as they really are, afterward you will teach him how they appear to us. He will then be able to make a comparison between popular ideas and truth, and be able to rise above the vulgar crowd; for you are unaware of the prejudices you adopt, and you do not lead a nation when you are like it. But if you begin to teach the opinions of other people before you teach how to judge of their worth, of one thing you may be sure, your pupil will adopt those opinions whatever you may do, and you will not succeed in uprooting them. I am therefore convinced that to make a young man judge rightly, you must form his judgment rather than teach him your own.

So far you see I have not spoken to my pupil about men; he would have too much sense to listen to me. His relations to other people are as yet not sufficiently apparent to him to enable him to judge others by himself. The only person he knows is himself, and his knowledge of himself is very imperfect. But if he forms few opinions about others, those opinions are correct. He knows nothing of another's place, but he knows his own and keeps to it. I have bound him with the strong cord of necessity, instead of social laws, which are beyond his knowledge. He is still little more than a body; let us treat him as such. . . .

As soon as Emile knows what life is, my first care will be to teach him to preserve his life. Hitherto I have made no distinction of condition, rank, station, or fortune; nor shall I distinguish between them in the future, since man is the same in every station; the rich man's stomach is no bigger than the poor man's, nor is his digestion any better; the master's arm is neither longer nor stronger than the slave's; a great man is no taller than one of the people, and indeed the natural needs are the same to all, and the means of satisfying them should be equally within the reach of all. Fit a man's education to his real self, not to what is no part of him. Do you not see that in striving to fit him merely for one station, you are unfitting him for anything else, so that some caprice of Fortune may make your work really harmful to him? What could be more absurd than a nobleman in rags who carries with him into his poverty the prejudices of his birth? What is more despicable than a rich man fallen into poverty who recalls the scorn with which he himself regarded the poor, and feels that he has sunk to the lowest depth of degradation? The one may become a professional thief, the other a cringing servant, with this fine saying, "I must live."

You reckon on the present order of society, without considering that this order is itself subject to inscrutable changes, and that you can neither foresee nor provide against the revolution which may affect your children. The great become small, the rich poor, the king a commoner. Does fate strike so seldom that you can count on immunity from her blows? The crisis is approaching, and we are on the edge of a revolution.* Who can answer for your fate? What man has made, man may destroy. Nature's characters alone are ineffaceable, and nature makes neither the prince, the rich man, nor the nobleman. This satrap whom you have educated for greatness, what will become of him in his degradation? This farmer of the taxes who can only live on gold, what will he do in poverty? This haughty fool who cannot use his own hands, who prides himself on what is not really his, what will he do when he is stripped of all? In that day, happy will he be who can give up the rank which is no longer his, and be still a man in Fate's despite. Let men praise as they will that conquered monarch who like a madman would be buried beneath the fragments of his throne; I behold him with scorn; to me he is merely a crown, and when that is gone he is nothing. But he who loses his crown and lives without it is more than a king; from the rank of a king, which may be held by a coward, a villain, or madman, he rises to the rank of a man, a position few can fill. Thus he triumphs over Fortune, he dares to look her in the face; he depends on himself alone, and when he has nothing left to show but himself he is not a nonentity, he is somebody. Better a thousandfold the king of Corinth a schoolmaster at Syracuse, than a wretched Tarquin, unable to be anything but a king, or the heir of the ruler of three kingdoms, the sport of all who would scorn his poverty, wandering from court to court in search of

---

* In my opinion it is impossible that the great kingdoms of Europe should last much longer. Each of them has had its period of splendor, after which it must inevitably decline. I have my own opinions as to the special applications of this general statement, but this is not the place to enter into details, and they are only too evident to everybody.

help, and finding nothing but insults, for want of knowing any trade but one which he can no longer practice.

The man and the citizen, whoever he may be, has no property to invest in society but himself, all his other goods belong to society in spite of himself, and when a man is rich, either he does not enjoy his wealth or the public enjoys it, too; in the first case he robs others as well as himself, in the second he gives them nothing. Thus his debt to society is still unpaid, while he pays only with his property. "But my father was serving society while he was acquiring his wealth." Just so; he paid his own debt, not yours. You owe more to others than if you had been born with nothing, since you were born under favorable conditions. It is not fair that what one man has done for society should pay another's debt, for since every man owes all that he is, he can pay only his own debt, and no father can transmit to his son any right to be of no use to mankind. "But," you say, "this is just what he does when he leaves me his wealth, the reward of his labor." The man who eats in idleness what he has not himself earned is a thief, and in my eyes the man who lives on an income paid him by the state for doing nothing differs little from a highwayman who lives on those who travel his way. Outside the pale of society, the solitary, owing nothing to any man, may live as he pleases, but in society either he lives at the cost of others or he owes them in labor the cost of his keep; there is no exception to this rule. Man in society is bound to work; rich or poor, weak or strong, every idler is a thief.

Now, of all the pursuits by which a man may earn his living, the nearest to a state of nature is manual labor; of all stations that of the artisan is least dependent on Fortune. The artisan depends on his labor alone, he is a free man while the plowman is a slave; for the latter depends on his field where the crops may be destroyed by others. An enemy, a prince, a powerful neighbor, or a lawsuit may deprive him of his field; through this field he may be harassed in all sorts of ways. But if the artisan is ill-treated, his goods are soon packed and he takes himself off. Yet agriculture is the earliest, the most honest of trades, and more useful than all the rest, and therefore more honorable for those who practice it. I do not say to Emile, "Study agriculture," he is already familiar with it. He is acquainted with every kind of rural labor, it was his first occupation, and he returns to it continually. So I say to him, "Cultivate your father's lands, but if you lose this inheritance, or if you have none to lose, what will you do? Learn a trade."

"A trade for my son! My son a workingman! What are you thinking of, sir?" Madam, my thoughts are wiser than yours; you want to make him fit for nothing but a lord, a marquis, or a prince; and someday he may be less than nothing. I want to give him a rank which he cannot lose, a rank which will always do him honor; I want to raise him to the status of a man, and, whatever you may say, he will have fewer equals in that rank than in your own.

The letter killeth, the spirit giveth life. Learning a trade matters less than overcoming the prejudices he despises. You will never be reduced to earning your livelihood; so much the worse for you. No matter; work for honor, not for need; stoop to the position of a workingman, to rise above your own. To conquer Fortune and everything else, begin by independence. To rule through public opinion, begin by ruling over it. . . .

FURTHER READING

Jean Château, *Jean-Jacques Rousseau: Sa Philosophie de l'éducation* (1962). Sound, sensible monograph.

Robert Derathé, "L'Homme selon Rousseau," in *Études sur le Contrat social de Jean-Jacques Rousseau* (1964), 203–17. Underlines, in a collection of essays devoted to the companion piece to *Émile,* the essential unity of Rousseau's view of man.

Ronald Grimsley, *Jean-Jacques Rousseau: A Study in Self-Awareness* (1961). A sensitive account of Rousseau's total development; pays due attention to *Émile.*

Georges Pire, *Stoïcisme et pédagogie; de Zénon à Marc-Aurèle, de Sénèque à Montaigne et à J.-J. Rousseau* (1958). Places Rousseau in the Stoic educational tradition; very valuable.

27 ✸ ROUSSEAU

Contrat Social

[From the book *The Social Contract and Discourses and Other Essays* by Jean-Jacques Rousseau, translated and with an introduction by G. D. H. Cole (1950), 3–32, 37–42, 49–52, 77–80, 93–94, 104–7, 139–41.*]

Rousseau's now most famous work, The Social Contract, *was not widely read in its own day, and its impact on the French Revolution (which was once thought to have been enormous) was highly selective. Yet we can see today what its contemporaries did not quite see: that the book is a complex document which belongs at once to Rousseau's biography, to the history of Geneva, to the pedagogical line of thinking most fully expressed in* Émile, *and to the history of masterpieces in political theory. The relation of* The Social Contract *to* Émile *is close and plain:* Émile *is the kind of person—clearheaded, hard-working, public-spirited, genuinely disinterested in the full, old sense of that now much-abused word— who can make the community delineated in* The Social Contract *work.*

The Social Contract *has been called many things: a paean to individualism, a prelude to collectivism, a justification of anarchy, of dictatorship, of democracy. Essentially, Rousseau's purpose was to solve the age-old conflict between the rights of the individual and the rights of the collectivity—not the state, for Rousseau, but the community. Political philosophers both before and after Rousseau have sought to resolve this difficulty by wholly subordinating the citizen to the collectivity, or wholly subordinating the collectivity to the citizen, or defining their respective spheres. This last solution,*

* Everyman's Library edition, published by E. P. Dutton & Company, Inc., and J. M. Dent & Sons, Ltd., and used with their permission.

with generous attention to the rights of the individual, was the solution of liberalism: the person has certain rights the state must never invade; the state must have only enough power to function— to defend itself, that is, against external and internal enemies. Rousseau, who was a democrat but not a liberal, tried to solve the tension between freedom and authority not by assigning to each a particular role, but by dissolving the dichotomy altogether. The good citizen, the Émile who thinks, when he votes, about the needs of his community first, is both ruler and ruled. As ruler, he makes the laws which, as subject, he obeys. Thus freedom and obedience appear simply as separate aspects of a single person.

It is debatable whether Rousseau solved the problem he had set himself, but The Social Contract *is a closely reasoned document. In its insistence on the rights of all to participate in the making of policy, that the assent of slaves is meaningless and that slavery is forever unlawful, the book is a landmark in the democratic tradition; in its contrary insistence on the overriding claims of the community, and the need to enforce consensus when none naturally exists, the book has more menacing potentialities, though these, in my judgment, are secondary. Whatever its final meaning, the* Contrat social *is important, and the argument it started goes on.*

BOOK I

CHAPTER I · SUBJECT OF THE FIRST BOOK

Man is born free; and everywhere he is in chains. One thinks himself the master of others, and still remains a greater slave than they. How did this change come about? I do not know. What can make it legitimate? That question I think I can answer.

If I took into account only force, and the effects derived from it, I should say: "As long as a people is compelled to obey, and obeys, it does well; as soon as it can shake off the yoke, and shakes it off, it does still better; for, regaining its liberty by the same right as took it away, either it is justified in resuming it or there was no justification for those who took it away." But the social order is a sacred right which is the basis of all rights. Nevertheless, this right does not come from nature, and must therefore be founded on conventions. Before coming to that, I have to prove what I have just asserted.

CHAPTER II · THE FIRST SOCIETIES

The most ancient of all societies, and the only one that is natural, is the family: and even so the children remain attached to the father only so long as they need him for their preservation. As soon as this need ceases, the natural bond is dissolved. The children, released from the obedience they owed to the father, and the father, released from the care he owed his children, return equally to independence. If they remain united, they continue so no longer naturally, but voluntarily; and the family itself is then maintained only by convention.

This common liberty results from the nature of man. His first law is to provide for his own preservation, his first cares are those which he owes to himself; and, as soon as he reaches years of discretion, he is the sole judge of the proper means of preserving himself, and consequently becomes his own master.

The family, then, may be called the first model of political societies: the ruler corresponds to the father, and the people to the children; and all, being born free and equal, alienate their liberty only for their own advantage. The whole difference is that in the family the love of the father for his children repays him for the care he takes of them, while in the State the pleasure of commanding takes the place of the love which the chief cannot have for the peoples under him.

Grotius denies that all human power is established in favor of the governed, and quotes slavery as an example. His usual method of reasoning is constantly to establish right by fact.* It would be possible to employ a more logical method, but none could be more favorable to tyrants.

It is, then, according to Grotius, doubtful whether the human race belongs to a hundred men or that hundred men to the human race: and, throughout his book, he seems to incline to the former

---

* "Learned inquiries into public right are often only the history of past abuses; and troubling to study them too deeply is a profitless infatuation" (*Essay on the Interests of France in Relation to its Neighbors,* by the Marquis d'Argenson). This is exactly what Grotius has done.

alternative, which is also the view of Hobbes. On this showing, the human species is divided into so many herds of cattle, each with its ruler, who keeps guard over them for the purpose of devouring them.

As a shepherd is of a nature superior to that of his flock, the shepherds of men, i.e. their rulers, are of a nature superior to that of the peoples under them. Thus, Philo tells us, the Emperor Caligula reasoned, concluding equally well either that kings were gods or that men were beasts.

The reasoning of Caligula agrees with that of Hobbes and Grotius. Aristotle, before any of them, had said that men are by no means equal naturally, but that some are born for slavery, and others for dominion.

Aristotle was right; but he took the effect for the cause. Nothing can be more certain than that every man born in slavery is born for slavery. Slaves lose everything in their chains, even the desire of escaping from them: they love their servitude, as the comrades of Ulysses loved their brutish condition.* If, then, there are slaves by nature, it is because there have been slaves against nature. Force made the first slaves, and their cowardice perpetuated the condition.

I have said nothing of King Adam, or Emperor Noah, father of the three great monarchs who shared out the universe, like the children of Saturn, whom some scholars have recognized in them. I trust to getting due thanks for my moderation; for, being a direct descendant of one of these princes, perhaps of the eldest branch, how do I know that a verification of titles might not leave me the legitimate king of the human race? In any case, there can be no doubt that Adam was sovereign of the world, as Robinson Crusoe was of his island, as long as he was its only inhabitant; and this empire had the advantage that the monarch, safe on his throne, had no rebellions, wars, or conspirators to fear.

CHAPTER III · THE RIGHT OF THE STRONGEST

The strongest is never strong enough to be always the master, unless he transforms strength into right, and obedience into duty. Hence the right of the strongest, which, though to all seeming meant ironically, is really laid down as a fundamental principle.

---

* See a short treatise of Plutarch's entitled "That Animals Reason."

But are we never to have an explanation of this phrase? Force is a physical power, and I fail to see what moral effect it can have. To yield to force is an act of necessity, not of will—at the most, an act of prudence. In what sense can it be a duty?

Suppose for a moment that this so-called "right" exists. I maintain that the sole result is a mass of inexplicable nonsense. For, if force creates right, the effect changes with the cause: every force that is greater than the first succeeds to its right. As soon as it is possible to disobey with impunity, disobedience is legitimate; and, the strongest being always in the right, the only thing that matters is to act so as to become the strongest. But what kind of right is that which perishes when force fails? If we must obey perforce, there is no need to obey because we ought; and if we are not forced to obey, we are under no obligation to do so. Clearly, the word "right" adds nothing to force: in this connection, it means absolutely nothing.

Obey the powers that be. If this means yield to force, it is a good precept, but superfluous: I can answer for its never being violated. All power comes from God, I admit; but so does all sickness: does that mean that we are forbidden to call in the doctor? A brigand surprises me at the edge of a wood: must I not merely surrender my purse on compulsion, but, even if I could withhold it, am I in conscience bound to give it up? For certainly the pistol he holds is also a power.

Let us then admit that force does not create right, and that we are obliged to obey only legitimate powers. In that case, my original question recurs.

CHAPTER IV · SLAVERY

Since no man has a natural authority over his fellow, and force creates no right, we must conclude that conventions form the basis of all legitimate authority among men.

If an individual, says Grotius, can alienate his liberty and make himself the slave of a master, why could not a whole people do the same and make itself subject to a king? There are in this passage plenty of ambiguous words which would need explaining; but let us confine ourselves to the word *alienate*. To alienate is to give or to sell. Now, a man who becomes the slave of another does not give himself; he sells himself, at the least for his subsistence: but for what does a people sell itself? A king is so far from furnishing his subjects with their subsistence that he gets his own only from them;

and, according to Rabelais, kings do not live on nothing. Do subjects then give their persons on condition that the king takes their goods also? I fail to see what they have left to preserve.

It will be said that the despot assures his subjects civil tranquillity. Granted; but what do they gain, if the wars his ambition brings down upon them, his insatiable avidity, and the vexatious conduct of his ministers press harder on them than their own dissensions would have done? What do they gain, if the very tranquillity they enjoy is one of their miseries? Tranquillity is found also in dungeons; but is that enough to make them desirable places to live in? The Greeks imprisoned in the cave of the Cyclops lived there very tranquilly while they were awaiting their turn to be devoured.

To say that a man gives himself gratuitously is to say what is absurd and inconceivable; such an act is null and illegitimate, from the mere fact that he who does it is out of his mind. To say the same of a whole people is to suppose a people of madmen; and madness creates no right.

Even if each man could alienate himself, he could not alienate his children: they are born men and free; their liberty belongs to them, and no one but they has the right to dispose of it. Before they come to years of discretion, the father can, in their name, lay down conditions for their preservation and well-being, but he cannot give them irrevocably and without conditions: such a gift is contrary to the ends of nature, and exceeds the rights of paternity. It would therefore be necessary, in order to legitimize an arbitrary government, that in every generation the people should be in a position to accept or reject it; but, were this so, the government would be no longer arbitrary.

To renounce liberty is to renounce being a man, to surrender the rights of humanity and even its duties. For him who renounces everything no indemnity is possible. Such a renunciation is incompatible with man's nature; to remove all liberty from his will is to remove all morality from his acts. Finally, it is an empty and contradictory convention that sets up, on the one side, absolute authority, and, on the other, unlimited obedience. Is it not clear that we can be under no obligation to a person from whom we have the right to exact everything? Does not this condition alone, in the absence of equivalence or exchange, in itself involve the nullity of the act? For what right can my slave have against me, when all that he has belongs to me, and, his right being mine, this right of mine against myself is a phrase devoid of meaning?

Grotius and the rest find in war another origin for the so-called right of slavery. The victor having, as they hold, the right of killing the vanquished, the latter can buy back his life at the price of his liberty; and this convention is the more legitimate because it is to the advantage of both parties.

But it is clear that this supposed right to kill the conquered is by no means deducible from the state of war. Men, from the mere fact that, while they are living in their primitive independence, they have no mutual relations stable enough to constitute either the state of peace or the state of war, cannot be naturally enemies. War is constituted by a relation between things, and not between persons; and, as the state of war cannot arise out of simple personal relations, but only out of real relations, private war, or war of man with man, can exist neither in the state of nature, where there is no constant property, nor in the social state, where everything is under the authority of the laws.

Individual combats, duels, and encounters are acts which cannot constitute a state; while the private wars authorized by the Establishments of Louis IX, King of France, and suspended by the Peace of God, are abuses of feudalism, in itself an absurd system if ever there was one, and contrary to the principles of natural right and to all good polity.

War, then, is a relation, not between man and man, but between State and State, and individuals are enemies only accidentally, not as men, nor even as citizens,* but as soldiers; not as members of their country, but as its defenders. Finally, each State can have for enemies only other States, and not men; for between things disparate in nature there can be no real relation.

Furthermore, this principle is in conformity with the established rules of all times and the constant practice of all civilized peoples. Declarations of war are intimations less to powers than to their subjects. The foreigner, whether king, individual, or people, who

---

* The Romans, who understood and respected the right of war more than any other nation on earth, carried their scruples on this head so far that a citizen was not allowed to serve as a volunteer without engaging himself expressly against the enemy, and against such and such an enemy by name. A legion in which the younger Cato was seeing his first service under Popilius having been reconstructed, the elder Cato wrote to Popilius that, if he wished his son to continue serving under him, he must administer to him a new military oath, because, the first having been annulled, he was no longer able to bear arms against the enemy. The same Cato wrote to his son telling him to take great care not to go into battle before taking this new oath. I know that the siege of Clusium and other isolated events can be quoted against me; but I am citing laws and customs. The Romans are the people that least often transgressed its laws; and no other people has had such good ones.

robs, kills, or detains the subjects, without declaring war on the prince, is not an enemy, but a brigand. Even in real war, a just prince, while laying hands, in the enemy's country, on all that belongs to the public, respects the lives and goods of individuals: he respects rights on which his own are founded. The object of the war being the destruction of the hostile State, the other side has a right to kill its defenders while they are bearing arms; but as soon as they lay them down and surrender, they cease to be enemies or instruments of the enemy, and become once more merely men, whose life no one has any right to take. Sometimes it is possible to kill the State without killing a single one of its members; and war gives no right which is not necessary to the gaining of its object. These principles are not those of Grotius: they are not based on the authority of poets, but derived from the nature of reality and based on reason.

The right of conquest has no foundation other than the right of the strongest. If war does not give the conqueror the right to massacre the conquered peoples, the right to enslave them cannot be based upon a right which does not exist. No one has a right to kill an enemy except when he cannot make him a slave, and the right to enslave him cannot therefore be derived from the right to kill him. It is accordingly an unfair exchange to make him buy at the price of his liberty his life, over which the victor holds no right. Is it not clear that there is a vicious circle in founding the right of life and death on the right of slavery, and the right of slavery on the right of life and death?

Even if we assume this terrible right to kill everybody, I maintain that a slave made in war, or a conquered people, is under no obligation to a master, except to obey him as far as he is compelled to do so. By taking an equivalent for his life, the victor has not done him a favor; instead of killing him without profit, he has killed him usefully. So far then is he from acquiring over him any authority in addition to that of force, that the state of war continues to subsist between them: their mutual relation is the effect of it, and the usage of the right of war does not imply a treaty of peace. A convention has indeed been made; but this convention, so far from destroying the state of war, presupposes its continuance.

So, from whatever aspect we regard the question, the right of slavery is null and void, not only as being illegitimate, but also because it is absurd and meaningless. The words *slave* and *right* contradict each other, and are mutually exclusive. It will always be equally foolish for a man to say to a man or to a people: "I make with you a convention wholly at your expense and wholly to my advantage; I shall keep it as long as I like, and you will keep it as long as I like."

CHAPTER VI · THE SOCIAL COMPACT

I suppose men to have reached the point at which the obstacles in the way of their preservation in the state of nature show their power of resistance to be greater than the resources at the disposal of each individual for his maintenance in that state. That primitive condition can then subsist no longer; and the human race would perish unless it changed its manner of existence.

But, as men cannot engender new forces, but only unite and direct existing ones, they have no other means of preserving themselves than the formation, by aggregation, of a sum of forces great enough to overcome the resistance. These they have to bring into play by means of a single motive power, and cause to act in concert.

This sum of forces can arise only where several persons come together: but, as the force and liberty of each man are the chief instruments of his self-preservation, how can he pledge them without harming his own interests, and neglecting the care he owes to himself? This difficulty, in its bearing on my present subject, may be stated in the following terms:

"The problem is to find a form of association which will defend and protect with the whole common force the person and goods of each associate, and in which each, while uniting himself with all, may still obey himself alone, and remain as free as before." This is the fundamental problem of which the *social contract* provides the solution.

The clauses of this contract are so determined by the nature of the act that the slightest modification would make them vain and ineffective; so that, although they have perhaps never been formally set forth, they are everywhere the same and everywhere tacitly admitted and recognized, until, on the violation of the social compact, each regains his original rights and resumes his natural liberty, while losing the conventional liberty in favor of which he renounced it.

These clauses, properly understood, may be reduced to one—the total alienation of each associate, together with all his rights, to the whole community; for, in the first place, as each gives himself absolutely, the conditions are the same for all; and, this being so, no one has any interest in making them burdensome to others.

Moreover, the alienation being without reserve, the union is as perfect as it can be, and no associate has anything more to demand: for, if the individuals retained certain rights, as there would be no common superior to decide between them and the public, each, being on one point his own judge, would ask to be so on all; the state of nature would thus continue, and the association would necessarily become inoperative or tyrannical.

Finally, each man, in giving himself to all, gives himself to nobody; and as there is no associate over which he does not acquire the same right as he yields others over himself, he gains an equivalent for everything he loses, and an increase of force for the preservation of what he has.

If then we discard from the social compact what is not of its essence, we shall find that it reduces itself to the following terms:

"Each of us puts his person and all his power in common under the supreme direction of the general will, and, in our corporate capacity, we receive each member as an indivisible part of the whole."

At once, in place of the individual personality of each contracting party, this act of association creates a moral and collective body, composed of as many members as the assembly contains voters, and receiving from this act its unity, its common identity, its life, and its will. This public person, so formed by the union of all other persons, formerly took the name of *city,* and now takes that of *Republic* or *body politic;* it is called by its members *State* when passive, *Sovereign* when active, and *Power* when compared with others like itself. Those who are associated in it take collectively the name of *people,* and severally are called *citizens,* as sharing in the sovereign power, and *subjects,* as being under the laws of the State. But these terms are often confused and taken one for another: it is enough to know how to distinguish them when they are being used with precision.

CHAPTER VII · THE SOVEREIGN

This formula shows us that the act of association comprises a mutual undertaking between the public and the individuals, and that each individual, in making a contract, as we may say, with himself, is bound in a double capacity; as a member of the Sovereign he is bound to the individuals, and as a member of the State to the Sovereign. But the maxim of civil right, that no one is bound by undertakings made to himself, does not apply in this case; for there is a great difference between incurring an obligation to yourself and incurring one to a whole of which you form a part.

Attention must further be called to the fact that public deliberation, while competent to bind all the subjects to the Sovereign, because of the two different capacities in which each of them may be regarded, cannot, for the opposite reason, bind the Sovereign to itself; and that it is consequently against the nature of the body politic for the Sovereign to impose on itself a law which it cannot infringe. Being able to regard itself in only one capacity, it is in the position of an individual who makes a contract with himself; and this makes it clear that there neither is nor can be any kind of fundamental law binding on the body of the people—not even the social contract itself. This does not mean that the body politic cannot enter into undertakings with others, provided the contract is not infringed by them; for in relation to what is external to it, it becomes a simple being, an individual.

But the body politic or the Sovereign, drawing its being wholly from the sanctity of the contract, can never bind itself, even to an outsider, to do anything derogatory to the original act, for instance to alienate any part of itself, or to submit to another Sovereign. Violation of the act by which it exists would be self-annihilation; and that which is itself nothing can create nothing.

As soon as this multitude is so united in one body, it is impossible to offend against one of the members without attacking the body, and still more to offend against the body without the members resenting it. Duty and interest therefore equally oblige the two contracting parties to give each other help; and the same men should seek to combine, in their double capacity, all the advantages dependent upon that capacity.

Again, the Sovereign, being formed wholly of the individuals who compose it, neither has nor can have any interest contrary to theirs; and consequently the sovereign power need give no guarantee to its subjects, because it is impossible for the body to wish to hurt all its members. We shall also see later on that it cannot hurt any in particular. The Sovereign, merely by virtue of what it is, is always what it should be.

This, however, is not the case with the relation of the subjects to the Sovereign, which, despite the common interest, would have no security that they would fulfill their undertakings, unless it found means to assure itself of their fidelity.

In fact, each individual, as a man, may have a particular will contrary or dissimilar to the general will which he has as a citizen. His particular interest may speak to him quite differently from the common interest: his absolute and naturally independent existence may make him look upon what he owes to the common cause as a gratuitous contribution, the loss of which will do less harm to others than the payment of it is burdensome to himself; and, regarding the moral person which constitutes the State as a *persona ficta,* because not a man, he may wish to enjoy the rights of citizenship without being ready to fulfill the duties of a subject. The continuance of such an injustice could not but prove the undoing of the body politic.

In order then that the social compact may not be an empty formula, it tacitly includes the undertakings, which alone can give force to the rest, that whoever refuses to obey the general will shall be compelled to do so by the whole body. This means nothing less than that he will be forced to be free; for this is the condition which, by giving each citizen to his country, secures him against all personal dependence. In this lies the key to the working of the political machine; this alone legitimizes civil undertakings, which, without it, would be absurd, tyrannical, and liable to the most frightful abuses.

CHAPTER VIII · THE CIVIL STATE

The passage from the state of nature to the civil state produces a very remarkable change in man, by substituting justice for instinct in his conduct, and giving his actions the morality they had formerly lacked. Then only, when the voice of duty takes the place of physical impulses and right of appetite, does man, who so far had considered only himself, find that he is forced to act on different principles, and to consult his reason before listening to his inclinations. Although, in this state, he deprives himself of some advantages which he got from nature, he gains in return others so great, his faculties are so stimulated and developed, his ideas so extended, his feelings so ennobled, and his whole soul so uplifted, that, did not the abuses of this new condition often degrade him below that which he left, he would be bound to bless continually the happy moment which took him from it forever, and, instead of a stupid and unimaginative animal, made him an intelligent being and a man.

Let us draw up the whole account in terms easily commensurable. What man loses by the social contract is his natural liberty and an unlimited right to everything he tries to get and succeeds in getting; what he gains is civil liberty and the proprietorship of all he possesses. If we are to avoid mistake in weighing one against the other, we must clearly distinguish natural liberty, which is bounded only by the strength of the individual, from civil liberty, which is limited by the general will; and possession, which is merely the effect of force or the right of the first occupier, from property, which can be founded only on a positive title.

We might, over and above all this, add, to what man acquires in the civil state, moral liberty, which alone makes him truly master of himself; for the mere impulse of appetite is slavery, while obedience to a law which we prescribe to ourselves is liberty. But I have already said too much on this head, and the philosophical meaning of the word "liberty" does not now concern us.

CHAPTER IX · REAL PROPERTY

Each member of the community gives himself to it, at the moment of its foundation, just as he is, with all the resources at his command, including the goods he possesses. This act does not make possession, in changing hands, change its nature, and becomes property in the hands of the Sovereign; but, as the forces of the city are incomparably greater than those of an individual, public possession is also, in fact, stronger and more irrevocable, without being any more legitimate, at any rate from the point of view of foreigners. For the State, in relation to its members, is master of all their goods by the social contract, which, within the State, is the basis of all rights; but, in relation to other powers, it is so only by the right of the first occupier, which it holds from its members.

The right of the first occupier, though more real than the right of the strongest, becomes a real right only when the right of property has already been established. Every man has naturally a right to everything he needs; but the positive act which makes him proprietor of one thing excludes him from everything else. Having his share, he ought to keep to it, and can have no further right against the community. This is why the right of the first occupier, which in the state of nature is so weak, claims the respect of every man in civil society. In this right we are respecting not so much what belongs to another as what does not belong to ourselves.

In general, to establish the right of the first occupier over a plot of ground, the following conditions are necessary: first, the land must not yet be inhabited; secondly, a man must occupy only the amount he needs for his subsistence; and, in the third place, possession must be taken, not by an empty ceremony, but by labor and cultivation, the only sign of proprietorship that should be respected by others, in default of a legal title.

In granting the right of first occupancy to necessity and labor, are we not really stretching it as far as it can go? Is it possible to leave such a right unlimited? Is it to be enough to set foot on a plot of common ground, in order to be able to call yourself at once the master of it? Is it to be enough that a man has the strength to expel others for a moment, in order to establish his right to prevent them from ever returning? How can a man or a people seize an immense territory and keep it from the rest of the world except by a punishable usurpation, since all others are being robbed, by such an act, of the place of habitation and the means of subsistence which nature gave them in common? When Nuñez Balboa, standing on the seashore, took possession of the South Seas and the whole of South America in the name of the crown of Castile, was that enough to dispossess all their actual inhabitants, and to shut out from them all the princes of the world? On such a showing, these ceremonies are idly multiplied, and the Catholic King need only take possession all at once, from his apartment, of the whole universe, merely making a subsequent reservation about what was already in the possession of other princes.

We can imagine how the lands of individuals, where they were contiguous and came to be united, became the public territory, and how the right of Sovereignty, extending from the subjects over the lands they held, became at once real and personal. The possessors were thus made more dependent, and the forces at their command used to guarantee their fidelity. The advantage of this does not seem to have been felt by ancient monarchs, who called themselves King of the Persians, Scythians, or Macedonians, and seemed to regard themselves more as rulers of men than as masters of a country. Those of the present day more cleverly call themselves Kings of France, Spain, England, etc.: thus holding the land, they are quite confident of holding the inhabitants.

The peculiar fact about this alienation is that, in taking over the goods of individuals, the community, so far from despoiling them, only assures them legitimate possession, and changes usurpation into a true right and enjoyment into proprietorship. Thus the possessors, being regarded as depositaries of the public good, and having their rights respected by all the members of the State and maintained against foreign aggression by all its forces, have, by a cession which benefits both the public and still more themselves, acquired, so to speak, all that they gave up. This paradox may easily be explained by the distinction between the rights which the Sovereign and the proprietor have over the same estate, as we shall see later on.

It may also happen that men begin to unite one with another before they possess anything, and that, subsequently occupying a tract of country which is enough for all, they enjoy it in common, or share it out among themselves, either equally or according to a scale fixed by the Sovereign. However the acquisition be made, the right which each individual has to his own estate is always subordinate to the right which the community has over all: without this, there would be neither stability in the social tie nor real force in the exercise of Sovereignty.

I shall end this chapter and this book by remarking on a fact on which the whole social system should rest: i.e. that, instead of destroying natural inequality, the fundamental compact substitutes, for such physical inequality as nature may have set up between men, an equality that is moral and legitimate, and that men, who may be unequal in strength or intelligence, become every one equal by convention and legal right.

BOOK II

CHAPTER I · THAT SOVEREIGNTY IS INALIENABLE

The first and most important deduction from the principles we have so far laid down is that the general will alone can direct the State according to the object for which it was instituted, i.e. the common good: for if the clashing of particular interests made the establishment of societies necessary, the agreement of these very interests made it possible. The common element in these different interests is what forms the social tie; and, were there no point of agreement between them all, no society could exist. It is solely on the basis of this common interest that every society should be governed.

I hold, then, that Sovereignty, being nothing less than the exercise of the general will, can never be alienated, and that the Sovereign, who is no less than a collective being, cannot be represented except by himself: the power indeed may be transmitted, but not the will.

In reality, if it is not impossible for a particular will to agree on some point with the general will, it is at least impossible for the agreement to be lasting and constant; for the particular will tends, by its very nature, to partiality, while the general will tends to equality. It is even more impossible to have any guarantee of this agreement; for even if it should always exist, it would be the effect not of art, but of chance. The Sovereign may indeed say: "I now will actually what this man wills, or at least what he says he wills"; but it cannot say: "What he wills tomorrow, I too shall will," because it is absurd for the will to bind itself for the future, nor is it incumbent on any will to consent to anything that is not for the good of the being who wills. If then the people promises simply to obey, by that very act it dissolves itself and loses what makes it a people; the moment a master exists, there is no longer a Sovereign, and from that moment the body politic has ceased to exist.

This does not mean that the commands of the rulers cannot pass for general wills, so long as the Sovereign, being free to oppose them, offers no opposition. In such a case, universal silence is taken to imply the consent of the people. This will be explained later on.

CHAPTER II · THAT SOVEREIGNTY IS INDIVISIBLE

Sovereignty, for the same reason as makes it inalienable, is indivisible; for will either is or is not general;* it is the will either of the body of the people, or only of a part of it. In the first case, the will, when declared, is an act of Sovereignty and constitutes law: in the second, it is merely a particular will, or act of magistracy—at the most a decree.

But our political theorists, unable to divide Sovereignty in prin-

---

* To be general, a will need not always be unanimous; but every vote must be counted: any exclusion is a breach of generality.

ciple, divide it according to its object: into force and will; into legislative power and executive power; into rights of taxation, justice, and war; into internal administration and power of foreign treaty. Sometimes they confuse all these sections, and sometimes they distinguish them; they turn the Sovereign into a fantastic being composed of several connected pieces: it is as if they were making man of several bodies, one with eyes, one with arms, another with feet, and each with nothing besides. We are told that the jugglers of Japan dismember a child before the eyes of the spectators; then they throw all the members into the air one after another, and the child falls down alive and whole. The conjuring tricks of our political theorists are very like that; they first dismember the body politic by an illusion worthy of a fair, and then join it together again we know not how.

This error is due to a lack of exact notions concerning the Sovereign authority, and to taking for parts of it what are only emanations from it. Thus, for example, the acts of declaring war and making peace have been regarded as acts of Sovereignty; but this is not the case, as these acts do not constitute law, but merely the application of a law, a particular act which decides how the law applies, as we shall see clearly when the idea attached to the word "law" has been defined.

If we examined the other divisions in the same manner, we should find that, whenever Sovereignty seems to be divided, there is an illusion: the rights which are taken as being part of Sovereignty are really all subordinate, and always imply supreme wills of which they sanction only the execution.

It would be impossible to estimate the obscurity this lack of exactness has thrown over the decisions of writers who have dealt with political right, when they have used the principles laid down by them to pass judgment on the respective rights of kings and peoples. Everyone can see, in Chapters III and IV of the first book of Grotius, how the learned man and his translator, Barbeyrac, entangle and tie themselves up in their own sophistries, for fear of saying too little or too much of what they think, and so offending the interests they have to conciliate. Grotius, a refugee in France, ill content with his own country, and desirous of paying his court to Louis XIII, to whom his book is dedicated, spares no pains to rob the peoples of all their rights and invest kings with them by every conceivable artifice. This would also have been much to the taste of Barbeyrac, who dedicated his translation to George I of England. But unfortunately the expulsion of James II, which he called his "abdication," compelled him to use all reserve, to shuffle and to tergiversate, in order to avoid making William out a usurper. If these two writers had adopted the true principles, all difficulties would have been removed, and they would have been always consistent; but it would have been a sad truth for them to tell, and would have paid court for them to no one save the people. Moreover, truth is no road to fortune, and the people dispenses neither ambassadorships nor professorships nor pensions.

CHAPTER III · WHETHER THE GENERAL WILL IS FALLIBLE

It follows from what has gone before that the general will is always right and tends to the public advantage; but it does not follow that the deliberations of the people are always equally correct. Our will is always for our own good, but we do not always see what that is; the people is never corrupted, but it is often deceived, and on such occasions only does it seem to will what is bad.

There is often a great deal of difference between the will of all and the general will; the latter considers only the common interest, while the former takes private interest into account, and is no more than a sum of particular wills: but take away from these same wills the pluses and minuses that cancel one another, and the general will remains as the sum of the differences.

If, when the people, being furnished with adequate information, held its deliberations, the citizens had no communication one with another, the grand total of the small differences would always give the general will, and the decision would always be good. But when factions arise, and partial associations are formed at the expense of the great association, the will of each of these associations becomes general in relation to its members, while it remains particular in relation to the State: it may then be said that there are no longer as many votes as there are men, but only as many as there are associations. The differences become less numerous and give a less general result. Lastly, when one of these associations is so great as to prevail over all the rest, the result is no longer a sum of small differences, but a single difference; in this case there is no longer a general will, and the opinion which prevails is purely particular.

It is therefore essential, if the general will is to be able to express itself, that there should be no partial society within the State, and that each citizen should think only his own thoughts; which was indeed the sublime and unique system established by the great Lycurgus. But if there are partial societies, it is best to have as many as possible and to prevent them from being unequal, as was done by Solon, Numa, and Servius. These precautions are the only ones that can guarantee that the general will shall be always enlightened, and that the people shall in no way deceive itself.

CHAPTER IV · THE LIMITS OF THE SOVEREIGN POWER

If the State is a moral person whose life is in the union of its members, and if the most important of its cares is the care for its own preservation, it must have a universal and compelling force, in order to move and dispose each part as may be most advantageous to the whole. As nature gives each man absolute power over all his members, the social compact gives the body politic absolute power over all its members also; and it is this power which, under the direction of the general will, bears, as I have said, the name of Sovereignty.

But, besides the public person, we have to consider the private persons composing it, whose life and liberty are naturally independent of it. We are bound then to distinguish clearly between the respective rights of the citizens and the Sovereign, and between the duties the former have to fulfill as subjects and the natural rights they should enjoy as men.

Each man alienates, I admit, by the social compact, only such part of his powers, goods, and liberty as it is important for the community to control; but it must also be granted that the Sovereign is sole judge of what is important.

Every service a citizen can render the State he ought to render as soon as the Sovereign demands it; but the Sovereign, for its part, cannot impose upon its subjects any fetters that are useless to the community, nor can it even wish to do so; for no more by the law of reason than by the law of nature can anything occur without a cause.

The undertakings which bind us to the social body are obligatory only because they are mutual; and their nature is such that in fulfilling them we cannot work for others without working for ourselves. Why is it that the general will is always in the right, and that all continually will the happiness of each one, unless it is because there is not a man who does not think of "each" as meaning him, and consider himself in voting for all? This proves that equality of rights and the idea of justice which such equality creates originate in the preference each man gives to himself, and accordingly in the very nature of man. It proves that the general will, to be really such, must be general in its object as well as its essence; that it must both come from all and apply to all; and that it loses its natural rectitude when it is directed to some particular and determinate object, because in such a case we are judging of something foreign to us, and have no true principle of equity to guide us.

Indeed, as soon as a question of particular fact or right arises on a point not previously regulated by a general convention, the matter becomes contentious. It is a case in which the individuals concerned are one party, and the public the other, but in which I can see neither the law that ought to be followed nor the judge who ought to give the decision. In such a case, it would be absurd to propose to refer the question to an express decision of the general will, which can be only the conclusion reached by one of the parties and in consequence will be, for the other party, merely an external and particular will, inclined on this occasion to injustice and subject to error. Thus, just as a particular will cannot stand for the general will, the general will, in turn, changes its nature when its object is particular, and, as general, cannot pronounce on a man or a fact. When, for instance, the people of Athens nominated or displaced its rulers, decreed honors to one, and imposed penalties on another, and, by a multitude of particular decrees, exercised all the functions of government indiscriminately, it had in such cases no longer a general will in the strict sense; it was acting no longer as Sovereign, but as magistrate. This will seem contrary to current views; but I must be given time to expound my own.

It should be seen from the foregoing that what makes the will general is less the number of voters than the common interest uniting them; for, under this system, each necessarily submits to the conditions he imposes on others: and this admirable agreement between interest and justice gives to the common deliberations an equitable character which at once vanishes when any particular question is discussed, in the absence of a common interest to unite and identify the ruling of the judge with that of the party.

From whatever side we approach our principle, we reach the same conclusion, that the social compact sets up among the citizens an equality of such a kind that they all bind themselves to observe the same conditions and should therefore all enjoy the same rights.

Thus, from the very nature of the compact, every act of Sovereignty, i.e. every authentic act of the general will, binds or favors all the citizens equally; so that the Sovereign recognizes only the body of the nation, and draws no distinctions between those of whom it is made up. What, then, strictly speaking, is an act of Sovereignty? It is not a convention between a superior and an inferior, but a convention between the body and each of its members. It is legitimate, because based on the social contract, and equitable, because common to all; useful, because it can have no other object than the general good, and stable, because guaranteed by the public force and the supreme power. So long as the subjects have to submit only to conventions of this sort, they obey no one but their own will; and to ask how far the respective rights of the Sovereign and the citizens extend is to ask up to what point the latter can enter into undertakings with themselves, each with all, and all with each.

We can see from this that the sovereign power, absolute, sacred, and inviolable as it is, does not and cannot exceed the limits of general conventions, and that every man may dispose at will of such goods and liberty as these conventions leave him; so that the Sovereign never has a right to lay more charges on one subject than on another, because, in that case, the question becomes particular, and ceases to be within its competency.

When these distinctions have once been admitted, it is seen to be so untrue that there is, in the social contract, any real renunciation on the part of the individuals, that the position in which they find themselves as a result of the contract is really preferable to that in which they were before. Instead of a renunciation, they have made an advantageous exchange; instead of an uncertain and precarious way of living they have got one that is better and more secure; instead of natural independence they have got liberty, instead of the power to harm others security for themselves, and instead of their strength, which others might overcome, a right which social union makes invincible. Their very life, which they have devoted to the State, is by it constantly protected; and when they risk it in the State's defense, what more are they doing than giving back what they have received from it? What are they doing that they would not do more often and with greater danger in the state of nature, in which they would inevitably have to fight battles at the peril of their lives in defense of that which is the means of their preservation? All have indeed to fight when their country needs them; but then no one has ever to fight for himself. Do we not gain something by running, on behalf of what gives us our security, only some of the risks we should have to run for ourselves, as soon as we lost it? . . .

CHAPTER VII · THE LEGISLATOR

In order to discover the rules of society best suited to nations, a superior intelligence beholding all the passions of men without experiencing any of them would be needed. This intelligence would have to be wholly unrelated to our nature, while knowing it through and through; its happiness would have to be independent of us, and yet ready to occupy itself with ours; and lastly, it would have, in the march of time, to look forward to a distant glory, and, working in one century, to be able to enjoy in the next. It would take gods to give men laws.

What Caligula argued from the facts, Plato, in the dialogue called the *Politicus,* argued in defining the civil or kingly man, on the basis of right. But if great princes are rare, how much more so are great legislators! The former have only to follow the pattern which the latter have to lay down. The legislator is the engineer who invents the machine, the prince merely the mechanic who sets it up and makes it go. "At the birth of societies," says Montesquieu, "the rulers of republics establish institutions and afterwards the institutions mould the rulers."

He who dares to undertake the making of a people's institutions ought to feel himself capable, so to speak, of changing human nature, of transforming each individual, who is by himself a complete and solitary whole, into part of a greater whole from which he in a manner receives his life and being; of altering man's constitution for the purpose of strengthening it; and of substituting a partial and moral existence for the physical and independent existence nature has conferred on us all. He must, in a word, take away from man his own resources and give him instead new ones alien to him, and incapable of being made use of without the help of other men. The more completely these natural resources are annihilated, the greater and the more lasting are those which he acquires, and the more stable and perfect the new institutions; so that if each citizen is nothing and can do nothing without the rest, and the resources acquired by the whole are equal or superior to the aggregate of the resources of all the individuals, it may be said that legislation is at the highest possible point of perfection.

The legislator occupies in every respect an extraordinary position in the State. If he should do so by reason of his genius, he does so no less by reason of his office, which is neither magistracy nor Sovereignty. This office, which sets up the Republic, nowhere enters into its constitution; it is an individual and superior function, which has nothing in common with human empire; for if he who holds command over men ought not to have command over the laws, he who has command over the laws ought not any more to have it over men; or else his laws would be the ministers of his passions and would often merely serve to perpetuate his injustices: his private aims would inevitably mar the sanctity of his work.

When Lycurgus gave laws to his country, he began by resigning the throne. It was the custom of most Greek towns to entrust the establishment of their laws to foreigners. The republics of modern Italy in many cases followed this example: Geneva did the same and profited by it. Rome, when it was most prosperous, suffered a revival of all the crimes of tyranny, and was brought to the verge of destruction, because it put the legislative authority and the sovereign power into the same hands.

Nevertheless, the decemvirs themselves never claimed the right to pass any law merely on their own authority. "Nothing we propose to you," they said to the people, "can pass into law without your consent. Romans, be yourselves the authors of the laws which are to make you happy."

He, therefore, who draws up the laws has, or should have, no right of legislation, and the people cannot, even if it wishes, deprive itself of this incommunicable right, because, according to the fundamental compact, only the general will can bind the individuals, and there can be no assurance that a particular will is in conformity with the general will, until it has been put to the free vote of the people. This I have said already; but it is worthwhile to repeat it.

Thus in the task of legislation we find together two things which appear to be incompatible: an enterprise too difficult for human powers, and, for its execution, an authority that is no authority.

There is a further difficulty that deserves attention. Wise men, if they try to speak their language to the common herd instead of its own, cannot possibly make themselves understood. There are a thousand kinds of ideas which it is impossible to translate into popular language. Conceptions that are too general and objects that are too remote are equally out of its range: each individual, having no taste for any other plan of government than that which suits his particular interest, finds it difficult to realize the advantages he might hope to draw from the continual privations good laws impose. For a young people to be able to relish sound principles of political theory and follow the fundamental rules of statecraft, the effect would have to become the cause: the social spirit which should be created by these institutions would have to preside over their very foundation and men would have to be before law what they should become by means of law. The legislator therefore, being unable to appeal to either force or reason, must have recourse to an authority of a different order, capable of constraining without violence and persuading without convincing.

This is what has, in all ages, compelled the fathers of nations to have recourse to divine intervention and credit the gods with their own wisdom, in order that the peoples, submitting to the laws of the State as to those of nature, and recognizing the same power in the formation of the city as in that of man, might obey freely, and bear with docility the yoke of the public happiness.

This sublime reason, far above the range of the common herd, is that whose decisions the legislator puts into the mouth of the immortals, in order to constrain by divine authority those whom human prudence could not move. But it is not anybody who can make the gods speak, or get himself believed when he proclaims himself their interpreter. The great soul of the legislator is the only miracle that can prove his mission. Any man may grave tablets of stone, or buy an oracle, or feign secret intercourse with some divinity, or train a bird to whisper in his ear, or find other vulgar ways of imposing on the people. He whose knowledge goes no further may perhaps gather round him a band of fools; but he will never found an empire, and his extravagances will quickly perish with him. Idle tricks form a passing tie; only wisdom can make it lasting. The Judaic law, which still subsists, and that of the child of Ishmael, which, for ten centuries has ruled half the world, still proclaim the great men who laid them down; and, while the pride of philosophy or the blind spirit of faction sees in them no more than lucky impostures, the true political theorist admires, in the institutions they set up, the great and powerful genius which presides over things made to endure.

We should not, with Warburton, conclude from this that politics and religion have among us a common object, but that, in the first periods of nations, the one is used as an instrument for the other. . . .

CHAPTER XI · THE VARIOUS SYSTEMS OF LEGISLATION

If we ask in what precisely consists the greatest good of all, which should be the end of every system of legislation, we shall find it reduce itself to two main objects, liberty and equality—liberty, because all particular dependence means so much force taken from the body of the State, and equality, because liberty cannot exist without it.

I have already defined civil liberty. By equality, we should understand, not that the degrees of power and riches are to be absolutely identical for everybody, but that power shall never be great enough for violence, and shall always be exercised by virtue of rank and law; and that, in respect of riches, no citizen shall ever be wealthy enough to buy another, and none poor enough to be forced to sell himself;* which implies, on the part of the great, moderation in goods and position, and, on the side of the common sort, moderation in avarice and covetousness.

Such equality, we are told, is an unpractical ideal that cannot actually exist. But if its abuse is inevitable, does it follow that we should not at least make regulations concerning it? It is precisely because the force of circumstances tends continually to destroy equality that the force of legislation should always tend to its maintenance.

But these general objects of every good legislative system need modifying in every country in accordance with the local situation and the temper of the inhabitants; and these circumstances should determine, in each case, the particular system of institutions which is best, not perhaps in itself, but for the State for which it is destined. If, for instance, the soil is barren and unproductive, or the land too crowded for its inhabitants, the people should turn to industry and the crafts, and exchange what they produce for the commodities they lack. If, on the other hand, a people dwells in rich plains and fertile slopes, or, in a good land, lacks inhabitants, it should give all its attention to agriculture, which causes men to multiply, and should drive out the crafts, which would only result

---

* If the object is to give the State consistency, bring the two extremes as near to each other as possible; allow neither rich men nor beggars. These two estates, which are naturally inseparable, are equally fatal to the common good; from the one come the friends of tyranny, and from the other tyrants. It is always between them that public liberty is put up to auction; the one buys and the other sells.

in depopulation, by grouping in a few localities the few inhabitants there are. If a nation dwells on an extensive and convenient coastline, let it cover the sea with ships and foster commerce and navigation: it will have a life that will be short and glorious. If, on its coasts, the sea washes nothing but almost inaccessible rocks, let it remain barbarous and ichthyphagous: it will have a quieter, perhaps a better, and certainly a happier life. In a word, besides the principles that are common to all, every nation has in itself something that gives them a particular application and makes its legislation peculiarly its own. Thus, among the Jews long ago and more recently among the Arabs, the chief object was religion, among the Athenians letters, at Carthage and Tyre commerce, at Rhodes shipping, at Sparta war, at Rome virtue. The author of *The Spirit of the Laws* has shown with many examples by what art the legislator directs the constitution toward each of these objects.

What makes the constitution of a State really solid and lasting is the due observance of what is proper, so that the natural relations are always in agreement with the laws on every point, and law serves only, so to speak, to assure, accompany and rectify them. But if the legislator mistakes his object and adopts a principle other than circumstances naturally direct, if his principle makes for servitude, while they make for liberty, or if it makes for riches, while they make for populousness, or if it makes for peace, while they make for conquest, the laws will insensibly lose their influence, the constitution will alter, and the State will have no rest from trouble till it is either destroyed or changed, and nature has resumed her invincible sway. . . .

BOOK III

CHAPTER VIII · THAT ALL FORMS OF GOVERNMENT DO NOT SUIT ALL COUNTRIES

Liberty, not being a fruit of all climates, is not within the reach of all peoples. The more this principle, laid down by Montesquieu, is considered, the more its truth is felt: the more it is combated, the more chance is given to confirm it by new proofs.

In all the governments that there are, the public person consumes without producing. Whence, then, does it get what it consumes?

From the labor of its members. The necessities of the public are supplied out of the superfluities of individuals. It follows that the civil State can subsist only so long as men's labor brings them a return greater than their needs.

The amount of this excess is not the same in all countries. In some it is considerable, in others middling, in yet others nil, in some even negative. The relation of product to subsistence depends on the fertility of the climate, on the sort of labor the land demands, on the nature of its products, on the strength of its inhabitants, on the greater or less consumption they find necessary, and on several further considerations of which the whole relation is made up.

On the other side, all governments are not of the same nature: some are less voracious than others, and the differences between them are based on this second principle, that the further from their source the public contributions are removed, the more burdensome they become. The charge should be measured not by the amount of the impositions, but by the path they have to travel in order to get back to those from whom they came. When the circulation is prompt and well established, it does not matter whether much or little is paid; the people is always rich and, financially speaking, all is well. On the contrary, however little the people gives, if that little does not return to it, it is soon exhausted by giving continually: the State is then never rich, and the people is always a people of beggars.

It follows that the more the distance between people and government increases, the more burdensome tribute becomes: thus, in a democracy, the people bears the least charge; in an aristocracy, a greater charge; and, in monarchy, the weight becomes heaviest. Monarchy therefore suits only wealthy nations; aristocracy, States of middling size and wealth; and democracy, States that are small and poor.

In fact, the more we reflect, the more we find the difference between free and monarchical States to be this: in the former, everything is used for the public advantage; in the latter, the public forces and those of individuals are affected by each other, and either increases as the other grows weak; finally, instead of governing subjects to make them happy, despotism makes them wretched in order to govern them.

We find then, in every climate, natural causes according to which the form of government which it requires can be assigned, and we can even say what sort of inhabitants it should have.

Unfriendly and barren lands, where the product does not repay the labor, should remain desert and uncultivated, or peopled only by savages; lands where men's labor brings in no more than the exact minimum necessary to subsistence should be inhabited by barbarous peoples: in such places all polity is impossible. Lands where the surplus of product over labor is only middling are suitable for free peoples; those in which the soil is abundant and fertile and gives a great product for a little labor call for monarchical government, in order that the surplus of superfluities among the subjects may be consumed by the luxury of the prince: for it is better for this excess to be absorbed by the government than dissipated among the individuals. I am aware that there are exceptions; but these exceptions themselves confirm the rule, in that sooner or later they produce revolutions which restore things to the natural order.

General laws should always be distinguished from individual causes that may modify their effects. If all the South were covered with republics and all the North with despotic States, it would be none the less true that, in point of climate, despotism is suitable to hot countries, barbarism to cold countries, and good polity to temperate regions. I see also that, the principle being granted, there may be disputes on its application; it may be said that there are cold countries that are very fertile, and tropical countries that are very unproductive. But this difficulty exists only for those who do not consider the question in all its aspects. We must, as I have already said, take labor, strength, consumption, etc., into account.

Take two tracts of equal extent, one of which brings in five and the other ten. If the inhabitants of the first consume four and those of the second nine, the surplus of the first product will be a fifth and that of the second a tenth. The ratio of these two surpluses will then be inverse to that of the products, and the tract which produces only five will give a surplus double that of the tract which produces ten.

But there is no question of a double product, and I think no one would put the fertility of cold countries, as a general rule, on an equality with that of hot ones. Let us, however, suppose this equality to exist: let us, if you will, regard England as on the same level as Sicily, and Poland as Egypt—farther south, we shall have Africa and the Indies: farther north, nothing at all. To get this equality of product, what a difference there must be in tillage: in Sicily, there is only need to scratch the ground; in England, how men must toil! but where more hands are needed to get the same product, the superfluity must necessarily be less. . . .

CHAPTER XV · DEPUTIES OR REPRESENTATIVES

As soon as public service ceases to be the chief business of the citizens and they would rather serve with their money than with their persons, the State is not far from its fall. When it is necessary to march out to war, they pay troops and stay at home: when it is necessary to meet in council, they name deputies and stay at home. By reason of idleness and money, they end by having soldiers to enslave their country and representatives to sell it.

It is through the hustle of commerce and the arts, through the greedy self-interest of profit, and through softness and love of amenities that personal services are replaced by money payments. Men surrender a part of their profits in order to have time to increase them at leisure. Make gifts of money, and you will not be long without chains. The word "finance" is a slavish word, unknown in the city-state. In a country that is truly free, the citizens do everything with their own arms and nothing by means of money; so far from paying to be exempted from their duties, they would even pay for the privilege of fulfilling them themselves. I am far from taking the common view: I hold enforced labor to be less opposed to liberty than taxes.

The better the constitution of a State is, the more do public affairs encroach on private in the minds of the citizens. Private affairs are even of much less importance, because the aggregate of the common happiness furnishes a greater proportion of that of each individual, so that there is less for him to seek in particular cares. In a well-ordered city every man flies to the assemblies; under a bad government no one cares to stir a step to get to them, because no one is interested in what happens there, because it is foreseen that the general will will not prevail, and lastly because domestic cares are all-absorbing. Good laws lead to the making of better ones; bad ones bring about worse. As soon as any man says of the affairs of the State, "What does it matter to me?," the State may be given up for lost. . . .

BOOK VI

CHAPTER II · VOTING

It may be seen, from the last chapter, that the way in which general business is managed may give a clear enough indication of the actual state of morals and the health of the body politic. The more concert reigns in the assemblies, that is, the nearer opinion approaches unanimity, the greater is the dominance of the general will. On the other hand, long debates, dissensions, and tumult proclaim the ascendancy of particular interests and the decline of the State.

This seems less clear when two or more orders enter into the constitution, as patricians and plebeians did at Rome; for quarrels between these two orders often disturbed the comitia, even in the best days of the Republic. But the exception is rather apparent than real; for then, through the defect that is inherent in the body politic, there were, so to speak, two States in one, and what is not true of the two together is true of either separately. Indeed, even in the most stormy times, the *plebiscita* of the people, when the Senate did not interfere with them, always went through quietly and by large majorities. The citizens having but one interest, the people had but a single will.

At the other extremity of the circle, unanimity recurs; this is the case when the citizens, having fallen into servitude, have lost both liberty and will. Fear and flattery then change votes into acclamation; deliberation ceases, and only worship or malediction is left. Such was the vile manner in which the Senate expressed its views under the emperors. It did so sometimes with absurd precautions. Tacitus observes that, under Otho, the senators, while they heaped curses on Vitellius, contrived at the same time to make a deafening noise, in order that, should he ever become their master, he might not know what each of them had said.

On these various considerations depend the rules by which the methods of counting votes and comparing opinions should be regulated, according as the general will is more or less easy to discover, and the State more or less in its decline.

There is but one law which, from its nature, needs unanimous consent. This is the social compact; for civil association is the most voluntary of all acts. Every man being born free and his own master, no one, under any pretext whatsoever, can make any man subject without his consent. To decide that the son of a slave is born a slave is to decide that he is not born a man.

If then there are opponents when the social compact is made, their opposition does not invalidate the contract, but merely prevents them from being included in it. They are foreigners among citizens. When the State is instituted, residence constitutes consent; to dwell within its territory is to submit to the Sovereign.

Apart from this primitive contract, the vote of the majority always binds all the rest. This follows from the contract itself. But it is asked how a man can be both free and forced to conform to wills that are not his own. How are the opponents at once free and subject to laws they have not agreed to?

I retort that the question is wrongly put. The citizen gives his consent to all the laws, including those which are passed in spite of his opposition, and even those which punish him when he dares to break any of them. The constant will of all the members of the State is the general will; by virtue of it they are citizens and free. When in the popular assembly a law is proposed, what the people is asked is not exactly whether it approves or rejects the proposal, but whether it is in conformity with the general will, which is their will. Each man, in giving his vote, states his opinion on that point; and the general will is found by counting votes. When therefore the opinion that is contrary to my own prevails, this proves neither more nor less than that I was mistaken, and that what I thought to be the general will was not so. If my particular opinion had carried the day I should have achieved the opposite of what was my will; and it is in that case that I should not have been free. . . .

CHAPTER VIII · CIVIL RELIGION

. . . There is therefore a purely civil profession of faith of which the Sovereign should fix the articles, not exactly as religious dogmas, but as social sentiments without which a man cannot be a good citizen or a faithful subject. While it can compel no one to believe them, it can banish from the State whoever does not believe them— it can banish him, not for impiety, but as an antisocial being, incapable of truly loving the laws and justice, and of sacrificing, at need, his life to his duty. If anyone, after publicly recognizing these dogmas, behaves as if he does not believe them, let him be punished by death: he has committed the worst of all crimes, that of lying before the law.

The dogmas of civil religion ought to be few, simple, and exactly worded, without explanation or commentary. The existence of a mighty, intelligent, and beneficent Divinity, possessed of foresight and providence, the life to come, the happiness of the just, the punishment of the wicked, the sanctity of the social contract and the laws: these are its positive dogmas. Its negative dogmas I confine to one, intolerance, which is a part of the cults we have rejected.

Those who distinguish civil from theological intolerance are, to my mind, mistaken. The two forms are inseparable. It is impossible to. live at peace with those we regard as damned; to love them would be to hate God who punishes them: we positively must either reclaim or torment them. Wherever theological intolerance is admitted, it must inevitably have some civil effect; and as soon as it has such an effect, the Sovereign is no longer Sovereign even in the temporal sphere: thenceforth priests are the real masters, and kings only their ministers.

Now that there is and can be no longer an exclusive national religion, tolerance should be given to all religions that tolerate others, so long as their dogmas contain nothing contrary to the duties of citizenship. But whoever dares to say, "Outside the Church is no salvation," ought to be driven from the State, unless the State is the Church, and the prince the pontiff. Such a dogma is good only in a theocratic government; in any other, it is fatal. The reason for which Henry IV is said to have embraced the Roman religion ought to make every honest man leave it, and still more any prince who knows how to reason. . . .

FURTHER READING

Alfred Cobban, *Rousseau and the Modern State* (1934). Though no longer new, worth reading (as everything that Cobban wrote is worth reading). A spirited defense of Rousseau's political ideas against his detractors.

Robert Derathé, *Jean-Jacques Rousseau et la science politique de son temps* (1950). A splendid, full analysis of the sources of Rousseau's political thought.

——, "La Religion civile selon Rousseau," *Annales de la Société Jean-Jacques Rousseau*, Vol. XXXV (1959–62), 161–70. An important appraisal of Rousseau's controversial "civic profession of faith," particularly notable since it is a criticism on the part of a staunch supporter of Rousseau.

John Plamenatz, "Rousseau," in *Man and Society*, Vol. I, *Machiavelli Through Rousseau* (1963) , 364–442. Clear, systematic exposition.

J. L. Talmon, *The Rise of Totalitarian Democracy* (1952) . An attack on Rousseau and his followers as the source of modern totalitarianism. Well-meaning but indefensible. (See R. A. Leigh, "Liberté et autorité dans le Contrat social," in *Jean-Jacques Rousseau et son oeuvre: problèmes et recherches* (1964) , 249–62. This essay overdoes the defense but demolishes the attacker.)

28 ❧ LESSING

The Education of the Human Race

[From *Lessing's Theological Writings*, translated and edited by Henry Chadwick, 82–98.*]

While in general, particularly in Western Europe, the Enlightenment moved to change the general way of thinking in a downright irreligious direction, in the German states theological modes of philosophizing retained their authority right through the eighteenth century, even among Aufklärer. *For balance, therefore, as well as to demonstrate the variety of ideas current in the Enlightenment, I have included this famous theological work by Lessing. Like all true* Aufklärer *Lessing had no patience with superstition and hated intolerance of all kinds.† At the same time, he found the theological modernism popular among advanced German theologians of his day unconvincing and empty. Thus he was happy to publish the posthumous deist fragments of Reimarus,‡ less happy with the open paganism of the likes of Voltaire. His own solution, characteristically highly individual, was to treat Christianity as a historical (and historic) step in mankind's educational history. Mankind, Lessing held, was evolving from stage to stage; the Christian stage had given humanity its primer. This was an essential and by no means unfortunate stage, but it had to be outgrown to permit mankind to discover its adult religion—humane, enlightened, free from all nonsense and intolerance. The crucial doctrine of Lessing's religious teaching was simple; as he put it in his moving brief dialogue of 1777,* Das Testament Johannis, *written when he had practically completed* Die Erziehung des Menschengeschlechts:

---

* Reprinted with the permission of the publishers, Stanford University Press, and A. and C. Black Ltd. Copyright 1956 by A. and C. Black Ltd.

† See below, pages 746–765.

‡ See above, pages 223–228.

"Little children, love each other"—that is the beginning and the end.

While the Erziehung *is Lessing's most ambitious attempt to bring clarity to his basic religious ideas, the continuing debate over his "true" convictions suggests that his attempt was not wholly successful. Yet the document (here reprinted practically complete) is important for what it tells us about Lessing, and about the variety of the Enlightenment as well.*

Gotthold Ephraim Lessing was born in 1729, in the small Saxon town of Kamenz, son of a Lutheran pastor whom he never ceased to respect. In 1746 he attended the University of Leipzig to study theology, but, while religious studies remained a strong interest all his life, literature had a stronger claim on him. By 1749 he was in Berlin, where he struck up a (then highly unusual) friendship with the Jew Moses Mendelssohn; he was already writing poetry and plays. But it was the 1760s, which he spent in Breslau and then in Hamburg, that saw his most important work: his treatise on aesthetics, Laocoön *(published in 1766),* his fine comedy* Minna von Barnhelm *(1767), a fable of reconciliation in which a Prussian officer and a charming Saxon lady symbolically overcome the quarrel between their two states recently at war, and his* Hamburgische Dramaturgie *(1767–69), a series of 104 papers on the theater. From 1770 he held the position of librarian at Wolfenbüttel, superintending the Duke of Brunswick's great library. It was there that he found and published the Reimarus fragments, and there that he wrote his great "tract" on toleration, the verse play* Nathan der Weise. *His contribution to German thought and literature was immense. When he began writing, the German language was clumsy and poverty-stricken, studded with French expressions; the German theater depended on banal farces and on translations from the English and French repertory. Lessing helped to change all this; when he died in 1781, there was a German language, a German theater, a German audience for books and plays, not least because Lessing had lived.*

1. What education is to the individual man, revelation is to the whole human race.

* See below, selection 35.

2. Education is revelation coming to the individual man; and revelation is education which has come, and is still coming, to the human race.

3. Whether it can be of any advantage to the science of instruction to consider education from this point of view I will not here inquire; but in theology it may unquestionably be of great advantage, and may remove many difficulties, if revelation be conceived of as an education of the human race.

4. Education gives man nothing which he could not also get from within himself; it gives him that which he could get from within himself, only quicker and more easily. In the same way too, revelation gives nothing to the human race which human reason could not arrive at on its own; only it has given, and still gives to it, the most important of these things sooner.

5. And just as in education, it is not a matter of indifference in what order the powers of a man are developed, as it cannot impart to a man everything at once; so also God had to maintain a certain order and a certain measure in his revelation.

6. Even though the first man was furnished at once with a conception of the One God; yet it was not possible that this conception, freely imparted and not won by experience, should subsist long in its clearness. As soon as human reason, left to itself, began to elaborate it, it broke up the one immeasurable into many measurables, and gave a distinguishing mark to every one of these parts.

7. Hence naturally arose polytheism and idolatry. And who can say for how many millions of years human reason would have been lost in these errors, even though at all places and times there were individual men who recognized them *as* errors, had it not pleased God to afford it a better direction by means of a new impulse?

8. But when he neither could, nor would, reveal himself any more to *each* individual man, he selected an individual people for his special education; and that the most rude and the most ferocious, in order to begin with it from the very beginning.

9. This was the Hebrew people, about whom we do not even know what kind of divine worship they had in Egypt. For so despised a race of slaves could not have been permitted to take part in the worship of the Egyptians; and the God of their fathers had become entirely unknown to them.

10. It is possible that the Egyptians had expressly prohibited the Hebrews from having a god or gods, and having destroyed their faith, had brought them to the belief that they had no god or gods

whatsoever; that to have a god or gods was the prerogative only of the superior Egyptians; this perhaps in order to be able to tyrannize over them with a greater show of fairness. Do Christians treat their slaves much differently even now?

11. To this rude people God caused himself to be announced at first simply as "the God of their fathers," in order to make them familiar and at home with the idea of a God belonging to them too.

12. Following this, through the miracles with which he led them out of Egypt and planted them in Canaan, he testified of himself to them as a God mightier than any other god.

13. And as he continued demonstrating himself to be the mightiest of all, which only one can be, he gradually accustomed them to the idea of the One.

14. But how far was this conception of the One below the true transcendental conception of the One, which reason, so late, teaches us only to conclude with certainty out of the conception of the infinite!

15. Although the best of the people were already more or less approaching the true conception of the One, the people as a whole could not for a long time elevate themselves to it. And this was the sole reason why they so often abandoned their one God, and expected to find the One, i.e. the mightiest, in some other god belonging to another people.

16. But of what kind of moral education was a people so raw, so incapable of abstract thoughts, and so entirely in their childhood, capable? Of none other but such as is adapted to the age of children, an education by rewards and punishments addressed to the senses.

17. Here too, then, education and revelation come together. As yet God could give to his people no other religion, no other law than one through obedience to which they might hope to be happy, or through disobedience to which they must fear to be unhappy. For as yet they envisaged nothing beyond this life. They knew of no immortality of the soul; they yearned after no life to come. But now to reveal these things, when their reason was so little prepared for them, what would it have been but the same fault in the divine rule as is committed by the vain schoolmaster who chooses to hurry his pupil too rapidly and boast of his progress, rather than thoroughly to ground him?

18. "But," it will be asked, "to what purpose was this education

of so rude a people, a people with whom God had to begin so entirely from the beginning?" I reply: "In order that in the process of time he might all the better employ particular members of this nation as the teachers of all other peoples. He was bringing up in them the future teachers of the human race. These were Jews, these could only be Jews, only men from a people which had been educated in this way."

19. Then further. When the child by dint of blows and caresses had grown and was now come to years of understanding, the Father sent it of a sudden into foreign lands: and here it recognized at once the good which in its Father's house it had possessed, and had not been conscious of.

20. While God guided his chosen people through all the degrees of a child's education, the other nations of the earth had gone on by the light of reason. The most part had remained far behind the chosen people. Only a few had got in front of them. And this, too, takes place with children, who are allowed to grow up on their own; many remain quite raw; some educate themselves to an astonishing degree.

21. But as these more fortunate few prove nothing against the use and necessity of education, so the few heathen nations, who hitherto seemed to be ahead of the chosen people even in the knowledge of God, prove nothing against a revelation. The child of education begins with slow but sure footsteps; it is late in overtaking many a more happily placed child of nature; but it *does* overtake it; and thenceforth can never be overtaken by it again.

22. Similarly—putting aside the doctrine of the unity of God, which in a way is found, and in a way is not found, in the books of the Old Testament—the fact that the doctrine of immortality at least is not to be found in it, but is wholly foreign to it, and all the related doctrine of reward and punishment in a future life, proves just as little against the divine origin of these books. For let us suppose that these doctrines were not only wanting there, but even that they were not even true; let us suppose that for mankind all was over in this life; would the being of God be for this reason less demonstrated? Would God on this account be less at liberty, would it less become him, to take immediate charge of the temporal fortunes of any people out of this perishable race? The miracles which he performed for the Jews, the prophecies which he caused to be recorded through them, were surely not for the few mortal Jews, in whose time they happened and were recorded; his intentions there concerned the whole Jewish people, the entire human race,

who, perhaps, are destined to remain forever here on earth, even though every individual Jew and every individual man dies and is gone forever.

23. Once more, the absence of those doctrines in the writings of the Old Testament proves nothing against their divinity. Moses was sent from God even though the sanction of his law extended only to this life. For why should it extend further? He was surely sent only to the Israelitish people, to the Israelitish people *of that time,* and his commission was perfectly adapted to the knowledge, capacities, inclinations of the *then existing* Israelitish people, as well as to the destiny of the people that was to come. And this is sufficient.

24. So far ought Warburton to have gone, and no further. But that learned man overdrew his bow. Not content that the absence of these doctrines did not *discredit* the divine mission of Moses, it must even be a *proof* to him of the divinity of the mission. If he had only sought this proof in the suitability of such a law for such a people!

But he took refuge in the hypothesis of a miraculous system continued in an unbroken line from Moses to Christ, according to which God had made every individual Jew just as happy or unhappy as his obedience or disobedience to the law deserved. This miraculous system, he said, had compensated for the lack of those doctrines [of eternal rewards and punishments] without which no state can subsist; and precisely this compensation proved what that lack at first sight appeared to deny.

25. How well it was that Warburton could by no argument prove or even make likely this continuous miracle, in which he placed the essence of the Israelitish theocracy. For could he have done so, then indeed, but not until then, he would have made the difficulty really insuperable, for me at least. For the truth which the divinity of Moses' mission was to restore, would, in fact, have been actually made doubtful by it: a truth which God, it is true, did not at that time want to reveal, but which, on the other hand, he certainly did not wish to make harder of attainment.

26. I will illustrate by something that is a counterpart to the process of revelation. A primer for children may fairly pass over in silence this or that important piece of the science or art which it expounds, when the teacher considers that it is not yet suitable for the capabilities of the children for whom he was writing. But it must contain absolutely nothing which bars the way to the knowledge which is held back, or which misleads the children away from it. Rather, all the approaches toward it must be carefully left open;

and to lead them away from even one of these approaches, or to cause them to enter it later than they need, would alone be enough to change the mere imperfection of the primer into an actual fault.

27. In the same way, in the writings of the Old Testament, those primers for the Israelitish people, rough, unpracticed in thought as they are, the doctrines of the immortality of the soul, and future recompense, might be fairly left out; but they were bound to contain nothing which could even have delayed the progress of the people for whom they were written, in their way to this great truth. And what, to say the least, could have delayed them more than the promise of such a miraculous recompense in this life—promised by him who makes no promise that he does not keep?

28. For even if the strongest proof of the immortality of the soul and of a life to come were not to be alleged from the inequality of the distribution of the material rewards in this life, in which so little account appears to be taken of virtue and vice; yet it is at least certain that without this difficulty—to be resolved in the life to come—human reason would still be far from any better and firmer proofs, and perhaps even would never have reached them. For what was to impel it to seek for these better proofs? Mere curiosity?

29. An Israelite here and there, no doubt, might have extended to every individual member of the entire state those promises and threatenings which applied to it as a whole, and been firmly persuaded that whosoever is pious must also be happy, and that whoever was unhappy must be bearing the penalty of his wrongdoing, which penalty would at once change itself into blessing, as soon as he abandoned his sin. One like this appears to have written Job, for the plan of it is entirely in this spirit.

30. But it was impossible that daily experience should confirm this conviction, or else it would have been all over, forever, with the people who had this experience, so far as all recognition and reception were concerned of the truth as yet unfamiliar to them. For if the pious man were absolutely happy, and it was also a necessary part of his happiness that his satisfaction should be broken by no uneasy thoughts of death, and that he should die old and "full of days," how could he yearn for another life? and how could he reflect upon a thing for which he did not yearn? But if the pious did not reflect on it, who then should reflect? The transgressor? he who felt the punishment of his misdeeds, and if he cursed this life must have so gladly renounced that other existence?

31. It was of much less consequence that an Israelite here and

there should directly and expressly have denied the immortality of the soul and future recompense, on the grounds that the law had no reference to it. The denial of an individual, had it even been a Solomon, did not arrest the progress of the common reason, and was in itself even a proof that the nation had now taken a great step nearer to the truth. For individuals only deny what the many are thinking over; and to think over an idea about which before no one troubled himself in the least is halfway to knowledge.

32. Let us also acknowledge that it is a heroic obedience to obey the laws of God simply because they are God's laws, and not because he has promised to reward those who obey them now and hereafter; to obey them even though there be an entire despair of future recompense, and uncertainty respecting a temporal one.

33. Must not a people educated in this heroic obedience toward God be destined, must they not be capable beyond all others of executing divine purposes of quite a special character? Let the soldier who pays blind obedience to his leader also become convinced of his leader's wisdom, and then say what that leader may not venture to do with his aid.

34. As yet the Jewish people had worshiped in their Jehovah rather the mightiest than the wisest of all gods; as yet they had rather feared him as a jealous God than loved him: this too is a proof that the conceptions which they had of their eternal One God were not exactly the right conceptions which we should have of God. However, now the time was come for these conceptions of theirs to be expanded, ennobled, rectified, to accomplish which God availed himself of a perfectly natural means, a better and more correct measure, by which they got the opportunity of appreciating him.

35. Instead of, as hitherto, appreciating him in contrast with the miserable idols of the small neighboring peoples, with whom they lived in constant rivalry, they began, in captivity under the wise Persians, to measure him against the "Being of all Beings" such as a more disciplined reason recognized and worshiped.

36. Revelation had guided their reason, and now, all at once, reason gave clearness to their revelation.

37. This was the first reciprocal influence which these two (reason and revelation) exercised on one another; and so far is such a mutual influence from being unbecoming to the author of them both, that without it either of them would have been useless.

38. The child, sent into foreign lands, saw other children who

knew more, who lived more becomingly, and asked itself, in confusion, "Why do I not know that, too? Why do I not live so, too? Ought I not to have learned and acquired all this in my Father's house?" Thereupon it again sought out its primer, which had long been thrown into a corner, in order to push the blame onto the primer. But behold, it discovers that the blame does not rest upon books, but the blame is solely its own, for not having long ago known this very thing, and lived in this very way.

39. Since the Jews, by this time, through the medium of the pure Persian doctrine, recognized in their Jehovah not simply the greatest of all national deities, but God; and since they could the more readily find him and show him to others in their sacred writings, inasmuch as he was really in them; and since they manifested as great an aversion for sensuous representations, or at all events were shown in these Scriptures as possessing an aversion as great as the Persians had always felt; it is not surprising that they found favor in the eyes of Cyrus with a divine worship which he recognized as being, no doubt, far below pure Sabeism, but yet far above the rude idolatries which in its stead had taken possession of the land of the Jews.

40. Thus enlightened respecting the treasures which they had possessed without knowing it, they returned, and became quite another people, whose first care it was to give permanence to this enlightenment amongst themselves. Soon apostasy and idolatry among them was out of the question. For it is possible to be faithless to a national deity, but never to God, after he has once been recognized.

41. The theologians have tried to explain this complete change in the Jewish people in different ways; and one who has well demonstrated the insufficiency of these explanations wanted finally to give, as the true reason, "the visible fulfillment of the prophecies which had been spoken and written respecting the Babylonian captivity and the restoration from it." But even this reason can be true only insofar as it presupposes the exalted ideas of God as they now are. The Jews must now, for the first time, have recognized that to do miracles and to predict the future belonged only to God, both of which powers they had formerly ascribed also to false idols; this precisely is the reason why miracles and prophecies had hitherto made so weak and fleeting an impression upon them.

42. Doubtless the Jews became better acquainted with the doctrine of immortality among the Chaldeans and Persians. They

became more familiar with it, too, in the schools of the Greek philosophers in Egypt.

43. However, as this doctrine did not correspond with their Scriptures in the same way that the doctrines of God's unity and attributes had done—since the former were entirely overlooked by that sensual people, while the latter would be sought for: and since, too, for the former, previous exercising was necessary, and as yet there had been only *hints* and *allusions,* the faith in the immortality of the soul could naturally never be the faith of the entire people. It was and continued to be only the creed of a certain section of them.

44. An example of what I mean by "previous exercising" in the doctrines of immortality is the divine threat of punishing the misdeeds of the father upon his children unto the third and fourth generation. This accustomed the fathers to live in thought with their remotest posterity, and to feel in advance the misfortunes which they had brought upon these innocents.

45. What I mean by an "allusion" is something which might merely excite curiosity or call forth a question. As, for instance, the common figure of speech which describes death by "he was gathered to his fathers."

46. By a "hint" I mean something which contains some sort of germ, from which the truth which up to now has been held back may be developed. Of this character was the inference of Christ from God's title as "the God of Abraham, Isaac, and Jacob." This hint appears to me to be undoubtedly capable of development into a strong proof.

47. In such exercises, allusions, hints, consists the *positive* perfection of a primer; just as the above-mentioned quality of not putting difficulties or hindrances in the way to the truths that have been withheld constitutes its *negative* perfection.

48. Add to all this the clothing and the style.

(1) The clothing of abstract truths which could scarcely be passed over, in allegories and instructive single circumstances, which were narrated as actual occurrences. Of this character are creation in the image of growing day; the origin of evil in the story of the forbidden tree; the source of the variety of languages in the story of the tower of Babel, etc.

49. (2) The style—sometimes plain and simple, sometimes poetical, throughout full of tautologies, but of such as call for a sharp wit, since they sometimes appear to be saying something else,

and yet say the same thing; sometimes seem to say the same thing over again, and yet to mean or to be capable of meaning, basically, something else:—

50. And there you have all the good qualities of a primer both for children and for a childlike people.

51. But every primer is only for a certain age. To delay the child, that has outgrown it, longer at it than was intended, is harmful. For to be able to do this in a way which is at all profitable, you must insert into it more than there is really in it, and extract from it more than it can contain. You must look for and make too much of allusions and hints; squeeze allegories too closely; interpret examples too circumstantially; press too much upon words. This gives the child a petty, crooked, hairsplitting understanding: it makes him full of mysteries, superstitious, full of contempt for all that is comprehensible and easy.

52. The very way in which the Rabbis handled *their* sacred books! The very character which they thereby imparted to the spirit of their people!

53. A better instructor must come and tear the exhausted primer from the child's hands—Christ came!

54. That portion of the human race which God had wished to embrace in one plan of education was ripe for the second great step. He had, however, only wished to embrace in such a plan that part of the human race which by language, habits, government, and other natural and political relationships was already united in itself.

55. That is, this portion of the human race had come so far in the exercise of its reason as to need, and to be able to make use of, nobler and worthier motives for moral action than temporal rewards and punishments, which had hitherto been its guides. The child has become a youth. Sweetmeats and toys have given place to an awakening desire to be as free, as honored, and as happy as its elder brother.

56. For a long time, already, the best individuals of that portion of the human race had been accustomed to let themselves be ruled by the shadow of such nobler motives. The Greek and Roman did everything to live on after this life, even if it were only in the memories of their fellow citizens.

57. It was time that another *true* life to be expected after this one should gain an influence over the youth's actions.

58. And so Christ was the first *reliable, practical* teacher of the immortality of the soul.

59. The first *reliable* teacher. Reliable, by reason of the prophecies which were fulfilled in him; reliable by reason of the miracles which he achieved; reliable by reason of his own revival after a death by which he had put the seal to his teaching. Whether we can still *prove* this revival, these miracles, I put aside, as I leave on one side *who* the person of Christ was. All *that* may have been at that time of great importance for the first acceptance of his teaching, but it is now no longer of the same importance for the recognition of the *truth* of his teaching.

60. The first *practical* teacher. For it is one thing to conjecture, to wish, and to believe in the immortality of the soul, as a philosophic speculation; quite another thing to direct one's inner and outer actions in accordance with it.

61. And this at least Christ was the first to teach. For although, before him, the belief had already been introduced among many nations that bad actions have yet to be punished in the life to come, yet they were only such actions as were injurious to civil society, and which had, therefore, already had their punishment in civil society, too. To preach an inward purity of heart in reference to another life was reserved for him alone.

62. His disciples have faithfully propagated this teaching: and even if they had had no other merit than that of having effected a more general publication among other nations of a truth which Christ had appeared to have destined for the Jews alone, yet if only on that account they would have to be reckoned among the benefactors and fosterers of the human race.

63. If, however, they mixed up this one great truth together with other doctrines whose truth was less enlightening, whose usefulness was less considerable, how could it be otherwise? Let us not blame them for this, but rather seriously examine whether these very commingled doctrines have not become a new directing impulse for human reason.

64. At least, it is already clear from our experience that the New Testament Scriptures, in which these doctrines after some time were found preserved, have afforded, and still afford, the second, better primer for the race of man.

65. For seventeen hundred years past they have occupied human reason more than all other books, and enlightened it more, were it even only through the light which human reason itself put into them.

66. It would have been impossible for any other book to become so generally known among such different nations; and, indisput-

ably, the fact that modes of thought so completely diverse from each other have turned their attention to this same book has assisted human reason on its way more than if every nation had had its *own* primer specially for itself.

67. It was also most necessary that each people should for a time consider this book as the *non plus ultra* of their knowledge. For the youth must believe his primer to be the first of all books, so that his impatience to be finished with it may not hurry him on to things for which he has not yet laid the foundations.

68. And that is also of the greatest importance now. You who are cleverer than the rest, who wait fretting and impatient on the last page of the prime, take care! Take care that you do not let your weaker classmates notice what you are beginning to scent, or even see!

69. Until these weaker fellows of yours have caught up with you it is better that you should return once more to this primer, and examine whether that which you take only for variations of method, for superfluous verbiage in the teaching, is not perhaps something more.

70. You have seen in the childhood of the human race, in the doctrine of the Unity of God, that God makes immediate revelations of mere truths of reason, or has permitted and caused pure truths of reason to be taught, for a time, as truths of immediate revelation, in order to promulgate them the more rapidly, and ground them the more firmly.

71. You learn in the childhood of the human race the same thing, in the doctrine of the immortality of the soul. It is *preached* in the second, better primer as revelation, not *taught* as a result of human reason.

72. As we by this time can dispense with the Old Testament for the doctrine of the unity of God, and as we are gradually beginning also to be less dependent on the New Testament for the doctrine of the immortality of the soul, might there not be mirrored in this book also other truths of the same kind, which we are to gaze at in awe as revelations, just until reason learns to deduce them from its other demonstrated truths, and to connect them with them?

73. For instance, the doctrine of the Trinity. How if this doctrine should in the end, after countless waverings to one side or the other, merely bring human reason on the path to recognizing that God cannot possibly be One in the sense in which finite things are one, that even his unity must be a transcendental unity which does not exclude a sort of plurality? Must not God at least have the most

perfect conception of himself, i.e. a conception which contains everything which is in him? But would everything be contained in it which is in him, if it contained merely a conception, merely the possibility even of his necessary reality, as well as of his other qualities? This possibility exhausts the being of his other qualities. Does it exhaust that of his necessary reality? I think not. Consequently either God can have no perfect conception of himself at all or this perfect conception is just as necessarily real (i.e. actually existent) as he himself is. Admittedly the image of myself in the mirror is nothing but an empty representation of me, because it has only that of me which is reflected by rays of light falling on its surface. If, however, this image contained everything, everything without exception, which is contained in me, would it then still be a mere empty representation, or not rather a true double of myself? When I believe that I recognize in God a similar reduplication, I perhaps do not so much err as that my language is insufficient for my ideas; and so much at least remains forever incontrovertible that those who want to make the idea acceptable to the popular intelligence could scarcely have expressed themselves in a more apt and comprehensible form than by giving the name of a Son whom God begets from eternity.

74. And the doctrine of original sin. How if finally everything were to convince us that man, standing on the first and lowest step of his humanity, is by no means so much master of his actions that he is *able* to obey moral laws?

75. And the doctrine of the Son's satisfaction. How if everything finally compelled us to assume that God, in spite of that original incapacity of man, chose rather to give him moral laws and forgive him all transgressions in consideration of his Son, i.e. in consideration of the living embodiment of all his own perfections, compared with which, and in which, all imperfections of the individual disappear, than *not* to give him those laws, and thus to exclude him from all moral bliss, which cannot be conceived of without moral laws?

76. Let it not be objected that speculations of this nature upon the mysteries of religion are forbidden. The word "mystery" signified, in the first age of Christianity, something quite different from what it means now; and the development of revealed truths into truths of reason is absolutely necessary if the human race is to be assisted by them. When they were revealed they were certainly not truths of reason, but they were revealed in order to become such. They were like the "facit" said to his boys by the mathematics

master; he goes on ahead of them in order to indicate to some extent the lines they should follow in their sums. If the scholars were to be satisfied with the "facit," they would never learn to do sums, and would frustrate the intention with which their good master gave them a guiding clue in their work.

77. And why should not we too, by means of a religion whose historical truth, if you will, looks dubious, be led in a similar way to closer and better conceptions of the divine Being, of our own nature, of our relation to God, which human reason would never have reached on its own?

78. It is not true that speculations upon these things have ever done harm or been injurious to civil society. Reproach is due, not to these speculations, but to the folly and tyranny which tried to keep them in bondage; a folly and tyranny which would not allow men to develop their own thoughts.

79. On the contrary, though they may in individual instances be found wanting, speculations of this sort are unquestionably the most fitting exercises of the human reason that exist, just as long as the human heart, as such, is capable to the highest degree of loving virtue for its eternal blessed consequences.

80. For this selfishness of the human heart, which wishes to exercise its understanding only on that which concerns our bodily needs, succeeds in blunting rather than in sharpening it. It is absolutely necessary for it to be exercised on spiritual objects, if it is to attain its perfect illumination, and bring out that purity of heart which makes us capable of loving virtue for its own sake alone.

81. Or is the human species never to arrive at this highest step of illumination and purity?—Never?

82. Never?—Let me not think this blasphemy, All Merciful! Education has its goal, in the race, no less than in the individual. That which is educated is educated for a purpose.

83. The flattering prospects which are opened to the youth, the honor and well-being which are held out to him, what are they more than means of educating him to become a man, who, when these prospects of honor and well-being have vanished, shall be able to do his *duty?*

84. This is the aim of *human* education, and does the divine education not extend as far? Is nature not to succeed with the whole, as art succeeded with the individual? Blasphemy! Blasphemy!

85. No! It will come! it will assuredly come! the time of the perfecting, when man, the more convinced his understanding feels about an ever better future, will nevertheless not need to borrow motives for his actions from this future; for he will do right because it *is* right, not because arbitrary rewards are set upon it, which formerly were intended simply to fix and strengthen his unsteady gaze in recognizing the inner, better rewards of well-doing.

86. It will assuredly come! the time of a new eternal gospel, which is promised us in the primers of the New Covenant itself!

87. Perhaps even some enthusiasts of the thirteenth and four-teenth centuries had caught a glimmer of this new eternal gospel, and erred only in that they predicted its arrival as so near to their own time.

88. Perhaps their "Three Ages of the World" were not so empty a speculation after all, and assuredly they had no bad intentions when they taught that the new covenant must become as antiquated as the old has become. There remained with them the same economy of the same God. Ever, to put my own expression into their mouths, ever the selfsame plan of the education of the human race.

89. Only they were premature. They believed that they could make their contemporaries, who had scarcely outgrown their child-hood, without enlightenment, without preparation, at one stroke men worthy of their *third age.*

90. And it was just this which made them enthusiasts. The enthusiast often casts true glances into the future, but for this future he cannot wait. He wants this future to come quickly, and to be made to come quickly through him. A thing over which nature takes thousands of years is to come to maturity just at the moment of his experience. For what part has he in it, if that which he recognizes as the best does not become the best in his lifetime? Does he come again? Does he expect to come again? It is strange that this enthusiasm is not more the fashion, if it were only among en-thusiasts.

91. Go thine inscrutable way, Eternal Providence! Only let me not despair of thee because of this inscrutableness. Let me not despair of thee, even if thy steps appear to me to be going back-ward. It is not true that the shortest line is always straight.

92. Thou hast on thine eternal way so much that thou must concern thyself with, so much to attend to! And what if it were as good as proved that the great, slow wheel which brings mankind nearer to its perfection is set in motion only by smaller, faster

wheels, each of which contributes its own individual part to the whole?

93. It is so! Must every individual man—one sooner, another later—have traveled along the very same path by which the race reaches its perfection? Have traveled along it in one and the same life? Can he have been, in one and the selfsame life, a sensual Jew and a spiritual Christian? Can he in the selfsame life have overtaken both?

94. Surely not that! But why should not every individual man have been present more than once in this world?

95. Is this hypothesis so laughable merely because it is the oldest? Because human understanding, before the sophistries of the Schools had dissipated and weakened it, lighted upon it at once?

96. Why may not even I have already performed all those steps toward my perfection which merely temporal penalties and rewards can bring man to?

97. And, once more, why not all those steps, to perform which the prospects of eternal rewards so powerfully assist us?

98. Why should I not come back as often as I am capable of acquiring new knowledge, new skills? Do I bring away so much from one visit that it is perhaps not worth the trouble of coming again?

99. Is this a reason against it? Or, because I forget that I have been here already? Happy is it for me that I do forget. The recollection of my former condition would permit me to make only a bad use of the present. And that which I must forget *now*, is that necessarily forgotten forever?

100. Or is it a reason against the hypothesis that so much time would have been lost to me? Lost?—And what then have I to lose?—Is not the whole of eternity mine?

FURTHER READING

Wilhelm Dilthey, "Gotthold Ephraim Lessing," in *Das Erlebnis und die Dichtung*, 8th edn. (1922). A penetrating account of Lessing's life and place in German literature.

H. B. Garland, *Lessing, the Founder of Modern German Literature* (1937). The best available biography of Lessing in English; it deserves to be superseded.

Franz Mehring, *Die Lessinglegende* (1893). Ancient but fascinating Marxist interpretation of the way the German bourgeoisie had appropriated Lessing.

Erich Schmidt, *Lessing: Geschichte seines Lebens und seiner Schriften*, 2 vols., 4th edn. (1923). While stodgy, it is very full and authoritative.

Benno von Wiese, *Lessing: Dichtung, Aesthetik, Philosophie* (1931). A thoughtful and suggestive essay.

29 ❁ HOLBACH

Système de la nature

[From "Mirabaud" (Holbach), *The System of Nature*, 4 vols. (1797), I, 17–32; IV, 676–79, 692–96.]

Doubtless the most consistent and most articulate atheist among the philosophes was Baron d'Holbach. To him and to his associates, changing the general way of thinking would be a success only when mankind had cast aside all religions of all description. Born in the Palatinate in 1723, Paul Henri Thiry, Baron d'Holbach, lived in and near Paris from his childhood; rich and moody, he associated with philosophes all his life, talking atheism and furthering the Cause. Diderot was for long Holbach's close friend, frequent guest, and valued collaborator: the hymn to nature with which our selection ends has been attributed to him. Not everyone, even in the Enlightened camp, cared for Holbach's style; Hume found Holbach's views too dogmatic for his tastes, and Goethe late in life remembered that when he had first come upon Holbach's writings their "arrogance" had put him off philosophy, "and especially metaphysics."

Be that as it may, the Holbachian circle had its impact. It was a small circle—smaller than hopeful philosophes and fearful Christians thought—but it was a busy one. The Holbachian "factory" rescued obscure English deists from oblivion by translating their works and abbreviating their polemics; it rescued, as well, even more obscure French antireligious manuscripts and gave them circulation in print. The specialty of the group was to publish their own unrespectable writings under respectable pseudonyms; sometimes they engaged in some rather heavy-handed humor, reserved for the insiders. Thus, Holbach attributed his main work, the Sys-tem of Nature (1770), to Mirabaud, a former secretary of the

French Academy, who had in fact been dead since 1760. Then, in 1772, Holbach published his Bon-sens *and slyly attributed it to the "author of the* Système de la nature." *In these advanced circles, even telling the truth was intended to deceive the authorities.*

The point of Holbach's System of Nature *is very simple—too simple for the taste of most philosophers; Ernst Cassirer, in his authoritative book on the Enlightenment, dismisses this materialist work as "an isolated phenomenon of no characteristic significance."* This overstates the case. The book and Holbach's other very similar works are effective variations on the theme that religion is a kind of "sacred contagion," fostered by self-interested priests and equally self-interested rulers. Once the fraud that is organized religion has been penetrated, men will be free and happy. It was precisely Holbach's simplicity that helped to get this message to its public.*

Man always deceives himself when he abandons experience to follow imaginary systems. Man is the work of nature: he exists in nature; he is submitted to her laws; he cannot deliver himself from them; he cannot step beyond them, even in thought; it is in vain that his mind would spring forward beyond the bounds of the visible world—he is always necessitated to return. For a being formed by nature and circumscribed by her, there exists nothing beyond the great whole of which he forms a part and of which he experiences the influence. The beings whom he supposes to be above nature or distinguished from her are always chimeras of which it is impossible he should ever form any just idea either of the place they occupy or of their manner of acting. There is nothing, there can be nothing, out of that nature, which includes all beings.

Let man cease, then, to search out of the world he inhabits for beings who can procure him a happiness that nature denies him; let him study this nature, let him learn her laws, let him contemplate her energies and the immutable rules by which she acts; let him apply these discoveries to his own felicity, and let him submit in silence to her laws, which nothing can alter; let him consent to be ignorant of causes hid from him under the most impenetrable veil;

* *Philosophy of the Enlightenment* (tr. 1951), 55.

let him submit without murmuring to the decrees of a universal necessity which can never be brought within his comprehension nor ever emancipate him from those rules his essence has imposed upon him.

The distinction that has so often been made betwixt the *physical* and *moral* man is evidently an abuse. Man is a being purely physical; the moral man is only this physical being considered under a certain point of view; that is to say relatively to some of his modes of action owing to his particular organization. But is not this organization the work of nature? The motion or impulse to action of which he is susceptible, is it not physical? His visible actions as well as the invisible motions interiorly excited, arising from his will or his thoughts, are equally the natural effects and necessary consequences of his peculiar mechanism, and the impulse he receives from those beings by whom he is surrounded. All that the human mind has successively invented to change or perfect his being, and to render himself happier, was never more than the necessary consequence of the peculiar essence of man and that of the beings who acted on him. All our institutions, all our reflections, all our knowledge, have nothing more for their object than to procure us that happiness toward which our peculiar nature has a tendency to impel us incessantly. All that we do or think, all that we are or that we shall be, is nothing more than the consequence of what universal nature has made us. All our ideas, our wills, our actions, are the necessary effects of those qualities and of the essence which nature has infused in us, and of those circumstances through which she has obliged us to pass and by which she regulates us. In short, ART is only nature acting with the tools she has made.

Nature sends man naked and destitute of succors into this world which is to be his abode; he quickly learns to cover his nakedness with the skins of wild beasts; by degrees, we see him establish manufactories of silk and of gold. To a being elevated above our globe, and who, from the height of the atmosphere, should contemplate the human species in all its progress and changes, man would not seem less subjected to the laws of nature when he is naked in the forest, painfully seeking his nutriment, than when he is living in civilized society—that is to say, enriched with greater experience and plunged in luxury, where he every day invents a thousand new wants and discovers a thousand means of satisfying them. All the steps we take to regulate our existence can only be regarded as a long succession of causes and effects which are no more than the development of the first impulse given us by nature. The same animal, by virtue of his organization, passes successively from the most simple to the most complicated wants, but it is nevertheless the consequence of its nature. It is thus that the butterfly whose beauty we so much admire commences by being an inanimate egg, out of which heat produces a worm; this becomes a chrysalis, and then changes into that winged insect which we see decorated with the most brilliant colors; arrived at this form, he reproduces and propagates; at last, despoiled of his ornaments, he is obliged to disappear, having fulfilled the task imposed upon him by nature, or having described the circle of mutation which she has marked out for the beings of his species.

We see similar progress and changes in all vegetables. It is by a succession of combinations which nature has interwoven in the original energies given to the aloe that this plant is insensibly regulated and enlarged, and produces, at the end of a great number of years, those flowers which announce its death.

It is the same with man, who in all his motions and all the changes he experiences never acts but after the laws peculiar to his organization, and to the matter of which nature has composed him. The physical man is he who acts by the impulse of causes which our senses make us understand. The moral man is he who acts by physical causes with which our prejudices prevent us from being acquainted. The wild man is a child destitute of experience and incapable of pursuing his happiness. The civilized man is he whom experience and social life have enabled to draw from nature the means of his own happiness. The enlightened man is man in his maturity, or in his perfection. The happy man is he who knows how to enjoy the benefits of nature. The unhappy man is he who finds himself incapacitated to profit by her bounty.

It is, then, to natural philosophy and to experience that man ought always to recur in his researches: these are what he ought to consult in his religion, in his morals, in his legislation, in his political government, in the arts and sciences, in his pleasures, and in his misfortunes. Experience enables us to know that nature acts by simple, uniform, and invariable laws. It is by our senses we are bound to universal nature; it is by our senses that we can experience and discover her secrets; whenever we quit experience, we fall into a gulf, and our imagination leads us astray.

All the errors of men are physical errors; they never deceive themselves but when they neglect to return to nature, to consult her rules, and to call experience to their aid. It is for want of experience that they form such imperfect ideas of matter, of its properties, of its combinations, of its force, of its manner of action, or of the energy which results from its essence; of course the whole universe becomes to them but a scene of illusions. They are ignorant of nature, they have mistaken her laws, they have not seen the necessary routine that she has marked out for all that she contains. What did I say? They have mistaken themselves: all their systems, all their conjectures, all their reasonings from which experience has been banished are but a long string of errors and absurdities.

All error is prejudicial to man; it is by deceiving itself that the human race has become miserable. For want of understanding nature, men have formed gods who have become the sole object of their hopes and their fears. Men have not felt that nature, equally destitute of goodness as of malice, follows only necessary and immutable laws in producing and destroying beings, in making those sometimes suffer whom she has endued with sensibility, in distributing to them good and evil, and in subjecting them to incessant change. They have not seen that it was in nature herself, and in her natural abundance, that man ought to seek for his wants, for remedies against his pains, and for the means of rendering himself happy; they have expected these things from some imaginary beings whom they have supposed to be the authors of their pleasures and their misfortunes; from whence we may see that it is to their ignorance of nature that must be attributed those unknown powers under which the human race has so long trembled, and that superstitious worship that has been the source of all its misery.

It is for want of knowing his peculiar nature, his proper tendency, his wants, and his rights, that man has fallen in society, from LIBERTY into SLAVERY. He had forgotten or believed himself obliged to smother the desires of his heart, and to sacrifice his well-being to the caprice of his chiefs; he was ignorant of the end of association and of government; he submitted himself without reserve to men like himself whom his prejudices made him regard as beings of a superior order, as gods upon earth; these, to enslave him, profited of his ignorance, corrupted him, rendered him vicious and miserable. It is thus, for having been ignorant of its peculiar nature, that the human race has fallen into servitude and has been wickedly governed.

It is for having mistaken himself, and for having been ignorant of the necessary affinity that subsisted between him and the beings of his own species, that man has mistaken his duty to others. He did not judge rightly what was necessary to his felicity, he did not see what he owed to himself: those excesses he ought to avoid to render him solidly happy; the passions he ought to resist, or follow for his comfort and advantage. In short, he did not know his true interest. Hence all his irregularities, his intemperance, his shameful voluptuousness, and all those vices to which he gave himself up at the expense of his preservation and his durable felicity. It is therefore the ignorance of human nature that has prevented man from enlightening his morals. Besides, the depraved governments to which he was submitted always prevented him from practicing them even when he knew them.

It is also for want of having studied nature and her laws, for want of having sought to discover her resources and her properties, that man has remained so long in ignorance, or that he has taken such slow and irresolute steps to ameliorate his condition. His sluggishness finds its account by letting him be guided by precedent, routine, or authority rather than by experience, which demands activity, and by his reason, which exacts reflection. Hence that aversion that men show for everything that makes them swerve from those rules to which they have been accustomed. Hence their stupid and scrupulous respect for antiquity and for the most foolish institutions of their fathers. Hence those fears that seize them when the most advantageous changes are proposed to them, or the most probable attempts. This is the reason why we see nations lingering in the most shameful lethargy, groaning under those abuses that have been transmitted from century to century, trembling at the very idea of what alone can remedy their misfortunes. It is by this want of energy, and for want of consulting experience, that medicine, natural philosophy, agriculture, and, in short, all the useful sciences, have made such little progress and have remained so long under the shackles of authority. Those who profess these sciences prefer rather to follow the beaten tracts than to trace out new ones; they prefer the ravings of their imagination, and their gratuitous conjectures to that laborious experience which alone is capable of extracting from nature her secrets.

In short, men, whether from sloth or from fear, having renounced the evidence of their senses, have only been guided in their actions and enterprises by imagination, enthusiasm, habit, prejudice, and, above all, authority, which well knew how to profit from their ignorance and to deceive them. Imaginary systems supplied the place of experience, reflection, and reason. Souls petrified with terror and inebriated with the marvelous, or benumbed with sloth and guided by credulity, which produces inexperience, created ridiculous opinions or else adopted without examination all those chimeras with which they wished to gorge themselves.

It is therefore for having forgotten nature and her ways, for having disdained experience, for having neglected reason, for having desired the marvelous and supernatural—in short, for having TREMBLED—that the human race has so long continued in a state of infancy, out of which there is so much trouble in conducting them. They have had only the most childish hypotheses, of which they have never dared to examine the principles and the proofs; they have been accustomed to hold them sacred, as the most perfect truths, of which they were not permitted to doubt even for an instant. The ignorance of man has rendered him credulous; his curiosity made him swallow, in large draughts, the marvelous; time confirmed him in his opinions, and he passed his conjectures from race to race for realities. A tyrannical force maintained him in his notions, now become so necessary for enslaving society. At length the whole science of man, of every kind, was but a heap of falsehoods, darkness, and contradictions, interspersed here and there with the faint glimmerings of truth furnished by nature, of which they can never totally divest themselves, because their necessities always bring them back to her.

Let us, then, raise ourselves above these clouds of prejudice. Let us leave this heavy atmosphere that envelops us, to consider the opinions of men, and their various systems. Let us distrust a disordered imagination and take experience for our guide. Let us consult nature. Let us draw our ideas from nature herself of those objects that she contains. Let us recur to our senses, which we have been made erroneously to suspect. Let us interrogate that reason which has been shamefully calumniated and disgraced. Let us contemplate attentively the visible world, and let us see if it will not suffice and enable us to judge of the unknown territory of the intellectual world; perhaps we shall find there has been no reason for distinguishing them, and that it was without motive that two empires have been separated which are equally the inheritance of nature.

The universe, that vast assemblage of all that exists, offers everywhere but matter and motion. The whole presents to us but an immense and uninterrupted succession of causes and effects. Some of these causes are known to us, because they strike immediately on our senses; others are unknown to us, because they act upon us by effects frequently very remote from their first cause.

A great variety of matter, combined in an infinity of forms, receives and communicates incessantly various motions. The different properties of this matter, its different combinations, its various methods of action which is the necessary consequence, constitute for us the *essence* of beings and it is from these diversified essences that result the different orders, classes, or systems that these beings occupy, and of which the sum total makes what we call NATURE.

Therefore, nature in its most extended signification is the great whole that results from the assemblage of different matter, of its different combinations, and of their different motions, which the universe presents to our view. Nature in a less extended sense, or considered in each being, is the whole that results from its essence, that is to say, of the properties, combinations, motions, or different modes of action by which it is distinguished from other beings. It is thus that man is, in the whole, the result of the combination of certain matter, endowed with peculiar properties, of which the arrangement is called *organization,* and of which the essence is to feel, to think, to act, and, in short, to move after a manner distinguished from other beings with which he can be compared. After this comparison man ranks in an order, a system, a class by himself, which differs from that of animals, in whom we see not the properties of which he is possessed. The different systems of beings, or, if they will, their *particular natures,* depend on the general system of the grand whole of universal nature of which they form a part, and to which everything that exists is necessarily attached. . . .

. . . Listen, then, to NATURE, she never contradicts herself.

"O ye" says she, "who, after the impulsion which I have given you, tend toward happiness in every instant of your existence, do not resist my sovereign law. Labor to your felicity; enjoy without fear, and be happy; you will find the means written in your heart. Vainly, O superstitious being, seekest thou thine happiness beyond the limits of the universe in which my hand hath placed thee. Vainly shalt thou ask it of those inexorable phantoms which thine imagination would establish upon my eternal throne; vainly dost thou expect it in those celestial regions which thy delirium hath created; vainly dost thou reckon upon those capricious deities with whose benevolence thou art in ecstacies, whilst they only fill thine abode with calamities, with fears, with groans, and with illusions. Dare, then, to affranchise thyself from this religion, my self-conceited rival who mistakes my rights; renounce these gods who are usurpers of my power, and return under the dominion of my laws. It is in my empire that liberty reigns. Tyranny and slavery are banished from it forever; equity watches over the security of my subjects and maintains them in their rights; benevolence and humanity connect them by amicable bonds; truth enlightens them; and never can imposture blind them with its dark clouds.

"Return, then, my child; deserter, return to Nature! She will console thee, she will drive from thine heart those fears which overwhelm thee, those inquietudes that distract thee, those transports which agitate thee, those hatreds which separate thee from man, whom thou shouldst love. Return to Nature, to Humanity, to thyself; strew flowers over the road of life; cease to contemplate the future; live for thyself, live for thy fellow creatures, descend into thine interior; consider afterward the sensitive beings that environ thee, and leave those gods who can do nothing for thy felicity. Enjoy and cause to be enjoyed those benefits which I have placed in common for all the children of the earth, who have all emanated equally from my bosom; assist them to support the sorrows to which destiny has submitted them as well as thee. I approve thy pleasures when, without injuring thyself, they are not fatal to thy brethren, whom I have rendered necessary to thine own peculiar happiness. These pleasures are permitted thee if thou usest them in that due proportion which I myself have fixed. Be, then, happy, O man, nature invites thee to it, but remember that thou canst not be so alone; I invite all mortals to happiness as well as thee, it is only in rendering them happy that thou wilt be so thyself; such is the order of destiny; if thou attemptest to withdraw thyself from it, remember that hatred, vengeance, and remorse are always ready to punish the infraction of its irrevocable decrees. . . ." . . .

The morality of nature is the only religion which the interpreter of nature offers to his fellow citizens, to nations, to the human species, to future races weaned from those prejudices which have so frequently disturbed the felicity of their ancestors. The friend of mankind cannot be the friend of the gods, who were in all times the real scourges of the earth. The apostle of nature will not be the instrument of deceitful chimeras, who make this world only an abode of illusions; the adorer of truth will not compromise with falsehood, he will make no covenant with error, of which the consequence will never be other than fatal to mortals; he knows that the happiness of the human species exacts that the dark and unsteady edifice of superstition should be destroyed from top to bottom, in order to elevate to nature, to peace, to virtue, the temple which is suitable to them. He knows that it is only by extirpating, even to the very roots, the poisonous tree which, during so many ages, has overshadowed the universe, that the eyes of the inhabitants of this world will be able to perceive that light which is suitable to illumine them, to guide them, and to warm their souls. If his efforts are vain, if he cannot inspire with courage those beings too much accustomed to tremble, he will applaud himself for having dared to make the attempt. Nevertheless, he will not judge his efforts useless if he has been able to make only one mortal happy, if his principles have calmed the transports of one honest soul, if his reasonings have cheered up some virtuous hearts. He will at least have the advantage of having banished from his mind the importunate terrors of the superstitious, of having driven from his heart the gall which exasperates zeal, of having trodden under his feet those chimeras with which the uninformed are tormented. Thus escaped from the tempest, he will contemplate from the summit of his rock those storms which the gods excite upon the earth; he will hold forth a succoring hand to those who shall be willing to accept it. He will encourage them with his voice, he will second them with his prayers, and in the warmth of his compassionate heart he will exclaim:

O NATURE, sovereign of all beings, and ye its adorable daughters, VIRTUE, REASON, and TRUTH, remain forever our only divinities; it is to you that belong the praises and the homage of the earth. Shew us, then, O NATURE, that which man ought to do in order to obtain the happiness which thou makest him desire. VIRTUE, animate him with thy beneficent fire. REASON, conduct his uncertain steps through the road of life. TRUTH, let thy flambeau illumine him. Unite, O assisting deities, your powers, in order to submit the hearts of men to your dominion. Banish from our mind error, wickedness, and confusion, and cause knowledge, goodness, and serenity to reign in their stead. Let imposture, confounded, never dare to shew itself. Fix our eyes, so long dazzled or blindfolded, at length upon those objects which we ought to seek. Dispel forever those hideous phantoms and those seducing chimeras which only serve to lead us astray. Draw us from those abysses into which superstition plunges us; overthrow the fatal empire of delusion and falsehood; wrest from them the power they have usurped over you. Command, without sharing it with mortals; break the chains which overwhelm them; tear the veil that covers them; allay that fury which intoxicates them; break in the bloody hands of tyranny that scepter with which it crushes them; exile forever, to the imaginary regions from whence fear has brought them forth, those gods who afflict them. Inspire the intelligent being with courage; give him energy, that at length he may dare to love himself, esteem himself, and feel his dignity; that he may dare enfranchise himself; that he may be happy and free; that he may never be a slave to any but your laws; that he may perfect his condition; that he may cherish his fellow creatures; that he may himself enjoy, and that he may also cause others to enjoy. Console the child of nature for those sorrows which destiny obliges him to undergo, by those pleasures of which wisdom permits him to taste; teach him to submit to necessity; conduct him without alarm to the period of all beings; and instruct him that HE IS MADE NEITHER TO AVOID IT NOR TO FEAR IT.

FURTHER READING

Pierre Naville, *D'Holbach*, 4th edn. (1943). A sympathetic account in French.
W. H. Wickwar, *Baron d'Holbach: A Prelude to the French Revolution* (1935).
An equally sympathetic account in English, full of useful and long quotations.

30 ❀ KANT

What Is Enlightenment?

[From Kant, "What Is Enlightenment?," translated by Peter Gay, in *Introduction to Contemporary Civilization in the West*, 2 vols., 2nd
edn. (1954), I, 1071–76.*]

*No one figure embodies the Enlightenment, but if one could be
singled out, it would be Immanuel Kant. Born at Königsberg, East
Prussia, in 1724, he was educated there, taught there, and died
there—he traveled, widely and deeply, but only in the mind. As a
young philosopher, he followed the dogmatic rationalism of the
German metaphysicians, notably Christian von Wolff. But his reading of Newton, Hume, and Rousseau caused him to revise his views
and look at philosophical questions in new, more radical ways.
Newton set him his life's task: to work out the philosophical implications of the Newtonian system of the world. Hume gave that task
its spice and shape: Hume's moderate but fundamental skepticism
about human certainty compelled Kant to justify the very possibility of scientific knowledge. And Rousseau showed him the relevance
of the common man for the political philosopher.*

*After publishing some impressive work on cosmology in the 1760s,
Kant was appointed to the chair of logic and metaphysics in 1770,
and began to work out his Critical system. In a celebrated trilogy,
the* Critique of Pure Reason *(published in 1781), the* Critique of
Practical Reason *(1788), and the* Critique of Judgment *(1790), he
gave a comprehensive account of human knowledge and the foundations of ethics and aesthetics. These books were critiques in the
largest possible meaning of the word; Kant saw it as his task to
establish the foundations on which men could build dependable
knowledge, to make it, in the best sense of that term, "scientific." It*

* By permission of Columbia University Press.

was a towering achievement, but Kant in addition wrote shorter elucidations of his ideas, including some popular articles. The best known of these, often quoted—and justifiably so—is the essay reprinted in large part below. Here Kant seeks to penetrate to the very heart of enlightenment, and finds it in human autonomy. No one was to state the case better than this.

The last years of Kant's career were a pathetic anticlimax to his glorious middle years. In 1793–94 he published his Religion Within the Bounds of Reason Alone *and was silenced by the Prussian government for his daring. He kept silence, at least on religious questions, from then on. In any event, his mind was declining, and even before his death in 1804 he was reduced to a shadow of his former self. But he lived, vigorously, long enough to experience and applaud the French Revolution.*

Enlightenment is man's emergence from his self-imposed nonage. Nonage is the inability to use one's own understanding without another's guidance. This nonage is self-imposed if its cause lies not in lack of understanding but in indecision and lack of courage to use one's own mind without another's guidance. *Dare to know!* (*Sapere aude.*) "Have the courage to use your own understanding," is therefore the motto of the enlightenment.

Laziness and cowardice are the reasons why such a large part of mankind gladly remain minors all their lives, long after nature has freed them from external guidance. They are the reasons why it is so easy for others to set themselves up as guardians. It is so comfortable to be a minor. If I have a book that thinks for me, a pastor who acts as my conscience, a physician who prescribes my diet, and so on—then I have no need to exert myself. I have no need to think, if only I can pay; others will take care of that disagreeable business for me. Those guardians who have kindly taken supervision upon themselves see to it that the overwhelming majority of mankind— among them the entire fair sex—should consider the step to maturity not only as hard, but as extremely dangerous. First, these guardians make their domestic cattle stupid and carefully prevent the docile creatures from taking a single step without the leading-strings to which they have fastened them. Then they show them the danger that would threaten them if they should try to walk by themselves. Now, this danger is really not very great; after stumbling a few times they would, at last, learn to walk. However, examples of such failures intimidate and generally discourage all further attempts.

Thus it is very difficult for the individual to work himself out of the nonage which has become almost second nature to him. He has even grown to like it and is at first really incapable of using his own understanding, because he has never been permitted to try it. Dogmas and formulas, these mechanical tools designed for reasonable use—or rather abuse—of his natural gifts, are the fetters of an everlasting nonage. The man who casts them off would make an uncertain leap over the narrowest ditch, because he is not used to such free movement. That is why there are only a few men who walk firmly, and who have emerged from nonage by cultivating their own minds.

It is more nearly possible, however, for the public to enlighten itself; indeed, if it is only given freedom, enlightenment is almost inevitable. There will always be a few independent thinkers, even among the self-appointed guardians of the multitude. Once such men have thrown off the yoke of nonage, they will spread about them the spirit of a reasonable appreciation of man's value and of his duty to think for himself. It is especially to be noted that the public which was earlier brought under the yoke by these men afterward forces these very guardians to remain in submission, if it is so incited by some of its guardians who are themselves incapable of any enlightenment. That shows how pernicious it is to implant prejudices: they will eventually revenge themselves upon their authors or their authors' descendants. Therefore, a public can achieve enlightenment only slowly. A revolution may bring about the end of a personal despotism or of avaricious and tyrannical oppression, but never a true reform of modes of thought. New prejudices will serve, in place of the old, as guidelines for the unthinking multitude.

This enlightenment requires nothing but *freedom*—and the most innocent of all that may be called "freedom": freedom to make public use of one's reason in all matters. Now I hear the cry from all sides: "Do not argue!" The officer says: "Do not argue—drill!" The tax collector: "Do not argue—pay!" The pastor: "Do not argue—believe!" Only one ruler in the world says: "Argue as much as you please, and about what you please, but obey!" We find restrictions on freedom everywhere. But which restriction is harmful to enlightenment? Which restriction is innocent, and which advances enlightenment? I reply: the public use of one's reason must be free at all times, and this alone can bring enlightenment to mankind.

On the other hand, the private use of reason may frequently be narrowly restricted without especially hindering the progress of enlightenment. By "public use of one's reason" I mean that use which a man, as *scholar,* makes of it before the reading public. I call "private use" that use which a man makes of his reason in a civic post that has been entrusted to him. In some affairs affecting the interest of the community a certain [governmental] mechanism is necessary in which some members of the community remain passive. This creates an artificial unanimity which will serve the fulfillment of public objectives, or at least keep these objectives from being destroyed. Here arguing is not permitted: one must obey. Insofar as a part of this machine considers himself at the same time a member of a universal community—a world society of citizens— (let us say that he thinks of himself as a scholar rationally addressing his public through his writings) he may indeed argue, and the affairs with which he is associated in part as a passive member will not suffer. Thus, it would be very unfortunate if an officer on duty and under orders from his superiors should want to criticize the appropriateness or utility of his orders. He must obey. But as a scholar he could not rightfully be prevented from taking notice of the mistakes in the military service and from submitting his views to his public for its judgment. The citizen cannot refuse to pay the taxes levied upon him; indeed, impertinent censure of such taxes could be punished as a scandal that might cause general disobedience. Nevertheless, this man does not violate the duties of a citizen if, as a scholar, he publicly expresses his objections to the impropriety or possible injustice of such levies. A pastor too is bound to preach to his congregation in accord with the doctrines of the church which he serves, for he was ordained on that condition. But as a scholar he has full freedom, indeed the obligation, to communicate to his public all his carefully examined and constructive thoughts concerning errors in that doctrine and his proposals concerning improvement of religious dogma and church institutions. This is nothing that could burden his conscience. For what he teaches in pursuance of his office as representative of the church, he represents as something which he is not free to teach as he sees it. He speaks as one who is employed to speak in the name and under the orders of another. He will say: "Our church teaches this or that; these are the proofs which it employs." Thus he will benefit his congregation as much as possible by presenting doctrines to which he may not subscribe with full conviction. He can commit himself to teach them because it is not completely impossible that they may contain hidden truth. In any event, he has found nothing in the doctrines that contradicts the heart of religion. For if he believed that such contradictions existed he would not be able to administer his office with a clear conscience. He would have to resign it. Therefore the use which a scholar makes of his reason before the congregation that employs him is only a private use, for, no matter how sizable, this is only a domestic audience. In view of this he, as preacher, is not free and ought not to be free, since he is carrying out the orders of others. On the other hand, as the scholar who speaks to his own public (the world) through his writings, the minister in the public use of his reason enjoys unlimited freedom to use his own reason and to speak for himself. That the spiritual guardians of the people should themselves be treated as minors is an absurdity which would result in perpetuating absurdities.

But should a society of ministers, say a Church Council, . . . have the right to commit itself by oath to a certain unalterable doctrine, in order to secure perpetual guardianship over all its members and through them over the people? I say that this is quite impossible. Such a contract, concluded to keep all further enlightenment from humanity, is simply null and void even if it should be confirmed by the sovereign power, by parliaments, and by the most solemn treaties. An epoch cannot conclude a pact that will commit succeeding ages, prevent them from increasing their significant insights, purging themselves of errors, and generally progressing in enlightenment. That would be a crime against human nature, whose proper destiny lies precisely in such progress. Therefore, succeeding ages are fully entitled to repudiate such decisions as unauthorized and outrageous. The touchstone of all those decisions that may be made into law for a people lies in this question: Could a people impose such a law upon itself? Now, it might be possible to introduce a certain order for a definite short period of time in expectation of a better order. But while this provisional order continues, each citizen (above all, each pastor acting as a scholar) should be left free to publish his criticisms of the faults of existing institutions. This should continue until public understanding of these matters has gone so far that, by uniting the voices of many (although not necessarily all) scholars, reform proposals could be brought before the sovereign to protect those congregations which had decided according to their best lights upon an altered religious

order, without, however, hindering those who want to remain true
to the old institutions. But to agree to a perpetual religious constitution which is not to be publicly questioned by anyone would be,
as it were, to annihilate a period of time in the progress of man's
improvement. This must be absolutely forbidden.

A man may postpone his own enlightenment, but only for a
limited period of time. And to give up enlightenment altogether,
either for oneself or one's descendants, is to violate and to trample
upon the sacred rights of man. What a people may not decide for
itself may even less be decided for it by a monarch, for his reputation as a ruler consists precisely in the way in which he unites the
will of the whole people within his own. If he only sees to it that all
true or supposed [religious] improvement remains in step with the
civic order, he can for the rest leave his subjects alone to do what
they find necessary for the salvation of their souls. Salvation is none
of his business; it *is* his business to prevent one man from forcibly
keeping another from determining and promoting his salvation to
the best of his ability. Indeed, it would be prejudicial to his majesty
if he meddled in these matters and supervised the writings in which
his subjects seek to bring their [religious] views into the open, even
when he does this from his own highest insight, because then he
exposes himself to the reproach: *Caesar non est supra grammaticos*
[Caesar is not above grammarians]. It is worse when he debases his
sovereign power so far as to support the spiritual despotism of a few
tyrants in his state over the rest of his subjects.

When we ask, Are we now living in an enlightened age? the
answer is, No, but we live in an age of enlightenment. As matters
now stand it is still far from true that men are already capable of
using their own reason in religious matters confidently and correctly
without external guidance. Still, we have some obvious indications
that the field of working toward the goal [of religious truth] is now
being opened. What is more, the hindrances against general enlightenment or the emergence from self-imposed nonage are gradually diminishing. In this respect this is the age of the enlightenment
and the century of Frederick [the Great].

A prince ought not to deem it beneath his dignity to state that he
considers it his duty not to dictate anything to his subjects in religious matters, but to leave them complete freedom. If he repudiates
the arrogant word *tolerant,* he is himself enlightened; he deserves to
be praised by a grateful world and posterity as that man who was
the first to liberate mankind from dependence, at least on the
government, and let everybody use his own reason in matters of

conscience. Under his reign, honorable pastors, acting as scholars and regardless of the duties of their office, can freely and openly publish their ideas to the world for inspection, although they deviate here and there from accepted doctrine. This is even more true of every other person not restrained by any oath of office. This spirit of freedom is spreading beyond the boundaries [of Prussia], even where it has to struggle against the external hindrances established by a government that fails to grasp its true interest. [Frederick's Prussia] is a shining example that freedom need not cause the least worry concerning public order or the unity of the community. When one does not deliberately attempt to keep men in barbarism, they will gradually work out of that condition by themselves.

I have emphasized the main point of the enlightenment—man's emergence from his self-imposed nonage—primarily in religious matters, because our rulers have no interest in playing the guardian to their subjects in the arts and sciences. Above all, nonage in religion is not only the most harmful but the most dishonorable. But the disposition of a sovereign ruler who favors freedom in the arts and sciences goes even further: he knows that there is no danger in permitting his subjects to make public use of their reason and to publish their ideas concerning a better constitution, as well as candid criticism of existing basic laws. We already have a striking example [of such freedom], and no monarch can match the one whom we venerate.

But only the man who is himself enlightened, who is not afraid of shadows, and who commands at the same time a well-disciplined and numerous army as guarantor of public peace—only he can say what [the sovereign of] a free state cannot dare to say: "Argue as much as you like, and about what you like, but obey!" Thus we observe here as elsewhere in human affairs, in which almost everything is paradoxical, a surprising and unexpected course of events: a large degree of civic freedom appears to be of advantage to the intellectual freedom of the people, yet at the same time it establishes insurmountable barriers. A lesser degree of civic freedom, however, creates room to let that free spirit expand to the limits of its capacity. Nature, then, has carefully cultivated the seed within the hard core—namely, the urge for and the vocation of free thought. And this free thought gradually reacts back on the modes of thought of the people, and men become more and more capable of acting in freedom. At last free thought acts even on the fundamentals of government, and the state finds it agreeable to treat man, who is now more than a machine, in accord with his dignity.

FURTHER READING

Ernst Cassirer, *Kants Leben und Lehre* (1918) . A full and appreciative biography by a brilliant Neo-Kantian.

Immanuel Kant, *Prolegomena to any Future Metaphysics,* ed. Lewis W. Beck (1950 edn.) . The best introduction to Kant's epistemology—by Kant himself.

A. D. Lindsay, *Kant* (1934) . A general account of Kant's thought.

H. J. Paton, *The Categorical Imperative: A Study in Kant's Moral Philosophy* (1948) . Among the best of modern commentaries on Kant's ethics.

Norman Kemp Smith, *A Commentary to Kant's Critique of Pure Reason,* 2nd edn. (1923) . Responsible but technical.

31 ✤ DIDEROT

Supplement to Bougainville's Voyage

[From Denis Diderot, *Rameau's Nephew and Other Works*, 187–92, 194–213.*]

In 1760, Denis Diderot wrote to his mistress, Sophie Volland: "If the spectacle of injustice sometimes rouses me to so much indignation that I lose my judgment over it, and that I'd kill, I'd destroy, during this delirium; so the spectacle of equity fills me with a sweetness, inflames me with such ardor and enthusiasm, that life would mean nothing to me if I had to yield it up. Then it seems to me that my heart expands beyond me, that it swims; an indescribably delicious and subtle sensation runs through me; I have difficulty breathing; the whole surface of my body is animated by something like a shudder; it is marked above all on my forehead, at the hairline; and then the symptoms of admiration and pleasure come to mingle on my face with those of joy, and my eyes fill with tears."† A writer who could feel a moral act with such orgastic force was well equipped to reconsider that most delicate of social questions—sensuality. Many of the philosophes thought it necessary to change the general way of thinking about sex, but few dared to discuss it openly, if at all. But the principle was plain enough: Christianity was, to their mind, the enemy not merely of reason, but of passion as well, and it was essential to rehabilitate them both. We have seen what the philosophes thought would rehabilitate reason; on the passions they were less explicit. But they gave hints:

---

* Translation copyright © 1956 by Jacques Barzun and Ralph H. Bowen. Reprinted by permission of Doubleday & Company, Inc.

† Oct. 18, 1760, in Diderot, *Correspondance*, ed. Georges Roth (1955–   ), III, 156. I have discussed this passage elsewhere, and called Diderot a "voyeur of virtue"; see *The Enlightenment: An Interpretation*, I, *The Rise of Modern Paganism*, 187–88, and II, *The Science of Freedom*, 206.

monastic *"virtues"* are, to the philosophes, nothing better than *"the deadly art of stifling nature."** Holbach, La Mettrie, and the other materialists saw sensuality as both natural and beneficial.

The most interesting and most amusing treatment of this question occurs in Diderot's Supplément au Voyage de Bougainville. Since the late *1750s*, Diderot had been writing reviews—of the biennial Salons, of new books—for that exclusive hand-written bimonthly newsletter, the Correspondance littéraire, edited by Diderot's friend Grimm. The *1760s* were a fertile period for Diderot: he wrote (though he did not publish) his little masterpiece Rameau's Nephew; he completed the Encyclopédie; and he wrote some splendid Salons for Grimm, notably those of *1765* and *1767*.

In the early *1770s* Diderot had another opportunity for inventing a new genre. Between *1766* and *1769* the French navigator Louis-Antoine de Bougainville traveled around the world, and in *1771–72* he published a two-volume account of his experiences. Diderot wrote a review of the work, doubtless for Grimm, but somehow it stimulated him into highly original speculations about comparative sensuality. It gave him a welcome chance to denigrate the dour *"hypocrisy"* of Christian sexual morality by comparing it invidiously with the healthy libertinism of the Tahitians. The work did not have any impact on the Enlightenment, for the simple reason that only a few select friends ever saw the manuscript. It was not published until *1796*. But it provides a glimpse of a non-Christian sexual Utopia, as idealized by the most openly sensual of the philosophes.

THE OLD MAN'S FAREWELL

He was the father of a numerous family. At the time of the Europeans' arrival, he cast upon them a look that was filled with scorn, though it revealed no surprise, no alarm and no curiosity. They approached him; he turned his back on them and retired into his hut. His thoughts were only too well revealed by his silence and his air of concern, for in the privacy of his thoughts he groaned inwardly over the happy days of his people, now gone forever. At

* Diderot to Sophie Volland, Aug. 16, 1759, *Correspondance*, II, 218.

the moment of Bougainville's departure, when all the natives ran swarming onto the beach, tugging at his clothing and throwing their arms around his companions and weeping, the old man stepped forward and solemnly spoke:

"Weep, wretched Tahitians, weep—but rather for the arrival than for the departure of these wicked and grasping men! The day will come when you will know them for what they are. Someday they will return, bearing in one hand that piece of wood you see suspended from this one's belt and in the other the piece of steel that hangs at the side of his companion. They will load you with chains, slit your throats and enslave you to their follies and vices. Someday you will be slaves to them, you will be as corrupt, as vile, as wretched as they are. But I have this consolation—my life is drawing to its close, and I shall not see the calamity that I foretell. O Tahitians, O my friends! You have the means of warding off a terrible fate, but I would die before I would advise you to make use of it. Let them leave, and let them live."

Then, turning to Bougainville, he went on: "And you, leader of these brigands who obey you, take your vessel swiftly from our shores. We are innocent and happy, and you can only spoil our happiness. We follow the pure instinct of nature, and you have tried to efface her imprint from our hearts. Here all things are for all, and you have preached to us I know not what distinctions between mine and thine. Our women and girls we possess in common; you have shared this privilege with us, and your coming has awakened in them a frenzy they have never known before. They have become mad in your arms; you have become ferocious in theirs. They have begun to hate one another; you have cut one another's throats for them, and they have come home to us stained with your blood.

"We are free—but see where you have driven into our earth the symbol of our future servitude. You are neither a god nor a devil— by what right, then, do you enslave people? Orou! You who understand the speech of these men, tell every one of us, as you have told me, what they have written on that strip of metal—'This land belongs to us.' This land belongs to you! And why? Because you set foot in it? If some day a Tahitian should land on your shores, and if he should engrave on one of your stones or on the bark of one of your trees 'This land belongs to the people of Tahiti,' what would you think? You are stronger than we are! And what does that signify? When one of our lads carried off some of the miserable trinkets with which your ship is loaded, what an uproar you made, and what revenge you took! And at that very moment you were plotting, in the depths of your hearts, to steal a whole country! You are not slaves; you would suffer death rather than be enslaved, yet you want to make slaves of us! Do you believe, then, that the Tahitian does not know how to die in defense of his liberty? This Tahitian, whom you want to treat as a chattel, as a dumb animal— this Tahitian is your brother. You are both children of Nature— what right do you have over him that he does not have over you?

"You came; did we attack you? Did we plunder your vessel? Did we seize you and expose you to the arrows of our enemies? Did we force you to work in the fields alongside our beasts of burden? We respected our own image in you. Leave us our own customs, which are wiser and more decent than yours. We have no wish to barter what you call our ignorance for your useless knowledge. We possess already all that is good or necessary for our existence. Do we merit your scorn because we have not been able to create superfluous wants for ourselves? When we are hungry, we have something to eat; when we are cold, we have clothing to put on. You have been in our huts—what is lacking there, in your opinion? You are welcome to drive yourselves as hard as you please in pursuit of what you call the comforts of life, but allow sensible people to stop when they see they have nothing to gain but imaginary benefits from the continuation of their painful labors. If you persuade us to go beyond the bounds of strict necessity, when shall we come to the end of our labor? When shall we have time for enjoyment? We have reduced our daily and yearly labors to the least possible amount, because to us nothing seemed more desirable than leisure. Go and bestir yourselves in your own country; there you may torment yourselves as much as you like; but leave us in peace, and do not fill our heads with a hankering after your false needs and imaginary virtues. Look at these men—see how healthy, straight and strong they are. See these women—how straight, healthy, fresh and lovely they are. Take this bow in your hands—it is my own—and call one, two, three, four of your comrades to help you try to bend it. I can bend it myself. I work the soil, I climb mountains, I make my way through the dense forest, and I can run four leagues on the plain in less than an hour. Your young comrades have been hard put to it to keep up with me, and yet I have passed my ninetieth year. . . .

"Woe to this island! Woe to all the Tahitians now living, and to all those yet to be born, woe from the day of your arrival! We used to know but one disease, the one to which all men, all animals and all plants are subject—old age. But you have brought us a new one:

you have infected our blood. We shall perhaps be compelled to exterminate with our own hands some of our young girls, some of our women, some of our children, those who have lain with your women, those who have lain with your men. Our fields will be spattered with the foul blood that has passed from your veins into ours. Or else our children, condemned to die, will nourish and perpetuate the evil disease that you have given their fathers and mothers, transmitting it forever to their descendants. Wretched men! You will bear the guilt either of the ravages that will follow your baneful caresses or of the murders we must commit to arrest the progress of the poison! You speak of crime! Can you conceive of a greater crime than the one you have committed? How do they punish, in your country, the man who has killed his neighbor? Death by the headsman's ax! How do you punish the man who has poisoned his neighbor? Burning at the stake! Compare the second crime with your own, and then tell us, you poisoner of whole nations, what tortures you deserve!

"But a little while ago, the young Tahitian girl blissfully abandoned herself to the embraces of a Tahitian youth and awaited impatiently the day when her mother, authorized to do so by her having reached the age of puberty, would remove her veil and uncover her breasts. She was proud of her ability to excite men's desires, to attract the amorous looks of strangers, of her own relatives, of her own brothers. In our presence, without shame, in the center of a throng of innocent Tahitians who danced and played the flute, she accepted the caresses of the young man whom her young heart and the secret promptings of her senses had marked out for her. The notion of crime and the fear of disease have come among us only with your coming. Now our enjoyments, formerly so sweet, are attended with guilt and terror. That man in black, who stands near to you and listens to me, has spoken to our young men, and I know not what he has said to our young girls, but our youths are hesitant and our girls blush. Creep away into the dark forest, if you wish, with the perverse companion of your pleasures, but allow the good, simple Tahitians to reproduce themselves without shame under the open sky and in broad daylight.

"What more noble or more wholesome feelings could you put in the place of the ones we have nurtured in them and by which they live? When they think the time has come to enrich the nation and the family with a new citizen, they glorify the occasion. They eat in order to live and grow; they grow in order that they may multiply, and in that they see neither vice nor shame. Listen to the consequences of your crimes. Scarcely had you shown yourselves among our people than they became thieves. Scarcely had you set foot upon our soil than it began to reek of blood. You killed the Tahitian who ran to greet you, crying '*Taïo*—friend!' And why did you kill him? Because he was tempted by the glitter of your little serpent's eggs. He gave you his fruit; he offered you his wife and daughter; he gave you his hut to live in—and you killed him for taking a handful of those little glass beads without asking your permission. And the others? At the sound of your murderous weapons they fled to the hills. But you should know that had it not been for me they would soon have come down again to destroy you. Oh, why did I appease their anger? Why did I calm their fury? Why do I still restrain them, even at this moment? I do not know, for you surely have no claim to pity. Your own soul is hard and will never feel any.

"You and your men have gone where you pleased, wandered over the whole island; you have been respected; you have enjoyed everything: no barrier nor refusal has been placed in your path. You have been invited into our homes; you have sat down at our tables; our people have spread before you the abundance of our land. If you wanted one of our young women, her mother presented her to you all naked, unless she was one of those who are not yet old enough to have the privilege of showing their faces and breasts. Thus you have enjoyed possession of these tender sacrificial victims to the duty of hospitality. For the girl and for you we have strewn the ground with leaves and flowers, the musicians have put their instruments in tune; nothing has troubled the sweetness nor interfered with the freedom of her caresses and yours. We chanted the hymn, the one that urges you to be a man, that urges our child to be a woman, a compliant and voluptuous woman. We danced around your couch. Yet you had hardly left this girl's embrace, having experienced in her arms the sweetest intoxication, than you killed her brother, her friend, or perhaps her father.

"And you have done worse still—look yonder at that enclosure, bristling with arrows, with weapons that heretofore have threatened only our foes—see them now turned against our own children. Look now upon the unhappy companions of your pleasures! See their sorrow! See the distress of their fathers and the despair of their mothers! That is where they are condemned to die at our hands or from the disease you gave them. So leave this place, unless your cruel eyes delight in the spectacle of death! Go! And may the guilty sea, that spared your lives when you came here, now absolve itself and avenge our wrongs by swallowing you up on your homeward way! And you, Tahitians, go back to your huts, go indoors, all of you, so that these unworthy strangers, as they depart, may hear nothing but the growling of the waves and may see nothing but the white spray dashing in fury on a desert coast!"

He finished speaking, and in an instant the throng of natives disappeared. A vast silence reigned over the whole extent of the island, and nothing was to be heard but the dry whistling of the wind and the dull pounding of the waves along the whole length of the coast. It was as though the winds and waters had heard the old man's voice and obeyed him.

B. Well, what do you think of that?

A. The oration strikes me as forceful enough, but in the midst of so much that is unmistakably abrupt and savage I seem to detect a few European ideas and turns of phrase.

B. You must remember that it is a translation from Tahitian into Spanish and from Spanish into French. The previous night, the old man made a visit to Orou, the one to whom he appealed while speaking, in whose family the knowledge of Spanish had been preserved for several generations. Orou wrote down the old man's harangue in Spanish, and Bougainville had a copy of it in his hand while the old man was speaking. . . .

CONVERSATION BETWEEN THE CHAPLAIN AND OROU

B. When the members of Bougainville's expedition were shared out among the native families, the ship's chaplain fell to the lot of Orou. The Tahitian and the chaplain were men of about the same age, that is, about thirty-five years old. At that time, Orou's family consisted of his wife and three daughters, who were called Asto, Palli and Thia. The women undressed their guest, washed his face, hands and feet, and put before him a wholesome though frugal meal. When he was about to go to bed, Orou, who had stepped outside with his family, reappeared and presented to him his wife and three girls—all naked as Eve—and said to him:

"You are young and healthy and you have just had a good supper. He who sleeps alone sleeps badly; at night a man needs a woman at his side. Here is my wife and here are my daughters.

Choose whichever one pleases you most, but if you would like to do me a favor, you will give your preference to my youngest girl, who has not yet had any children."

The mother said: "Poor girl! I don't hold it against her. It's no fault of hers."

The chaplain replied that his religion, his holy orders, his moral standards and his sense of decency all prevented him from accepting Orou's invitation.

Orou answered: "I don't know what this thing is that you call 'religion,' but I can only have a low opinion of it because it forbids you to partake of an innocent pleasure to which Nature, the sovereign mistress of us all, invites everybody. It seems to prevent you from bringing one of your fellow creatures into the world, from doing a favor asked of you by a father, a mother and their children, from repaying the kindness of a host, and from enriching a nation by giving it an additional citizen. I don't know what it is that you call 'holy orders,' but your chief duty is to be a man and to show gratitude. I am not asking you to take my moral standards back with you to your own country, but Orou, your host and your friend, begs you merely to lend yourself to the morality of Tahiti. Is our moral code a better or a worse one than your own? This is an easy question to answer. Does the country you were born in have more people than it can support? If it does, then your morals are neither better nor worse than ours. Or can it feed more people than it now has? Then our morals are better than yours. As for the sense of propriety that leads you to object to my proposal, that I understand, and I freely admit that I am in the wrong. I ask your pardon. I cannot ask you to do anything that might harm your health; if you are too tired, you should by all means go to sleep at once. But I hope that you will not persist in disappointing us. Look at the distress you have caused to appear on the faces of these four women—they are afraid you have noticed some defect in them that arouses your distaste. But even if that were so, would it not be possible for you to do a good deed and have the pleasure of honoring one of my daughters in the sight of her sisters and friends? Come, be generous!"

THE CHAPLAIN. You don't understand—it's not that. They are all four of them equally beautiful. But there is my religion! My holy orders!

OROU. They are mine and I offer them to you; they are all of age and they give themselves to you. However clear a conscience may be demanded of you by this thing 'religion,' or by those 'holy orders' of yours, you need have no scruples about accepting these women. I am making no abuse of my paternal authority, and you may be sure that I recognize and respect the rights of individuals to their own persons.

At this point in his account, the truthful chaplain has to admit that up to that moment Providence had never exposed him to such strong temptation. He was young, he was excited, he was in torment. He turned his eyes away from the four lovely suppliants, then let his gaze wander back to them again. He lifted his hands and his countenance to Heaven. Thia, the youngest of the three girls, threw her arms around his knees and said to him: "Stranger, do not disappoint my father and mother. Do not disappoint me! Honor me in this hut and among my own family! Raise me to the dignity enjoyed by my sisters, for they make fun of me. Asto, my eldest sister, already has three children; Palli, the second oldest of us, has two; and Thia has none! Stranger, good stranger, do not reject me! Make me a mother! Give me a child whom I can someday lead by the hand as he walks at my side, to be seen by all Tahiti—a little one to nurse at my breast nine months from now, a child of whom I can be proud, and who will be part of my dowry when I go from my father's hut into that of another. Perhaps I shall be more fortunate with you than I have been with our Tahitian young men. If you will only grant me this favor, I will never forget you; I will bless you all my life; I will write your name on my arm and on that of my child; we will always pronounce it with joy; and when you leave this shore, my prayers will go with you across the seas all the way to your own country."

The poor chaplain records that she pressed his hands, that she fastened her eyes on his with the most expressive and touching gaze, that she wept, that her father, mother and sisters went out, leaving him alone with her, and that despite his repetition of "But there is my religion and my holy orders," he awoke the next morning to find the young girl lying at his side. She overwhelmed him with more caresses, and when her father, mother and sisters came in, she called upon them to add their gratitude to hers.

Asto and Palli, who had left the room briefly, soon returned bearing native food, drink and fruits. They embraced their sister and wished her good fortune. They all ate breakfast together; then, when Orou was left alone with the chaplain, he said to him: "I see that my daughter is pleased with you, and I thank you. But would you be good enough to tell me the meaning of this word 'religion' which you have spoken so frequently and so mournfully?"

After considering for a moment what to say, the chaplain replied: "Who made your hut and all the furnishings in it?"

OROU. I did.

THE CHAPLAIN. Well, we believe that this world and everything in it is the work of a maker.

OROU. Then he must have hands and feet, and a head.

THE CHAPLAIN. No.

OROU. Where is his dwelling place?

THE CHAPLAIN. Everywhere.

OROU. In this place too?

THE CHAPLAIN. In this place too.

OROU. But we have never seen him.

THE CHAPLAIN. He cannot be seen.

OROU. He sounds to me like a father that doesn't care very much for his children. He must be an old man, because he must be at least as old as the things he made.

THE CHAPLAIN. No, he never grows old. He spoke to our ancestors and gave them laws; he prescribed to them the way in which he wishes to be honored; he ordained that certain actions are good, and others he forbade them to do as being evil.

OROU. I see. And one of these evil actions which he has forbidden is that of a man who goes to bed with a woman or girl. But in that case, why did he make two sexes?

THE CHAPLAIN. In order that they might come together—but only when certain conditions are satisfied and only after certain initial ceremonies have been performed. By virtue of these ceremonies one man belongs to one woman and only to her; one woman belongs to one man and only to him.

OROU. For their whole lives?

THE CHAPLAIN. For their whole lives.

OROU. So that if it should happen that a woman should go to bed with some man who was not her husband, or some man should go to bed with a woman that was not his wife . . . but that could never happen, because the workman would know what was going on, and since he doesn't like that sort of thing, he wouldn't let it occur.

THE CHAPLAIN. No. He lets them do as they will, and they sin against the law of God (for that is the name by which we call the great workman) and against the law of the country; they commit a crime.

OROU. I should be sorry to give offense by anything I might say, but if you don't mind, I'll tell you what I think.

THE CHAPLAIN. Go ahead.

OROU. I find these strange precepts contrary to nature, and contrary to reason. I think they are admirably calculated to increase the number of crimes and to give endless annoyance to the old workman—who made everything without hands, head or tools, who is everywhere but can be seen nowhere, who exists today and tomorrow but grows not a day older, who gives commands and is not obeyed, who can prevent what he dislikes but fails to do so. His commands are contrary to nature because they assume that a thinking being, one that has feelings and a sense of freedom, can be the property of another being like himself. On what could such a right of ownership be founded? Do you not see that in your country you have confused things that have no feelings, thoughts, desires or wills—things one takes or leaves, keeps or sells, without them suffering or complaining—with things that can neither be bought nor sold, which have freedom, volition, and desires of their own, which have the ability to give or to withhold themselves for a moment or forever, which suffer and complain? These latter things can never be treated like a trader's stock of goods unless one forgets what their true character is and does violence to nature. Furthermore, your laws seem to me to be contrary to the general order of things. For in truth is there anything so senseless as a precept that forbids us to heed the changing impulses that are inherent in our being, or commands that require a degree of constancy which is not possible, that violate the liberty of both male and female by chaining them perpetually to one another? Is there anything more unreasonable than this perfect fidelity that would restrict us, for the enjoyment of pleasures so capricious, to a single partner, than an oath of immutability taken by two individuals made of flesh and blood under a sky that is not the same for a moment, in a cavern that threatens to collapse upon them, at the foot of a cliff that is crumbling into dust, under a tree that is withering, on a bench of stone that is being worn away? Take my word for it, you have reduced human beings to a worse condition than that of the animals. I don't know what your great workman is, but I am very happy that he never spoke to our forefathers, and I hope that he never speaks to our children, for if he does, he may tell them the same foolishness, and they may be foolish enough to believe it. Yesterday, as we were having supper, you told us all about your "magistrates" and "priests." I do not know who these characters are whom you call magistrates and priests and who have the authority to govern your conduct—but tell me, are they really masters of good and evil? Can they transform justice into injustice and contrariwise? Is it within their power to attach the name of "good" to harmful actions or the name of "evil" to harmless or useful deeds? One can hardly think so, because in that case there would no longer be any difference between true and false, between good and bad, between beautiful and ugly—only such differences as it pleased your great workman, your magistrates or your priests to define as such. You would then have to change your ideas and behavior from one moment to the next. One day you would be told, on behalf of one of your three masters, "Kill," and in all good conscience you would be obliged to kill. Another day they might say, "Steal," and you would be bound to steal. Or: "Do not eat of this fruit," and would not dare to eat of it; "I forbid you to eat this vegetable or this meat," and you would be careful never to touch them. There is not a single good thing they could not forbid you to enjoy, and no wickedness they could not order you to commit. And where would you be if your three masters, disagreeing among themselves, took it into their heads to permit, enjoin and forbid you to do the same thing, as I am sure must occasionally happen? Then, in order to please your priest, you would have to get yourself into hot water with the magistrate; to satisfy the magistrate, you would have to risk the displeasure of the great workman; and to make yourself agreeable to the great workman, you would have to fly in the face of your own nature. And do you know what will finally happen? You will come to despise all three, and you will be neither man nor citizen nor pious believer; you will be nothing at all; you will be at odds with all the authorities, at odds with yourself, malicious, disturbed by your own conscience, persecuted by your witless masters, and miserable, as you were yesterday evening when I offered you my wife and daughters and you could only wail, "What about my religion? What about my holy orders?" Would you like to know what is good and what is bad in all times and places? Pay close attention to the nature of things and actions, to your relations with your fellow creatures, to the effect of your behavior on your own well-being and on the general welfare. You are mad if you believe that there is anything in the universe, high or low, that can add or subtract from the laws of nature. Her eternal will is that good shall be chosen rather than evil, and the general welfare rather than the individual's well-being. You may decree the opposite, but you will not be obeyed. By threats, punishment and guilt you can make more wretches and rascals, make more depraved consciences and more corrupted characters. People will no longer know what they ought or ought not to do. They will feel guilty when they are doing nothing wrong and proud of themselves in the midst of crime; they will have lost the North Star that should guide their course. Give me an honest answer: in spite of the express commands of your three legislators, do the young men in your country never go to bed with a young woman without having received permission?

THE CHAPLAIN. I would be lying if I said they never do.

OROU. And the women, once they have sworn an oath to belong to only one husband, do they never give themselves to another man?

THE CHAPLAIN. Nothing happens more often.

OROU. And are your legislators severe in handing out punishment to such disobedient people, or are they not? If they are, then they are wild animals who make war against nature; if they are not severe, they are fools who risk bringing their authority into contempt by issuing futile prohibitions.

THE CHAPLAIN. The guilty ones, if they escape the rigor of the laws, are punished by public opinion.

OROU. That's like saying that justice is done by means of the whole nation's lack of common sense, and that public folly is the substitute for law.

THE CHAPLAIN. A girl who has lost her honor cannot find a husband.

OROU. Lost her honor! And for what cause?

THE CHAPLAIN. An unfaithful woman is more or less despised.

OROU. Despised! Why should that be?

THE CHAPLAIN. And the young man is called a cowardly seducer.

OROU. Coward? Seducer? Why that?

THE CHAPLAIN. The father and mother and their dishonored child are desolate. An erring husband is called a libertine; a husband who has been betrayed shares the shame of his wife.

OROU. What monstrous foolishness you're talking! And still you must be holding something back, because when people take it upon themselves to rearrange all ideas of justice and propriety to suit their own whims, to apply or remove the names of things in a completely arbitrary manner, to associate the ideas of good and evil with certain actions or to dissociate them for no reason save caprice —then of course people will blame each other, accuse each other, suspect each other, tyrannize, become jealous and envious, deceive and wound one another, conceal, dissimulate, and spy on one another, catch each other out, quarrel and tell lies. Girls will deceive their parents, husbands their wives and wives their husbands. Unmarried girls—yes, I am sure of it—unmarried girls will suffocate their babies; suspicious fathers will neglect or show contempt for their own rightful children; mothers will abandon their infants and leave them to the mercy of fate. Crime and debauchery will appear in every imaginable shape and form. I see all that as plainly as if I had lived among you. These things are so because they must be so, and your society, whose well-ordered ways your chief boasts to you about, can't be anything but a swarm of hypocrites who secretly trample the laws under foot, or a multitude of wretched beings who serve as instruments for inflicting willing torture upon themselves; or imbeciles in whom prejudice has utterly silenced the voice of nature, or ill-fashioned creatures in whom nature cannot claim her rights.

THE CHAPLAIN. That is a close likeness. But do you never marry?

OROU. Oh yes, we marry.

THE CHAPLAIN. Well, how does it work?

OROU. It consists only of an agreement to occupy the same hut and to sleep in the same bed for so long as both partners find the arrangement good.

THE CHAPLAIN. And when they find it bad?

OROU. Then they separate.

THE CHAPLAIN. But what becomes of the children?

OROU. Oh, stranger! That last question of yours finally reveals to me the last depths of your country's wretchedness. Let me tell you, my friend, that the birth of a child is always a happy event, and its death is an occasion for weeping and sorrow. A child is a precious thing because it will grow up to be a man or a woman. Therefore we take infinitely better care of our children than of our plants and animals. The birth of a child is the occasion for public celebration and a source of joy for its entire family. For the hut it means an increase in wealth, while for the nation it signifies additional strength. It means another pair of hands and arms for Tahiti—we see in the newborn baby a future farmer, fisherman, hunter, soldier, husband or father. When a woman goes from her husband's hut back to that of her family, she takes with her all the children she brought with her as her dowry; those born during the marriage are divided equally between the two spouses, and care is taken to give each an equal number of boys and girls whenever possible.

THE CHAPLAIN. But children are a burden for many years before they are old enough to make themselves useful.

OROU. We set aside for them and for the support of the aged one part in six of all our harvests; wherever the child goes, this support follows him. And so, you see, the larger the family a Tahitian has, the richer he is.

THE CHAPLAIN. One part in six!

OROU. Yes. It's a dependable method for encouraging the growth of population, for promoting respect for our old people and for safeguarding the welfare of our children.

THE CHAPLAIN. And does it ever happen that a couple who have separated decide to live together again?

OROU. Oh, yes. It happens fairly often. Also, the shortest time any marriage can last is one month.

THE CHAPLAIN. Assuming, of course, that the wife is not with child, for in that case, wouldn't the marriage have to last at least nine months?

OROU. Not at all. The child keeps the name of its mother's husband at the time it was conceived, and its paternity, like its means of support, follows it wherever it goes.

THE CHAPLAIN. You spoke about the children that a wife brings to her husband as dowry.

OROU. To be sure. Take my eldest daughter, who has three children. They are able to walk, they are healthy and attractive, and they promise to be strong when they are grown up. If she should take it into her head to get married, she would take them along, for they belong to her, and her husband would be extremely happy to have them in his hut. He would think all the better of his wife if she were carrying still a fourth child at the time of her wedding.

THE CHAPLAIN. *His* child?

OROU. His or another's. The more children our young women have had, the more desirable they are as wives. The stronger and lustier our young men are, the richer they become. Therefore, careful as we are to protect our young girls from male advances, and our young boys from intercourse with women, before they reach sexual maturity, once they have passed the age of puberty we exhort them all the more strongly to have as many children as possible. You probably haven't fully realized what an important service you will have rendered my daughter Thia if you have succeeded in getting her with child. Her mother will no longer plague her every month by saying, "But, Thia, what is the matter with you? You never get pregnant, and here you are nineteen years old. You should have had at least a couple of babies by this time, and you have none. Who is going to look after you in your old age if you throw away your youth in this way? Thia, I begin to think there is something wrong with you, some defect that puts men off. Find out what it is, my child, and correct it if you can. At your age, I was already three times a mother!"

THE CHAPLAIN. What precautions do you take to safeguard your boys and girls before they reach maturity?

OROU. That's the main object of our children's education within the family circle, and it's the main important point in our code of public morality. Our boys, until the age of twenty-two, that is for two to three years after they reach maturity, must wear a long tunic that covers their bodies completely, and they must wear a little chain around their loins. Before they reach nubile age, our girls would not dare to go out without white veils. The two misdeeds of taking off one's chain or of raising one's veil are rarely met with, because we teach our children at a very early age what harmful results will ensue. But when the proper time comes—when the male has attained his full strength, when the principal indication of virility lasts for a sufficient time, and when we are confirmed in our judgment by the quality and by the frequent emission of the seminal fluid—and when the young girl seems wilted and suffers from boredom, when she seems mature enough to feel passion, to inspire it and to satisfy it, then the father unfastens his son's chain and cuts the nail on the middle finger of the boy's right hand. The mother removes her daughter's veil. The young man can now ask a woman for her favors or be asked by her to grant his. The girl may walk about freely in public places with her face and breast uncovered; she may accept or reject men's caresses. All we do is to point out in advance to the boy certain girls and to the girl certain boys that they might well choose as partners. The day when a boy or girl is emancipated is a gala holiday. In the case of a girl, the young men assemble the night before around her hut and the air is filled all night long with singing and the sound of musical instruments. When the sun has risen, she is led by her father and mother into an enclosure where dancing is going on and where games of wrestling, running and jumping are in progress. A naked man is paraded in front of her, allowing her to examine his body from all aspects and in all sorts of attitudes. For a young man's initiation, the young girls do the honors of the occasion by letting him look at the nude female body unadorned and unconcealed. The remainder of the ceremony is enacted on a bed of leaves, just as you saw it on your arrival here. At sunset the girl returns to her parents' hut or else moves to the hut of the young man she has chosen and remains there as long as she pleases.

THE CHAPLAIN. But is this celebration a marriage ceremony or is it not?

OROU. Well, as you have said . . .

A. What do I see written there in the margin?

B. It is a note in which the good chaplain says that the parents' advice on how to choose wives and husbands was full of common sense and contained many acute and useful observations, but that he could not bring himself to quote the catechism itself because it would have seemed intolerably licentious to corrupt, superstitious people like us. He adds, nevertheless, that he was sorry to have left out certain details that would have shown, in the first place, what vast progress a nation can make in some important matter without the assistance of physics and anatomy if it busies itself continually with it, and, in the second place, the different ideals of beauty that prevail in a country where one judges forms in the light of momentary pleasures, as contrasted with a nation where they are appreciated for their usefulness over a longer period of time. To be considered beautiful in the former country a woman must have a high color, a wide forehead, a small mouth, large eyes, finely modeled features, a narrow waist, and small hands and feet. . . . With the Tahitians, however, scarcely one of these things is of any account. The woman who attracts the most admirers and the most lovers is the one who seems most likely to bear many children (like the wife of Cardinal d'Ossat) and whose children seem likely to be active, intelligent, brave, healthy and strong. The Athenian Venus has next to nothing in common with the Venus of Tahiti—the former is a flirtatious Venus, the latter a fertile Venus. A woman of Tahiti said scornfully one day to a woman of her acquaintance: "You are beautiful enough, but the children you bear are ugly; I am ugly, but my children are beautiful, so the men prefer me."

Following this note by the chaplain, Orou continues:

OROU. What a happy moment it is for a young girl and her parents when it is discovered that she is with child! She jumps up and runs about, she throws her arms around her father's and mother's necks. She tells them the wonderful news amidst outcries of mutual joy. "Mother! Father! kiss me! I am pregnant!" "Is it really true?" "Really and truly!" "And who got you with child?" "Such-and-such a one."

THE CHAPLAIN. How can she know who the father of her child is?

OROU. How could she not know? With us the same rule that applies to marriage applies also to love affairs—each lasts at least from one moon to the next.

THE CHAPLAIN. And is the rule strictly observed?

OROU. You can judge for yourself. First, the interval between two moons isn't long, but when it appears that two men have well-founded claims to be the father of a child, it no longer belongs to the mother.

THE CHAPLAIN. To whom does it belong?

OROU. To whichever of the two men the mother chooses to give it. This is the only right she has, and since a child is an object of both interest and value, you can understand that among us loose women are rare and that our young men keep away from them.

THE CHAPLAIN. Then you do have a few licentious women? That makes me feel better.

OROU. Yes, we have some, and more than one kind—but that is another subject. When one of our girls gets pregnant, she is twice as pleased with herself if the child's father is a handsome, well-built, brave, intelligent, industrious young man, because she has reason to hope that the child will inherit its father's good qualities. The only thing a girl would be ashamed of would be a bad choice. You have no idea how much store we set by good health, beauty, strength, industry and courage; you have no notion what a tendency there is, even without our having to pay any particular attention to it, for good physical inheritance to be passed on from generation to generation among us. You are a person who has traveled in all sorts of countries—tell me if you have seen anywhere else so many handsome men and beautiful women as in Tahiti. Look at me. What do you think of me? Well, there are ten thousand men on this island who are taller than I am and just as strong; but there is none braver, and for that reason mothers very often point me out to their girls as a good father for their children.

THE CHAPLAIN. And out of all these children you have sired outside your own hut, how many fall to your share?

OROU. Every fourth, be it a boy or a girl. You see, we have developed a kind of circulation of men, women and children—that is, of able-bodied workers of all ages and occupations—which is much more important than trade in foodstuffs (which are only the products of human labor) in your country.

THE CHAPLAIN. I can easily believe it. What is the significance of those black veils that I have seen a few persons wearing?

OROU. They indicate barrenness, either congenital or that which comes with advanced age. Any woman who lays aside such a veil and mingles with men is considered dissolute, and so is any man who raises such a veil and has commerce with a barren woman.

THE CHAPLAIN. And the gray veils?

OROU. That shows that the woman is having her monthly period. Failure to wear this veil when it should be worn also stigmatizes a woman as dissolute if she has relations with men during that time, and likewise the man who has relations with her.

THE CHAPLAIN. Do you punish this libertinism?

OROU. Only with public disapproval.

THE CHAPLAIN. May a father sleep with his daughter, a mother with her son, a brother with his sister, a husband with someone else's wife?

OROU. Why not?

THE CHAPLAIN. Well! To say nothing of the fornication, what of the incest, the adultery?

OROU. What do you mean by those words, "fornication, incest" and "adultery"?

THE CHAPLAIN. They are crimes, horrible crimes for which people are burned at the stake in my country.

OROU. Well, whether they burn or don't burn in your country is nothing to me. But you cannot condemn the morals of Europe for not being those of Tahiti, nor our morals for not being those of Europe. You need a more dependable rule of judgment than that. And what shall it be? Do you know a better one than general welfare and individual utility? Well, now, tell me in what way your crime of incest is contrary to the two aims of our conduct; if you think that everything is settled once and for all because a law has been promulgated, a derogatory word invented, and a punishment established. Why don't you tell me what you mean by "incest."

THE CHAPLAIN. Why, incest . . .

OROU. Yes, incest . . . ? Has it been a long time since your great workman without hands, head or tools made the world?

THE CHAPLAIN. No.

OROU. Did he make the whole human race at one time?

THE CHAPLAIN. No, he made only one man and one woman.

OROU. Had they children?

THE CHAPLAIN. Of course.

OROU. Let's suppose that these two original parents had no sons—only daughters—and that the mother was the first to die. Or that they had only sons and that the wife lost her husband.

THE CHAPLAIN. You embarrass me. But in spite of anything you may say, incest is a horrible crime, so let's talk about something else.

OROU. That's all very well for you to say. But as for me, I won't speak another word until you tell me why incest is such a horrible crime.

THE CHAPLAIN. All right, I'll grant you that perhaps incest does not offend nature, but isn't it objection enough that it threatens the political order? What would happen to the security of the chief of state, and what would become of a nation's tranquillity, if millions of people should come to be under the thumbs of fifty or so fathers of families?

OROU. That would be the lesser of two evils. There would be no single great society, but fifty or so little ones, more happiness and one crime the less.

THE CHAPLAIN. I should think, though, that even here it must not be very common for a son to sleep with his mother.

OROU. No, not unless he has a great deal of respect for her, or a degree of tenderness that makes him forget the disparity in their ages and prefer a woman of forty to a girl of nineteen.

THE CHAPLAIN. What about intercourse between fathers and daughters?

OROU. Hardly more frequent, unless the girl is ugly and little sought after. If her father has a great deal of affection for her, he helps her in getting ready her dowry of children.

THE CHAPLAIN. What you say suggests to me that in Tahiti the women on whom nature has not smiled have a rather hard time of it.

OROU. What you say only shows that you haven't a high opinion of the generosity of our young men.

THE CHAPLAIN. As for unions between brothers and sisters, I imagine they are very common.

OROU. Yes, and very strongly approved of.

THE CHAPLAIN. According to you, the same passion that gives rise to so many evils and crimes in our countries is completely innocent here.

OROU. Stranger, you have poor judgment and a faulty memory. Poor judgment, because whenever something is forbidden, it is inevitable that people should be tempted to do that thing, and do it. Faulty memory, because you have already forgotten what I told you. We do have dissolute old women who sneak out at night without their black veils and offer themselves to men, even though nothing can come of it. If they are recognized or surprised, the punishment is either exile to the northern tip of the island or slavery. There are precocious girls who lift their white veils without their parents' knowledge—for them we have a locked room in the hut. There are young boys who take off their chain before the time established by nature and our laws—in that case the parents get a strong reprimand. There are women who find the nine months of pregnancy a long time; women and girls who are careless about wearing their gray veils—but as a matter of fact we attach little importance to all these lapses. You would find it hard to believe how much our morals have been improved on these points by the fact that we have come to identify in our minds the idea of public and private wealth with the idea of increasing the population.

THE CHAPLAIN. But don't disturbances ever arise when two men have a passion for the same woman, or when two girls desire the same man?

OROU. I haven't seen as many as four instances. The choice of the woman or man settles the matter. If a man should commit any act of violence, that would be a serious misdemeanor, but even then no one would take any notice unless the injured party were to make a public complaint, and it is almost unheard of for a girl or woman to do so. The only thing I have noticed is that our women are a little less considerate of homely men than our young men are of ill-favored women; but no one is worried with this state of affairs.

THE CHAPLAIN. So far as I can see, jealousy is practically unknown here in Tahiti. But tenderness between husband and wife, and maternal love, which are strong, beautiful emotions—if they exist here at all, they must be fairly lukewarm.

OROU. We have put in their place another impulse, which is more universal, powerful and lasting—self-interest. Examine your conscience in all candor, put aside the hypocritical parade of virtue which is always on the lips of your companions, though not in their hearts, and tell me if there is anywhere on the face of the earth a man who, if he were not held back by shame, would not prefer to lose his child—a husband who would not prefer to lose his wife—rather than lose his fortune and all the amenities of life? You may be sure that if ever a man can be led to care as much about his fellow men as he does about his own bed, his own health, his leisure, his house, his harvests or his fields, he can be depended upon to do his utmost to look out for the well-being of other people. Then you will see him shedding tears over the bed of a sick child or taking care of a mother when she is ill. Then you will find fruitful women, nubile girls and handsome young men highly regarded.

Then you will find a great deal of attention paid to the education of the young, because the nation grows stronger with their growth, and suffers a material loss if their well-being is impaired.

THE CHAPLAIN. I am afraid there is some reason in what this savage says. The poor peasant of our European lands wears out his wife in order to spare his horse, lets his child die without help and calls the veterinary to look after his ox.

OROU. I didn't quite hear what you were just saying. But when you get back to your own country where everything is so well managed, try to teach them how well our method works. Then they will begin to realize how precious a newborn baby is and how important it is to increase the population. Shall I tell you a secret? But take care that you don't let it out. When you came, we let you do what you liked with our women and girls. You were astonished and your gratitude made us laugh. You thanked us, even though we were levying the heaviest of all taxes on you and your companions. We asked no money of you; we didn't loot your ship; we didn't give a hang for any of your stores of food—but our women and girls came to draw the blood out of your veins. When you go away, you will leave with us a brood of children. Do you think we could have extracted a more valuable tribute from you than this tax collected from your own bodies and from your own substance? If you would care to try and estimate its value, imagine that you have yet to sail along two hundred leagues of coastline, and that every twenty miles they collect the same tribute from you! We have vast areas of land yet to be put under the plow; we need workers, and we have tried to get you to give them to us. We have epidemics from time to time, and these losses must be made up; we have sought your aid to fill up the gaps in our population. We have external enemies to deal with, and for this we need soldiers, so we have allowed you to give them to us. We have a surplus of women and girls over men, and we have enlisted your services to help us out. Among these women and girls there are some with whom our men have thus far been unable to beget any children, and these were the ones we first assigned to receive your embraces. A neighboring nation holds us in vassalage, and we have to pay an annual tribute to them in men; you and your friends have helped us to pay off this debt, and in five or six years we shall send them your sons if they turn out to be inferior in some way to our own. Although we are stronger and healthier than you, we have observed that you have the edge on us when it comes to intelligence. So we immediately marked out some of our most beautiful women and girls to collect the seed of a race superior to ours. This is an experiment we have tried, and that we hope will succeed. We have taken from you and your fellows the only thing we could get from you. Just because we are savages, don't think we are incapable of calculating where our best advantage lies. Go wherever you will, and you will always find a man as shrewd as you are. He will give you what he has no use for, and he will always ask for something he has need of. If he offers to trade you a piece of gold for a scrap of iron, that is because he doesn't care a hang for gold, and desires iron. By the way, why is it that you are not dressed like the others? What is the significance of the long robe that covers you from head to foot, and what is that pointed bag that you let hang over your shoulders and sometimes draw up around your ears?

THE CHAPLAIN. The reason I dress as I do is that I am a member of a society of men who are called monks in my country. The most sacred of their vows is never to have intercourse with any woman and never to beget any children.

OROU. Then what kind of work do you do?

THE CHAPLAIN. None.

OROU. And your magistrates allow that sort of idleness—the worst of all?

THE CHAPLAIN. They more than allow it: they honor it and make others do the same.

OROU. My first thought was that nature, or some accident, or some cruel form of sorcery, had deprived you of the ability to reproduce your kind, and that out of pity they had let you go on living instead of killing you. But my daughter tells me that you are a man as robust as any Tahitian and that she has high hopes of getting good results from your repeated caresses. Well, at last I know why you kept mumbling yesterday evening, "But there's my religion, my holy orders!" Could you explain to me why it is that your magistrates show you such favor and treat you with so much respect?

THE CHAPLAIN. I don't know.

OROU. Still, you must know why it was that, although you are a man, you have condemned yourself of your own free will to be one no longer?

THE CHAPLAIN. That's hard to explain, and it would take too long.

OROU. Are monks faithful to their vows of sterility?

THE CHAPLAIN. No.

OROU. I was sure of it. Do you also have female monks?

THE CHAPLAIN. Yes.

OROU. As well behaved as the male monks?

THE CHAPLAIN. They are kept more strictly in seclusion, they dry up from unhappiness and die of boredom.

OROU. So Nature is avenged for the injury done to her! Ugh! What a country! If everything is managed the way you say, you are more barbarous than we are.

The good chaplain tells us that he spent the rest of the day wandering about the island, visiting a number of huts, and that in the evening, after supper, the father and mother begged him to go to bed with Palli, the second eldest daughter. She offered herself in the same undress as Thia's, and he tells us that several times during the night he cried out, "My religion! My holy orders!" The third night he suffered the same guilty torments in the arms of Asto, the eldest, and the fourth night, not to be unfair, he devoted to his hostess. . . .

FURTHER READING

David Foxon, "Libertine Literature in England, 1660–1745," *The Book Collector*, Vol. XII, Nos. 1, 2, 3 (Spring, Summer, Winter 1963), 21–36, 159–77, 294–307. A bibliographical analysis of dirty books. Similar appraisals for the rest of the enlightened world are needed before we can place such books as Diderot's *Supplement* in perspective.

Robert Mauzi, *L'Idée de la bonheur au XVIIIᵉ siècle* (1960). An exhaustive French thesis throwing much light on the idea of happiness, including Diderot's, in the Age of the Enlightenment.

Leo Spitzer, "The Style of Diderot," in his *Linguistics and Literary History: Essays in Stylistics* (1948), 135–91. A brilliant, original, and convincing essay arguing for the fundamentally sensual nature of all of Diderot's writings.

The Line
of Beauty

In the natural and the social sciences, and in the search for good government and rational philosophy, the men of the Enlightenment were confident of success. They thought, not without self-satisfaction, that they were presiding over an age of breathtaking innovation. In the arts, on the other hand, they saw themselves as shadows of their forebears; Voltaire and the others kept reiterating that they were living in a mere Silver Age, pale after the Golden Age of the seventeenth century. While his audiences applauded Voltaire's dramas as equal in stature to those of Corneille and Racine, Voltaire deprecated them as inferior to his imperishable models—and Voltaire was right. While the English public celebrated Sir Joshua Reynolds as a great painter, Reynolds held up the immortal name of "Michael Angelo" as beyond reach, certainly on his part—and Reynolds was right.

Yet, while the philosophes were right to think of their century as a kind of Silver Age in the arts, they witnessed, and made, a transformation in the philosophy of literature and art. At the beginning of the eighteenth century the civilized world was still in the grip of neoclassical dogma. Its tenets were, briefly, that art is a science, that it elevates its audience as it entertains, that it obeys strict standards of decorum. This last implied classification and hierarchy: in the theater, Neoclassicism insisted on the Aristotelian unities of time, place, and action, on the dignity of speech, and on the separation of genres—the macabre humor of the gravedigger in the tragedy of Hamlet was, for Neoclassical taste, a grievous breach of taste. In painting, it granted elevated subjects—great moments in man's religious, military, or political history—the highest prestige, to be followed down the ladder of regard by portraits, landscapes, genre scenes, and still lifes. And the proposition that art is a science brought with it the demand that art must imitate nature, not as it is, but as it might be.

As writers and critics, and in their personal preferences, the philosophes never wholly shook off this burden of the past. But in their far-ranging writings on the arts they began to discover alterna-

tives. Theirs was an immensely active time of exploration into the meaning of the arts and their relation to one another; it is hardly an accident that the very word aesthetics *should enter the language at midcentury, with the writings of the German philosopher Alexander Gottlieb Baumgarten. The Neoclassical claim that art is scientific had implied the existence of an objective standard of beauty, which men discover and apply; the philosophes first damaged and then destroyed this claim and replaced it with a far more relativist, wholly modern, appraisal of aesthetic perception. And, of course, to our continuing delight, the philosophes did not confine themselves to philosophizing: they practiced literature, and in their most interesting work—Diderot's* Neveu de Rameau, *or Voltaire's* Candide—*they changed its face. As Count Algarotti, scientific popularizer and professional hanger-on, put it in 1756, "The philosophical spirit which has made such progress in our times and has penetrated all the domains of knowledge, has in a certain manner become the censor of all the arts."**

As elsewhere, so in aesthetics the philosophes had assiduous allies. It was Edmund Burke, scarcely a philosophe, who as a young man wrote an inquiry into the Origin of our Ideas of the Sublime and the Beautiful *(1756). The book seems slight to us today, but it was influential in its time, and contributed to the discussion of that astonishing phenomenon: the aesthetic pleasure men take from confronting scenes of certain types of horror and ugliness. And it was William Hogarth, combative chauvinist, scourge of modern vice, and certainly no philosophe, who published, in 1753, an essay called* The Analysis of Beauty, *in which he extolled the pleasing qualities of the serpentine line—the line of beauty. The philosophes did much to analyze that line of beauty, and to trace its meaning for those who created and those who enjoyed it. In aesthetics—in the history, the criticism, the psychology and the philosophy of art—the philosophes decisively changed the general way of thinking.*

* Quoted in Rémy G. Saisselin, "Neo-Classicism: Virtue, Reason and Nature," in Henry Hawley, ed., *Neo-Classicism: Style and Motif* (1964), 5.

FURTHER READING

Frederick Antal, *Hogarth and His Place in European Art* (1962). A stimulating, informative appraisal of Hogarth, though handicapped by its Marxist simplifications.

Walter Jackson Bate, *From Classic to Romantic: Premises of Taste in Eighteenth Century England* (1946). Short, masterly; goes beyond England to discuss Kant's important aesthetic writings.

Herbert Dieckmann, *Esthetic Theory and Criticism in the Enlightenment: Some Examples of Modern Trends* (1965). Erudite, economical, indispensable.

A. Dresdner, *Die Kunstkritik: Ihre Geschichte und Theorie*, Vol. I, *Die Entstehung der Kunstkritik* (1915—the only volume to appear). A splendid analysis of art criticism in the eighteenth century; rightly stresses the role of Diderot and sets him off from his precursors.

Wladyslaw Folkierski, *Entre le classicisme et le romantisme: Étude sur l'esthétique et les esthéticiens du XVIIIᵉ siècle* (1925). A dependable old warhorse.

Paul Oskar Kristeller, "The Modern System of the Arts: A Study in the History of Aesthetics," *Journal of the History of Ideas*, Vol. XII, No. 4 (October 1951), 296–327, and Vol. XIII, No. 1 (January 1952), 17–46. Learned survey of the rise of modern thinking about art; important for the role of the Enlightenment.

Raymond Naves, *Le Goût de Voltaire* (1938). Examines the literary and aesthetic taste (mainly literary) of the most famous of philosophes.

René Wellek, "Aesthetics and Criticism," in C. W. Hendel, ed., *The Philosophy of Kant and Our Modern World* (1957). Excellent presentation.

———, *A History of Modern Criticism*, Vol. I, *The Later Eighteenth Century* (1955). Impeccable in scholarship, superb in judgment, this is an invaluable history.

32 ❀ WINCKELMANN

Reflections on the Painting and Sculpture of the Greeks

[From Johann Joachim Winckelmann, *Reflexions on the Imitation of the Painting and Sculpture of the Greeks,* translated by Henry Fusseli (*sic*) (1765), 1–19. The style has been slightly modernized.]

Of all the birds in the philosophic aviary, Johann Joachim Winckelmann was distinctly the oddest. Born in 1717 in the poorest circumstances, Winckelmann was from his earliest years possessed by the lust for Greek art—which, to him, meant the masculine ideal of Greek beauty as embodied in its statuary. Impecunious and dependent, Winckelmann was determined to go to the source of that beauty; in 1754, largely from calculation, he converted to Roman Catholicism, and he went to Italy in the following year. Before he reached the South he published his Gedanken über die Nachahmung der griechischen Werke in Malerei und Bildhauerkunst, *in which he first adumbrated his ideal of Greek sculptural beauty, and his controversial definition of the Greek aesthetic ideal as "noble simplicity and quiet grandeur."**

Once in Rome, Winckelmann spent his time studying classical remains, and reading in the extensive Vatican Library. The chief result of his passionate labors was the pioneering Geschichte der Kunst des Altertums *(1764). This "history of art in antiquity," like everything else Winckelmann did, is studded with contradictions. It is an epoch-making work devoted to periodizing the art of ancient Greece and to relating the Greek artistic achievement to its political*

---

* See below, Lessing, *Laocoön* (selection 35), in which Lessing takes off from this definition and quotes the pamphlet of 1755 at some length.

institutions and its physical setting. But much of its dating is wrong; worse, this history, ostensibly dedicated to historical understanding, is propaganda for male beauty. Winckelmann had no sympathy for Egyptian art, since its figures, he thought, were ugly. His aesthetic preferences were grounded in his sexual preferences. Even his death dramatized the sexual origins of his artistic taste: he was murdered in 1768 over some gold coins by a dubious acquaintance he had picked up. Yet Winckelmann, partisan, emotionally crippled, and half informed as he was, put the history of art on truly historical grounds by insisting that style—its birth, evolution, and decay—is a historical phenomenon. He may have been (as Herder put it) less interested in history than in "a historical metaphysics of history,"* but it was the byproduct that gave him influence and immortality.

I. NATURE

To the Greek climate we owe the production of Taste, and from thence it spread at length over all the politer world. Every invention communicated by foreigners to that nation was but the seed of what it became afterwards, changing both its nature and size in a country chosen, as Plato says, by Minerva to be inhabited by the Greeks, as productive of every kind of genius.

But this Taste was not only original among the Greeks, but seemed also quite peculiar to their country: it seldom went abroad without loss, and was long ere it imparted its kind influences to more distant climes. It was, doubtless, a stranger to the northern zones, when Painting and Sculpture, those offsprings of Greece, were despised there to such a degree that the most valuable pieces of Correggio served only for blinds to the windows of the royal stables at Stockholm.

There is but one way for the moderns to become great, and perhaps unequalled; I mean, by imitating the ancients. And what we are told of Homer, that whoever understands him well, admires him, we find no less true in matters concerning the ancient, espe-

---

* Quoted in Carl Justi, *Winckelmann und seine Zeitgenossen*, 3 vols., 5th edn. (1956), III, 129–30.

cially the Greek, arts. But then we must be as familiar with them as with a friend, to find Laocoön as inimitable as Homer. By such intimacy our judgment will be that of Nicomachus: "Take these eyes," replied he to some paltry critic censuring the Helen of Zeuxis, "Take my eyes, and she will appear a goddess."

With such eyes Michael Angelo, Raphael, and Poussin considered the performances of the ancients. They imbibed taste at its source; and Raphael particularly in its native country. We know that he sent young artists to Greece, to copy there, for his use, the remains of antiquity.

An ancient Roman statue compared to a Greek one will generally appear like Virgil's Diana amidst her Oreads in comparison of the Nausicaa of Homer, whom he imitated.

Laocoön was the standard of the Roman artists as well as ours; and the rules of Polycletus became the rules of art.

I need not put the reader in mind of the negligences to be met with in the most celebrated ancient performances: the Dolphin at the feet of the Medicean Venus, with the children, and the Parerga of the Diomedes by Dioscorides, being commonly known. The reverse of the best Egyptian and Syrian coins seldom equals the head, in point of workmanship. Great artists are wisely negligent, and even their errors instruct. Behold their works as Lucian bids you behold the Zeus of Phidias: Zeus himself, not his footstool.

It is not only Nature which the votaries of the Greeks find in their works, but still more, something superior to Nature: ideal beauties, brain-born images, as Proclus says.

The most beautiful body of ours would perhaps be as much inferior to the most beautiful Greek one as Iphicles was to his brother Hercules. The forms of the Greeks, prepared to beauty by the influence of the mildest and purest sky, became perfectly elegant by their early exercises. Take a Spartan youth, sprung from heroes, undistorted by swaddling-cloths; whose bed, from his seventh year, was the earth, familiar with wrestling and swimming from his infancy; and compare him with one of our young Sybarites, and then decide which of the two would be deemed worthy by an artist to serve for the model of a Theseus, an Achilles, or even a Bacchus. The latter would produce a Theseus fed on roses, the former a Theseus fed on flesh, to borrow the expression of Euphranor.

The grand games were always a very strong incentive for every Greek youth to exercise himself. Whoever aspired to the honours of these was obliged, by the laws, to submit to a trial of ten months at

Elis, the general rendezvous; and there the first rewards were commonly won by youths, as Pindar tells us. *To be like the God-like Diagoras* was the fondest wish of every youth.

Behold the swift Indian outstripping in pursuit the hart: how briskly his juices circulate! how flexible, how elastic his nerves and muscles! how easy his whole frame! Thus Homer draws his heroes, and his Achilles he eminently marks for "being swift of foot."

By these exercises the bodies of the Greeks got the great and manly contour observed in their statues, without any bloated corpulency. The young Spartans were bound to appear every tenth day naked before the Ephori, who, when they perceived any inclinable to fatness, ordered them a scantier diet; nay, it was one of Pythagoras's precepts to beware of growing too corpulent; and, perhaps for the same reason, youths aspiring to wrestling-games were, in the remoter ages of Greece, during their trial, confined to a milk diet.

They were particularly cautious in avoiding every deforming custom; and Alcibiades, when a boy, refusing to learn to play on the flute, for fear of its discomposing his features, was followed by all the youth of Athens.

In their dress they were professed followers of Nature. No modern stiffening habit, no squeezing stays hindered Nature from forming easy beauty; the fair knew no anxiety about their attire, and from their loose and short habits the Spartan girls got the epithet of Phaenomirides.

We know what pains they took to have handsome children, but want to be acquainted with their methods: for certainly Quillet, in his Callipaedy, falls short of their numerous expedients. They even attempted changing blue eyes to black ones, and games of beauty were exhibited at Elis, the rewards consisting of arms consecrated to the temple of Minerva. How could they miss of competent and learned judges when, as Aristotle tells us, the Grecian youths were taught drawing expressly for that purpose? From their fine complexion, which, though mingled with a vast deal of foreign blood, is still preserved in most of the Greek islands, and from the still enticing beauty of the fair sex, especially at Chios, we may easily form an idea of the beauty of the former inhabitants, who boasted of being aborigines, nay, more ancient than the moon.

And are not there several modern nations among whom beauty is too common to give any title to pre-eminence? Such are unanimously accounted the Georgians and the Kabardinski in the Crim.

Those diseases which are destructive of beauty were moreover unknown to the Greeks. There is not the least hint of the smallpox in the writings of their physicians; and Homer, whose portraits are always so truly drawn, mentions not one pitted face. Venereal plagues, and their daughter the English malady, had not yet names.

And must we not then, considering every advantage which Nature bestows, or art teaches, for forming, preserving, and improving beauty, enjoyed and applied by the Grecians; must we not then confess there is the strongest probability that the beauty of their persons excelled all we can have an idea of?

Art claims liberty: in vain would Nature produce her noblest offsprings in a country where rigid laws would choke her progressive growth, as in Egypt, that pretended parent of sciences and arts; but in Greece, where, from their earliest youth, the happy inhabitants were devoted to mirth and pleasure, where narrow-spirited formality never restrained the liberty of manners, the artist enjoyed Nature without a veil.

The gymnasies, where, sheltered by public modesty, the youths exercised themselves naked, were the schools of art. These the philosopher frequented, as well as the artist: Socrates for the instruction of a Charmides, Autolycas, Lysis; Phidias for the improvement of his art by their beauty. Here he studied the elasticity of the muscles, the ever varying motions of the frame, the outlines of fair forms, or the contour left by the young wrestler on the sand. Here beautiful nakedness appeared with such a liveliness of expression, such truth and variety of situations, such a noble air of the body, as it would be ridiculous to look for in any hired model of our academies.

Truth springs from the feelings of the heart. What shadow of it therefore can the modern artist hope for by relying upon a vile model whose soul is either too base to feel or too stupid to express the passions, the sentiment his object claims? Unhappy he! if experience and fancy fail him.

The beginning of many of Plato's dialogues, supposed to have been held in the gymnasies, cannot raise our admiration of the generous souls of the Athenian youth without giving us, at the same time, a strong presumption of a suitable nobleness in their outward carriage and bodily exercises.

The fairest youths danced undressed on the theatre; and Sophocles, the great Sophocles, when young, was the first who dared to entertain his fellow-citizens in this manner. Phryne went to bathe at the Eleusinian games, exposed to the eyes of all Greece, and, rising from the water, became the model of Venus Anadyomene. During certain solemnities the young Spartan maidens danced naked before the young men: strange this may seem, but will appear more probable when we consider that the Christians of the primitive Church, both men and women, were dipped together in the same font.

Then every solemnity, every festival, afforded the artist opportunity to familiarize himself with all the beauties of Nature.

In the most happy times of their freedom, the humanity of the Greeks abhorred bloody games, which even in the Ionic Asia had ceased long before, if, as some guess, they had once been usual there. Antiochus Epiphanes, by ordering shows of Roman gladiators, first presented them with such unhappy victims; and custom and time, weakening the pangs of sympathizing humanity, changed even these games into schools of art. There Ctesias studied his dying gladiator, in whom you might descry "how much life was still left in him."*

These frequent occasions of observing Nature taught the Greeks to go on still farther. They began to form certain general ideas of beauty, with regard to the proportions of the inferior parts as well as of the whole frame: these they raised above the reach of mortality, according to the superior model of some ideal Nature.

Thus Raphael formed his Galatea, as we learn by his letter to Count Baltazar Castiglione, where he says, "Beauty being so seldom found among the fair, I avail myself of a certain ideal image."

According to those ideas, exalted above the pitch of material models, the Greeks formed their gods and heroes: the profile of the brow and nose of gods and goddesses is almost a straight line. The same they gave on their coins to queens, etc., but without indulging their fancy too much. Perhaps this profile was as peculiar to the ancient Greeks as flat noses and little eyes to the Calmucks and Chinese; a supposition which receives some strength from the large eyes of all the heads on Greek coins and gems.

From the same ideas the Romans formed their Empresses on their coins. Livia and Agrippina have the profile of Artemisia and Cleopatra.

We observe, nevertheless, that the Greek artists in general submitted to the law prescribed by the Thebans: "to do, under a penalty, their best in imitating Nature." For, where they could not possibly apply their easy profile without endangering the resem-

---

* Some are of opinion, that the celebrated Ludovisian gladiator, now in the great salon of the Capitol, is this same whom Pliny mentions.

blance, they followed Nature, as we see instanced in the beauteous head of Julia, the daughter of Titus, done by Euodus.

But to form a "just resemblance, and, at the same time, a handsomer one," being always the chief rule they observed, and which Polygnotus constantly went by, they must, of necessity, be supposed to have had in view a more beauteous and more perfect Nature. And when we are told that some artists imitated Praxiteles, who took his concubine Cratina for the model of his Cnidian Venus, or that others formed the Graces from Lais, it is to be understood that they did so without neglecting these great laws of the art. Sensual beauty furnished the painter with all that Nature could give; ideal beauty, with the awful and sublime; from that he took the humane, from this the divine.

Let anyone sagacious enough to pierce into the depths of art compare the whole system of the Greek figures with that of the moderns, by which, as they say, Nature alone is imitated; good heaven! what a number of neglected beauties will he not discover!

For instance, in most of the modern figures, if the skin happens to be anywhere pressed, you see there several little smart wrinkles; when, on the contrary, the same parts, pressed in the same manner on Greek statues, by their soft undulations form at last but one noble pressure. These masterpieces never show us the skin forcibly stretched, but softly embracing the firm flesh, which fills it up without any tumid expansion, and harmoniously follows its direction. There the skin never, as on modern bodies, appears in plaits distinct from the flesh.

Modern works are likewise distinguished from the ancient by parts: a crowd of small touches and dimples too sensibly drawn. In ancient works you find these distributed with sparing sagacity, and, as relative to a completer and more perfect Nature, offered but as hints, nay, often perceived only by the learned.

The probability still increases that the bodies of the Greeks as well as the works of their artists were framed with more unity of system, a nobler harmony of parts, and a completeness of the whole, above our lean tensions and hollow wrinkles.

Probability, it is true, is all we can pretend to; but it deserves the attention of our artists and connoisseurs the rather as the veneration professed for the ancient monuments is commonly imputed to prejudice and not to their excellence; as if the numerous ages during which they have mouldered were the only motive for bestowing on them exalted praises and setting them up for the standards of imitation.

Such as would fain deny to the Greeks the advantages both of a more perfect Nature and of ideal beauties boast of the famous Bernini as their great champion. He was of opinion, besides, that Nature was possessed of every requisite beauty; the only skill being to discover that. He boasted of having got rid of a prejudice concerning the Medicean Venus, whose charms he at first thought peculiar ones, but, after many careful researches, discovered now and then in Nature.

He was taught then, by the Venus, to discover beauties in common Nature which he had formerly thought peculiar to that statue, and but for it he never would have searched for them. Follows it not from thence that the beauties of the Greek statues, being discovered with less difficulty than those of Nature, are of course more affecting; not so diffused, but more harmoniously united? And if this be true, the pointing out of Nature as chiefly imitable is leading us into a more tedious and bewildered road to the knowledge of perfect beauty than setting up the ancients for that purpose; consequently Bernini, by adhering too strictly to Nature, acted against his own principles, as well as obstructed the progress of his disciples.

The imitation of beauty is either reduced to a single object, and is *individual*, or, gathering observations from single ones, *composes of these one whole*. The former we call copying, drawing a portrait; it is the straight way to Dutch forms and figures; whereas the other leads to general beauty and its ideal images, and is the way the Greeks took. But there is still this difference between them and us: they, enjoying daily occasions of seeing beauty (suppose even not superior to ours), acquired those ideal riches with less toil than we, confined as we are to a few and often fruitless opportunities, ever can hope for. It would be no easy matter, I fancy, for our Nature to produce a frame equal in beauty to that of Antinous; and surely no idea can soar above the more than human proportions of a deity in the Apollo of the Vatican, which is a compound of the united force of Nature, Genius, and Art.

Their imitation, discovering in the one every beauty diffused through Nature, showing in the other the pitch to which the most perfect Nature can elevate herself when soaring above the senses, will quicken the genius of the artist, and shorten his discipleship: he will learn to think and draw with confidence, seeing here the fixed limits of human and divine beauty.

Building on this ground, his hand and senses directed by the Greek rule of beauty, the modern artist goes on the surest way to the imitation of Nature. The ideas of unity and perfection which he acquired in meditating on antiquity will help him to combine and to ennoble the more scattered and weaker beauties of our Nature. . . .

FURTHER READING

E. M. Butler, *The Tyranny of Greece over Germany* (1935). A brilliant diatribe against the German penchant for getting the wrong ideas from the classics; Winckelmann is the first exhibit in the case for the prosecution (see Hatfield, below).

Henry Hatfield, *Winckelmann and His German Critics* (1943). A sensible, informative survey of the German literature.

———, *Aesthetic Paganism in German Literature* (1964). Excellent and judicious analysis of eighteenth-century German literary attitudes toward the classical world; Winckelmann is prominent. (A fine corrective to Butler, above.)

Carl Justi, *Winckelmann und seine Zeitgenossen,* 3 vols., 5th edn. (1956). Though old, and a little coy on Winckelmann's homosexuality, still enormously useful.

33 ❀ REYNOLDS

Discourses on Art

[From *The Literary Works of Sir Joshua Reynolds*,
2 vols. (1892), I, 406–16, 423–27, 435–37.]

*Joshua Reynolds—Sir Joshua Reynolds after 1769—is an exhibit of
critical importance to this anthology. He represents a new type so
congenial to the Enlightenment: the self-respecting bourgeois, the
man of letters or artist who makes a good living, takes pride in his
work, and does not cringe before the great. I suggested in the Introduction that the philosophes, if they were optimists at all, had
optimism forced upon them by their experience. And that experience prominently included professional success. While some of the
leading and most prosperous philosophes, like Voltaire, never quite
believed it, and never quite shed that courtier's flattery more
appropriate to the seventeenth century than the eighteenth, many
of them stood in their world as sturdy, independent men. Reynolds
splendidly embodies this new attitude.*

*Reynolds is best known, of course, as a painter, as an elegant
maker of neoclassical portraits. But he himself liked to think more
of his literary endeavors and studiously cultivated his literary associations. He preferred, it was said, praise for his writing to praise for
his painting. Born the son of a Devonshire clergyman in 1723, he
studied painting first in London and then, from 1749 on, in Italy.
In 1752 he established himself in London and was soon the rage; by
the late 1750s, when he had to limit his commissions, he was earning
more than £6,000 a year. In 1764, with Dr. Samuel Johnson, he
founded the famous "Club," a select group of brilliant talkers that
numbered among its members Edmund Burke, Edward Gibbon,
James Boswell and others. When, in 1768, the Royal Academy was
founded, Reynolds was its logical, one might say its inevitable,
president. It was at the Academy, year after year, between 1769 and*

1790, that Reynolds delivered his magisterial discourses on art. When he died two years later, full of honors, he left more than £100,000.

The discourses, of which I reprint most of the seventh, are injunctions to honor reason and good sense alike, and to respect both the past and the painter's craft. They end, touchingly, as the aging Reynolds invokes, for the last time, "the name of—MICHAEL ANGELO." Painting is not a handicraft but an intellectual enterprise. Reynolds insisted that the old Roman practice of honoring the art while despising the artist was no longer valid. This too was part of the message the Enlightenment impressed on its century.

DISCOURSE VII

DELIVERED TO THE STUDENTS OF THE ROYAL ACADEMY, ON THE DISTRIBUTION OF THE PRIZES, DECEMBER 10, 1776

The reality of a standard of taste, as well as of corporal beauty.— Beside this immediate truth, there are secondary truths, which are variable; both requiring the attention of the artist, in proportion to their stability or their influence.

GENTLEMEN,

It has been my uniform endeavour, since I first addressed you from this place, to impress you strongly with one ruling idea. I wished you to be persuaded, that success in your art depends almost entirely on your own industry; but the industry which I principally recommended, is not the industry of the *hands,* but of the *mind.*

As our art is not a divine *gift,* so neither is it a mechanical *trade.* Its foundations are laid in solid science; and practice, though essential to perfection, can never attain that to which it aims, unless it works under the direction of principle.

Some writers upon art carry this point too far, and suppose that such a body of universal and profound learning is requisite, that the very enumeration of its kinds is enough to frighten a beginner. Vitruvius, after going through the many accomplishments of nature, and the many acquirements of learning, necessary to an architect, proceeds with great gravity to assert that he ought to be well skilled in the civil law, that he may not be cheated in the title of the ground he builds on. But without such exaggeration, we may go so far as to assert, that a painter stands in need of more knowledge than is to be picked off his pallet, or collected by looking on his model, whether it be in life or in picture. He can never be a great artist who is grossly illiterate.

Every man whose business is description, ought to be tolerably conversant with the poets, in some language or other; that he may imbibe a poetical spirit, and enlarge his stock of ideas. He ought to acquire an habit of comparing and digesting his notions. He ought not to be wholly unacquainted with that part of philosophy which gives an insight into human nature, and relates to the manners, characters, passions, and affections. He ought to know *something* concerning the mind, as well as *a great deal* concerning the body of man. For this purpose, it is not necessary that he should go into such a compass of reading, as must, by distracting his attention, disqualify him for the practical part of his profession, and make him sink the performer in the critic. Reading, if it can be made the favourite recreation of his leisure hours, will improve and enlarge his mind, without retarding his actual industry. What such partial and desultory reading cannot afford, may be supplied by the conversation of learned and ingenious men, which is the best of all substitutes for those who have not the means or opportunities of deep study. There are many such men in this age; and they will be pleased with communicating their ideas to artists, when they see them curious and docile, if they are treated with that respect and deference which is so justly their due. Into such society, young artists, if they make it the point of their ambition, will, by degrees, be admitted. There, without formal teaching, they will insensibly come to feel and reason like those they live with, and find a rational and systematic taste imperceptibly formed in their minds, which they will know how to reduce to a standard, by applying general truth to their own purposes, better, perhaps, than those to whom they owned the original sentiment.

Of these studies, and this conversation, the desire and legitimate offspring is a power of distinguishing right from wrong; which power applied to works of art, is denominated TASTE. Let me then, without further introduction, enter upon an examination, whether taste be so far beyond our reach, as to be unattainable by care; or be so very vague and capricious, that no care ought to be employed about it.

It has been the fate of arts to be enveloped in mysterious and incomprehensible language, as if it was thought necessary that even the terms should correspond to the idea entertained of the instability and uncertainty of the rules which they expressed.

To speak of genius and taste, as in any way connected with reason or common sense, would be, in the opinion of some towering talkers, to speak like a man who possessed neither; who had never felt that enthusiasm, or, to use their own inflated language, was never warmed by that Promethean fire, which animates the canvass and vivifies the marble.

If, in order to be intelligible, I appear to degrade art by bringing her down from the visionary situation in the clouds, it is only to give her a more solid mansion upon the earth. It is necessary that at some time or other we should see things as they really are, and not impose on ourselves by that false magnitude with which objects appear when viewed indistinctly as through a mist.

We will allow a poet to express his meaning, when his meaning is not well known to himself, with a certain degree of obscurity, as it is one sort of the sublime. But when, in plain prose, we gravely talk of courting the Muse in shady bowers; waiting the call and inspiration of Genius, finding out where he inhabits, and where he is to be invoked with the greatest success; of attending to times and seasons when the imagination shoots with the greatest vigour, whether at the summer solstice or the vernal equinox; sagaciously observing how much the wild freedom and liberty of imagination is cramped by attention to established rules; and how this same imagination begins to grow dim in advanced age, smothered and deadened by too much judgment; when we talk such language, or entertain such sentiments as these, we generally rest contented with mere words, or at best entertain notions not only groundless but pernicious.

If all this means, what it is very possible was originally intended only to be meant, that in order to cultivate an art, a man secludes himself from the commerce of the world, and retires into the country at particular seasons; or that at one time of the year his body is in better health, and consequently his mind fitter for the business of hard thinking than at another time; or that the mind may be fatigued and grow confused by long and unremitted application; this I can understand. I can likewise believe, that a man eminent when young for possessing poetical imagination, may, from having taken another road, so neglect its cultivation, as to show less of its powers in his latter life. But I am persuaded, that scarce a poet is to be found, from Homer down to Dryden, who preserved a sound mind in a sound body, and continued practising his profession to the very last, whose latter works are not as replete with the fire of imagination, as those which were produced in his more youthful days.

To understand literally these metaphors, or ideas expressed in poetical language, seems to be equally absurd as to conclude, that because painters sometimes represent poets writing from the dictates of a little winged boy or genius, that this same genius did really inform him in a whisper what he was to write; and that he is himself but a mere machine, unconscious of the operations of his own mind. . . .

Genius and taste, in their common acceptation, appear to be very nearly related; the difference lies only in this, that genius has superadded to it a habit or power of execution; or we may say, that taste, when this power is added, changes its name, and is called genius. They both, in the popular opinion, pretend to an entire exemption from the restraint of rules. It is supposed that their powers are intuitive; that under the name of genius great works are produced, and under the name of taste an exact judgment is given, without our knowing why, and without our being under the least obligation to reason, precept, or experience.

One can scarce state these opinions without exposing their absurdity; yet they are constantly in the mouths of men, and particularly of artists. They who have thought seriously on this subject, do not carry the point so far; yet I am persuaded, that even among those few who may be called thinkers, the prevalent opinion allows less than it ought to the powers of reason; and considers the principles of taste, which give all their authority to the rules of art, as more fluctuating, and as having less solid foundations, than we shall find, upon examination, they really have.

The common saying, that *tastes are not to be disputed,* owes its influence, and its general reception, to the same error which leads us to imagine this faculty of too high an original to submit to the authority of an earthly tribunal. It likewise corresponds with the notions of those who consider it as a mere phantom of the imagination, so devoid of substance as to elude all criticism. . . .

We apply the term Taste to that act of the mind by which we like or dislike, whatever be the subject. Our judgment upon an airy nothing, a fancy which has no foundation, is called by the same name which we give to our determination concerning those truths which refer to the most general and most unalterable principles of human nature; to the works which are only to be produced by the greatest efforts of the human understanding. However inconvenient this may be, we are obliged to take words as we find them; all we can do is to distinguish the THINGS to which they are applied.

We may let pass those things which are at once subjects of taste and sense, and which, having as much certainty as the senses themselves, give no occasion to inquiry or dispute. The natural appetite or taste of the human mind is for TRUTH; whether that truth results from the real agreement or equality of original ideas among themselves; from the agreement of the representation of any object with the thing represented; or from the correspondence of the several parts of any arrangement with each other. It is the very same taste which relishes a demonstration in geometry, that is pleased with the resemblance of a picture to an original and touched with the harmony of music.

All these have unalterable and fixed foundations in nature, and are therefore equally investigated by reason, and known by study; some with more, some with less clearness, but all exactly in the same way. A picture that is unlike, is false. Disproportionate ordonnance of parts is not right; because it cannot be true, until it ceases to be a contradiction to assert, that the parts have no relation to the whole. Colouring is true, when it is naturally adapted to the eye, from brightness, from softness, from harmony, from resemblance; because these agree with their object, NATURE, and therefore are true; as true as mathematical demonstration; but known to be true only to those who study these things.

But besides real, there is also apparent truth, or opinion, or prejudice. With regard to real truth, when it is known, the taste which conforms to it is, and must be, uniform. With regard to the second sort of truth, which may be called truth upon sufferance, or truth by courtesy, it is not fixed, but variable. However, whilst these opinions and prejudices, on which it is founded, continue, they operate as truth; and the art, whose office it is to please the mind, as well as instruct it, must direct itself according to opinion, or it will not attain its end.

In proportion as these prejudices are known to be generally diffused, or long received, the taste which conforms to them approaches nearer to certainty, and to a sort of resemblance to real science, even where opinions are found to be no better than prejudices. And since they deserve, on account of their duration and extent, to be considered as really true, they become capable of no small degree of stability and determination, by their permanent and uniform nature.

As these prejudices become more narrow, more local, more transitory, this secondary taste becomes more and more fantastical; recedes from real science; is less to be approved by reason, and less followed by practice: though in no case perhaps to be wholly neglected, where it does not stand, as it sometimes does, in direct defiance of the most respectable opinions received amongst mankind.

Having laid down these positions, I shall proceed with less method, because less will serve to explain and apply them.

We will take it for granted, that reason is something invariable, and fixed in the nature of things; and without endeavouring to go back to an account of first principles, which for ever will elude our search, we will conclude, that whatever goes under the name of taste, which we can fairly bring under the dominion of reason, must be considered as equally exempt from change. If, therefore, in the course of this enquiry, we can show that there are rules for the conduct of the artist which are fixed and invariable, it follows of course, that the art of the connoisseur, or, in other words, taste, has likewise invariable principles.

Of the judgment which we make on the works of art, and the preference that we give to one class of art over another, if a reason be demanded, the question is perhaps evaded by answering, I judge from my taste; but it does not follow that a better answer cannot be given, though, for common gazers, this may be sufficient. Every man is not obliged to investigate the cause of his approbation or dislike.

The arts would lie open for ever to caprice and casualty, if those who are to judge of their excellencies had no settled principles by which they are to regulate their decisions, and the merit or defect of performances were to be determined by unguided fancy. And indeed we may venture to assert, that whatever speculative knowledge is necessary to the artist, is equally and indispensably necessary to the connoisseur.

The first idea that occurs in the consideration of what is fixed in art, or in taste, is that presiding principle of which I have so frequently spoken in former discourses,—the general idea of nature. The beginning, the middle, and the end of every thing that is valuable in taste, is comprised in the knowledge of what is truly nature; for whatever notions are not conformable to those of nature, or universal opinion, must be considered as more or less capricious.

My notion of nature comprehends not only the forms which nature produces, but also the nature and internal fabric and organization, as I may call it, of the human mind and imagination.

The terms beauty, or nature, which are general ideas, are but different modes of expressing the same thing, whether we apply these terms to statues, poetry, or pictures. Deformity is not nature, but an accidental deviation from her accustomed practice. This general idea therefore ought to be called Nature; and nothing else, correctly speaking, has a right to that name. But we are sure so far from speaking, in common conversation, with any such accuracy, that, on the contrary, when we criticise Rembrandt and other Dutch painters, who introduced into their historical pictures exact representations of individual objects with all their imperfections, we say,—though it is not in a good taste, yet it is nature.

This misapplication of terms must be very often perplexing to the young student. Is not art, he may say, an imitation of nature? Must he not therefore who imitates her with the greatest fidelity be the best artist? By this mode of reasoning Rembrandt has a higher place than Raffaelle. But a very little reflection will serve to show us that these particularities cannot be nature; for how can that be the nature of man, in which no two individuals are the same?

It plainly appears, that as a work is conducted under the influence of general ideas, or partial, it is principally to be considered as the effect of a good or a bad taste.

As beauty therefore does not consist in taking what lies immediately before you, so neither, in our pursuit of taste, are those opinions which we first received and adopted, the best choice, or the most natural to the mind and imagination. In the infancy of our knowledge we seize with greediness the good that is within our reach; it is by after-consideration, and in consequence of discipline, that we refuse the present for a greater good at a distance. The nobility or elevation of all arts, like the excellency of virtue itself, consists in adopting this enlarged and comprehensive idea; and all criticism built upon the more confined view of what is natural, may properly be called *shallow* criticism, rather than false: its defect is, that the truth is not sufficiently extensive. . . .

I shall now say something on that part of *taste,* which as I have hinted to you before, does not belong so much to the external form of things, but is addressed to the mind, and depends on its original frame, or, to use the expression, the organisation of the soul; I mean the imagination and the passions. The principles of these are as invariable as the former, and are to be known and reasoned upon in the same manner, by an appeal to common sense deciding upon the common feelings of mankind. This sense, and these feelings appear to me of equal authority, and equally conclusive. Now this appeal implies a general uniformity and agreement in the minds of men. It would be else an idle and vain endeavour to establish rules of art; it would be pursuing a phantom, to attempt to move affections with which we were entirely unacquainted. We have no reason to suspect there is a greater difference between our minds than between our forms; of which, though there are no two alike, yet there is a general similitude that goes through the whole race of mankind; and those who have cultivated their taste, can distinguish what is beautiful or deformed, or, in other words, what agrees with or deviates from the general idea of nature, in one case, as well as in the other.

The internal fabric of our minds, as well as the external form of our bodies, being nearly uniform; it seems then to follow of course, that as the imagination is incapable of producing anything originally of itself, and can only vary and combine those ideas with which it is furnished by means of the senses, there will be necessarily an agreement in the imaginations, as in the senses of men. There being this agreement, it follows, that in all cases, in our lightest amusements, as well as in our most serious actions and engagements of life, we must regulate our affections of every kind by that of others. The well-disciplined mind acknowledges this authority, and submits its own opinion to the public voice. It is from knowing what are the general feelings and passions of mankind, that we acquire a true idea of what imagination is; though it appears as if we had nothing to do but to consult our own particular sensations, and these were sufficient to ensure us from all error and mistake.

A knowledge of the disposition and character of the human mind can be acquired only by experience; a great deal will be learned, I admit, by a habit of examining what passes in our bosoms, what are our own motives of action, and of what kind of sentiments we are conscious on any occasion. We may suppose an uniformity, and conclude that the same effect will be produced by the same cause in the mind of others. This examination will contribute to suggest to us matters of inquiry; but we can never be sure that our own sentiments are true and right, till they are confirmed by more extensive observation. One man opposing another determines nothing; but a general union of minds, like a general combination of the forces of all mankind, makes a strength that is irresistible. In fact, as he who does not know himself, does not know others, so it may be said with equal truth, that he who does not know others, knows himself but very imperfectly.

A man who thinks he is guarding himself against prejudices by resisting the authority of others, leaves open every avenue to singularity, vanity, self-conceit, obstinacy, and many other vices, all tending to warp the judgment, and prevent the natural operation of his faculties. This submission to others is a deference which we owe, and indeed are forced involuntarily to pay. In fact, we never are satisfied with our opinions, whatever we may pretend, till they are ratified and confirmed by the suffrages of the rest of mankind. We dispute and wrangle for ever; we endeavour to get men to come to us, when we do not go to them.

He therefore who is acquainted with the works which have pleased different ages and different countries, and has formed his opinion on them, has more materials, and more means of knowing what is analogous to the mind of man, than he who is conversant only with the works of his own age or country. What has pleased, and continues to please, is likely to please again: hence are derived the rules of art, and on this immoveable foundation they must ever stand.

This search and study of the history of the mind, ought not to be confined to one art only. It is by the analogy that one art bears to another, that many things are ascertained, which either were but faintly seen, or, perhaps, would not have been discovered at all, if the inventor had not received the first hints from the practices of a sister art on a similar occasion. The frequent allusions which every man who treats of any art is obliged to make to others, in order to illustrate and confirm his principles, sufficiently show their near connection and inseparable relation.

All arts having the same general end, which is to please; and addressing themselves to the same faculties through the medium of the senses; it follows that their rules and principles must have as great affinity, as the different materials and the different organs or vehicles by which they pass to the mind, will permit them to retain.

We may therefore conclude, that the real substance, as it may be called, of what goes under the name of taste, is fixed and established in the nature of things; that there are certain and regular causes by which the imagination and passions of men are affected; and that the knowledge of these causes is acquired by a laborious and diligent investigation of nature, and by the same slow progress as wisdom or knowledge of every kind, however instantaneous its operations may appear when thus acquired. . . .

Gentlemen, it has been the main scope and principal end of this discourse to demonstrate the reality of a standard in taste, as well as in corporeal beauty; that a false or depraved taste is a thing as well known, as easily discovered, as any thing that is deformed, misshapen, or wrong, in our form or outward make; and that this knowledge is derived from the uniformity of sentiments among mankind, from whence proceeds the knowledge of what are the general habits of nature; the result of which is an idea of perfect beauty.

If what has been advanced be true,—that beside this beauty or truth, which is formed on the uniform, eternal, and immutable laws of nature, and which of necessity can be but *one;* that beside this one immutable verity there are likewise what we have called apparent or secondary truths, proceeding from local and temporary prejudices, fancies, fashions or accidental connection of ideas; if it appears that these last have still their foundation, however slender, in the original fabric of our minds; it follows that all these truths or beauties deserve and require the attention of the artist, in proportion to their stability or duration, or as their influence is more or less extensive. And let me add, that as they ought not to pass their just bounds, so neither do they, in a well-regulated taste, at all prevent or weaken the influence of those general principles, which alone can give to art its true and permanent dignity.

To form this just taste is undoubtedly in your own power, but it is to reason and philosophy that you must have recourse; from them you must borrow the balance, by which is to be weighed and estimated the value of every pretension that intrudes itself on your notice.

The general objection which is made to the introduction of Philosophy into the regions of taste, is, that it checks and restrains the flights of the imagination, and gives that timidity, which an over-carefulness not to err or act contrary to reason is likely to produce. It is not so. Fear is neither reason nor philosophy. The true spirit of philosophy, by giving knowledge, gives a manly confidence, and substitutes rational firmness in the place of vain presumption. A man of real taste is always a man of judgment in other respects; and those inventions which either disdain or shrink from reason, are generally, I fear, more like the dreams of a distempered brain, than the exalted enthusiasm of a sound and true genius. In the midst of the highest flights of fancy or imagination, reason ought to preside from first to last, though I admit her more powerful operation is upon reflection.

Let me add, that some of the greatest names of antiquity, and those who have most distinguished themselves in works of genius and imagination, were equally eminent for their critical skill. Plato, Aristotle, Cicero, and Horace; and among the moderns, Boileau, Corneille, Pope, and Dryden, are at least instances of genius not being destroyed by attention or subjection to rules and science. I should hope, therefore, that the natural consequence of what has been said, would be, to excite in you a desire of knowing the principles and conduct of the great masters of our art, and respect and veneration for them when known.

FURTHER READING

Frederick W. Hilles, *The Literary Career of Sir Joshua Reynolds* (1936). Indispensable to an understanding of Reynolds as a writer.

———, ed., *Portraits by Sir Joshua Reynolds* (1952). A valuable collection of minor writings—essays, character sketches, dialogues.

Sir Joshua Reynolds, *Discourses on Art,* ed. Robert R. Wark (1959). The best critical edition.

Ellis K. Waterhouse, *Reynolds* (1941). A good modern Life.

Edgar Wind, "Humanitätsidee und heroisiertes Porträt in der englischen Kultur des 18ten Jahrhunderts," *Warburg Vorträge, 1930–1* (1932), 156–229. A remarkable essay, connecting art and culture; Reynolds figures prominently.

34 ❀ HUME

"Of the Standard of Taste"

[From *The Philosophical Works of
David Hume,* edited by T. H. Green and
T. H. Grose, 4 vols. (1882), III, 266, 268–81.]

*The preceding selection from Sir Joshua Reynolds' Discourses shows
that as late as the 1770s, writers on art could treat taste—that is,
sound taste—as unchanging and universal. This was the neoclassical position in all its purity. But there were chinks even in
Reynolds' armor, and long before he had begun to deliver his discourses other philosophes had thrown doubt on this kind of rationalism. While Winckelmann searched for the objective proofs
demonstrating the laws of beauty which, once found, good taste
would then seek out and imitate, Montesquieu in the 1750s and
Voltaire in the 1760s laid stress on the subjective element in the
perception and appreciation of the beautiful. Indeed, in 1764, the
very year that Winckelmann published his epoch-making* History of
Art in Antiquity, *Voltaire published an article on "Beauté" in the
first edition of his* Dictionnaire philosophique *that took a perfectly
relativist view of beauty. It is a trivial essay, but all the more
revealing of a drastic shift of opinion for that. Beauty, Voltaire
insisted, depends on the standpoint of the beholder: a toad thinks
the lady toad (whom we consider hideous) nothing less than beautiful, "with her two big round eyes coming out of her little head,
her large flat snout, yellow belly, brown back." And while a French
audience may applaud a tragedy that an English audience yawns at,
this does not mean that either the one or the other is deficient in
good taste.*

*It is in this relativizing tradition, though still confident that the
educated are likely to agree on what to read, what to applaud, and
what to hang on their walls, that we must place David Hume's fine*

essay. It was published in 1757, the year of Burke's inquiry into the
sublime and the beautiful, and it states the emerging view about
taste with Hume's customary lucidity and moderation.

The great variety of Taste, as well as of opinion, which prevails in
the world, is too obvious not to have fallen under everyone's observation. Men of the most confined knowledge are able to remark a
difference of taste in the narrow circle of their acquaintance, even
where the persons have been educated under the same government,
and have early imbibed the same prejudices. But those, who can
enlarge their view to contemplate distant nations and remote ages,
are still more surprized at the great inconsistence and contrariety.
We are apt to call *barbarous* whatever departs widely from our own
taste and apprehension: But soon find the epithet of reproach re-
torted on us. And the highest arrogance and self-conceit is at last
startled, on observing an equal assurance on all sides, and scruples,
amidst such a contest of sentiment, to pronounce positively in its
own favour.

As this variety of taste is obvious to the most careless enquirer; so
will it be found, on examination, to be still greater in reality than
in appearance. The sentiments of men often differ with regard to
beauty and deformity of all kinds, even while their general discourse is the same. There are certain terms in every language, which
import blame, and others praise; and all men, who use the same
tongue, must agree in their application of them. Every voice is
united in applauding elegance, propriety, simplicity, spirit in writing; and in blaming fustian, affectation, coldness, and a false brilliancy: But when critics come to particulars, this seeming unanimity
vanishes; and it is found, that they had affixed a very different
meaning to their expressions. In all matters of opinion and science,
the case is opposite: The difference among men is there oftener
found to lie in generals than in particulars; and to be less in reality
than in appearance. An explanation of the terms commonly ends
the controversy; and the disputants are surprized to find, that they
had been quarrelling, while at bottom they agreed in their judgment. . . .

It is natural for us to seek a *Standard of Taste;* a rule, by which
the various sentiments of men may be reconciled; at least, a deci-

sion, afforded, confirming one sentiment, and condemning another.

There is a species of philosophy, which cuts off all hopes of success in such an attempt, and represents the impossibility of ever attaining any standard of taste. The difference, it is said, is very wide between judgment and sentiment. All sentiment is right; because sentiment has a reference to nothing beyond itself, and is always real, wherever a man is conscious of it. But all determinations of the understanding are not right; because they have a reference to something beyond themselves, to wit, real matter of fact; and are not always conformable to that standard. Among a thousand different opinions which different men may entertain of the same subject, there is one, and but one, that is just and true; and the only difficulty is to fix and ascertain it. On the contrary, a thousand different sentiments, excited by the same object, are all right: Because no sentiment represents what is really in the object. It only marks a certain conformity or relation between the object and the organs or faculties of the mind; and if that conformity did not really exist, the sentiment could never possibly have being. Beauty is no quality in things themselves: It exists merely in the mind which contemplates them; and each mind perceives a different beauty. One person may even perceive deformity, where another is sensible of beauty; and every individual ought to acquiesce in his own sentiment, without pretending to regulate those of others. To seek the real beauty, or real deformity, is as fruitless an enquiry, as to pretend to ascertain the real sweet or real bitter. According to the disposition of the organs, the same object may be both sweet and bitter; and the proverb has justly determined it to be fruitless to dispute concerning tastes. It is very natural, and even quite necessary, to extend this axiom to mental, as well as bodily taste; and thus common sense, which is so often at variance with philosophy, especially with the sceptical kind, is found, in one instance at least, to agree in pronouncing the same decision.

But though this axiom, by passing into a proverb, seems to have attained the sanction of common sense; there is certainly a species of common sense which opposes it, at least serves to modify and restrain it. Whoever would assert an equality of genius and elegance between Ogilby and Milton, or Bunyan and Addison, would be thought to defend no less an extravagance, than if he had maintained a mole-hill to be as high as Teneriffe, or a pond as extensive as the ocean. Though there may be found persons, who give the preference to the former authors; no one pays attention to such a taste; and we pronounce without scruple the sentiment of these pretended critics to be absurd and ridiculous. The principle of the natural equality of tastes is then totally forgot, and while we admit it on some occasions, where the objects seem near an equality, it appears an extravagant paradox, or rather a palpable absurdity, where objects so disproportioned are compared together.

It is evident that none of the rules of composition are fixed by reasonings *a priori,* or can be esteemed abstract conclusions of the understanding, from comparing those habitudes and relations of ideas, which are eternal and immutable. Their foundation is the same with that of all the practical sciences, experience; nor are they any thing but general observations, concerning what has been universally found to please in all countries and in all ages. Many of the beauties of poetry and even of eloquence are founded on false-hood and fiction, on hyperboles, metaphors, and an abuse or perversion of terms from their natural meaning. To check the sallies of the imagination, and to reduce every expression to geometrical truth and exactness, would be the most contrary to the laws of criticism; because it would produce a work, which, by universal experience, has been found the most insipid and disagreeable. But though poetry can never submit to exact truth, it must be confined by rules of art, discovered to the author either by genius or observation. If some negligent or irregular writers have pleased, they have not pleased by their transgressions of rule or order, but in spite of these transgressions: They have possessed other beauties, which were conformable to just criticism; and the force of these beauties has been able to overpower censure, and give the mind a satisfaction superior to the disgust arising from the blemishes. Ariosto pleases; but not by his monstrous and improbable fictions, by his bizarre mixture of the serious and comic styles, by the want of coherence in his stories, or by the continual interruptions of his narration. He charms by the force and clearness of his expression, by the readiness and variety of his inventions, and by his natural pictures of the passions, especially those of the gay and amorous kind: And however his faults may diminish our satisfaction, they are not able entirely to destroy it. Did our pleasure really arise from those parts of his poem, which we denominate faults, this would be no objection to criticism in general: It would only be an objection to those particular rules of criticism, which would establish such circumstances to be faults, and would represent them as universally blameable. If they are found to please, they cannot be faults; let the pleasure, which they produce, be ever so unexpected and unaccountable.

But though all the general rules of art are founded only on experience and on the observation of the common sentiments of human nature, we must not imagine that, on every occasion, the feelings of men will be conformable to these rules. Those finer emotions of the mind are of a very tender and delicate nature, and require the concurrence of many favourable circumstances to make them play with facility and exactness, according to their general and established principles. The least exterior hindrance to such small springs, or the least internal disorder, disturbs their motion, and confounds the operation of the whole machine. When we would make an experiment of this nature, and would try the force of any beauty or deformity, we must choose with care a proper time and place, and bring the fancy to a suitable situation and disposition. A perfect serenity of mind, a recollection of thought, a due attention to the object; if any of these circumstances be wanting, our experiment will be fallacious, and we shall be unable to judge of the catholic and universal beauty. The relation, which nature has placed between the form and the sentiment, will at least be more obscure; and it will require greater accuracy to trace and discern it. We shall be able to ascertain its influence not so much from the operation of each particular beauty, as from the durable admiration, which attends those works, that have survived all the caprices of mode and fashion, all the mistakes of ignorance and envy.

The same Homer, who pleased at Athens and Rome two thousand years ago, is still admired at Paris and at London. All the changes of climate, government, religion, and language, have not been able to obscure his glory. Authority or prejudice may give a temporary vogue to a bad poet or orator; but his reputation will never be durable or general. When his compositions are examined by posterity or by foreigners, the enchantment is dissipated, and his faults appear in their true colours. On the contrary, a real genius, the longer his works endure, and the more wide they are spread, the more sincere is the admiration which he meets with. Envy and jealousy have too much place in a narrow circle; and even familiar acquaintance with his person may diminish the applause due to his performances: But when these obstructions are removed, the beauties, which are naturally fitted to excite agreeable sentiments, immediately display their energy; and while the world endures, they maintain their authority over the minds of men.

It appears then, that, amidst all the variety and caprice of taste, there are certain general principles of approbation or blame, whose influence a careful eye may trace in all operations of the mind. Some particular forms or qualities, from the original structure of the internal fabric, are calculated to please, and others to displease; and if they fail of their effect in any particular instance, it is from some apparent defect or imperfection in the organ. A man in a fever would not insist on his palate as able to decide concerning flavours; nor would one, affected with the jaundice, pretend to give a verdict with regard to colours. In each creature, there is a sound and a defective state; and the former alone can be supposed to afford us a true standard of taste and sentiment. If, in the sound state of the organ, there be an entire or a considerable uniformity of sentiment among men, we may thence derive an idea of the perfect beauty; in like manner as the appearance of objects in day-light, to the eye of a man in health, is denominated their true and real colour, even while colour is allowed to be merely a phantasm of the senses. . . .

One obvious cause, why many feel not the proper sentiment of beauty, is the want of that *delicacy* of imagination, which is requisite to convey a sensibility of those finer emotions. This delicacy every one pretends to: Every one talks of it; and would reduce every kind of taste or sentiment to its standard. But as our intention in this essay is to mingle some light of the understanding with the feelings of sentiment, it will be proper to give a more accurate definition of delicacy, than has hitherto been attempted. And not to draw our philosophy from too profound a source, we shall have recourse to a noted story in *Don Quixote*.

It is with good reason, says Sancho to the squire with the great nose, that I pretend to have a judgment in wine: This is a quality hereditary in our family. Two of my kinsmen were once called to give their opinion of a hogshead, which was supposed to be excellent, being old and of a good vintage. One of them tastes it; considers it; and after mature reflection pronounces the wine to be good, were it not for a small taste of leather, which he perceived in it. The other, after using the same precautions, gives also his verdict in favour of the wine: but with the reserve of a taste of iron, which he could easily distinguish. You cannot imagine how much they were both ridiculed for their judgment. But who laughed in the end? On emptying the hogshead, there was found at the bottom, an old key with a leathern thong tied to it.

The great resemblance between mental and bodily taste will easily teach us to apply this story. Though it be certain, that beauty and deformity, more than sweet and bitter, are not qualities in objects, but belong entirely to the sentiment, internal or external; it must be allowed, that there are certain qualities in objects, which are fitted by nature to produce those particular feelings. Now as these qualities may be found in a small degree, or may be mixed and confounded with each other, it often happens, that the taste is not affected with such minute qualities, or is not able to distinguish all the particular flavours, amidst the disorder, in which they are presented. Where the organs are so fine, as to allow nothing to escape them; and at the same time so exact as to perceive every ingredient in the composition: This we call delicacy of taste, whether we employ these terms in the literal or metaphorical sense. Here then the general rules of beauty are of use; being drawn from established models, and from the observation of what pleases or displeases, when presented singly and in a high degree: And if the same qualities, in a continued composition and in a smaller degree, affect not the organs with a sensible delight or uneasiness, we exclude the person from all pretensions to this delicacy. To produce these general rules or avowed patterns of composition is like finding the key with the leathern thong; which justified the verdict of Sancho's kinsmen, and confounded those pretended judges who had condemned them. Though the hogshead had never been emptied, the taste of the one was still equally delicate, and that of the other equally dull and languid: But it would have been more difficult to have proved the superiority of the former, to the conviction of every by-stander. In like manner, though the beauties of writing had never been methodized, or reduced to general principles; though no excellent models had ever been acknowledged; the different degrees of taste would still have subsisted, and the judgment of one man been preferable to that of another; but it would not have been so easy to silence the bad critic, who might always insist upon his particular sentiment, and refuse to submit to his antagonist. But when we show him an avowed principle of art; when we illustrate this principle by examples, whose operation, from his own particular taste, he acknowledges to be conformable to the principle; when we prove, that the same principle may be applied to the present case, where he did not perceive or feel its influence: He must conclude, upon the whole, that the fault lies in himself, and that he wants the delicacy, which is requisite to make him sensible of every beauty and every blemish, in any composition or discourse. . . .

But though there be naturally a wide difference in point of delicacy between one person and another, nothing tends further to increase and improve this talent, than *practice* in a particular art, and the frequent survey or contemplation of a particular species of beauty. When objects of any kind are first presented to the eye or imagination, the sentiment, which attends them is obscure and confused; and the mind is, in a great measure, incapable of pronouncing concerning their merits or defects. The taste cannot perceive the several excellences of the performance; much less distinguish the particular character of each excellency, and ascertain its quality and degree. If it pronounce the whole in general to be beautiful or deformed, it is the utmost that can be expected; and even this judgment, a person, so unpractised, will be apt to deliver with great hesitation and reserve. But allow him to acquire experience in those objects, his feeling becomes more exact and nice: He not only perceives the beauties and defects of each part, but marks the distinguishing species of each quality, and assigns it suitable praise or blame. A clear and distinct sentiment attends him through the whole survey of the objects; and he discerns that very degree and kind of approbation or displeasure, which each part is naturally fitted to produce. The mist dissipates, which seemed formerly to hang over the object: The organ acquires greater perfection in its operations; and can pronounce, without danger of mistake, concerning the merits of every performance. In a word, the same address and dexterity, which practice gives to the execution of any work, is also acquired by the same means, in the judging of it.

So advantageous is practice to the discernment of beauty, that, before we can give judgment on any work of importance, it will even be requisite, that that very individual performance be more than once perused by us, and be surveyed in different lights with attention and deliberation. There is a flutter or hurry of thought which attends the first perusal of any piece, and which confounds the genuine sentiment of beauty. The relation of the parts is not discerned: The true characters of style are little distinguished: The several perfections and defects seem wrapped up in a species of confusion, and present themselves indistinctly to the imagination. Not to mention, that there is a species of beauty, which, as it is florid and superficial, pleases at first; but being found incompatible with a just expression either of reason or passion, soon palls upon the taste, and is then rejected with disdain, at least rated at a much lower value.

It is impossible to continue in the practice of contemplating any order of beauty, without being frequently obliged to form *comparisons* between the several species and degrees of excellence, and estimating their proportion to each other. A man, who has had no opportunity of comparing the different kinds of beauty, is indeed totally unqualified to pronounce an opinion with regard to any object presented to him. By comparison alone we fix the epithets of praise or blame, and learn how to assign the due degree of each. The coarsest daubing contains a certain lustre of colours and exactness of imitation, which are so far beauties, and would affect the mind of a peasant or Indian with the highest admiration. The most vulgar ballads are not entirely destitute of harmony or nature; and none but a person, familiarized to superior beauties, would pronounce their numbers harsh, or narration uninteresting. A great inferiority of beauty gives pain to a person conversant in the highest excellence of the kind, and is for that reason pronounced a deformity: As the most finished object, with which we are acquainted, is naturally supposed to have reached the pinnacle of perfection, and to be entitled to the highest applause. One accustomed to see, and examine, and weigh the several performances, admired in different ages and nations, can only rate the merits of a work exhibited to his view, and assign its proper rank among the productions of genius.

But to enable a critic the more fully to execute this undertaking, he must preserve his mind free from all *prejudice,* and allow nothing to enter into his consideration, but the very object which is submitted to his examination. We may observe, that every work of art, in order to produce its due effect on the mind, must be surveyed in a certain point of view, and cannot be fully relished by persons, whose situation, real or imaginary, is not conformable to that which is required by the performance. An orator addresses himself to a particular audience, and must have a regard to their particular genius, interests, opinions, passions, and prejudices; otherwise he hopes in vain to govern their resolutions, and inflame their affections. Should they even have entertained some prepossessions against him, however unreasonable, he must not overlook this disadvantage; but, before he enters upon the subject, must endeavour to conciliate their affection, and acquire their good graces. A critic of a different age or nation, who should peruse this discourse, must have all these circumstances in his eye, and must place himself in the same situation as the audience, in order to form a true judgment of the oration. In like manner, when any work is addressed to the public, though I should have a friendship or enmity with the author, I must depart from this situation; and considering myself as a man in general, forget, if possible, my individual being and my peculiar circumstances. A person influenced by prejudice, complies not with this condition; but obstinately maintains his natural position, without placing himself in that point of view, which the performance supposes. If the work be addressed to persons of a different age or nation, he makes no allowance for their peculiar views and prejudices; but, full of the manners of his own age and country, rashly condemns what seemed admirable in the eyes of those for whom alone the discourse was calculated. If the work be executed for the public, he never sufficiently enlarges his comprehension, or forgets his interest as a friend or enemy, as a rival or commentator. By this means, his sentiments are perverted; nor have the same beauties and blemishes the same influence upon him, as if he had imposed a proper violence on his imagination, and had forgotten himself for a moment. So far his taste evidently departs from the true standard; and of consequence loses all credit and authority.

It is well known, that in all questions, submitted to the understanding, prejudice is destructive of sound judgment, and perverts all operations of the intellectual faculties: It is no less contrary to good taste; nor has it less influence to corrupt our sentiment of beauty. It belongs to *good sense* to check its influence in both cases; and in this respect, as well as in many others, reason, if not an essential part of taste, is at least requisite to the operations of this latter faculty. In all the nobler productions of genius, there is a mutual relation and correspondence of parts; nor can either the beauties or blemishes be perceived by him, whose thought is not capacious enough to comprehend all those parts, and compare them with each other, in order to perceive the consistence and uniformity of the whole. Every work of art has also a certain end or purpose, for which it is calculated; and is to be deemed more or less perfect, as it is more or less fitted to attain this end. . . .

. . . [the] same excellence of faculties which contributes to the improvement of reason, the same clearness of conception, the same exactness of distinction, the same vivacity of apprehension, are essential to the operations of true taste, and are its infallible concomitants. It seldom, or never happens, that a man of sense, who has experience in any art, cannot judge of its beauty; and it is no less rare to meet with a man who has a just taste without a sound understanding.

Thus, though the principles of taste be universal, and nearly, if not entirely the same in all men; yet few are qualified to give judgment on any work of art, or establish their own sentiment as the standard of beauty. The organs of internal sensation are seldom so perfect as to allow the general principles their full play, and produce a feeling correspondent to those principles. They either labour under some defect, or are vitiated by some disorder; and by that means, excite a sentiment, which may be pronounced erroneous. When the critic has no delicacy, he judges without any distinction, and is only affected by the grosser and more palpable qualities of the object: The finer touches pass unnoticed and disregarded. Where he is not aided by practice, his verdict is attended with confusion and hesitation. Where no comparison has been employed, the most frivolous beauties, such as rather merit the name of defects, are the object of his admiration. Where he lies under the influence of prejudice, all his natural sentiments are perverted. Where good sense is wanting, he is not qualified to discern the beauties of design and reasoning, which are the highest and most excellent. Under some or other of these imperfections, the generality of men labour; and hence a true judge in the finer arts is observed, even during the most polished ages, to be so rare a character: Strong sense, united to delicate sentiment, improved by practice, perfected by comparison, and cleared of all prejudice, can alone entitle critics to this valuable character; and the joint verdict of such, wherever they are to be found, is the true standard of taste and beauty.

But where are such critics to be found? By what marks are they to be known? How distinguish them from pretenders? These questions are embarrassing; and seem to throw us back into the same uncertainty, from which, during the course of this essay, we have endeavoured to extricate ourselves.

But if we consider the matter aright, these are questions of fact, not of sentiment. Whether any particular person be endowed with good sense and a delicate imagination, free from prejudice, may often be the subject of dispute, and be liable to great discussion and enquiry: But that such a character is valuable and estimable will be agreed in by all mankind. Where these doubts occur, men can do no more than in other disputable questions, which are submitted to the understanding: They must produce the best arguments, that their invention suggests to them; they must acknowledge a true and decisive standard to exist somewhere, to wit, real existence and matter of fact; and they must have indulgence to such as differ from them in their appeals to this standard. It is sufficient for our present purpose, if we have proved, that the taste of all individuals is not upon an equal footing, and that some men in general, however difficult to be particularly pitched upon, will be acknowledged by universal sentiment to have a preference above others.

But in reality the difficulty of finding, even in particulars, the standard of taste, is not so great as it is represented. Though in speculation, we may readily avow a certain criterion in science and deny it in sentiment, the matter is found in practice to be much more hard to ascertain in the former case than in the latter. Theories of abstract philosophy, systems of profound theology, have prevailed during one age: In a successive period, these have been universally exploded: Their absurdity has been detected: Other theories and systems have supplied their place, which again gave place to their successors: And nothing has been experienced more liable to the revolutions of chance and fashion than these pretended decisions of science. The case is not the same with the beauties of eloquence and poetry. Just expressions of passion and nature are sure, after a little time, to gain public applause, which they maintain for ever. Aristotle, and Plato, and Epicurus, and Descartes, may successively yield to each other: But Terence and Virgil maintain an universal, undisputed empire over the minds of men. The abstract philosophy of Cicero has lost its credit: The vehemence of his oratory is still the object of our admiration.

Though men of delicate taste be rare, they are easily to be distinguished in society, by the soundness of their understanding and the superiority of their faculties above the rest of mankind. The ascendant, which they acquire, gives a prevalence to that lively approbation, with which they receive any productions of genius, and renders it generally predominant. Many men, when left to themselves, have but a faint and dubious perception of beauty, who yet are capable of relishing any fine stroke, which is pointed out to them. Every convert to the admiration of the real poet or orator is the cause of some new conversion. And though prejudices may prevail for a time, they never unite in celebrating any rival to the true genius, but yield at last to the force of nature and just sentiment. Thus, though a civilized nation may easily be mistaken in the choice of their admired philosopher, they never have been found long to err, in their affection for a favorite epic or tragic author.

But notwithstanding all our endeavours to fix a standard of taste, and reconcile the discordant apprehensions of men, there still remain two sources of variation, which are not sufficient indeed to confound all the boundaries of beauty and deformity, but will often serve to produce a difference in the degrees of our approbation or blame. The one is the different humours of particular men; the other, the particular manners and opinions of our age and country. The general principles of taste are uniform in human nature:

Where men vary in their judgments, some defect or perversion in the faculties may commonly be remarked; proceeding either from prejudice, from want of practice, or want of delicacy; and there is just reason for approving one taste, and condemning another. But where there is such a diversity in the internal frame or external situation as is entirely blameless on both sides, and leaves no room to give one the preference above the other; in that case a certain degree of diversity in judgment is unavoidable, and we seek in vain for a standard, by which we can reconcile the contrary sentiments.

A young man, whose passions are warm, will be more sensibly touched with amorous and tender images, than a man more advanced in years, who takes pleasure in wise, philosophical reflections concerning the conduct of life and moderation of the passions. At twenty, Ovid may be the favourite author; Horace at forty; and perhaps Tacitus at fifty. Vainly would we, in such cases, endeavour to enter into the sentiments of others, and divest ourselves of those propensities, which are natural to us. We choose our favourite author as we do our friend, from a conformity of humour and disposition. Mirth or passion, sentiment or reflection; whichever of these most predominates in our temper, it gives us a peculiar sympathy with the writer who resembles us. . . .

FURTHER READING

Charles Jacques Beyer, "Montesquieu et le relativisme esthétique," *Studies on Voltaire and the Eighteenth Century*, Vol. XXIV (1963), 171–82. A clear and brief analysis of an important eighteenth-century aesthetic relativist.

Olivier Brunet, *Philosophie et esthétique chez David Hume* (1965). The only thoroughgoing analysis of Hume's ideas on the arts; far too long and too humorless.

Jean Ehrard, *Montesquieu: Critique d'Art* (1965). Good study of the evolution of Montesquieu's taste through his voyages.

A. Lombard, *L'Abbè Du Bos, un initiateur de la pensée moderne (1670–1742)* (1913). Excellent, full monograph on a French aesthetician whose *Réfléxions critiques sur la poésie et la peinture* (1719) pioneered the modern position.

35 ❈ LESSING

Laocoön

[From Gotthold Ephraim Lessing, *Laocoön*,
translated by Edward Allen McCormick,
7–18.*]

In his great autobiography, Dichtung und Wahrheit, *Goethe recalled how strongly Lessing's* Laocoön *had struck him in 1766, when he was a young man of eighteen: "One must be a young man," he wrote, "to recognize what effect Lessing's* Laocoön *had upon us. It carried us from the region of poverty-stricken notions to the open country of thought."† What made* Laocoön *so impressive was not that it started a new debate, but that it brought clarity into an old one. Its self-proclaimed task was to determine "the boundaries of painting and poetry"; it was an attempt, so close to the heart of the philosophes, to apply intelligence to an area in which the real issues had been so long obscured.*

The real issue was this: in his Ars poetica, *the Roman poet Horace had proclaimed, "Ut pictura poesis"—as painting is, so is poetry. From the Renaissance on, writers on aesthetic questions had accepted the authority of the ancient without cavil, as was their custom. They had derivative, repetitive discussions of the painterly quality of poetry and the poetic quality of painting, to the detriment of both poetry and painting. By the middle of the eighteenth century, isolated adventurous spirits like Diderot—who had much in common with Lessing on this point—had begun to question this antique wisdom. In 1767, in his great* Salon *of that year, Diderot broke with the accepted view once and for all: it is not* true *that*

---

† In Goethe, *Gedenkausgabe der Werke, Briefe, und Gespräche,* ed. Ernst Beutler, 24 vols. (1948–54), X, 348.

poetry is like painting; quite the contrary, he insisted, the two are wholly distinct—"Ut pictura poesis non erit."*

This point Lessing had tried to spell out, with awesome erudition and weighty logical apparatus, a year before, in the substantial fragment of a work intended to embrace the definition of all the arts. Laocoön *is a flawed book: Lessing never saw the sculpture on which he hangs his central argument, but had to depend on inaccurate engravings. And his own taste is oddly narrow—he had little knowledge of painting and no interest in lyrical poetry. What makes his essay, incomplete and partisan as it is, so important is, as Goethe remembered, that it moved to "the open country of thought." It is a superb piece of constructive criticism—the kind of general philosophical reconsideration that inquires into the foundations of the arts; while its practical criticism (its judgment of individual paintings or poems) is of very limited value, its constructive effort was to bring flexibility where there had been dogma, and a willingness to experiment where there had been abject dependence on tradition. In its own limited sphere,* Laocoön *was a blow for freedom.*

CHAPTER ONE

The general and distinguishing characteristics of the Greek masterpieces of painting and sculpture are, according to Herr Winckelmann, noble simplicity and quiet grandeur, both in posture and in expression. "As the depths of the sea always remain calm," he says, "however much the surface may be agitated, so does the expression in the figures of the Greeks reveal a great and composed soul in the midst of passions."

Such a soul is depicted in Laocoön's face—and not only in his face—under the most violent suffering. The pain is revealed in every muscle and sinew of his body, and one can almost feel it oneself in the painful contraction of the abdomen without looking at the face or other parts of the body at all. However, this pain expresses itself without any sign of rage either in his face or in his

* Diderot, *Salons*, ed. Jean Seznec and Jean Adhémar, 4 vols. (1957–67), III, 108.

posture. He does not raise his voice in a terrible scream, which Virgil describes his Laocoön as doing; the way in which his mouth is open does not permit it. Rather he emits the anxious and subduced sigh described by Sadolet. The pain of body and the nobility of soul are distributed and weighed out, as it were, over the entire figure with equal intensity. Laocoön suffers, but he suffers like the Philoctetes of Sophocles; his anguish pierces our very soul, but at the same time we wish that we were able to endure our suffering as well as this great man does.

Expressing so noble a soul goes far beyond the formation of a beautiful body. This artist must have felt within himself that strength of spirit which he imparted to his marble. In Greece artists and philosophers were united in one person, and there was more than one Metrodorus. Philosophy extended its hand to art and breathed into its figures more than common souls. . . .

The remark on which the foregoing comments are based, namely that the pain in Laocoön's face is not expressed with the same intensity that its violence would lead us to expect, is perfectly correct. It is also indisputable that this very point shows truly the wisdom of the artist. Only the ill-informed observer would judge that the artist had fallen short of nature and had not attained the true pathos of suffering.

But as to the reasons on which Herr Winckelmann bases this wisdom, and the universality of the rule which he derives from it, I venture to be of a different opinion.

I must confess that the disparaging reference to Virgil was the first cause of my doubts, and the second was the comparison with Philoctetes. I shall proceed from this point and record my thoughts as they developed in me.

"Laocoön suffers like the Philoctetes of Sophocles." But how does Philoctetes suffer? It is strange that his suffering should have left such different impressions. The laments, the cries, the wild curses with which his anguish filled the camp and interrupted all the sacrifices and sacred rites resounded no less terribly through the desert island, and it was this that brought about his banishment there. What sounds of despondency, of sorrow and despair in the poet's presentation ring through the theater! It has been found that the third act of his work is much shorter than the others. From this, the critics claim, we may conclude that the ancients were little concerned with having acts of equal length. I agree with this, but I should prefer to rely on some other example than this for support. The cries of anguish, the moaning, the disjointed ἆ ἆ φεῦ, ἀπαταῖ, ὤμοι μοι! the hole lines of παπᾶ, παπᾶ of which this act consists and which must be spoken with prolonged stresses and with pauses quite different from those of connected speech, have in actual performance doubtless made this act just about as long as the others. It seems much shorter on paper to the reader than it probably did to a theater audience.

A cry is the natural expression of physical pain. Homer's wounded warriors not infrequently fall to the ground with a cry. Venus shrieks aloud at a mere scratch, not because she must be made to represent the tender goddess of sensuality, but because suffering nature must have her due. Even iron Mars screams so horribly on feeling the lance of Diomedes that it sounds like the shouting of ten thousand raging warriors and fills both armies with terror.

High as Homer raises his heroes above human nature in other respects, he still has them remain faithful to it in their sensitiveness to pain and injury and in the expression of this feeling by cries, tears, or invectives. In their deeds they are beings of a higher order, in their feelings true men.

I know that we more refined Europeans of a wiser, later age know better how to govern our mouths and our eyes. Courtesy and propriety force us to restrain our cries and tears. The aggressive bravery of the rough, early ages has become in our time a passive courage of endurance. Yet even our ancestors were greater in the latter than the former. But our ancestors were barbarians. To master all pain, to face death's stroke with unflinching eye, to die laughing under the adder's bite, to weep neither at the loss of one's dearest friend nor at one's own sins: these are the traits of old Nordic heroism. Palnatoko decreed that his Jomsburghers were not to fear anything nor even so much as mention the word "fear."

Not so the Greek! He felt and feared, and he expressed his pain and grief. He was not ashamed of any human weakness, but it must not prevent him from attaining honor nor from fulfilling his duty. The Greek acted from principles whereas the barbarian acted out of his natural ferocity and callousness. In the Greek, heroism was like the spark hidden in the flint, which sleeps quietly as long as no external force awakens it and robs it of its clarity or its coldness. In the barbarian, heroism was a bright, consuming, and ever-raging flame which devoured, or at least blackened, every other fine qual-

ity in him. When Homer makes the Trojans march to battle with
wild cries, while the Greeks go in resolute silence, the commentators
rightly observe that the poet thereby intends to depict the former as
barbarians and the latter as civilized peoples. I am surprised that
they did not notice a similar contrast of character in another
passage. Here the opposing armies have agreed to a truce and are
busy burning their dead, which does not take place without the
shedding of hot tears on both sides (δάκρυα θερμὰ χέοντες). But
Priam forbids his Trojans to weep (οὐδ᾿ εἴα κλαίειν Πρίαμος μέγας).
He does this, Madame Dacier says, because he is afraid they may
grow too softhearted and take up the battle on the following
day with less courage. True! But why, may I ask, should only Priam
fear this? Why does Agamemnon not issue the same command to
the Greeks? The poet's meaning goes deeper: he wants to tell us
that only the civilized Greek can weep and yet be brave at the same
time, while the uncivilized Trojan, to be brave, must first stifle all
human feeling. Νεμεσσῶμαί γε μὲν οὐδὲν κλάιειν ["Weeping does not
make me indignant"] is the remark that Homer has the sensible son
of wise Nestor make on another occasion.

It is worthy of note that among the few tragedies which have
come down to us from antiquity there are two in which physical
pain is not the least part of the misfortune that befalls the suffering
heroes, Philoctetes and the dying Hercules. And Sophocles lets even
the latter wail and moan, weep and cry out. Thanks to our well-
mannered neighbors, those masters of propriety, a wailing Philoctetes or a bawling Hercules today would be the most ridiculous and
unbearable figure on stage. One of their most recent poets [Chateau-
brun] has, to be sure, ventured on a Philoctetes, but did he dare to
show his audience the *true* Philoctetes?

There is even a Laocoön among the lost plays of Sophocles. If
only fate had saved this one for us! From the slight references of
some of the ancient grammarians we cannot determine how the
poet treated his subject. But of this much I am certain: he did not
portray Laocoön as more stoical than Philoctetes and Hercules.
Stoicism is not dramatic, and our sympathy is in direct proportion
to the suffering of the object of our interest. If we see him bearing
his misery with nobility of soul, he will, to be sure, excite our
admiration; but admiration is only a cold sentiment whose barren
wonderment excludes not only every warmer passion but every
other clear conception as well.

I come now to my conclusion: if, according to the ancient Greeks, crying aloud when in physical pain is compatible with nobility of soul, then the desire to express such nobility could not have prevented the artist from representing the scream in his marble. There must be another reason why he differs on this point from his rival the poet, who expresses this scream with deliberate intention.

CHAPTER TWO

Whether it be fact or fiction that Love inspired the first artistic effort in the fine arts, this much is certain: she never tired of guiding the hands of the old masters. Painting, as practiced today, comprises all representations of three-dimensional bodies on a plane. The wise Greek, however, confined it to far narrower limits by restricting it to the imitation of beautiful bodies only. The Greek artist represented only the beautiful; and ordinary beauty, the beauty of a lower order, was only his accidental subject, his exercise, his relaxation. The perfection of the object itself in his work had to give delight, and he was too great to demand of his audience that they be satisfied with the barren pleasure that comes from looking at a perfect resemblance, or from consideration of his skill as a craftsman. Nothing in his art was dearer to him or seemed nobler than its ultimate purpose.

"Who would want to paint you when no one even wants to look at you?" an old epigrammatist asks of an exceedingly deformed man. Many an artist of our time would say, "Be as ugly as possible, I will paint you nevertheless. Even though no one likes to look at you, they will still be glad to look at my picture, not because it portrays you but because it is a proof of my art, which knows how to present such a monster so faithfully."

To be sure, the propensity to this wanton boasting of mere skills, not ennobled by the intrinsic worth of their subjects, is too natural for even the Greeks not to have had their Pauson and their Pyreicus. They had them, but they treated them with stern justice. Pauson, whose subjects did not even have the beauty of ordinary nature and whose low taste made him enjoy best the portrayal of what is faulty and ugly in the human form, lived in the most abject poverty. And Pyreicus, who painted barbershops, filthy workshops, asses, and kitchen herbs with all the zeal of a Dutch artist—as if such things in nature had so much charm or were so rare!—acquired the name of Rhyparographer, or the painter of filth. Indeed, the debauched rich paid their weight in gold for his paintings, as if to offset their intrinsic worthlessness by putting a fictitious value upon them.

The authorities themselves did not deem it beneath their dignity to force the artist to remain in his proper sphere. It is well known that the law of the Thebans commanded idealization in art and threatened digression toward ugliness with punishment. This was no law against bunglers, which has been generally supposed, even by Junius himself. It condemned the Greek Ghezzis, that unworthy artistic device through which a likeness is obtained by exaggerating the ugly parts of the original—in a word, the caricature.

The law of the Olympic judges sprang from the same idea of the beautiful. Every victor in the Olympic games received a statue, but only the three-time winner had a portrait-statue erected in his honor. This was to prevent the increase of mediocre portraits among works of art, for a portrait, although admitting idealization, is dominated by likeness. It is the ideal of one particular man and not of man in general.

We laugh when we hear that among the ancients even the arts were subject to the civil code. But we are not always right when we do so. Unquestionably, laws must not exercise any constraint on the sciences, for the ultimate goal of knowledge is truth. Truth is a necessity to the soul, and it is tyranny to impose the slightest constraint on the satisfaction of this essential need. But the ultimate goal of the arts is pleasure, and this pleasure is not indispensable. Hence it may be for the lawmaker to determine what kind of pleasure and how much of each kind he will permit.

The plastic arts in particular—aside from the inevitable influence they exert on the character of a nation—have an effect that demands close supervision by the law. If beautiful men created beautiful statues, these statues in turn affected the men, and thus the state owed thanks also to beautiful statues for beautiful men. (With us the highly susceptible imagination of mothers seems to express itself only in producing monsters.)

From this point of view I believe I can find some truth in some of the ancient tales which are generally rejected as outright lies. The mothers of Aristomenes, Aristodamas, Alexander the Great, Scipio, Augustus, and Galerius all dreamed during pregnancy that they had relations with a serpent. The serpent was a symbol of divinity, and the beautiful statues and paintings depicting Bacchus, Apollo, Mercury, or Hercules were seldom without one. Those honest mothers had feasted their eyes on the god during the day, and their confused dreams recalled the image of the reptile. Thus I save the dream and abandon the interpretation born of the pride of their sons and the impudence of the flatterer. For there must be some reason why the adulterous fantasy was always a serpent.

But I am digressing. I wanted simply to establish that among the ancients beauty was the supreme law of the visual arts. Once this has been established, it necessarily follows that whatever else these arts may include must give way completely if not compatible with beauty, and, if compatible, must at least be subordinate to it.

Let us consider expression. There are passions and degrees of passion which are expressed by the most hideous contortions of the face and which throw the whole body into such unnatural positions as to lose all the beautiful contours of its natural state. The ancient artists either refrained from depicting such emotions or reduced them to a degree where it is possible to show them with a certain measure of beauty.

Rage and despair did not degrade any of their works. I venture to say that they never depicted a Fury. Wrath was reduced to seriousness. In poetry it was the wrathful Jupiter who hurled the thunderbolt; in art it was only the stern Jupiter.

Anguish was softened into sadness. Where this softening was impossible, where anguish would have been disparaging as well as distorting—what did Timanthes do? We know the answer from his painting of the sacrifice of Iphigenia: he imparted to each bystander the particular degree of sadness appropriate to him but concealed the face of the father, which should have shown the most intense suffering. Many clever things have been said about this. One critic, for instance, says that he had so exhausted himself in depicting the sorrowful faces of the bystanders that he despaired of his ability to give a still more sorrowful one to the father. Another says that by so doing he admitted that the anguish of a father in such circumstances is beyond expressing. For my part, I see no incapacity on the part of either the artist or his art. The intensity of the emotions intensifies the corresponding expression in the features of the face; the highest degree will cause the most extreme expression, and nothing is easier in art than to express this. But Timanthes knew the limits which the Graces had set for his art. He knew that the anguish appropriate to Agamemnon as the father would have to be expressed through distortions, which are always ugly. He went as far as he could in combining beauty and dignity with the expression of anguish. He would have preferred to pass over the ugly or to soften it, but since his composition did not permit him to do either, there was nothing left him but to veil it. What he might not paint he left to conjecture. In short, this concealment is a sacrifice that the artist has made to beauty; it is an example, not of how one pushes expression beyond the limits of art, but how one should subject it to the first law of art, the law of beauty.

If we apply this now to the Laocoön, the principle which I am seeking becomes apparent. The master strove to attain the highest beauty possible under the given condition of physical pain. The demands of beauty could not be reconciled with the pain in all its disfiguring violence, so it had to be reduced. The scream had to be softened to a sigh, not because screaming betrays an ignoble soul, but because it distorts the features in a disgusting manner. Simply imagine Laocoön's mouth forced wide open, and then judge! Imagine him screaming, and then look! From a form which inspired pity because it possessed beauty and pain at the same time, it has now become an ugly, repulsive figure from which we gladly turn away. For the sight of pain provokes distress; however, the distress should be transformed, through beauty, into the tender feeling of pity.

The wide-open mouth, aside from the fact that the rest of the face is thereby twisted and distorted in an unnatural and loathsome manner, becomes in painting a mere spot and in sculpture a cavity, with most repulsive effect. Montfaucon showed little taste when he pronounced an old bearded head with gaping mouth to be Jupiter uttering oracles. Must a god shout when he reveals the future? Would a pleasing outline of the mouth cast suspicion on his words? Nor do I believe Valerius when he says that Ajax was represented as screaming in the abovementioned picture of Timanthes. Far inferior painters, in a period when art was already in decay, did not allow even the most savage barbarians to open their mouths wide enough to scream though they were seized with terror and fear of death beneath the victor's sword.

It is certain that this softening of extreme physical pain to a less intense degree is observable in a number of ancient art works. The suffering Hercules in the poisoned garment, by an unknown master, was not the Hercules of Sophocles, who screamed so horribly that the rocks of Locris and the headlands of Euboea resounded. He was sullen rather than wild. The Philoctetes of Pythagoras Leontinus seemed to communicate his pain to the spectator, and yet the effect of this pain would have been destroyed by any feature even slightly suggestive of horror. One might ask how I know that this master made a statue of Philoctetes. From a passage in Pliny, which is so obviously interpolated or mutilated that it should not have had to wait for me to emend it.

FURTHER READING

Ernst Gombrich, "Lessing," *Proceedings of the British Academy*, Vol. XXXXV (1957), 133–56. A thoughtful essay.

Gotthold Ephraim Lessing, *Laocoön*, ed. Hugo Blümner, 2nd edn. (1880). The best critical edition, with long introduction.

Rensselaer W. Lee, *"Ut Pictura Poesis: The Humanistic Theory of Painting,"* *The Art Bulletin*, Vol. XXII, No. 4 (December 1940), 197–269. The classic treatment of the antique and hardy cliché about painting being like poetry.

Roland Mortier, *Diderot en Allemagne: 1750–1850* (1954). An interesting survey of the impact of Diderot's ideas in Lessing's Germany and after.

J. G. Robertson, *Lessing's Dramatic Theory: Being an Introduction to and Commentary on his Hamburgische Dramaturgie* (1939). While (as the title shows) this book concentrates on Lessing's writings about the theater, it sheds light on Lessing's aesthetic ideas as well—which, in a thin field in English, is doubtless welcome.

36 ❋ DIDEROT

The Paradox of Acting

[From Denis Diderot, *The Paradox of Acting,*
translated by Walter Herries Pollock (1883),
4–9, 13–14.]

*Diderot never ceases to astonish us. He began his philosophical
career an unambiguous pleader for the passions, and in his own life,
as I have indicated, passion—especially sensuality—held a favored
place. Then, in the 1760s, he began to reconsider his position. It
would be vulgar to explain this shift exclusively on psychological or
physiological grounds; it is true that he was getting older—he was
fifty in 1763—but it is true, too, that he was growing wiser. Besides,
he would never deny the power, or the value, of passion even in his
last writings; but he found ways of integrating passion into the
psychic economy of man, and to find a place for calculation and
sober thought.*

*Sometime in the mid-1760s, he began to apply his new, enlarged
views to the craft of acting. "An actor who has only good sense and
judgment is cold," he wrote* to Mademoiselle Jodin, a young
actress in whom he took a fatherly interest, "the one who has only
verve and sensibility is mad." The* Paradoxe sur le comédien, *which
he began to write in 1769, is a serious attempt to deal with this
problem, in Diderot's favorite genre—the dialogue. Neither passion
nor discipline alone is enough; both belong together. In watching
his favorite actress, Mademoiselle Clairon, Diderot found her em-
bodying two personalities at the same time: on the stage, "in that
moment, she is double: the little Clairon and the great Agrippina."
The great English actor Garrick, whom Diderot also watched with
admiration, made the same point for him.*

I must only add that Diderot was not alone in these ideas. Sir

---

* Probably in 1766; *Correspondance,* ed. Georges Roth (1955–   ), VI, 168.

Joshua Reynolds, who knew Garrick even better than Diderot did, came to the same conclusion. "Garrick's trade was to represent passion, not to feel it," and so, "Garrick left nothing to chance. Every gesture, every expression of countenance and variation of voice, was settled in his closet before he set his foot upon the stage." *This convergence is worth noting. That Reynolds, the old Neoclassicist, should have praised artfulness and deliberation is hardly surprising; but Diderot's insistence on discipline and intelligence must compel those who think of Diderot simply as a creature of the emotions to revise their estimate of him.*

THE FIRST. . . . . It is Nature who bestows personal gifts—appearance, voice, judgment, tact. It is the study of the great models, the knowledge of the human heart, the habit of society, earnest work, experience, close acquaintance with the boards, which perfect Nature's gifts. The actor who is merely a mimic can count upon being always tolerable; his playing will call neither for praise nor for blame.

THE SECOND. Or else for nothing but blame.

THE FIRST. Granted. The actor who goes by Nature alone is often detestable, sometimes excellent. But in whatever line, beware of a level mediocrity. No matter how harshly a beginner is treated, one may easily foretell his future success. It is only the incapables who are stifled by cries of "Off! off!" How should Nature without Art make a great actor when nothing happens on the stage exactly as it happens in nature, and when dramatic poems are all composed after a fixed system of principles? And how can a part be played in the same way by two different actors when, even with the clearest, the most precise, the most forceful of writers, words are no more, and never can be more, than symbols, indicating a thought, a feeling, or an idea; symbols which need action, gesture, intonation, expression, and a whole context of circumstance, to give them their full significance? When you have heard these words—

> *Que fait là votre main?*
> *Je tâte votre habit, l'étoffe en est moelleuse,*

* Frederick W. Hilles, ed., *Portraits by Sir Joshua Reynolds* (1952), 51-52, 104-5.

what do you know of their meaning? Nothing. Weigh well what follows, and remember how often and how easily it happens that two speakers may use the same words to express entirely different thoughts and matters. The instance I am going to cite is a very singular one; it is the very work of your friend that we have been discussing. Ask a French actor what he thinks of it; he will tell you that every word of it is true. Ask an English actor, and he will swear that, *"By God,* there's not a sentence to change! It is the very gospel of the stage!" However, since there is nothing in common between the way of writing comedy and tragedy in England and the way of writing stage poems in France; since, according to Garrick himself, an actor who will play you a scene of Shakespeare to perfection is ignorant of the first principles of declamation needed for Racine; since, entwined by Racine's musical lines as if by so many serpents whose folds compress his head, his feet, his hands, his legs, and his arms, he would, in attempting these lines, lose all liberty of action; it follows obviously that the French and the English actors, entirely at one as to the soundness of your author's principles, are yet at variance, and that the technical terms of the stage are so broad and so vague that men of judgment, and of diametrically opposite views, yet find in them the light of conviction. Now hold closer than ever to your maxim, *"Avoid explanation if what you want is a mutual understanding."*

THE SECOND. You think that in every work, and especially in this, there are two distinct meanings, both expressed in the same terms, one understood in London, the other in Paris?

THE FIRST. Yes; and that these terms express so clearly the two meanings that your friend himself has fallen into a trap. In associating the names of English with those of French actors, applying to both the same precepts, giving to both the same praise and the same reproofs, he has doubtless imagined that what he said of the one set was equally true of the other.

THE SECOND. According to this, never before was author so wrongheaded.

THE FIRST. I am sorry to admit that this is so, since he uses the same words to express one thing at the Crossroads of Buffy and another thing at Drury Lane. Of course, I may be wrong. But the important point on which your author and I are entirely at variance concerns the qualities above all necessary to a great actor. In my view he must have a deal of judgment. He must have in himself an unmoved and disinterested onlooker. He must have, consequently, penetration and no sensibility; the art of mimicking everything, or, which comes to the same thing, the same aptitude for every sort of character and part.

THE SECOND. No sensibility?

THE FIRST. None. I have not yet arranged my ideas logically, and you must let me tell them to you as they come to me, with the same want of order that marks your friend's book. If the actor were full, really full, of feeling, how could he play the same part twice running with the same spirit and success? Full of fire at the first performance, he would be worn out and cold as marble at the third. But take it that he is an attentive mimic and thoughtful disciple of Nature, then the first time he comes on the stage as Augustus, Cinna, Orosmanes, Agamemnon, or Mahomet, faithful copying of himself and the effects he has arrived at, and constantly observing human nature, will so prevail that his acting, far from losing in force, will gather strength with the new observations he will make from time to time. He will increase or moderate his effects, and you will be more and more pleased with him. If he is himself while he is playing, how is he to stop being himself? If he wants to stop being himself, how is he to catch just the point where he is to stay his hand?

What confirms me in this view is the unequal acting of players who play from the heart. From them you must expect no unity. Their playing is alternately strong and feeble, fiery and cold, dull and sublime. Tomorrow they will miss the point they have excelled in today, and to make up for it will excell in some passage where last time they failed. On the other hand, the actor who plays from thought, from study of human nature, from constant imitation of some ideal type, from imagination, from memory, will be one and the same at all performances, will be always at his best mark; he has considered, combined, learned and arranged the whole thing in his head; his diction is neither monotonous nor dissonant. His passion has a definite course—it has bursts, and it has reactions; it has a beginning, a middle, and an end. The accents are the same, the positions are the same, the movements are the same; if there is any difference between two performances, the latter is generally the better. He will be invariable; a looking-glass, as it were, ready to reflect realities, and to reflect them ever with the same precision, the same strength, and the same truth. Like the poet, he will dip forever into the inexhaustible treasure-house of Nature, instead of coming very soon to an end of his own poor resources. . . .

Your fiery, extravagant, sensitive fellow is forever on the boards; he acts the play, but he gets nothing out of it. It is in him that the man of genius finds his model. Great poets, great actors, and, I may add, all great copyists of Nature, in whatever art, beings gifted with fine imagination, with broad judgment, with exquisite tact, with a sure touch of taste, are the least sensitive of all creatures. They are too apt for too many things, too busy with observing, considering, and reproducing, to have their inmost hearts affected with any liveliness. To me such a one always has his portfolio spread before him and his pencil in his fingers.

It is we who feel; it is they who watch, study, and give us the result. And then . . . well, why should I not say it? Sensibility is by no means the distinguishing mark of a great genius. He will have, let us say, an abstract love of justice, but he will not be moved to temper it with mercy. It is the head, not the heart, which works in and for him. Let some unforeseen opportunity arise, the man of sensibility will lose it; he will never be a great king, a great minister, a great commander, a great advocate, a great physician. Fill the front of a theater with tearful creatures, but I will none of them on the boards. . . .

FURTHER READING

Yvon Bélaval, *L'Esthétique sans paradoxe de Diderot* (1950). A fine essay that moves beyond the *Paradoxe* to Diderot's aesthetic ideas in general.

Herbert Dieckmann, *Cinq Leçons sur Diderot* (1959). A brilliant brief book on Diderot; two excellent chapters deal with his aesthetics.

Louis Jouvet, *Le Comédien désincarné* (1954). One of several books by men of the theater on the *Paradoxe,* a work that has consistently fascinated them.

Arthur M. Wilson, "The Biographical Implications of Diderot's *Paradoxe sur le comédien,*" *Diderot Studies,* Vol. III (1961), 369–83. Diderot's best biographer sets the *Paradoxe* into the context of Diderot's life.

37 ❈ GLUCK

Letters

[From *Letters of Distinguished Musicians,*
edited by Ludwig Nohe, translated by
Lady Wallace (1867), 2–14.]

*The Enlightenment was, of course, principally a movement of ideas,
and it is notoriously hard to establish a sensible connection between
such a movement and music. Still, it is reasonable to see the ferment
of Enlightenment in the history of music in the eighteenth century.
It was an age of innovation in instrumentation and in the fixing of
forms: genres like the sonata or the concerto, names that had been
loosely affixed to all sorts of compositions in the seventeenth century, were now subjected to rule.*

*But the Enlightenment entered music also quite explicitly in the
work of Christoph Willibald Gluck. His immortal predecessors
Bach and Handel had innovated, when they did innovate, by instinct. Gluck innovated on principle, and his efforts on behalf of
reforming the opera belong in any comprehensive anthology of the
Enlightenment. The opera was, by its very nature, a most vulner-
able form: it invited parody with its palpable incompatibility of
words and music. In opera, lovers rushed off into the night after
long recitatives, heroes died after equally long and undeniably
vigorous arias. To make things worse, by the middle of the eighteenth century, composers and impresarios had made a virtue of
operatic necessities and trumpeted instead of apologizing for artifi-
ciality. The typical opera had become a vehicle for the star, designed to display the technical virtuosity of the singer, the invention
of the composer, or the imagination of the designer. In consequence, the quality of the music was indifferent, librettos were put
together for effect. One did not have to be a philistine to laugh at
the endless coloratura passages in which vocally agile sopranos*

469

repeated a single word. As Addison put it in The Spectator: *"There is nothing that has more startled our English audience, than the Italian* recitativo *at its first entrance upon the stage. People were wonderfully surprised to hear generals singing the word of command, and ladies delivering messages in music."*

The first blow for good sense was John Gay's Beggar's Opera of 1728, an immense success with its broad political satire but also with its lampoon of the Italian opera. The second blow came in the early 1750s in Paris, when the French philosophes and especially Rousseau championed the simple, natural comic opera La serva padrona, by Pergolesi, in opposition to the pompous productions then highly favored. This was the so-called Buffoons' War—a serious engagement in trivial guise. The third and decisive blow was delivered in 1762, when Gluck's opera Orfeo ed Euridice opened in Vienna.

Christoph Willibald Gluck was born in Bavaria in 1714, and studied first in Prague and then, like other operatic composers, in Italy. His compositions were immediate successes, and he served as conductor in various distinguished posts, including the court opera in Vienna, after 1754. He died, rich and famous, in 1787. While his first operas had been in the traditional Italian style, he came to revise his views in the most drastic possible way—in part because he was fortunate to encounter the poet Raniero da Calzabigi, with whom he collaborated in his greatest operas. The two were equally weary of the elaborate plots, hectic actions, and meaningless recitatives of conventional operatic performances; with Orfeo, for which Calzabigi wrote the libretto, Gluck tried out his newfound classical simplicity. Orfeo simplified the action, united words and music, eliminated recitatives, and gave arias new dignity. In 1767 the two reformers followed up the success of Orfeo with Alceste, another masterpiece. To explain their reform, Gluck published (though Calzabigi doubtless wrote) a preface for Alceste, which served as a dedication to his patron, the music-loving Leopold, Grand Duke of Tuscany, the future Emperor Leopold II. This is the first letter by "Gluck" in the selections below; it makes the reformers' intentions unmistakably clear. It is surely justified to see this appeal to reason as part of the Enlightenment's way of changing the general way of thinking.

To the Grand Duke Leopold of Tuscany (*Written in Italian*)

YOUR ROYAL HIGHNESS,

When I undertook to compose music for *Alceste,* I proposed entirely to abolish all those abuses introduced by the injudicious vanity of singers, or by the excessive complaisance of masters, which have so long disfigured the Italian opera, and instead of the most splendid and beautiful of all entertainments, thus rendered it the most ridiculous and tiresome. My purpose was to restrict music to its true office, that of ministering to the expression of the poetry, and to the situations of the plot, without interrupting the action, or chilling it by superfluous and needless ornamentation; I thought that it should accomplish what brilliancy of colour and a skilfully adapted contrast of light and shade effect for a correct and well-designed drawing, by animating the figures without distorting their contours. I wished, therefore, to avoid arresting an actor in the most excited moment of his dialogue, by causing him to wait for a tiresome *ritournelle,* or in the midst of half-uttered words, to detain him on a favourable note, either for the purpose of displaying his fine voice and flexibility in some long passage, or causing him to pause till the orchestra gave him time to take breath for a cadence. It did not appear to me that I ought to hurry rapidly over the second part of an aria, possibly the most impassioned and important of all, in order to have the opportunity of repeating regularly four times over the words of the first part, causing the aria to end where in all probability the sense did not end, merely for the convenience of the singer, and to enable him to vary a passage according to his caprice; in short, I have striven to banish the abuses against which reason and good sense have so long protested in vain.

My idea was that the overture should prepare the spectators for the plot to be represented, and give some indication of its nature; that the concerted instruments ought to be regulated according to the interest and passion of the drama, and not leave a void in the dialogue between the air and the recitative, so that the meaning of a passage might not be perverted, nor the force and warmth of the action improperly interrupted.

Further, I thought that my most strenuous efforts must be directed in search of a noble simplicity, thus avoiding a parade of difficulty at the expense of clearness. I did not consider a mere display of novelty valuable, unless naturally suggested by the situation and the expression, and on this point no rule in composition exists that I would not have gladly sacrificed in favor of the effect produced.

Such are my principles. Fortunately, the *libretto* was wonderfully adapted to my purpose, in which the celebrated author [Calzabigi], having imagined a new dramatic plan, replaced flowery descriptions, superfluous similes, and cold sententious morality by the language of the heart, strong passions, interesting situations, and an ever varying *spectacle*.

Success has justified my maxims, and the unanimous approval of so enlightened a city [Vienna] clearly shows that simplicity, truth, and nature are the great fundamental principles of the beautiful in all artistic creations. Nevertheless, in spite of the repeated entreaties of the most highly respected persons to publish my opera, I am so fully aware of the risks I incur in combating prejudices so widely spread, and so deeply rooted, that I am under the necessity of arming myself with the mighty protection of your Royal Highness, and therefore entreat the favour of being permitted to prefix to my opera your august name, which so justly unites the suffrages of enlightened Europe.

A great protector of the fine arts, reigning over a nation which enjoys the renown of having rescued these from universal oppression, and producing the grandest models in them all, in a city [Florence] always the first to cast off the yoke of vulgar prejudice in order to proceed onwards to perfection—can alone undertake the reform of the noble Drama, in which all the fine arts bear so large a share. When this is effected, the glory will at least be mine of having set in motion the first stone, and obtained the public testimony of your illustrious patronage.

I have the honour to subscribe myself, with the utmost devotion,
Your Royal Highness's grateful and obedient servant,
CHRISTOPH GLUCK

To the Duke of Braganza * (Written in Italian)

Vienna, Oct. 30, 1770

YOUR HIGHNESS,

In dedicating this my new work [*Paride ed Elena (Paris and Helen)*] to Your Highness, I seek rather a judge than a patron. A

* The English traveller Dr. Burney writes, in his *Journal of a Musical Tour,* the following about the Duke of Braganza:—"This prince is an excellent judge of music; he is a great traveller, having visited England, France, and Italy, before his arrival in Germany. He is very lively, and occasioned much mirth by his pleasantries, which were all seasoned with good humour."—L.N.

soul superior to commonplace prejudices, with an adequate knowledge of the great principles of art, a taste formed not so much on grand models, as on the immutable foundations of the beautiful and the true—such are the qualities that I look for in my Maecenas, and which I find combined in Your Highness. The sole reason that induced me to publish my music of *Alceste* was the hope of finding successors, who, following the path already opened, and encouraged by the full suffrages of an enlightened public, should take courage to destroy the abuses introduced on the Italian stage, and bring it as far as possible to perfection. I bitterly feel that I have hitherto striven after this in vain. Pedants and critics, an infinite multitude, who form the greatest obstacle to the progress of the fine arts, loudly protesting against a method which, were it actually to take root, would at once destroy all their pretensions to supremacy of judgment, and injure their sphere of influence. They thought themselves entitled to pronounce a verdict on *Alceste* from some informal rehearsals, badly conducted, and even worse executed; the effect to be produced in a theatre being calculated from that in a room, with the same sagacity as in a certain city of Greece where judgment was passed on statues at the distance of a few feet, originally intended to be erected on the most lofty columns.

A fastidious ear perhaps found a vocal passage too harsh, or another too impassioned, or not sufficiently studied, forgetting that, in their proper places, such forcible expression and striking contrasts were absolutely required. One pedant took advantage of an evident oversight, or perhaps an error of the press, to condemn it as if it had been some irremediable sin against the mysteries of harmony; it was likewise decided in full conclave that this style of music was barbarous and extravagant. It is true that other scores are judged by a similar criterion, and judged too with almost the certainty of infallibility; but Your Highness will at once perceive the cause of this. The more truth and perfection are sought after, the more necessary are precision and exactness.

The differences are almost imperceptible that distinguish Raphael from the common herd of painters, and the slightest alteration in an outline, that would not destroy the likeness in a caricature, entirely disfigures the portrait of a lovely woman. Very little would suffice, by merely changing something in the expression of my aria "Che farò senza Euridice?" to turn it into a *saltarello* for *fantoccini*. A note more or less sustained, a neglected *rinforzo* in the time or voice carelessly omitted, an *appoggiatura* out of place, a shake, a passage, a run, may ruin a whole scene in such an opera;

whereas such things do no harm, or, indeed, rather embellish the common run of operas. The presence, therefore, of the composer at the performance of this class of music is as indispensable, so to speak, as the presence of the sun to the works of nature. He is its absolute soul and life, and without him all must be confusion and darkness. But we must be prepared for such obstacles so long as there are in the world people who consider themselves authorised to decide on the fine arts, because they enjoy the privilege of possessing eyes and ears, no matter what the quality of these may be. The mania of discussing those very subjects which they least understand is unhappily a failing only too prevalent among men.

Your Highness has no doubt read the drama of *Paride,* and must have observed that it does not offer to the composer those violent passions, those grand images, or tragic situations, which agitate the spectators in *Alceste,* furnishing such opportunities for great effects in harmony; thus the same power and energy cannot assuredly be expected in the music,—just as in a picture in a full blaze of light, the same force of *chiaroscuro* and the same sharp contrasts are not to be exacted, that the painter can employ on a subject which permits him to choose a subdued light. This opera does not treat of a wife about to lose her husband, and who, in order to save him, has the courage to invoke the infernal gods in a wild forest, amid the black shades of night, trembling even in her last death-struggle for the fate of her children, and forced to tear herself away from the husband whom she adores. In the present work we see a loving youth combating for a time the conscientious scruples of a haughty and noble woman, and at last triumphing over them by all the arts of a vehement passion. I have striven to find some variety of colouring, seeking it in the diverse characters of the two nations, Phrygia and Sparta, contrasting the wild and rude nature of the one with the delicate and indolent nature of the other. I thought that singing in an opera being only a substitute for declamation, ought to imitate in Elena the native ruggedness of her country; and that, in order to preserve this character in the music, it would not be thought a defect on my part to descend even to trivialities. When truth is sought, it must be varied in accordance with the subject we have to work out, and the greatest beauties of melody and harmony become defects and imperfections when out of place. I do not expect greater success from my *Paride* than from *Alceste,* at least in my purpose to effect the desired change in musical composers; on the contrary, I anticipate greater opposition than ever; but, for my part, this shall never deter me from making fresh attempts to accomplish my good design; and, if I gain the approval of Your Highness, I shall gladly say, *Tolle siparium; sufficit mihi unus Plato pro cuncto populo* [Raise the curtain; to me one Plato is worth an entire people].

I have the honour to be, with the most profound respect,

Your Highness's humble, devoted, and obliged servant,

LE CHEVALIER CHRISTOPH GLUCK

To the Editor of the Mercure de France *(Written in French)*

LE CHEVALIER CHRISTOPH GLUCK

SIR,

I might justly be reproached by others, and should also severely reproach myself, after reading the letter written to one of the directors of the Royal Academy of Music, inserted in your *Mercure* of last October, the subject of which is *Iphigénie* and, after expressing my gratitude to the author of that letter for the praise which he had been pleased to lavish on me—were I not eager to declare that his friendship, and far too favourable impressions of me, have no doubt carried him away, and I am very far from flattering myself that I merit the eulogies he bestows on me.* I should reproach myself even more keenly, were I to allow the invention of this new style of Italian opera, the success of which has justified the attempt, to be attributed to myself. The principal merit is due to M. Calzabigi; and if my music has produced any sensation, I ought to acknowledge that it is he who has enabled me to develop the resources of my art. This author, full of genius and talent, has followed a path little known by Italians in his *libretti* of *Orpheus, Alceste,* and *Paride.* These works are overflowing with those happy situations, and terrible and pathetic events, which supply the composer with the

---

* The letter in question was addressed to one of the directors of the opera at Paris, and dated August 1, 1772, and written by M. Bailly du Rollet, secretary to the French Embassy in Vienna, to M. le Chevalier Antoine d'Auvergne, in order to pave the way for the reception at the Grand Opera of *Iphigénie en Aulide,* the text of which Du Rollet himself had written to suit the French taste, thus encouraging Gluck to compose music in the French dramatic style. Gluck's answer to this letter, which could scarcely have been written without his knowledge, and the appearance of which in the *Mercure* no doubt caused him much satisfaction, bears evident traces of Du Rollet's helping hand. The flattering expressions, too, applied to the French, are only designed to awaken the attention of the public, and to render the performance of the opera possible.—L.N.

means of expressing ardent passion, and creating energetic and touching music. Whatever talent a composer may possess, he can only write indifferent music if the poet does not excite in him that enthusiasm without which the productions of every art must be feeble and languid. The imitation of nature is the acknowledged aim which all ought to seek. This it is that I strive to attain; always simple and natural, so far as I can possibly make it so, my music only tends to enhance the expression, and to add force to the declamation of the poetry. For this reason I do not employ those *shakes, passages,* and *cadences,* of which Italians are so lavish. Their language, therefore, which quite suits this style, is, in this respect, by no means advantageous for me: no doubt it has many other merits, but, born in Germany, I do not consider that any study on my part, of either Italian or French, entitles me to appreciate the delicate shades which cause a preference for one beyond the other, and I think that a foreigner ought to abstain from judging between them; but I may be allowed to say that the language which suits me best is that which enables the poet to furnish me with the most varied means of expressing the passions; and such is the advantage I found in the words of *Iphigénie,* the poetry of which appeared to me to have all the energy calculated to inspire good music. Though I never had occasion to offer my works to any theatre, I cannot be displeased with the writer of the letter in question to one of the directors, for having proposed my *Iphigénie* to your academy of music. I must confess that I would gladly have brought it out in Paris, because, by its effect and with the aid of the celebrated M. Rousseau of Geneva, whom I purposed to consult, we might perhaps, acting in concert, and seeking a noble, touching, and natural melody—the declamation too being in exact accordance with the prosody of each language, and the character of each people—have succeeded in establishing the system I have in view, that of producing music appropriate to all nations, and thus abolishing the ridiculous distinctions of national music. My studies of the works of this great man on music, and among others the letter in which he analyses the monologue in Lully's *Armide,* prove to me the sublimity of his knowledge and the accuracy of his taste, and fill me with admiration. The result is the most entire conviction on my part, that if he had chosen to apply himself to the exercise of this art, he might have realised the prodigious effects that antiquity attributes to music. I am charmed to take advantage of the present occasion to render to him publicly that tribute of praise which I think he deserves.

I request, Sir, that you will be so obliging as to insert this letter in your next *Mercure*.

I have the honour to be, Sir, etc.,
CHEVALIER GLUCK

FURTHER READING

Manfred F. Bukofzer, *Music in the Baroque Era* (1947). An authoritative survey which ends with Bach but sets the background for the Age of the Enlightenment.

Alfred Einstein, *Gluck* (1962 edn.). Short and dependable.

Paul Henry Lang, *Music in Western Civilization* (1941). A large-scale general history, whose relevant chapters place music in the cultural setting of the eighteenth century.

VI

The Science of
Man and
Society

Despite the central place of the human sciences in the thought of the Enlightenment, they have not received the prominence they deserve. These sciences—the sciences of man and society—were central because in them the two aims of the Enlightenment, knowledge and reform, became one. It is therefore wholly appropriate that it was in the Age of the Enlightenment, and by the agency of the philosophes, that the foundations of the modern social sciences were put down. The philosophes, in a sense, had to write these books; they were implicit in their view of the function and range of knowledge, and their view of the method and possibility for reform. To list these books is to list the first modern classics in the social sciences: I mention only Montesquieu's De L'Esprit des lois, Hume's Populousness of Ancient Nations, Gibbon's Decline and Fall of the Roman Empire, Voltaire's Essai sur les moeurs, Ferguson's History of Civil Society, and Adam Smith's Wealth of Nations.

The philosophes were aware that their enterprise concealed a deep tension: knowledge did not always lead to improvement. They knew, and indeed insisted, that what Bentham would later call "sinister interests" often abused knowledge for the sake not of improvement for all, but of power and profit for the few. Besides, they recognized that the true and the desirable were not always the same. Matters of fact and matters of value—on this point David Hume particularly insisted—are distinct and must be kept distinct. Yet the philosophes saw no intellectual trap in pursuing true facts and true theories: the path of fancy, of metaphysics, of organized error had been tried and had failed. Knowledge would not automatically make man happy, but ignorance always made him unhappy. This conviction, coupled with the philosophes' disenchanted view of the world, made them the natural founders of the social sciences. We live off their ideas still.

In this commitment to the utilization of knowledge, the philosophes differ from many of their twentieth-century heirs in a decisive respect. They differ from these heirs in yet another respect: the philosophes were not specialists. We must read their works in the *social sciences, therefore, as fragments of a larger tapestry: Adam Smith was never simply a political economist, but a moralist and an aesthetician; Voltaire was a playwright quite as much as a pioneering social historian; David Hume was, in everything he did, a philosopher.*

FURTHER READING

J. B. Black, *The Art of History: A Study of Four Great Historians in the Eighteenth Century* (1926). An elegant set of essays on Hume, Voltaire, Robertson and Gibbon, to be supplemented with special studies.

Louis I. Bredvold, *The Brave New World of the Enlightenment* (1961). Diatribe by a frightened humanist against the philosophes' commitment to social science; worth reading mainly as a symptom.

Gladys Bryson, *Man and Society: The Scottish Inquiry of the Eighteenth Century* (1945). Useful survey of the leading social scientists of the age, most of whom were Scots.

J. W. Burrow, *Evolution and Society: A Study in Victorian Social Theory* (1966). Begins, in defiance of its title, with a lucid analysis of eighteenth-century social speculation.

Paul F. Lazarsfeld, "Notes on the History of Quantification in Sociology—Trends, Sources and Problems," in *Quantification,* ed. Harry Woolf (1961), 147–203. Tentative but very illuminating on the origins of social quantitative thinking.

Claude Lévy-Strauss, "Jean-Jacques Rousseau, fondateur des sciences de l'homme," in Samuel Baud-Bovy *et al., Jean-Jacques Rousseau* (1962), 239–48. Private, almost perverse, but fascinating treatment of Rousseau as founder of the human sciences.

38 ❀ HUME

A Treatise of Human Nature

[From David Hume, *A Treatise of Human Nature,* edited by L. A. Selby-Bigge (1888), xvii–
xxiii.]

*No document better illustrates the philosophes' sense of hope for a
"science of man" than Hume's introduction to his first philosophical masterpiece, the* Treatise of Human Nature *(1739–40). I here
reprint it in its entirety. We must not dismiss this introduction as a
young man's ebullition; it introduces, after all, a sustained philosophy of skepticism. Hume, as he never tired of saying, was a
moderate skeptic, convinced that absolute skepticism was both
psychologically impossible and philosophically impermissible. Yet,
however moderate, it was from a skeptical position that he expressed his conviction that the science of man is a possibility, in
principle as capable of certainty as physics or astronomy. Hume, to
be sure, linked the sciences of nature and of man by affirming not
the easiness of the latter, but the difficulty of the former. But from
his philosophical vantage point, the argument is unassailable—how
unassailable we can appreciate only if we read the* Treatise
*through: man's knowledge of stars, like man's knowledge of man, is
about matters of fact, and about matters of fact absolute certainty is
impossible. Having said this, though, Hume goes on to more cheerful news: given patience, caution, persistence, and intelligence, we
may construct a reliable science of man, and a science of the highest
utility. This was the conviction on which Hume and the other
philosophes built sociology, demography, political science, social
history, and economics.*

❀

INTRODUCTION

Nothing is more usual and more natural for those, who pretend to discover any thing new to the world in philosophy and the sciences, than to insinuate the praises of their own systems, by decrying all those, which have been advanced before them. And indeed were they content with lamenting that ignorance, which we still lie under in the most important questions, that can come before the tribunal of human reason, there are few, who have an acquaintance with the sciences, that would not readily agree with them. 'Tis easy for one of judgment and learning, to perceive the weak foundation even of those systems, which have obtained the greatest credit, and have carried their pretensions highest to accurate and profound reasoning. Principles taken upon trust, consequences lamely deduced from them, want of coherence in the parts, and of evidence in the whole, these are every where to be met with in the systems of the most eminent philosophers, and seem to have drawn disgrace upon philosophy itself.

Nor is there requir'd such profound knowledge to discover the present imperfect condition of the sciences, but even the rabble without doors may judge from the noise and clamour, which they hear, that all goes not well within. There is nothing which is not the subject of debate, and in which men of learning are not of contrary opinions. The most trivial question escapes not our controversy, and in the most momentous we are not able to give any certain decision. Disputes are multiplied, as if every thing was uncertain; and these disputes are managed with the greatest warmth, as if every thing was certain. Amidst all this bustle 'tis not reason, which carries the prize, but eloquence; and no man needs ever despair of gaining proselytes to the most extravagant hypothesis, who has art enough to represent it in any favourable colours. The victory is not gained by the men at arms, who manage the pike and the sword; but by the trumpeters, drummers, and musicians of the army.

From hence in my opinion arises that common prejudice against metaphysical reasonings of all kinds, even amongst those, who profess themselves scholars, and have a just value for every other part of literature. By metaphysical reasonings, they do not understand those on any particular branch of science, but every kind of argument, which is any way abstruse, and requires some attention to be comprehended. We have so often lost our labour in such researches, that we commonly reject them without hesitation, and resolve, if we must for ever be a prey to errors and delusions, that they shall at least be natural and entertaining. And indeed nothing but the most determined scepticism, along with a great degree of indolence, can justify this aversion to metaphysics. For if truth be at all within the reach of human capacity, 'tis certain it must lie very deep and abstruse; and to hope we shall arrive at it without pains, while the greatest geniuses have failed with the utmost pains, must certainly be esteemed sufficiently vain and presumptuous. I pretend to no such advantage in the philosophy I am going to unfold, and would esteem it a strong presumption against it, were it so very easy and obvious.

'Tis evident, that all the sciences have a relation, greater or less, to human nature; and that however wide any of them may seem to run from it, they still return back by one passage or another. Even *Mathematics, Natural Philosophy, and Natural Religion,* are in some measure dependent on the science of Man; since they lie under the cognizance of men, and are judged of by their powers and faculties. 'Tis impossible to tell what changes and improvements we might make in these sciences were we thoroughly acquainted with the extent and force of human understanding, and cou'd explain the nature of the ideas we employ, and of the operations we perform in our reasonings. And these improvements are the more to be hoped for in natural religion, as it is not content with instructing us in the nature of superior powers, but carries its views farther, to their disposition towards us, and our duties towards them; and consequently we ourselves are not only the beings, that reason, but also one of the objects, concerning which we reason.

If therefore the sciences of Mathematics, Natural Philosophy, and Natural Religion, have such a dependence on the knowledge of man, what may be expected in the other sciences, whose connexion with human nature is more close and intimate? The sole end of logic is to explain the principles and operations of our reasoning faculty, and the nature of our ideas: morals and criticism regard our tastes and sentiments: and politics consider men as united in society, and dependent on each other. In these four sciences of *Logic, Morals, Criticism, and Politics,* is comprehended almost every thing, which it can any way import us to be acquainted with, or which can tend either to the improvement or ornament of the human mind.

Here then is the only expedient, from which we can hope for success in our philosophical researches, to leave the tedious ling'ring method, which we have hitherto followed, and instead of taking now and then a castle or village on the frontier, to march up directly to the capital or center of these sciences, to human nature itself; which being once masters of, we may every where else hope for an easy victory. From this station we may extend our conquests over all those sciences, which more intimately concern human life, and may afterwards proceed at leisure to discover more fully those, which are the objects of pure curiosity. There is no question of importance, whose decision is not compriz'd in the science of man; and there is none, which can be decided with any certainty, before we become acquainted with that science. In pretending therefore to explain the principles of human nature, we in effect propose a compleat system of the sciences, built on a foundation almost entirely new, and the only one upon which they can stand with any security.

And as the science of man is the only solid foundation for the other sciences, so the only solid foundation we can give to this science itself must be laid on experience and observation. 'Tis no astonishing reflection to consider, that the application of experimental philosophy to moral subjects should come after that to natural at the distance of above a whole century; since we find in fact, that there was about the same interval betwixt the origins of these sciences; and that reckoning from Thales to Socrates, the space of time is nearly equal to that betwixt my Lord Bacon and some late philosophers in *England,** who have begun to put the science of man on a new footing, and have engaged the attention, and excited the curiosity of the public. So true it is, that however other nations may rival us in poetry, and excel us in some other agreeable arts, the improvements in reason and philosophy can only be owing to a land of toleration and of liberty.

Nor ought we to think, that this latter improvement in the science of man will do less honour to our native country than the former in natural philosophy, but ought rather to esteem it a greater glory, upon account of the greater importance of that science, as well as the necessity it lay under of such a reformation. For to me it seems evident, that the essence of the mind being equally unknown to us with that of external bodies, it must be equally impossible to form any notion of its powers and qualities otherwise than from careful and exact experiments, and the observation of those particular effects, which result from its different circumstances and situations. And tho' we must endeavour to

* Mr. Locke, my Lord Shaftsbury, Dr. Mandeville, Mr. Hutchinson, Dr. Butler, &c.

render all our principles as universal as possible, by tracing up our experiments to the utmost, and explaining all effects from the simplest and fewest causes, 'tis still certain we cannot go beyond experience; and any hypothesis, that pretends to discover the ultimate original qualities of human nature, ought at first to be rejected as presumptuous and chimerical.

I do not think a philosopher, who would apply himself so earnestly to the explaining the ultimate principles of the soul, would show himself a great master in that very science of human nature, which he pretends to explain, or very knowing in what is naturally satisfactory to the mind of man. For nothing is more certain, than that despair has almost the same effect upon us with enjoyment, and that we are no sooner acquainted with the impossibility of satisfying any desire, than the desire itself vanishes. When we see, that we have arrived at the utmost extent of human reason, we sit down contented; tho' we be perfectly satisfied in the main of our ignorance, and perceive that we can give no reason for our most general and most refined principles, beside our experience of their reality; which is the reason of the mere vulgar, and what it required no study at first to have discovered for the most particular and most extraordinary phaenomenon. And as this impossibility of making any farther progress is enough to satisfy the reader, so the writer may derive a more delicate satisfaction from the free confession of his ignorance, and from his prudence in avoiding that error, into which so many have fallen, of imposing their conjectures and hypotheses on the world for the most certain principles. When this mutual contentment and satisfaction can be obtained betwixt the master and scholar, I know not what more we can require of our philosophy.

But if this impossibility of explaining ultimate principles should be esteemed a defect in the science of man, I will venture to affirm, that 'tis a defect common to it with all the sciences, and all the arts, in which we can employ ourselves, whether they be such as are cultivated in the schools of the philosophers, or practised in the shops of the meanest artizans. None of them can go beyond experience, or establish any principles which are not founded on that authority. Moral philosophy has, indeed, this peculiar disadvantage, which is not found in natural, that in collecting its experiments, it cannot make them purposely, with premeditation, and after such a manner as to satisfy itself concerning every particular difficulty which may arise. When I am at a loss to know the effects of one body upon another in any situation, I need only put them in that situation, and observe what results from it. But should I endeavour to clear up after the same manner any doubt in moral philosophy, by placing myself in the same case with that which I consider, 'tis evident this reflection and premeditation would so disturb the operation of my natural principles, as must render it impossible to form any just conclusion from the phaenomenon. We must therefore glean up our experiments in this science from a cautious observation of human life, and take them as they appear in the common course of the world, by men's behaviour in company, in affairs, and in their pleasures. Where experiments of this kind are judiciously collected and compared, we may hope to establish on them a science, which will not be inferior in certainty, and will be much superior in utility to any other of human comprehension.

FURTHER READING

Rachael M. Kydd, *Reason and Conduct in Hume's Treatise* (1946). A technical examination.

D. F. Pears, ed., *David Hume, A Symposium* (1963). A number of essays and radio talks, brief and non-technical but suggestive; see especially, for the *Treatise* and its ambitions, the chapters by S. N. Hampshire, "Hume's Place in Philosophy," D. F. Pears, "Hume's Empiricism and Modern Empiricism," and G. J. Warnock, "Hume on Causation."

H. H. Price, *Hume's Theory of the External World* (1940). A brilliant treatment of a special problem raised in the *Treatise*.

39 ❊ MONTESQUIEU

The Spirit of the Laws

[From Montesquieu, *The Spirit of the Laws,*
translated by Thomas Nugent, revised by J. V.
Pritchard, 2 vols. (1900), I, 9–34, 182–95, 265–
69.]

In the 1730s, having achieved fame with his Lettres Persanes *of 1721
and cemented it with his election to the* Académie Française *seven
years later,* Montesquieu settled down at his ancestral château at
La Brède, not far from Bordeaux, and began to work on his greatest
and most influential book,* De l'Esprit des lois. *It appeared in 1748,
but first generally circulated two years later, to embroil him in
controversy and gain him new admirers. When he died in 1755, he
knew himself to be a pioneer in a new discipline, for which the
name—sociology—was not to be coined for another three quarters
of a century.*

Montesquieu's Spirit of the Laws *is a hard book to judge. It is, for
one thing, disorganized, or strangely organized; long chapters (like
that famous Chapter 6 of Book XI on the British Constitution)
alternate with short chapters, sometimes containing only the title
and one remark. The style is witty, aphoristic, often brilliant, while
the discussion seems rambling, often disjointed; the facts, culled
from the classics, Montesquieu's own experience, and travelers'
tales, are thrown at the reader quite indiscriminately. Voltaire,
who, like everyone else, admired Montesquieu greatly but who,
unlike most others, ventured also to differ, found the* Spirit of the
Laws *"a labyrinth without a clue, lacking all method."† What
made it admirable to Voltaire was its scattered insights, and its*

---

* See above, page 123.

† "A, B, C," in Voltaire, *Philosophical Dictionary,* tr. Peter Gay (1962), II,
500.

*uncompromising devotion to decency, to reasonableness, to humanity.**

Roughly, this ungainly masterpiece is divided into three parts: in the first and most significant portion of the book Montesquieu analyzes the form and spirit of government, and the rights of the subject; in the second portion he turns to the impact of environment on constitutions and political behavior; in the third portion he offers an ill-arranged mixture including speculations on French medieval history, legal theory and related matters.

To complicate our appraisal further, Montesquieu's treatise, though wide-ranging in subject matter and generous in thought, was also part of the great political combat dividing the France of his time.† *Those who thought that security and social improvement lay in the assertion of royal power discerned the legal roots of that power in medieval French history; that party, articulately represented by Voltaire, championed the so-called* thèse *royale. But the proponents of this "royal thesis" were vigorously opposed by the champions of the* thèse *nobiliaire, which claimed that the exercise of royal prerogative, especially over legislation, was nothing better than a usurpation on the part of modern French kings. The proponents of this "noble thesis" argued that a strong nobility was grounded in French history and French law, and essential to the preservation of time-honored freedoms. Montesquieu's* Spirit of the Laws *speaks for this latter party, a party, we may note, wrong in its reading of history and selfish in its proposals for political organization.*

Yet if Montesquieu's Spirit of the Laws *had spoken only, or even mainly, for the* thèse *nobiliaire, it would not have become a classic. With all its very obvious faults, the book is also an epoch-making work in the social sciences. The early parts are particularly noteworthy for their departure from the formal analysis of types of government, and for their concern with the substance and substructure of political morale. The section on climate, though palpably absurd in its physiology, is noteworthy as well for its attempt to link the physical with the psychological and political aspects of social life. In these books we can see modern sociology in the making.*

* For an instance of that humanity, see below, pages 699–709.

† For some general comments on this combat, see above, pages 119–120.

BOOK II

Of Laws Directly Derived from the Nature of Government

I. THERE are three species of government: republican, monarchical, and despotic. In order to discover their nature, it is sufficient to recollect the common notion, which supposes three definitions, or rather three facts: that a republican government is that in which the body, or only a part of the people, is possessed of the supreme power; monarchy, that in which a single person governs by fixed and established laws; a despotic government, that in which a single person directs everything by his own will and caprice.

This is what I call the nature of each government; we must now inquire into those laws which directly conform to this nature, and consequently are the fundamental institutions.

II. When the body of the people is possessed of the supreme power, it is called a democracy. When the supreme power is lodged in the hands of a part of the people, it is then an aristocracy.

In a democracy the people are in some respects the sovereign, and in others the subject.

There can be no exercise of sovereignty but by their suffrages, which are their own will; now the sovereign's will is the sovereign himself. The laws therefore which establish the right of suffrage are fundamental to this government. And indeed it is as important to regulate in a republic, in what manner, by whom, to whom, and concerning what, suffrages are to be given, as it is in a monarchy to know who is the prince, and after what manner he ought to govern.

Libanius says that at "Athens a stranger who intermeddled in the assemblies of the people was punished with death." This is because such a man usurped the rights of sovereignty.

It is an essential point to fix the number of citizens who are to form the public assemblies; otherwise it would be uncertain whether the whole, or only a part of the people, had given their votes. At Sparta the number was fixed at ten thousand. But Rome, designed by Providence to rise from the weakest beginnings to the highest pitch of grandeur; Rome, doomed to experience all the vicissitudes of fortune; Rome, who had sometimes all her inhabitants without her walls, and sometimes all Italy and a considerable part of the world within them; Rome, I say, never fixed the number; and this was one of the principal causes of her ruin.

The people, in whom the supreme power resides, ought to have the management of everything within their reach: that which exceeds their abilities must be conducted by their ministers.

But they cannot properly be said to have their ministers, without the power of nominating them: it is, therefore, a fundamental maxim in this government, that the people should choose their ministers—that is, their magistrates.

They have occasion, as well as monarchs, and even more so, to be directed by a council or senate. But to have a proper confidence in these, they should have the choosing of the members; whether the election be made by themselves, as at Athens, or by some magistrate deputed for that purpose, as on certain occasions was customary at Rome.

The people are extremely well qualified for choosing those whom they are to intrust with part of their authority. They have only to be determined by things to which they cannot be strangers, and by facts that are obvious to sense. They can tell when a person has fought many battles, and been crowned with success; they are, therefore, capable of electing a general. They can tell when a judge is assiduous in his office, gives general satisfaction, and has never been charged with bribery: this is sufficient for choosing a praetor. They are struck with the magnificence or riches of a fellow citizen; no more is requisite for electing an aedile. These are facts of which they can have better information in a public forum than a monarch in his palace. But are they capable of conducting an intricate affair, of seizing and improving the opportunity and critical moment of action? No; this surpasses their abilities.

Should we doubt the people's natural capacity, in respect to the discernment of merit, we need only cast an eye on the series of surprising elections made by the Athenians and Romans; which no one surely will attribute to hazard.

We know that though the people of Rome assumed the right of raising plebeians to public offices, yet they never would exert this power; and though at Athens the magistrates were allowed, by the law of Aristides, to be elected from all the different classes of inhabitants, there never was a case, says Xenophon, when the common people petitioned for employments which could endanger either their security or their glory.

As most citizens have sufficient ability to choose, though unqualified to be chosen, so the people, though capable of calling others to an account for their administration, are incapable of conducting the administration themselves.

The public business must be carried on with a certain motion, neither too quick nor too slow. But the motion of the people is always either too remiss or too violent. Sometimes with a hundred thousand arms they overturn all before them; and sometimes with a hundred thousand feet they creep like insects.

In a popular state the inhabitants are divided into certain classes. It is in the manner of making this division that great legislators have signalized themselves; and it is on this that the duration and prosperity of democracy have ever depended.

Servius Tullius followed the spirit of aristocracy in the distribution of his classes. We find in Livy and in Dionysius Halicarnassus in what manner he lodged the right of suffrage in the hands of the principal citizens. He had divided the people of Rome into one hundred and niney-three centuries, which formed six classes; and, ranking the rich, who were in smaller numbers, in the first centuries, and those in middling circumstances, who were more numerous, in the next, he flung the indigent multitude into the last; and as each century had but one vote, it was property rather than numbers that decided the election.

Solon divided the people of Athens into four classes. In this he was directed by the spirit of democracy, his intention not being to fix those who were to choose, but such as were eligible: therefore, leaving to every citizen the right of election, he made the judges eligible from each of those four classes; but the magistrates he ordered to be chosen only out of the first three, consisting of persons of easy fortunes.

As the division of those who have a right of suffrage is a fundamental law in republics, so the manner of giving this suffrage is another fundamental.

The suffrage by lot is natural to democracy; as that by choice is to aristocracy.

The suffrage by lot is a method of electing that offends no one, but animates each citizen with the pleasing hope of serving his country.

Yet as this method is in itself defective, it has been the endeavor of the most eminent legislators to regulate and amend it.

Solon made a law at Athens, that military employments should be conferred by choice; but that senators and judges should be elected by lot.

The same legislator ordained that civil magistracies, attended with great expense, should be given by choice; and the others by lot.

In order, however, to amend the suffrage by lot, he made a rule, that none but those who presented themselves should be elected; that the person elected should be examined by judges, and that everyone should have a right to accuse him if he were unworthy of the office; this participated at the same time of the suffrage by lot, and of that by choice. When the time of their magistracy had expired, they were obliged to submit to another judgment in regard to their conduct. Persons utterly unqualified must have been extremely backward in giving in their names to be drawn by lot.

The law which determines the manner of giving suffrage is likewise fundamental in a democracy. It is a question of some importance whether the suffrages ought to be public or secret. Cicero observes that the laws which rendered them secret toward the close of the republic were the cause of its decline. But as this is differently practiced in different republics, I shall offer here my thoughts concerning this subject.

The people's suffrages ought doubtless to be public; and this should be considered as a fundamental law of democracy. The lower class ought to be directed by those of higher rank, and restrained within bounds by the gravity of eminent personages. Hence, by rendering the suffrages secret in the Roman Republic, all was lost; it was no longer possible to direct a populace that sought its own destruction. But when the body of the nobles are to vote in an aristocracy, or in a democracy the senate, as the business is then only to prevent intrigues, the suffrages cannot be too secret.

Intriguing in a senate is dangerous; it is dangerous also in a body of nobles; but not so among the people, whose nature is to act through passion. In countries where they have no share in the government, we often see them as much inflamed on account of an actor as ever they could be for the welfare of the state. The misfortune of a republic is when intrigues are at an end; which happens when the people are gained by bribery and corruption: in this case they grow indifferent to public affairs, and avarice becomes their predominant passion. Unconcerned about the government and everything belonging to it, they quietly wait for their hire.

It is likewise a fundamental law in democracies, that the people should have the sole power to enact laws. And yet there are a thousand occasions on which it is necessary the senate should have the power of decreeing; nay, it is frequently proper to make some trial of a law before it is established. The constitutions of Rome and Athens were excellent. The decrees of the Senate had the force of laws for the space of a year, but did not become perpetual till they were ratified by the consent of the people.

III. In an aristocracy the supreme power is lodged in the hands of a certain number of persons. These are invested both with the legislative and executive authority; and the rest of the people are, in respect to them, the same as the subjects of a monarchy in regard to the sovereign.

They do not vote here by lot, for this would be productive of inconveniences only. And indeed, in a government where the most mortifying distinctions are already established, though they were to be chosen by lot, still they would not cease to be odious; it is the nobleman they envy, and not the magistrate.

When the nobility are numerous, there must be a senate to regulate the affairs which the body of the nobles are incapable of deciding, and to prepare others for their decision. In this case it may be said that the aristocracy is in some measure in the senate, the democracy in the body of the nobles, and the people are a cipher.

It would be a very happy thing in an aristocracy if the people, in some measure, could be raised from their state of annihilation. Thus at Genoa, the Bank of St. George being administered by the people gives them a certain influence in the government, whence their whole prosperity is derived.

The senators ought by no means to have the right of naming their own members; for this would be the only way to perpetuate abuses. At Rome, which in its early years was a kind of artistocracy, the Senate did not fill up the vacant places in their own body; the new members were nominated by the censors.

In a republic, the sudden rise of a private citizen to exorbitant power produces monarchy, or something more than monarchy. In the latter the laws have provided for, or in some measure adapted themselves to, the constitution; and the principle of government checks the monarch: but in a republic, where a private citizen has obtained an exorbitant power, the abuse of this power is much greater, because the laws foresaw it not, and consequently made no provision against it.

There is an exception to this rule, when the constitution is such as to have immediate need of a magistrate invested with extraordinary power. Such was Rome with her dictators, such is Venice with her state inquisitors; these are formidable magistrates, who restore, as it were by violence, the state to its liberty. But how comes it that these magistracies are so very different in these two republics? It is because Rome supported the remains of her aristocracy against the people; whereas Venice employs her state inquisitors to maintain her aristocracy against the nobles. The consequence was, that at Rome the dictatorship could be only of short duration, as the people acted through passion and not with design. It was necessary that a magistracy of this kind should be exercised with luster and pomp, the business being to intimidate, and not to punish, the multitude. It was also proper that the dictator should be created only for some particular affair, and for this only should have an unlimited authority, as he was always created upon some sudden emergency. On the contrary, at Venice they have occasion for a permanent magistracy; for here it is that schemes may be set on foot, continued, suspended, and resumed; that the ambition of a single person becomes that of a family, and the ambition of one family that of many. They have occasion for a secret magistracy, the crimes they punish being hatched in secrecy and silence. This magistracy must have a general inquisition, for their business is not to remedy known disorders, but to prevent the unknown. In a word, the latter is designed to punish suspected crimes; whereas the former used rather menaces than punishment even for crimes that were openly avowed.

In all magistracies the greatness of the power must be compensated by the brevity of the duration. This most legislators have fixed to a year; a longer space would be dangerous, and a shorter would be contrary to the nature of government. For who is it that in the management even of his domestic affairs would be thus confined? At Ragusa the chief magistrate of the republic is changed every month, the other officers every week, and the governor of the castle every day. But this can take place only in a small republic environed by formidable powers, who might easily corrupt such petty and insignificant magistrates.

The best aristocracy is that in which those who have no share in the legislature are so few and inconsiderable that the governing party have no interest in oppressing them. Thus when Antipater made a law at Athens, that whosoever was not worth two thousand drachmas should have no power to vote, he formed by this method the best aristocracy possible; because this was so small a sum as to exclude very few, and not one of any rank or consideration in the city.

Aristocratic families ought therefore, as much as possible, to level themselves in appearance with the people. The more an aristocracy borders on democracy, the nearer it approaches perfection: and, in proportion as it draws toward monarchy, the more is it imperfect.

But the most imperfect of all is that in which the part of the people that obeys is in a state of civil servitude to those who command, as the aristocracy of Poland, where the peasants are slaves to the nobility.

IV. The intermediate, subordinate, and dependent powers constitute the nature of monarchical government; I mean of that in which a single person governs by fundamental laws. I said, the intermediate, subordinate, and dependent powers. And indeed, in monarchies the prince is the source of all power, political and civil. These fundamental laws necessarily suppose the intermediate channels through which the power flows: for if there be only the momentary and capricious will of a single person to govern the state, nothing can be fixed, and of course there is no fundamental law.

The most natural, intermediate, and subordinate power is that of the nobility. This in some measure seems to be essential to a monarchy, whose fundamental maxim is, "No monarch, no nobility; no nobility, no monarch"; but there may be a despotic prince.

There are men who have endeavored in some countries in Europe to suppress the jurisdiction of the nobility, not perceiving that they were driving at the very thing that was done by the Parliament of England. Abolish the privileges of the lords, the clergy, and cities in a monarchy, and you will soon have a popular state, or else a despotic government.

The courts of a considerable kingdom in Europe have, for many ages, been striking at the patrimonial jurisdiction of the lords and clergy. We do not pretend to censure these sage magistrates; but we leave it to the public to judge how far this may alter the constitution.

Far am I from being prejudiced in favor of the privileges of the clergy; however, I should be glad if their jurisdiction were once fixed. The question is not whether their jurisdiction was justly established, but whether it be really established; whether it constitutes a part of the laws of the country, and is in every respect in relation to those laws; whether between two powers acknowledged independent, the conditions ought not to be reciprocal; and whether it be not equally the duty of a good subject to defend the prerogative of the prince, and to maintain the limits which from time immemorial have been prescribed to his authority.

Though the ecclesiastic power be so dangerous in a republic, yet it is extremely proper in a monarchy, especially of the absolute kind. What would become of Spain and Portugal, since the subversion of their laws, were it not for this only barrier against the incursions of arbitrary power? A barrier ever useful when there is no other: for since a despotic government is productive of the most dreadful calamities to human nature, the very evil that restrains it is beneficial to the subject.

In the same manner as the ocean, threatening to overflow the whole earth, is stopped by weeds and pebbles that lie scattered along the shore, so monarchs, whose power seems unbounded, are restrained by the smallest obstacles, and suffer their natural pride to be subdued by supplication and prayer.

The English, to favor their liberty, have abolished all the intermediate powers of which their monarchy was composed. They have a great deal of reason to be jealous of this liberty; were they ever to be so unhappy as to lose it, they would be one of the most servile nations upon earth.

Mr. Law, through ignorance both of a republican and monarchical constitution, was one of the greatest promoters of absolute power ever known in Europe. Besides the violent and extraordinary changes owing to his direction, he would fain suppress all the intermediate ranks, and abolish the political communities. He was dissolving the monarchy by his chimerical reimbursements, and seemed as if he even wanted to redeem the constitution.

It is not enough to have intermediate powers in a monarchy; there must be also a depositary of the laws. This depositary can only be the judges of the supreme courts of justice, who promulgate the new laws, and revive the obsolete. The natural ignorance of the nobility, their indolence and contempt of civil government, require that there should be a body invested with the power of reviving and executing the laws, which would be otherwise buried in oblivion. The prince's council are not a proper depositary. They are naturally the depositary of the momentary will of the prince, and not of the fundamental laws. Besides, the prince's council is continually changing; it is neither permanent nor numerous; neither has it a sufficient share of the confidence of the people; consequently it is incapable of setting them right in difficult conjunctures, or of reducing them to proper obedience.

Despotic governments, where there are no fundamental laws, have no such kind of depositary. Hence it is that religion has generally so much influence in those countries, because it forms a kind of permanent depositary; and if this cannot be said of religion, it may of the customs that are respected instead of laws.

V. From the nature of despotic power it follows that the single person, invested with this power, commits the execution of it also to a single person. A man whom his senses continually inform that he himself is everything and that his subjects are nothing, is naturally lazy, voluptuous, and ignorant. In consequence of this, he neglects the management of public affairs. But were he to commit the administration to many, there would be continual disputes among them; each would form intrigues to be his first slave; and he would be obliged to take the reins into his own hands. It is, therefore, more natural for him to resign it to a vizier, and to invest him with the same power as himself. The creation of a vizier is a fundamental law of this government.

It is related of a Pope, that he had started an infinite number of difficulties against his election, from a thorough conviction of his incapacity. At length he was prevailed on to accept of the pontificate, and resigned the administration entirely to his nephew. He was soon struck with surprise, and said, "I should never have thought that these things were so easy." The same may be said of the princes of the East, who, being educated in a prison where eunuchs corrupt their hearts and debase their understandings, and where they are frequently kept ignorant even of their high rank, when drawn forth in order to be placed on the throne, are at first confounded: but as soon as they have chosen a vizier, and abandoned themselves in their seraglio to the most brutal passions, pursuing, in the midst of a prostituted court, every capricious extravagance, they would never have dreamed that they could find matters so easy.

The more extensive the empire, the larger the seraglio; and consequently the more voluptuous the prince. Hence the more nations such a sovereign has to rule, the less he attends to the cares of government; the more important his affairs, the less he makes them the subject of his deliberations.

BOOK III

Of the Principles of the Three Kinds of Government

I. HAVING examined the laws in relation to the nature of each government, we must investigate those which relate to its principle.

There is this difference between the nature and principle of government, that the former is that by which it is constituted, the latter that by which it is made to act. One is its particular structure, and the other the human passions which set it in motion.

Now, laws ought no less to relate to the principle than to the nature of each government. We must, therefore, inquire into this principle, which shall be the subject of this third book.

II. I have already observed that it is the nature of a republican government, that either the collective body of the people, or particular families, should be possessed of the supreme power; of a monarchy, that the prince should have this power, but in the execution of it should be directed by established laws; of a despotic government, that a single person should rule according to his own will and caprice. This enables me to discover their three principles, which are thence naturally derived. I shall begin with a republican government, and in particular with that of democracy.

III. There is no great share of probity necessary to support a monarchical or despotic government. The force of laws in one, and the prince's arm in the other, are sufficient to direct and maintain the whole. But in a popular state, one spring more is necessary—namely, virtue.

What I have here advanced is confirmed by the unanimous testimony of historians, and is extremely agreeable to the nature of things. For it is clear that in a monarchy, where he who commands the execution of the laws generally thinks himself above them, there is less need of virtue than in a popular government, where the person intrusted with the execution of the laws is sensible of his being subject to their direction.

Clear is it also that a monarch who, through bad advice or indolence, ceases to enforce the execution of the laws, may easily repair the evil; he has only to follow other advice, or to shake off his indolence. But when, in a popular government, there is a suspension of the laws, as this can proceed only from the corruption of the republic, the state is certainly undone.

A very droll spectacle it was in the last century to behold the impotent efforts of the English toward the establishment of democracy. As they who had a share in the direction of public affairs were void of virtue; as their ambition was inflamed by the success of the most daring of their members; as the prevailing parties were successively animated by the spirit of faction, the government was continually changing: the people, amazed at so many revolutions, in vain attempted to erect a commonwealth. At length, when the country had undergone the most violent shocks, they were obliged to have recourse to the very government which they had so wantonly proscribed.

When Sylla thought of restoring Rome to her liberty, this unhappy city was incapable of receiving that blessing. She had only the feeble remains of virtue, which were continually diminishing. Instead of being roused from her lethargy by Caesar, Tiberius, Caius Claudius, Nero, and Domitian, she riveted every day her chains; if she struck some blows, her aim was at the tyrant, not at the tyranny.

The politic Greeks, who lived under a popular government, knew no other support than virtue. The modern inhabitants of that country are entirely taken up with manufacture, commerce, finances, opulence, and luxury.

When virtue is banished, ambition invades the minds of those who are disposed to receive it, and avarice possesses the whole community. The objects of their desires are changed; what they were fond of before has become indifferent; they were free while under the restraint of laws, but they would fain now be free to act against law; and as each citizen is like a slave who has run away from his master, that which was a maxim of equity he calls rigor; that which was a rule of action he styles constraint; and to precaution he gives the name of fear. Frugality, and not the thirst of gain, now passes for avarice. Formerly the wealth of individuals constituted the public treasure; but now this has become the patrimony of private persons. The members of the commonwealth riot on the public spoils, and its strength is only the power of a few, and the license of many.

Athens was possessed of the same number of forces when she triumphed so gloriously as when with such infamy she was enslaved. She had twenty thousand citizens, when she defended the Greeks against the Persians, when she contended for empire with Sparta, and invaded Sicily. She had twenty thousand when Demetrius Phalereus numbered them, as slaves are told by the head in a marketplace. When Philip attempted to lord it over Greece, and appeared at the gates of Athens, she had even then lost nothing but time. We may see in Demosthenes how difficult it was to awaken her; she dreaded Philip, not as the enemy of her liberty, but of her pleasures. This famous city, which had withstood so many defeats, and having been so often destroyed had as often risen out of her ashes, was overthrown at Chaeronea, and at one blow deprived of all hopes of resource. What does it avail her that Philip sends back her prisoners, if he does not return her men? It was ever after as easy to triumph over the forces of Athens as it had been difficult to subdue her virtue.

How was it possible for Carthage to maintain her ground? When Hannibal, upon his being made praetor, endeavored to hinder the magistrates from plundering the republic, did not they complain of him to the Romans? Wretches, who would fain be citizens without a city, and be beholden for their riches to their very destroyers! Rome soon insisted upon having three hundred of their principal citizens as hostages; she obliged them next to surrender their arms and ships; and then she declared war. From the desperate efforts of his defenseless city, one may judge of what she might have performed in her full vigor, and assisted by virtue.

IV. As virtue is necessary in a popular government, it is requisite also in an aristocracy. True it is that in the latter it is not so absolutely requisite.

The people, who in respect to the nobility are the same as the subjects with regard to a monarch, are restrained by their laws. They have, therefore, less occasion for virtue than the people in a democracy. But how are the nobility to be restrained? They who are to execute the laws against their colleagues will immediately perceive that they are acting against themselves. Virtue is therefore necessary in this body, from the very nature of the constitution.

An aristocratic government has an inherent vigor, unknown to democracy. The nobles form a body, who by their prerogative, and for their own particular interest, restrain the people; it is sufficient that there are laws in being to see them executed.

But easy as it may be for the body of the nobles to restrain the people, it is difficult to restrain themselves. Such is the nature of this constitution, that it seems to subject the very same persons to the power of the laws, and at the same time to exempt them.

Now, such a body as this can restrain itself only in two ways:

either by a very eminent virtue, which puts the nobility in some measure on a level with the people, and may be the means of forming a great republic; or by an inferior virtue, which puts them at least upon a level with one another, and upon this their preservation depends.

Moderation is therefore the very soul of this government; a moderation, I mean, founded on virtue, not that which proceeds from indolence and pusillanimity.

V. In monarchies, policy effects great things with as little virtue as possible. Thus in the nicest machines, art has reduced the number of movements, springs, and wheels.

The state subsists independently of the love of our country, of the thirst of true glory, of self-denial, of the sacrifice of our dearest interests, and of all those heroic virtues which we admire in the ancients, and to us are known only by tradition.

The laws supply here the place of those virtues; they are by no means wanted, and the state dispenses with them: an action performed here in secret is in some measure of no consequence.

Though all crimes be in their own nature public, yet there is a distinction between crimes really public and those that are private, which are so called because they are more injurious to individuals than to the community.

Now, in republics private crimes are more public—that is, they attack the constitution more than they do individuals; and in monarchies, public crimes are more private—that is, they are more prejudicial to private people than to the constitution.

I beg that no one will be offended with what I have been saying; my observations are founded on the unanimous testimony of historians. I am not ignorant that virtuous princes are so very rare; but I venture to affirm, that in a monarchy it is extremely difficult for the people to be virtuous.

Let us compare what the historians of all ages have asserted concerning the courts of monarchs; let us recollect the conversations and sentiments of people of all countries, in respect to the wretched character of courtiers, and we shall find that these are not airy speculations, but truths confirmed by a sad and melancholy experience.

Ambition in idleness; meanness mixed with pride; a desire of riches without industry; aversion to truth; flattery, perfidy, violation of engagements, contempt of civil duties, fear of the prince's virtue, hope from his weakness, but, above all, a perpetual ridicule cast upon virtue, are, I think, the characteristics by which most courtiers in all ages and countries have been constantly distinguished. Now, it is exceedingly difficult for the leading men of the nation to be knaves, and the inferior sort to be honest; for the former to be cheats, and the latter to rest satisfied with being only dupes.

But if there should chance to be some unlucky honest man among the people, Cardinal Richelieu, in his political testament, seems to hint that a prince should take care not to employ him. So true is it that virtue is not the spring of this government! It is not indeed excluded, but it is not the spring of government.

VI. But it is high time for me to have done with this subject, lest I should be suspected of writing a satire against monarchical government. Far be it from me; if monarchy wants one spring, it is provided with another. Honor—that is, the prejudice of every person and rank—supplies the place of the political virtue of which I have been speaking, and is everywhere her representative: here it is capable of inspiring the most glorious actions, and, joined with the force of laws, may lead us to the end of government as well as virtue itself.

Hence, in well-regulated monarchies, they are almost all good subjects, and very few good men; for to be a good man, a good intention is necessary, and we should love our country, not so much on our own account, as out of regard to the community.

VII. A monarchical government supposes, as we have already observed, preeminences and ranks, as likewise a noble descent. Now, since it is the nature of honor to aspire to preferments and titles, it is properly placed in this government.

Ambition is pernicious in a republic. But in a monarchy it has some good effects; it gives life to the government, and is attended with this advantage, that it is in no way dangerous, because it may be continually checked.

It is with this kind of government as with the system of the universe, in which there is a power that constantly repels all bodies from the center, and a power of gravitation that attracts them to it. Honor sets all the parts of the body politic in motion, and by its very action connects them; thus each individual advances the public good, while he only thinks of promoting his own interest.

True it is, that philosophically speaking it is a false honor which moves all the parts of the government; but even this false honor is as useful to the public as true honor could possibly be to private persons.

Is it not very exacting to oblige men to perform the most difficult actions, such as require an extraordinary exertion of fortitude and resolution, without other recompense than that of glory and applause?

VIII. Honor is far from being the principle of despotic government: mankind being here all upon a level, no one person can prefer himself to another; and as on the other hand they are all slaves, they can give themselves no sort of preference.

Besides, as honor has its laws and rules, as it knows not how to submit; as it depends in a great measure on a man's own caprice, and not on that of another person, it can be found only in countries in which the constitution is fixed, and where they are governed by settled laws.

How can despotism abide with honor? The one glories in the contempt of life, and the other is founded on the power of taking it away. How can honor, on the other hand, bear with despotism? The former has its fixed rules and peculiar caprices, but the latter is directed by no rule, and its own caprices are subversive of all others.

Honor, therefore, a thing unknown in arbitrary governments, some of which have not even a proper word to express it, is the prevailing principle in monarchies; here it gives life to the whole body politic, to the laws, and even to the virtues themselves.

IX. As virtue is necessary in a republic, and in a monarchy honor, so fear is necessary in a despotic government: with regard to virtue, there is no occasion for it, and honor would be extremely dangerous.

Here the immense power of the prince devolves entirely upon those whom he is pleased to intrust with the administration. Persons capable of setting a value upon themselves would be likely to create disturbances. Fear must therefore depress their spirits, and extinguish even the least sense of ambition.

A moderate government may, whenever it pleases, and without the least danger, relax its springs. It supports itself by the laws, and by its own internal strength. But when a despotic prince ceases for one single moment to uplift his arm, when he cannot instantly demolish those whom he has intrusted with the first employments, all is over: for as fear, the spring of this government, no longer subsists, the people are left without a protector.

It is probably in this sense the Cadis maintained that the Grand Seignior was not obliged to keep his word or oath when he limited thereby his authority.

It is necessary that the people should be judged by laws, and the great men by the caprice of the prince, that the lives of the lowest subject should be safe, and the pasha's head ever in danger. We cannot mention these monstrous governments without horror. The Sophi of Persia, dethroned in our days by Mahomet, the son of Miriveis, saw the constitution subverted before this resolution, because he had been too sparing of blood.

History informs us that the horrid cruelties of Domitian struck such a terror into the governors that the people recovered themselves a little during his reign. Thus a torrent overflows one side of a country, and on the other leaves fields untouched where the eye is refreshed by the prospect of fine meadows.

X. In despotic states, the nature of government requires the most passive obedience; and when once the prince's will is made known, it ought infallibly to produce its effect.

Here they have no limitations or restrictions, no mediums, terms, equivalents, or remonstrances; no change to propose: man is a creature that blindly submits to the absolute will of the sovereign.

In a country like this they are no more allowed to represent their apprehensions of a future danger than to impute their miscarriage to the capriciousness of fortune. Man's portion here, like that of beasts, is instinct, compliance, and punishment.

Little does it then avail to plead the sentiments of Nature, filial respect, conjugal or parental tenderness, the laws of honor, or want of health; the order is given, and that is sufficient.

In Persia, when the king has condemned a person, it is no longer lawful to mention his name, or to intercede in his favor. Even if the prince were intoxicated, or non compos, the decree must be executed, otherwise he would contradict himself, and the law admits of no contradiction. This has been the way of thinking in that country in all ages: as the order which Ahasuerus gave, to exterminate the Jews, could not be revoked, they were allowed the liberty of defending themselves.

One thing, however, may be sometimes opposed to the prince's will, namely, religion. They will abandon, nay, they will slay a parent, if the prince so commands; but he cannot oblige them to drink wine. The laws of religion are of a superior nature, because they bind the sovereign as well as the subject. But with respect to the law of Nature, it is otherwise; the prince is no longer supposed to be a man.

In monarchical and moderate states, the power is limited by its very spring; I mean by honor, which, like a monarch, reigns over the prince and his people. They will not allege to their sovereign the laws of religion; a courtier would be apprehensive of rendering himself ridiculous. But the laws of honor will be appealed to on all occasions. Hence arise the restrictions necessary to obedience; honor is naturally subject to whims, by which the subject's submission will be ever directed.

Though the manner of obeying be different in these two kinds of government, the power is the same. On which side soever the monarch turns, he inclines the scale, and is obeyed. The whole difference is that in a monarchy the prince receives instruction, at the same time that his ministers have greater abilities, and are more versed in public affairs, than the ministers of a despotic government.

XI. Such are the principles of the three sorts of government: which does not imply that in a particular republic they actually are, but that they ought to be, virtuous; nor does it prove that in a particular monarchy they are actuated by honor, or in a particular despotic government by fear; but that they ought to be directed by these principles, otherwise the government is imperfect.

BOOK XI

Of the Laws Which Establish Political Liberty with Regard to the Constitution

VI. In every government there are three sorts of power: the legislative; the executive in respect to things dependent on the law of nations; and the executive in regard to matters that depend on the civil law.

By virtue of the first, the prince or magistrate enacts temporary or perpetual laws, and amends or abrogates those that have been already enacted. By the second, he makes peace or war, sends or receives embassies, establishes the public security, and provides against invasions. By the third he punishes criminals, or determines the disputes that arise between individuals. The latter we shall call the judiciary power, and the other simply the executive power of the state.

The political liberty of the subject is a tranquillity of mind arising from the opinion each person has of his safety. In order to have this liberty, it is requisite that the government be so constituted that one man need not be afraid of another.

When the legislative and executive powers are united in the same person, or in the same body of magistrates, there can be no liberty, because apprehensions may arise lest the same monarch or senate should enact tyrannical laws, to execute them in a tyrannical manner.

Again, there is no liberty if the judiciary power be not separated from the legislative and executive. Were it joined with the legislative, the life and liberty of the subject would be exposed to arbitrary control; for the judge would be then the legislator. Were it joined to the executive power, the judge might behave with violence and oppression.

There would be an end of everything, were the same man or the same body, whether of the nobles or of the people, to exercise these three powers: that of enacting laws, that of executing the public resolutions, and of trying the causes of individuals.

Most kingdoms in Europe enjoy a moderate government because the prince who is invested with the first two powers leaves the third to his subjects. In Turkey, where these three powers are united in the Sultan's person, the subjects groan under the most dreadful oppression.

In the republics of Italy, where these three powers are united, there is less liberty than in our monarchies. Hence their government is obliged to have recourse to as violent methods for its support as even that of the Turks; witness the state inquisitors, and the lion's mouth into which every informer may at all hours throw his written accusations.

In what a situation must the poor subject be in those republics! The same body of magistrates are possessed, as executors of the laws, of the whole power they have given themselves in quality of legislators. They may plunder the state by their general determinations, and as they have likewise the judiciary power in their hands, every private citizen may be ruined by their particular decisions.

The whole power is here united in one body; and though there is no external pomp that indicates a despotic sway, yet the people feel the effects of it every moment.

Hence it is that many of the princes of Europe, whose aim has been leveled at arbitrary power, have constantly set out with uniting in their own persons all the branches of magistracy and all the great offices of state.

I allow, indeed, that the mere hereditary aristocracy of the Italian republics does not exactly answer to the despotic power of the

Eastern princes. The number of magistrates sometimes moderates the power of the magistracy; the whole body of the nobles do not always concur in the same design; and different tribunals are erected, that temper each other. Thus at Venice the legislative power is in the Council, the executive in the Pregadi, and the judiciary in the Quarantia. But the mischief is, that these different tribunals are composed of magistrates all belonging to the same body, which constitutes almost one and the same power.

The judiciary power ought not to be given to a standing senate; it should be exercised by persons taken from the body of the people at certain times of the year, and consistently with a form and manner prescribed by law, in order to erect a tribunal that should last only so long as necessity requires.

By this method the judicial power, so terrible to mankind, not being annexed to any particular state or profession, becomes, as it were, invisible. People have not then the judges continually present to their view; they fear the office, but not the magistrate.

In accusations of a deep and criminal nature, it is proper that the person accused should have the privilege of choosing, in some measure, his judges, in concurrence with the law; or at least he should have a right to except against so great a number that the remaining part may be deemed his own choice.

The other two powers may be given rather to magistrates or permanent bodies, because they are not exercised on any private subject; one being no more than the general will of the state, and the other the execution of that general will.

But though the tribunals ought not to be fixed, the judgments ought; and to such a degree as to be ever conformable to the letter of the law. Were they to be the private opinion of the judge, people would then live in society without exactly knowing the nature of their obligations.

The judges ought likewise to be of the same rank as the accused, or, in other words, his peers; to the end that he may not imagine he is fallen into the hands of persons inclined to treat him with rigor.

If the legislature leaves the executive power in possession of a right to imprison those subjects who can give security for their good behavior, there is an end of liberty; unless they are taken up, in order to answer without delay to a capital crime, in which case they are really free, being subject only to the power of the law.

But should the legislature think itself in danger by some secret conspiracy against the state, or by a correspondence with a foreign enemy, it might authorize the executive power, for a short and limited time, to imprison suspected persons, who in that case would lose their liberty only for a while, to preserve it forever.

And this is the only reasonable method that can be substituted to the tyrannical magistracy of the Ephori, and to the state inquisitors of Venice, who are also despotic.

As in a country of liberty, every man who is supposed a free agent ought to be his own governor; the legislative power should reside in the whole body of the people. But since this is impossible in large states, and in small ones is subject to many inconveniences, it is fit that the people should transact by their representatives what they cannot transact by themselves.

The inhabitants of a particular town are much better acquainted with its wants and interests than with those of other places; and are better judges of the capacity of their neighbors than of that of the rest of their countrymen. The members, therefore, of the legislature should not be chosen from the general body of the nation; but it is proper that in every considerable place a representative should be elected by the inhabitants.

The great advantage of representatives is their capacity of discussing public affairs. For this the people collectively are extremely unfit, which is one of the chief inconveniences of a democracy.

It is not at all necessary that the representatives who have received a general instruction from their constituents should wait to be directed on each particular affair, as is practiced in the Diets of Germany. True it is that by this way of proceeding the speeches of the deputies might with greater propriety be called the voice of the nation; but, on the other hand, this would occasion infinite delays; would give each deputy a power of controlling the assembly; and, on the most urgent and pressing occasions, the wheels of government might be stopped by the caprice of a single person.

When the deputies, as Mr. Sidney well observes, represent a body of people, as in Holland, they ought to be accountable to their constituents; but it is a different thing in England, where they are deputed by boroughs.

All the inhabitants of the several districts ought to have a right of voting at the election of a representative, except such as are in so mean a situation as to be deemed to have no will of their own.

One great fault there was in most of the ancient republics, that the people had a right to active resolutions, such as require some execution, a thing of which they are absolutely incapable. They ought to have no share in the government but for the choosing of representatives, which is within their reach; for though few can tell the exact degree of men's capacities, yet there are none but are capable of knowing in general whether the person they choose is better qualified than most of his neighbors.

Neither ought the representative body to be chosen for the executive part of government, for which it is not so fit; but for the enacting of laws, or to see whether the laws in being are duly executed, a thing suited to their abilities, and which none indeed but themselves can properly perform.

In such a state there are always persons distinguished by their birth, riches, or honors; but were they to be confounded with the common people, and to have only the weight of a single vote like the rest, the common liberty would be their slavery, and they would have no interest in supporting it, as most of the popular resolutions would be against them. The share they have, therefore, in the legislature ought to be proportioned to their other advantages in the state, which happens only when they form a body that has a right to check the licentiousness of the people, as the people have a right to oppose any encroachment of theirs.

The legislative power is therefore committed to the body of the nobles, and to that which represents the people, each having their assemblies and deliberations apart, each their separate views and interests.

Of the three powers above mentioned, the judiciary is in some measure next to nothing; there remain, therefore, only two, and as these have need of a regulating power to moderate them, the part of the legislative body composed of the nobility is extremely proper for this purpose.

The body of the nobility ought to be hereditary. In the first place it is so in its own nature; and in the next there must be a considerable interest to preserve its privileges—privileges that in themselves are obnoxious to popular envy, and of course in a free state are always in danger.

But as a hereditary power might be tempted to pursue its own particular interests, and forget those of the people, it is proper that where a singular advantage may be gained by corrupting the nobility, as in the laws relating to the supplies, they should have no other share in the legislation than the power of rejecting, and not that of resolving.

By the power of resolving I mean the right of ordaining by their own authority, or of amending what has been ordained by others. By the power of rejecting I would be understood to mean the right of annulling a resolution taken by another, which was the power of the tribunes at Rome. And though the person possessed of the privilege of rejecting may likewise have the right of approving, yet this approbation passes for no more than a declaration, that he intends to make no use of his privilege of rejecting, and is derived from that very privilege.

The executive power ought to be in the hands of a monarch, because this branch of government, having need of dispatch, is better administered by one than by many; on the other hand, whatever depends on the legislative power is oftentimes better regulated by many than by a single person.

But if there were no monarch, and the executive power should be committed to a certain number of persons selected from the legislative body, there would be an end then of liberty; by reason that the two powers would be united, as the same persons would sometimes possess, and would be always able to possess, a share in both.

Were the legislative body to be a considerable time without meeting, this would likewise put an end to liberty. For of two things one would naturally follow: either that there would be no longer any legislative resolutions, and then the state would fall into anarchy; or that these resolutions would be taken by the executive power, which would render it absolute.

It would be needless for the legislative body to continue always assembled. This would be troublesome to the representatives, and, moreover, would cut out too much work for the executive power, so as to take off its attention to its office, and oblige it to think only of defending its own prerogatives, and the right it has to execute.

Again, were the legislative body to be always assembled, it might happen to be kept up only by filling the places of the deceased members with new representatives; and in that case, if the legislative body were once corrupted, the evil would be past all remedy. When different legislative bodies succeed one another, the people who have a bad opinion of that which is actually sitting may reasonably entertain some hopes of the next; but were it to be always the same body, the people upon seeing it once corrupted would no longer expect any good from its laws; and of course they would either become desperate or fall into a state of indolence.

The legislative body should not meet of itself. For a body is supposed to have no will but when it is met; and besides, were it not to meet unanimously, it would be impossible to determine which was really the legislative body: the part assembled, or the other. And if it had a right to prorogue itself, it might happen never to be prorogued; which would be extremely dangerous, in case it should ever attempt to encroach on the executive power. Besides, there are seasons, some more proper than others, for assembling the legislative body; it is fit, therefore, that the executive power should regulate the time of meeting, as well as the duration of those assemblies, according to the circumstances and exigencies of a state known to itself.

Were the executive power not to have a right of restraining the encroachments of the legislative body, the latter would become despotic; for as it might arrogate to itself what authority it pleased, it would soon destroy all the other powers.

But it is not proper, on the other hand, that the legislative power should have a right to stay the executive; for as the execution has its natural limits, it is useless to confine it; besides, the executive power is generally employed in momentary operations. The power, therefore, of the Roman tribunes was faulty, as it put a stop not only to the legislation, but likewise to the executive part of government, which was attended with infinite mischief.

But if the legislative power in a free state has no right to stay the executive, it has a right and ought to have the means of examining in what manner its laws have been executed; an advantage which this government has over that of Crete and Sparta, where the Cosmi and the Ephori gave no account of their administration.

But whatever may be the issue of that examination, the legislative body ought not to have a power of arraigning the person, nor, of course, the conduct, of him who is intrusted with the executive power. His person should be sacred, because as it is necessary for the good of the state to prevent the legislative body from rendering themselves arbitrary, the moment he is accused or tried there is an end of liberty.

In this case the state would be no longer a monarchy, but a kind of republic, though not a free government. But as the person intrusted with the executive power cannot abuse it without bad counselors, and such as have the laws as ministers, though the laws protect them as subjects, these men may be examined and punished —an advantage which this government has over that of Gnidus, where the law allowed of no such thing as calling the Amymones to an account, even after their administration; and therefore the people could never obtain any satisfaction for the injuries done them.

Though, in general, the judiciary power ought not to be united with any part of the legislative, yet this is liable to three exceptions, founded on the particular interest of the party accused.

The great are always obnoxious to popular envy; and were they to be judged by the people, they might be in danger from their judges, and would, moreover, be deprived of the privilege which the meanest subject is possessed of in a free state, of being tried by his peers. The nobility, for this reason, ought not to be cited before the ordinary courts of judicature, but before that part of the legislature which is composed of their own body.

It is possible that the law, which is clear-sighted in one sense, and blind in another, might, in some cases, be too severe. But, as we have already observed, the national judges are no more than the mouth that pronounces the words of the law, mere passive beings, incapable of moderating either its force or rigor. That part, therefore, of the legislative body which we have just now observed to be a necessary tribunal on another occasion, is also a necessary tribunal in this; it belongs to its supreme authority to moderate the law in favor of the law itself, by mitigating the sentence.

It might also happen that a subject intrusted with the administration of public affairs may infringe the rights of the people, and be guilty of crimes which the ordinary magistrates either could not or would not punish. But, in general, the legislative power cannot try causes; and much less can it try this particular case, where it represents the party aggrieved, which is the people. It can only, therefore, impeach. But before what court shall it bring its impeachment? Must it go and demean itself before the ordinary tribunals, which are its inferiors, and, being composed, moreover, of men who are chosen from the people as well as itself, will naturally be swayed by the authority of so powerful an accuser? No; in order to preserve the dignity of the people, and the security of the subject, the legislative part which represents the people must bring in its charge before the legislative part which represents the nobility, who have neither the same interests nor the same passions.

Here is an advantage which this government has over most of the ancient republics, where this abuse prevailed, that the people were at the same time both judge and accuser.

The executive power, pursuant of what has been already said, ought to have a share in the legislature by the power of rejecting, otherwise it would soon be stripped of its prerogative. But should the legislative power usurp a share of the executive, the latter would be equally undone.

If the prince were to have a part in the legislature by the power of resolving, liberty would be lost. But as it is necessary he should have a share in the legislature for the support of his own prerogative, this share must consist in the power of rejecting.

The change of government at Rome was owing to this, that neither the Senate, who had one part of the executive power, nor the magistrates, who were intrusted with the other, had the right of rejecting, which was entirely lodged in the people.

Here, then, is the fundamental constitution of the government we are treating of. The legislative body being composed of two parts, they check one another by the mutual privilege of rejecting. They are both restrained by the executive power, as the executive is by the legislative.

These three powers should naturally form a state of repose or inaction. But as there is a necessity for movement in the course of human affairs, they are forced to move, but still in concert.

As the executive power has no other part in the legislative than the privilege of rejecting, it can have no share in the public debates. It is not even necessary that it should propose, because as it may always disapprove of the resolutions that shall be taken, it may likewise reject the decisions on those proposals which were made against its will.

In some ancient commonwealths, where public debates were carried on by the people in a body, it was natural for the executive power to propose and debate in conjunction with the people, otherwise their resolutions must have been attended with a strange confusion.

Were the executive power to determine the raising of public money otherwise than by giving its consent, liberty would be at an end, because it would become legislative in the most important point of legislation.

If the legislative power was to settle the subsidies, not from year to year, but forever, it would run the risk of losing its liberty, because the executive power would be no longer dependent; and when once it was possessed of such a perpetual right, it would be a matter of indifference whether it held it of itself or of another. The same may be said if it should come to a resolution of intrusting, not an annual but a perpetual command of the fleets and armies to the executive power.

To prevent the executive power from being able to oppress, it is requisite that the armies with which it is intrusted should consist of the people, and have the same spirit as the people, as was the case at Rome till the time of Marius. To obtain this end, there are only two ways: either that the persons employed in the army should have sufficient property to answer for their conduct to their fellow subjects, and be enlisted only for a year, as was customary at Rome; or if there should be a standing army, composed chiefly of the most despicable part of the nation, the legislative power should have a right to disband them as soon as it pleased; the soldiers should live in common with the rest of the people; and no separate camp, barracks, or fortress should be suffered.

When once an army is established, it ought not to depend immediately on the legislative but on the executive power; and this from the very nature of the thing, its business consisting more in action than in deliberation.

It is natural for mankind to set a higher value upon courage than timidity, on activity than prudence, on strength than counsel. Hence the army will ever despise a senate, and respect their own officers. They will naturally slight the orders sent them by a body of men whom they look upon as cowards, and therefore unworthy to command them. So that as soon as the troops depend entirely on the legislative body, it becomes a military government; and if the contrary has ever happened, it has been owing to some extraordinary circumstances. It is because the army was always kept divided; it is because it was composed of several bodies that depended each on a particular province; it is because the capital towns were strong places, defended by their natural situation, and not garrisoned with regular troops. Holland, for instance, is still safer than Venice; she might drown or starve the revolted troops, for as they are not quartered in towns capable of furnishing them with necessary subsistence, this subsistence is of course precarious.

In perusing the admirable treatise of Tacitus "On the Manners of the Germans," we find it is from that nation that the English have borrowed the idea of their political government. This beautiful system was invented first in the woods.

As all human things have an end, the state we are speaking of will lose its liberty, will perish. Have not Rome, Sparta, and Carthage perished? It will perish when the legislative power shall be more corrupt than the executive.

It is not my business to examine whether the English actually enjoy this liberty or not. Sufficient it is for my purpose to observe that it is established by their laws; and I inquire no further.

Neither do I pretend by this to undervalue other governments, nor to say that this extreme political liberty ought to give uneasiness to those who have only a moderate share of it. How should I have any such design, I who think that even the highest refinement of reason is not always desirable, and that mankind generally find their account better in mediums than in extremes?

Harrington, in his "Oceana," has also inquired into the utmost degree of liberty to which the constitution of a state may be carried. But of him, indeed, it may be said that for want of knowing the nature of real liberty he busied himself in pursuit of an imaginary one; and that he built a Chalcedon, though he had a Byzantium before his eyes.

BOOK XIV

Of Laws in Relation to the Nature of the Climate

I. If it be true that the temper of the mind and the passions of the heart are extremely different in different climates, the laws ought to be in relation both to the variety of these passions and to the variety of these tempers.

II. Cold air constringes the extremities of the external fibers of the body; this increases their elasticity, and favors the return of the blood from the extreme parts to the heart. It contracts those very fibers; consequently it increases also their force. On the contrary, warm air relaxes and lengthens the extremes of the fibers; of course, it diminishes their force and elasticity.

People are therefore more vigorous in cold climates. Here the action of the heart and the reaction of the extremities of the fibers are better performed, the temperature of the humors is greater, the blood moves more freely toward the heart, and reciprocally the heart has more power. This superiority of strength must produce various effects: for instance, a greater boldness—that is, more courage; a greater sense of superiority—that is, less desire of revenge; a greater opinion of security—that is, more frankness, less suspicion, policy, and cunning. In short, this must be productive of very different tempers. Put a man into a close, warm place, and for reasons above given he will feel a great faintness. If under this circumstance you propose a bold enterprise to him, I believe you will find him very little disposed toward it; his present weakness will throw him into despondency; he will be afraid of everything,

being in a state of total incapacity. The inhabitants of warm countries are, like old men, timorous; the people in cold countries are,
like young men, brave. If we reflect on the late wars, which are
more recent in our memory, and in which we can better distinguish
some particular effects that escape us at a greater distance of time,
we shall find that the northern people transplanted into southern
regions did not perform such exploits as their countrymen, who,
fighting in their own climate, possessed their full vigor and courage.

This strength of the fibers in northern nations is the cause that
the coarser juices are extracted from their aliments. Hence two
things result: one, that the parts of the chyle or lymph are more
proper, by reason of their large surface, to be applied to and to
nourish the fibers; the other, that they are less proper, from their
coarseness, to give a certain subtilty to the nervous juice. Those
people have therefore large bodies and but little vivacity.

The nerves that terminate from all parts in the cutis form each a
nervous bundle; generally speaking, the whole nerve is not moved,
but a very minute part. In warm climates, where the cutis is relaxed, the ends of the nerves are expanded and laid open to the
weakest action of the smallest objects. In cold countries the cutis is
constringed and the papillae compressed; the miliary glands are in
some measure paralytic, and the sensation does not reach the brain,
except when it is very strong and proceeds from the whole nerve at
once. Now, imagination, taste, sensibility, and vivacity depend on
an infinite number of small sensations.

I have observed the outermost part of a sheep's tongue, where, to
the naked eye, it seems covered with papillae. On these papillae I
have discerned through a microscope small hairs, or a kind of down;
between the papillae were pyramids shaped toward the ends like
pincers. Very likely these pyramids are the principal organs of taste.

I caused the half of this tongue to be frozen, and observing it
with the naked eye I found the papillae considerably diminished;
even some rows of them were sunk into their sheath. The outermost
part I examined with the microscope, and perceived no pyramids.
In proportion as the frost went off, the papillae seemed to the naked
eye to rise, and with the microscope the miliary glands began to
appear.

This observation confirms what I have been saying, that in cold
countries the nervous glands are less expanded; they sink deeper
into their sheaths, or they are sheltered from the action of external
objects; consequently they have not such lively sensations.

In cold countries they have very little sensibility for pleasure; in temperate countries they have more; in warm countries their sensibility is exquisite. As climates are distinguished by degrees of latitude, we might distinguish them also in some measure by those of sensibility. I have been at the opera in England and in Italy, where I have seen the same pieces and the same performers; and yet the same music produces such different effects on the two nations: one is so cold and phlegmatic, and the other so lively and enraptured that it seems almost inconceivable.

It is the same with regard to pain, which is excited by the laceration of some fiber of the body. The author of Nature has made it an established rule that this pain should be more acute in proportion as the laceration is greater; now it is evident that the large bodies and coarse fibers of the people of the north are less capable of laceration than the delicate fibers of the inhabitants of warm countries; consequently the soul is there less sensible of pain. You must flay a Muscovite alive to make him feel.

From this delicacy of organs peculiar to warm climates it follows that the soul is most sensibly moved by whatever relates to the union of the two sexes; here everything leads to this object.

In northern climates scarcely has the animal part of love a power of making itself felt. In temperate climates, love, attended by a thousand appendages, endeavors to please by things that have at first the appearance, though not the reality, of this passion. In warmer climates it is liked for its own sake, it is the only cause of happiness, it is life itself.

In southern countries a machine of a delicate frame but strong sensibility resigns itself either to a love which rises and is incessantly laid in a seraglio, or to a passion which leaves women in a greater independence, and is consequently exposed to a thousand inquietudes. In northern regions a machine robust and heavy finds pleasure in whatever is apt to throw the spirits into motion, such as hunting, traveling, war, and wine. If we travel toward the north we meet with people who have few vices, many virtues, and a great share of frankness and sincerity. If we draw near the south, we fancy ourselves entirely removed from the verge of morality; here the strongest passions are productive of all manner of crimes, each man endeavoring, let the means be what they will, to indulge his inordinate desires. In temperate climates we find the inhabitants inconstant in their manners, as well as in their vices and virtues; the climate has not a quality determinate enough to fix them.

The heat of the climate may be so excessive as to deprive the body of all vigor and strength. Then the faintness is communicated to the mind; there is no curiosity, no enterprise, no generosity of sentiment; the inclinations are all passive; indolence constitutes the utmost happiness; scarcely any punishment is so severe as mental employment; and slavery is more supportable than the force and vigor of mind necessary for human conduct.

III. The Indians are naturally a pusillanimous people; even the children of Europeans born in India lose the courage peculiar to their own climate. But how shall we reconcile this with their customs and penances so full of barbarity? The men voluntarily undergo the greatest hardships, and the women burn themselves; here we find a very odd compound of fortitude and weakness.

Nature, having framed these people of a texture so weak as to fill them with timidity, has formed them at the same time of an imagination so lively that every object makes the strongest impression upon them. That delicacy of organs which renders them apprehensive of death contributes likewise to make them dread a thousand things more than death; the very same sensibility induces them to fly and dare all dangers. . . .

FURTHER READING

Raymond Aron, *Main Currents in Sociological Thought,* Vol. I, *Montesquieu, Comte, Marx, Tocqueville, the Sociologists and the Revolution of 1848* (tr. 1965). The opening chapter on Montesquieu is judicious.

Emile Durkheim, *Montesquieu and Rousseau: Precursors of Sociology* (tr. 1960). Important pioneer appraisal, which makes Montesquieu into a forerunner of positivism; a view criticized by Neumann (see just below).

Franz Neumann, introduction to Montesquieu, *Spirit of the Laws* (1945 edn.). Comprehensive and brilliant.

40 ❈ CONDILLAC

Treatise on Sensations

[From Condillac, *Oeuvres*, 3 vols. (1777), III,
282–86. Translated by Peter Gay.]

*For reasons implicit in the very structure of its thought, the En-
lightenment was strongly oriented toward psychology. Neither theology (the science of God) nor metaphysics (the science of being)
answered man's most urgent questions. Perhaps, as Pope had put it
in his famous line, the proper study of mankind is man. Of course,
to ask questions about man himself is, in itself, not a new idea; it
goes back to the Platonic dialogues and beyond. But until the
middle of the seventeenth century, with the rigorous inquiries of
Descartes, Spinoza and Locke, man's search for self-knowledge had
been in the hands of essayists, aphorists, and poets. Locke, as Voltaire gratefully noted in his* Philosophical Letters, *had modestly
refrained from inquiring into the essence of the soul and instead
written its natural history. The philosophes pursued this line of
inquiry much further.*

*Perhaps the leading psychologist of the eighteenth century was
Étienne Bonnot de Condillac (1714–80), a typical philosophe in his
versatility. Condillac wrote on philosophical and pedagogical questions, on history and economics. But among his large corpus of
writings, his books on psychology stand out for their power and
originality. Locke was Condillac's model: he did much to naturalize
Locke's ideas on epistemology and psychology in France. But he
went beyond that model. Locke had postulated two sources for
ideas, sensations and reflection. Condillac, using the ingenious
metaphor of a lifeless statue which acquires senses, emotions, psychological activities one by one, reduced these two sources to
sensation alone.*

Condillac's extended metaphor of the awakening statue was

imaginative in the extreme; his antimetaphysical attitude toward the human psyche was a forerunner of the psychological experimentation of the nineteenth century.

PART IV

IX. CONCLUSION

I. We cannot apply all the suppositions I have made; but at least they prove that all our knowledge [*connoissances*] comes from the senses, and especially from that of touch, because that teaches the others. If, in supposing our statue to have nothing but sensations, it has yet acquired ideas both particular and general, and has made itself capable of performing all the operations of the understanding; if it has formed desires, and made itself passions that it resists or obeys; finally, if pleasure and pain are the single principle of the development of its faculties, then it is reasonable to conclude that we had only sensations at the outset, and that our knowledge and our passions are the effects of the pleasures and pains that accompany sense impressions.

Indeed, the more one thinks about it, the more convinced one will be, that the single source of our information [*lumière*] and of our feelings lies there. Let us consider information: we instantly—if I may so express myself—enjoy a new life, very different from the one that our raw sensations had previously procured for us. Let us consider feeling, let us observe it chiefly when it is supplied with all the judgments which we customarily confuse with sense impressions: instantly, these sensations, which initially gave us only a small number of coarse pleasures, now give rise to delicate pleasures succeeding one another in an astonishing variety. Thus, the farther away we move from what our feelings were at the beginning, the more our existence develops, the more varied it grows. It will extend to so many things that we will hardly be able to understand how all our faculties could have a common beginning in sensation.

II. As long as men only see in sense impressions sensations almost wholly devoid of judgments, the life of one individual is much like that of another: there is practically no difference between them except in the degree of liveliness with which they feel. For them, experience and reflection will be what the chisel is in the hands of the sculptor who discovers a perfect statue in the unformed stone; and, according to the skill with which they employ that chisel, they will see arising from their sensations new knowledge and new pleasures.

If we observe them, we will see how these materials remain crude or are shaped; and, considering the difference between men, we will be astonished to see how, in the same space of time, some live more than others: for to live is, properly speaking, to enjoy life, and life is longer for the one who knows how to multiply the objects of his enjoyment.

We have seen that enjoyment may begin with the first agreeable sensation. The first time, for instance, that we endowed our statue with sight, it was enjoying itself: its eyes were no longer struck with the color black alone. For we must not judge its pleasures by ours. A number of sensations are indifferent to us, or even disagreeable, whether because they have nothing new for us or because we know livelier ones. But the situation of the statue is quite different: it can be entranced when it experiences feelings that we do not deign to notice, or notice only with disgust.

Let us observe light, when touch teaches the eye to spread colors across all of nature: there are as many feelings, and consequently as many new pleasures, as there are new enjoyments.

We must reason in the same way about all the other senses, and about all the operations of the mind. For we enjoy not merely through sight, hearing, taste, smell, and touch; we enjoy also through memory, imagination, reflection, the passions, hope; in a word, through all our faculties. But these sources are not equally active in all men.

III. It is pleasures and pains compared, that is to say our needs, that activate our faculties. Consequently it is to them that we owe the happiness it is ours to enjoy. There are as many different enjoyments as there are needs; there are as many degrees in enjoyment as there are degrees in need. Here is the germ of all that we are, the source of our misery or our happiness. Observe the influence of this principle, for it is the single means we have for studying ourselves.

The history of the faculties of our statue makes the course of all these things plain. When it was limited to fundamental feeling, a uniform sensation made up all its being, all its knowledge, all its pleasure. In successively endowing it with new ways of being and with new senses, we have seen it form desires, learn from experience to dominate or satisfy them, and move from needs to needs, from knowledge to knowledge, from pleasures to pleasures. It is therefore nothing but all that it has acquired. Why should this not be true of man?

FURTHER READING

Isabel F. Knight, *The Geometric Spirit: The Abbé de Condillac and the French Enlightenment* (1968). A competent though not conclusive monograph.

Paul Kuehner, *Theories on the Origin and Formation of Language in the Eighteenth Century in France* (1944). A useful treatment of an important theme in Condillac and the Enlightenment in general.

Georges Le Roy, *La Psychologie de Condillac* (1937). A fair-minded analysis of Condillac's psychology by the modern editor of his works.

Roger Lefèvre, *Condillac, ou La Joie de vivre* (1966). Short and sensible; the elliptical subtitle doubtless refers to the statue.

41 ❀ HUME

"Of National Characters"

[From "Of National Characters," in *The
Philosophical Works of David Hume*, edited by
T. H. Green and T. H. Grose, 4 vols. (1882), III
244–54.]

*Generalization is the lifeblood and the nemesis of social scientists.
Without it, they must fall into biography or anecdotes; with it, they
may fall into bias or superficiality. The problem is still with us, and
it is Hume's merit to have perceived it as a problem. His essay "Of
National Characters," first published in 1748, confines itself to the
influence of national and racial heritage on the individual. But his
essay "Of the Standard of Taste"* shows that Hume also thought
age a factor in the formation of opinion and character. Class differences, to which we pay so much attention today, do not appear
prominently in Hume's work, but it would be unhistorical in the
extreme to blame him for this "neglect." There were steep gradations in the hierarchy of eighteenth-century society, but no classes in
the modern sense.*

*Two other matters deserve notice: the confidence with which
Hume assigns inferior status to the black race, and his disagreement
with the position of Montesquieu. In criticizing the notion that
"physical causes" such as climate actually affect national character,
Hume is at the opposite pole from Montesquieu's* Spirit *of the*
Laws, *which also appeared in 1748. We are here therefore witness-
ing one of the first debates in the social sciences.*

* See above, selection 34.

The vulgar are apt to carry all *national characters* to extremes; and having once established it as a principle, that any people are knavish, or cowardly, or ignorant, they will admit of no exception, but comprehend every individual under the same censure. Men of sense condemn these undistinguishing judgments: Though at the same time, they allow, that each nation has a peculiar set of manners, and that some particular qualities are more frequently to be met with among one people than among their neighbours. The common people in Switzerland have probably more honesty than those of the same rank in Ireland; and every prudent man will, from that circumstance alone, make a difference in the trust which he reposes in each. We have reason to expect greater wit and gaiety in a Frenchman than in a Spaniard; though Cervantes was born in Spain. An Englishman will naturally be supposed to have more knowledge than a Dane; though Tycho Brahe was a native of Denmark.

Different reasons are assigned for these *national characters;* while some account for them from *moral,* others from *physical* causes. By *moral* causes, I mean all circumstances, which are fitted to work on the mind as motives or reasons, and which render a peculiar set of manners habitual to us. Of this kind are, the nature of the government, the revolutions of public affairs, the plenty or penury in which the people live, the situation of the nation with regard to its neighbours, and such like circumstances. By *physical* causes I mean those qualities of the air and climate, which are supposed to work insensibly on the temper, by altering the tone and habit of the body, and giving a particular complexion, which, though reflection and reason may sometimes overcome it, will yet prevail among the generality of mankind, and have an influence on their manners.

That the character of a nation will much depend on *moral* causes, must be evident to the most superficial observer; since a nation is nothing but a collection of individuals, and the manners of individuals are frequently determined by these causes. As poverty and hard labour debase the minds of the common people, and render them unfit for any science and ingenious profession; so where any government becomes very oppressive to all its subjects, it must have a proportional effect on their temper and genius, and must banish all the liberal arts from among them.

The same principle of moral causes fixes the character of different professions, and alters even that disposition, which the particular members receive from the hand of nature. A *soldier* and a *priest* are different characters, in all nations, and all ages; and this difference is founded on circumstances, whose operation is eternal and unalterable.

The uncertainty of their life makes soldiers lavish and generous, as well as brave: Their idleness, together with the large societies, which they form in camps or garrisons, inclines them to pleasure and gallantry: By their frequent change of company, they acquire good breeding and an openness of behaviour: Being employed only against a public and an open enemy, they become candid, honest, and undesigning: And as they use more the labour of the body than that of the mind, they are commonly thoughtless and ignorant.

It is a trite, but not altogether a false maxim, that *priests of all religions are the same;* and though the character of the profession will not, in every instance, prevail over the personal character, yet it is sure always to predominate with the greater number. For as chymists observe, that spirits, when raised to a certain height, are all the same, from whatever material they be extracted; so these men, being elevated above humanity, acquire a uniform character, which is entirely their own, and which, in my opinion, is, generally speaking, not the most amiable that is to be met with in human society. It is, in most points, opposite to that of a soldier; as is the way of life, from which it is derived.*

* Though all mankind have a strong propensity to religion at certain times and in certain dispositions; yet are there few or none, who have it to that degree, and with that constancy, which is requisite to support the character of this profession. It must, therefore, happen, that clergymen, being drawn from the common mass of mankind, as people are to other employments, by the views of profit, the greater part, though no atheists or free-thinkers, will find it necessary, on particular occasions, to feign more devotion than they are, at that time, possessed of, and to maintain the appearance of fervor and seriousness, even when jaded with the exercises of their religion, or when they have their minds engaged in the common occupations of life. They must not, like the rest of the world, give scope to their natural movements and sentiments: They must set a guard over their looks and words and actions: And in order to support the veneration paid them by the multitude, they must not only keep a remarkable reserve, but must promote the spirit of superstition, by a continued grimace and hypocrisy. This dissimulation often destroys the candor and ingenuity of their temper, and makes an irreparable breach in their character.

If by chance any of them be possessed of a temper more susceptible of devo-

There are few questions more curious than this, or which will oftener occur in our enquiries concerning human affairs; and therefore it may be proper to give it a full examination.

The human mind is of a very imitative nature; nor is it possible for any set of men to converse often together, without acquiring a similitude of manners, and communicating to each other their vices as well as virtues. The propensity to company and society is strong in all rational creatures; and the same disposition, which gives us

---

tion than usual, so that he has but little occasion for hypocrisy to support the character of his profession; it is so natural for him to over-rate this advantage, and to think that it atones for every violation of morality, that frequently he is not more virtuous than the hypocrite. And though few dare openly avow those exploded opinions, *that every thing is lawful to the saints*, and *that they alone have property in their goods;* yet may we observe, that these principles lurk in every bosom, and represent a zeal for religious observances as so great a merit, that it may compensate for many vices and enormities. This observation is so common, that all prudent men are on their guard, when they meet with any extraordinary appearance of religion; though at the same time, they confess, that there are many exceptions to this general rule, and that probity and superstition, or even probity and fanaticism, are not altogether and in every instance incompatible.

Most men are ambitious; but the ambition of other men may commonly be satisfied, by excelling in their particular profession, and thereby promoting the interests of society. The ambition of the clergy can often be satisfied only by promoting ignorance and superstition and implicit faith and pious frauds. And having got what Archimedes only wanted, (namely, another world, on which he could fix his engines) no wonder they move this world at their pleasure.

Most men have an overweening conceit of themselves; but *these* have a peculiar temptation to that vice, who are regarded with such veneration, and are even deemed sacred, by the ignorant multitude.

Most men are apt to bear a particular regard for members of their own profession; but as a lawyer, or physician, or merchant, does, each of them, follow out his business apart, the interests of men of these professions are not so closely united as the interests of clergymen of the same religion; where the whole body gains by the veneration, paid to their common tenets, and by the suppression of antagonists.

Few men can bear contradiction with patience; but the clergy too often proceed even to a degree of fury on this head: Because all their credit and livelihood depend upon the belief, which their opinions meet with; and they alone pretend to a divine and supernatural authority, or have any colour for representing their antagonists as impious and prophane. The *Odium Theologicum*, or Theological Hatred, is noted even to a proverb, and means that degree of rancour, which is the most furious and implacable.

Revenge is a natural passion to mankind; but seems to reign with the greatest force in priests and women: Because, being deprived of the immediate exertion of anger, in violence and combat, they are apt to fancy themselves despised on that account; and their pride supports their vindictive disposition. [This paragraph was added in 1753–54.]

this propensity, makes us enter deeply into each other's sentiments, and causes like passions and inclinations to run, as it were, by contagion, through the whole club or knot of companions. Where a number of men are united into one political body, the occasions of this intercourse must be so frequent, for defence, commerce, and government, that, together with the same speech or language, they must acquire a resemblance in their manners, and have a common or national character, as well as a personal one, peculiar to each individual. Now though nature produces all kinds of temper and understanding in great abundance, it does not follow, that she always produces them in like proportions, and that in every society the ingredients of industry and indolence, valour and cowardice, humanity and brutality, wisdom and folly, will be mixed after the same manner. In the infancy of society, if any of these dispositions be found in greater abundance than the rest, it will naturally prevail in the composition, and give a tincture to the national character. Or should it be asserted, that no species of temper can reasonably be presumed to predominate, even in those contracted societies, and that the same proportions will always be preserved in the mixture; yet surely the persons in credit and authority, being still a more contracted body, cannot always be presumed to be of the same character; and their influence on the manners of the people, must, at all times, be very considerable. If on the first establishment of a republic, a Brutus should be placed in authority, and be transported with such an enthusiasm for liberty and public good, as to overlook all the ties of nature, as well as private interest, such an illustrious example will naturally have an effect on the whole society, and kindle the same passion in every bosom. Whatever it be that forms the manners of one generation, the next must imbibe a deeper tincture of the same dye; men being more susceptible of all impressions during infancy, and retaining these impressions as long as they remain in the world. I assert, then, that all national characters, where they depend not on fixed *moral* causes, proceed from such accidents as these, and that physical causes have no discernible operation on the human mind.

If we run over the globe, or revolve the annals of history, we shall discover every where signs of a sympathy or contagion of manners, none of the influence of air or climate.

First. We may observe, that, where a very extensive government has been established for many centuries, it spreads a national character over the whole empire, and communicates to every part a similarity of manners. Thus the Chinese have the greatest uniformity of character imaginable: though the air and climate in different parts of those vast dominions, admit of very considerable variations.

Secondly. In small governments, which are contiguous, the people have notwithstanding a different character, and are often as distinguishable in their manners as the most distant nations. Athens and Thebes were but a short day's journey from each other; though the Athenians were as remarkable for ingenuity, politeness, and gaiety, as the Thebans for dullness, rusticity, and a phlegmatic temper. Plutarch, discoursing of the effects of air on the minds of men, observes, that the inhabitants of the Piraeum possessed very different tempers from those of the higher town in Athens, which was distant about four miles from the former: But I believe no one attributes the difference of manners in Wapping and St. James's, to a difference of air or climate.

Thirdly. The same national character commonly follows the authority of government to a precise boundary; and upon crossing a river or passing a mountain, one finds a new set of manners, with a new government. The Languedocians and Gascons are the gayest people in France; but whenever you pass the Pyrenees, you are among Spaniards. Is it conceivable, that the qualities of the air should change exactly with the limits of an empire, which depend so much on the accidents of battles, negociations, and marriages?

Fourthly. Where any set of men, scattered over distant nations, maintain a close society or communication together, they acquire a similitude of manners, and have but little in common with the nations amongst whom they live. Thus the Jews in Europe, and the Armenians in the east, have a peculiar character; and the former are as much noted for fraud, as the latter for probity. The Jesuits, in all Roman-catholic countries, are also observed to have a character peculiar to themselves.

Fifthly. Where any accident, as a difference in language or religion, keeps two nations inhabiting the same country, from mixing with each other, they will preserve, during several centuries, a distinct and even opposite set of manners. The integrity, gravity, and bravery of the Turks, form an exact contrast to the deceit, levity, and cowardice of the modern Greeks.

Sixthly. The same set of manners will follow a nation, and adhere to them over the whole globe, as well as the same laws and language. The Spanish, English, French and Dutch colonies are all distinguishable even between the tropics.

Seventhly. The manners of a people change very considerably from one age to another, either by great alterations in their government, by the mixtures of new people, or by that inconstancy, to which all human affairs are subject. The ingenuity, industry, and activity of the ancient Greeks have nothing in common with the stupidity and indolence of the present inhabitants of those regions. Candour, bravery, and love of liberty formed the character of the ancient Romans; as subtilty, cowardice, and a slavish disposition do that of the modern. The old Spaniards were restless, turbulent, and so addicted to war, that many of them killed themselves, when deprived of their arms by the Romans. One would find an equal difficulty at present, (at least one would have found it fifty years ago) to rouze up the modern Spaniards to arms. The Batavians were all soldiers of fortune, and hired themselves into the Roman armies. Their posterity make use of foreigners for the same purpose that the Romans did their ancestors. Though some few strokes of the French character be the same with that which Caesar has ascribed to the Gauls: yet what comparison between the civility humanity, and knowledge of the modern inhabitants of that country, and the ignorance, barbarity, and grossness of the ancient?

Eighthly. Where several neighbouring nations have a very close communication together, either by policy, commerce, or travelling, they acquire a similitude of manners, proportioned to the communication. Thus all the Franks appear to have a uniform character to the eastern nations. The differences among them are like the peculiar accents of different provinces, which are not distinguishable, except by an ear accustomed to them, and which commonly escape a foreigner.

Ninthly. We may often remark a wonderful mixture of manners and characters in the same nation, speaking the same language, and subject to the same government: And in this particular the English are the most remarkable of any people, that perhaps ever were in the world. Nor is this to be ascribed to the mutability and uncertainty of their climate, or to any other *physical* causes; since all these causes take place in the neighbouring country of Scotland, without having the same effect. Where the government of a nation is altogether republican, it is apt to beget a peculiar set of manners. Where it is altogether monarchical, it is more apt to have the same effect; the imitation of superiors spreading the national manners faster among the people. If the governing part of a state consists altogether of merchants, as in Holland, their uniform way of life will fix their character. If it consists chiefly of nobles and landed gentry, like Germany, France, and Spain, the same effect follows.

The genius of a particular sect or religion is also apt to mould the manners of a people. But the English government is a mixture of monarchy, aristocracy, and democracy. The people in authority are composed of gentry and merchants. All sects of religion are to be found among them. And the great liberty and independency, which every man enjoys, allows him to display the manners peculiar to him. Hence the English, of any people in the universe, have the least of a national character; unless this very singularity may pass for such.

If the characters of men depend on the air and climate, the degrees of heat and cold should naturally be expected to have a mighty influence; since nothing has a greater effect on all plants and irrational animals. And indeed there is some reason to think, that all the nations, which live beyond the polar circles or between the tropics, are inferior to the rest of the species, and are incapable of all the higher attainments of the human mind. The poverty and misery of the northern inhabitants of the globe, and the indolence of the southern, from their few necessities, may, perhaps, account for this remarkable difference, without our having recourse to *physical* causes. This however is certain, that the characters of nations are very promiscuous in the temperate climates, and that almost all the general observations, which have been formed of the more southern or more northern people in these climates, are found to be uncertain and fallacious.*

Shall we say, that the neighbourhood of the sun inflames the imagination of men, and gives it a peculiar spirit and vivacity. The French, Greeks, Egyptians, and Persians are remarkable for gaiety. The Spaniards, Turks, and Chinese are noted for gravity and a

---

* I am apt to suspect the negroes, and in general all the other species of men (for there are four or five different kinds) to be naturally inferior to the whites. There never was a civilized nation of any other complexion than white, nor even any individual eminent either in action or speculation. No ingenious manufactures amongst them, no arts, no sciences. On the other hand, the most rude and barbarous of the whites, such as the ancient Germans, the present Tartars, have still something eminent about them, in their valour, form of government, or some other particular. Such a uniform and constant difference could not happen, in so many countries and ages, if nature had not made an original distinction betwixt these breeds of men. Not to mention our colonies, there are negroe slaves dispersed all over Europe, of which none ever discovered any symptoms of ingenuity; tho' low people, without education, will start up amongst us, and distinguish themselves in every profession. In Jamaica indeed they talk of one negroe as a man of parts and learning; but 'tis likely he is admired for very slender accomplishments, like a parrot, who speaks a few words plainly. [This note was added in 1753–54.]

serious deportment, without any such difference of climate as to produce this difference of temper.

The Greeks and Romans, who called all other nations barbarians, confined genius and a fine understanding to the more southern climates, and pronounced the northern nations incapable of all knowledge and civility. But our island has produced as great men, either for action or learning, as Greece or Italy has to boast of.

It is pretended, that the sentiments of men become more delicate as the country approaches nearer to the sun; and that the taste of beauty and elegance receives proportional improvements in every latitude; as we may particularly observe of the languages, of which the more southern are smooth and melodious, the northern harsh and untuneable. But this observation holds not universally. The Arabic is uncouth and disagreeable: The Muscovite soft and musical. Energy, strength, and harshness form the character of the Latin tongue: The Italian is the most liquid, smooth, and effeminate language that can possibly be imagined. Every language will depend somewhat on the manners of the people; but much more on that original stock of words and sounds, which they received from their ancestors, and which remain unchangeable, even while their manners admit of the greatest alterations. Who can doubt, but the English are at present a more polite and knowing people than the Greeks were for several ages after the siege of Troy? Yet is there no comparison between the language of Milton and that of Homer. Nay, the greater are the alterations and improvements, which happen in the manners of a people, the less can be expected in their language. A few eminent and refined geniuses will communicate their taste and knowledge to a whole people, and produce the greatest improvements; but they fix the tongue by their writings, and prevent, in some degree, its farther changes.

Lord Bacon has observed, that the inhabitants of the south are, in general, more ingenious than those of the north; but that, where the native of a cold climate has genius, he rises to a higher pitch than can be reached by the southern wits. This observation a late writer confirms, by comparing the southern wits to cucumbers, which are commonly all good in their kind; but at best are an insipid fruit: While the northern geniuses are like melons, of which not one in fifty is good; but when it is so, it has an exquisite relish. I believe this remark may be allowed just, when confined to the European nations, and to the present age, or rather to the preceding one: But I think it may be accounted for from moral causes. All the sciences and liberal arts have been imported to us from the south; and it is easy to imagine, that, in the first order of application, when excited by emulation and by glory, the few, who were addicted to them, would carry them to the greatest height, and stretch every nerve, and every faculty, to reach the pinnacle of perfection. Such illustrious examples spread knowledge everywhere, and begot an universal esteem for the sciences: After which it is no wonder, that industry relaxes; while men meet not with suitable encouragement, nor arrive at such distinction by their attainments. The universal diffusion of learning among a people, and the entire banishment of gross ignorance and rusticity, is, therefore, seldom attended with any remarkable perfection in particular persons. This state of learning is remarkable; because Juvenal is himself the last of the Roman writers, that possessed any degree of genius. Those, who succeeded, are valued for nothing but the matters of fact, of which they give us information. I hope the late conversion of Muscovy to the study of the sciences will not prove a like prognostic to the present period of learning. . . .

FURTHER READING

Alex Inkeles and Daniel J. Levinson, "National Character: The Study of Modal Personality and Sociocultural Systems," in Gardner Lindzey, ed., *Handbook of Social Psychology,* Vol. II (1954) , 977–1020.

Otto Klineberg, "A Science of National Character," *Bulletin of the Society for the Psychological Study of Social Issues,* No. 19 (1944) , 147–62.

Ralph Linton, *The Cultural Background of Personality* (1945). A general analysis of the relation of culture to the individual mind. Should be read in conjunction with the first two items, which are more technical.

42 ❦ HUME

"Of the Populousness of Ancient Nations"

[From "Of the Populousness of Ancient
Nations," in *The Philosophical Works of David
Hume,* edited by T. H. Green and T. H. Grose,
4 vols. (1882), III, 381–89.]

*Hume's essay on the populousness of ancient nations, first published
in 1752, is a tribute to his empiricism, and to his learning as well.
The idea of the scientific study of population was in the air, though
still rather haltingly pursued. In 1662, the English researcher John
Graunt had published his* Natural and Political Observations upon
the Bills of Mortality, *which analyzed the records for christenings
and burials in and around London; modern demography was to be
constructed on such studies. But in the first half of the eighteenth
century such widely read students of society as Montesquieu could
offer the most improbable estimates of population as established
fact—it was Montesquieu's claim, in* The Spirit of the Laws, *that
the ancient world was far more heavily populated than the modern
world that set Hume off to inquire into the matter more closely,
and in a more scientific spirit. For what mattered in this (good-
tempered) debate was not Montesquieu's conclusions so much as his
reasoning. In purely deductive fashion, Montesquieu had established this implicit syllogism: antiquity was unquestionably a
greater age than ours; greatness and populousness go together;
hence antiquity must have been more populous than modern times.
In discarding this logic and disproving its conclusion, Hume took
occasion to cite more than fifty ancient authors, Greek as well as
Latin, and to move beyond the circle of famous writers to the*

*obscure authors of forgotten treatises. In preparing "Of the Popu-
lousness of Ancient Nations," Hume wrote a friend, he "read over
almost all the Classics, both Greek and Latin."* Hume may have
lacked the sophisticated statistical techniques that are the common
property of demographers today, but he had a classical erudition,
and a fund of penetrating good sense, that made modern demography possible.*

There is very little ground, either from reason or observation, to
conclude the world eternal or incorruptible. The continual and
rapid motion of matter, the violent revolutions with which every
part is agitated, the changes remarked in the heavens, the plain
traces as well as tradition of an universal deluge, or general convulsion of the elements; all these prove strongly the mortality of this
fabric of the world, and its passage, by corruption or dissolution,
from one state or order to another. It must therefore, as well as each
individual form which it contains, have its infancy, youth, manhood, and old age; and it is probable, that, in all these variations,
man, equally with every animal and vegetable, will partake. In the
flourishing age of the world, it may be expected, that the human
species should possess greater vigour both of mind and body, more
prosperous health, higher spirits, longer life, and a stronger inclination and power of generation. But if the general system of things,
and human society of course, have any such gradual revolutions,
they are too slow to be discernible in that short period which is
comprehended by history and tradition. Stature and force of body,
length of life, even courage and extent of genius, seem hitherto to
have been naturally, in all ages, pretty much the same. The arts and
sciences, indeed, have flourished in one period, and have decayed in
another: But we may observe, that, at the time when they rose to
greatest perfection among one people, they were perhaps totally
unknown to all the neighbouring nations; and though they universally decayed in one age, yet in a succeeding generation they again
revived, and diffused themselves over the world. As far, therefore, as
observation reaches, there is no universal difference discernible in

---

* Hume to Gilbert Elliott, Feb. 18, 1751, *Letters,* ed. J. Y. T. Greig, 2 vols.
(1932), I, 152.

the human species; and though it were allowed, that the universe, like an animal body, had a natural progress from infancy to old age; yet as it must still be uncertain, whether, at present, it be advancing to its point of perfection, or declining from it, we cannot thence presuppose any decay in human nature.* To prove, therefore, or account for that superior populousness of antiquity, which is commonly supposed, by the imaginary youth or vigour of the world, will scarcely be admitted by any just reasoner. These *general physical* causes ought entirely to be excluded from this question.

There are indeed some more *particular physical* causes of importance. Diseases are mentioned in antiquity, which are almost unknown to modern medicine; and new diseases have arisen and propagated themselves, of which there are no traces in ancient history. In this particular we may observe, upon comparison, that the disadvantage is much on the side of the moderns. Not to mention some others of less moment, the small-pox commits such ravages, as would almost alone account for the great superiority ascribed to ancient times. The tenth or the twelfth part of mankind, destroyed every generation, should make a vast difference, it may be thought, in the numbers of the people; and when joined to venereal distempers, a new plague diffused every where, this disease is perhaps equivalent, by its constant operation, to the three great scourges of mankind, war, pestilence, and famine. Were it certain, therefore, that ancient times were more populous than the present, and could no moral causes be assigned for so great a change; these physical causes alone, in the opinion of many, would be sufficient to give us satisfaction on that head.

But is it certain, that antiquity was so much more populous, as is pretended? The extravagancies of Vossius, with regard to this subject, are well known. But an author of much greater genius and discernment [Montesquieu] has ventured to affirm, that, according to the best computations which these subjects will admit of, there are not now, on the face of the earth, the fiftieth part of mankind, which existed in the time of Julius Caesar. It may easily be observed, that the comparison, in this case, must be imperfect, even

* Columella says . . . that in Egypt and Africa, the bearing of twins was frequent, and even customary; . . . If this was true, there is a physical difference both in countries and ages. For travellers make no such remarks on these countries at present. On the contrary, we are apt to suppose the northern nations more prolific. As those two countries were provinces of the Roman empire, it is difficult, though not altogether absurd, to suppose that such a man as Columella might be mistaken with regard to them.

though we confine ourselves to the scene of ancient history; Europe, and the nations round the Mediterranean. We know not exactly the numbers of any European kingdom, or even city, at present: How can we pretend to calculate those of ancient cities and states, where historians have left us such imperfect traces? For my part, the matter appears to me so uncertain, that, as I intend to throw together some reflections on that head, I shall intermingle the enquiry concerning *causes* with that concerning *facts;* which ought never to be admitted, where the facts can be ascertained with any tolerable assurance. We shall, *first,* consider whether it be probable, from what we know of the situation of society in both periods, that antiquity must have been more populous; *secondly,* whether in reality it was so. If I can make it appear, that the conclusion is not so certain as is pretended, in favour of antiquity, it is all I aspire to.

In general, we may observe, that the question, with regard to the comparative populousness of ages or kingdoms, implies important consequences, and commonly determines concerning the preference of their whole police, their manners, and the constitution of their government. For as there is in all men, both male and female, a desire and power of generation, more active than is ever universally exerted, the restraints, which they lie under, must proceed from some difficulties in their situation, which it belongs to a wise legislature carefully to observe and remove. Almost every man who thinks he can maintain a family will have one; and the human species, at this rate of propagation, would more than double every generation. How fast do mankind multiply in every colony or new settlement; where it is an easy matter to provide for a family; and where men are nowise straitened or confined, as in long established governments? History tells us frequently of plagues, which have swept away the third or fourth part of a people: Yet in a generation or two, the destruction was not perceived; and the society had again acquired their former number. The lands which were cultivated, the houses built, the commodities raised, the riches acquired, enabled the people, who escaped, immediately to marry, and to rear families, which supplied the place of those who had perished. And for a like reason, every wise, just, and mild government, by rendering the condition of its subjects easy and secure, will always abound most in people, as well as in commodities and riches. A country, indeed, whose climate and soil are fitted for vines, will naturally be more populous than one which produces corn only, and that more populous than one which is only fitted for pasturage. In general, warm climates, as the necessities of the inhabitants are there fewer, and vegetation more powerful, are likely to be most populous: But if everything else be equal, it seems natural to expect, that, wherever there are most happiness and virtue, and the wisest institutions, there will also be most people.

The question, therefore, concerning the populousness of ancient and modern times, being allowed of great importance, it will be requisite, if we would bring it to some determination, to compare both the *domestic* and *political* situation of these two periods, in order to judge of the facts by their moral causes; which is the *first* view in which we proposed to consider them.

The chief difference between the *domestic* economy of the ancients and that of the moderns consists in the practice of slavery, which prevailed among the former, and which has been abolished for some centuries throughout the greater part of Europe. Some passionate admirers of the ancients, and zealous partizans of civil liberty (for these sentiments, as they are, both of them, in the main, extremely just, are found to be almost inseparable) cannot forbear regretting the loss of this institution; and whilst they brand all submission to the government of a single person with the harsh denomination of slavery, they would gladly reduce the greater part of mankind to real slavery and subjection. But to one who considers coolly on the subject it will appear, that human nature, in general, really enjoys more liberty at present, in the most arbitrary government of Europe, than it ever did during the most flourishing period of ancient times. As much as submission to a petty prince, whose dominions extend not beyond a single city, is more grievous than obedience to a great monarch; so much is domestic slavery more cruel and oppressive than any civil subjection whatsoever. The more the master is removed from us in place and rank, the greater liberty we enjoy; the less are our actions inspected and controled; and the fainter that cruel comparison becomes between our own subjection, and the freedom, and even dominion of another. The remains which are found of domestic slavery, in the American colonies, and among some European nations, would never surely create a desire of rendering it more universal. The little humanity, commonly observed in persons, accustomed, from their infancy, to exercise so great authority over their fellow-creatures, and to trample upon human nature, were sufficient alone to disgust us with that unbounded dominion. Nor can a more probable reason be assigned for the severe, I might say, barbarous manners of ancient times, than the practice of domestic slavery; by which every man of rank was rendered a petty tyrant, and educated amidst the flattery, submission, and low debasement of his slaves.

According to ancient practice, all checks were on the inferior, to restrain him to the duty of submission; none on the superior, to engage him to the reciprocal duties of gentleness and humanity. In modern times, a bad servant finds not easily a good master, nor a bad master a good servant; and the checks are mutual, suitably to the inviolable and eternal laws of reason and equity.

The custom of exposing old, useless, or sick slaves in an island of the Tyber, there to starve, seems to have been pretty common in Rome; and whoever recovered, after having been so exposed, had his liberty given him, by an edict of the emperor Claudius; in which it was likewise forbidden to kill any slave merely for old age or sickness. But supposing that this edict was strictly obeyed, would it better the domestic treatment of slaves, or render their lives much more comfortable? We may imagine what others would practise, when it was the professed maxim of the elder Cato, to sell his superannuated slaves for any price, rather than maintain what he esteemed a useless burden.

The *ergastula,* or dungeons, where slaves in chains were forced to work, were very common all over Italy. Columella advises, that they be always built under ground; and recommends it as the duty of a careful overseer, to call over every day the names of these slaves, like the mustering of a regiment or ship's company, in order to know presently when any of them had deserted. A proof of the frequency of these *ergastula,* and of the great number of slaves usually confined in them.

A chained slave for a porter, was usual in Rome, as appears from Ovid, and other authors. Had not these people shaken off all sense of compassion towards that unhappy part of their species, would they have presented their friends, at the first entrance, with such an image of the severity of the master, and misery of the slave?

Nothing so common in all trials, even of civil causes, as to call for the evidence of slaves; which was always extorted by the most exquisite torments. Demosthenes says, that, where it was possible to produce, for the same fact, either freemen or slaves, as witnesses, the judges always preferred the torturing of slaves, as a more certain evidence.*

Seneca draws a picture of that disorderly luxury, which changes

---

* The same practice was very common in Rome; but Cicero seems not to think this evidence so certain as the testimony of free-citizens.

day into night, and night into day, and inverts every stated hour of every office in life. Among other circumstances, such as displacing the meals and times of bathing, he mentions, that, regularly about the third hour of the night, the neighbours of one, who indulges this false refinement, hear the noise of whips and lashes; and, upon enquiry, find that he is then taking an account of the conduct of his servants, and giving them due correction and discipline. This is not remarked as an instance of cruelty, but only of disorder, which even in actions the most usual and methodical, changes the fixed hours that an established custom had assigned for them.*

But our present business is only to consider the influence of slavery on the populousness of a state. It is pretended, that, in this particular, the ancient practice had infinitely the advantage, and was the chief cause of that extreme populousness, which is supposed in those times. At present, all masters discourage the marrying of their male servants, and admit not by any means the marriage of the female, who are then supposed altogether incapacitated for their service. But where the property of the servants is lodged in the master, their marriage forms his riches, and brings him a succession of slaves that supply the place of those whom age and infirmity have disabled. He encourages, therefore, their propagation as much as that of his cattle; rears the young with the same care; and educates them to some art or calling, which may render them more useful or valuable to him. The opulent are, by this policy, interested in the being at least, though not in the well-being of the poor; and enrich themselves, by encreasing the number and industry of those who are subjected to them. Each man, being a sovereign in his own family, has the same interest with regard to it, as the prince with regard to the state; and has not, like the prince, any opposite motives of ambition or vainglory, which may lead him to depopulate his little

---

* Epist. 122. The inhuman sports exhibited at Rome, may justly be considered too as an effect of the people's contempt for slaves, and was also a great cause of the general inhumanity of their princes and rulers. Who can read the accounts of the amphitheatrical entertainments without horror? Or who is surprized, that the emperors should treat that people in the same way the people treated their inferiors? One's humanity, on that occasion, is apt to renew the barbarous wish of Caligula, that the people had but one neck. A man could almost be pleased, by a single blow, to put an end to such a race of monsters. You may thank God, says the author above cited, (Epist. 7) addressing himself to the Roman people, that you have a master, (*viz.* the mild and merciful Nero) who is incapable of learning cruelty from your example. This was spoke in the beginning of his reign: But he fitted them very well afterwards; and no doubt was considerably improved by the sight of the barbarous objects, to which he had, from his infancy, been accustomed.

sovereignty. All of it is, at all times, under his eye; and he has leisure to inspect the most minute detail of the marriage and education of his subjects.*

Such are the consequences of domestic slavery, according to the first aspect and appearance of things: But if we enter more deeply into the subject, we shall perhaps find reason to retract our hasty determinations. The comparison is shocking between the management of human creatures and that of cattle; but being extremely just, when applied to the present subject, it may be proper to trace the consequences of it. At the capital, near all great cities, in all populous, rich, industrious provinces, few cattle are bred. Provisions, lodging, attendance, labour are there dear; and men find their account better in buying the cattle, after they come to a certain age, from the remoter and cheaper countries. These are consequently the only breeding countries for cattle; and by a parity of reason, for men too, when the latter are put on the same footing with the former. To rear a child in London, till he could be serviceable, would cost much dearer, than to buy one of the same age from Scotland or Ireland; where he had been bred in a cottage, covered with rags, and fed on oatmeal or potatoes. Those who had slaves, therefore, in all the richer and more populous countries, would discourage the pregnancy of the females, and either prevent or destroy the birth. The human species would perish in those places where it ought to encrease the fastest; and a perpetual recruit be wanted from the poorer and more desert provinces. Such a continued drain would tend mightily to depopulate the state, and render great cities ten times more destructive than with us; where every man is master of himself, and provides for his children from the powerful instinct of nature, not the calculations of sordid interest. If London, at present, without much encreasing, needs a yearly recruit from the country, of 5000 people, as is usually computed, what must it require, if the greater part of the tradesmen and common people were slaves, and were hindered from breeding by their avaricious masters?

All ancient authors tell us, that there was a perpetual flux of slaves to Italy from the remoter provinces, particularly Syria, Cilicia,

---

* We may here observe, that if domestic slavery really encreased populousness, it would be an exception to the general rule, that the happiness of any society and its populousness are necessary attendants. A master, from humour or interest, may make his slaves very unhappy, yet be careful, from interest, to increase their number. Their marriage is not a matter of choice with them, more than any other action of their life.

Cappadocia, and the Lesser Asia, Thrace, and Egypt: Yet the number of people did not encrease in Italy; and writers complain of the continual decay of industry and agriculture. Where then is that extreme fertility of the Roman slaves, which is commonly supposed? So far from multiplying, they could not, it seems, so much as keep up the stock, without immense recruits. And though great numbers were continually manumitted and converted into Roman citizens, the numbers even of these did not encrease, till the freedom of the city was communicated to foreign provinces.

FURTHER READING

Phillis Deane, *The First Industrial Revolution* (1965). Summarizes recent research into conditions of life in the Age of the Enlightenment and includes population growth.

D. V. Glass and D. E. C. Eversley, eds., *Population in History: Essays in Historical Demography* (1965). Immensely useful, with its numerous articles on facts and ideas about population in the eighteenth century.

Philip M. Hauser and Otis Dudley Duncan, eds., *The Study of Population: An Inventory and Appraisal* (1964 edn.). A collection of essays that includes treatment of the history of demography.

William Petersen, *Population* (1964 edn.). A clear textbook introducing the subject.

43 ❧ FERGUSON

An Essay on the History of Civil Society

[From Adam Ferguson, *An Essay on the History
of Civil Society* (Philadelphia, 1819), 1–21,
35–45, 324–37.]

*Though by no means averse to political theorizing, the philosophes
were deeply suspicious of theorizing on the basis of political myths.
(Rousseau was, in this, as in so much else, an exception). One such
myth, which engaged their sustained attention for decades, was the
social contract, according to which individuals, living free and
solitary lives in a state of nature, construct a social order by concluding a contract with one another. The philosophes knew that
this myth, which had risen to prominence late in the sixteenth and
dominated political theory in the seventeenth century, took many
forms and had many uses. It was one way of asserting the rights of
the individual against the collectivity; moreover, not all those
writers who postulated a social contract thought it an actual historical event, but treated it as an indispensable fiction.*

*While the political thinkers of the Enlightenment applauded the
libertarian sentiments that inspired most of the theorists of social
contract, they preferred to ground these sentiments in more reliable
soil. Once again, David Hume performed the role of a catalyst for
the philosophes. His late essay on the origins of government sums
up the debate; but Hume had taken the same view in the third
book of his* Treatise of Human Nature, *published as early as 1740.
In "Of the Origin of Government," Hume gave the speculative
question of political institutions a functionalist orientation:*

Man, born in a family, is compelled to maintain society, from necessity, from natural inclination, and from habit. The same creature, in his farther progress, is engaged to establish political society, in order to administer justice; without which there can be no peace among them, nor safety, nor mutual intercourse. We are, therefore, to look upon all the vast apparatus of our government, as having ultimately no other object or purpose but the distribution of justice, or, in other words, the support of the twelve judges. Kings and parliaments, fleets and armies, officers of the court and revenue, ambassadors, ministers, and privy-counsellors, are all subordinate in their end to this part of administration. Even the clergy, as their duty leads them to inculcate morality, may justly be thought, so far as regards this world, to have no other useful object of their institution.

All men are sensible of the necessity of justice to maintain peace and order; and all men are sensible of the necessity of peace and order for the maintenance of society. Yet, notwithstanding this strong and obvious necessity, such is the frailty or perverseness of our nature! it is impossible to keep men, faithfully and unerringly, in the paths of justice. Some extraordinary circumstances may happen, in which a man finds his interests to be more promoted by fraud or rapine, than hurt by the breach which his injustice makes in the social union. But much more frequently, he is seduced from his great and important, but distant interests, by the allurement of present, though often very frivolous temptations. This great weakness is incurable in human nature.

Men must, therefore, endeavour to palliate what they cannot cure. They must institute some persons, under the appellation of magistrates, whose peculiar office it is, to point out the decrees of equity, to punish transgressors, to correct fraud and violence, and to oblige men, however reluctant, to consult their own real and permanent interests. In a word, Obedience is a new duty which must be invented to support that of Justice; and the tyes of equity must be corroborated by those of allegiance.

But still, viewing matters in an abstract light, it may be thought, that nothing is gained by this alliance, and that the factitious duty of obedience, from its very nature, lays as feeble a hold of the human mind, as the primitive and natural duty of justice. Peculiar interests and present temptations may overcome the one as well as the other. They are equally exposed to the same inconvenience. And the man, who is inclined to be a bad neighbour, must be led by the same motives, well or ill understood, to be a bad citizen and subject. Not to mention, that the magistrate himself may often be negligent, or partial, or unjust in his administration.

Experience, however, proves, that there is a great difference between the cases. Order in society, we find, is much better maintained by means of government; and our duty to the magistrate is more strictly guarded by the principles of human nature, than our duty to our fellow-citizens. The love of dominion is so strong in the breast of man, that many, not only submit to, but court all the dangers, and fatigues, and cares of government; and men, once raised to that station, though often led astray by private passions, find, in ordinary cases, a visible interest in the impartial administration of justice. The persons, who first attain this distinction by the consent, tacit or express, of the people, must be endowed with superior personal qualities of valour, force, integrity, of prudence, which command respect and confidence: and after government is established, a regard to birth, rank, and station has a mighty influence over men, and enforces the decrees of the magistrate. The prince or leader exclaims against every disorder, which disturbs his society. He summons all his partizans and all men of probity to aid him in correcting and redressing it: and he is readily followed by all indifferent persons in the execution of his office. He soon acquires the power of rewarding these services; and in the progress of society, he establishes subordinate ministers and often a military force, who find an immediate and a visible interest, in supporting his authority. Habit soon consolidates what other principles of human nature had imperfectly founded; and men, once accustomed to obedience, never think of departing from that path, in which they and their ancestors have constantly trod, and to which they are confined by so many urgent and visible motives.

But though this progress of human affairs may appear certain and inevitable, and though the support which allegiance brings to justice, be founded on obvious principles of human nature, it cannot be expected that men should beforehand be able to discover them, or foresee their operation. Government commences more casually and more imperfectly. It is probable, that the first ascendant of one man over multitudes began during a state of war; where the superiority of courage and of genius discovers itself most visibly, where unanimity and concert are most requisite, and where the pernicious effects of disorder are most sensibly felt. The long continuance of that state, an incident common among savage tribes, enured the people to submission; and if the chieftain possessed as much equity as prudence and valour, he became, even during peace, the arbiter of all differences, and could gradually, by a mixture of force and consent, establish his authority. The benefit sensibly felt from his influence, made it be cherished by the people, at least by the peaceable and well disposed among them; and if his son enjoyed the same good qualities, government advanced the sooner to maturity and perfection; but was still in a feeble state, till the farther progress of improvement procured the magistrate a revenue, and enabled him to bestow rewards on the several instruments of his administration, and to inflict punishments on the refractory and disobedient. Before that period, each exertion of his influence must have been particular, and founded on the peculiar circumstances of the case. After it, submission was no longer a matter of choice in the bulk of the community, but was rigorously exacted by the authority of the supreme magistrate.

In all governments, there is a perpetual intestine struggle, open or secret, between Authority and Liberty; and neither of them can ever absolutely prevail in the contest. A great sacrifice of liberty must necessarily be made in every government; yet even the authority, which confines liberty, can never, and perhaps ought never, in any constitution, to become quite entire and uncontrollable. The sultan is master of the life and fortune of any individual; but will not be permitted to impose new taxes on his subjects: a French monarch can impose taxes at pleasure; but would find it dangerous to attempt the lives and fortunes of individuals. Religion also, in most countries, is commonly found to be a very intractable principle; and other principles or prejudices frequently resist all the authority of the civil magistrate; whose power, being founded on opinion, can never subvert other opinions, equally rooted with that of his title to dominion. The government, which, in common appellation, receives the appellation of free, is that which admits of a partition of power among several members, whose united authority is no less, or is commonly greater than that of any monarch; but who, in the usual course of administration, must act by general and equal laws, that are previously known to all the members and to all their subjects. In this sense, it must be owned, that liberty is the perfection of civil society; but still authority must be acknowledged essential to its very existence: and in those contests, which so often take place between the one and the other, the latter may, on that account, challenge the preference. Unless perhaps one may say (and it may be said with some reason) that a circumstance, which is essential to the existence of civil society, must always support itself, and needs be guarded with less jealousy, than one that contributes only to its perfection, which the indolence of men is so apt to neglect, or their ignorance to overlook.*

The thinker who dealt with social origins most systematically was the Scottish philosophe Adam Ferguson. Born in 1723, he came early under the influence of Montesquieu and, like all intelligent Scotsmen not devoutly religious, under the spell of Hume. It was David Hume who had insisted that societies are not the fruit of calculation, but of passion, habit and desperate need: "Reason, history, and experience show us, that all political societies have had an origin much less accurate and regular."† Overcoming his diffident conviction that Montesquieu had said everything worth saying, Ferguson tackled the question Hume had raised, and in 1767 published his greatest work, the Essay on the History of Civil Society. *Its main intention was to put the study of society on an empirical basis. Toward that end, Ferguson rejected all talk of a social contract, and refused to speculate beyond the available evidence. Human nature, the evidence shows, is inherently social.*

It is also inherently combative. Ferguson gives a cool, even approving, account of the role of conflict in human affairs; studies, and applauds, a certain measure of aggressiveness; and pursues social conflicts into that little-explored region, the division of labor, a subject that his friend Adam Smith was to pursue with far greater brilliance a few years later, in his Wealth of Nations.‡ *Hume did not wholly like Ferguson's book; perhaps it was too insistent in tone, too pedantic. Yet its importance for the sober study of society is great. While, by the time of his death in 1816, Ferguson's fame had been eclipsed by more elegant stylists, he deserves a prominent place in the history of the social sciences.*

* "Of the Origin of Government," in *The Philosophical Works of David Hume,* ed. T. H. Green and T. H. Grose, 4 vols. (1882), III, 113–17.
† "Of the Original Contract," *Philosophical Works,* III, 450.
‡ See below, page 571.

PART FIRST OF THE GENERAL CHARACTERISTICS OF HUMAN NATURE

SECTION I · OF THE QUESTION RELATING TO THE STATE OF NATURE

Natural productions are generally formed by degrees. Vegetables are raised from a tender shoot, and animals from an infant state. The latter, being active, extend together their operations and their powers, and have a progress in what they perform, as well as in the faculties they acquire. This progress in the case of man is continued to a greater extent than in that of any other animal. Not only the individual advances from infancy to manhood, but the species itself from rudeness to civilization. Hence the supposed departure of mankind from the state of their nature; hence our conjectures and different opinions of what man must have been in the first age of his being. The poet, the historian, and the moralist frequently allude to this ancient time; and under the emblems of gold, or of iron, represent a condition, and a manner of life, from which mankind have either degenerated, or on which they have greatly improved. On either supposition, the first state of our nature must have borne no resemblance to what men have exhibited in any subsequent period; historical monuments, even of the earliest date, are to be considered as novelties; and the most common establishments of human society are to be classed among the encroachments which fraud, oppression, or a busy invention, have made upon the reign of nature, by which the chief of our grievances or blessings were equally withheld.

Among the writers who have attempted to distinguish, in the human character, its original qualities, and to point out the limits between nature and art, some have represented mankind in their first condition, as possessed of mere animal sensibility, without any exercise of the faculties that render them superior to the brutes, without any political union, without any means of explaining their sentiments, and even without possessing any of the apprehensions and passions which the voice and the gesture are so well fitted to express. Others have made the state of nature to consist in perpetual wars kindled by competition for dominion and interest, where every individual had a separate quarrel with his kind, and where the presence of a fellow creature was the signal of battle.

The desire of laying the foundation of a favourite system, or a fond expectation, perhaps, that we may be able to penetrate the secrets of nature, to the very source of existence, have, on this subject, led to many fruitless inquiries, and given rise to many wild suppositions. Among the various qualities which mankind possess, we select one or a few particulars on which to establish a theory, and in framing our account of what man was in some imaginary state of nature, we overlook what he has always appeared within the reach of our own observation, and in the records of history.

In every other instance, however, the natural historian thinks himself obliged to collect facts, not to offer conjectures. When he treats of any particular species of animals, he supposes that their present dispositions and instincts are the same which they originally had, and that their present manner of life is a continuance of their first destination. He admits, that his knowledge of the material system of the world consists in a collection of facts, or at most, in general tenets derived from particular observations and experiments. It is only in what relates to himself, and in matters the most important and the most easily known, that he substitutes hypothesis instead of reality, and confounds the provinces of imagination and reason, of poetry and science.

But without entering any further on questions either in moral or physical subjects, relating to the manner or to the origin of our knowledge; without any disparagement to that subtilty which would analyze every sentiment, and trace every mode of being to its source; it may be safely affirmed, that the character of man, as he now exists, that the laws of his animal and intellectual system, on which his happiness now depends, deserve our principal study; and that general principles relating to this or any other subject, are useful only so far as they are founded on just observation, and lead to the knowledge of important consequences, or so far as they enable us to act with success when we would apply either the intellectual or the physical powers of nature, to the purposes of human life.

If both the earliest and the latest accounts collected from every quarter of the earth, represent mankind as assembled in troops and companies; and the individual always joined by affection to one party, while he is possibly opposed to another; employed in the exercise of recollection and foresight; inclined to communicate his own sentiments, and to be made acquainted with those of others; these facts must be admitted as the foundation of all our reasoning relative to man. His mixed disposition to friendship or enmity, his reason, his use of language and articulate sounds, like the shape and the erect position of his body, are to be considered as so many attributes of his nature: they are to be retained in his description, as the wing and the paw are in that of the eagle and the lion, and as different degress of fierceness, vigilance, timidity, or speed, have a place in the natural history of different animals.

If the question be put, What the mind of man could perform, when left to itself, and without the aid of any foreign direction? we are to look for our answer in the history of mankind. Particular experiments which have been found so useful in establishing the principles of other sciences, could probably, on this subject, teach us nothing important, or new: we are to take the history of every active being from his conduct in the situation to which he is formed, not from his appearance in any forced or uncommon condition; a wild man therefore, caught in the woods, where he had always lived apart from his species, is a singular instance, not a specimen of any general character. As the anatomy of an eye which had never received the impressions of light, or that of an ear which had never felt the impulse of sounds, would probably exhibit defects in the very structure of the organs themselves, arising from their not being applied to their proper functions; so any particular case of this sort would only show in what degree the powers of apprehension and sentiment could exist where they had not been employed, and what would be the defects and imbecilities of a heart in which the emotions that arise in society had never been felt.

Mankind are to be taken in groups, as they have always subsisted. The history of the individual is but a detail of the sentiments and the thoughts he has entertained in the view of his species: and every experiment relative to this subject should be made with entire societies, not with single men. We have every reason, however, to believe, that in the case of such an experiment made, we shall suppose, with a colony of children transplanted from the nursery, and left to form a society apart, untaught, and undisciplined, we should only have the same things repeated, which, in so many different parts of the earth, have been transacted already. The members of our little society would feed and sleep, would herd together and play, would have a language of their own, would quarrel and divide, would be to one another the most important objects of the scene, and, in the ardour of their friendships and competitions, would overlook their personal danger, and suspend the care of their self-preservation. Has not the human race been planted like the colony in question? Who has directed their course? whose instruction have they heard? or whose example have they followed?

Nature, therefore, we shall presume, having given to every animal its mode of existence, its dispositions and manner of life, has dealt equally with the human race; and the natural historian who would collect the properties of this species, may fill up every article now as well as he could have done in any former age. The attainments of the parent do not descend in the blood of his children, nor is the progress of man to be considered as a physical mutation of the species. The individual, in every age, has the same race to run from infancy to manhood, and every infant, or ignorant person, now, is a model of what man was in his original state. He enters on his career with advantages peculiar to his age; but his natural talent is probably the same. The use and application of this talent is changing, and men continue their works in progression through many ages together: they build on foundations laid by their ancestors; and in a succession of years, tend to a perfection in the application of their faculties, to which the aid of long experience is required, and to which many generations must have combined their endeavours. We observe the progress they have made; we distinctly enumerate many of its steps; we can trace them back to a distant antiquity, of which no record remains, nor any monument is preserved, to inform us what were the openings of this wonderful scene. The consequence is, that instead of attending to the character of our species, where the particulars are vouched by the surest authority, we endeavour to trace it through ages and scenes unknown; and, instead of supposing that the beginning of our story was nearly of a piece with the sequel, we think ourselves warranted to reject every circumstance of our present condition and frame, as adventitious, and foreign to our nature. The progress of mankind, from a supposed state of animal sensibility, to the attainment of reason, to the use of language, and to the habit of society, has been accordingly painted with a force of imagination, and its steps have been marked with a boldness of invention, that would tempt us to admit, among the materials of history, the suggestions of fancy, and to receive, perhaps, as the model of our nature in its original state, some of the animals whose shape has the greatest resemblance to ours.*

It would be ridiculous to affirm, as a discovery, that the species of the horse was probably never the same with that of the lion; yet, in opposition to what has dropped from the pens of eminent writers, we are obliged to observe, that men have always appeared among animals a distinct and a superior race; that neither the possession of similar organs, nor the approximation of shape, nor the use of the hand,† nor the continued intercourse with this sovereign artist, has enabled any other species to blend their nature or their inventions with his; that, in his rudest state, he is found to be above them; and in his greatest degeneracy, never descends to their level. He is, in short, a man in every condition; and we can learn nothing of his nature from the analogy of other animals. If we would know him, we must attend to himself, to the course of his life, and the tenor of his conduct. With him the society appears to be as old as the individual, and the use of the tongue as universal as that of the hand or the foot. If there was a time in which he had his acquaintance with his own species to make, and his faculties to acquire, it is a time of which we have no record, and in relation to which our opinions can serve no purpose, and are supported by no evidence.

We are often tempted into these boundless regions of ignorance or conjecture, by a fancy which delights in creating rather than in merely retaining the forms which are presented before it: we are the dupes of a subtilty, which promises to supply every defect of our knowledge, and, by filling up a few blanks in the story of nature, pretends to conduct our apprehension nearer to the source of existence. On the credit of a few observations, we are apt to presume, that the secret may soon be laid open, and that what is termed *wisdom* in nature, may be referred to the operation of physical powers. We forget that physical powers employed in succession or together, and combined to a salutary purpose, constitute those very proofs of design from which we infer the existence of God; and that this truth being once admitted, we are no longer to search for the source of existence; we can only collect the laws which the Author of nature has established; and in our latest as well as our earliest discoveries, only perceive a mode of creation or providence before unknown.

We speak of art as distinguished from nature; but art itself is natural to man. He is in some measure the artificer of his own

* Rousseau, *Sur l'origine de l'inégalité parmi les hommes.*
† [Helvétius], *Traité de l'esprit.*

frame, as well as of his fortune, and is destined, from the first age of his being, to invent and contrive. He applies the same talents to a variety of purposes, and acts nearly the same part in very different scenes. He would be always improving on his subject, and he carries this intention wherever he moves, through the streets of the populous city, or the wilds of the forest. While he appears equally fitted to every condition, he is upon this account unable to settle in any. At once obstinate and fickle, he complains of innovations, and is never sated with novelty. He is perpetually busied in reformations, and is continually wedded to his errors. If he dwells in a cave, he would improve it into a cottage; if he has already built, he would still build to a greater extent. But he does not propose to make rapid and hasty transitions; his steps are progressive and slow; and his force, like the power of a spring, silently presses on every resistance; an effect is sometimes produced before the cause is perceived; and with all his talent for projects, his work is often accomplished before the plan is devised. It appears, perhaps, equally difficult to retard or to quicken his pace; if the projector complain he is tardy, the moralist thinks him unstable; and whether his motions be rapid or slow, the scenes of human affairs perpetually change in his management: his emblem is a passing stream, not a stagnating pool. We may desire to direct his love of improvement to its proper object, we may wish for stability of conduct; but we mistake human nature, if we wish for a termination of labour, or a scene of repose.

The occupations of men, in every condition, bespeak their freedom of choice, their various opinions, and the multiplicity of wants by which they are urged: but they enjoy, or endure, with a sensibility, or a phlegm, which are nearly the same in every situation. They possess the shores of the Caspian, or the Atlantic, by a different tenure, but with equal ease. On the one they are fixed to the soil, and seem to be formed for settlement, and the accommodation of cities: the names they bestow on a nation, and on its territory, are the same. On the other they are mere animals of passage, prepared to roam on the face of the earth, and with their herds, in search of new pasture and favourable seasons, to follow the sun in his annual course.

Man finds his lodgment alike in the cave, the cottage, and the palace; and his subsistence equally in the woods, in the dairy, or the farm. He assumes the distinction of titles, equipage, and dress; he devises regular systems of government, and a complicated body of laws; or naked in the woods has no badge of superiority but the strength of his limbs and the sagacity of his mind; no rule of conduct but choice; no tie with his fellow creatures but affection, the love of company, and the desire of safety. Capable of a great variety of arts, yet dependent on none in particular for the preservation of his being; to whatever length he has carried his artifice, there he seems to enjoy the conveniences that suit his nature, and to have found the condition to which he is destined. The tree which an American on the banks of the Oroonoko,* has chosen to climb for the retreat, and the lodgment of his family, is to him a convenient dwelling. The sopha, the vaulted dome, and the colonade, do not more effectually content their native inhabitant.

If we are asked therefore, where the state of nature is to be found? we may answer, it is here; and it matters not whether we are understood to speak in the island of Great Britain, at the Cape of Good Hope, or the Straits of Magellan. While this active being is in the train of employing his talents, and of operating on the subjects around him, all situations are equally natural. If we are told, that vice, at least, is contrary to nature; we may answer, it is worse; it is folly and wretchedness. But if nature is only opposed to art, in what situation of the human race are the footsteps of art unknown? In the condition of the savage, as well as in that of the citizen, are many proofs of human invention; and in either is not any permanent station, but a mere stage through which this travelling being is destined to pass. If the palace be unnatural, the cottage is so no less; and the highest refinements of political and moral apprehension, are not more artificial in their kind, than the first operations of sentiment and reason.

If we admit that man is susceptible of improvement, and has in himself a principle of progression, and a desire of perfection, it appears improper to say, that he has quitted the state of his nature, when he has begun to proceed; or that he finds a station for which he was not intended, while, like other animals, he only follows the disposition, and employs the powers that nature has given.

The latest efforts of human invention are but a continuation of certain devices which were practised in the earliest ages of the world, and in the rudest state of mankind. What the savage projects, or observes, in the forest, are the steps which led nations, more advanced, from the architecture of the cottage to that of the palace, and conducted the human mind from the perceptions of sense, to the general conclusions of science.

Acknowledged defects are to man in every condition matter of dislike. Ignorance and imbecility are objects of contempt: penetra-

---

* Lafitau, *Mœurs des sauvages.*

tion and conduct give eminence and procure esteem. Whither should his feelings and apprehensions on these subjects lead him? To a progress, no doubt, in which the savage, as well as the philosopher, is engaged; in which they have made different advances, but in which their ends are the same. The admiration which Cicero entertained for literature, eloquence, and civil accomplishments, was not more real than that of a Scythian for such a measure of similar endowments as his own apprehension could reach. "Were I to boast," says a Tartar prince,* "it would be of that wisdom I have received from God. For as, on the one hand, I yield to none in the conduct of war, in the disposition of armies, whether of horse or of foot, and in directing the movements of great or small bodies; so, on the other, I have my talent in writing, inferior perhaps only to those who inhabit the great cities of Persia or India. Of other nations, unknown to me, I do not speak."

Man may mistake the objects of his pursuit; he may misapply his industry, and misplace his improvements. If, under a sense of such possible errors, he would find a standard by which to judge of his own proceedings, and arrive at the best state of his nature, he cannot find it perhaps in the practice of any individual, or of any nation whatever; not even in the sense of the majority, or the prevailing opinion of his kind. He must look for it in the best conceptions of his understanding, in the best movements of his heart; he must thence discover what is the perfection and the happiness of which he is capable. He will find, on the scrutiny, that the proper state of his nature, taken in this sense, is not a condition from which mankind are for ever removed, but one to which they may now attain; not prior to the exercise of their faculties, but procured by their just application.

Of all the terms that we employ in treating of human affairs, those of *natural* and *unnatural* are the least determinate in their meaning. Opposed to affectation, frowardness, or any other defect of the temper or character, the natural is an epithet of praise; but employed to specify a conduct which proceeds from the nature of man, can serve to distinguish nothing; for all the actions of men are equally the result of their nature. At most, this language can only refer to the general and prevailing sense or practice of mankind; and the purpose of every important enquiry on this subject may be served by the use of a language equally familiar and more precise.

---

* Abulgaze Bahadur Chan, *History of the Tartars.*

What is just, or unjust? What is happy or wretched, in the manners of men? What, in their various situations, is favourable or adverse to their amiable qualities? are questions to which we may expect a satisfactory answer; and whatever may have been the original state of our species, it is of more importance to know the condition to which we ourselves should aspire, than that which our ancestors may be supposed to have left.

SECTION II · OF THE PRINCIPLES OF SELF PRESERVATION

If in human nature there are qualities by which it is distinguished from every other part of the animal creation, this nature itself is in different climates and in different ages greatly diversified. The varieties merit our attention, and the course of every stream into which this mighty current divides, deserves to be followed to its source. It appears necessary, however, that we attend to the universal qualities of our nature, before we regard its varieties, or attempt to explain differences consisting in the unequal possession or application of dispositions and powers that are in some measure common to all mankind.

Man, like the other animals, has certain instinctive propensities, which, prior to the perception of pleasure or pain, and prior to the experience of what is pernicious or useful, lead him to perform many functions which terminate in himself, or have a relation to his fellow creatures. He has one set of dispositions which tend to his animal preservation, and to the continuance of his race; another which lead to society, and by inlisting him on the side of one tribe or community, frequently engage him in war and contention with the rest of mankind. His powers of discernment, or his intellectual faculties, which, under the appellation of *reason,* are distinguished from the analogous endowments of other animals, refer to the objects around him, either as they are subjects of mere knowledge, or as they are subjects of approbation or censure. He is formed not only to know, but likewise to admire and to contemn; and these proceedings of his mind have a principal reference to his own character, and to that of his fellow creatures, as being the subjects on which he is chiefly concerned to distinguish what is right from what is wrong. He enjoys his felicity likewise on certain fixed and determinate conditions; and either as an individual apart, or as a member of civil society, must take a particular course, in order to reap the advantages of his nature. He is, withal, in a very high degree susceptible of habits; and can, by forbearance or exercise, so far weaken, confirm, or even diversify his talents, and his dispositions, as to appear, in a great measure, the arbiter of his own rank in nature, and the author of all the varieties which are exhibited in the actual history of his species. The universal characteristics, in the mean time, to which we have now referred, must, when we would treat of any part of this history, constitute the first subject of our attention; and they require not only to be enumerated, but to be distinctly considered.

The dispositions which tend to the preservation of the individual, while they continue to operate in the manner of instinctive desires, are nearly the same in man that they are in the other animals; but in him they are sooner or later combined with reflection and foresight; they give rise to his apprehensions on the subject of property, and make him acquainted with that object of care which he calls his interest. Without the instincts which teach the beaver and the squirrel, the ant and the bee, to make up their little hoards for winter, at first improvident, and where no immediate object of passion is near, addicted to sloth, he becomes, in process of time, the great storemaster among animals. He finds in a provision of wealth, which he is probably never to employ, an object of his greatest solicitude, and the principal idol of his mind. He apprehends a relation between his person and his property, which renders what he calls his own in a manner a part of himself, a constituent of his rank, his condition, and his character, in which, independent of any real enjoyment, he may be fortunate or unhappy; and, independent of any personal merit, he may be an object of consideration or neglect; and in which he may be wounded and injured, while his person is safe, and every want of his nature is completely supplied.

In these apprehensions, while other passions only operate occasionally, the interested find the object of their ordinary cares; their motive to the practice of mechanic and commercial arts; their temptation to trespass on the laws of justice; and, when extremely corrupted, the price of their prostitutions, and the standard of their opinions on the subject of good and of evil. Under this influence, they would enter, if not restrained by the laws of civil society, on a scene of violence or meanness, which would exhibit our species, by turns, under an aspect more terrible and odious, or more vile and contemptible, than that of any animal which inherits the earth.
. . .

SECTION IV · OF THE PRINCIPLES OF WAR AND DISSENTION

"There are some circumstances in the lot of mankind," says Socrates, "that show them to be destined to friendship and amity: Those are, their mutual need of each other; their mutual compassion; their sense of mutual benefit; and the pleasures arising in company. There are other circumstances which prompt them to war and dissention; the admiration and the desire which they entertain for the same subjects; their opposite pretensions; and the provocations which they mutually offer in the course of their competitions."

When we endeavour to apply the maxims of natural justice to the solution of difficult questions, we find that some cases may be supposed, and actually happen, where oppositions take place, and are lawful, prior to any provocation, or act of injustice; that where the safety and preservation of numbers are mutually inconsistent, one party may employ his right of defence, before the other has begun an attack. And when we join with such examples, the instances of mistake, and misunderstanding, to which mankind are exposed, we may be satisfied that war does not always proceed from an intention to injure; and that even the best qualities of men, their candour, as well as their resolution, may operate in the midst of their quarrels.

There is still more to be observed on this subject. Mankind not only find in their condition the sources of variance and dissention; they appear to have in their minds the seeds of animosity, and to embrace the occasions of mutual opposition, with alacrity and pleasure. In the most pacific situation, there are few who have not their enemies, as well as their friends; and who are not pleased with opposing the proceedings of one, as much as with favouring the designs of another. Small and simple tribes, who in their domestic society have the firmest union, are in their state of opposition as separate nations, frequently animated with the most implacable hatred. Among the citizens of Rome, in the early ages of that republic, the name of a foreigner, and that of an enemy, were the same. Among the Greeks, the name of Barbarian, under which that people comprehended every nation that was of a race, and spoke a language, different from their own, became a term of indiscriminate contempt and aversion. Even where no particular claim to superiority is formed, the repugnance to union, the frequent wars, or rather the perpetual hostilities which take place among rude nations and separate clans, discover how much our species is disposed to opposition, as well as to concert.

Late discoveries have brought to our knowledge almost every situation in which mankind are placed. We have found them spread over large and extensive continents, where communications are open, and where national confederacy might be easily formed. We have found them in narrower districts, circumscribed by mountains, great rivers, and arms of the sea. They have been found in small islands, where the inhabitants might be easily assembled, and derive an advantage from their union. But in all those situations, alike, they were broke into cantons, and affected a distinction of name and community. The titles of *fellow citizen* and *countryman,* unopposed to those of *alien* and *foreigner,* to which they refer, would fall into disuse, and lose their meaning. We love individuals on account of personal qualities; but we love our country, as it is a party in the divisions of mankind; and our zeal for its interest, is a predilection in behalf of the side we maintain.

In the promiscuous concourse of men, it is sufficient that we have an opportunity of selecting our company. We turn away from those who do not engage us, and we fix our resort where the society is more to our mind. We are fond of distinctions; we place ourselves in opposition, and quarrel under the denominations of faction and party, without any material subject of controversy. Aversion, like affection, is fostered by a continued direction to its particular object. Separation and estrangement, as well as opposition, widen a breach which did not owe its beginnings to any offence. And it would seem, that till we have reduced mankind to the state of a family, or found some external consideration to maintain their connection in greater numbers, they will be for ever separated into bands, and form a plurality of nations.

The sense of a common danger, and the assaults of an enemy, have been frequently useful to nations, by uniting their members more firmly together, and by preventing the secessions and actual separations in which their civil discord might otherwise terminate. And this motive to union which is offered from abroad, may be necessary, not only in the case of large and extensive nations, where coalitions are weakened by distance, and the distinction of provincial names; but even in the narrow society of the smallest states. Rome itself was founded by a small party which took its flight from Alba; her citizens were often in danger of separating; and if the villages and cantons of the Volsci had been further removed from the scene of their dissentions, the Mons Sacer might have received a new colony before the mother country was ripe for such a discharge. She continued long to feel the quarrels of her nobles and her people; and kept open the gates of Janus, to remind those parties of the duties they owed to their country.

Societies, as well as individuals, being charged with the care of their own preservation, and having separate interests, which give rise to jealousies and competitions, we cannot be surprised to find hostilities arise from this source. But were there no angry passions of a different sort, the animosities which attend an opposition of interest, should bear a proportion to the supposed value of the subject. "The Hottentot nations," says Kolben, "trespass on each other by thefts of cattle and of women; but such injuries are seldom committed, except with a view to exasperate their neighbours, and bring them to a war." Such depredations then, are not the foundation of a war, but the effects of a hostile intention already conceived. The nations of North America, who have no herds to preserve, nor settlements to defend, are yet engaged in almost perpetual wars, for which they can assign no reason, but the point of honour, and a desire to continue the struggle their fathers maintained. They do not regard the spoils of an enemy; and the warrior who has seized any booty, easily parts with it to the first person who comes in his way.*

But we need not cross the Atlantic to find proofs of animosity, and to observe, in the collision of separate societies, the influence of angry passions, that do not arise from an opposition of interest. Human nature has no part of its character of which more flagrant examples are given on this side of the globe. What is it that stirs in the breasts of ordinary men when the enemies of their country are named? Whence are the prejudices that subsist between different provinces, cantons, and villages, of the same empire and territory? What is it that excites one half of the nations of Europe against the other? The statesman may explain his conduct on motives of national jealousy and caution, but the people have dislikes and antipathies, for which they cannot account. Their mutual reproaches of perfidy and injustice, like the Hottentot depredations, are but symptoms of an animosity, and the language of a hostile disposition, already conceived. The charge of cowardice and pusillanimity, qualities which the interested and cautious enemy should, of all others, like best to find in his rival, is urged with aversion, and made the ground of dislike. Hear the peasants on different sides of the Alps, and the Pyrenees, the Rhine, or the British channel,

* See Charlevoix's *History of Canada.*

give vent to their prejudices and national passions; it is among them that we find the materials of war and dissention laid without the direction of government, and sparks ready to kindle into a flame, which the statesman is frequently disposed to extinguish. The fire will not always catch where his reasons of state would direct, nor stop where the concurrence of interest has produced an alliance. "My father," said a Spanish peasant, "would rise from his grave, if he could foresee a war with France." What interest had he, or the bones of his father, in the quarrels of princes?

These observations seem to arraign our species, and to give an unfavourable picture of mankind; and yet the particulars we have mentioned are consistent with the most amiable qualities of our nature, and often furnish a scene for the exercise of our greatest abilities. They are sentiments of generosity and self denial that animate the warrior in defence of his country; and they are dispositions most favourable to mankind, that become the principles of apparent hostility to men. Every animal is made to delight in the exercise of his natural talents and forces. The lion and the tyger sport with the paw; the horse delights to commit his mane to the wind, and forgets his pasture to try his speed in the field; the bull even before his brow is armed, and the lamb while yet an emblem of innocence, have a disposition to strike with the forehead, and anticipate, in play, the conflicts they are doomed to sustain. Man too is disposed to opposition, and to employ the forces of his nature against an equal antagonist; he loves to bring his reason, his eloquence, his courage, even his bodily strength to the proof. His sports are frequently an image of war; sweat and blood are freely expended in play; and fractures or death are often made to terminate the pastime of idleness and festivity. He was not made to live for ever, and even his love of amusement has opened a way to the grave.

Without the rivalship of nations, and the practice of war, civil society itself could scarcely have found an object, or a form. Mankind might have traded without any formal convention, but they cannot be safe without a national concert. The necessity of a public defence, has given rise to many departments of state, and the intellectual talents of men have found their busiest scene in wielding their national forces. To overawe, or intimidate, or, when we cannot persuade with reason, to resist with fortitude, are the occupations which give its most animating exercise, and its greatest triumphs, to a vigorous mind; and he who has never struggled with his fellow creatures, is a stranger to half the sentiments of mankind.

The quarrels of individuals, indeed, are frequently the operations of unhappy and detestable passions, malice, hatred, and rage. If such passions alone possess the breast, the scene of dissention becomes an object of horror; but a common opposition maintained by numbers, is always allayed by passions of another sort. Sentiments of affection and friendship mix with animosity; the active and strenuous become the guardians of their society; and violence itself is, in their case, an exertion of generosity, as well as of courage. We applaud, as proceeding from a national or party spirit, what we could not endure as the effect of a private dislike; and, amidst the competitions of rival states, think we have found, for the patriot and the warrior, in the practice of violence and stratagem, the most illustrious career of human virtue. Even personal opposition here does not divide our judgment on the merits of men. The rival names of Agesilaus and Epaminondas, of Scipio and Hannibal, are repeated with equal praise; and war itself, which in one view appears so fatal, in another is the exercise of a liberal spirit; and in the very effects which we regret, is but one distemper more, by which the Author of nature has appointed our exit from human life.

These reflections may open our view into the state of mankind; but they tend to reconcile us to the conduct of Providence, rather than to make us change our own; where, from a regard to the welfare of our fellow creatures, we endeavour to pacify their animosities, and unite them by the ties of affection. In the pursuit of this amiable intention, we may hope, in some instances, to disarm the angry passions of jealousy and envy; we may hope to instil into the breasts of private men sentiments of candour towards their fellow creatures, and a disposition to humanity and justice. But it is vain to expect that we can give to the multitude of a people a sense of union among themselves, without admitting hostility to those who oppose them. Could we at once, in the case of any nation, extinguish the emulation which is excited from abroad, we should probably break or weaken the bands of society at home, and close the busiest scenes of national occupations and virtues.

PART FOURTH
OF CONSEQUENCES THAT RESULT FROM THE ADVANCEMENT OF CIVIL AND COMMERCIAL ARTS

SECTION I · OF THE SEPARATION OF ARTS AND PROFESSIONS

It is evident, that, however urged by a sense of necessity, and a desire of convenience, or favoured by any advantages of situation and policy, a people can make no great progress in cultivating the arts of life, until they have separated, and committed to different persons, the several tasks which require a peculiar skill and attention. The savage, or the barbarian, who must build and plant, and fabricate for himself, prefers, in the interval of great alarms and fatigues, the enjoyments of sloth to the improvement of his fortune: he is, perhaps, by the diversity of his wants, discouraged from industry; or, by his divided attention, prevented from acquiring skill in the management of any particular subject.

The enjoyment of peace, however, and the prospect of being able to exchange one commodity for another, turns, by degrees, the hunter and the warrior into a tradesman and a merchant. The accidents which distribute the means of subsistence unequally, inclination, and favourable opportunities, assign the different occupations of men; and a sense of utility leads them, without end, to subdivide their professions.

The artist finds, that the more he can confine his attention to a particular part of any work, his productions are the more perfect, and grow under his hands in the greater quantities. Every undertaker in manufacture finds, that the more he can subdivide the tasks of his workmen, and the more hands he can employ on separate articles, the more are his expenses diminished, and his profits increased. The consumer too requires, in every kind of commodity, a workmanship more perfect than hands employed on a variety of subjects can produce; and the progress of commerce is but a continued subdivision of the mechanical arts.

Every craft may engross the whole of a man's attention, and has a mystery which must be studied or learned by a regular apprenticeship. Nations of tradesmen come to consist of members, who, beyond their own particular trade, are ignorant of all human affairs, and who may contribute to the preservation and enlargement of their commonwealth, without making its interest an object of their regard or attention. Every individual is distinguished by his calling, and has a place to which he is fitted. The savage, who knows no distinction but that of his merit, of his sex, or of his species, and to whom his community is the sovereign object of affection, is astonished to find, that in a scene of this nature, his being a man does not qualify him for any station whatever: he flies to the woods with amazement, distaste, and aversion.

By the separation of arts and professions, the sources of wealth are laid open; every species of material is wrought up to the greatest perfection, and every commodity is produced in the greatest abundance. The state may estimate its profits and its revenues by the number of its people. It may procure, by its treasure, that national consideration and power, which the savage maintains at the expense of his blood.

The advantage gained in the inferior branches of manufacture by the separation of their parts, seem to be equalled by those which arise from a similar device in the higher departments of policy and war. The soldier is relieved from every care but that of his service; statesmen divide the business of civil government into shares; and the servants of the public, in every office, without being skilful in the affairs of state, may succeed, by observing forms which are already established on the experience of others. They are made, like the parts of an engine, to concur to a purpose, without any concert of their own: and equally blind with the trader to any general combination, they unite with him, in furnishing to the state its resources, its conduct, and its force.

The artifices of the beaver, the ant, and the bee, are ascribed to the wisdom of nature. Those of polished nations are ascribed to themselves, and are supposed to indicate a capacity superior to that of rude minds. But the establishments of men, like those of every animal, are suggested by nature, and are the result of instinct, directed by the variety of situations in which mankind are placed. Those establishments arose from successive improvements that were made, without any sense of their general effect; and they bring human affairs to a state of complication, which the greatest reach of capacity with which human nature was ever adorned, could not have projected; nor even when the whole is carried into execution, can it be comprehended in its full extent.

Who could anticipate, or even enumerate, the separate occupations and professions by which the members of any commercial state are distinguished; the variety of devices which are practised in separate cells, and which the artist, attentive to his own affair, has invented, to abridge or to facilitate his separate task? In coming to this mighty end, every generation, compared to its predecessors, may have appeared to be ingenious; compared to its followers, may have appeared to be dull: and human ingenuity, whatever heights it may have gained in a succession of ages, continues to move with an equal pace, and to creep in making the last, as well as the first, step of commercial or civil improvement.

It may even be doubted, whether the measure of national capacity increases with the advancement of arts. Many mechanical arts, indeed, require no capacity; they succeed best under a total suppression of sentiment and reason; and ignorance is the mother of industry as well as of superstition. Reflection and fancy are subject to err; but a habit of moving the hand, or the foot, is independent of either. Manufactures, accordingly, prosper most where the mind is least consulted, and where the workshop may, without any great effort of imagination, be considered as an engine, the parts of which are men.

The forest has been felled by the savage without the use of the axe, and weights have been raised without the aid of the mechanical powers. The merit of the inventor, in every branch, probably deserves a preference to that of the performer; and he who invented a tool, or could work without its assistance, deserved the praise of ingenuity in a much higher degree than the mere artist, who, by its assistance, produces a superior work.

But if many parts in the practice of every art, and in the detail of every department, require no abilities, or actually tend to contract and to limit the views of the mind, there are others which lead to general reflections, and to enlargement of thought. Even in manufacture, the genius of the master, perhaps, is cultivated, while that of the inferior workman lies waste. The statesman may have a wide comprehension of human affairs, while the tools he employs are ignorant of the system in which they are themselves combined. The general officer may be a great proficient in the knowledge of war, while the skill of the soldier is confined to a few motions of the hand and the foot. The former may have gained what the latter has lost; and being occupied in the conduct of disciplined armies, may practise on a larger scale all the arts of preservation, of deception, and of stratagem, which the savage exerts in leading a small party, or merely in defending himself.

The practitioner of every art and profession may afford matter of general speculation to the man of science; and thinking itself, in this age of separations, may become a peculiar craft. In the bustle of civil pursuits and occupations, men appear in a variety of lights, and suggest matter of inquiry and fancy, by which conversation is enlivened, and greatly enlarged. The productions of ingenuity are brought to the market; and men are willing to pay for whatever has a tendency to inform or amuse. By this means the idle, as well as the busy, contribute to forward the progress of arts, and bestow on polished nations that air of superior ingenuity, under which they appear to have gained the ends that were pursued by the savage in his forest, knowledge, order, and wealth.

SECTION II · OF THE SUBORDINATION CONSEQUENT TO THE SEPARATION OF ARTS AND PROFESSIONS

There is one ground of subordination in the difference of natural talents and dispositions; a second in the unequal division of property; and a third, not less sensible, in the habits which are acquired by the practice of different arts.

Some employments are liberal, others mechanic. They require different talents, and inspire different sentiments; and whether or not this be the cause of the preference we actually give, it is certainly reasonable to form our opinion of the rank that is due to men of certain professions and stations, from the influence of their manner of life in cultivating the powers of the mind, or in preserving the sentiments of the heart.

There is an elevation natural to man, by which he would be thought, in his rudest state, however urged by necessity, to rise above the consideration of mere subsistence, and the regards of interest: he would appear to act only from the heart, in its engagements of friendship or opposition; he would shew himself only upon occasions of danger or difficulty, and leave ordinary cares to the weak or the servile.

The same apprehensions, in every situation, regulate his notions of meanness or of dignity. In that of polished society, his desire to avoid the character of sordid, makes him conceal his regard for what relates merely to his preservation or his livelihood. In his estimation, the beggar, who depends upon charity; the labourer, who toils that he may eat; the mechanic, whose art requires no exertion of genius, are degraded by the object they pursue, and by the means they employ to attain it. Professions requiring more knowledge and study; proceeding on the exercise of fancy, and the love of perfection; leading to applause as well as to profit, place the artist in a superior class, and bring him nearer to that station in which men are supposed to be highest; because in it they are bound to no task, because they are left to follow the disposition of the mind, and to take that part in society to which they are led by the sentiments of the heart, or by the calls of the public.

This last was the station, which, in the distinction betwixt freemen and slaves, the citizens of every ancient republic strove to gain, and to maintain for themselves. Women, or slaves, in the earliest ages, had been set apart for the purposes of domestic care, or bodily labour; and in the progress of lucrative arts, the latter were bred to mechanical professions, and were even intrusted with merchandise for the benefit of their masters. Freemen would be understood to have no object beside those of politics and war. In this manner, the honours of one half of the species were sacrificed to those of the other; as stones from the same quarry are buried in the foundation, to sustain the blocks which happen to be hewn for the superior parts of the pile. In the midst of our encomiums bestowed on the Greeks and the Romans, we are, by this circumstance, made to remember, that no human institution is perfect.

In many of the Grecian states, the benefits arising to the free from this cruel distinction, were not conferred equally on all the citizens. Wealth being unequally divided, the rich alone were exempted from labour; the poor were reduced to work for their own subsistence: interest was a reigning passion in both, and the possession of slaves, like that of any other lucrative property, became an object of avarice, not an exemption from sordid attentions. The entire effects of the institution were obtained, or continued to be enjoyed for any considerable time, at Sparta alone. We feel its injustice; we suffer for the helot, under the severities and unequal treatment to which he was exposed: but when we think only of the superior order of men in this state; when we attend to that elevation and magnanimity of spirit, for which danger had no terror, interest no means to corrupt; when we consider them as friends, or as citizens, we are apt to forget, like themselves, that slaves have a title to be treated like men.

We look for elevation of sentiment, and liberality of mind, among those orders of citizens, who, by their condition, and their fortunes, are relieved from sordid cares and attentions. This was the description of a free man at Sparta; and if the lot of a slave among the ancients was really more wretched than that of the indigent labourer and the mechanic among the moderns, it may be doubted whether the superior orders, who are in possession of consideration and honours, do not proportionally fail in the dignity which befits their condition. If the pretension to equal justice and freedom should terminate in rendering every class equally servile and mercenary, we make a nation of helots, and have no free citizens.

In every commercial state, notwithstanding any pretension to equal rights, the exaltation of a few must depress the many. In this arrangement, we think that the extreme meanness of some classes must arise chiefly from the defect of knowledge, and of liberal education; and we refer to such classes, as to an image of what our species must have been in its rude and uncultivated state. But we forget how many circumstances, especially in populous cities, tend to corrupt the lowest orders of men. Ignorance is the least of their failings. An admiration of wealth unpossessed, becoming a principle of envy, or of servility; a habit of acting perpetually with a view to profit, and under a sense of subjection; the crimes to which they are allured, in order to feed their debauch, or to gratify their avarice, are examples, not of ignorance, but of corruption and baseness. If the savage has not received our instructions, he is likewise unacquainted with our vices. He knows no superior, and cannot be servile; he knows no distinctions of fortune, and cannot be envious; he acts from his talents in the highest station which human society can offer, that of the counsellor, and the soldier of his country. Towards forming his sentiments, he knows all that the heart requires to be known; he can distinguish the friend whom he loves, and the public interest which awakens his zeal.

The principal objections to democratical or popular government, are taken from the inequalities which arise among men in the result of commercial arts. And it must be confessed, that popular assemblies, when composed of men whose dispositions are sordid, and whose ordinary applications are illiberal, however they may be intrusted with the choice of their masters and leaders, are certainly, in their own persons, unfit to command. How can he who has confined his views to his own subsistence or preservation, be intrusted with the conduct of nations? Such men, when admitted to deliberate on matters of state, bring to its councils confusion and tumult, or servility and corruption; and seldom suffer it to repose from ruinous factions, or the effect of resolutions ill formed or ill conducted.

The Athenians retained their popular government under all

these defects. The mechanic was obliged, under a penalty, to appear in the public market-place, and to hear debates on the subjects of war and of peace. He was tempted by pecuniary rewards, to attend on the trial of civil and criminal causes. But, notwithstanding an exercise tending so much to cultivate their talents, the indigent came always with minds intent upon profit, or with the habits of an illiberal calling. Sunk under the sense of their personal disparity and weakness, they were ready to resign themselves entirely to the influence of some popular leader, who flattered their passions, and wrought on their fears; or, actuated by envy, they were ready to banish from the state whomsoever was respectable and eminent in the superior order of citizens; and whether from their neglect of the public at one time, or their mal-administration at another, the sovereignty was every moment ready to drop from their hands.

The people, in this case, are, in fact, frequently governed by one, or a few, who know how to conduct them. Pericles possessed a species of princely authority at Athens; Crassus, Pompey, and Caesar, either jointly or successively, possessed for a considerable period the sovereign direction at Rome.

Whether in great or in small states, democracy is preserved with difficulty, under the disparities of condition, and the unequal cultivation of the mind, which attend the variety of pursuits, and applications, that separate mankind in the advanced state of commercial arts. In this, however, we do but plead against the form of democracy, after the principle is removed; and see the absurdity of pretensions to equal influence and consideration, after the characters of men have ceased to be similar.

FURTHER READING

Duncan Forbes, ed., Adam Ferguson, *An Essay on the History of Civil Society* (1966). A fine critical edition with a fine introductory essay.

David Kettler, *The Social and Political Thought of Adam Ferguson* (1965). Fair-minded and informative.

William C. Lehmann, *Adam Ferguson and the Beginnings of Modern Sociology* 1930). Pioneering introduction to Ferguson's thought, written at a time when he was rather neglected; somewhat superseded by the later titles cited above.

44 ❃ ADAM SMITH

The Wealth of Nations

[From Adam Smith, *An Inquiry into the Nature
and Causes of the Wealth of Nations*, 2 vols.
(1904), I, 5–15, 66–84, 395, 418–22, 456–62; II,
207, 266–68.]

*In the nineteenth century, the social science of economics became
known, in Thomas Carlyle's words, as the "Dismal Science." It was
dismal because it seemed to preach the futility of reform; if the rich
were rich and the poor were poor, and if workers existed to be
exploited by their employers, this state of affairs was natural and
permanent. This jaundiced view of economics, pushed forward by
Marxist critics of capitalism and its defenders, is somewhat too
unrelieved. But there was something in it; the classical economists
of the early nineteenth century did preach a kind of comfortable
fatalism—comfortable, that is, for the beneficiaries of the system.*
*Adam Smith is often treated as the father of classical economics,
but if he was indeed its father, his children did not grow to be like
him. In his hands, political economy was the science of wealth and
of welfare. "It proposes," he wrote, "to enrich both the people and
the sovereign."* I have insisted before that Smith was above all a
philosopher, and while* The Wealth of Nations *is his most famous
work—justly so—it does not represent the whole of his output. Nor
does it portray the whole of man as Smith saw him: he was concerned, in this long treatise, to treat of man acting as a trading
animal. No wonder it was partial; it was meant to be. Adam Smith's*
Wealth of Nations *is thus a triumph not merely in its chosen field,
political economy, but on a far larger scale as well. It transformed
discussions of economics, but it also raised questions about stand-*

---

* *Wealth of Nations*, ed. Edwin Cannan (1937) , 397.

ards of living, the division of labor, and the need to control rapacious monopolists to which we have not yet found the answer today.

One of the many things The Wealth of Nations *has to offer is a devastating attack on mercantilism, that rather unsystematic set of ideas about economic power that had governed states and statesmen since the beginning of the modern era. Mercantilists had insisted on a surplus of exports over imports (tendentiously known as "a favorable balance of trade"), the hoarding of bullion against foreigners, the keeping of trade secrets, prohibitions on the emigration of scarce labor combined with a positive population policy. It would be too simple to define mercantilism as a system designed to amass power; many of its votaries in the seventeenth century were interested also in profits. But they insisted that by and large profit was power; and they admitted that when power and profits clashed, profits must yield. As Sir Josiah Child frankly conceded late in the seventeenth century: "All trade" is "a kind of warfare."* Behind this harsh conception of economics lay a harsh view of the world: the total amount of resources seemed limited and fixed; if one nation got more, it must get it from another.*

The philosophes changed all this, in part because they were more humane, in part because they found it realistic to be more humane: the world economy, it seemed in the eighteenth century, was not forever doomed to be static. The pie of wealth to be divided might actually grow, giving more to all.

Adam Smith did not ruin mercantilism all by himself. It had long been crumbling; and there were other economists besides Smith, including that Italian wit, the Abbé Galiani, and that odd school of French enthusiasts, the Physiocrats, who sniped at mercantilist policies. It is true that Smith was in France from 1764 to 1766, and absorbed a number of ideas from his French colleagues; but he had been on his free-trading tack since the late 1740s, and, besides, he had his older friend, David Hume, whose brilliant essays on economic questions echo through the pages of Adam Smith's Wealth of Nations.

As so often, we must praise Hume's penetration and uncommon common sense. In several essays, he rehearsed most of the arguments that Smith would later put more systematically. One of these essays, "Of the Jealousy of Trade," is one of Hume's most pungent productions, and deserves to be reprinted practically in its entirety:

---

* Quoted in William Letwin, *The Origins of Scientific Economics* (1963), 44.

. . . Nothing is more usual, among states which have made some advances in commerce, than to look on the progress of their neighbours with a suspicious eye, to consider all trading states as their rivals, and to suppose that it is impossible for any of them to flourish, but at their expence. In opposition to this narrow and malignant opinion, I will venture to assert, that the encrease of riches and commerce in any one nation, instead of hurting, commonly promotes the riches and commerce of all its neighbours; and that a state can scarcely carry its trade and industry very far, where all the surrounding states are buried in ignorance, sloth, and barbarism.

It is obvious, that the domestic industry of a people cannot be hurt by the greatest prosperity of their neighbours; and as this branch of commerce is undoubtedly the most important in any extensive kingdom, we are so far removed from all reason of jealousy. But I go farther, and observe, that where an open communication is preserved among nations, it is impossible but the domestic industry of every one must receive an encrease from the improvements of the others. Compare the situation of Great Britain at present, with what it was two centuries ago. All the arts both of agriculture and manufactures were then extremely rude and imperfect. Every improvement, which we have since made, has arisen from our imitation of foreigners; and we ought so far to esteem it happy, that they had previously made advances in arts and ingenuity. But this intercourse is still upheld to our great advantage: Notwithstanding the advanced state of our manufactures, we daily adopt, in every art, the inventions and improvements of our neighbours. The commodity is first imported from abroad, to our great discontent, while we imagine that it drains us of our money: Afterwards, the art itself is gradually imported, to our visible advantage: Yet we continue still to repine, that our neighbours should possess any art, industry, and invention; forgetting that, had they not first instructed us, we should have been at present barbarians; and did they not still continue their instructions, the arts must fall into a state of languor, and lose that emulation and novelty, which contribute so much to their advancement.

The encrease of domestic industry lays the foundation of foreign commerce. Where a great number of commodities are raised and perfected for the home-market, there will always be found some which can be exported with advantage. But if our neighbours have no art or cultivation, they cannot take them; because they will have nothing to give in exchange. In this respect, states are in the same condition as individuals. A single man can scarcely be industrious, where all his fellow-citizens are idle. The riches of the several members of a community contribute to encrease my riches, whatever profession I may follow. They consume the produce of my industry, and afford me the produce of theirs in return.

Nor needs any state entertain apprehensions, that their neighbours will improve to such a degree in every art and manufacture, as to have no demand from them. Nature, by giving a diversity of geniuses, climates, and soils, to different nations, has secured their mutual intercourse and commerce, as long as they all remain industrious and civilized. Nay, the more the arts encrease in any state, the more will be its demands from its industrious neighbours. The inhabitants, having become opulent and skilful, desire to have every commodity in the utmost perfection; and as they have plenty of commodities to give in exchange, they make large importations from every foreign country. The industry of the nations, from whom they import, receives encouragement: Their own is also encreased, by the sale of the commodities which they give in exchange.

But what if a nation has any staple commodity, such as the woollen manufacture is in England? Must not the interfering of our neighbours in that manufacture be a loss to us? I answer, that, when any commodity is denominated the staple of a kingdom, it is supposed that this kingdom has some peculiar and natural advantages for raising the commodity; and if, notwithstanding these advantages, they lose such a manufacture, they ought to blame their own idleness, or bad government, not the industry of their neighbours. It ought also to be considered, that, by the encrease of industry among the neighbouring nations, the consumption of every particular species of commodity is also encreased; and though foreign manufactures interfere with them in the market, the demand for their product may still continue, or even encrease. And should it diminish, ought the consequence to be esteemed so fatal? If the spirit of industry be preserved, it may easily be diverted from one branch to another; and the manufacturers of wool, for instance, be employed in linen, silk, iron, or any other commodities, for which there appears to be a demand. We need not apprehend, that all the objects of industry will be exhausted, or that our manufacturers, while they remain on an equal footing with those of our neighbours, will be in danger of wanting employment. The emulation among rival nations serves rather to keep industry alive in all of them: And any people is happier who possess a variety of manufactures, than if they enjoyed one single great manufacture, in which they are all employed. Their situation is less precarious; and they will feel less sensibly those revolutions and uncertainties, to which every particular branch of commerce will always be exposed.

The only commercial state, that ought to dread the improvements and industry of their neighbours, is such a one as the Dutch, who, enjoying no extent of land, nor possessing any number of native commodities, flourish only by their being the brokers, and factors, and carriers of others. Such a people may naturally apprehend, that, as soon as the neighbouring states come to know and pursue their interest, they will take into their own hands the management of their affairs, and deprive their brokers of that profit, which they formerly reaped from it. But though this consequence may naturally be dreaded, it is very long before it takes place; and by art and industry it may be warded off for many generations, if not wholly eluded. The advantage of superior stocks and correspondence is so great, that it is not easily overcome; and as all the transactions encrease by the encrease of industry in the neighbouring states, even a people whose commerce stands on this precarious basis, may at first reap a considerable profit from the flourishing condition of their neighbours. The Dutch, having mortgaged all their revenues, make not such a figure in political transactions as formerly; but their commerce is surely equal to what it was in the middle of the last century, when they were reckoned among the great powers of Europe.

Were our narrow and malignant politics to meet with success, we should reduce all our neighbouring nations to the same state of sloth and ignorance that prevails in Morocco and the coast of Barbary. But what would be the consequence? They could send us no commodities: They could take none from us: Our domestic commerce itself would languish for want of emulation, example and instruction: And we ourselves should soon fall into the same abject condition, to which we had reduced them. I shall therefore venture to acknowledge, that, not only as a man, but as a British subject, I pray for the flourishing commerce of Germany, Spain, Italy, and even France itself. I am at least certain, that Great Britain, and all those nations, would flourish more, did their sovereigns and ministers adopt such enlarged and benevolent sentiments towards each other.*

Adam Smith's essential attitude toward the economic world as a peaceful market in which traders compete for the benefit of all is quite explicitly anticipated here.

Adam Smith was born in 1723, and educated at Glasgow and Oxford. In 1752 he was appointed professor of moral philosophy at the University of Glasgow, but his title inadequately conveys the range of his interests and his lectures; they include political theory and political administration, aesthetics, the history of ethics, and, of course, political economy. In 1759 he published a remarkable ethical treatise, The Theory of Moral Sentiments, *which constructs a moral system by depending heavily on ancient pagan doctrine; it was in this book that Smith developed his all-too-famous notion of the invisible hand: individuals within society, laboring to advance their own interests, actually, without intending it, also advance the interests of society as a whole. This plea for* laissez-faire *also appears in* The Wealth of Nations, *but it is far less prominent there: that Adam Smith opposed governmental intervention in the economy is a tenacious but misleading myth.*

Adam Smith spent much time reflecting on, and polishing, his ideas; his Inquiry into the Nature and Causes of the Wealth of Nations, *which appeared in 1776, was an immediate and immense success; when Smith died in 1790, his masterpiece was in its fifth edition, and his international reputation was secure.*

The Wealth of Nations *is in general such a lucid book that it requires simply careful reading. But it is worth insisting that the book is at all points more complex than summaries usually make it. It is often said that it celebrates the division of labor. So it does; but it also warns against its dehumanizing effects. It is often said that it champions a free economy against government restrictions. So it does; but it also insists that merchants and manufacturers, being born monopolists, must be subjected to public supervision. It is often said, finally, that it urges that wages be allowed to find their own natural level. So it does; but it says also that the higher the real wages of the working force, the happier the country. Adam Smith was a true philosophe: a scientist who hoped his science would make life a little easier.*

* "Of the Balance of Trade," in *The Philosophical Works of David Hume*, ed. T. H. Green and T. H. Grose, 4 vols. (1882), III, 345–48.

❧

BOOK I
Of the Causes of Improvement in the Productive Powers of Labour, and of the Order According to Which its Produce is Naturally Distributed among the Different Ranks of the People

CHAPTER I · OF THE DIVISION OF LABOUR

The greatest improvement in the productive powers of labour, and the greater part of the skill, dexterity, and judgment with which it is any where directed, or applied, seem to have been the effects of the division of labour.

The effects of the division of labour, in the general business of society, will be more easily understood, by considering in what manner it operates in some particular manufactures. It is commonly supposed to be carried furthest in some very trifling ones; not perhaps that it really is carried further in them than in others of more importance: but in those trifling manufactures which are destined to supply the small wants of but a small number of people, the whole number of workmen must necessarily be small; and those employed in every different branch of the work can often be collected into the same workhouse, and placed at once under the view of the spectator. In those great manufactures, on the contrary, which are destined to supply the great wants of the great body of the people, every different branch of the work employs so great a number of workmen, that it is impossible to collect them all into the same workhouse. We can seldom see more, at one time, than those employed in one single branch. Though in such manufactures, therefore, the work may really be divided into a much greater number of parts, than in those of a more trifling nature, the division is not near so obvious, and has accordingly been much less observed.

To take an example, therefore, from a very trifling manufacture; but one in which the division of labour has been very often taken notice of, the trade of the pin-maker; a workman not educated to this business (which the division of labour has rendered a distinct trade) nor acquainted with the use of the machinery employed in it (to the invention of which the same division of labour has probably given occasion), could scarce, perhaps, with his utmost industry, make one pin in a day, and certainly could not make twenty. But in the way in which this business is now carried on, not only the whole work is a peculiar trade, but it is divided into a number of branches, of which the greater part are likewise peculiar trades. One man draws out the wire, another straights it, a third cuts it, a fourth points it, a fifth grinds it at the top for receiving the head; to make the head requires two or three distinct operations; to put it on, is a peculiar business, to whiten the pins is another; it is even a trade by itself to put them into the paper; and the important business of making a pin is, in this manner, divided into about eighteen distinct operations, which, in some manufactories, are all performed by distinct hands, though in others the same man will sometimes perform two or three of them. I have seen a small manufactory of this kind where ten men only were employed, and where some of them consequently performed two or three distinct operations. But though they were very poor, and therefore but indifferently accommodated with the necessary machinery, they could, when they exerted themselves, make among them about twelve pounds of pins in a day. There are in a pound upwards of four thousand pins of a middling size. Those ten persons, therefore, could make among them upwards of forty-eight thousand pins in a day. Each person, therefore, making a tenth part of forty-eight thousand pins, might be considered as making four thousand eight hundred pins in a day. But if they had all wrought separately and independently, and without any of them having been educated to this peculiar business, they certainly could not each of them have made twenty, perhaps not one pin in a day; that is, certainly, not the two hundred and fortieth, perhaps not the four thousand eight hundredth part of what they are at present capable of performing, in consequence of a proper division and combination of their different operations.

In every other art and manufacture, the effects of the division of labour are similar to what they are in this very trifling one; though, in many of them, the labour can neither be so much subdivided, nor reduced to so great a simplicity of operation. The division of labour, however, so far as it can be introduced, occasions, in every art, a proportionable increase of the productive powers of labour. The separation of different trades and employments from one another, seems to have taken place, in consequence of this advantage. This separation too is generally carried furthest in those countries which enjoy the highest degree of industry and improvement; what is the work of one man in a rude state of society, being generally that of several in an improved one. In every improved society, the farmer is generally nothing but a farmer; the manufacturer, nothing but a manufacturer. The labour too which is necessary to produce any one complete manufacture, is almost always divided among a great number of hands. How many different trades are employed in each branch of the linen and woollen manufactures, from the growers of the flax and the wool, to the bleachers and smoothers of the linen, or to the dyers and dressers of the cloth! The nature of agriculture, indeed, does not admit of so many subdivisions of labour, nor of so complete a separation of one business from another, as manufactures. It is impossible to separate so entirely, the business of the grazier from that of the corn-farmer, as the trade of the carpenter is commonly separated from that of the smith. The spinner is almost always a distinct person from the weaver; but the ploughman, the harrower, the sower of the seed, and the reaper of the corn, are often the same. The occasions for those different sorts of labour returning with the different seasons of the year, it is impossible that one man should be constantly employed in any one of them. This impossibility of making so complete and entire a separation of all the different branches of labour employed in agriculture, is perhaps the reason why the improvement of the productive powers of labour in this art, does not always keep pace with their improvement in manufactures. The most opulent nations, indeed, generally excel all their neighbours in agriculture as well as in manufactures; but they are commonly more distinguished by their superiority in the latter than in the former. Their lands are in general better cultivated, and having more labour and expence bestowed upon them, produce more in proportion to the extent and natural fertility of the ground. But this superiority of produce is seldom much more than in proportion to the superiority of labour and expence. In agriculture, the labour of the rich country is not always much more productive than that of the poor; or, at least, it is never so much more productive, as it commonly is in manufactures. The corn of the rich country, therefore, will not always, in the same degree of goodness, come cheaper to market than that of the poor. The corn of Poland, in the same degree of goodness, is as cheap as that of France, notwithstanding the superior opulence and improvement of the latter country. The corn of France is, in the corn provinces, fully as good, and in most years nearly about the same price with the corn of England, though, in opulence and improvement, France is perhaps inferior to England. The corn-lands of England, however, are better cultivated than those of France, and the corn-lands of France are said to be much better cultivated than those of Poland. But though the poor country, notwithstanding the inferiority of its cultivation, can, in some measure, rival the rich in the cheapness and goodness of its corn, it can pretend to no such competition in its manufactures; at least if those manufactures suit the soil, climate, and situation of the rich country. The silks of France are better and cheaper than those of England, because the silk manufacture, at least under the present high duties upon the importation of raw silk, does not so well suit the climate of England as that of France. But the hardware and the coarse woollens of England are beyond all comparison superior to those of France, and much cheaper too in the same degree of goodness. In Poland there are said to be scarce any manufactures of any kind, a few of those coarser household manufactures excepted, without which no country can well subsist.

This great increase of the quantity of work, which, in consequence of the division of labour, the same number of people are capable of performing, is owing to three different circumstances; first, to the increase of dexterity in every particular workman; secondly, to the saving of the time which is commonly lost in passing from one species of work to another; and lastly, to the invention of a great number of machines which facilitate and abridge labour, and enable one man to do the work of many.

First, the improvement of the dexterity of the workman necessarily increases the quantity of the work he can perform; and the division of labour, by reducing every man's business to some one simple operation, and by making this operation the sole employment of his life, necessarily increases very much the dexterity of the workman. A common smith, who, though accustomed to handle the hammer, has never been used to make nails, if upon some particular occasion he is obliged to attempt it, will scarce, I am assured, be able to make above two or three hundred nails in a day, and those too very bad ones. A smith who has been accustomed to make nails, but whose sole or principal business has not been that of a nailer, can seldom with his utmost diligence make more than eight hundred or a thousand nails in a day. I have seen several boys under twenty years of age who had never exercised any other trade but that of making nails, and who, when they exerted themselves, could make, each of them, upwards of two thousand three hundred nails in a day. The making of a nail, however, is by no means one of the simplest operations. The same person blows the bellows, stirs or mends the fire as there is occasion, heats the iron, and forges every part of the nail: In forging the head too he is obliged to change his tools. The different operations into which the making of a pin, or of a metal button, is subdivided, are all of them much more simple, and the dexterity of the person, of whose life it has been the sole business to perform them, is usually much greater. The rapidity with which some of the operations of those manufactures are performed, exceeds what the human hand could, by those who had never seen them, be supposed capable of acquiring.

Secondly, the advantage which is gained by saving the time commonly lost in passing from one sort of work to another, is much greater than we should at first view be apt to imagine it. It is impossible to pass very quickly from one kind of work to another, that is carried on in a different place, and with quite different tools. A country weaver, who cultivates a small farm, must lose a good deal of time in passing from his loom to the field, and from the field to his loom. When the two trades can be carried on in the same workhouse, the loss of time is no doubt much less. It is even in this case, however, very considerable. A man commonly saunters a little in turning his hand from one sort of employment to another. When he first begins the new work he is seldom very keen and hearty; his mind, as they say, does not go to it, and for some time he rather trifles than applies to good purpose. The habit of sauntering and of indolent careless application, which is naturally, or rather necessarily acquired by every country workman who is obliged to change his work and his tools every half hour, and to apply his hand in twenty different ways almost every day of his life, renders him almost always slothful and lazy, and incapable of any vigorous application even on the most pressing occasions. Independent, therefore, of his deficiency in point of dexterity, this cause alone must always reduce considerably the quantity of work which he is capable of performing.

Thirdly, and lastly, every body must be sensible how much labour is facilitated and abridged by the application of proper machinery. It is unnecessary to give any example. I shall only observe, therefore, that the invention of all those machines by which labour is so much facilitated and abridged, seems to have been originally owing to the division of labour. Men are much more likely to discover easier and readier methods of attaining any object, when the whole attention of their minds is directed towards that single object, than when it is dissipated among a great variety of things. But in consequence of the division of labour, the whole of every man's attention comes naturally to be directed towards some one very simple object. It is naturally to be expected, therefore, that some one or other of those who are employed in each particular branch of labour should soon find out easier and readier methods of performing their own particular work, wherever the nature of it admits of such improvement. A great part of the machines made use of in those manufactures in which labour is most subdivided, were originally the inventions of common workmen, who, being each of them employed in some very simple operation, naturally turned their thoughts towards finding out easier and readier methods of performing it. Whoever has been much accustomed to visit such manufactures, must frequently have been shewn very pretty machines, which were the inventions of such workmen, in order to facilitate and quicken their own particular part of the work. In the first fire-engines, a boy was constantly employed to open and shut alternately the communication between the boiler and the cylinder, according as the piston either ascended or descended. One of those boys, who loved to play with his companions, observed that, by tying a string from the handle of the valve which opened this communication to another part of the machine, the valve would open and shut without his assistance, and leave him at liberty to divert himself with his play-fellows. One of the greatest improvements that has been made upon this machine, since it was first invented, was in this manner the discovery of a boy who wanted to save his own labour.

All the improvements in machinery, however, have by no means been the inventions of those who had occasion to use the machines. Many improvements have been made by the ingenuity of the makers of the machines, when to make them became the business of a peculiar trade; and some by that of those who are called philosophers or men of speculation, whose trade it is not to do any thing, but to observe every thing; and who, upon that account, are often capable of combining together the powers of the most distant and dissimilar objects. In the progress of society, philosophy or speculation becomes, like every other employment, the principal or sole trade and occupation of a particular class of citizens. Like every other employment too, it is subdivided into a great number of different branches, each of which affords occupation to a peculiar tribe or class of philosophers; and this subdivision of employment in philosophy, as well as in every other business, improves dexterity, and saves time. Each individual becomes more expert in his own peculiar branch, more work is done upon the whole, and the quantity of science is considerably increased by it.

It is the great multiplication of the productions of all the different arts, in consequence of the division of labour, which occasions, in a well-governed society, that universal opulence which extends itself to the lowest ranks of the people. Every workman has a great quantity of his own work to dispose of beyond what he himself has occasion for; and every other workman being exactly in the same situation, he is enabled to exchange a great quantity of his own goods for a great quantity, or, what comes to the same thing, for the price of a great quantity of theirs. He supplies them abundantly with what they have occasion for, and they accommodate him as amply with what he has occasion for, and a general plenty diffuses itself through all the different ranks of the society.

Observe the accommodation of the most common artificer or day-labourer in a civilized and thriving country, and you will perceive that the number of people of whose industry a part, though but a small part, has been employed in procuring him this accommodation, exceeds all computation. The woollen coat, for example, which covers the day-labourer, as coarse and rough as it may appear, is the produce of the joint labour of a great multitude of workmen. The shepherd, the sorter of the wool, the wool-comber or carder, the dyer, the scribbler, the spinner, the weaver, the fuller, the dresser, with many others, must all join their different arts in order to complete even this homely production. How many merchants and carriers, besides, must have been employed in transporting the materials from some of those workmen to others who often live in a very distant part of the country! how much commerce and navigation in particular, how many ship-builders, sailors, sail-makers, rope-makers, must have been employed in order to bring together the different drugs made use of by the dyer, which often come from the remotest corners of the world! What a variety of labour too is necessary in order to produce the tools of the meanest of those workmen! To say nothing of such complicated machines as the ship of the sailor, the mill of the fuller, or even the loom of the weaver, let us consider only what a variety of labour is requisite in order to form that very simple machine, the shears with which the shepherd clips the wool. The miner, the builder of the furnace for smelting the ore, the feller of the timber, the burner of the charcoal to be made use of in the smelting-house, the brick-maker, the brick-layer, the workmen who attend the furnace, the mill-wright, the forger, the smith, must all of them join their different arts in order to produce them. Were we to examine, in the same manner, all the different parts of his dress and household furniture, the coarse linen shirt which he wears next his skin, the shoes which cover his feet, the bed which he lies on, and all the different parts which compose it, the kitchen-grate at which he prepares his victuals, the coals which he makes use of for that purpose, dug from the bowels of the earth, and brought to him perhaps by a long sea and a long land carriage, all the other utensils of his kitchen, all the furniture of his table, the knives and forks, the earthen or pewter plates upon which he serves up and divides his victuals, the different hands employed in preparing his bread and his beer, the glass window which lets in the heat and the light, and keeps out the wind and the rain, with all the knowledge and art requisite for preparing that beautiful and happy invention, without which these northern parts of the world could scarce have afforded a very comfortable habitation, together with the tools of all the different workmen employed in producing those different conveniencies; if we examine, I say, all these things, and consider what a variety of labour is employed about each of them, we shall be sensible that without the assistance and co-operation of many thousands, the very meanest person in a civilized country could not be provided, even according to, what we very falsely imagine, the easy and simple manner in which he is commonly accommodated. Compared, indeed, with the more extravagant luxury of the great, his accommodation must no doubt appear extremely simple and easy; and yet it may be true, perhaps, that the accommodation of an European prince does not always so much exceed that of an industrious and frugal peasant, as the accommodation of the latter exceeds that of many an African king, the absolute master of the lives and liberties of ten thousand naked savages.

CHAPTER II · OF THE PRINCIPLE WHICH GIVES OCCASION TO THE DIVISION OF LABOUR

This division of labour, from which so many advantages are derived, is not originally the effect of any human wisdom, which foresees and intends that general opulence to which it gives occasion. It is the necessary, though very slow and gradual, consequence of a certain propensity in human nature which has in view no such extensive utility; the propensity to truck, barter, and exchange one thing for another.

Whether this propensity be one of those original principles in human nature, of which no further account can be given; or whether, as seems more probable, it be the necessary consequence of the faculties of reason and speech, it belongs not to our present subject to enquire. It is common to all men, and to be found in no other race of animals, which seem to know neither this nor any other species of contracts. Two greyhounds, in running down the same hare, have sometimes the appearance of acting in some sort of concert. Each turns her towards his companion, or endeavours to intercept her when his companion turns her towards himself. This, however, is not the effect of any contract, but of the accidental concurrence of their passions in the same object at that particular time. Nobody ever saw a dog make a fair and deliberate exchange of one bone for another with another dog. Nobody ever saw one animal by its gestures and natural cries signify to another, this is mine, that yours; I am willing to give this for that. . . .

CHAPTER VIII · OF THE WAGES OF LABOUR

The produce of labour constitutes the natural recompence or wages of labour.

In that original state of things, which precedes both the appropriation of land and the accumulation of stock, the whole produce of labour belongs to the labourer. He has neither landlord nor master to share with him.

Had this state continued, the wages of labour would have augmented with all those improvements in its productive powers, to which the division of labour gives occasion. All things would gradually have become cheaper. They would have been produced by a smaller quantity of labour; and as the commodities produced by equal quantities of labour would naturally in this state of things be exchanged for one another, they would have been purchased likewise with the produce of a smaller quantity.

But though all things would have become cheaper in reality, in appearance many things might have become dearer than before, or have been exchanged for a greater quantity of other goods. Let us suppose, for example, that in the greater part of employments the productive powers of labour had been improved to tenfold, or that a day's labour could produce ten times the quantity of work which it had done originally; but that in a particular employment they had been improved only to double, or that a day's labour could produce only twice the quantity of work which it had done before. In exchanging the produce of a day's labour in the greater part of employments, for that of a day's labour in this particular one, ten times the original quantity of work in them would purchase only twice the original quantity in it. Any particular quantity in it, therefore, a pound weight, for example, would appear to be five times dearer than before. In reality, however, it would be twice as cheap. Though it required five times the quantity of other goods to purchase it, it would require only half the quantity of labour either to purchase or to produce it. The acquisition, therefore, would be twice as easy as before.

But this original state of things, in which the labourer enjoyed the whole produce of his own labour, could not last beyond the first introduction of the appropriation of land and the accumulation of stock. It was at an end, therefore, long before the most considerable improvements were made in the productive powers of labour, and it would be to no purpose to trace further what might have been its effects upon the recompence or wages of labour.

As soon as land becomes private property, the landlord demands a share of almost all the produce which the labourer can either raise, or collect from it. His rent makes the first deduction from the produce of the labour which is employed upon land.

It seldom happens that the person who tills the ground has wherewithal to maintain himself till he reaps the harvest. His maintenance is generally advanced to him from the stock of a master, the farmer who employs him, and who would have no interest to employ him, unless he was to share in the produce of his labour, or unless his stock was to be replaced to him with a profit. This profit makes a second deduction from the produce of the labour which is employed upon land.

The produce of almost all other labour is liable to the like deduction of profit. In all arts and manufactures the greater part of the workmen stand in need of a master to advance them the materials of their work, and their wages and maintenance till it be compleated. He shares in the produce of their labour, or in the value which it adds to the materials upon which it is bestowed; and in this share consists his profit.

It sometimes happens, indeed, that a single independent workman has stock sufficient both to purchase the materials of his work, and to maintain himself till it be compleated. He is both master and workman, and enjoys the whole produce of his own labour, or the whole value which it adds to the materials upon which it is bestowed. It includes what are usually two distinct revenues, belonging to two distinct persons, the profits of stock, and the wages of labour.

Such cases, however, are not very frequent, and in every part of Europe, twenty workmen serve under a master for one that is independent; and the wages of labour are every where understood to be, what they usually are, when the labourer is one person, and the owner of the stock which employs him another.

What are the common wages of labour, depends every where upon the contract usually made between those two parties, whose interests are by no means the same. The workmen desire to get as much, the masters to give as little as possible. The former are disposed to combine in order to raise, the latter in order to lower the wages of labour.

It is not, however, difficult to foresee which of the two parties must, upon all ordinary occasions, have the advantage in the dispute, and force the other into a compliance with their terms. The masters, being fewer in number, can combine much more easily; and the law, besides, authorises, or at least does not prohibit their combinations, while it prohibits those of the workmen. We have no acts of parliament against combining to lower the price of work; but many against combining to raise it. In all such disputes the masters can hold out much longer. A landlord, a farmer, a master manufacturer, or merchant, though they did not employ a single workman, could generally live a year or two upon the stocks which they have already acquired. Many workmen could not subsist a week, few could subsist a month, and scarce any a year without employment. In the long-run the workman may be as necessary to his master as his master is to him, but the necessity is not so immediate.

We rarely hear, it has been said, of the combinations of masters, though frequently of those of workmen. But whoever imagines, upon this account, that masters rarely combine, is as ignorant of the world as of the subject. Masters are always and every where in a sort of tacit, but constant and uniform combination, not to raise the wages of labour above their actual rate. To violate this combination is every where a most unpopular action, and a sort of reproach to a master among his neighbours and equals. We seldom, indeed, hear of this combination, because it is the usual, and one may say, the natural state of things which nobody ever hears of.

Masters too sometimes enter into particular combinations to sink the wages of labour even below this rate. These are always conducted with the utmost silence and secrecy, till the moment of execution, and when the workmen yield, as they sometimes do, without resistance, though severely felt by them, they are never heard of by other people. Such combinations, however, are frequently resisted by a contrary defensive combination of the workmen; who sometimes too, without any provocation of this kind, combine of their own accord to raise the price of their labour. Their usual pretences are, sometimes the high price of provisions; sometimes the great profit which their masters make by their work. But whether their combinations be offensive or defensive, they are always abundantly heard of. In order to bring the point to a speedy decision, they have always recourse to the loudest clamour, and sometimes to the most shocking violence and outrage. They are desperate, and act with the folly and extravagance of desperate men, who must either starve, or frighten their masters into an immediate compliance with their demands. The masters upon these occasions are just as clamorous upon the other side, and never cease to call aloud for the assistance of the civil magistrate, and the rigorous execution of those laws which have been enacted with so much severity against the combinations of servants, labourers, and journeymen. The workmen, accordingly, very seldom derive any advantage from the violence of those tumultuous combinations, which, partly from the interposition of the civil magistrate, partly from the superior steadiness of the masters, partly from the necessity which the greater part of the workmen are under of submitting for the sake of present subsistence, generally end in nothing, but the punishment or ruin of the ring-leaders.

But though in disputes with their workmen, masters must generally have the advantage, there is however a certain rate below which it seems impossible to reduce, for any considerable time, the ordinary wages even of the lowest species of labour.

A man must always live by his work, and his wages must at least be sufficient to maintain him. They must even upon most occasions be somewhat more; otherwise it would be impossible for him to bring up a family, and the race of such workmen could not last beyond the first generation. Mr. Cantillon seems, upon this account, to suppose that the lowest species of common labourers must every where earn at least double their own maintenance, in order that one with another they may be enabled to bring up two children; the labour of the wife, on account of her necessary attendance on the children, being supposed no more than sufficient to provide for herself. But one-half the children born, it is computed, die before the age of manhood. The poorest labourers, therefore, according to this account, must, one with another, attempt to rear at least four children, in order that two may have an equal chance of living to that age. But the necessary maintenance of four children, it is supposed, may be nearly equal to that of one man. The labour of an able-bodied slave, the same author adds, is computed to be worth double his maintenance; and that of the meanest labourer, he thinks, cannot be worth less than that of an able-bodied slave. Thus far at least seems certain, that, in order to bring up a family, the labour of the husband and wife together must, even in the lowest species of common labour, be able to earn something more than what is precisely necessary for their own maintenance; but in what proportion, whether in that above mentioned, or in any other, I shall not take upon me to determine.

There are certain circumstances, however, which sometimes give the labourers an advantage, and enable them to raise their wages considerably above this rate; evidently the lowest which is consistent with common humanity.

When in any country the demand for those who live by wages: labourers, journeymen, servants of every kind, is continually increasing; when every year furnishes employment for a greater number than had been employed the year before, the workmen have no occasion to combine in order to raise their wages. The scarcity of hands occasions a competition among masters, who bid against one another, in order to get workmen, and thus voluntarily break through the natural combination of masters not to raise wages.

The demand for those who live by wages, it is evident, cannot increase but in proportion to the increase of the funds which are destined for the payment of wages. These funds are of two kinds; first, the revenue which is over and above what is necessary for the maintenance; and, secondly, the stock which is over and above what is necessary for the employment of their masters.

When the landlord, annuitant, or monied man, has a greater revenue than what he judges sufficient to maintain his own family, he employs either the whole or a part of the surplus in maintaining one or more menial servants. Increase this surplus, and he will naturally increase the number of those servants.

When an independent workman, such as a weaver or shoe-maker, has got more stock than what is sufficient to purchase the materials of his own work, and to maintain himself till he can dispose of it, he naturally employs one or more journeymen with the surplus, in order to make a profit by their work. Increase this surplus, and he will naturally increase the number of his journeymen.

The demand for those who live by wages, therefore, necessarily increases with the increase of the revenue and stock of every country, and cannot possibly increase without it. The increase of revenue and stock is the increase of national wealth. The demand for those who live by wages, therefore, naturally increases with the increase of national wealth, and cannot possibly increase without it.

It is not the actual greatness of national wealth, but its continual increase, which occasions a rise in the wages of labour. It is not, accordingly, in the richest countries, but in the most thriving, or in those which are growing rich the fastest, that the wages of labour are highest. England is certainly, in the present times, a much richer country than any part of North America. The wages of labour, however, are much higher in North America than in any part of England. In the province of New York, common labourers earn three shillings and sixpence currency, equal to two shillings sterling, a day; ship carpenters, ten shillings and sixpence currency, with a pint of rum worth sixpence sterling, equal in all to six shillings and sixpence sterling; house carpenters and bricklayers, eight shillings currency, equal to four shillings and sixpence sterling; journeymen taylors, five shillings currency, equal to about two shillings and ten pence sterling. These prices are all above the London price; and wages are said to be as high in the other colonies as in New York. The price of provisions is every where in North America much lower than in England. A dearth has never been known there. In the worst seasons, they have always had a sufficiency for themselves, though less for exportation. If the money price of labour, therefore, be higher than it is any where in the mother country, its real price, the real command of the necessaries and conveniencies of life which it conveys to the labourer, must be higher in a still greater proportion.

But though North America is not yet so rich as England, it is much more thriving, and advancing with much greater rapidity to the further acquisition of riches. The most decisive mark of the prosperity of any country is the increase of the number of its inhabitants. In Great Britain, and most other European countries, they are not supposed to double in less than five hundred years. In the British colonies in North America, it has been found, that they double in twenty or five-and-twenty years. Nor in the present times is this increase principally owing to the continual importation of new inhabitants, but to the great multiplication of the species. Those who live to old age, it is said, frequently see there from fifty to a hundred, and sometimes many more, descendants from their own body. Labour is there so well rewarded that a numerous family of children, instead of being a burthen is a source of opulence and prosperity to the parents. The labour of each child, before it can leave their house, is computed to be worth a hundred pounds clear gain to them. A young widow with four or five young children, who among the middling or inferior ranks of people in Europe, would have so little chance for a second husband, is there frequently courted as a sort of fortune. The value of children is the greatest of all encouragements to marriage. We cannot, therefore, wonder that the people in North America should generally marry very young. Notwithstanding the great increase occasioned by such early marriages, there is a continual complaint of the scarcity of hands in North America. The demand for labourers, the funds destined for maintaining them, increase, it seems, still faster than they can find labourers to employ.

Though the wealth of a country should be very great, yet if it has been long stationary, we must not expect to find the wages of labour very high in it. The funds destined for the payment of wages, the revenue and stock of its inhabitants, may be of the greatest extent; but if they have continued for several centuries of the same, or very nearly of the same extent, the number of labourers employed every year could easily supply, and even more than supply, the number wanted the following year. There could seldom be any scarcity of hands, nor could the masters be obliged to bid against one another in order to get them. The hands, on the contrary, would, in this case, naturally multiply beyond their employment. There would be a constant scarcity of employment, and the labourers would be obliged to bid against one another in order to get it. If in such a country the wages of labour had ever been more than sufficient to maintain the labourer, and to enable him to bring up a family, the competition of the labourers and the interest of the masters would soon reduce them to this lowest rate which is consistent with common humanity. China has been long one of the richest, that is, one of the most fertile, best cultivated, most industrious, and most populous countries in the world. It seems, however, to have been long stationary. Marco Polo, who visited it more than five hundred years ago, describes its cultivation, industry, and populousness, almost in the same terms in which they are described by travellers in the present times. It had perhaps, even long before his time, acquired that full complement of riches which the nature of its laws and institutions permits it to acquire. The accounts of all travellers, inconsistent in many other respects, agree in the low wages of labour, and in the difficulty which a labourer finds in bringing up a family in China. If by digging the ground a whole day he can get what will purchase a small quantity of rice in the evening, he is contented. The condition of artificers is, if possible, still worse. Instead of waiting indolently in their work-houses, for the calls of their customers, as in Europe, they are continually running about the streets with the tools of their respective trades, offering their service, and as it were begging employment. The poverty of the lower ranks of people in China far surpasses that of the most beggarly nations in Europe. In the neighbourhood of Canton many hundred, it is commonly said, many thousand families have no habitation on the land, but live constantly in little fishing boats upon the rivers and canals. The subsistence which they find there is so scanty that they are eager to fish up the nastiest garbage thrown overboard from any European ship. Any carrion, the carcase of a dead dog or cat, for example, though half putrid and stinking, is as welcome to them as the most wholesome food to the people of other countries. Marriage is encouraged in China, not by the profitableness of children, but by the liberty of destroying them. In all great towns several are every night exposed in the street, or drowned like puppies in the water. The performance of this horrid office is even said to be the avowed business by which some people earn their subsistence.

China, however, though it may perhaps stand still, does not seem to go backwards. Its towns are no-where deserted by their inhabitants. The lands which had once been cultivated are no-where neglected. The same or very nearly the same annual labour must therefore continue to be performed, and the funds destined for maintaining it must not, consequently, be sensibly diminished. The lowest class of labourers, therefore, notwithstanding their scanty subsistence, must some way or another make shift to continue their race so far as to keep up their usual numbers.

But it would be otherwise in a country where the funds destined for the maintenance of labour were sensibly decaying. Every year the demand for servants and labourers would, in all the different classes of employments, be less than it had been the year before. Many who had been bred in the superior classes, not being able to find employment in their own business, would be glad to seek it in the lowest. The lowest class being not only overstocked with its own workmen, but with the overflowings of all the other classes, the competition for employment would be so great in it, as to reduce the wages of labour to the most miserable and scanty subsistence of the labourer. Many would not be able to find employment even upon these hard terms, but would either starve, or be driven to seek a subsistence either by begging, or by the perpetration perhaps of the greatest enormities. Want, famine, and mortality would immediately prevail in that class, and from thence extend themselves to all the superior classes, till the number of inhabitants in the country was reduced to what could easily be maintained by the revenue and stock which remained in it, and which had escaped either the tyranny or calamity which had destroyed the rest. This perhaps is nearly the present state of Bengal, and of some other of the English settlements in the East Indies. In a fertile country which had before been much depopulated, where subsistence, consequently, should not be very difficult, and where, notwithstanding, three or four hundred thousand people die of hunger in one year, we may be assured that the funds destined for the maintenance of the labouring poor are fast decaying. The difference between the genius of the British constitution which protects and governs North America, and that of the mercantile company which oppresses and domineers in the East Indies, cannot perhaps be better illustrated than by the current state of those countries.

The liberal reward of labour, therefore, as it is the necessary effect, so it is the natural symptom of increasing national wealth. The scanty maintenance of the labouring poor, on the other hand, is the natural symptom that things are at a stand, and their starving condition that they are going fast backwards.

In Great Britain the wages of labour seem, in the present times, to be evidently more than what is precisely necessary to enable the labourer to bring up a family. In order to satisfy ourselves upon this point it will not be necessary to enter into any tedious or doubtful calculation of what may be the lowest sum upon which it is possible to do this. There are many plain symptoms that the wages of labour are no-where in this country regulated by this lowest rate which is consistent with common humanity.

First, in almost every part of Great Britain there is a distinction, even in the lowest species of labour, between summer and winter wages. Summer wages are always highest. But on account of the extraordinary expence of fuel, the maintenance of a family is most expensive in winter. Wages, therefore, being highest when this expence is lowest, it seems evident that they are not regulated by what is necessary for this expence; but by the quantity and supposed value of the work. A labourer, it may be said indeed, ought to save part of his summer wages in order to defray his winter expence; and that through the whole year they do not exceed what is necessary to maintain his family through the whole year. A slave, however, or one absolutely dependent on us for immediate subsistence, would not be treated in this manner. His daily subsistence would be proportioned to his daily necessities.

Secondly, the wages of labour do not in Great Britian fluctuate with the price of provisions. These vary every where from year to year, frequently from month to month. But in many places the money price of labour remains uniformly the same sometimes for half a century together. If in these places, therefore, the labouring poor can maintain their families in dear years, they must be at their ease in times of moderate plenty, and in affluence in those of extraordinary cheapness. The high price of provisions during these ten years past has not in many parts of the kingdom been accompanied with any sensible rise in the money price of labour. It has, indeed, in some; owing probably more to the increase of the demand for labour than to that of the price of provisions.

Thirdly, as the price of provisions varies more from year to year than the wages of labour, so, on the other hand, the wages of labour vary more from place to place than the price of provisions. The prices of bread and butcher's meat are generally the same or very nearly the same through the greater part of the united kingdom. These and most other things which are sold by retail, the way in which the labouring poor buy all things, are generally fully as cheap or cheaper in great towns than in the remoter parts of the country, for reasons which I shall have occasion to explain hereafter. But the wages of labour in a great town and its neighbourhood are frequently a fourth or a fifth part, twenty or five-and-twenty per cent, higher than at a few miles distance. Eighteen pence a day may be reckoned the common price of labour in London and its neighbourhood. At a few miles distance it falls to fourteen and fifteen pence. Ten pence may be reckoned its price in Edinburgh and its neighbourhood. At a few miles distance it falls to eight pence, the usual price of common labour through the greater part of the low country of Scotland, where it varies a good deal less than in England. Such a difference of prices, which it seems is not always sufficient to transport a man from one parish to another, would necessarily occasion so great a transportation of the most bulky commodities, not only from one parish to another, but from one end of the kingdom, almost from one end of the world to the other, as would soon reduce them more nearly to a level. After all that has been said of the levity and inconstancy of human nature, it appears evidently from experience that a man is of all sorts of luggage the most difficult to be transported. If the labouring poor, therefore, can maintain their families in those parts of the kingdom where the price of labour is lowest, they must be in affluence where it is highest.

Fourthly, the variations in the price of labour not only do not correspond either in place or time with those in the price of provisions, but they are frequently quite opposite.

Grain, the food of the common people, is dearer in Scotland than in England, whence Scotland receives almost every year very large supplies. But English corn must be sold dearer in Scotland, the country to which it is brought, than in England, the country from which it comes; and in proportion to its quality it cannot be sold dearer in Scotland than the Scotch corn that comes to the same market in competition with it. The quality of grain depends chiefly upon the quantity of flour or meal which it yields at the mill, and in this respect English grain is so much superior to the Scotch, that, though often dearer in appearance, or in proportion to the measure of its bulk, it is generally cheaper in reality, or in proportion to its quality, or even to the measure of its weight. The price of labour, on the contrary, is dearer in England than in Scotland. If the labouring poor, therefore, can maintain their families in the one part of the united kingdom, they must be in affluence in the other. Oatmeal indeed supplies the common people in Scotland with the greatest and the best part of their food, which is in general much inferior to that of their neighbours of the same rank in England. This difference, however, in the mode of their subsistence is not the cause, but the effect, of the difference in their wages; though, by a strange misapprehension, I have frequently heard it represented as the cause. It is not because one man keeps a coach while his neighbour walks a-foot, that the one is rich and the other poor; but because the one is rich he keeps a coach, and because the other is poor he walks a-foot.

During the course of the last century, taking one year with another, grain was dearer in both parts of the united kingdom than during that of the present. This is a matter of fact which cannot now admit of any reasonable doubt; and the proof of it is, if possible, still more decisive with regard to Scotland than with regard to

England. It is in Scotland supported by the evidence of the public
fiars, annual valuations made upon oath, according to the actual
state of the markets, of all the different sorts of grain in every
different county of Scotland. If such direct proof could require any
collateral evidence to confirm it, I would observe that this has
likewise been the case in France, and probably in most other parts
of Europe. With regard to France there is the clearest proof. But
though it is certain that in both parts of the united kingdom grain
was somewhat dearer in the last century than in the present, it is
equally certain that labour was much cheaper. If the labouring
poor, therefore, could bring up their families then, they must be
much more at their ease now. In the last century, the most usual
day-wages of common labour through the greater part of Scotland
were sixpence in summer and five-pence in winter. Three shillings a
week, the same price very nearly, still continues to be paid in some
parts of the Highlands and Western Islands. Through the greater
part of the low country the most usual wages of common labour are
now eight-pence a day; ten-pence, sometimes a shilling about Edinburgh, in the counties which border upon England, probably on
account of that neighbourhood, and in a few other places where
there has lately been a considerable rise in the demand for labour,
about Glasgow, Carron, Ayr-shire, &c. In England the improvements of agriculture, manufactures and commerce began much
earlier than in Scotland. The demand for labour, and consequently
its price, must necessarily have increased with those improvements.
In the last century, accordingly, as well as in the present, the wages
of labour were higher in England than in Scotland. They have risen
too considerably since that time, though, on account of the greater
variety of wages paid there in different places, it is more difficult to
ascertain how much. In 1614, the pay of a foot soldier was the same
as in the present times, eight pence a day. When it was first established it would naturally be regulated by the usual wages of common labourers, the rank of people from which foot soldiers are
commonly drawn. Lord Chief Justice Hales, who wrote in the time
of Charles II, computes the necessary expence of a labourer's family,
consisting of six persons, the father and mother, two children able
to do something, and two not able, at ten shillings a week, or
twenty-six pounds a year. If they cannot earn this by their labour,
they must make it up, he supposes, either by begging or stealing. He
appears to have enquired very carefully into this subject. In 1688,
Mr. Gregory King, whose skill in political arithmetic is so much
extolled by Doctor Davenant, computed the ordinary income of

labourers and out-servants to be fifteen pounds a year to a family, which he supposed to consist, one with another, of three and a half persons. His calculation, therefore, though different in appearance, corresponds very nearly at bottom with that of judge Hales. Both suppose the weekly expence of such families to be about twenty pence a head. Both the pecuniary income and expence of such families have increased considerably since that time through the greater part of the kingdom; in some places more, and in some less; though perhaps scarce any where so much as some exaggerated accounts of the present wages of labour have lately represented them to the public. The price of labour, it must be observed, cannot be ascertained very accurately any where, different prices being often paid at the same place and for the same sort of labour, not only according to the different abilities of the workmen, but according to the easiness or hardness of the masters. Where wages are not regulated by law, all that we can pretend to determine is what are the most usual; and experience seems to show that law can never regulate them properly, though it has often pretended to do so.

The real recompence of labour, the real quantity of the necessaries and conveniencies of life which it can procure to the labourer, has, during the course of the present century, increased perhaps by a still greater proportion than its money price. Not only grain has become somewhat cheaper, but many other things, from which the industrious poor derive an agreeable and wholesome variety of food, have become a great deal cheaper. Potatoes, for example, do not at present, through the greater part of the kingdom, cost half the price which they used to do thirty or forty years ago. The same thing may be said of turnips, carrots, cabbages; things which were formerly never raised but by the spade, but which are now commonly raised by the plough. All sort of garden stuff too has become cheaper. The greater part of the apples and even of the onions consumed in Great Britain were in the last century imported from Flanders. The great improvements in the coarser manufactures of both linen and woollen cloth furnish the labourers with cheaper and better cloathing; and those in the manufactures of the coarser metals, with cheaper and better instruments of trade, as well as with many agreeable and convenient pieces of household furniture. Soap, salt, candles, leather, and fermented liquors, have, indeed, become a good deal dearer; chiefly from the taxes which have been laid upon them. The quantity of these, however, which the labouring poor are under any necessity of consuming, is so very small, that the increase in their price does not compensate the diminution in that of so many other things. The common complaint that luxury extends itself even to the lowest ranks of the people, and that the labouring poor will not now be contented with the same food, cloathing and lodging which satisfied them in former times, may convince us that it is not the money price of labour only, but its real recompence, which has augmented.

Is this improvement in the circumstances of the lower ranks of the people to be regarded as an advantage or as an inconveniency to the society? The answer seems at first sight abundantly plain. Servants, labourers and workmen of different kinds, make up the far greater part of every great political society. But what improves the circumstances of the greater part can never be regarded as an inconveniency to the whole. No society can surely be flourishing and happy, of which the far greater part of the members are poor and miserable. It is but equity, besides, that they who feed, cloath and lodge the whole body of the people, should have such a share of the produce of their own labour as to be themselves tolerably well fed, cloathed and lodged.

Poverty, though it no doubt discourages, does not always prevent marriage. It seems even to be favourable to generation. A half-starved Highland woman frequently bears more than twenty children, while a pampered fine lady is often incapable of bearing any, and is generally exhausted by two or three. Barrenness, so frequent among women of fashion, is very rare among those of inferior station. Luxury in the fair sex, while it inflames perhaps the passion for enjoyment, seems always to weaken, and frequently to destroy altogether, the powers of generation.

But poverty, though it does not prevent the generation, is extremely unfavourable to the rearing of children. The tender plant is produced, but in so cold a soil, and so severe a climate, soon withers and dies. It is not uncommon, I have been frequently told, in the Highlands of Scotland for a mother who has borne twenty children not to have two alive. Several officers of great experience have assured me, that so far from recruiting their regiment, they have never been able to supply it with drums and fifes from all the soldiers' children that were born in it. A greater number of fine children, however, is seldom seen any where than about a barrack of soldiers. Very few of them, it seems, arrive at the age of thirteen or fourteen. In some places one half the children born die before they are four years of age; in many places before they are seven; and in almost all places before they are nine or ten. This great mortality, however, will every where be found chiefly among the children of the common people, who cannot afford to tend them with the same care as those of better station. Though their marriages are generally more fruitful than those of people of fashion, a smaller proportion of their children arrive at maturity. In foundling hospitals, and among the children brought up by parish charities, the mortality is still greater than among those of the common people.

Every species of animals naturally multiplies in proportion to the means of their subsistence, and no species can ever multiply beyond it. But in civilized society it is only among the inferior ranks of people that the scantiness of subsistence can set limits to the further multiplication of the human species; and it can do so in no other way than by destroying a great part of the children which their fruitful marriages produce.

The liberal reward of labour, by enabling them to provide better for their children, and consequently to bring up a greater number, naturally tends to widen and extend those limits. It deserves to be remarked too, that it necessarily does this as nearly as possible in the proportion which the demand for labour requires. If this demand is continually increasing, the reward of labour must necessarily encourage in such a manner the marriage and multiplication of labourers, as may enable them to supply that continually increasing demand by a continually increasing population. If the reward should at any time be less than what was requisite for this purpose, the deficiency of hands would soon raise it; and if it should at any time be more, their excessive multiplication would soon lower it to this necessary rate. The market would be so much under-stocked with labour in the one case, and so much over-stocked in the other, as would soon force back its price to that proper rate which the circumstances of the society required. It is in this manner that the demand for men, like that for any other commodity, necessarily regulates the production of men; quickens it when it goes on too slowly, and stops it when it advances too fast. It is this demand which regulates and determines the state of propagation in all the different countries of the world, in North America, in Europe, and in China; which renders it rapidly progressive in the first, slow and gradual in the second, and altogether stationary in the last.

The wear and tear of a slave, it has been said, is at the expence of his master; but that of a free servant is at his own expence. The wear and tear of the latter, however, is, in reality, as much at the expence of his master as that of the former. The wages paid to journeymen and servants of every kind must be such as may enable them, one with another, to continue the race of journeymen and servants, according as the increasing, diminishing, or stationary demand of the society may happen to require. But though the wear and tear of a free servant be equally at the expence of his master, it generally costs him much less than that of a slave. The fund destined for replacing or repairing, if I may say so, the wear and tear of the slave, is commonly managed by a negligent master or careless overseer. That destined for performing the same office with regard to the free man, is managed by the free man himself. The disorders which generally prevail in the economy of the rich, naturally introduce themselves into the management of the former: The strict frugality and parsimonious attention of the poor as naturally establish themselves in that of the latter. Under such different management, the same purpose must require very different degrees of expence to execute it. It appears, accordingly, from the experience of all ages and nations, I believe, that the work done by freemen comes cheaper in the end than that performed by slaves. It is found to do so even at Boston, New York, and Philadelphia, where the wages of common labour are so very high.

The liberal reward of labour, therefore, as it is the effect of increasing wealth, so it is the cause of increasing population. To complain of it, is to lament over the necessary effect and cause of the greatest public prosperity.

It deserves to be remarked, perhaps, that it is in the progressive state, while the society is advancing to the further acquisition, rather than when it has acquired its full complement of riches, that the condition of the labouring poor, of the great body of the people, seems to be the happiest and the most comfortable. It is hard in the stationary, and miserable in the declining state. The progressive state is in reality the cheerful and the hearty state to all the different orders of the society. The stationary is dull; the declining melancholy.

The liberal reward of labour, as it encourages the propagation, so it increases the industry of the common people. The wages of labour are the encouragement of industry, which, like every other human quality, improves in proportion to the encouragement it receives. A plentiful subsistence increases the bodily strength of the labourer, and the comfortable hope of bettering his condition, and of ending his days perhaps in ease and plenty, animates him to exert that strength to the utmost. Where wages are high, accordingly, we shall always find the workmen more active, diligent, and expeditious, than where they are low; in England, for example, than in Scotland; in the neighbourhood of great towns, than in remote country places. Some workmen, indeed, when they can earn in four days what will maintain them through the week, will be idle the other three. This, however, is by no means the case with the greater part. Workmen, on the contrary, when they are liberally paid by the piece, are very apt to over-work themselves, and to ruin their health and constitution in a few years. A carpenter in London, and in some other places, is not supposed to last in his utmost vigour above eight years. Something of the same kind happens in many other trades, in which the workmen are paid by the piece; as they generally are in manufactures, and even in country labour, wherever wages are higher than ordinary. Almost every class of artificers is subject to some peculiar infirmity occasioned by excessive application to their peculiar species of work. Ramuzzini, an eminent Italian physician, has written a particular book concerning such diseases. We do not reckon our soldiers the most industrious set of people among us. Yet when soldiers have been employed in some particular sorts of work, and liberally paid by the piece, their officers have frequently been obliged to stipulate with the undertaker, that they should not be allowed to earn above a certain sum every day, according to the rate at which they were paid. Till this stipulation was made, mutual emulation and the desire of greater gain, frequently prompted them to over-work themselves, and to hurt their health by excessive labour. Excessive application during four days of the week, is frequently the real cause of the idleness of the other three, so much and so loudly complained of. Great labour, either of mind or body, continued for several days together, is in most men naturally followed by a great desire of relaxation, which, if not restrained by force or by some strong necessity, is almost irresistible. It is the call of nature, which requires to be relieved by some indulgence, sometimes of ease only, but sometimes too of dissipation and diversion. If it is not complied with, the consequences are often dangerous, and sometimes fatal, and such as almost always, sooner or later, bring on the peculiar infirmity of the trade. If masters would always listen to the dictates of reason and humanity, they have frequently occasion rather to moderate, than to animate the application of many of their workmen. It will be found, I believe, in every sort of trade, that the man who works so moderately, as to be able to work constantly, not only preserves his health the longest, but, in the course of the year, executes the greatest quantity of work.

BOOK IV
Of Systems of Political Economy

INTRODUCTION

Political economy, considered as a branch of the science of a statesman or legislator, proposes two distinct objects: first, to provide a plentiful revenue or subsistence for the people, or more properly to enable them to provide such a revenue or subsistence for themselves; and secondly, to supply the state or commonwealth with a revenue sufficient for the public services. It proposes to enrich both the people and the sovereign.

CHAPTER II · OF RESTRAINTS UPON THE IMPORTATION FROM FOREIGN COUNTRIES OF SUCH GOODS AS CAN BE PRODUCED AT HOME

The general industry of the society never can exceed what the capital of the society can employ. As the number of workmen that can be kept in employment by any particular person must bear a certain proportion to his capital, so the number of those that can be continually employed by all the members of a great society, must bear a certain proportion to the whole capital of that society, and never can exceed that proportion. No regulation of commerce can increase the quantity of industry in any society beyond what its capital can maintain. It can only divert a part of it into a direction into which it might not otherwise have gone; and it is by no means certain that this artificial direction is likely to be more advantageous to the society than that into which it would have gone of its own accord.

Every individual is continually exerting himself to find out the most advantageous employment for whatever capital he can command. It is his own advantage, indeed, and not that of the society, which he has in view. But the study of his own advantage naturally, or rather necessarily leads him to prefer that employment which is most advantageous to the society.

First, every individual endeavours to employ his capital as near home as he can, and consequently as much as he can in the support of domestic industry; provided always that he can thereby obtain the ordinary, or not a great deal less than the ordinary profits of stock.

Thus, upon equal or nearly equal profits, every wholesale merchant naturally prefers the home-trade to the foreign trade of consumption, and the foreign trade of consumption to the carrying trade. In the home-trade his capital is never so long out of his sight as it frequently is in the foreign trade of consumption. He can know better the character and situation of the persons whom he trusts, and if he should happen to be deceived, he knows better the laws of the country from which he must seek redress. In the carrying trade, the capital of the merchant is, as it were, divided between two foreign countries, and no part of it is ever necessarily brought home, or placed under his own immediate view and command. The capital which an Amsterdam merchant employs in carrying corn from Konnigsberg to Lisbon, and fruit and wine from Lisbon to Konnigsberg, must generally be the one-half of it at Konnigsberg and the other half at Lisbon. No part of it need ever come to Amsterdam. The natural residence of such a merchant should either be at Konnigsberg or Lisbon, and it can only be some very particular circumstances which can make him prefer the residence of Amsterdam. The uneasiness, however, which he feels at being separated so far from his capital, generally determines him to bring part both of the Konnigsberg goods which he destines for the market of Lisbon, and of the Lisbon goods which he destines for that of Konnigsberg, to Amsterdam: and though this necessarily subjects him to a double charge of loading and unloading, as well as to the payment of some duties and customs, yet for the sake of having some part of his capital always under his own view and command, he willingly submits to this extraordinary charge; and it is in this manner that every country which has any considerable share of the carrying trade, becomes always the emporium, or general market, for the goods of all the different countries whose trade it carries on. The merchant, in order to save a second loading and unloading, endeavours always to sell in the home-market as much of the goods of all those different countries as he can, and thus, so far as he can, to convert his carrying trade into a foreign trade of consumption. A merchant, in the same manner, who is engaged in the foreign trade of consumption, when he collects goods for foreign markets, will always be glad, upon equal or nearly equal profits, to sell as great a part of them at home as he can. He saves himself the risk and trouble of exportation, when, so far as he can, he thus converts his foreign trade of consumption into a home-trade. Home is in this manner the center, if I may say so, round which the capitals of the inhabitants of every country are continually circulating, and towards which they are always tending, though by particular causes they may sometimes be driven off and repelled from it towards more distant employments. But a capital employed in the home-trade, it has already been shown, necessarily puts into motion a greater quantity of domestic industry, and gives revenue and employment to a greater number of the inhabitants of the country, than an equal capital employed in the foreign trade of consumption: and one employed in the foreign trade of consumption has the same advantage over an equal capital employed in the carrying trade. Upon equal, or only nearly equal profits, therefore, every individual naturally inclines to employ his capital in the manner in which it is likely to afford the greatest support to domestic industry, and to give revenue and employment to the greatest number of people of his own country.

Secondly, every individual who employs his capital in the support of domestic industry, necessarily endeavours so to direct that industry, that its produce may be of the greatest possible value.

The produce of industry is what it adds to the subject or materials upon which it is employed. In proportion as the value of this produce is great or small, so will likewise be the profits of the employer. But it is only for the sake of profit that any man employs a capital in the support of industry; and he will always, therefore, endeavour to employ it in the support of that industry of which the produce is likely to be of the greatest value, or to exchange for the greatest quantity either of money or of other goods.

But the annual revenue of every society is always precisely equal to the exchangeable value of the whole annual produce of its industry, or rather is precisely the same thing with that exchangeable value. As every individual, therefore, endeavours as much as he can both to employ his capital in the support of domestic industry, and so to direct that industry that its produce may be of the greatest value; every individual necessarily labours to render the annual revenue of the society as great as he can. He generally, indeed, neither intends to promote the public interest, nor knows how much he is promoting it. By preferring the support of domestic to that of foreign industry, he intends only his own security; and by directing that industry in such a manner as its produce may be of the greatest value, he intends only his own gain, and he is in this, as in many other cases, led by an invisible hand to promote an end which was no part of his intention. Nor is it always the worse for the society that it was no part of it. By pursuing his own interest he frequently promotes that of the society more effectually than when he really intends to promote it. I have never known much good done by those who affected to trade for the public good. It is an affectation, indeed, not very common among merchants, and very few words need be employed in dissuading them from it.

What is the species of domestic industry which his capital can employ, and of which the produce is likely to be of the greatest value, every individual, it is evident, can, in his local situation, judge much better than any statesman or lawgiver can do for him. The statesman, who should attempt to direct private people in what manner they ought to employ their capitals, would not only load himself with a most unnecessary attention, but assume an authority which could safely be trusted, not only to no single person, but to no council or senate whatever, and which would no-where be so dangerous as in the hands of a man who had folly and presumption enough to fancy himself fit to exercise it.

To give the monopoly of the home-market to the produce of domestic industry, in any particular art or manufacture, is in some measure to direct private people in what manner they ought to employ their capitals, and must, in almost all cases, be either a useless or a hurtful regulation. If the produce of domestic can be brought there as cheap as that of foreign industry, the regulation is evidently useless. If it cannot, it must generally be hurtful. It is the maxim of every prudent master of a family, never to attempt to make at home what it will cost him more to make than to buy. The taylor does not attempt to make his own shoes, but buys them of the shoemaker. The shoemaker does not attempt to make his own clothes, but employs a taylor. The farmer attempts to make neither the one nor the other, but employs those different artificers. All of them find it for their interest to employ their whole industry in a way in which they have some advantage over their neighbours, and to purchase with a part of its produce, or what is the same thing, with the price of a part of it, whatever else they have occasion for.

What is prudence in the conduct of every private family, can scarce be folly in that of a great kingdom. If a foreign country can supply us with a commodity cheaper than we ourselves can make it, better buy it of them with some part of the produce of our own industry, employed in a way in which we have some advantage. The general industry of the country, being always in proportion to the capital which employs it, will not thereby be diminished, no more than that of the above-mentioned artificers; but only left to find out the way in which it can be employed with the greatest advantage. It is certainly not employed to the greatest advantage, when it is thus directed towards an object which it can buy cheaper than it can make. The value of its annual produce is certainly more or less diminished, when it is thus turned away from producing commodities evidently of more value than the commodity which it is directed to produce. According to the supposition, that commodity could be purchased from foreign countries cheaper than it can be made at home. It could, therefore, have been purchased with a part only of the commodities, or, what is the same thing, with a part only of the price of the commodities, which the industry employed by an equal capital would have produced at home, had it been left to follow its natural course. The industry of the country, therefore, is thus turned away from a more, to a less advantageous employment, and the exchangeable value of its annual produce, instead of being increased, according to the intention of the lawgiver, must necessarily be diminished by every such regulation. . . .

CHAPTER III · OF THE EXTRAORDINARY RESTRAINTS UPON THE IMPORTATION OF GOODS OF ALMOST ALL KINDS . . .

. . . No goods are sent abroad but those for which the demand is supposed to be greater abroad than at home, and of which the returns consequently, it is expected, will be of more value at home than the commodities exported. If the tobacco which, in England, is worth only a hundred thousand pounds, when sent to France will purchase wine which is, in England, worth a hundred and ten thousand pounds, the exchange will augment the capital of England by ten thousand pounds. If a hundred thousand pounds of English gold, in the same manner, purchase French wine, which, in England, is worth a hundred and ten thousand, this exchange will equally augment the capital of England by ten thousand pounds. As a merchant who has a hundred and ten thousand pounds' worth of wine in his cellar, is a richer man than he who has only a hundred thousand pounds' worth of tobacco in his warehouse, so is he likewise a richer man than he who has only a hundred thousand pounds' worth of gold in his coffers. He can put into motion a greater quantity of industry, and give revenue, maintenance, and employment, to a greater number of people than either of the other two. But the capital of the country is equal to the capitals of all its different inhabitants, and the quantity of industry which can be annually maintained in it, is equal to what all those different capitals can maintain. Both the capital of the country, therefore, and the quantity of industry which can be annually maintained in it, must generally be augmented by this exchange. It would, indeed, be more advantageous for England that it could purchase the wines of France with its own hard-ware and broad-cloth, than with either the tobacco of Virginia, or the gold and silver of Brazil and Peru. A direct foreign trade of consumption is always more advantageous than a round-about one. But a round-about foreign trade of consumption, which is carried on with gold and silver, does not seem to be less advantageous than any other equally round-about one. Neither is a country which has no mines, more likely to be exhausted of gold and silver by this annual exportation of those metals, than one which does not grow tobacco by the like annual exportation of that plant. As a country which has wherewithal to buy tobacco will never be long in want of it, so neither will one be long in want of gold and silver which has wherewithal to purchase those metals.

It is a losing trade, it is said, which a workman carries on with the alehouse; and the trade which a manufacturing nation would naturally carry on with a wine country, may be considered as a trade of the same nature. I answer, that the trade with the alehouse is not necessarily a losing trade. In its own nature it is just as advantageous as any other, though, perhaps, somewhat more liable to be abused. The employment of a brewer, and even that of a retailer of fermented liquors, are as necessary divisions of labour as any other. It will generally be more advantageous for a workman to buy of the brewer the quantity he has occasion for, than to brew it himself, and if he is a poor workman, it will generally be more advantageous for him to buy it, by little and little, of the retailer, than a large quantity of the brewer. He may no doubt buy too much of either, as he may of any other dealers in his neighbourhood, of the butcher, if he is a glutton, or of the draper, if he affects to be a beau among his companions. It is advantageous to the great body of workmen, notwithstanding, that all these trades should be free, though this freedom may be abused in all of them, and is more likely to be so, perhaps, in some than in others. Though individuals, besides, may sometimes ruin their fortunes by an excessive consumption of fermented liquors, there seems to be no risk that a nation should do so. Though in every country there are many people who spend upon such liquors more than they can afford, there are always many more who spend less. It deserves to be remarked too, that, if we consult experience, the cheapness of wine seems to be a cause, not of drunkenness, but of sobriety. The inhabitants of the wine countries are in general the soberest people in Europe; witness the Spaniards, the Italians, and the inhabitants of the southern provinces of France. People are seldom guilty of excess in what is their daily fare. Nobody affects the character of liberality and good fellowship, by being profuse of a liquor which is as cheap as small beer. On the contrary, in the countries which, either from excessive heat or cold, produce no grapes, and where wine consequently is dear and a rarity, drunkenness is a common vice, as among the northern nations, and all those who live between the tropics, the negroes, for example, on the coast of Guinea. When a French regiment comes from some of the northern provinces of France, where wine is somewhat dear, to be quartered in the southern, where it is very cheap, the soldiers, I have frequently heard it observed, are at first debauched by the cheapness and novelty of good wine; but after a few months' residence, the greater part of them become as sober as the rest of the inhabitants. Were the duties upon foreign wines, and the excises upon malt, beer, and ale, to be taken away all at once, it might, in the same manner, occasion in Great Britain a pretty general and temporary drunkenness among the middling and inferior ranks of people, which would probably be soon followed by a permanent and almost universal sobriety. At present drunkenness is by no means the vice of people of fashion, or of those who can easily afford the most expensive liquors. A gentleman drunk with ale, has scarce ever been seen among us. The restraints upon the wine trade in Great Britain, besides, do not so much seem calculated to hinder the people from going, if I may say so, to the alehouse, as from going where they can buy the best and cheapest liquor. They favour the wine trade of Portugal, and discourage that of France. The Portuguese, it is said, indeed, are better customers for our manufactures than the French, and should therefore be encouraged in preference to them. As they give us their custom, it is pretended, we should give them ours. The sneaking arts of underling tradesmen are thus erected into political maxims for the conduct of a great empire; for it is the most underling tradesmen only who make it a rule to employ chiefly their own customers. A great trader purchases his goods always where they are cheapest and best, without regard to any little interest of this kind.

By such maxims as these, however, nations have been taught that their interest consisted in beggaring all their neighbours. Each nation has been made to look with an invidious eye upon the prosperity of all the nations with which it trades, and to consider their gain as its own loss. Commerce, which ought naturally to be, among nations, as among individuals, a bond of union and friendship, has become the most fertile source of discord and animosity. The capricious ambition of kings and ministers has not, during the present and the preceding century, been more fatal to the repose of Europe, than the impertinent jealousy of merchants and manufacturers. The violence and injustice of the rulers of mankind is an ancient evil, for which, I am afraid, the nature of human affairs can scarce admit of a remedy. But the mean rapacity, the monopolizing spirit of merchants and manufacturers, who neither are, nor ought to be, the rulers of mankind, though it cannot perhaps be corrected, may very easily be prevented from disturbing the tranquillity of any body but themselves.

That it was the spirit of monopoly which originally both invented and propagated this doctrine, cannot be doubted; and they who first taught it were by no means such fools as they who believed it. In every country it always is and must be the interest of the great body of the people to buy whatever they want of those who sell it cheapest. The proposition is so very manifest, that it seems ridiculous to take any pains to prove it; nor could it ever have been called in question, had not the interested sophistry of merchants and manufacturers confounded the common sense of mankind. Their interest is, in this respect, directly opposite to that of the great body of the people. As it is the interest of the freemen of a corporation to hinder the rest of the inhabitants from employing any workmen but themselves, so it is the interest of the merchants and manufacturers of every country to secure to themselves the monopoly of the home-market. Hence in Great Britain, and in most other European countries, the extraordinary duties upon almost all goods imported by alien merchants. Hence the high duties and prohibitions upon all those foreign manufactures which can come into competition with our own. Hence too the extraordinary restraints upon the importation of almost all sorts of goods from those countries with which the balance of trade is supposed to be disadvantageous; that is, from those against whom national animosity happens to be most violently inflamed.

The wealth of a neighbouring nation, however, though dangerous in war and politics, is certainly advantageous in trade. In a state of hostility it may enable our enemies to maintain fleets and armies superior to our own; but in a state of peace and commerce it must likewise enable them to exchange with us to a greater value, and to afford a better market, either for the immediate produce of our own industry, or for whatever is purchased with that produce. As a rich man is likely to be a better customer to the industrious people in his neighbourhood, than a poor, so is likewise a rich nation. A rich man, indeed, who is himself a manufacturer, is a very dangerous neighbour to all those who deal in the same way. All the rest of the neighbourhood, however, by far the greatest number, profit by the good market which his expence affords them. They even profit by his underselling the poorer workmen who deal in the same way with him. The manufacturers of a rich nation, in the same manner, may no doubt be very dangerous rivals to those of their neighbours. This very competition, however, is advantageous to the great body of the people, who profit greatly besides by the good market which the great expence of such a nation affords them in every other way. Private people who want to make a fortune, never think of retiring to the remote and poor provinces of the country, but resort either to the capital, or to some of the great commercial towns. They know, that, where little wealth circulates, there is little to be got, but that where a great deal is in motion, some share of it may fall to them. The same maxims which would in this manner direct the common sense of one, or ten, or twenty individuals, should regulate the judgment of one, or ten, or twenty millions, and should make a whole nation regard the riches of its neighbours, as a probable cause and occasion for itself to acquire riches. A nation that would enrich itself by foreign trade, is certainly most likely to do so when its neighbours are all rich, industrious, and commercial nations. A great nation surrounded on all sides by wandering savages and poor barbarians might, no doubt, acquire riches by the cultivation of its own lands, and by its own interior commerce, but not by foreign trade. It seems to have been in this manner that the ancient Egyptians and the modern Chinese acquired their great wealth. The ancient Egyptians, it is said, neglected foreign commerce, and the modern Chinese, it is known, hold it in the utmost contempt, and scarce deign to afford it the decent protection of the laws. The modern maxims of foreign commerce, by aiming at the impoverishment of all our neighbours, so far as they are capable of producing their intended effect, tend to render that very commerce insignificant and contemptible.

It is in consequence of these maxims that the commerce between France and England has in both countries been subjected to so many discouragements and restraints. If those two countries, however, were to consider their real interest, without either mercantile jealousy or national animosity, the commerce of France might be more advantageous to Great Britain than that of any other country, and for the same reason that of Great Britain to France. France is the nearest neighbour to Great Britain. In the trade between the southern coast of England and the northern and north-western coasts of France, the returns might be expected, in the same manner as in the inland trade, four, five, or six times in the year. The capital, therefore, employed in this trade, could in each of the two countries keep in motion four, five, or six times the quantity of industry, and afford employment and subsistence to four, five, or six times the number of people, which an equal capital could do in the greater part of the other branches of foreign trade. Between the parts of France and Great Britain most remote from one another, the returns might be expected, at least, once in the year, and even this trade would so far be at least equally advantageous as the greater part of the other branches of our foreign European trade. It would be, at least, three times more advantageous, than the boasted trade with our North American colonies, in which the returns were seldom made in less than three years, frequently not in less than four or five years. France, besides, is supposed to contain twenty-four millions of inhabitants. Our North American colonies were never supposed to contain more than three millions: And France is a much richer country than North America; though, on account of the more unequal distribution of riches, there is much more poverty and beggary in the one country, than in the other. France therefore could afford a market at least eight times more extensive, and, on account of the superior frequency of the returns, four and twenty times more advantageous, than that which our North American colonies ever afforded. The trade of Great Britain would be just as advantageous to France, and, in proportion to the wealth, population and proximity of the respective countries, would have the same superiority over that which France carries on with her own colonies. Such is the very great difference between that trade which the wisdom of both nations has thought proper to discourage, and that which it has favoured the most.

But the very same circumstances which would have rendered an open and free commerce between the two countries so advantageous to both, have occasioned the principal obstructions to that commerce. Being neighbours, they are necessarily enemies, and the wealth and power of each becomes, upon that account, more formidable to the other; and what would increase the advantage of national friendship, serves only to inflame the violence of national animosity. They are both rich and industrious nations; and the merchants and manufacturers of each, dread the competition of the skill and activity of those of the other. Mercantile jealousy is excited, and both inflames, and is itself inflamed, by the violence of national animosity: And the traders of both countries have announced, with all the passionate confidence of interested falsehood, the certain ruin of each, in consequence of that unfavourable balance of trade, which, they pretend, would be the infallible effect of an unrestrained commerce with the other.

There is no commercial country in Europe of which the approaching ruin has not frequently been foretold by the pretended doctors of this system, from an unfavourable balance of trade. After all the anxiety, however, which they have excited about this, after all the vain attempts of almost all trading nations to turn that balance in their own favour and against their neighbours, it does not appear that any one nation in Europe has been in any respect impoverished by this cause. Every town and country, on the contrary, in proportion as they have opened their ports to all nations, instead of being ruined by this free trade, as the principles of the commercial system would lead us to expect, have been enriched by it. Though there are in Europe, indeed, a few towns which in some respects deserve the name of free ports, there is no country which does so. Holland, perhaps, approaches the nearest to this character of any, though still very remote from it; and Holland, it is acknowledged, not only derives its whole wealth, but a great part of its necessary subsistence, from foreign trade.

There is another balance, indeed, which has already been explained, very different from the balance of trade, and which, according as it happens to be either favourable or unfavourable, necessarily occasions the prosperity or decay of every nation. This is the balance of the annual produce and consumption. If the exchangeable value of the annual produce, it has already been observed, exceeds that of the annual consumption, the capital of the society must annually increase in proportion to this excess. The society in this case lives within its revenue, and what is annually saved out of its revenue, is naturally added to its capital, and employed so as to increase still further the annual produce. If the exchangeable value of the annual produce, on the contrary, fall short of the annual consumption, the capital of the society must annually decay in proportion to this deficiency. The expence of the society in this case exceeds its revenue, and necessarily encroaches upon its capital. Its capital, therefore, must necessarily decay, and, together with it, the exchangeable value of the annual produce of its industry.

This balance of produce and consumption is entirely different from, what is called, the balance of trade. It might take place in a nation which had no foreign trade, but which was entirely separated from all the world. It may take place in the whole globe of the earth, of which the wealth, population, and improvement may be either gradually increasing or gradually decaying.

The balance of produce and consumption may be constantly in favour of a nation, though what is called the balance of trade be generally against it. A nation may import to a greater value than it exports for half a century, perhaps, together; the gold and silver which comes into it during all this time may be all immediately sent out of it; its circulating coin may gradually decay, different sorts of paper money being substituted in its place, and even the debts too which it contracts in the principal nations with whom it deals, may be gradually increasing; and yet its real wealth, the exchangeable value of the annual produce of its lands and labour, may, during the same period, have been increasing in a much greater proportion. The state of our North American colonies, and of the trade which they carried on with Great Britain, before the commencement of the present disturbances, may serve as a proof that this is by no means an impossible supposition.

BOOK V
Of the Revenue of the Sovereign or Commonwealth

CHAPTER I · OF THE EXPENCES OF THE SOVEREIGN OR COMMONWEALTH

. . . It is in the age of shepherds, in the second period of society, that the inequality of fortune first begins to take place, and introduces among men a degree of authority and subordination which could not possibly exist before. It thereby introduces some degree of that civil government which is indispensably necessary for its own preservation: and it seems to do this naturally, and even independent of the consideration of that necessity. The consideration of that necessity comes no doubt afterwards to contribute very much to maintain and secure that authority and subordination. The rich, in particular, are necessarily interested to support that order of things, which can alone secure them in the possession of their own advantages. Men of inferior wealth combine to defend those of superior wealth in the possession of their property, in order that men of superior wealth may combine to defend them in the possession of theirs. All the inferior shepherds and herdsmen feel that the security of their own herds and flocks depends upon the security of those of the great shepherd or herdsman; that the maintenance of their lesser authority depends upon that of his greater authority, and that upon their subordination to him depends his power of keeping their inferiors in subordination to them. They constitute a sort of little nobility, who feel themselves interested to defend the property and to support the authority of their own little sovereign, in order that he may be able to defend their property and to support their authority. Civil government, so far as it is instituted for the security of property, is in reality instituted for the defence of the rich against the poor, or of those who have some property against those who have none at all. . . .

. . . There are no public institutions for the education of women, and there is accordingly nothing useless, absurd, or fantastical in the common course of their education. They are taught what their parents or guardians judge it necessary or useful for them to learn; and they are taught nothing else. Every part of their education tends evidently to some useful purpose; either to improve the natural attractions of their person, or to form their mind to reserve, to modesty, to chastity, and to economy; to render them both likely to become the mistresses of a family, and to behave properly when they have become such. In every part of her life a woman feels some conveniency or advantage from every part of her education. It seldom happens that a man, in any part of his life, derives any conveniency or advantage from some of the most laborious and troublesome parts of his education.

Ought the public, therefore, to give no attention, it may be asked, to the education of the people? Or if it ought to give any, what are the different parts of education which it ought to attend to in the different orders of the people? and in what manner ought it to attend to them?

In some cases the state of the society necessarily places the greater part of individuals in such situations as naturally form in them, without any attention of government, almost all the abilities and virtues which that state requires, or perhaps can admit of. In other cases the state of the society does not place the greater part of individuals in such situations, and some attention of government is necessary in order to prevent the almost entire corruption and degeneracy of the great body of the people.

In the progress of the division of labour, the employment of the far greater part of those who live by labour, that is, of the great body of the people, comes to be confined to a few very simple operations, frequently to one or two. But the understandings of the greater part of men are necessarily formed by their ordinary employments. The man whose whole life is spent in performing a few simple operations, of which the effects too are, perhaps, always the same, or very nearly the same, has no occasion to exert his understanding, or to exercise his invention in finding out expedients for removing difficulties which never occur. He naturally loses, therefore, the habit of such exertion, and generally becomes as stupid and ignorant as it is possible for a human creature to become. The torpor of his mind renders him, not only incapable of relishing or bearing a part in any rational conversation, but of conceiving any generous, noble, or tender sentiment, and consequently of forming any just judgment concerning many even of the ordinary duties of private life. Of the great and extensive interests of his country he is altogether incapable of judging; and unless very particular pains have been taken to render him otherwise, he is equally incapable of defending his country in war. The uniformity of his stationary life naturally corrupts the courage of his mind, and makes him regard with abhorrence the irregular, uncertain, and adventurous life of a soldier. It corrupts even the activity of his body, and renders him incapable of exerting his strength with vigour and perseverance, in any other employment than that to which he has been bred. His dexterity at his own particular trade seems, in this manner, to be acquired at the expence of his intellectual, social, and martial virtues. But in every improved and civilized society this is the state into which the labouring poor, that is, the great body of the people, must necessarily fall, unless government takes some pains to prevent it.

It is otherwise in the barbarous societies, as they are commonly called, of hunters, of shepherds, and even of husbandmen in that rude state of husbandry which precedes the improvement of manufactures, and the extension of foreign commerce. In such societies the varied occupations of every man oblige every man to exert his capacity, and to invent expedients for removing difficulties which are continually occurring. Invention is kept alive, and the mind is not suffered to fall into that drowsy stupidity, which, in a civilized society, seems to benumb the understanding of almost all the inferior ranks of people. In those barbarous societies, as they are called, every man, it has already been observed, is a warrior. Every man too is in some measure a statesman, and can form a tolerable judgment concerning the interest of the society, and the conduct of those who govern it. How far their chiefs are good judges in peace, or good leaders in war, is obvious to the observation of almost every single man among them. In such a society indeed, no man can well acquire that improved and refined understanding, which a few men sometimes possess in a more civilized state. Though in a rude society there is a good deal of variety in the occupations of every individual, there is not a great deal in those of the whole society. Every man does, or is capable of doing, almost every thing which any other man does, or is capable of doing. Every man has a considerable degree of knowledge, ingenuity, and invention; but scarce any man has a great degree. The degree, however, which is commonly possessed, is generally sufficient for conducting the whole simple business of the society. . . .

FURTHER READING

C. R. Fay, *Adam Smith and the Scotland of His Day* (1956). A useful study.

William Letwin, *The Origins of Scientific Economics: English Economic Thought 1660–1776* (1963). A very interesting history of Adam Smith's precursors.

Ronald L. Meek, *The Economics of Physiocracy* (1962). A thoughtful collection of publications by a school of economists that lack of space alone kept me from including here; Meek's introduction is splendidly informative.

Glenn R. Morrow, *The Ethical and Economic Theories of Adam Smith: A Study in the Social Philosophy of the Eighteenth Century* (1923). A trenchant critique of the German inclination to create intellectual problems—here the supposed contradictions between the *Theory of Moral Sentiments* and *The Wealth of Nations*.

Eugene Rotwein, *David Hume: Writings on Economics* (1955). A handy anthology complete with long, good introduction.

Jacob Viner, *The Long View and the Short: Studies in Economic Theory and Policy* (1958). A collection of important articles, notably "Power versus Plenty as Objectives of Foreign Policy in the Seventeenth and Eighteenth Centuries" (pp. 277–305), and "Adam Smith and Laissez Faire" (pp. 213–45). Both essays will serve to change their readers' minds.

45 ❊ GIBBON

The Decline and Fall of the Roman Empire

[From Edward Gibbon, *The History of the
Decline and Fall of the Roman Empire,* edited
by J. B. Bury, 7 vols. (1896–1902), I, 1–11,
28–35, 53–66; IV, 160–69.]

*The contribution of the philosophes to the science of history has
been obscured by the denigration of their nineteenth-century successors. The nineteenth century was the age of historical classics; it
was the age of Ranke and Burckhardt, Taine and Mommsen, an
age that lavished the most refined scholarship, generous cross-
cultural empathy, and striking literary craftsmanship on the study
of the past; it was the age, finally, in which the craft of history
became a profession and was naturalized in the university. From its
perspective, the historians of the Age of the Enlightenment had
failed in two important respects: they had been too aggressive—
which is to say, inadequately historical—with their own Christian
past;* and they had refused to respect, let alone improve, the
scholarly foundations on which all reliable history must rest.*

*These charges are not baseless. It is true, first of all, that the
philosophes did not shed their hostility to "superstition and fanaticism" when they turned to history—though it must be added that
historical probity, sheer curiosity about the past, and love of variety
encouraged the philosophes to move, often enough, beyond the*

---

* A related charge was that the philosophe-historians could not appreciate
historical variety because they were crippled by their conception of a uniform
human nature. This charge, though familiar, will not withstand examination:
in the philosophes' view, this single human nature was capable of the most
enormous variety of expression.

limitations that their polemical intentions normally imposed on them. And it is true, secondly, that in their eagerness to escape the "pedantry" of seventeenth-century scholars they did little of that tedious but indispensable labor of gathering and evaluating raw materials—though it must be added, once again, that the philosophes disdained the pedants more than the results of their pedantry. They called for more and better archives, skeptically weighed improbable tales, and sought for the truth: they were, if not the producers, the consumers of scholarship.

These defects once admitted, the philosophes' historical work was nothing less than epoch-making, and their share in advancing the discipline nothing less than decisive. To summarize this share briefly: (1) The philosophes secularized historical causation. While around them pious chroniclers continued to see the hand of God in the affairs of man, the philosophes concentrated on the human and physical causes—religion, geography, power, the passions—for the true causes of events. This, though it seems obvious to us, was a radical step in a century in which the miraculous still served many as the universal cause. (2) The philosophes enormously enlarged the canvas of the historically interesting. Along with retaining respect for the intervention of God in history, Christian historians retained their concern for the history of a few individuals, nations, and institutions. Bossuet's "so-called Universal History," *Voltaire complained, was "nothing but the history of four or five peoples, and above all of the little Jewish nation, either ignored or justly despised by the rest of the world"*—and that history, though old (it had been published in 1681) retained its influence. It may be that the philosophes substituted for the parochialism of the Christians a parochialism of their own; but in including the histories of Asian peoples, paying new attention to secular events, and shifting their focus away from Biblical times, the philosophes vastly increased the size of their parish. (3) The philosophes found not only new historical nations, but new historical subjects; modern cultural history, with its interest in the arts, the economy, social life, the rise and fall of population, had its origins in eighteenth-century historical works, especially those of Voltaire. The philosophes' intentions were perhaps more far-ranging than their performance, but that performance, as Voltaire's* Essai sur les moeurs *demonstrates, was a striking improvement over the constricted horizons of their predecessors. And their intentions served as valuable pointers to what might yet be done: "A lock on a canal that joins the two seas, a*

---

* Quoted in J. H. Brumfitt, *Voltaire Historian* (1958) , 32.

painting by Poussin, a fine tragedy," wrote Voltaire, "are things a thousand times more precious than all the court annals and all the campaign reports put together." * Voltaire did not despise archives; on the contrary, he demanded their multiplication. But the questions that really interested him were questions like these: What was the strength of a country before a war and after it? Was Spain richer before the conquest of the New World or after? Why did the population of Amsterdam grow within two hundred years from twenty thousand to two hundred and forty thousand? Older historians had forgotten Terence's much-quoted saying, "I am a man; nothing human is alien to me"; none of them, Voltaire complained, "has taken for his motto,* Homo sum, humani nil a me alienum puto. *Yet it seems to me that one must skillfully incorporate this useful kind of knowledge into the tissue of events."†* If we put together these three contributions—secularization of historical cause, enlargement of the historical canvas, deepening of historical interest—they constitute nothing less than a revolution in historical writing, and a giant step toward the philosophes' own ideal: the science of history.*

To speak of history in the Enlightenment is to speak principally of four historians: Robertson, Hume, Voltaire, and Gibbon. William Robertson (1721–93), Scot, friend of Hume, rationalist cleric, and principal of the University of Edinburgh, wrote a number of remarkable histories, characterized by wide reading, diligent scholarship, and a deeper sympathy for the Christian Middle Ages than his fellow philosophes could muster. His History of Scotland During the Reigns of Queen Mary and King James VI, *which appeared in two volumes in 1759, was his first major work; but it is his* History of the Reign of Charles V *(three volumes, 1769) and his* History of the Discovery and Settlement of America *(two volumes, 1777) on which his fame rests. Hume's large-scale history of England, published in six volumes between 1754 and 1762, was far more controversial. Hume himself asserted that he had written a "Tory" history. But his political views served his search for true historical explanations. Earlier historians of England had denigrated the Stuarts, and treated the English past as a simple combat between the forces of freedom, represented by Parliament, and the forces of slavery, represented by such strong kings as Charles I. For Hume, life (and, hence, history) was not so simple, and his percep-*

---

* *Ibid.,* 46.

† *Nouvelles Considérations sur l'histoire,* in Voltaire, *Oeuvres historiques,* ed. René Pomeau (1957), 46–48.

tion of complexity, coupled with his unsurpassed style, made his voluminous work the standard history of England for almost a century. Voltaire, who greatly admired Hume, thought his History of England *"perhaps the best ever written in any language." And it was the best because it was so objective: "Mr. Hume, in his* History, *is neither parliamentarian, nor royalist, nor Anglican, nor Presbyterian—he is simply judicial."**

This, from Voltaire, was a remarkable tribute, for if anyone aspired to writing the best history anywhere, it was Voltaire himself. He came to history during his English stay in the late 1720s; the result was a biography of that quixotic king of Sweden, Charles XII, first published in 1731. It was brilliant but still conventional. Then, during his years with Madame du Châtelet, he began writing two other histories, both enormously ambitious. The first was the Siècle de Louis XIV *of 1751, written, as he said in the opening chapter, to paint not merely the life of a single man, but "the spirit of men in the most enlightened century that ever was." His other historical masterpiece, the* Essai sur les moeurs, *published in 1756, is equally far-ranging in subject matter, and far more far-ranging in time span: it goes back to the ancients. With Voltaire, history was elegant, fascinating, generally reliable; it was authentic history, but it was always history* en philosophe—*history that partook of the philosophes' mission to* écraser l'infâme.

The most philosophical of all the philosophe-historians was Edward Gibbon. But he was also, unlike the other philosophes, attuned to the most recondite scholarship of his day. He respected the "pedants" in the certainty that he would never be a pedant himself. How right he was, both in his respect and in his certainty, the following selections will make plain.†

CHAPTER I · THE EXTENT AND MILITARY FORCE OF THE EMPIRE IN THE AGE OF THE ANTONINES

In the second century of the Christian Era, the empire of Rome comprehended the fairest part of the earth, and the most civilized

---

* From a review of Hume's *History*, quoted in Ernest Campbell Mossner, *The Life of David Hume* (1954), 318.

† For a brief survey of his life and character, see above, pages 255-262.

portion of mankind. The frontiers of that extensive monarchy were guarded by ancient renown and disciplined valour. The gentle, but powerful, influence of laws and manners had gradually cemented the union of the provinces. Their peaceful inhabitants enjoyed and abused the advantages of wealth and luxury. The image of a free constitution was preserved with decent reverence. The Roman senate appeared to possess the sovereign authority, and devolved on the emperors all the executive powers of government. During a happy period of more than fourscore years, the public administration was conducted by the virtue and abilities of Nerva, Trajan, Hadrian, and the two Antonines. It is the design of this and of the two succeeding chapters, to describe the prosperous condition of their empire; and afterwards, from the death of Marcus Antoninus, to deduce the most important circumstances of its decline and fall: a revolution which will ever be remembered, and is still felt by the nations of the earth.

The principal conquests of the Romans were achieved under the republic; and the emperors, for the most part, were satisfied with preserving those dominions which had been acquired by the policy of the senate, the active emulation of the consuls, and the martial enthusiasm of the people. The seven first centuries were filled with a rapid succession of triumphs; but it was reserved for Augustus to relinquish the ambitious design of subduing the whole earth, and to introduce a spirit of moderation into the public councils. Inclined to peace by his temper and situation, it was easy for him to discover that Rome, in her present exalted situation, had much less to hope than to fear from the chance of arms; and that, in the prosecution of remote wars, the undertaking became every day more difficult, the event more doubtful, and the possession more precarious and less beneficial. The experience of Augustus added weight to these salutary reflections, and effectually convinced him that, by the prudent vigour of his counsels, it would be easy to secure every concession which the safety or the dignity of Rome might require from the most formidable barbarians. Instead of exposing his person and his legions to the arrows of the Parthians, he obtained, by an honourable treaty, the restitution of the standards and prisoners which had been taken in the defeat of Crassus.*

His generals, in the early part of his reign, attempted the reduc-

---

* Dion Cassius (l. liv. p. 736) with the annotations of Reimar, who has collected all that Roman vanity has left upon the subject. The marble of Ancyra, on which Augustus recorded his own exploits, asserts that *he compelled* the Parthians to restore the ensigns of Crassus.

tion of Ethiopia and Arabia Felix. They marched near a thousand miles to the south of the tropic; but the heat of the climate soon repelled the invaders and protected the unwarlike natives of those sequestered regions.* The northern countries of Europe scarcely deserved the expense and labour of conquest. The forests and morasses of Germany were filled with a hardy race of barbarians, who despised life when it was separated from freedom; and though, on the first attack, they seemed to yield to the weight of the Roman power, they soon, by a signal act of despair, regained their independence, and reminded Augustus of the vicissitude of fortune.† On the death of that emperor his testament was publicly read in the senate. He bequeathed, as a valuable legacy to his successors, the advice of confining the empire within those limits which nature seemed to have placed as its permanent bulwarks and boundaries: on the west the Atlantic ocean; the Rhine and Danube on the north; the Euphrates on the east; and towards the south the sandy deserts of Arabia and Africa.‡

Happily for the repose of mankind, the moderate system recommended by the wisdom of Augustus was adopted by the fears and vices of his immediate successors. Engaged in the pursuit of pleasure or in the exercise of tyranny, the first Caesars seldom showed themselves to the armies, or to the provinces; nor were they disposed to suffer that those triumphs which *their* indolence neglected should be usurped by the conduct and valour of their lieutenants. The military fame of a subject was considered as an insolent invasion of the Imperial prerogative; and it became the duty, as well as interest, of every Roman general, to guard the frontiers intrusted to his care, without aspiring to conquests which might have proved no less fatal to himself than to the vanquished barbarians.§

* Strabo (l. xvi. p. 780), Pliny the elder (Hist. Natur. l. vi. 32, 35) and Dion Cassius (l. liii. p. 723, and l. liv. p. 734) have left us very curious details concerning these wars. The Romans made themselves masters of Mariaba, or Merab, a city of Arabia Felix, well known to the Orientals (see Abulfeda and the Nubian geography, p. 52). They were arrived within three days' journey of the Spice country, the rich object of their invasion.

† By the slaughter of Varus and his three legions. See the first book of the Annals of Tacitus. Sueton. in August. c. 23, and Velleius Paterculus, l. ii. c. 117, &c. Augustus did not receive the melancholy news with all the temper and firmness that might have been expected from his character.

‡ Tacit. Annal. l, ii. Dion Cassius, l. lvi. p. 832, and the speech of Augustus himself, in Julian's Caesars. It receives great light from the learned notes of his French translator, M. Spanheim.

§ Germanicus, Suetonius Paulinus, and Agricola were checked and recalled in the course of their victories. Corbulo was put to death. Military merit, as it

The only accession which the Roman empire received during the first century of the Christian era was the province of Britain. In this single instance the successors of Caesar and Augustus were persuaded to follow the example of the former, rather than the precept of the latter. The proximity of its situation to the coast of Gaul seemed to invite their arms; the pleasing, though doubtful, intelligence of a pearl fishery attracted their avarice;* and as Britain was viewed in the light of a distinct and insulated world, the conquest scarcely formed any exception to the general system of continental measures. After a war of about forty years, undertaken by the most stupid,† maintained by the most dissolute, and terminated by the most timid of all the emperors, the far greater part of the island submitted to the Roman yoke.‡ The various tribes of Britons possessed valour without conduct, and the love of freedom without the spirit of union. They took up arms with savage fierceness, they laid them down, or turned them against each other, with wild inconstancy; and while they fought singly, they were successively subdued. Neither the fortitude of Caractacus, nor the despair of Boadicea, nor the fanaticism of the Druids, could avert the slavery of their country, or resist the steady progress of the Imperial generals, who maintained the national glory, when the throne was disgraced by the weakest or the most vicious of mankind. At the very time when Domitian, confined to his palace, felt the terrors which he inspired, his legions, under the command of the virtuous Agricola, defeated the collected force of the Caledonians at the foot of the Grampian hills; and his fleets, venturing to explore an unknown and dangerous navigation, displayed the Roman arms round every part of the island. The conquest of Britain was considered as already achieved; and it was the design of Agricola to complete and ensure his success by the easy reduction of Ireland, for

---

is admirably expressed by Tacitus, was, in the strictest sense of the word, *imperatoria virtus.*

* Caesar himself conceals that ignoble motive; but it is mentioned by Suetonius, c. 47. The British pearls proved, however, of little value, on account of their dark and livid colour. Tacitus observes, with reason (in Agricola, c. 12), that it was an inherent defect. "*Ego facilius crediderim, naturam margaritis deesse quam nobis avaritiam.*"

† Claudius, Nero, and Domitian. A hope is expressed by Pomponius Mela, l. iii. c. 6 (he wrote under Claudius), that, by the success of the Roman arms, the island and its savage inhabitants would soon be better known. It is amusing enough to peruse such passages in the midst of London.

‡ See the admirable abridgment, given by Tacitus, in the Life of Agricola, and copiously, though perhaps not completely, illustrated by our own antiquarians Camden and Horsley.

which, in his opinion, one legion and a few auxiliaries were sufficient.* The western isle might be improved into a valuable possession, and the Britons would wear their chains with the less reluctance, if the prospect and example of freedom was on every side removed from before their eyes.

But the superior merit of Agricola soon occasioned his removal from the government of Britain; and for ever disappointed this rational, though extensive, scheme of conquest. Before his departure the prudent general had provided for security as well as for dominion. He had observed that the island is almost divided into two unequal parts by the opposite gulfs or, as they are now called, the Friths of Scotland. Across the narrow interval of about forty miles he had drawn a line of military stations, which was afterwards fortified, in the reign of Antoninus Pius, by a turf rampart, erected on foundations of stone.† This wall of Antoninus, at a small distance beyond the modern cities of Edinburgh and Glasgow, was fixed as the limit of the Roman province. The native Caledonians preserved, in the northern extremity of the island, their wild independence, for which they were not less indebted to their poverty than to their valour. Their incursions were frequently repelled and chastised; but their country was never subdued.‡ The masters of the fairest and most wealthy climates of the globe turned with contempt from gloomy hills assailed by the winter tempest, from lakes concealed in a blue mist, and from cold and lonely heaths, over which the deer of the forest were chased by a troop of naked barbarians.§

Such was the state of the Roman frontiers, and such the maxims of Imperial policy, from the death of Augustus to the accession of Trajan. That virtuous and active prince had received the education of a soldier, and possessed the talents of a general.|| The peaceful system of his predecessors was interrupted by scenes of war and conquest; and the legions, after a long interval, beheld a military emperor at their head. The first exploits of Trajan were against the

* The Irish writers, jealous of their national honour, are extremely provoked on this occasion, both with Tacitus and with Agricola.

† See Horsley's *Britannia Romana*, l. i. c. 10.

‡ The poet Buchanan celebrates, with elegance and spirit (see his Sylvae, v.), the unviolated independence of his native country. But, if the single testimony of Richard of Cirencester was sufficient to create a Roman province of Vespasiana to the north of the wall, that independence would be reduced within very narrow limits.

§ See Appian (in Proem.) and the uniform imagery of Ossian's poems, which according to every hypothesis, were composed by a native Caledonian.

|| See Pliny's Panegyric, which seems founded on facts.

Dacians, the most warlike of men, who dwelt beyond the Danube, and who, during the reign of Domitian, had insulted, with impunity, the majesty of Rome.* To the strength and fierceness of barbarians they added a contempt for life, which was derived from a warm persuasion of the immortality and transmigration of the soul.† Decebalus, the Dacian king, approved himself a rival not unworthy of Trajan; nor did he despair of his own and the public fortune, till, by the confession of his enemies, he had exhausted every resource both of valour and policy.‡ This memorable war, with a very short suspension of hostilities, lasted five years; and as the emperor could exert, without control, the whole force of the state, it was terminated by the absolute submission of the barbarians.§ The new province of Dacia, which formed a second exception to the precept of Augustus, was about thirteen hundred miles in circumference. Its natural boundaries were the Dniester, the Theiss or Tibiscus, the Lower Danube, and the Euxine Sea. The vestiges of a military road may still be traced from the banks of the Danube to the neighbourhood of Bender, a place famous in modern history, and the actual frontier of the Turkish and Russian Empires.||

Trajan was ambitious of fame; and as long as mankind shall continue to bestow more liberal applause on their destroyers than on their benefactors, the thirst of military glory will ever be the vice of the most exalted characters. The praises of Alexander, transmitted by a succession of poets and historians, had kindled a dangerous emulation in the mind of Trajan. Like him, the Roman emperor undertook an expedition against the nations of the east, but he lamented with a sigh that his advanced age scarcely left him any hopes of equalling the renown of the son of Philip.¶ Yet the success of Trajan, however transient, was rapid and specious. The degenerate Parthians, broken by intestine discord, fled before his arms. He descended the river Tigris in triumph, from the mountains of Armenia to the Persian gulf. He enjoyed the honour of being the first, as he was the last, of the Roman generals, who ever

* Dion Cassius, l. lxvii.
† Herodotus, l. iv. c. 94. Julian in the Caesars, with Spanheim's observations.
‡ Plin. Epist. viii. 9.
§ Dion Cassius, l. lxviii. p. 1123, 1131. Julian, in Caesaribus. Eutropius, viii. 2, 6. Aurelius Victor in Epitome.
|| See a Memoir of M. d'Anville, on the Province of Dacia, in the Académie des Inscriptions, tom. xxviii. p. 444–468.
¶ Trajan's sentiments are represented in a very just and lively manner in the Caesars of Julian.

navigated that remote sea. His fleets ravished the coasts of Arabia; and Trajan vainly flattered himself that he was approaching towards the confines of India.* Every day the astonished senate received the intelligence of new names and new nations that acknowledged his sway. They were informed that the kings of Bosphorus, Colchos, Iberia, Albania, Osrhoene, and even the Parthian monarch himself, had accepted their diadems from the hands of the emperor; that the independent tribes of the Median and Carduchian hills had implored his protection; and that the rich countries of Armenia, Mesopotamia, and Assyria, were reduced into the state of provinces.† But the death of Trajan soon clouded the splendid prospect; and it was justly to be dreaded that so many distant nations would throw off the unaccustomed yoke, when they were no longer restrained by the powerful hand which had imposed it.

It was an ancient tradition that, when the Capitol was founded by one of the Roman kings, the god Terminus (who presided over boundaries, and was represented according to the fashion of that age by a large stone) alone, among all the inferior deities, refused to yield his place to Jupiter himself. A favourable inference was drawn from his obstinacy, which was interpreted by the augurs as a sure presage that the boundaries of the Roman power would never recede.‡ During many ages, the prediction, as it is usual, contributed to its own accomplishment. But though Terminus had resisted the majesty of Jupiter, he submitted to the authority of the emperor Hadrian.§ The resignation of all the eastern conquests of Trajan was the first measure of his reign. He restored to the Parthians the election of an independent sovereign; withdrew the Roman garrisons from the provinces of Armenia, Mesopotamia, and Assyria; and, in compliance with the precepts of Augustus, once more established the Euphrates as the frontier of the empire.‖ Censure, which arraigns the public actions and the private motives of princes, has ascribed to envy a conduct which might be attributed

---

* Eutropius and Sextus Rufus have endeavoured to perpetuate the illusion. See a very sensible dissertation of M. Freret, in the Académie des Inscriptions, tom. xxi. p. 55.

† Dion Cassius, l. lxviii; and the Abbreviators.

‡ Ovid Fast. l. ii. ver. 667. See Livy, and Dionysius of Halicarnassus, under the reign of Tarquin.

§ St. Augustin is highly delighted with the proof of the weakness of Terminus, and the vanity of the Augurs. See De Civitate Dei, iv. 29.

‖ See the Augustan History, p. 5. Jerome's Chronicle, and all the Epitomisers. It is somewhat surprising, that this memorable event should be omitted by Dion, or rather by Xiphilin.

to the prudence and moderation of Hadrian. The various character of that emperor, capable, by turns, of the meanest and the most generous sentiments, may afford some colour to the suspicion. It was, however, scarcely in his power to place the superiority of his predecessor in a more conspicuous light than by thus confessing himself unequal to the task of defending the conquests of Trajan.

The martial and ambitious spirit of Trajan formed a very singular contrast with the moderation of his successor. The restless activity of Hadrian was not less remarkable when compared with the gentle repose of Antoninus Pius. The life of the former was almost a perpetual journey; and as he possessed the various talents of the soldier, the statesman, and the scholar, he gratified his curiosity in the discharge of his duty. Careless of the difference of seasons and of climates, he marched on foot, and bareheaded, over the snows of Caledonia, and the sultry plains of the Upper Egypt; nor was there a province of the empire which, in the course of his reign, was not honoured with the presence of the monarch.* But the tranquil life of Antoninus Pius was spent in the bosom of Italy; and, during the twenty-three years that he directed the public administration, the longest journeys of that amiable prince extended no farther than from his palace in Rome to the retirement of his Lanuvian villa.†

Notwithstanding this difference in their personal conduct, the general system of Augustus was equally adopted and uniformly pursued by Hadrian and by the two Antonines. They persisted in the design of maintaining the dignity of the empire, without attempting to enlarge its limits. By every honourable expedient they invited the friendship of the barbarians; and endeavoured to convince mankind that the Roman power, raised above the temptation of conquest, was actuated only by the love of order and justice. During a long period of forty-three years their virtuous labours were crowned with success; and, if we except a few slight hostilities that served to exercise the legions of the frontier, the reigns of Hadrian and Antoninus Pius offer the fair prospect of universal peace.‡ The Roman name was revered among the most remote

---

* Dion, l. lxix. p. 115. Hist. August. p. 5, 8. If all our historians were lost, medals, inscriptions, and other monuments, would be sufficient to record the travels of Hadrian.

† See the Augustan History and the Epitomes.

‡ We must, however, remember that, in the time of Hadrian, a rebellion of the Jews raged with religious fury, though only in a single province. Pausanias (l. viii. c. 43) mentions two necessary and successful wars, conducted by the

nations of the earth. The fiercest barbarians frequently submitted their differences to the arbitration of the emperor; and we are informed by a contemporary historian that he had seen ambassadors who were refused the honour which they came to solicit, of being admitted into the rank of subjects.*

The terror of the Roman arms added weight and dignity to the moderation of the emperors. They preserved peace by a constant preparation for war; and, while justice regulated their conduct, they announced to the nations on their confines that they were as little disposed to endure as to offer an injury. The military strength, which it had been sufficient for Hadrian and the elder Antoninus to display, was exerted against the Parthians and the Germans by the emperor Marcus. The hostilities of the barbarians provoked the resentment of that philosophic monarch, and, in the prosecution of a just defence, Marcus and his generals obtained many signal victories, both on the Euphrates and on the Danube.† The military establishment of the Roman empire, which thus assured either its tranquillity or success, will now become the proper and important object of our attention.

In the purer ages of the commonwealth, the use of arms was reserved for those ranks of citizens who had a country to love, a property to defend, and some share in enacting those laws which it was their interest, as well as duty, to maintain. But in proportion as the public freedom was lost in extent of conquest, war was gradually improved into an art, and degraded into a trade.‡ The legions themselves, even at the time when they were recruited in the most distant provinces, were supposed to consist of Roman citizens. That distinction was generally considered either as a legal qualification or as a proper recompense for the soldier; but a more serious regard was paid to the essential merit of age, strength, and military

---

generals of Pius. 1st, Against the wandering Moors, who were driven into the solitudes of Atlas. 2d, Against the Brigantes of Britain, who had invaded the Roman province. Both these wars (with several other hostilities) are mentioned in the Augustan History, p 19.

* Appian of Alexandria, in the preface to his History of the Roman Wars.

† Dion, l. lxxi. Hist. August. in Marco. The Parthian victories gave birth to a crowd of contemptible historians, whose memory has been rescued from oblivion, and exposed to ridicule, in a very lively piece of criticism of Lucian.

‡ The poorest rank of soldiers possessed above forty pounds sterling (Dionys. Halicarn. iv. 17), a very high qualification, at a time when money was so scarce, that an ounce of silver was equivalent to seventy pound weight of brass. The populace, excluded by the ancient constitution, were indiscriminately admitted by Marius. See Sallust. de Bell. Jugurth. c. 91.

stature.* In all levies, a just preference was given to the climates of the north over those of the south; the race of men born to the exercise of arms was sought for in the country rather than in cities, and it was very reasonably presumed that the hardy occupations of smiths, carpenters, and huntsmen would supply more vigour and resolution than the sedentary trades which are employed in the service of luxury.† After every qualification of property had been laid aside, the armies of the Roman emperors were still commanded, for the most part, by officers of a liberal birth and education; but the common soldiers, like the mercenary troops of modern Europe, were drawn from the meanest, and very frequently from the most profligate, of mankind.

That public virtue, which among the ancients was denominated patriotism, is derived from a strong sense of our own interest in the preservation and prosperity of the free government of which we are members. Such a sentiment, which had rendered the legions of the republic almost invincible, could make but a very feeble impression on the mercenary servants of a despotic prince; and it became necessary to supply that defect by other motives, of a different, but not less forcible nature,—honour and religion. The peasant, or mechanic, imbibed the useful prejudice that he was advanced to the more dignified profession of arms, in which his rank and reputation would depend on his own valour; and that, although the prowess of a private soldier must often escape the notice of fame, his own behaviour might sometimes confer glory or disgrace on the company, the legion, or even the army, to whose honours he was associated. On his first entrance into the service, an oath was administered to him with every circumstance of solemnity. He promised never to desert his standard, to submit his own will to the commands of his leaders, and to sacrifice his life for the safety of the emperor and the empire.‡ The attachment of the Roman troops to their standards was inspired by the united influence of religion and of honour. The golden eagle, which glittered in the front of the legion, was the object of their fondest devotion; nor was it esteemed less impious than it was ignominious, to abandon that sacred ensign in the hour of danger.§ These motives, which derived their strength

---

* Caesar formed his legion Alauda of Gauls and strangers; but it was during the licence of civil war; and after the victory he gave them the freedom of the city for their reward.

† See Vegetius de Re Militari, l. i. c. 2–7.

‡ The oath of service and fidelity to the emperor was annually renewed by the troops, on the first of January.

§ Tacitus calls the Roman Eagles, Bellorum Deos. They were placed in a

from the imagination, were enforced by fears and hopes of a more substantial kind. Regular pay, occasional donatives, and a stated recompense, after the appointed term of service, alleviated the hardships of the military life,* whilst, on the other hand, it was impossible for cowardice or disobedience to escape the severest punishment. The centurions were authorized to chastise with blows, the generals had a right to punish with death; and it was an inflexible maxim of Roman discipline that a good soldier should dread his officers far more than the enemy. From such laudable arts did the valour of the Imperial troops receive a degree of firmness and docility, unattainable by the impetuous and irregular passions of barbarians. . . .

CHAPTER II · OF THE UNION AND INTERNAL PROSPERITY OF THE ROMAN EMPIRE, IN THE AGE OF THE ANTONINES

It is not alone by the rapidity or extent of conquest that we should estimate the greatness of Rome. The sovereign of the Russian deserts commands a larger portion of the globe. In the seventh summer after his passage of the Hellespont, Alexander erected the Macedonian trophies on the banks of the Hyphasis.† Within less than a century, the irresistible Zingis, and the Mogul princes of his race, spread their cruel devastations and transient empire from the sea of China to the confines of Egypt and Germany.‡ But the firm edifice of Roman power was raised and preserved by the wisdom of ages. The obedient provinces of Trajan and the Antonines were united by laws and adorned by arts. They might occasionally suffer from the partial abuse of delegated au-

---

chapel in the camp, and with the other deities received the religious worship of the troops.

* See Gronovius de Pecunia vetere, 1. iii. p. 120 &c. The emperor Domitian raised the annual stipend of the legionaries to twelve pieces of gold, which, in his time, was equivalent to about ten of our guineas. This pay, somewhat higher than our own, had been, and was afterwards, gradually increased, according to the progress of wealth and military government. After twenty years' service, the veteran received three thousand denarii (about one hundrd pounds sterling) , or a proportionable allowance of land. The pay and advantages of the guards were, in general, about double those of the legions.

† They were erected about the midway between Lahor and Dehli. The conquests of Alexander in Hindostan were confined to the Punjab, a country watered by the five great streams of the Indus.

‡ See M. de Guignes, Histoire des Huns, 1. xv. xvi. and xvii.

thority; but the general principle of government was wise, simple, and beneficent. They enjoyed the religion of their ancestors, whilst in civil honours and advantages they were exalted, by just degrees, to an equality with their conquerors.

1. The policy of the emperors and the senate, as far as it concerned religion, was happily seconded by the reflections of the enlightened, and by the habits of the superstitious, part of their subjects. The various modes of worship which prevailed in the Roman world were all considered by the people as equally true; by the philosopher as equally false; and by the magistrate as equally useful. And thus toleration produced not only mutual indulgence, but even religious concord.

The superstition of the people was not embittered by any mixture of theological rancour; nor was it confined by the chains of any speculative system. The devout polytheist, though fondly attached to his national rites, admitted with implicit faith the different religions of the earth.* Fear, gratitude, and curiosity, a dream or an omen, a singular disorder, or a distant journey, perpetually disposed him to multiply the articles of his belief, and to enlarge the list of his protectors. The thin texture of the pagan mythology was interwoven with various but not discordant materials. As soon as it was allowed that sages and heroes, who had lived or who had died for the benefit of their country, were exalted to a state of power and immortality, it was universally confessed that they deserved, if not the adoration, at least the reverence of all mankind. The deities of a thousand groves and a thousand streams possessed in peace their local and respective influence; nor could the Roman who deprecated the wrath of the Tiber deride the Egyptian who presented his offering to the beneficent genius of the Nile. The visible powers of Nature, the planets, and the elements, were the same throughout the universe. The invisible governors of the moral world were inevitably cast in a similar mould of fiction and allegory. Every virtue, and even vice, acquired its divine representative; every art and profession its patron, whose attributes in the most distant ages and countries were uniformly derived from the character of their

---

* There is not any writer who describes in so lively a manner as Herodotus the true genius of Polytheism. The best commentary may be found in Mr. Hume's Natural History of Religion; and the best contrast in Bossuet's Universal History. Some obscure traces of an intolerant spirit appear in the conduct of the Egyptians (see Juvenal, Sat. xv.) ; and the Christians as well as Jews, who lived under the Roman empire, formed a very important exception; so important indeed, that the discussion will require a distinct chapter of this work.

peculiar votaries. A republic of gods of such opposite tempers and interests required, in every system, the moderating hand of a supreme magistrate, who, by the progress of knowledge and of flattery, was gradually invested with the sublime perfections of an Eternal Parent and Omnipotent Monarch.* Such was the mild spirit of antiquity, that the nations were less attentive to the difference than to the resemblance of their religious worship. The Greek, the Roman, and the Barbarian, as they met before their respective altars, easily persuaded themselves that, under various names and with various ceremonies, they adored the same deities. The elegant mythology of Homer gave a beautiful and almost a regular form to the polytheism of the ancient world.†

The philosophers of Greece deduced their morals from the nature of man rather than from that of God. They meditated, however, on the Divine Nature as a very curious and important speculation, and in the profound inquiry they displayed the strength and weakness of the human understanding.‡ Of the four most celebrated schools, the Stoics and the Platonists endeavoured to reconcile the jarring interests of reason and piety. They have left us the most sublime proofs of the existence and perfections of the first cause; but, as it was impossible for them to conceive the creation of matter, the workman in the Stoic philosophy was not sufficiently distinguished from the work; whilst, on the contrary, the spiritual God of Plato and his disciples resembled an idea rather than a substance. The opinions of the Academics and Epicureans were of a less religious cast; but, whilst the modest science of the former induced them to doubt, the positive ignorance of the latter urged them to deny, the providence of a Supreme Ruler. The spirit of inquiry, prompted by emulation and supported by freedom, had divided the public teachers of philosophy into a variety of contending sects; but the ingenuous youth, who from every part resorted to Athens and the other seats of learning in the Roman empire, were alike instructed in every school to reject and to despise the religion of the multitude. How, indeed, was it possible that a philosopher should accept as divine truths the idle tales of the poets, and the incoherent

---

* The rights, power, and pretensions of the sovereign of Olympus are very clearly described in the xvth book of the Iliad: in the Greek original, I mean; for Mr. Pope, without perceiving it, has improved the theology of Homer.

† See, for instance, Caesar de Bell. Gall. vi. 17. Within a century or two the Gauls themselves applied to their gods the names of Mercury, Mars, Apollo, &c.

‡ The admirable work of Cicero de Natura Deorum is the best clue we have to guide us through the dark and profound abyss. He represents with candour, and confutes with subtlety, the opinions of the philosophers.

traditions of antiquity; or that he should adore, as gods, those imperfect beings whom he must have despised, as men! Against such unworthy adversaries, Cicero condescended to employ the arms of reason and eloquence; but the satire of Lucian was a much more adequate as well as more efficacious weapon. We may be well assured that a writer conversant with the world would never have ventured to expose the gods of his country to public ridicule, had they not already been the objects of secret contempt among the polished and enlightened orders of society.*

Notwithstanding the fashionable irreligion which prevailed in the age of the Antonines, both the interests of the priests and the credulity of the people were sufficiently respected. In their writings and conversation the philosophers of antiquity asserted the independent dignity of reason; but they resigned their actions to the commands of law and of custom. Viewing with a smile of pity and indulgence the various errors of the vulgar, they diligently practised the ceremonies of their fathers, devoutly frequented the temples of the gods; and, sometimes condescending to act a part on the theatre of superstition, they concealed the sentiments of an Atheist under the sacerdotal robes. Reasoners of such a temper were scarcely inclined to wrangle about their respective modes of faith or of worship. It was indifferent to them what shape the folly of the multitude might choose to assume; and they approached, with the same inward contempt and the same external reverence, the altars of the Libyan, the Olympian, or the Capitoline Jupiter.†

It is not easy to conceive from what motives a spirit of persecution could introduce itself into the Roman councils. The magistrates could not be actuated by a blind though honest bigotry, since the magistrates were themselves philosophers; and the schools of Athens had given laws to the senate. They could not be impelled by ambition or avarice, as the temporal and ecclesiastical powers were united in the same hands. The pontiffs were chosen among the most illustrious of the senators; and the office of Supreme Pontiff was constantly exercised by the emperors themselves. They knew and valued the advantages of religion, as it is connected with civil government. They encouraged the public festivals which humanize the manners of the people. They managed the arts of divination as

---

* I do not pretend to assert that, in this irreligious age, the natural terrors of superstition, dreams, omens, apparitions, &c., had lost their efficacy.

† Socrates, Epicurus, Cicero, and Plutarch, always inculcated a decent reverence for the religion of their own country, and of mankind. The devotion of Epicurus was assiduous and exemplary. Diogen. Laert. x. 10.

a convenient instrument of policy; and they respected, as the firmest bond of society, the useful persuasion that, either in this or in a future life, the crime of perjury is most assuredly punished by the avenging gods.* But, whilst they acknowledged the general advantages of religion, they were convinced that the various modes of worship contributed alike to the same salutary purposes; and that, in every country, the form of superstition which had received the sanction of time and experience was the best adapted to the climate and to its inhabitants. Avarice and taste very frequently despoiled the vanquished nations of the elegant statues of their gods and the rich ornaments of their temples;† but, in the exercise of the religion which they derived from their ancestors, they uniformly experienced the indulgence, and even protection, of the Roman conquerors. The province of Gaul seems, and indeed only seems, an exception to this universal toleration. Under the specious pretext of abolishing human sacrifices, the emperors Tiberius and Claudius suppressed the dangerous power of the Druids;‡ but the priests themselves, their gods, and their altars, subsisted in peaceful obscurity till the final destruction of Paganism.§

Rome, the capital of a great monarchy, was incessantly filled with subjects and strangers from every part of the world,‖ who all introduced and enjoyed the favourite superstitions of their native country.¶ Every city in the empire was justified in maintaining the purity of its ancient ceremonies; and the Roman senate, using the common privilege, sometimes interposed to check this inundation of foreign rites. The Egyptian superstition, of all the most contemptible and abject, was frequently prohibited; the temples of Serapis and Isis demolished, and their worshippers banished from Rome and Italy.** But the zeal of fanaticism prevailed over the cold and

* Polybus, l. vi. c. 56. Juvenal, Sat. xiii., laments that in his time this apprehension had lost much of its effect.

† See the fate of Syracuse, Tarentum, Ambracia, Corinth, &c., the conduct of Verres, in Cicero (Actio ii. Orat. 4) , and the usual practice of governors, in the viiith Satire of Juvenal.

‡ Sueton. in Claud. Plin. Hist. Nat. xxx. i.

§ Pelloutier, Histoire des Celtes, tom. vi. p. 230–252.

‖ Seneca Consolat. ad Helviam, p. 74. Edit. Lips.

¶ Dionysius Halicarn. Antiquitat. Roman. l. ii.

** In the year of Rome 701, the temple of Iris and Serapis was demolished by the order of the senate (Dion Cassius, l. xl. p. 252) , and even by the hands of the consul (Valerius Maximus, 1, 3). After the death of Caesar, it was restored at the public expense (Dion, l. xlvii. p. 501). When Augustus was in Egypt, he revered the majesty of Serapis (Dion, l. li. p. 647) ; but in the Pomaerium of Rome, and a mile around it, he prohibited the worship of the Egyptian gods

feeble efforts of policy. The exiles returned, the proselytes multiplied, the temples were restored with increasing splendour, and Isis and Serapis at length assumed their place among the Roman deities.* Nor was this indulgence a departure from the old maxims of government. In the purest ages of the commonwealth, Cybele and Aesculapius had been invited by solemn embassies;† and it was customary to tempt the protectors of besieged cities by the promise of more distinguished honours than they possessed in their native country.‡ Rome gradually became the common temple of her subjects; and the freedom of the city was bestowed on all the gods of mankind.§

II. The narrow policy of preserving without any foreign mixture the pure blood of the ancient citizens, had checked the fortune, and hastened the ruin, of Athens and Sparta. The aspiring genius of Rome sacrificed vanity to ambition, and deemed it more prudent, as well as honourable, to adopt virtue and merit for her own wheresoever they were found, among slaves or strangers, enemies or barbarians.‖ During the most flourishing era of the Athenian commonwealth the number of citizens gradually decreased from about thirty¶ to twenty-one thousand.** If, on the contrary, we study the growth of the Roman republic, we may discover that, notwithstanding the incessant demands of wars and colonies, the citizens, who, in the first census of Servius Tullius, amounted to no more than eighty-three thousand, were multiplied, before the commencement of the social war, to the number of four hundred and sixty-three thousand men able to bear arms in the service of their country.†† When the allies of Rome claimed an equal share of

---

(Dion, l. liii. p. 697, l. liv. p. 735). They remained, however, very fashionable under his reign (Ovid. de Art. Amand. l. i.) and that of his successor, till the justice of Tiberius was provoked to some acts of severity. (See Tacit. Annal. ii. 85, Joseph Antiquit. l. xviii. c. 3.)

* Tertullian, in Apologetic. c. 6, p. 74. Edit. Havercamp. I am inclined to attribute their establishment to the devotion of the Flavian family.

† See Livy, l. xi. and xxix.

‡ Macrob. Saturnalia, l. iii. c. 9. He gives us a form of evocation.

§ Minucius Felix in Octavio, p. 54. Arnobius, l. vi. p. 115.

‖ Tacit. Annal. xi. 24. The Orbis Romanus of the learned Spanheim is a complete history of the progressive admission of Latium, Italy, and the provinces to the freedom of Rome.

¶ Herodotus, v. 97. It should seem, however, that he followed a large and popular estimation.

** Athenaeus Deipnosophist, l. vi. p. 272, Edit. Casaubon. Meursius de Fortuna Attica, c. 4.

†† See a very accurate collection of the numbers of each Lustrum in M. de Beaufort, République Romaine, l. iv. c. 4.

honours and privileges, the senate indeed preferred the chance of arms to an ignominious concession. The Samnites and the Lucanians paid the severe penalty of their rashness; but the rest of the Italian states, as they successively returned to their duty, were admitted into the bosom of the republic,* and soon contributed to the ruin of public freedom. Under a democratical government the citizens exercise the powers of sovereignty; and those powers will be first abused, and afterwards lost, if they are committed to an unwieldy multitude. But, when the popular assemblies had been suppressed by the administration of the emperors, the conquerors were distinguished from the vanquished nations only as the first and most honourable order of subjects; and their increase, however rapid, was no longer exposed to the same dangers. Yet the wisest princes who adopted the maxims of Augustus guarded with the strictest care the dignity of the Roman name, and diffused the freedom of the city with a prudent liberality.†

Till the privileges of Romans had been progressively extended to all the inhabitants of the empire, an important distinction was preserved between Italy and the provinces. The former was esteemed the centre of public unity, and the firm basis of the constitution. Italy claimed the birth, or at least the residence, of the emperors and the senate.‡ The estates of the Italians were exempt from taxes, their persons from the arbitrary jurisdiction of governors. Their municipal corporations, formed after the perfect model of the capital, were intrusted, under the immediate eye of the supreme power, with the execution of the laws. From the foot of the Alps to the extremity of Calabria, all the natives of Italy were born citizens of Rome. Their partial distinctions were obliterated, and they insensibly coalesced into one great nation, united by language, manners, and civil institutions, and equal to the weight of a powerful empire. The republic gloried in her generous policy, and was frequently rewarded by the merit and services of her adopted sons. Had she always confined the distinction of Romans to the ancient families within the walls of the city, that immortal name would have been deprived of some of its noblest ornaments. Virgil

* Appian de Bell. Civil. l. i. Velleius Paterculus, l. ii. c. 15, 16, 17.

† Maecenas had advised him to declare, by one edict, all his subjects citizens. But we may justly suspect that the historian Dion was the author of a counsel, so much adapted to the practice of his own age, and so little to that of Augustus.

‡ The senators were obliged to have one-third of their own landed property in Italy. See Plin. l. vi. ep. 19. The qualification was reduced by Marcus to one-fourth. Since the reign of Trajan, Italy had sunk nearer to the level of the provinces.

was a native of Mantua; Horace was inclined to doubt whether he should call himself an Apulian or a Lucanian; it was in Padua that an historian was found worthy to record the majestic series of Roman victories. The patriot family of the Catos emerged from Tusculum; and the little town of Arpinum claimed the double honour of producing Marius and Cicero, the former of whom deserved, after Romulus and Camillus, to be styled the Third Founder of Rome; and the latter, after saving his country from the designs of Catiline, enabled her to contend with Athens for the palm of eloquence.*

The provinces of the empire (as they have been described in the preceding chapter) were destitute of any public force or constitutional freedom. In Etruria, in Greece,† and in Gaul,‡ it was the first care of the senate to dissolve those dangerous confederacies which taught mankind that, as the Roman arms prevailed by division, they might be resisted by union. Those princes whom the ostentation of gratitude or generosity permitted for a while to hold a precarious sceptre were dismissed from their thrones, as soon as they had performed their appointed task of fashioning to the yoke the vanquished nations. The free states and cities which had embraced the cause of Rome were rewarded with a nominal alliance, and insensibly sunk into real servitude. The public authority was everywhere exercised by the ministers of the senate and of the emperors, and that authority was absolute and without control. But the same salutary maxims of government, which had secured the peace and obedience of Italy, were extended to the most distant conquests. A nation of Romans was gradually formed in the provinces, by the double expedient of introducing colonies, and of admitting the most faithful and deserving of the provincials to the freedom of Rome. . . .

Agriculture is the foundation of manufactures; since the productions of nature are the materials of art. Under the Roman empire, the labour of an industrious and ingenious people was variously, but incessantly, employed in the service of the rich. In their dress, their table, their houses, and their furniture, the favourites of fortune united every refinement of conveniency, of elegance, and of

* The first part of the Verona Illustrata of the Marquis Maffei gives the clearest and most comprehensive view of the state of Italy under the Caesars.

† See Pausanias, l. vii. The Romans condescended to restore the names of those assemblies, when they could no longer be dangerous.

‡ They are frequently mentioned by Caesar. The Abbé Dubos attempts, with very little success, to prove that the assemblies of Gaul were continued under the emperors. Histoire de l'Establissement de la Monarchi Françoise l. i. c. 4.

splendour, whatever could soothe their pride or gratify their sensuality. Such refinements, under the odious name of luxury, have been severely arraigned by the moralists of every age; and it might perhaps be more conducive to the virtue, as well as happiness, of mankind, if all possessed the necessaries, and none the superfluities, of life. But in the present imperfect condition of society, luxury, though it may proceed from vice or folly, seems to be the only means that can correct the unequal distribution of property. The diligent mechanic, and the skilful artist, who have obtained no share in the division of the earth, receive a voluntary tax from the possessors of land; and the latter are prompted, by a sense of interest, to improve those estates, with whose produce they may purchase additional pleasures. This operation, the particular effects of which are felt in every society, acted with much more diffusive energy in the Roman world. The provinces would soon have been exhausted of their wealth, if the manufactures and commerce of luxury had not insensibly restored to the industrious subjects the sums which were exacted from them by the arms and authority of Rome. As long as the circulation was confined within the bounds of the empire, it impressed the political machine with a new degree of activity, and its consequences, sometimes beneficial, could never become pernicious.

But it is no easy task to confine luxury within the limits of an empire. The most remote countries of the ancient world were ransacked to supply the pomp and delicacy of Rome. The forest of Scythia afforded some valuable furs. Amber was brought over land from the shores of the Baltic to the Danube; and the barbarians were astonished at the price which they received in exchange for so useless a commodity.* There was a considerable demand for Babylonian carpets, and other manufactures of the East; but the most important and unpopular branch of foreign trade was carried on with Arabia and India. Every year, about the time of the summer solstice, a fleet of an hundred and twenty vessels sailed from Myoshormos, a port of Egypt, on the Red Sea. By the periodical assistance of the monsoons, they traversed the ocean in about forty days. The coast of Malabar, or the island of Ceylon,† was the usual term of

---

* Tacit, Germania, c. 45. Plin. Hist. Natur. xxxvii. 11. The latter observed, with some humour, that even fashion had not yet found out the use of amber. Nero sent a Roman knight to purchase great quantities on the spot, where it was produced; the coast of modern Prussia.

† Called Taprobana by the Romans, and Serendib by the Arabs. It was discovered under the reign of Claudius, and gradually became the principal mart of the east.

their navigation, and it was in those markets that the merchants from the more remote countries of Asia expected their arrival. The return of the fleet of Egypt was fixed to the months of December or January; and as soon as their rich cargo had been transported on the backs of camels from the Red Sea to the Nile, and had descended that river as far as Alexandria, it was poured, without delay, into the capital of the empire.* The objects of oriental traffic were splendid and trifling: silk, a pound of which was esteemed not inferior in value to a pound of gold;† precious stones, among which the pearl claimed the first rank after the diamond;‡ and a variety of aromatics, that were consumed in religious worship and the pomp of funerals. The labour and risk of the voyage was rewarded with almost incredible profit; but the profit was made upon Roman subjects, and a few individuals were enriched at the expense of the public. As the natives of Arabia and India were contented with the productions and manufactures of their own country, silver, on the side of the Romans, was the principal, if not the only, instrument of commerce. It was a complaint worthy of the gravity of the senate, that, in the purchase of female ornaments, the wealth of the state was irrecoverably given away to foreign and hostile nations.§ The annual loss is computed, by a writer of an inquisitive but censorious temper, at upwards of eight hundred thousand pounds sterling.‖ Such was the style of discontent, brooding over the dark prospect of approaching poverty. And yet, if we compare the proportion between gold and silver, as it stood in the time of Pliny, and as it was fixed in the reign of Constantine, we shall discover within that period a very considerable increase.¶ There is not the least reason to suppose that gold was become more scarce; it is therefore evident that silver was grown more common; that whatever might be the amount of the Indian and Arabian exports, they were far from exhausting the wealth of the Roman world; and that the produce of the mines abundantly supplied the demands of commerce.

* Plin. Hist. Natur. l. vi. Strabo, l. xvii.

† Hist. August. p. 224. A silk garment was considered as an ornament to a woman, but as a disgrace to a man.

‡ The two great pearl fisheries were the same as at present, Ormuz and Cape Comorin. As well as we can compare ancient with modern geography, Rome was supplied with diamonds from the mine of Sumelpur, in Bengal, which is described in the Voyages de Tavernier, tom. ii. p. 281.

§ Tacit. Annal. iii. 53. In a speech of Tiberius.

‖ Plin. Hist. Natur. xii. 18. In another place he computes half that sum; Quingenties HS for India exclusive of Arabia.

¶ The proportion, which was 1 to 10, and 12½, rose to 14⅘, the legal regulation of Constantine. See Arbuthnot's Table of ancient Coins, c. v.

Notwithstanding the propensity of mankind to exalt the past, and to depreciate the present, the tranquil and prosperous state of the empire was warmly felt, and honestly confessed, by the provincials as well as Romans. "They acknowledged that the true principles of social life, laws, agriculture, and science, which had been first invented by the wisdom of Athens, were now firmly established by the power of Rome, under whose auspicious influence the fiercest barbarians were united by an equal government and common language. They affirm that, with the improvement of arts, the human species was visibly multiplied. They celebrate the increasing splendour of the cities, the beautiful face of the country, cultivated and adorned like an immense garden; and the long festival of peace, which was enjoyed by so many nations, forgetful of their ancient animosities, and delivered from the apprehension of future danger."* Whatever suspicions may be suggested by the air of rhetoric and declamation which seems to prevail in these passages, the substance of them is perfectly agreeable to historic truth.

It was scarcely possible that the eyes of contemporaries should discover in the public felicity the latent causes of decay and corruption. This long peace, and the uniform government of the Romans, introduced a slow and secret poison into the vitals of the empire. The minds of men were gradually reduced to the same level, the fire of genius was extinguished, and even the military spirit evaporated. The natives of Europe were brave and robust. Spain, Gaul, Britain, and Illyricum supplied the legions with excellent soldiers, and constituted the real strength of the monarchy. Their personal valour remained, but they no longer possessed that public courage which is nourished by the love of independence, the sense of national honour, the presence of danger, and the habit of command. They received laws and governors from the will of their sovereign, and trusted for their defence to a mercenary army. The posterity of their boldest leaders was contented with the rank of citizens and subjects. The most aspiring spirits resorted to the court or standard of the emperors; and the deserted provinces, deprived of political strength or union, insensibly sunk into the languid indifference of private life.

The love of letters, almost inseparable from peace and refinement, was fashionable among the subjects of Hadrian and the Antonines, who were themselves men of learning and curiosity. It was diffused over the whole extent of their empire; the most north-

---

* Among many other passages, see Pliny (Hist. Natur. iii. 5), Aristides (de Urbe Roma) and Tertullian (de Anima, c. 30).

ern tribes of Britons had acquired a taste for rhetoric; Homer as well as Virgil were transcribed and studied on the banks of the Rhine and Danube; and the most liberal rewards sought out the faintest glimmerings of literary merit.* The sciences of physic and astronomy were successfully cultivated by the Greeks; the observations of Ptolemy and the writings of Galen are studied by those who have improved their discoveries and corrected their errors; but, if we except the inimitable Lucian, this age of indolence passed away without having produced a single writer of original genius or who excelled in the arts of elegant composition. The authority of Plato and Aristotle, of Zeno and Epicurus, still reigned in the schools, and their systems, transmitted with blind deference from one generation of disciples to another, precluded every generous attempt to exercise the powers, or enlarge the limits, of the human mind. The beauties of the poets and orators, instead of kindling a fire like their own, inspired only cold and servile imitations: or, if any ventured to deviate from those models, they deviated at the same time from good sense and propriety. On the revival of letters, the youthful vigour of the imagination after a long repose, national emulation, a new religion, new languages, and a new world, called forth the genius of Europe. But the provincials of Rome, trained by a uniform artificial foreign education, were engaged in a very unequal competition with those bold ancients, who, by expressing their genuine feelings in their native tongue, had already occupied every place of honour. The name of Poet was almost forgotten; that of Orator was usurped by the sophists. A cloud of critics, of compilers, of commentators, darkened the face of learning, and the decline of genius was soon followed by the corruption of taste.

The sublime Longinus, who in somewhat a later period, and in the court of a Syrian queen, preserved the spirit of ancient Athens, observes and laments this degeneracy of his contemporaries, which debased their sentiments, enervated their courage, and depressed their talents. "In the same manner," says he, "as some children

---

* Herodes Atticus gave the sophist Polemo above eight thousand pounds for three declamations. See Philostrat. l. i. p. 558. The Antonines founded a school at Athens, in which professors of grammar, rhetoric, politics, and the four great sects of philosophy, were maintained at the public expense for the instruction of youth. The salary of a philosopher was ten thousand drachmae, between three and four hundred pounds a year. Similar establishments were formed in the other great cities of the empire. See Lucian in Eunuch. tom. ii. p. 353, edit. Reitz. Philostrat. l. ii. p. 566. Hist. August. p. 21. Dion Cassius, l. lxxxi. p. 1195. Juvenal himself, in a morose satire, which in every line betrays his own disappointment and envy, is obliged, however, to say, "*O Juvenes, circumspicit et agitat vos, Materiamque sibi Ducis indulgentia quaerit.*"—Satir. vii. 20.

always remain pigmies, whose infant limbs have been too closely confined; thus our tender minds, fettered by the prejudices and habits of a just servitude, are unable to expand themselves, or to attain that well-proportioned greatness which we admire in the ancients, who, living under a popular government, wrote with the same freedom as they acted."* This diminutive stature of mankind, if we pursue the metaphor, was daily sinking below the old standard, and the Roman world was indeed peopled by a race of pigmies, when the fierce giants of the north broke in and mended the puny breed. They restored a manly spirit of freedom; and, after the revolution of ten centuries, freedom became the happy parent of taste and science.

CHAPTER III · OF THE CONSTITUTION OF THE ROMAN EMPIRE, IN THE AGE OF THE ANTONINES

The obvious definition of a monarchy seems to be that of a state, in which a single person, by whatsoever name he may be distinguished, is intrusted with the execution of the laws, the management of the revenue, and the command of the army. But unless public liberty is protected by intrepid and vigilant guardians, the authority of so formidable a magistrate will soon degenerate into despotism. The influence of the clergy, in an age of superstition, might be usefully employed to assert the rights of mankind; but so intimate is the connexion between the throne and the altar, that the banner of the church has very seldom been seen on the side of the people. A martial nobility and stubborn commons, possessed of arms, tenacious of property, and collected into constitutional assemblies, form the only balance capable of preserving a free constitution against enterprises of an aspiring prince.

Every barrier of the Roman constitution had been levelled by the vast ambition of the dictator; every fence had been extirpated by the cruel hand of the triumvir. After the victory of Actium, the fate of the Roman world depended on the will of Octavianus, surnamed Caesar by his uncle's adoption, and afterwards Augustus, by the flattery of the senate. The conqueror was at the head of forty-four

---

* Longin. de Sublim. c. 43, p. 229, edit. Toll. Here too we may say of Longinus, "his own example strengthens all his laws." Instead of proposing his sentiments with a manly boldness, he insinuates them with the most guarded caution, puts them into the mouth of a friend, and, as far as we can collect from a corrupted text, makes a show of refuting them himself.

veteran legions,* conscious of their own strength and of the weakness of the constitution, habituated during twenty years' civil war to every act of blood and violence, and passionately devoted to the house of Caesar, from whence alone they had received and expected the most lavish rewards. The provinces, long oppressed by the ministers of the republic, sighed for the government of a single person, who would be the master, not the accomplice, of those petty tyrants. The people of Rome, viewing with a secret pleasure the humiliation of the aristocracy, demanded only bread and public shows, and were supplied with both by the liberal hand of Augustus. The rich and polite Italians, who had almost universally embraced the philosophy of Epicurus, enjoyed the present blessings of ease and tranquillity, and suffered not the pleasing dream to be interrupted by the memory of their old tumultuous freedom. With its power, the senate had lost its dignity; many of the most noble families were extinct. The republicans of spirit and ability had perished in the field of battle, or in the proscription. The door of the assembly had been designedly left open for a mixed multitude of more than a thousand persons, who reflected disgrace upon their rank, instead of deriving honour from it.†

The reformation of the senate, was one of the first steps in which Augustus laid aside the tyrant, and professed himself the father of his country. He was elected censor; and, in concert with his faithful Agrippa, he examined the list of the senators, expelled a few members, whose vices or whose obstinacy required a public example, persuaded near two hundred to prevent the shame of an expulsion by a voluntary retreat, raised the qualification of a senator to about ten thousand pounds, created a sufficient number of patrician families, and accepted for himself the honourable title of Prince of the Senate, which had always been bestowed by the censors on the citizen the most eminent for his honours and services.‡ But, whilst he thus restored the dignity, he destroyed the independence, of the senate. The principles of a free constitution are irrecoverably lost, when the legislative power is nominated by the executive.

Before an assembly thus modelled and prepared, Augustus pronounced a studied oration, which displayed his patriotism, and

---

* Orosius, vi. 18.

† Julius Caesar introduced soldiers, strangers and half-barbarians, into the senate. (Sueton. in Caesar. c. 80.) The abuse became still more scandalous after his death.

‡ Dion Cassius, l. iii. p. 693, Suetonius in August. c. 35.

disguised his ambition. He lamented, yet excused, his past conduct. Filial piety had required at his hands the revenge of his father's murder; the humanity of his own nature had sometimes given way to the stern laws of necessity, and to a forced connexion with two unworthy colleagues: as long as Antony lived, the republic forbad him to abandon her to a degenerate Roman and a barbarian queen. He was now at liberty to satisfy his duty and his inclination. He solemnly restored the senate and people to all their ancient rights; and wished only to mingle with the crowd of his fellow-citizens, and to share the blessings which he had obtained for his country.*

It would require the pen of Tacitus (if Tacitus had assisted at this assembly) to describe the various emotions of the senate; those that were suppressed, and those that were affected. It was dangerous to trust the sincerity of Augustus; to seem to distrust it was still more dangerous. The respective advantages of monarchy and a republic have often divided speculative inquirers; the present greatness of the Roman state, the corruption of manners, and the licence of the soldiers, supplied new arguments to the advocates of monarchy; and these general views of government were again warped by the hopes and fears of each individual. Amidst this confusion of sentiments, the answer of the senate was unanimous and decisive. They refused to accept the resignation of Augustus; they conjured him not to desert the republic which he had saved. After a decent resistance the crafty tyrant submitted to the orders of the senate; and consented to receive the government of the provinces, and the general command of the Roman armies, under the well-known names of Proconsul and Imperator.† But he would receive them only for ten years. Even before the expiration of that period, he hoped that the wounds of civil discord would be completely healed, and that the republic, restored to its pristine health and vigour, would no longer require the dangerous interposition of so extraordinary a magistrate. The memory of this comedy, repeated several times during the life of Augustus, was preserved to the last ages of the empire by the peculiar pomp with which the perpetual

---

* Dion, l. liii. p. 698$_3$, gives us a prolix and bombastic speech on this great occasion. I have borrowed from Suetonius and Tacitus the general language of Augustus.

† *Imperator* (from which we have derived *emperor*) signified under the republic no more than *general*, and was emphatically bestowed by the soldiers, when on the field of battle they proclaimed their victorious leader worthy of that title. When the Roman *emperors* assumed it in that sense, they placed it after their name, and marked how often they had taken it.

monarchs of Rome always solemnized the tenth years of their reign.*

Without any violation of the principles of the constitution, the general of the Roman armies might receive and exercise an authority almost despotic over the soldiers, the enemies, and the subjects of the republic. With regard to the soldiers, the jealousy of freedom had, even from the earliest ages of Rome, given way to the hopes of conquest and a just sense of military discipline. The dictator, or consul, had a right to command the service of the Roman youth, and to punish an obstinate or cowardly disobedience by the most severe and ignominious penalties, by striking the offender out of the list of citizens, by confiscating his property, and by selling his person into slavery.† The most sacred rights of freedom, confirmed by the Porcian and Sempronian laws, were suspended by the military engagement. In his camp the general exercised an absolute power of life and death; his jurisdiction was not confined by any forms of trial or rules of proceeding, and the execution of the sentence was immediate and without appeal.‡ The choice of the enemies of Rome was regularly decided by the legislative authority. The most important resolutions of peace and war were seriously debated in the senate, and solemnly ratified by the people. But when the arms of the legions were carried to a great distance from Italy, the generals assumed the liberty of directing them against whatever people, and in whatever manner, they judged most advantageous for the public service. It was from the success, not from the justice, of their enterprises, that they expected the honours of a triumph. In the use of victory, especially after they were no longer controlled by the commissioners of the senate, they exercised the most unbounded despotism. When Pompey commanded in the East, he rewarded his soldiers and allies, dethroned princes, divided kingdoms, founded colonies, and distributed the treasures of Mithridates. On his return to Rome he obtained, by a single act of the senate and people, the universal ratification of all his proceedings.§ Such was the power

---

* Dion, l. liii. p. 703, &c.

† Liv. Epitom. l. xiv. Valer. Maxim. vi. 3.

‡ See in the viiith book of Livy, the conduct of Manlius Torquatus and Papirius Cursor. They violated the laws of nature and humanity, but they asserted those of military discipline; and the people, who abhorred the action, were obliged to respect the principle.

§ By the lavish but unconstrained suffrages of the people, Pompey had obtained a military command scarcely inferior to that of Augustus. Among the extraordinary acts of power executed by the former, we may remark the foundation of twenty-nine cities, and the distribution of three or four millions sterling

over the soldiers, and over the enemies of Rome, which was either granted to, or assumed by, the generals of the republic. They were, at the same time, the governors, or rather monarchs, of the conquered provinces, united the civil with the military character, administered justice as well as the finances, and exercised both the executive and legislative power of the state.

From what has been already observed in the first chapter of this work, some notion may be formed of the armies and provinces thus intrusted to the ruling hand of Augustus. But, as it was impossible that he could personally command the legions of so many distant frontiers, he was indulged by the senate, as Pompey had already been, in the permission of devolving the execution of his great office on a sufficient number of lieutenants. In rank and authority these officers seemed not inferior to the ancient proconsuls; but their station was dependent and precarious. They received and held their commissions at the will of a superior, to whose *auspicious* influence the merit of their action was legally attributed.* They were the representatives of the emperor. The emperor alone was the general of the republic, and his jurisdiction, civil as well as military, extended over all the conquests of Rome. It was some satisfaction, however, to the senate that he always delegated his power to the members of their body. The imperial lieutenants were of consular or praetorian dignity; the legions were commanded by senators, and the praefecture of Egypt was the only important trust committed to a Roman knight.

Within six days after Augustus had been compelled to accept so very liberal a grant, he resolved to gratify the pride of the senate by an easy sacrifice. He represented to them that they had enlarged his powers, even beyond that degree which might be required by the melancholy condition of the times. They had not permitted him to refuse the laborious command of the armies and the frontiers; but he must insist on being allowed to restore the more peaceful and secure provinces to the mild administration of the civil magistrate. In the division of the provinces Augustus provided for his own

---

to his troops. The ratification of his acts met with some opposition and delays in the senate. See Plutarch, Appian, Dion Cassius, and the first book of the epistles to Atticus.

* Under the commonwealth, a triumph could only be claimed by the general, who was authorized to take the Auspices in the name of the people. By an exact consequence, drawn from this principle of policy and religion, the triumph was reserved to the emperor, and his most successful lieutenants were satisfied with some marks of distinction, which, under the name of triumphal honours, were invented in their favour.

power and for the dignity of the republic. The proconsuls of the senate, particularly those of Asia, Greece, and Africa, enjoyed a more honourable character than the lieutenants of the emperor, who commanded in Gaul or Syria. The former were attended by lictors, the latter by soldiers. A law was passed that, wherever the emperor was present, his extraordinary commission should supersede the ordinary jurisdiction of the governor; a custom was introduced that the new conquests belonged to the imperial portion; and it was soon discovered that the authority of the *Prince,* the favourite epithet of Augustus, was the same in every part of the empire.

In return for this imaginary concession, Augustus obtained an important privilege, which rendered him master of Rome and Italy. By a dangerous exception to the ancient maxims, he was authorized to preserve his military command, supported by a numerous body of guards, even in time of peace, and in the heart of the capital. His command, indeed, was confined to those citizens who were engaged in the service by the military oath; but such was the propensity of the Romans to servitude, that the oath was voluntarily taken by the magistrates, the senators, and the equestrian order, till the homage of flattery was insensibly converted into an annual and solemn protestation of fidelity.

Although Augustus considered a military force as the firmest foundation, he wisely rejected it as a very odious instrument, of government. It was more agreeable to his temper, as well as to his policy, to reign under the venerable names of ancient magistracy, and artfully to collect in his own person all the scattered rays of civil jurisdiction. With this view, he permitted the senate to confer upon him, for his life, the powers of the consular* and tribunitian offices,† which were, in the same manner, continued to all his successors. The consuls had succeeded to the kings of Rome, and represented the dignity of the state. They superintended the ceremonies of religion, levied and commanded the legions, gave audience to foreign ambassadors, and presided in the assemblies both of the senate and people. The general control of the finances was intrusted to their care; and, though they seldom had leisure to administer

---

* Cicero (de Legibus, iii. 3) gives the consular office the name of *Regia potestas:* and Polybius (l. vi. c. 3) observes three powers in the Roman constitution. The monarchical was represented and exercised by the consuls.

† As the tribunitian power (distinct from the annual office) was first invented for the dictator Caesar (Dion, l. xliv. p. 384) , we may easily conceive, that it was given as a reward for having so nobly asserted, by arms, the sacred rights of the tribunes and people. See his own commentaries, de Bell. Civil. l. i.

justice in person, they were considered as the supreme guardians of law, equity, and the public peace. Such was their ordinary jurisdiction; but, whenever the senate empowered the first magistrate to consult the safety of the commonwealth, he was raised by that decree above the laws, and exercised, in the defence of liberty, a temporary despotism.* The character of the tribunes was, in every respect, different from that of the consuls. The appearance of the former was modest and humble; but their persons were sacred and inviolable. Their force was suited rather for opposition than for action. They were instituted to defend the oppressed, to pardon offences, to arraign the enemies of the people, and, when they judged it necessary, to stop, by a single word, the whole machine of government. As long as the republic subsisted, the dangerous influence which either the consul or the tribune might derive from their respective jurisdiction was diminished by several important restrictions. Their authority expired with the year in which they were elected; the former office was divided between two, the latter among ten, persons; and, as both in their private and public interest they were adverse to each other, their mutual conflicts contributed, for the most part, to strengthen rather than to destroy the balance of the constitution. But when the consular and tribunitian powers were united, when they were vested for life in a single person, when the general of the army was, at the same time, the minister of the senate and the representative of the Roman people, it was impossible to resist the exercise, nor was it easy to define the limits, of his imperial prerogative.

To these accumulated honours the policy of Augustus soon added the splendid as well as important dignities of supreme pontiff, and of censor. By the former he acquired the management of the religion, and by the latter a legal inspection over the matters and fortunes, of the Roman people. If so many distinct and independent powers did not exactly unite with each other, the complaisance of the senate was prepared to supply every deficiency by the most ample and extraordinary concessions. The emperors, as the first ministers of the republic, were exempted from the obligation and penalty of many inconvenient laws: they were authorized to con-

---

* Augustus exercised nine annual consulships without interruption. He then most artfully refused that magistracy as well as the dictatorship, absented himself from Rome, and waited till the fatal effects of tumult and faction forced the senate to invest him with a perpetual consulship. Augustus, as well as his successors, affected, however, to conceal so invidious a title.

voke the senate, to make several motions in the same day, to recommend candidates for the honours of the state, to enlarge the bounds of the city, to employ the revenue at their discretion, to declare peace and war, to ratify treaties; and, by a most comprehensive clause, they were empowered to execute whatsoever they should judge advantageous to the empire, and agreeable to the majesty of things private or public, human or divine.*

When all the various powers of executive government were committed to the *Imperial magistrate,* the ordinary magistrates of the commonwealth languished in obscurity, without vigour, and almost without business. The names and forms of the ancient administration were preserved by Augustus with the most anxious care. The usual number of consuls, praetors, and tribunes† were annually invested with their respective ensigns of office, and continued to discharge some of their least important functions. Those honours still attracted the vain ambition of the Romans; and the emperors themselves, though invested for life with the powers of the consulship, frequently aspired to the title of that annual dignity, which they condescended to share with the most illustrious of their fellow-citizens.‡ In the election of these magistrates, the people, during the reign of Augustus, were permitted to expose all the inconveniences of a wild democracy. That artful prince, instead of discovering the least symptom of impatience, humbly solicited their suffrages for himself or his friends, and scrupulously practised all the duties of an ordinary candidate.§ But we may venture to ascribe

---

* See a fragment of a Decree of the Senate, conferring on the Emperor Vespasian all the powers granted to his predecessors, Augustus, Tiberius, and Claudius. This curious and important monument is published in Gruter's Inscriptions, No. ccxlii.

† Two consuls were created on the Calends of January; but in the course of the year others were substituted in their places, till the annual number seems to have amounted to no less than twelve. The praetors were usually sixteen or eighteen (Lipsius in Excurs. D. ad Tacit. Annal. l. i.). I have not mentioned the Aediles or Quaestors. Officers of the police or revenue easily adapt themselves to any form of government. In the time of Nero the tribunes legally possessed the right of intercession, though it might be dangerous to exercise it (Tacit. Annal. xvi. 26). In the time of Trajan, it was doubtful whether the tribuneship was an office or a name (Plin. Epist. 123).

‡ The tyrants themselves were ambitious of the consulship. The virtuous princes were moderate in the pursuit, and exact in the discharge, of it. Trajan revived the ancient oath, and swore before the consul's tribunal that he would observe the laws (Plin. Panegyric. c. 64).

§ *Quoties magistratuum comitiis interesset, tribus cum candidatis suis circuibat; supplicabatque more solemni. Ferebat et ipse suffragium in tribubus, ut unus e populo.* Suetonius in August. c. 56.

to his councils the first measure of the succeeding reign, by which the elections were transferred to the senate. . . .*

CHAPTER XXXVIII · GENERAL OBSERVATIONS ON THE FALL OF THE ROMAN EMPIRE IN THE WEST

The Greeks, after their country had been reduced into a province, imputed the triumphs of Rome, not to the merit, but to the fortune, of the republic. The inconstant goddess, who so blindly distributes and resumes her favours, had *now* consented (such was the language of envious flattery) to resign her wings, to descend from her globe, and to fix her firm and immutable throne on the banks of the Tiber.† A wiser Greek, who has composed, with a philosophic spirit, the memorable history of his own times, deprived his countrymen of this vain and delusive comfort by opening to their view the deep foundations of the greatness of Rome.‡ The fidelity of the citizens to each other, and to the state, was confirmed by the habits of education and the prejudices of religion. Honour, as well as virtue, was the principle of the republic; the ambitious citizens laboured to deserve the solemn glories of a triumph; and the ardour of the Roman youth was kindled into active emulation, as often as they beheld the domestic images of their ancestors.§ The temperate struggles of the patricians and plebeians had finally established the firm and equal balance of the constitution; which united the freedom of popular assemblies with the authority and wisdom of a senate and the executive powers of a regal magistrate.

* *Tum primun Comitia e campo ad patres translata sunt.* Tacit. Annal. l. 15. The word *primum* seems to allude to some faint and unsuccessful efforts, which were made towards restoring them to the people.

† Such are the figurative expressions of Plutarch (Opera, tom. ii. p. 318, edit. Wechel), to whom, on the faith of his son Lamprias (Fabricius, Bibliot. Graec. tom. iii. p. 341), I shall boldly impute the malicious declamation, περὶ τῆς Ῥωμαίων τύχης. The same opinions had prevailed among the Greeks two hundred and fifty years before Plutarch; and to confute them is the professed intention of Polybius (Hist. l. i. p. 90, edit. Gronov. Amstel, 1670).

‡ See the inestimable remains of the sixth book of Polybius, and many other parts of his general history, particularly a disgression in the seventeenth book, in which he compares the phalanx and the legion.

§ Sallust, de Bell. Jugurthin. c. 4. Such were the generous professions of P. Scipio and Q. Maximus. The Latin historian had read, and most probably transcribed, Polybius, their contemporary and friend.

When the consul displayed the standard of the republic, each citizen bound himself, by the obligation of an oath, to draw his sword in the cause of his country, till he had discharged the sacred duty by a military service of ten years. This wise institution continually poured into the field the rising generations of freemen and soldiers; and their numbers were reinforced by the warlike and populous states of Italy, who, after a brave resistance, had yielded to the valour, and embraced the alliance, of the Romans. The sage historian, who excited the virtue of the younger Scipio and beheld the ruin of Carthage,* has accurately described their military system; their levies, arms, exercises, subordination, marches, encampments; and the invincible legion, superior in active strength to the Macedonian phalanx of Philip and Alexander. From these institutions of peace and war, Polybius has deduced the spirit and success of a people incapable of fear and impatient of repose. The ambitious design of conquest, which might have been defeated by the seasonable conspiracy of mankind, was attempted and achieved; and the perpetual violation of justice was maintained by the political virtues of prudence and courage. The arms of the republic, sometimes vanquished in battle, always victorious in war, advanced with rapid steps to the Euphrates, the Danube, the Rhine, and the Ocean; and the images of gold, or silver, or brass, that might serve to represent the nations and their kings, were successively broken by the *iron* monarchy of Rome.†

The rise of a city, which swelled into an Empire, may deserve, as a singular prodigy, the reflection of a philosophic mind. But the decline of Rome was the natural and inevitable effect of immoderate greatness. Prosperity ripened the principle of decay; the causes of destruction multiplied with the extent of conquest; and, as soon as time or accident had removed the artificial supports, the stupendous fabric yielded to the pressure of its own weight. The story of its ruin is simple and obvious; and, instead of inquiring why the

* While Carthage was in flames, Scipio repeated two lines of the Iliad, which express the destruction of Troy, acknowledging to Polybius, his friend and preceptor (Polyb. in Excerpt. de Virtut. et Vit. tom. ii. p. 1455–1465) , that, while he recollected the vicissitudes of human affairs, he inwardly applied them to the future calamities of Rome (Appian. in Libycis, p. 136, edit. Toll.) .

† See Daniel, ii. 31–40. "And the fourth kingdom shall be strong as *iron;* forasmuch as iron breaketh in pieces, and subdueth all things." The remainder of the prophecy (the mixture of iron and *clay*) was accomplished, according to St. Jerom, in his own time. *Sicut enim in principio nihil Romano Imperio fortius et durius, ita in fine rerum nihil imbecillius: quum et in bellis civilibus et adversus diversas nationes aliarum gentium barbararum auxilio indigemus.* (Opera, tom. v. p. 572) .

Roman empire was destroyed, we should rather be surprised that it had subsisted so long. The victorious legions, who, in distant wars, acquired the vices of strangers and mercenaries, first oppressed the freedom of the republic, and afterwards violated the majesty of the purple. The emperors, anxious for their personal safety and the public peace, were reduced to the base expedient of corrupting the discipline which rendered them alike formidable to their sovereign and to the enemy; the vigour of the military government was relaxed, and finally dissolved, by the partial institutions of Constantine; and the Roman world was overwhelmed by a deluge of Barbarians.

The decay of Rome has been frequently ascribed to the translation of the seat of empire; but this history has already shewn that the powers of government were *divided* rather than *removed*. The throne of Constantinople was erected in the East; while the West was still possessed by a series of emperors who held their residence in Italy and claimed their equal inheritance of the legions and provinces. This dangerous novelty impaired the strength, and fomented the vices, of a double reign; the instruments of an oppressive and arbitrary system were multiplied; and a vain emulation of luxury, not of merit, was introduced and supported between the degenerate successors of Theodosius. Extreme distress, which unites the virtue of a free people, embitters the factions of a declining monarchy. The hostile favourites of Arcadius and Honorius betrayed the republic to its common enemies; and the Byzantine court beheld with indifference, perhaps with pleasure, the disgrace of Rome, the misfortunes of Italy, and the loss of the West. Under the succeeding reigns, the alliance of the two empires was restored; but the aid of the Oriental Romans was tardy, doubtful, and ineffectual; and the national schism of the Greeks and Latins was enlarged by the perpetual difference of language and manners, of interest, and even of religion. Yet the salutary event approved in some measure the judgment of Constantine. During a long period of decay, his impregnable city repelled the victorious armies of Barbarians, protected the wealth of Asia, and commanded, both in peace and war, the important straits which connect the Euxine and Mediterranean seas. The foundation of Constantinople more essentially contributed to the preservation of the East than to the ruin of the West.

As the happiness of a *future* life is the great object of religion, we may hear, without surprise or scandal, that the introduction, or at least the abuse, of Christianity had some influence on the decline and fall of the Roman empire. The clergy successfully preached the doctrines of patience and pusillanimity; the active virtues of society were discouraged; and the last remains of the military spirit were buried in the cloister; a large portion of public and private wealth was consecrated to the specious demands of charity and devotion; and the soldiers' pay was lavished on the useless multitudes of both sexes, who could only plead the merits of abstinence and chastity. Faith, zeal, curiosity, and the more earthly passions of malice and ambition kindled the flame of theological discord; the church, and even the state, were distracted by religious factions, whose conflicts were sometimes bloody, and always implacable; the attention of the emperors was diverted from camps to synods; the Roman world was oppressed by a new species of tyranny; and the persecuted sects became the secret enemies of their country. Yet party-spirit, however pernicious or absurd, is a principle of union as well as of dissension. The bishops, from eighteen hundred pulpits, inculcated the duty of passive obedience to a lawful and orthodox sovereign; their frequent assemblies, and perpetual correspondence, maintained the communion of distant churches: and the benevolent temper of the gospel was strengthened, though confined, by the spiritual alliance of the Catholics. The sacred indolence of the monks was devoutly embraced by a servile and effeminate age; but, if superstition had not afforded a decent retreat, the same vices would have tempted the unworthy Romans to desert, from baser motives, the standard of the republic. Religious precepts are easily obeyed, which indulge and sanctify the natural inclinations of their votaries; but the pure and genuine influence of Christianity may be traced in its beneficial, though imperfect, effects on the Barbarian proselytes of the North. If the decline of the Roman empire was hastened by the conversion of Constantine, his victorious religion broke the violence of the fall, and mollified the ferocious temper of the conquerors.

This awful revolution may be usefully applied to the instruction of the present age. It is the duty of a patriot to prefer and promote the exclusive interest and glory of his native country; but a philosopher may be permitted to enlarge his views, and to consider Europe as one great republic, whose various inhabitants have attained almost the same level of politeness and cultivation. The balance of power will continue to fluctuate, and the prosperity of our own or the neighbouring kingdoms may be alternately exalted or depressed; but these partial events cannot essentially injure our general state of happiness, the system of arts, and laws, and manners, which so advantageously distinguish, above the rest of mankind, the Europeans and their colonies. The savage nations of the globe are the common enemies of civilized society; and we may inquire with anxious curiosity, whether Europe is still threatened with a repetition of those calamities which formerly oppressed the arms and institutions of Rome. Perhaps the same reflections will illustrate the fall of that mighty empire, and explain the probable causes of our actual security.

I. The Romans were ignorant of the extent of their danger, and the number of their enemies. Beyond the Rhine and Danube, the northern countries of Europe and Asia were filled with innumerable tribes of hunters and shepherds, poor, voracious, and turbulent; bold in arms, and impatient to ravish the fruits of industry. The Barbarian world was agitated by the rapid impulse of war; and the peace of Gaul or Italy was shaken by the distant revolutions of China. The Huns, who fled before a victorious enemy, directed their march towards the West; and the torrent was swelled by the gradual accession of captives and allies. The flying tribes who yielded to the Huns assumed in *their* turn the spirit of conquest; the endless column of Barbarians pressed on the Roman empire with accumulated weight; and, if the foremost were destroyed, the vacant space was instantly replenished by new assailants. Such formidable emigrations can no longer issue from the North; and the long repose, which has been imputed to the decrease of population, is the happy consequence of the progress of arts and agriculture. Instead of some rude villages, thinly scattered among its woods and morasses, Germany now produces a list of two thousand three hundred walled towns; the Christian kingdoms of Denmark, Sweden, and Poland, have been successively established; and the Hanse merchants, with the Teutonic knights, have extended their colonies along the coast of the Baltic, as far as the Gulf of Finland. From the Gulf of Finland to the Eastern Ocean, Russia now assumes the form of a powerful and civilized empire. The plough, the loom, and the forge, are introduced on the banks of the Volga, the Oby, and the Lena; and the fiercest of the Tartar hordes have been taught to tremble and obey. The reign of independent Barbarism is now contracted to a narrow span; and the remnant of Calmucks or Uzbecks, whose forces may be almost numbered, cannot seriously excite the apprehensions of the great republic of Europe.* Yet this apparent security should not tempt us to forget that new enemies, and unknown dangers, may *possibly* arise from

* The French and English editors of the Genealogical History of the Tartars have subjoined a curious, though imperfect, description of their present state.

some obscure people, scarcely visible in the map of the world. The Arabs or Saracens, who spread their conquests from India to Spain, had languished in poverty and contempt, till Mahomet breathed into those savage bodies the soul of enthusiasm.

II. The empire of Rome was firmly established by the singular and perfect coalition of its members. The subject nations, resigning the hope, and even the wish, of independence, embraced the character of Roman citizens; and the provinces of the West were reluctantly torn by the Barbarians from the bosom of their mother-country.* But this union was purchased by the loss of national freedom and military spirit; and the servile provinces, destitute of life and motion, expected their safety from the mercenary troops and governors, who were directed by the orders of a distant court. The happiness of an hundred millions depended on the personal merit of one or two men, perhaps children, whose minds were corrupted by education, luxury, and despotic power. The deepest wounds were inflicted on the empire during the minorities of the sons and grandsons of Theodosius; and, after those incapable princes seemed to attain the age of manhood, they abandoned the church to the bishops, the state to the eunuchs, and the provinces to the Barbarians. Europe is now divided into twelve powerful, though unequal, kingdoms, three respectable commonwealths, and a variety of smaller, though independent, states; the chances of royal and ministerial talents are multiplied, at least with the number of its rulers; and a Julian, or Semiramis, may reign in the North, while Arcadius and Honorius again slumber on the thrones of the South. The abuses of tyranny are restrained by the mutual influence of fear and shame; republics have acquired order and stability; monarchies have imbibed the principles of freedom, or, at least, of moderation; and some sense of honour and justice is introduced into the most defective constitutions by the general manners of the times. In peace, the progress of knowledge and industry is accelerated by the emulation of so many active rivals: in war, the Euro-

---

We might question the independence of the Calmucks, or Eluths, since they have been recently vanquished by the Chinese, who, in the year 1759, subdued the lesser Bucharia, and advanced into the country of Badakshan, near the sources of the Oxus (Mémoires sur les Chinois, tom. i. p. 325–400) . But these conquests are precarious, nor will I venture to ensure the safety of the Chinese empire.

* The prudent reader will determine how far this general proposition is weakened by the revolt of the Isaurians, the independence of Britain and Armorica, the Moorish tribes, or the Bagandae of Gaul and Spain (vol. i. p. 280, vol. iii. p. 352, 402, 480) .

pean forces are exercised by temperate and undecisive contests. If a savage conqueror should issue from the deserts of Tartary, he must repeatedly vanquish the robust peasants of Russia, the numerous armies of Germany, the gallant nobles of France, and the intrepid freemen of Britain; who, perhaps, might confederate for their common defence. Should the victorious Barbarians carry slavery and desolation as far as the Atlantic Ocean, ten thousand vessels would transport beyond their pursuit the remains of civilized society; and Europe would revive and flourish in the American world which is already filled with her colonies and institutions.*

III. Cold, poverty, and a life of danger and fatigue, fortify the strength and courage of Barbarians. In every age they have oppressed the polite and peaceful nations of China, India, and Persia, who neglected, and still neglect, to counterbalance these natural powers by the resources of military art. The war-like states of antiquity, Greece, Macedonia, and Rome, educated a race of soldiers; exercised their bodies, disciplined their courage, multiplied their forces by regular evolutions, and converted the iron which they possessed into strong and serviceable weapons. But this superiority insensibly declined with their laws and manners; and the feeble policy of Constantine and his successors armed and instructed, for the ruin of the empire, the rude valour of the Barbarian mercenaries. The military art has been changed by the invention of gunpowder; which enables man to command the two most powerful agents of nature, air and fire. Mathematics, chemistry, mechanics, architecture, have been applied to the service of war; and the adverse parties oppose to each other the most elaborate modes of attack and of defence. Historians may indignantly observe that the preparations of a siege would found and maintain a flourishing colony;† yet we cannot be displeased that the subver-

---

* America now contains about six millions of European blood and descent; and their numbers, at least in the North, are continually increasing. Whatever may be the changes of their political situation, they must preserve the manners of Europe; and we may reflect with some pleasure that the English language will probably be diffused over an immense and populous continent.

† *On avoit fait venir* [for the siege of Turin] *140 pièces de canon; et il est à remarquer que chaque gros canon monté revient à environ 2000 écus; il y avoit 110,000 boulets; 106,000 cartouches d'une façon, et 300,000 d'une autre; 21,000 bombes; 27,700 grenades, 15,000 sacs à terre, 30,000 instruments pour le pionnage; 1,200,000 livres de poudre. Ajoutez à ces munitions, le plomb, le fer, et le fer blanc, les cordages, tout ce qui sert aux mineurs, le souphre, le salpêtre, les outils de toute espèce. Il est certain que les frais de tous ces préparatifs de destruction suffiroient pour fonder et pour faire fleurir la plus nombreuse colonie.*—Voltaire, Siècle de Louis XIV, c. xx. in his Works, tom. xi. p. 391.

sion of a city should be a work of cost and difficulty, or that an industrious people should be protected by those arts, which survive and supply the decay of military virtue. Cannon and fortifications now form an impregnable barrier against the Tartar horse; and Europe is secure from any future irruption of Barbarians; since, before they can conquer, they must cease to be barbarous. Their gradual advances in the science of war would always be accompanied, as we may learn from the example of Russia, with a proportionable improvement in the arts of peace and civil policy; and they themselves must deserve a place among the polished nations whom they subdue.

Should these speculations be found doubtful or fallacious, there still remains a more humble source of comfort and hope. The discoveries of ancient and modern navigators, and the domestic history, or tradition, of the most enlightened nations, represent the *human savage,* naked both in mind and body, and destitute of laws, of arts, of ideas, and almost of language.* From this abject condition, perhaps the primitive and universal state of man, he has gradually arisen to command the animals, to fertilise the earth, to traverse the ocean, and to measure the heavens. His progress in the improvement and exercise of his mental and corporeal faculties† has been irregular and various, infinitely slow in the beginning, and increasing by degrees with redoubled velocity; ages of laborious ascent have been followed by a moment of rapid downfall; and the several climates of the globe have felt the vicissitudes of light and darkness. Yet the experience of four thousand years should enlarge our hopes, and diminish our apprehensions; we cannot determine to what height the human species may aspire in their advances towards perfection; but it may safely be presumed that no people, unless the face of nature is changed, will relapse into their original barbarism. The improvements of society may be viewed under a

---

* It would be an easy though tedious task to produce the authorities of poets, philosophers, and historians. I shall therefore content myself with appealing to the decisive and authentic testimony of Diodorus Siculus (tom. i. l. i. p. 11, 12, l. iii. p. 184, &c., edit. Wesseling). The Ichthyophagi, who in his time wandered along the shores of the Red Sea, can only be compared to the natives of New Holland (Dampier's Voyages, vol. i. p. 464–469). Fancy or perhaps reason may still suppose an extreme and absolute state of nature far below the level of these savages, who had acquired some arts and instruments.

† See the learned and rational work of the President Goguet, de l'Origine des Loix, des Arts, et des Sciences. He traces from facts or conjectures (tom. i. p. 147–337, edit. 12mo) the first and most difficult steps of human invention.

threefold aspect. 1. The poet or philosopher illustrates his age and country by the efforts of a *single* mind; but these superior powers of reason or fancy are rare and spontaneous productions, and the genius of Homer, or Cicero, or Newton, would excite less admiration, if they could be created by the will of a prince or the lessons of a preceptor. 2. The benefits of law and policy, of trade and manufactures, of arts and sciences, are more solid and permanent; and *many* individuals may be qualified, by education and discipline, to promote, in their respective stations, the interest of the community. But this general order is the effect of skill and labour; and the complex machinery may be decayed by time or injured by violence. 3. Fortunately for mankind, the more useful, or, at least, more necessary arts can be performed without superior talents, or national subordination; without the powers of *one* or the union of *many*. Each village, each family, each individual, must always possess both ability and inclination to perpetuate the use of fire* and of metals; the propagation and service of domestic animals; the methods of hunting and fishing; the rudiments of navigation; the imperfect cultivation of corn or other nutritive grain; and the simple practice of the mechanic trades. Private genius and public industry may be extirpated; but these hardy plants survive the tempest, and strike an everlasting root into the most unfavourable soil. The splendid days of Augustus and Trajan were eclipsed by a cloud of ignorance; and the Barbarians subverted the laws and palaces of Rome. But the scythe, the invention or emblem of Saturn,† still continued annually to mow the harvests of Italy: and the human feasts of the Laestrygons‡ have never been renewed on the coast of Campania.

Since the first discovery of the arts, war, commerce, and religious zeal have diffused, among the savages of the Old and New World, those inestimable gifts: they have been successively propagated;

* It is certain, however strange, that many nations have been ignorant of the use of fire. Even the ingenious natives of Otaheite, who are destitute of metals, have not invented any earthen vessels capable of sustaining the action of fire and of communicating the heat to the liquids which they contain.

† Plutarch. Quaest. Rom. in tom. ii. p. 275. Macrob. Saturnal. l. i. c. 8, p. 152 edit. London. The arrival of Saturn (or his religious worship) in a ship may indicate that the savage coast of Latium was first discovered and civilized by the Phoenicians.

‡ In the ninth and tenth books of the Odyssey, Homer has embellished the tales of fearful and credulous sailors, who transformed the cannibals of Italy and Sicily into monstrous giants.

they can never be lost. We may therefore acquiesce in the pleasing conclusion that every age of the world has increased, and still increases, the real wealth, the happiness, the knowledge, and perhaps the virtue, of the human race.*

FURTHER READING

Arnaldo Momigliano, "Gibbon's Contribution to Historical Method," in *Studies in Historiography* (1966) , 40–55. Brilliant, indispensable.

Thomas P. Peardon, *The Transition in English Historical Writing, 1760–1830* (1933) . Puts Gibbon into his place and time.

* The merit of discovery has too often been stained with avarice, cruelty, and fanaticism; and the intercourse of nations has produced the communication of disease and prejudice. A singular exception is due to the virtue of our own times and country. The five great voyages successively undertaken by the command of his present Majesty were inspired by the pure and generous love of science and of mankind. The same prince, adapting his benefactions to the different stages of society, has founded a school of painting in his capital, and has introduced into the islands of the South Sea the vegetables and animals most useful to human life.

46 ❋ BENTHAM

An Introduction to the Principles of Morals and Legislation

[From *The Works of Jeremy Bentham*, edited by
John Bowring, 11 vols. (1843), I, 1–6, 83–86.]

*For the student of the Enlightenment, Jeremy Bentham is doubly
interesting. He represents, in his work, the purest expression of the
Enlightenment's rejection of natural law and of its advocacy of
utilitarian principles. In his long and polemic-ridden life—he was
born in 1748 and died in 1832—he transmitted the ideas and, even
more, the techniques of enlightened social science from the eighteenth to the nineteenth century.*

*Bentham was, and remains, controversial. His own appraisal was
that his work meant a radical attack on all fictions, all sentimental
gush, in social inquiry for the sake of clarity and humane action.
But his critics have charged him with insensitivity to the finer
nuances and the higher achievements of civilization, and of a program for social engineering so ruthless that Benthamite humaneness
actually becomes a new, and harsher, form of slavery. His notorious
design for prisons so built that a warder can see the prisoners'
activities from a central station suggests that the critics have a
point. On the other hand, it is unhistorical to judge Bentham's
work, and even his mentality, from the dreadful experiences of our
own century, with its massive brutality, its brainwashing, its manip-
ulation of the public. Bentham would have regarded totalitarianism, no matter how "public-spirited," as just another vicious fiction.*

*Educated at Oxford, Bentham practiced law for a time, and
published his first book, the* Fragment on Government, *in 1776.
Soon he devoted himself to discovering the psychological principles*

of human action, and to unmasking the fictions that kept mankind
in thrall to superstition, legal obscurantism, and the rule of the few.
Following the French philosophe and psychologist Helvétius, and
the Scottish philosopher Hume—Hume, it seems, is everywhere!—
Bentham argued essentially for two closely related points, hedonism
and Utilitarianism. Hedonism we may define as the psychological
position, hinted at by Locke, adumbrated by Condillac, and pushed
to its conclusion by Helvétius, that holds man to be exclusively
driven by pleasure and pain. Pleasure is what man wants to secure,
pain is what man acts to avoid. On this simple foundation the
whole complex of human action can be constructed, without recourse to impressive-sounding but untenable myths like selflessness
or asceticism. And Utilitarianism we may define as the social
application of hedonism: since the largest amount of pleasure is
clearly the goal of the individual, the largest amount of pleasure for
all must be the goal of society. This is generally known as the
"greatest-happiness principle."

Two obvious difficulties present themselves, and Bentham was
not unaware of them: how do we measure pleasures, and how do we
reconcile the pleasures of one with the pain of another? As to the
first, Bentham worked out what he called the "felicific calculus": we
may rationally estimate a pleasure by seven criteria—its intensity,
duration, certainty, propinquity, fecundity, purity, and extent.
This may sound mechanical and even absurd, but the felicific calculus is, in essence, an appeal to reason, or rather reasonableness: to
enjoy a pleasure (for example, taking drugs) intensely may not be
worthwhile, since its duration will be short and its known penalties
great. On the second difficulty, Bentham suggested that other social
theorists had recommended policies on fictive or speculative bases;
the best social policy was one that distributed pleasures as widely as
possible, and reduced pain as much as possible. While this does not
seem too specific a guide to policy, it points the state in a humane
direction: punishment, for instance, must be as small as is compatible with security. And it points, also, to the need for close empirical research into the consequences of policy. From this perspective,
Bentham's Utilitarianism was not merely humane, but intensely
practical as well.*

Bentham wrote incessantly, and many of his manuscripts still
await publication. Among the books he published, The Principles of

---

* That it was a system dubious in its application became clear when Bentham's
disciples (and he had many) helped to push through a new Poor Law in
England in 1834, with its harsh "incentives" to work.

Morals and Legislation *(1789)*, *here excerpted, is the best known, and the best. It lays down the principles of Utilitarianism with all of Bentham's clarity, and lack of elegance.*

CHAPTER I · OF THE PRINCIPLE OF UTILITY

I. Nature has placed mankind under the governance of two sovereign masters, *pain* and *pleasure*. It is for them alone to point out what we ought to do, as well as to determine what we shall do. On the one hand the standard of right and wrong, on the other the chain of causes and effects, are fastened to their throne. They govern us in all we do, in all we say, in all we think: every effort we can make to throw off our subjection, will serve but to demonstrate and confirm it. In words a man may pretend to abjure their empire: but in reality he will remain subject to it all the while. The *principle of utility** recognises this subjection, and assumes it for the foundation of that system, the object of which is to rear the fabric of felicity by the hands of reason and of law. Systems which attempt to question it, deal in sounds instead of sense, in caprice instead of reason, in darkness instead of light.

But enough of metaphor and declamation: it is not by such means that moral science is to be improved.

II. The principle of utility is the foundation of the present

* NOTE BY THE AUTHOR, JULY 1822:

To this denomination has of late been added, or substituted, the *greatest happiness* or *greatest felicity* principle: this for shortness, instead of saying at length *that principle* which states the greatest happiness of all those whose interest is in question, as being the right and proper, and only right and proper and universally desirable, end of human action: of human action in every situation, and in particular in that of a functionary or set of functionaries exercising the powers of Government. The word *utility* does not so clearly point to the ideas of *pleasure* and *pain* as the words *happiness* and *felicity* do: nor does it lead us to the consideration of the *number,* of the interests affected; to the *number,* as being the circumstance, which contributes, in the largest proportion, to the formation of the standard here in question; the *standard of right and wrong,* by which alone the propriety of human conduct, in every situation, can with propriety be tried. This want of a sufficiently manifest connexion between the ideas of *happiness* and *pleasure* on the one hand, and the idea of *utility* on the other, I have every now and then found operating, and with but too much efficiency, as a bar to the acceptance, that might otherwise have been given, to this principle.

work: it will be proper therefore at the outset to give an explicit and determinate account of what is meant by it. By the principle of utility is meant that principle which approves or disapproves of every action whatsoever, according to the tendency which it appears to have to augment or diminish the happiness of the party whose interest is in question: or, what is the same thing in other words, to promote or to oppose that happiness. I say of every action whatsoever; and therefore not only of every action of a private individual, but of every measure of government.

III. By utility is meant that property in any object, whereby it tends to produce benefit, advantage, pleasure, good, or happiness, (all this in the present case comes to the same thing) or (what comes again to the same thing) to prevent the happening of mischief, pain, evil, or unhappiness to the party whose interest is considered: if that party be the community in general, then the happiness of the community: if a particular individual, then the happiness of that individual.

IV. The interest of the community is one of the most general expressions that can occur in the phraseology of morals: no wonder that the meaning of it is often lost. When it has a meaning, it is this. The community is a fictitious *body*, composed of the individual persons who are considered as constituting as it were its *members*. The interest of the community then is, what?—the sum of the interests of the several members who compose it.

V. It is in vain to talk of the interest of the community, without understanding what is the interest of the individual. A thing is said to promote the interest, or to be *for* the interest, of an individual, when it tends to add to the sum total of his pleasures: or, what comes to the same thing, to diminish the sum total of his pains.

VI. An action then may be said to be conformable to the principle of utility, or, for shortness sake, to utility, (meaning with respect to the community at large) when the tendency it has to augment the happiness of the community is greater than any it has to diminish it.

VII. A measure of government (which is but a particular kind of action, performed by a particular person or persons) may be said to be conformable to or dictated by the principle of utility, when in like manner the tendency which it has to augment the happiness of the community is greater than any which it has to diminish it.

VIII. When an action, or in particular a measure of government, is supposed by a man to be conformable to the principle of utility, it may be convenient, for the purposes of discourse, to imagine a kind of law or dictate, called a law or dictate of utility: and to speak of the action in question, as being conformable to such law or dictate.

IX. A man may be said to be a partizan of the principle of utility, when the approbation or disapprobation he annexes to any action, or to any measure, is determined by and proportioned to the tendency which he conceives it to have to augment or to diminish the happiness of the community: or in other words, to its conformity or unconformity to the laws or dictates of utility.

X. Of an action that is conformable to the principle of utility one may always say either that it is one that ought to be done, or at least that it is not one that ought not to be done. One may say also, that it is right it should be done; at least that it is not wrong it should be done: that it is a right action; at least that it is not a wrong action. When thus interpreted, the words *ought,* and *right* and *wrong,* and others of that stamp, have a meaning: when otherwise, they have none.

XI. Has the rectitude of this principle been ever formally contested? It should seem that it had, by those who have not known what they have been meaning. Is it susceptible of any direct proof? it should seem not: for that which is used to prove every thing else, cannot itself be proved: a chain of proofs must have their commencement somewhere. To give such proof is as impossible as it is needless.

XII. Not that there is or ever has been that human creature breathing, however stupid or perverse, who has not on many, perhaps on most occasions of his life, deferred to it. By the natural constitution of the human frame, on most occasions of their lives men in general embrace this principle, without thinking of it: if not for the ordering of their own actions, yet for the trying of their own actions, as well as of those of other men. There have been, at the same time, not many, perhaps, even of the most intelligent, who have been disposed to embrace it purely and without reserve. There are even few who have not taken some occasion or other to quarrel with it, either on account of their not understanding always how to apply it, or on account of some prejudice or other which they were afraid to examine into, or could not bear to part with. For such is the stuff that man is made of: in principle and in practice, in a right track and in a wrong one, the rarest of all human qualities is consistency.

XIII. When a man attempts to combat the principle of utility, it is with reasons drawn, without his being aware of it, from that very

principle itself.* His arguments, if they prove any thing, prove not
that the principle is *wrong*, but that, according to the applications
he supposes to be made of it, it is *misapplied*. Is it possible for a
man to move the earth? Yes; but he must first find out another earth
to stand upon.

XIV. To disprove the propriety of it by arguments is impossible;
but, from the causes that have been mentioned, or from some confused or partial view of it, a man may happen to be disposed not to

* "The principle of utility, [I have heard it said] is a dangerous principle:
it is dangerous on certain occasions to consult it." This is as much as to say,
what? that it is not consonant to utility, to consult utility: in short, that it is
not consulting it, to consult it.

ADDITION BY THE AUTHOR, JULY 1822:

Not long after the publication of the Fragment on Government, anno 1776,
in which, in the character of an all-comprehensive and all-commanding principle, the principle of *utility* was brought to view, one person by whom observation to the above effect was made was Alexander Wedderburn, at that time
Attorney or Solicitor General, afterwards successively Chief Justice of the
Common Pleas, and Chancellor of England, under the successive titles of Lord
Loughborough and Earl of Rosslyn. It was made—not indeed in my hearing,
but in the hearing of a person by whom it was almost immediately communicated to me. So far from being self-contradictory, it was a shrewd and perfectly
true one. By that distinguished functionary, the state of the Government was
thoroughly understood: by the obscure individual, at that time not so much as
supposed to be so: his disquisitions had not been as yet applied, with any thing
like a comprehensive view, to the field of Constitutional Law, nor therefore to
those features of the English Government, by which the greatest happiness of
the ruling *one* with or without that of a favoured few, are now so plainly seen
to be the only ends to which the course of it has at any time been directed.
The *principle of utility* was an appellative, at that time employed—employed by
me, as it had been by others, to designate that which, in a more perspicuous
and instructive manner, may, as above, be designated by the name of the
greatest happiness principle. "This principle [said Wedderburn] is a dangerous
one." Saying so, he said that which, to a certain extent, is strictly true: a principle, which lays down, as the only *right* and justifiable end of Government, the
greatest happiness of the greatest number—how can it be denied to be a
dangerous one? dangerous it unquestionably is, to every government which has
for its *actual* end or object, the greatest happiness of a certain *one*, with or
without the addition of some comparatively small number of others, whom
it is matter of pleasure or accommodation to him to admit, each of them, to a
share in the concern, on the footing of so many junior partners. *Dangerous* it
therefore really was, to the interest—the sinister interest—of all those functionaries, himself included, whose interest it was, to maximize delay, vexation, and
expense, in judicial and other modes of procedure, for the sake of the profit,
extractible out of the expense. In a Government which had for its end in view
the greatest happiness of the greatest number, Alexander Wedderburn might
have been Attorney General and then Chancellor: but he would not have been
Attorney General with £15,000 a year, nor Chancellor, with a peerage with a
veto upon all justice, with £25,000 a year, and with 500 sinecures at his disposal,
under the name of Ecclesiastical Benefices, besides *et caeteras*.

relish it. Where this is the case, if he thinks the settling of his opinions on such a subject worth the trouble, let him take the following steps, and at length, perhaps, he may come to reconcile himself to it.

1. Let him settle with himself, whether he would wish to discard this principle altogether; if so, let him consider what it is that all his reasonings (in matters of politics especially) can amount to?

2. If he would, let him settle with himself, whether he would judge and act without any principle, or whether there is any other he would judge and act by?

3. If there be, let him examine and satisfy himself whether the principle he thinks he has found is really any separate intelligible principle; or whether it be not a mere principle in words, a kind of phrase, which at bottom expresses neither more nor less than the mere averment of his own unfounded sentiments; that is, what in another person he might be apt to call caprice?

4. If he is inclined to think that his own approbation or disapprobation, annexed to the idea of an act, without any regard to its consequences, is a sufficient foundation for him to judge and act upon, let him ask himself whether his sentiment is to be a standard of right and wrong, with respect to every other man, or whether every man's sentiment has the same privilege of being a standard to itself?

5. In the first case, let him ask himself whether his principle is not despotical, and hostile to all the rest of human race?

6. In the second case, whether it is not anarchial, and whether at this rate there are not as many different standards of right and wrong as there are men? and whether even to the same man, the same thing, which is right to-day, may not (without the least change in its nature) be wrong to-morrow? and whether the same thing is not right and wrong in the same place at the same time? and in either case, whether all argument is not at an end? and whether, when two men have said, "I like this," and "I don't like it," they can (upon such a principle) have any thing more to say?

7. If he should have said to himself, No: for that the sentiment which he proposes as a standard must be grounded on reflection, let him say on what particulars the reflection is to turn? if on particulars having relation to the utility of the act, then let him say whether this is not deserting his own principle, and borrowing assistance from that very one in opposition to which he sets it up: or if not on those particulars, on what other particulars?

8. If he should be for compounding the matter, and adopting his

own principle in part, and the principle of utility in part, let him say how far he will adopt it?

9. When he has settled with himself where he will stop, then let him ask himself how he justifies to himself the adopting it so far? and why he will not adopt it any farther?

10. Admitting any other principle than the principle of utility to be a right principle, a principle that it is right for a man to pursue; admitting (what is not true) that the word *right* can have a meaning without reference to utility, let him say whether there is any such thing as a *motive* that a man can have to pursue the dictates of it: if there is, let him say what that motive is, and how it is to be distinguished from those which enforce the dictates of utility: if not, then lastly let him say what it is this other principle can be good for?

CHAPTER II · OF PRINCIPLES ADVERSE TO THAT OF UTILITY

I. If the principle of utility be a right principle to be governed by, and that in all cases, it follows from what has been just observed, that whatever principle differs from it in any case must necessarily be a wrong one. To prove any other principle, therefore, to be a wrong one, there needs no more than just to show it to be what it is, a principle of which the dictates are in some point or other different from those of the principle of utility: to state it is to confute it.

II. A principle may be different from that of utility in two ways: 1. By being constantly opposed to it: this is the case with a principle which may be termed the principle of *asceticism*. 2. By being sometimes opposed to it, and sometimes not, as it may happen: this is the case with another, which may be termed the principle of *sympathy* and *antipathy*.

III. By the principle of asceticism I mean that principle, which, like the principle of utility, approves or disapproves of any action, according to the tendency which it appears to have to augment or diminish the happiness of the party whose interest is in question; but in an inverse manner: approving of actions in as far as they tend to diminish his happiness; disapproving of them in as far as they tend to augment it.

IV. It is evident that any one who reprobates any the least particle of pleasure, as such, from whatever source derived, is *pro tanto* a partizan of the principle of asceticism. It is only upon that principle, and not from the principle of utility, that the most abominable pleasure which the vilest of malefactors ever reaped from his crime would be to be reprobated, if it stood alone. The case is, that it never does stand alone; but is necessarily followed by such a quantity of pain (or, what comes to the same thing, such a chance for a certain quantity of pain) that the pleasure in comparison of it, is as nothing: and this is the true and sole, but perfectly sufficient, reason for making it a ground for punishment.

V. There are two classes of men of very different complexions, by whom the principle of asceticism appears to have been embraced; the one a set of moralists, the other a set of religionists. Different accordingly have been the motives which appear to have recommended it to the notice of these different parties. Hope, that is the prospect of pleasure, seems to have animated the former: hope, the aliment of philosophic pride: the hope of honour and reputation at the hands of men. Fear, that is the prospect of pain, the latter: fear, the offspring of superstitious fancy: the fear of future punishment at the hands of a splenetic and revengeful Deity. I say in this case fear: for of the invisible future, fear is more powerful than hope. These circumstances characterize the two different parties among the partizans of the principle of asceticism; the parties and their motives different, the principle the same.

VI. The religious party, however, appear to have carried it farther than the philosophical: they have acted more consistently and less wisely. The philosophical party have scarcely gone farther than to reprobate pleasure: the religious party have frequently gone so far as to make it a matter of merit and of duty to court pain. The philosophical party have hardly gone farther than the making pain a matter of indifference. It is no evil, they have said: they have not said, it is a good. They have not so much as reprobated all pleasure in the lump. They have discarded only what they have called the gross; that is, such as are organical, or of which the origin is easily traced up to such as are organical: they have even cherished and magnified the refined. Yet this, however, not under the name of pleasure: to cleanse itself from the sordes of its impure original, it was necessary it should change its name: the honourable, the glorious, the reputable, the becoming, the *honestum,* the *decorum,* it was to be called: in short, any thing but pleasure.

VII. From these two sources have flowed the doctrines from which the sentiments of the bulk of mankind have all along received a tincture of this principle; some from the philosophical, some from the religious, some from both. Men of education more frequently from the philosophical, as more suited to the elevation of their sentiments: the vulgar more frequently from the superstitious, as more suited to the narrowness of their intellect, undilated by knowledge: and to the abjectness of their condition, continually open to the attacks of fear. The tinctures, however, derived from the two sources, would naturally intermingle, insomuch that a man would not always know by which of them he was most influenced: and they would often serve to corroborate and enliven one another. It was this conformity that made a kind of alliance between parties of a complexion otherwise so dissimilar: and disposed them to unite upon various occasions against the common enemy, the partizan of the principle of utility, whom they joined in branding with the odious name of Epicurean.

VIII. The principle of asceticism, however, with whatever warmth it may have been embraced by its partizans as a rule of private conduct, seems not to have been carried to any considerable length, when applied to the business of government. In a few instances it has been carried a little way by the philosophical party: witness the Spartan regimen. Though then, perhaps, it may be considered as having been a measure of security: and an application, though a precipitate and perverse application, of the principle of utility. Scarcely in any instances, to any considerable length, by the religious: for the various monastic orders, and the societies of the Quakers, Dumplers, Moravians, and other religionists, have been free societies, whose regimen no man has been astricted to without the intervention of his own consent. Whatever merit a man may have thought there would be in making himself miserable, no such notion seems ever to have occurred to any of them, that it may be a merit, much less a duty, to make others miserable: although it should seem, that if a certain quantity of misery were a thing so desirable, it would not matter much whether it were brought by each man upon himself, or by one man upon another. It is true, that from the same source from whence, among the religionists, the attachment to the principle of asceticism took its rise, flowed other doctrines and practices, from which misery in abundance was produced in one man by the instrumentality of another: witness the holy wars, and the persecutions for religion. But the passion for producing misery in these cases proceeded upon some special ground: the exercise of it was confined to persons of particular descriptions: they were tormented, not as men, but as heretics and infidels. To have inflicted the same miseries on their fellow-believers and fellow-sectaries, would have been as blameable in the eyes even of these religionists, as in those of a partizan of the principle of utility. For a man to give himself a certain number of stripes was indeed meritorious: but to give the same number of stripes to another man, not consenting, would have been a sin. We read of saints, who for the good of their souls, and the mortification of their bodies, have voluntarily yielded themselves a prey to vermin: but though many persons of this class have wielded the reins of empire, we read of none who have set themselves to work, and made laws on purpose, with a view of stocking the body politic with the breed of highwaymen, housebreakers, or incendiaries. If at any time they have suffered the nation to be preyed upon by swarms of idle pensioners, or useless placemen, it has rather been from negligence and imbecility, than from any settled plan for oppressing and plundering of the people. If at any time they have sapped the sources of national wealth, by cramping commerce, and driving the inhabitants into emigration, it has been with other views, and in pursuit of other ends. If they have declaimed against the pursuit of pleasure, and the use of wealth, they have commonly stopped at declamation: they have not, like Lycurgus, made express ordinances for the purpose of banishing the precious metals. If they have established idleness by a law, it has been not because idleness, the mother of vice and misery, is itself a virtue, but because idleness (say they) is the road to holiness. If under the notion of fasting, they have joined in the plan of confining their subjects to a diet, thought by some to be of the most nourishing and prolific nature, it has been not for the sake of making them tributaries to the nations by whom that diet was to be supplied, but for the sake of manifesting their own power, and exercising the obedience of the people. If they have established, or suffered to be established, punishments for the breach of celibacy, they have done no more than comply with the petitions of those deluded rigorists, who, dupes to the ambitious and deep-laid policy of their rulers, first laid themselves under that idle obligation by a vow.

IX. The principle of asceticism seems originally to have been the reverie of certain hasty speculators, who having perceived, or fancied, that certain pleasures, when reaped in certain circumstances, have, at the long run, been attended with pains more than equivalent to them, took occasion to quarrel with every thing that offered itself under the name of pleasure. Having then got thus far, and having forgot the point which they set out from, they pushed on, and went so much further as to think it meritorious to fall in love with pain. Even this, we see, is at bottom but the principle of utility misapplied.

X. The principle of utility is capable of being consistently pursued; and it is but tautology to say, that the more consistently it is pursued, the better it must ever be for human kind. The principle of asceticism never was, nor ever can be, consistently pursued by any living creature. Let but one tenth part of the inhabitants of this earth pursue it consistently, and in a day's time they will have turned it into a hell.

CHAPTER XV

§ I. *General view of cases unmeet for punishment.*

I. The general object which all laws have, or ought to have, in common, is to augment the total happiness of the community; and therefore, in the first place, to exclude, as far as may be, every thing that tends to subtract from that happiness: in other words, to exclude mischief.

II. But all punishment is mischief: all punishment in itself is evil. Upon the principle of utility, if it ought at all to be admitted, it ought only to be admitted in as far as it promises to exclude some greater evil.

III. It is plain, therefore, that in the following cases punishment ought not to be inflicted.

1. Where it is *groundless:* where there is no mischief for it to prevent; the act not being mischievous upon the whole.

2. Where it must be *inefficacious:* where it cannot act so as to prevent the mischief.

3. Where it is *unprofitable,* or too *expensive:* where the mischief it would produce would be greater than what it prevented.

4. Where it is *needless:* where the mischief may be prevented, or cease of itself, without it: that is, at a cheaper rate.

§ 2. *Cases in which punishment is groundless.*

These are,

IV. 1. Where there has never been any mischief: where no mischief has been produced to any body by the act in question. Of this number are those in which the act was such as might, on some occasions, be mischievous or disagreeable, but the person whose interest it concerns gave his *consent* to the performance of it. This consent, provided it be free, and fairly obtained, is the best proof that can be produced, that, to the person who gives it, no mischief, at least no immediate mischief, upon the whole, is done. For no man can be so good a judge as the man himself, what it is gives him pleasure or displeasure.

V. 2. Where the mischief was *outweighed*: although a mischief was produced by that act, yet the same act was necessary to the production of a benefit which was of greater value than the mischief. This may be the case with any thing that is done in the way of precaution against instant calamity, as also with any thing that is done in the exercise of the several sorts of powers necessary to be established in every community, to wit, domestic, judicial, military, and supreme.

VI. 3. Where there is a certainty of an adequate compensation: and that in all cases where the offence can be committed. This supposes two things: 1. That the offence is such as admits of an adequate compensation: 2. That such a compensation is sure to be forthcoming. Of these suppositions, the latter will be found to be a merely ideal one: a supposition that cannot, in the universality here given to it, be verified by fact. It cannot, therefore, in practice, be numbered amongst the grounds of absolute impunity. It may, however, be admitted as a ground for an abatement of that punishment, which other considerations, standing by themselves, would seem to dictate.

§ 3. *Cases in which punishment must be inefficacious.*

These are,

VII. 1. Where the penal provision is *not established* until after the act is done. Such are the cases, 1. Of an *ex-post-facto* law; where the legislator himself appoints not a punishment till after the act is done. 2. Of a sentence beyond the law; where the judge, of his own authority, appoints a punishment which the legislator had not appointed.

VIII. 2. Where the penal provision, though established, is *not conveyed* to the notice of the person on whom it seems intended that it should operate. Such is the case where the law has omitted to employ any of the expedients which are necessary, to make sure that every person whatsoever, who is within the reach of the law, be apprized of all the cases whatsoever, in which (being in the station of life he is in) he can be subjected to the penalties of the law.

IX. 3. Where the penal provision, though it were conveyed to a man's notice, *could produce no effect* on him, with respect to the preventing him from engaging in any act of the *sort* in question. Such is the case, 1. In extreme *infancy;* where a man has not yet attained that state or disposition of mind in which the prospect of evils so distant as those which are held forth by the law, has the effect of influencing his conduct. 2. In *insanity;* where the person, if he has attained to that disposition, has since been deprived of it through the influence of some permanent though unseen cause. 3. In *intoxication;* where he has been deprived of it by the transient influence of a visible cause: such as the use of wine, or opium, or other drugs, that act in this manner on the nervous system: which condition is indeed neither more nor less than a temporary insanity produced by an assignable cause.

X. 4. Where the penal provision (although, being conveyed to the party's notice, it might very well prevent his engaging in acts of the sort in question, provided he knew that it related to those acts) could not have this effect, with regard to the *individual* act he is about to engage in: to wit, because he knows not that it is of the number of those to which the penal provision relates. This may happen, 1. In the case of *unintentionality;* where he intends not to engage, and thereby knows not that he is about to engage, in the *act* in which eventually he is about to engage. 2. In the case of *unconsciousness;* where, although he may know that he is about to engage in the *act* itself, yet, from not knowing all the material *circumstances* attending it, he knows not of the *tendency* it has to produce that mischief, in contemplation of which it has been made penal in most instances. 3. In the case of *missupposal;* where, although he may know of the tendency the act has to produce that degree of mischief, he supposes it, though mistakenly, to be attended with some circumstance, or set of circumstances, which, if it had been attended with, it would either not have been productive of that mischief, or have been productive of such a greater degree of good, as has determined the legislator in such a case not to make it penal.

XI. 5. Where, though the penal clause might exercise a full and prevailing influence, were it to act alone, yet by the *predominant* influence of some opposite cause upon the will, it must necessarily be ineffectual; because the evil which he sets himself about to undergo, in the case of his *not* engaging in the act, is so great, that the evil denounced by the penal clause, in case of his engaging in it, cannot appear greater. This may happen, 1. In the case of *physical danger;* where the evil is such as appears likely to be brought about by the unassisted powers of *nature.* 2. In the case of a *threatened mischief;* where it is such as appears likely to be brought about through the intentional and conscious agency of *man.**

XII. 6. Where (though the penal clause may exert a full and prevailing influence over the *will* of the party) yet his *physical faculties* (owing to the predominant influence of some physical cause) are not in a condition to follow the determination of the will: insomuch that the act is absolutely *involuntary.* Such is the case of physical *compulsion* or *restraint,* by whatever means brought about; where the man's hand, for instance, is pushed against some object which his will disposes him *not* to touch; or tied down from touching some object which his will disposes him to touch.

§ 4. *Cases where punishment is unprofitable.*

These are,

XIII. 1. Where, on the one hand, the nature of the offence, on the other hand, that of the punishment, are, *in the ordinary state of things,* such, that when compared together, the evil of the latter will turn out to be greater than that of the former.

XIV. Now the evil of the punishment divides itself into four branches, by which so many different sets of persons are affected.

1. The evil of *coercion* or *restraint:* or the pain which it gives a man not to be able to do the act, whatever it be, which by the apprehension of the punishment he is deterred from doing. This is felt by those by whom the law is *observed.* 2. The evil of *apprehension:* or the pain which a man, who has exposed himself to punishment, feels at the thoughts of undergoing it. This is felt by those by whom the law has been *broken,* and who feel themselves in *danger* of its being executed upon them. 3. The evil of *sufferance:* or the pain which a man feels, in virtue of the punishment itself, from the time when he begins to undergo it. This is felt by those by whom the law is broken, and upon whom it comes actually to be executed. 4. The pain of sympathy, and the other *derivative* evils resulting to

---

* The influences of the *moral* and *religious* sanctions, or, in other words, of the motives of *love of reputation* and *religion,* are other causes, the force of which may, upon particular occasions, come to be greater than that of any punishment which the legislator is *able,* or at least which he will *think proper,* to apply. These, therefore, it will be proper for him to have his eye upon. But the force of these influences is variable and different in different times and places: the force of the foregoing influences is constant and the same, at all times and every where. These, therefore, it can never be proper to look upon as safe grounds for establishing absolute impunity: owing (as in the above-mentioned cases of infancy and intoxication) to the impracticability of ascertaining the matter of fact.

the persons who are in *connection* with the several classes of original sufferers just mentioned. Now of these four lots of evil, the first
will be greater or less, according to the nature of the act from which
the party is restrained: the second and third according to the nature
of the punishment which stands annexed to that offence.

XV. On the other hand, as to the evil of the offence, this will
also, of course, be greater or less, according to the nature of each
offence. The proportion between the one evil and the other will
therefore be different in the case of each particular offence. The
cases, therefore, where punishment is unprofitable on this ground,
can by no other means be discovered, than by an examination of
each particular offence; which is what will be the business of the
body of the work.

XVI. 2. Where, although in the *ordinary state* of things, the evil
resulting from the punishment is not greater than the benefit which
is likely to result from the force with which it operates, during the
same space of time, towards the excluding the evil of the offences,
yet it may have been rendered so by the influence of some *occasional circumstances*. In the number of these circumstances may be,
1. The multitude of delinquents at a particular juncture; being
such as would increase, beyond the ordinary measure, the *quantum*
of the second and third lots, and thereby also of a part of the fourth
lot, in the evil of the punishment. 2. The extraordinary value of
the services of some one delinquent; in the case where the effect of
the punishment would be to deprive the community of the benefit
of those services. 3. The displeasure of the *people;* that is, of an
indefinite number of the members of the *same* community, in cases
where (owing to the influence of some occasional incident) they
happen to conceive, that the offence or the offender ought not to be
punished at all, or at least ought not to be punished in the way in
question. 4. The displeasure of *foreign powers;* that is, of the
governing body, or a considerable number of the members of some
foreign community or communities, with which the community in
question is connected.

§ 5. *Cases where punishment is needless.*

These are,

XVII. 1. Where the purpose of putting an end to the practice
may be attained as effectually at a cheaper rate: by instruction, for
instance, as well as by terror: by informing the understanding, as
well as by exercising an immediate influence on the will. This seems

to be the case with respect to all those offences which consist in the disseminating pernicious principles in matters of *duty;* of whatever kind the duty be; whether political, or moral, or religious. And this, whether such principles be disseminated *under,* or even *without,* a sincere persuasion of their being beneficial. I say, even *without:* for though in such a case it is not instruction that can prevent the writer from endeavouring to inculcate his principles, yet it may the readers from adopting them: without which, his endeavouring to inculcate them will do no harm. In such a case, the sovereign will commonly have little need to take an active part: if it be the interest of *one* individual to inculcate principles that are pernicious, it will as surely be the interest of *other* individuals to expose them. But if the sovereign must needs take a part in the controversy, the pen is the proper weapon to combat error with, not the sword. . . .

FURTHER READING

Charles W. Everett, *The Education of Jeremy Bentham* (1931). A highly favorable appraisal.

Élie Halévy, *The Growth of Philosophical Radicalism* (1928). A pioneering and sympathetic examination of Utilitarianism by a great French historian of England.

Gertrude Himmelfarb, "The Haunted House of Jeremy Bentham," in *Victorian Minds* (1970 edn.). A harsh indictment of Bentham that charges his supporters with gullibility. Important but not wholly convincing.

Mary P. Mack, *Jeremy Bentham: An Odyssey of Ideas* (1963). The most significant defense of Bentham's ideas; goes only to 1792.

VII

The Party of Humanity

Whatever the flaws of the philosophes' analytical schemes and the defects of their intentions, the general aim of their movement was to increase the quantity of humanity in the world. Not all of the philosophes were crusaders, and some of the crusaders among them kept an eye on their reputation—which is to say that they were individuals and that they were human. And some of the good causes they adopted, they came to champion quite late in the game— which is to say that they were part of their culture and, however rebellious, enmeshed in its values. Yet when all this has been conceded, we must insist that the philosophes wanted a world more tolerant, more peaceful, and more prosperous, less cruel, less superstitious, and less parochial—a world of free and reasonable men.

The event that did most to put the humanitarian goals of the Enlightenment into the forefront of public attention was the Calas case. This is briefly the story: In the evening of October 13, 1761, a young Huguenot named Marc-Antoine Calas was found hanged in his father's shop in Toulouse. As a Huguenot, Marc-Antoine had been prevented from entering the legal career he craved, and he was known to be moody, but at first the family testified that he had been murdered by a stranger. Only later, after pressing questions, did the Calas family concede that the young man had in fact committed suicide. The family was arrested, subjected to the extensive and intensive interrogations characteristic of French law; the local magistrates made immense efforts to find out the truth about the affair. Finally, on March 9, 1762, Marc-Antoine's elderly father, Jean Calas, was convicted of murdering his son, presumably to prevent him from converting to Roman Catholicism. Before his execution, Jean Calas was subjected to the question ordinaire *and the* question extraordinaire—*two innocuous-sounding phrases which meant, in a word, torture—but throughout his ordeal the old man reasserted his innocence and refused to name accomplices to a crime he insisted he had never committed. On March 10, he was broken on the wheel, and strangled by the executioner.*

Later that month, Voltaire, at Ferney, heard of the case, and was grimly amused: if Calas was in fact guilty, this demonstrated the fanaticism of Protestants ready to commit the most heinous crime to keep any of their number from embracing the True Faith; if Calas was in fact innocent, this demonstrated the fanaticism of Catholics ready to commit judicial murder on the basis of the fantastic charge of ritual murder. By the end of the month, Voltaire was no longer amused. Almost obsessively, he asked for more information. He interviewed surviving members of the Calas family. He used his extensive connections to find out more about the legal procedures the Toulouse magistrates had used. What he found appalled him. For one thing, he became convinced that Jean Calas was an innocent victim of local prejudice and parochial stupidity; there was no evidence for the murder, and powerful evidence against the possibility of an old man stringing up a vigorous young man all by himself. And if he had help from his family, why had the authorities let them go? There was one awkward fact: the family had obviously lied about that stranger killing Marc-Antoine. But this was easily explained: under French law a suicide was an infamous criminal whose dead body was subjected to a degrading mock trial, dragged naked through the streets by the heels, and hanged as a murderer. Fear of disgrace, combined with shock, had produced a fatal lie—but this did not excuse the authorities.

Here was another thing Voltaire found out: the French legal system, based on a Criminal Ordinance passed in 1670, was hardly calculated to discover the truth in difficult cases. The law was savage in its punishments, brutal in its permissible forms of interrogation, favorable to the prosecution and hostile to the defense. Unlike English trials, of which Voltaire as an Anglomaniac had a most favorable impression, French "trials" seemed like theatrical rituals intent on finding the accused guilty, even if he was innocent. Elderly but energetic, Voltaire went to work, deluging his friends and influential acquaintances with letters, and mobilizing public opinion by writing pamphlet after pamphlet in Jean Calas's behalf. Jean Calas was dead; but it might be possible to rehabilitate his memory and his family, and to prevent similar cases.

Voltaire's campaign was partly a success, partly a failure: in 1763 the Conseil d'État decided to reopen the case; in 1764 the Conseil Privé du Roi set aside the verdict; and in March 1765, three years after the execution, the Calas family was rehabilitated, the sentence stricken from the record, and the family indemnified. Yet similar trials went on: in 1766, a not-very-bright adolescent named the Chevalier de La Barre was executed for some fairly innocent anticlerical pranks. *Voltaire took on the La Barre case as well, and others that were brought to his attention. Beginning with an intervention in a single miscarriage of justice, Voltaire broadened his public campaign to reform French justice as a whole. Voltaire, once aroused, was a formidable campaigner, successful, be it noted, where he was successful, in part because he had powerful support among liberal and humane Catholics.*

The Calas case dramatized the cause of the Enlightenment. And it spurred on the philosophes themselves to unprecedented efforts of public propaganda. Some of their work, mainly theoretical, will occupy the pages that follow. But then, for the philosophes, the terrains of theory and practice were contiguous, and the boundaries between them easy to cross.

FURTHER READING

David D. Bien, *The Calas Affair: Persecution, Toleration, and Heresy in Eighteenth-Century Toulouse* (1960). An imaginative and most informative monograph that places a sensational legal case in its social setting.

James Heath, *Eighteenth Century Penal Theory* (1963). A helpful anthology.

Dorothy Marshall, *The English Poor in the Eighteenth Century* (1926). A wide-ranging survey of a subject getting more and more attention from historians.

Shelby T. McCloy, *The Humanitarian Movement in Eighteenth-Century France* (1957). Pedestrian but informative.

47 ❊ SCHLÖZER

Neujahrs-Geschenk aus Jamaika

[From August Ludwig von Schlözer, *Neujahrs-
Geschenk aus Jamaika* (1780), 35–40. Translated
by Ruth Gay.* The existence of this book was
first called to my attention by Joan Karle.]

*For many in the eighteenth century, slavery seemed a vaguely
obnoxious but economically indispensable institution. "The
Quakers of Pennsylvania," the noted Scottish sociologist John Millar noted in 1771, "are the first body of men" to have "discovered
any scruples" about slavery, and to have "thought that the abolition of this practice is a duty they owe to religion and humanity."†
Among the philosophes too there was serious doubt that slavery was
compatible with law or with humanity. Montesquieu hinted at this
position as early as 1721, in his* Persian Letters; *Rousseau rejected
slavery in principle in 1762, in the* Social Contract; *other humanitarians expressed their outrage. In 1773, when British commercial
interests centered in the West Indies managed to have a threatened
inquiry called off, Horace Walpole exploded in fury: "Caribs, black
Caribs, have no representatives in Parliament; they have no agent
but God, and he is seldom called to the bar of the House to defend
their cause; 206 to 88 gave them up to the mercy of their persecutors . . . Alas! dare I complain of gout and rheumatism, when so
much a bitterer cup is brewed for men as good as myself in every
quarter of the globe!"‡ A year later he professed himself ready to*

* Reprinted with the kind permission of Dr. Haenel, Handschriftenabteilung,
Niedersächsische Staats- und Universitätsbibliothek, Göttingen.

† *The Origins of the Distinction of Ranks,* 2nd edn. (1779), reprinted in its
entirety in William C. Lehmann, *John Millar of Glasgow, 1735–1801* (1960);
the quotation is from p. 311.

‡ To Sir Horace Mann, Feb. 17, 1773, in Walpole, *Letters,* ed. Mrs. Paget
Toynbee, 16 vols. (1904–5), VIII, 241.

welcome and to support a general slave rebellion. "I should think,"
he wrote prophetically, "the souls of the Africans would sit heavily
on the swords of the Americans."*

But there was also another strand in the philosophes' growing
objection to the Peculiar Institution: in addition to being inhumane it was unprofitable. This, though it seemed a cooler argument
for abolition than the humanitarian and legal ones, was more
effective since there were many with little love for slavery who saw
no way out of it because they thought it essential to commercial
prosperity. The Scottish social scientists took the lead: John Millar
argued that slavery is "equally inconvenient and pernicious,"†
while Adam Smith proved with detailed psychological and economic arguments that slavery was wasteful, and profitable only to a
small minority of entrepreneurs. "The work done by slaves," he
insisted, "though it appears to cost only their maintenance, is in the
end the dearest of any."‡ Once again, the philosophes called science
to the aid of humanity.

Among the antislavery appeals perhaps not the least effective was
the sentimental. Our selection from Schlözer's Neurjahrs-Geschenk
aus Jamaika (1780), one of the first children's books ever published, is a fine example of this kind of appeal. August Ludwig von
Schlözer (1735–1809) was an erudite scholar, a specialist in Scandinavian and Russian history; in 1769, after a time in the Russia of
Catherine the Great, he was appointed professor at the University
of Göttingen, where he lectured on the new social science of statis-
tics, on the history of countries he knew best, and, in later years, on
universal history. In addition, he was an indefatigable journalist
who for some years published a journal of his own. A difficult man
but a friend of freedom, he intended to reach not merely adults but
children. It was, in his day, a much neglected audience.

To illustrate the sort of information on which the antislavery
cause could draw, I am reprinting§ a broadside "Description of a
Slave Ship," printed in London in 1789.

---

* To Rev. William Mason, Feb. 14, 1774, *ibid.*, 423.

† *Distinction of Ranks*, in Lehmann, *Millar*, 316.

‡ *The Wealth of Nations*, Modern Library edn., 365. It is obvious from his
writings, though, that this economic argument, though serious and in Adam
Smith's mind conclusive, only accompanies the humanitarian argument that
slavery is—or should be—unthinkable in a civilized world.

§ From a copy in the Beinecke Rare Book and Manuscript Library at Yale
University.

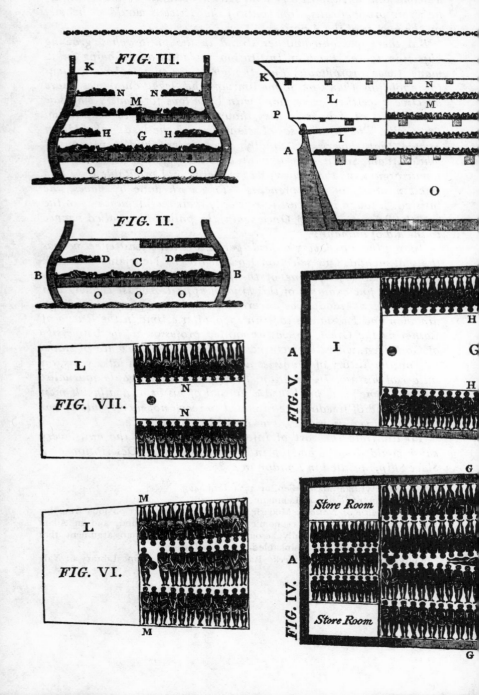

FIG. III.

FIG. II.

FIG. VII.

FIG. VI.

FIG. V.

FIG. IV.

Store Room

Store Room

OF A SLAVE SHIP.

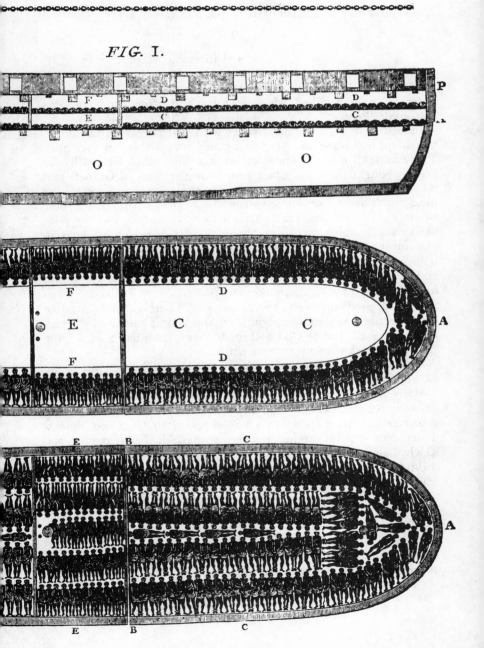

FIG. I.

A New Year's Letter from Jamaica

Kingston, December 7, 1778

Early this morning a Negro went through all the streets ringing a little bell. He had a slip of paper in his hand and called out something for sale. I asked what he was calling out, and someone answered: "People."

Indeed, last week a ship arrived with 550 Negroes. Just think, Christian, 550 stout, fat Negroes penned into a ship, in that heat. There must have been a fine smell on that ship . . . ! Originally the French bought these 550 black people on the coast of Guinea, and wanted to ship them to Martinique. On their way, the French were intercepted by an English privateer who boarded them (since there is a war going on) and took off their cargo of people. But the poor blacks won nothing by this exchange. Instead of becoming slaves in Martinique, they will be slaves in Jamaica. These blacks were now being advertised by the Negro with the bell as if they were oysters and dried cod. Whoever had the interest and the taste for it was invited to go to the Negro market and pick out what he liked.

I got dressed and went to the market. There a whole mass of black people was standing about, old and young, men and women, all stark naked, just as God had made them. Each had a card hung around his neck with a number written on it.

Dear God, I thought, here people sell human beings just as we sell geese and pigs.

Many buyers were walking about; they examined and felt the blacks to see whether they had anything wrong with them. A strong young fellow in his best years was expected to fetch 600 Reichsthaler. For others varying prices were asked: from 450 to 200 Reichsthaler. Old men and women were not worth more than little children.

I saw Madame vom Blocksberge's steward. He was buying for his mistress a thirty-year-old, robust Negro for 580 Reichsthaler. Thrown in, for nothing, was a little black boy, about your size and age. This child is going to wait on Madame. Every morning he will get up at four o'clock and climb the mountain to the coffee plantation to pick up the fallen coffee berries. And for all this, he will get nothing more than plantains to eat.

A sugar planter bought his sister, a little girl of about twelve years of age, for 150 Reichsthaler. So these poor children were separated and may never see one another again for the rest of their lives.

By nine o'clock, everything was sold, and everyone made his preparations to carry off his newly acquired goods. The little black girl kissed her little brother once again and cried; the old Negroes embraced one another and howled their goodbyes. As they were going, there suddenly started up a dull roaring among them. At first I thought it was just more howling. Then I realized they were singing a song in their Guinea language which would go something as follows:

> Far from my homeland
> I must languish and die,
> Without comfort, amidst struggle and shame.
> O the white men, so clever and handsome!
> Yet I have done these pitiless white men no harm.
> You, there, in heaven, help me, a poor black man!

FURTHER READING

David Brion Davis, *The Problem of Slavery in Western Culture* (1966). The first volume of a projected three, concentrating on *ideas.*

Frank J. Klingberg, *The Anti-Slavery Movement in England: A Study in English Humanitarianism* (1926). Comprehensive, informative.

Leonard Krieger, *The German Idea of Freedom: History of a Political Tradition* (1957). Analytical and sophisticated; illuminating about Schlözer and his age.

C. L. Locke, *France and the Colonial Question: A Study of Contemporary French Opinion, 1763–1801* (1932). Useful survey of public opinion.

Daniel P. Mannix (in collaboration with Malcolm Cowley), *Black Cargoes: A History of the Atlantic Slave Trade, 1518–1865* (1962). Popular, reliable, a good specimen of a growing literature.

48 ❦ BOSWELL

The Life of Samuel Johnson

[From James Boswell, *The Life of Samuel
Johnson, LL.D.*, 4 vols. (1807), III, 219–22
(September 23, 1777)].

*On abolition, as on other issues, the philosophes had support from
many in their time who were not philosophes by any stretch of that
term. I have made that point before; I illustrate it here: Samuel
Johnson, implacable adversary of the Humes and Rousseaus of his
world, was an equally implacable adversary of slavery. In a discussion with Boswell, whose complacency on the subject could not be
surpassed, Johnson made his views unmistakably clear. They are
worth preserving.*

After supper I accompanied him to his apartment, and at my
request he dictated to me an argument in favour of the negro who
was then claiming his liberty, in an action in the Court of Session in
Scotland. He had always been very zealous against slavery in every
form, in which I with all deference thought that he discovered "a
zeal without knowledge." Upon one occasion, when in company
with some very grave men at Oxford, his toast was, "Here's to the
next insurrection of the negroes in the West Indies." His violent
prejudice against our West Indian and American settlers appeared
whenever there was an opportunity. Towards the conclusion of his
"Taxation no Tyranny," he says, "how is it that we hear the loudest
yelps for liberty among the drivers of negroes?"

The argument dictated by Dr. Johnson, was as follows:

"It must be agreed that in most ages many countries have had part of their inhabitants in a state of slavery; yet it may be doubted whether slavery can ever be supposed the natural condition of man. It is impossible not to conceive that men in their original state were equal; and very difficult to imagine how one would be subjected to another but by violent compulsion. An individual may, indeed, forfeit his liberty by a crime; but he cannot by that crime forfeit the liberty of his children. What is true of a criminal seems true likewise of a captive. A man may accept life from a conquering enemy on condition of perpetual servitude; but it is very doubtful whether he can entail that servitude on his descendants; for no man can stipulate without commission for another. The condition which he himself accepts, his son or grandson perhaps would have rejected. If we should admit, what perhaps may with more reason be denied, that there are certain relations between man and man which may make slavery necessary and just, yet it can never be proved that he who is now suing for his freedom ever stood in any of those relations. He is certainly subject by no law, but that of violence, to his present master; who pretends no claim to his obedience, but that he bought him from a merchant of slaves, whose right to sell him never was examined. It is said that according to the constitutions of Jamaica he was legally enslaved; these constitutions are merely positive; and apparently injurious to the rights of mankind, because whoever is exposed to sale is condemned to slavery without appeal; by whatever fraud or violence he might have been originally brought into the merchant's power. In our own time Princes have been sold, by wretches to whose care they were entrusted, that they might have an European education; but when once they were brought to a market in the plantations, little would avail either their dignity or their wrongs. The laws of Jamaica afford a Negro no redress. His colour is considered as a sufficient testimony against him. It is to be lamented that moral right should ever give way to political convenience. But if temptations of interest are sometimes too strong for human virtue, let us at least retain a virtue where there is no temptation to quit it. In the present case there is apparent right on one side, and no convenience on the other. Inhabitants of this island can neither gain riches nor power by taking away the liberty of any part of the human species. The sum of the argument is this:—No man is by nature the property of another: The defendant is, therefore, by nature free: The rights of nature must be some way forfeited before they can be justly taken away: That the defendant has by any act forfeited the rights of nature we require to be proved; and if no proof of such forfeiture can be given, we doubt not but the justice of the court will declare him free."

I record Dr. Johnson's argument fairly upon this particular case; where, perhaps, he was in the right. But I beg leave to enter my most solemn protest against his general doctrine with respect to the *Slave Trade.* For I will resolutely say—that his unfavourable notion of it was owing to prejudice, and imperfect or false information. The wild and dangerous attempt which has for some time been persisted in to obtain an act of our Legislature, to abolish so very important and necessary a branch of commercial interest, must have been crushed at once, had not the insignificance of the zealots who vainly took the lead in it, made the vast body of Planters, Merchants, and others, whose immense properties are involved in that trade, reasonably enough suppose that there could be no danger. The encouragement which the attempt has received excites my wonder and indignation; and though some men of superiour abilities have supported it; whether from a love of temporary popularity, when prosperous; or a love of general mischief when desperate, my opinion is unshaken. To abolish a *status,* which in all ages God has sanctioned, and man has continued, would not only be *robbery* to an innumerable class of our fellow-subjects; but it would be extreme cruelty to the African Savages, a portion of whom it saves from massacre, or intolerable bondage in their own country, and introduces into a much happier state of life; especially now when their passage to the West-Indies and their treatment there is humanely regulated. To abolish that trade would be to "shut the gates of mercy on mankind.". . .

FURTHER READING

Walter Jackson Bate, *The Achievement of Samuel Johnson* (1955). A clear analysis of a complex man.

Donald J. Greene, *The Politics of Samuel Johnson* (1960). Bellicose and revisionist; sees Johnson as anything but a "crusty" conservative; an important monograph.

Robert Voitle, *Samuel Johnson the Moralist* (1961). A persuasive analysis; recommended.

49 ❀ MACKENZIE

The Man of Feeling

[From Henry Mackenzie, *The Man of Feeling*
(*1771*).]

*The new sensitivity to suffering (some of which was to issue in
sentimentality or romantic sensibility) gave new prominence to
tears. Addison—or, at least his spokesman, Mr. Spectator—was
touched to tears at the spectacle of the London stock exchange;
novelists like Richardson and Rousseau made their readers weep
over parting lovers, dying declarations, or unforeseen reunions.
Much of this lachrymosity is maudlin and offensive today, but it
was both cause and consequence of an important cultural development. Tears were sometimes an escape from giving serious consideration to social problems, but often they were a sign that
something was being recognized as a problem in the first place.*

*Henry Mackenzie (1745–1831), a distinguished Edinburgh attor-
ney and popular novelist, has the hero of his* Man of Feeling
*weeping on every page, and readers have had good sport counting
tears in that novel. But in the chapter here reproduced, Harley
weeps for the insane whom, as he points out, it has been fashionable
to show off to the curious visitor on a Sunday afternoon. Hogarth
had recorded this dreadful scene in* A Rake's Progress. *Mackenzie
records his abhorrence of this callous practice, and thus a shift
toward greater awareness of the wretched insane, traditionally regarded as sacred figures or, more often, as figures of fun.*

*This shift of attitude appears in the scanty writings of the philos-
ophes on the subject. Skeptical of the notion of sacred fools, unwilling to consider the mad as outcasts to be freely mistreated,
incredulous of talk about madness as a divine punishment or a
divine sign, the secular philosophes saw it simply as a disorder in*

*the human machine. "A madman," wrote Voltaire, "is a sick man
whose brain is in distress, as the gouty man is a sick man who suffers
in his feet and hands."* From this view to the medical treatment of
the insane was but one, admittedly large, step.*

CHAPTER XX · HE VISITS BEDLAM.—THE DISTRESSES OF A DAUGHTER.

Of those things called Sights in London, which every stranger is
supposed desirous to see, Bedlam is one. To that place, therefore, an
acquaintance of Harley's, after having accompanied him to several
other shows, proposed a visit. Harley objected to it, "because," said
he, "I think it an inhuman practice to expose the greatest misery
with which our nature is afflicted, to every idle visitant, who can
afford a trifling perquisite to the keeper; especially as it is a distress
which the humane must see with the painful reflection, that it is not
in their power to alleviate it." He was overpowered, however, by the
solicitations of his friend and the other persons of the party,
(amongst whom were several ladies;) and they went in a body to
Moorfields.

Their conductor led them first to the dismal mansions of those
who are in the most horrid state of incurable madness. The clank-
ing of chains, the wildness of their cries, and the imprecations which
some of them uttered, formed a scene inexpressibly shocking.
Harley and his companions, especially the female part of them,
begged their guide to return: he seemed surprised at their uneasiness, and was with difficulty prevailed on to leave that part of the
house without showing them some others; who, as he expressed it, in
the phrase of those who keep wild beasts for show, were much better
worth seeing than any they had passed, being ten times more fierce
and unmanageable.

He led them next to that quarter where those reside, who, as they
are not dangerous to themselves or others, enjoy a certain degree of
freedom, according to the state of their distemper.

Harley had fallen behind his companions, looking at a man who

* "Madness," in *Philosophical Dictionary*, tr. Peter Gay (1962), 277–78.

was making pendulums with bits of thread, and little balls of clay. He had delineated a segment of a circle on the wall with chalk, and marked their different vibrations, by intersecting it with cross lines. A decent looking man came up, and smiling at the maniac, turned to Harley, and told him, that gentleman had once been a very celebrated mathematician. "He fell a sacrifice," said he, "to the theory of comets; for having, with infinite labor, formed a table on the conjectures of Sir Isaac Newton, he was disappointed in the return of one of those luminaries, and was very soon after obliged to be placed here by his friends. If you please to follow me, Sir," continued the stranger, "I believe I shall be able to give you a more satisfactory account of the unfortunate people you see here, than the man who attends your companions." Harley bowed and accepted the offer.

The next person they came up to had scrawled a variety of figures on a piece of slate. Harley had the curiosity to take a nearer view of them. They consisted of different columns, on the top of which were marked South Sea annuities, India stock, and Three per cent. annuities consol. "This," said Harley's instructer, "was a gentleman well known in Change-alley. He was once worth fifty thousand pounds, and had actually agreed for the purchase of an estate in the West, in order to realize his money; but he quarrelled with the proprietor about the repairs of the garden-wall, and so returned to town to follow his old trade of stock-jobbing a little longer; when an unlucky fluctuation of stock, in which he was engaged to an immense extent, reduced him at once to poverty and to madness. Poor wretch! he told me t'other day, that against the next payment of differences, he should be some hundreds above a plum." "It is a spondee, and I will maintain it," interrupted a voice on his left hand. This assertion was followed by a very rapid recital of some verses from Homer. "That figure," said the gentleman, "whose clothes are so bedaubed with snuff, was a schoolmaster of some reputation: he came hither to be resolved of some doubts he entertained concerning the genuine pronunciation of the Greek vowels. In his highest fits, he makes frequent mention of one Mr. Bentley.

"But delusive ideas, Sir, are the motives of the greatest part of mankind, and a heated imagination the power by which their actions are incited: the world, in the eye of a philosopher, may be said to be a large madhouse." "It is true," answered Harley, "the passions of men are temporary madness; and sometimes very fatal in their effects,

"From Macedonia's madman to the Swede."

"It was, indeed," said the stranger, "a very mad thing in Charles, to think of adding so vast a country as Russia to his dominions; that would have been fatal indeed; the balance of the North would then have been lost; but the Sultan and I would never have allowed it."—"Sir!" said Harley, with no small surprise on his countenance. "Why, yes," answered the other, "the Sultan and I; do you know me? I am the Chan of Tartary."

Harley was a good deal struck by this discovery; he had prudence enough, however, to conceal his amazement, and, bowing as low to the monarch as his dignity required, left him immediately, and joined his companions.

He found them in a quarter of the house set apart for the insane of the other sex, several of whom had gathered about the female visiters, and were examining, with rather more accuracy than might have been expected, the particulars of their dress.

Separate from the rest stood one, whose appearance had something of superior dignity. Her face, though pale and wasted, was less squalid than those of the others, and showed a dejection of that decent kind, which moves our pity unmixed with horror: upon her, therefore, the eyes of all were immediately turned. The keeper, who accompanied them, observed it: "This," said he, "is a young lady, who was born to ride in her coach and six. She was beloved, if the story I have heard be true, by a young gentleman, her equal in birth, though by no means her match in fortune: but love, they say, is blind, and so she fancied him as much as he did her. Her father, it seems, would not hear of their marriage, and threatened to turn her out of doors, if ever she saw him again. Upon this, the young gentleman took a voyage to the West Indies, in hopes of bettering his fortune, and obtaining his mistress; but he was scarce landed, when he was seized with one of the fevers, which are common in those islands, and died in a few days, lamented by every one that knew him. This news soon reached his mistress, who was at the same time pressed by her father to marry a rich miserly fellow, who was old enough to be her grandfather. The death of her lover had no effect on her inhuman parent: he was only the more earnest for her marriage with the man he had provided for her; and what between her despair at the death of the one, and her aversion to the other, the poor young lady was reduced to the condition you see her in. But God would not prosper such cruelty: her father's affairs soon after went to wreck, and he died almost a beggar."

Though this story was told in very plain language, it had particularly attracted Harley's notice; he had given it the tribute of some tears. The unfortunate young lady had, till now, seemed entranced in thought, with her eyes fixed on a little garnet ring she wore on her finger: she turned them now upon Harley. "My Billy is no more!" said she; "Do you weep for my Billy? Blessings on your tears! I would weep too, but my brain is dry; and it burns, it burns, it burns!" She drew nearer to Harley. "Be comforted, young lady," said he, "your Billy is in heaven." "Is he, indeed? and shall we meet again? and shall that frightful man (pointing to the keeper) not be there? Alas! I am grown naughty of late; I have almost forgotten to think of heaven: yet I pray sometimes; when I can, I pray, and sometimes I sing; when I am saddest, I sing. You shall hear me—hush!

> "Light be the earth on Billy's breast,
> And green the sod that wraps his grave."

There was a plaintive wildness in the air not to be withstood; and, except the keeper's, there was not an unmoistened eye around her.

"Do you weep again?" said she; "I would not have you weep. You are like my Billy: you are, believe me; just so he looked, when he gave me this ring; poor Billy! 'twas the last time ever we met!

> " 'Twas when the seas were roaring"—

"I love you for resembling my Billy; but I shall never love any man like him." She stretched out her hand to Harley; he pressed it between both of his, and bathed it with his tears. "Nay, that is Billy's ring," said she, "you cannot have it, indeed; but here is another, look here, which I plated, to-day, of some gold-thread from this bit of stuff; will you keep it for my sake? I am a strange girl; but my heart is harmless: my poor heart! it will burst some day; feel how it beats!" She pressed his hand to her bosom, then holding her head in the attitude of listening,—"Hark! one, two, three! be quiet, thou little trembler; my Billy's is cold!—but I had forgotten the ring." She put it on his finger. "Farewell! I must leave you now." She would have withdrawn her hand; Harley held it to his lips. "I dare not stay longer; my head throbs sadly: farewell!" She walked with a hurried step to a little apartment at some distance. Harley stood fixed in astonishment and pity; his friend gave money to the keeper. Harley looked on his ring. He put a couple of guineas into the man's hand:—"Be kind to that unfortunate." He burst into tears, and left them.

FURTHER READING

Michel Foucault, *Madness and Civilization: A History of Insanity in the Age of Reason* (tr. 1965) . Full of fascinating lore, this modish book, which indicts civilization as madder than its madmen, must be used with great care.

Richard Hunter and Ida McAlpine, *Three Hundred Years of Psychiatry, 1535–1860* (1963) . Substantial and reliable.

H. W. Thompson, *A Scottish Man of Feeling* (1931) . A good life of Mackenzie.

50 ❧ MONTESQUIEU

The Spirit of the Laws

[From Montesquieu, *The Spirit of the Laws*,
translated by Thomas Nugent, revised by
J. V. Pritchard, 2 vols. (1900), I, 220–34.]

*In the early modern period, with the rise of the nation state, penal
laws had grown harsher than ever. Traditional conceptions of
communities needing protection from contagion, and religious
bodies needing vengeance against insults from heretics or the
impious, were stretched to justify codes of unprecedented ferocity.
The first of the philosophes to break with this conception of law was
Montesquieu. In his* Persian Letters *he had already shown his distaste for legal cruelty; in* The Spirit of the Laws *he devoted the
whole of Book XII to the rights of the accused. His treatment
breathes good sense and decency. What is needed, he argues, is not
piecemeal reform but wholesale reconsideration: some so-called
crimes are not crimes at all, some "heinous" crimes are unimportant
infractions. What counts is not the dignity of the king or the priest,
but the security of the community, and acts that demonstrably do
not hurt it should not be repressed; similarly, antisocial acts that
damage individuals only slightly should be punished slightly. The
idea of proportionality, which Beccaria made into the central principle of his jurisprudence,* was central also to Montesquieu's writings on the subject. No wonder they have been called "the Magna
Carta of the citizen."†*

* See below, page 710.
† Franz Neumann, introduction to Montesquieu, *Spirit of the Laws* (1945
edn.) , lix.

❧

BOOK XII
Of the Laws that Establish Political Liberty, in Relation to the Subject

I. It is not sufficient to have treated of political liberty in relation to the constitution; we must examine it likewise in the relation it bears to the subject.

We have observed that in the former case it arises from a certain distribution of the three powers; but in the latter we must consider it in another light. It consists in security, or in the opinion people have of their country.

The constitution may happen to be free, and the subject not. The subject may be free, and not the constitution. In those cases, the constitution will be free by right, and not in fact; the subject will be free in fact, and not by right.

It is the disposition only of the laws, and even of the fundamental laws, that constitutes liberty in relation to the constitution. But as it regards the subject: manners, customs, or received examples may give rise to it, and particular civil laws may encourage it, as we shall presently observe.

Further, as in most states liberty is more checked or depressed than their constitution requires, it is proper to treat of the particular laws that in each constitution are apt to assist or check the principle of liberty which each state is capable of receiving.

II. Philosophic liberty consists in the free exercise of the will; or at least, if we must speak agreeably to all systems, in an opinion that we have the free exercise of our will. Political liberty consists in securing, or, at least, in the opinion that we enjoy security.

This security is never more dangerously attacked than in public or private accusations. It is, therefore, on the goodness of criminal laws that the liberty of the subject principally depends.

Criminal laws did not receive their full perfection all at once. Even in places where liberty has been most sought after, it has not been always found. Aristotle informs us that at Cumae the parents of the accuser might be witnesses. So imperfect was the law under the kings of Rome, that Servius Tullius pronounced sentence against the children of Ancus Martius, who were charged with having assassinated the king, his father-in-law. Under the first kings of France, Clotarius made a law that nobody should be condemned without being heard, which shows that a contrary custom had prevailed in some particular case or among some barbarous people. It was Charondas that first established penalties against false witnesses. When the subject has no fence to secure his innocence, he has none for his liberty.

The knowledge already acquired in some countries, or that may be hereafter attained in others, concerning the surest rules to be observed in criminal judgments, is more interesting to mankind than any other thing in the world.

Liberty can be founded on the practice of this knowledge only; and supposing a state to have the best laws imaginable in this respect, a person tried under that state, and condemned to be hanged the next day, would have much more liberty than a pasha enjoys in Turkey.

Those laws which condemn a man to death on the deposition of a single witness are fatal to liberty. In reason there should be two, because a witness who affirms, and the accused who denies, make an equal balance, and a third must incline the scale.

The Greeks and Romans required one voice more to condemn; but our French laws insist upon two. The Greeks pretend that their custom was established by the gods; but this more justly may be said of ours.

III. Liberty is in perfection when criminal laws derive each punishment from the particular nature of the crime. There are then no arbitrary decisions; the punishment does not flow from the capriciousness of the legislator, but from the very nature of the thing; and man uses no violence to man.

There are four sorts of crimes. Those of the first species are prejudicial to religion, the second to morals, the third to the public tranquillity, and the fourth to the security of the subject. The punishments inflicted for these crimes ought to proceed from the nature of each of these species.

In the class of crimes that concern religion, I rank only those which attack it directly, such as all simple sacrileges. For as to crimes that disturb the exercise of it, they are of the nature of those which prejudice the tranquillity or security of the subject, and ought to be referred to those classes.

In order to derive the punishment of simple sacrileges from the nature of the thing, it should consist in depriving people of the advantages conferred by religion in expelling them out of the temples, in a temporary or perpetual exclusion from the society of the faithful, in shunning their presence, in execrations, comminations, and conjurations.

In things that prejudice the tranquillity or security of the state, secret actions are subject to human jurisdiction. But in those which offend the Deity, where there is no public act, there can be no criminal matter; the whole passes between man and God, who knows the measure and time of his vengeance. Now, if magistrates confounding things should inquire also into hidden sacrileges, this inquisition would be directed to a kind of action that does not at all require it; the liberty of the subject would be subverted by arming the zeal of timorous as well as of presumptuous consciences against him.

The mischief arises from a notion which some people have entertained of revenging the cause of the Deity. But we must honor the Deity and leave him to avenge his own cause. And, indeed, were we to be directed by such a notion, where would be the end of punishments? If human laws are to avenge the cause of an infinite Being, they will be directed by his infinity, and not by the weakness, ignorance, and caprice of man.

A historian of Provence relates a fact which furnishes us with an excellent description of the consequences that may arise in weak capacities from the notion of avenging the Deity's cause. A Jew was accused of having blasphemed against the Virgin Mary, and upon conviction was condemned to be flayed alive. A strange spectacle was then exhibited: gentlemen masked, with knives in their hands, mounted the scaffold, and drove away the executioner, in order to be the avengers themselves of the honor of the blessed Virgin. I do not here choose to anticipate the reflections of the reader.

The second class consists of those crimes which are prejudicial to morals. Such is the violation of public or private continence—that is, of the police directing the manner in which the pleasure annexed to the conjunction of the sexes is to be enjoyed. The punishment of those crimes ought to be also derived from the nature of the thing; the privation of such advantages as society has attached to the purity of morals, fines, shame, necessity of concealment, public infamy, expulsion from home and society, and, in fine, all such punishments as belong to a corrective jurisdiction, are sufficient to repress the temerity of the two sexes. In effect these things are less founded on malice than on carelessness and self-neglect.

We speak here of none but crimes which relate merely to morals, for as to those that are also prejudicial to the public security, such as rapes, they belong to the fourth species.

The crimes of the third class are those which disturb the public tranquillity. The punishments ought therefore to be derived from the nature of the thing, and to be in relation to this tranquillity: such as imprisonment, exile, and other like chastisements, proper for reclaiming turbulent spirits, and obliging them to conform to the established order.

I confine those crimes that injure the public tranquillity to things which imply a bare offense against the police; for as to those which by disturbing the public peace attack at the same time the security of the subject, they ought to be ranked in the fourth class.

The punishments inflicted upon the latter crimes are such as are properly distinguished by that name. They are a kind of retaliation, by which the society refuses security to a member who has actually or intentionally deprived another of his security. These punishments are derived from the nature of the thing, founded on reason, and drawn from the very source of good and evil. A man deserves death when he has violated the security of the subject so far as to deprive, or attempt to deprive, another man of his life. This punishment of death is the remedy, as it were, of a sick society. When there is a breach of security with regard to property, there may be some reasons for inflicting a capital punishment; but it would be much better, and perhaps more natural, that crimes committed against the security of property should be punished with the loss of property; and this ought, indeed, to be the case if men's fortunes were common or equal. But as those who have no property of their own are generally the readiest to attack that of others, it has been found necessary, instead of a pecuniary, to substitute a corporal, punishment.

All that I have here advanced is founded in Nature, and extremely favorable to the liberty of the subject.

IV. It is an important maxim that we ought to be very circumspect in the prosecution of witchcraft and heresy. The accusation of these two crimes may be vastly injurious to liberty, and productive of infinite oppression, if the legislator knows not how to set bounds to it. For as it does not directly point at a person's actions, but at his character, it grows dangerous in proportion to the ignorance of the people; and then a man is sure to be always in danger, because the most exceptional conduct, the purest morals, and the constant practice of every duty in life are not a sufficient security against the suspicion of his being guilty of the like crimes.

Under Manuel Comnenus, the Protestator was accused of having conspired against the emperor, and of having employed for that purpose some secrets that render men invisible. It is mentioned in the life of this emperor that Aaron was detected as he was poring over a book of Solomon's, the reading of which was sufficient to conjure up whole legions of devils. Now, by supposing a power in witchcraft to rouse the infernal spirits to arms, people look upon a man whom they call a sorcerer as the person in the world most likely to disturb and subvert society, and of course they are disposed to punish him with the utmost severity.

But their indignation increases when witchcraft is supposed to have the power of subverting religion. The history of Constantinople informs us that in consequence of a revelation made to a bishop of a miracle having ceased because of the magic practices of a certain person, both that person and his son were put to death. On how many surprising things did not this single crime depend!— that revelations should not be uncommon, that the bishop should be favored with one, that it was real, that there had been a miracle in the case, that this miracle had ceased, that there was an art magic, that magic could subvert religion, that this particular person was a magician, and, in fine, that he had committed that magic act.

The Emperor Theodorus Lascarus attributed his illness to witchcraft. Those who were accused of this crime had no other resource left than to handle a red-hot iron without being hurt. Thus among the Greeks a person ought to have been a sorcerer to be able to clear himself of the imputation of witchcraft. Such was the excess of their stupidity that to the most dubious crime in the world they joined the most dubious proofs of innocence.

Under the reign of Philip the Long, the Jews were expelled from France, being accused of having poisoned the springs with their lepers. So absurd an accusation ought to make us doubt all those that are founded on public hatred.

I have not here asserted that heresy ought not to be punished; I said only that we ought to be extremely circumspect in punishing it.

V. God forbid that I should have the least inclination to diminish the public horror against a crime which religion, morality, and civil government equally condemn. It ought to be proscribed, were it only for its communicating to one sex the weaknesses of the other, and for leading people by a scandalous prostitution of their youth to an ignominious old age. What I shall say concerning it will in no way diminish its infamy, being leveled only against the tyranny that may abuse the very horror we ought to have against the vice.

As a natural circumstance of this crime is secrecy, there are frequent instances of its having been punished by legislators upon the deposition of a child. This was opening a very wide door to calumny. "Justinian," says Procopius, "published a law against this crime; he ordered an inquiry to be made not only against those who were guilty of it, after the enacting of that law, but even before. The deposition of a single witness, sometimes of a child, sometimes of a slave, was sufficient, especially against such as were rich, and against those of the green faction."

It is very odd that these three crimes—witchcraft, heresy, and that against Nature, of which the first might easily be proved not to exist, the second to be susceptible of an infinite number of distinctions, interpretations, and limitations, the third to be often obscure and uncertain—it is very odd, I say, that these three crimes should among us be punished with fire.

I may venture to affirm that the crime against Nature will never make any great progress in society, unless people are prompted to it by some particular custom, as among the Greeks, where the youths of that country performed all their exercises naked; as among us, where domestic education is disused; as among the Asiatics, where particular persons have a great number of women whom they despise, while others can have none at all. Let there be no customs preparatory to this crime; let it, like every other violation of morals, be severely proscribed by the civil magistrate; and Nature will soon defend or resume her rights. Nature, that fond, that indulgent parent, has strewed her pleasures with a bounteous hand, and while she fills us with delights she prepares us, by means of our issue, in whom we see ourselves, as it were, reproduced—she prepares us, I say, for future satisfactions of a more exquisite kind than those very delights.

VI. It is determined by the laws of China that whosoever shows any disrespect to the emperor is to be punished with death. As they do not mention in what this disrespect consists, everything may furnish a pretext to take away a man's life, and to exterminate any family whatsoever.

Two persons of that country who were employed to write the court gazette, having inserted some circumstances relating to a certain fact that was not true, it was pretended that to tell a lie in the court gazette was a disrespect shown to the court, in consequence of which they were put to death. A prince of the blood having inadvertently made some mark on a memorial signed with the red pencil by the emperor, it was determined that he had behaved disrespectfully to the sovereign, which occasioned one of the most terrible persecutions against that family that ever was recorded in history.

If the crime of high treason be indeterminate, this alone is sufficient to make the government degenerate into arbitrary power. I shall descant more largely on this subject when I come to treat of the composition of laws.

VII. It is likewise a shocking abuse to give the appellation of high treason to an action that does not deserve it. By an imperial law it was decreed that those who called in question the prince's judgment, or doubted the merit of such as he had chosen for a public office, should be prosecuted as guilty of sacrilege. Surely it was the cabinet council and the prince's favorites who invented that crime. By another law it was determined that whosoever made any attempt to injure the ministers and officers belonging to the sovereign should be deemed guilty of high treason, as if he had attempted to injure the sovereign himself. This law is owing to two princes remarkable for their weaknesses—princes who were led by their ministers as flocks by shepherds; princes who were slaves in the palace, children in the council, strangers to the army; princes, in fine, who preserved their authority only by giving it away every day. Some of those favorites conspired against their sovereigns. Nay, they did more, they conspired against the empire—they called in barbarous nations; and when the emperors wanted to stop their progress the state was so enfeebled as to be under a necessity of infringing the law, and of exposing itself to the crime of high treason in order to punish those favorites.

And yet this is the very law which the judge of Monsieur de Cinq-Mars built upon when endeavoring to prove that the latter was guilty of the crime of high treason for attempting to remove Cardinal Richelieu from the ministry. He says: "Crimes that aim at the persons of ministers are deemed by the imperial constitutions of equal consequence with those which are leveled against the emperor's own person. A minister discharges his duty to his prince and to his country; to attempt, therefore, to remove him is endeavoring to deprive the former one of his arms, and the latter of part of its power." It is impossible for the meanest tools of power to express themselves in more servile language.

By another law of Valentinian, Theodosius, and Arcadius, false coiners are declared guilty of high treason. But is not this confounding the ideas of things? Is not the very horror of high treason diminished by giving that name to another crime?

Paulinus having written to the Emperor Alexander that "he was preparing to prosecute for high treason a judge who had decided contrary to his edict," the emperor answered that "under his reign there was no such thing as indirect high treason."

Faustinian wrote to the same emperor, that as he had sworn by the prince's life never to pardon his slave, he found himself thereby obliged to perpetuate his wrath, lest he should incur the guilt of *laesa majestas*. Upon which the emperor made answer, "Your fears are groundless, and you are a stranger to my principles."

It was determined by a senatus-consultum that whosoever melted down any of the emperor's statues which happened to be rejected should not be deemed guilty of high treason. The Emperors Severus and Antoninus wrote to Pontius that those who sold unconsecrated statues of the emperor should not be charged with high treason. The same princes wrote to Julius Cassianus that if a person in flinging a stone should by chance strike one of the emperor's statues he should not be liable to a prosecution for high treason. The Julian law requires this sort of limitations; for in virtue of this law the crime of high treason was charged not only upon those who melted down the emperor's statues, but likewise on those who committed any suchlike action, which made it an arbitrary crime. When a number of crimes of *laesa majestas* had been established, they were obliged to distinguish the several sorts. Hence Ulpian, the civilian, after saying that the accusation of *laesa majestas* did not die with the criminal, adds that this does not relate to all the treasonable acts established by the Julian law, but only to that which implies an attempt against the empire, or against the emperor's life.

There was a law passed in England under Henry VIII, by which whoever predicted the king's death was declared guilty of high treason. This law was extremely vague; the terror of despotic power is so great that it recoils upon those who exercise it. In this king's last illness, the physicians would not venture to say he was in danger; and surely they acted very right.

VIII. Marsyas dreamed that he had cut Dionysius' throat. Dionysius put him to death, pretending that he would never have dreamed of such a thing by night if he had not thought of it by day. This was a most tyrannical action, for though it had been the subject of his thoughts, yet he had made no attempt toward it. The laws do not take upon them to punish any other than overt acts.

IX. Nothing renders the crime of high treason more arbitrary than declaring people guilty of it for indiscreet speeches. Speech is so subject to interpretation; there is so great a difference between indiscretion and malice; and frequently so little is there of the latter in the freedom of expression, that the law can hardly subject people to a capital punishment for words unless it expressly declares what words they are.

Words do not constitute an overt act; they remain only in idea. When considered by themselves, they have generally no determinate signification, for this depends on the tone in which they are uttered. It often happens that in repeating the same words they have not the same meaning; this depends on their connection with other things, and sometimes more is signified by silence than by any expression whatever. Since there can be nothing so equivocal and ambiguous as all this, how is it possible to convert it into a crime of high treason? Wherever this law is established, there is an end not only of liberty, but even of its very shadow.

In the manifesto of the late Czarina [Anna Ivanovna] against the family of the Dolgorukis, one of these princes is condemned to death for having uttered some indecent words concerning her person; another, for having maliciously interpreted her imperial laws, and for having offended her sacred person by disrespectful expressions.

Not that I pretend to diminish the just indignation of the public against those who presume to stain the glory of their sovereign; what I mean is, that if despotic princes are willing to moderate their power, a milder chastisement would be more proper on those occasions than the charge of high treason—a thing always terrible even to innocence itself.

Overt acts do not happen every day; they are exposed to the eye of the public, and a false charge with regard to matters of fact may be easily detected. Words carried into action assume the nature of that action. Thus a man who goes into a public marketplace to incite the subject to revolt incurs the guilt of high treason, because the words are joined to the action, and partake of its nature. It is not the words that are punished, but an action in which words are employed. They do not become criminal but when they are annexed to a criminal action; everything is confounded if words are construed into a capital crime, instead of considering them only as a mark of that crime.

The Emperors Theodosius, Arcadius, and Honorius wrote thus to Rufinus, who was *praefectus praetorio:* "Though a man should happen to speak amiss of our person or government, we do not intend to punish him. If he has spoken through levity, we must despise him; if through folly, we must pity him; and if he wrongs us, we must forgive him. Therefore, leaving things as they are, you are to inform us accordingly, that we may be able to judge of words by persons, and that we may duly consider whether we ought to punish or overlook them."

X. In writings there is something more permanent than in words, but when they are in no way preparative to high treason they cannot amount to that charge. . . .

FURTHER READING

Robert Anchel, *Crimes et châtiments au XVIIIe siècle,* 2nd edn. (1933). A useful study.

A. Esmein, *Histoire de la procédure criminelle en France* (1882). Old, but very informative.

Leon Radzinowicz, *A History of English Criminal Law and Its Administration,* 3 vols. (1948–56). Extremely illuminating, very full; despite its name, rich in comparisons with the Continent.

51 ❋ BECCARIA

On Crimes and Punishments

[From Cesare Beccaria, *On Crimes and Punishments,* translated by Henry Paolucci, 7–20, 30–36, 42–52.*]

Cesare Bonesana, Marchese di Beccaria (1738–94), is the principal representative of the Italian Enlightenment. Gifted but diffident, passionate but depressed, Beccaria had to be goaded into his best work by his devoted associates. When his little Dei delitti e delle pene *of 1764 reached France, the leading philosophes hailed it as a masterpiece; Voltaire took the lead in saluting its author as a laborer "in behalf of reason and humanity"†—and he expressed himself in the same way when he wrote to his intimates. Indeed, Beccaria's influence was enormous; he was translated quickly into French and English; Voltaire and other legal reformers borrowed from his laconic formulations with commendable enthusiasm. The message of his treatise is simplicity itself: cruel punishments, like the death penalty, are never justified; harsh treatment of the accused, including torture, is always detestable; the only principle the maker of laws must always remember is the Utilitarian one:* "the greatest happiness divided among the greatest number—la massima felicità divisa nel maggior numero."

Unlike his optimistic admirers, Beccaria was not particularly hopeful about the effect of his work. His main hope was that a handful would understand him: "A philosopher's voice is too weak for the tumults and the shouting of so many men guided by blind habit. But the few wise men scattered over the face of the earth will

---

* Copyright © 1963 by The Bobbs-Merrill Company, Inc. Reprinted by permission of the publisher.

† Voltaire to Beccaria, May 30, 1768, *Voltaire's Correspondence,* ed. Theodore Besterman, 107 vols. (1953–65), LXIX, 159.

echo me in their hearts." History, at least in the short range, confirmed not the cheer of his followers but the gloom of Beccaria. In England, year by year, new offenses were added to the list of capital crimes—all of these offenses against property. And conditions in the prisons did not improve for a very long time to come. In 1777 John Howard published a famous bleak report, The State of the Prisons in England and Wales, *which summarized his harrowing investigations. I reproduce its opening pages here, to illustrate the extent of the problem, and the distance that the most vigorous, most enlightened statesman would have to travel to ameliorate these conditions.*

There are prisons, into which whoever looks will, at first sight of the people confined there, be convinced, that there is some great error in the management of them: the sallow meagre countenances declare, without words, that they are very miserable: many who went in healthy, are in a few months changed to emaciated dejected objects. Some are seen pining under diseases, *"sick and in prison;"* expiring on the floors, in loathsome cells, of pestilential fevers, and the confluent small-pox: victims, I must not say to the cruelty, but I will say to the inattention, of sheriffs, and gentlemen in the commission of the peace.

The cause of this distress is, that many prisons are scantily supplied, and some almost totally unprovided with the necessaries of life.

There are several Bridewells* (to begin with them) in which prisoners have no allowance of FOOD at all. In some, the keeper farms what little is allowed them: and where he engages to supply each prisoner with one or two pennyworth of bread a day, I have known this shrunk to half, sometimes less than half the quantity, cut or broken from his own loaf.

It will perhaps be asked, does not their work maintain them? for every one knows that those offenders are committed to *hard labour.* The answer to that question, though true, will hardly be believed. There are very few Bridewells in which any work is done, or can be done. The prisoners have neither tools, nor materials of any kind; but spend their time in sloth, profaneness and debauchery, to a degree which, in some of those houses that I have seen, is extremely shocking.

* [House of correction, for minor offenses—P.G.]

Some keepers of these houses, who have represented to the magistrates the wants of their prisoners, and desired for them necessary food, have been silenced with these inconsiderate words, *Let them work or starve*. When those gentlemen know the former is impossible, do they not by that sentence, inevitably doom poor creatures to the latter?

I have asked some keepers, since the late act for preserving the health of prisoners, why no care is taken of their sick: and have been answered, that the magistrates tell them *the act does not extend to Bridewells*.

In consequence of this, at the quarter sessions you see prisoners, covered (hardly covered) with rags; almost famished; and sick of diseases, which the discharged spread wherever they go, and with which those who are sent to the County-Gaols infect these prisons.

The same complaint, *want of food*, is to be found in many COUNTY-GAOLS. In about half these, debtors have no bread; although it is granted to the highwayman, the house-breaker, and the murderer; and medical assistance, which is provided for the latter, is withheld from the former. In many of these Gaols, debtors who would work are not permitted to have any tools, lest they should furnish felons with them for escape or other mischief. I have often seen those prisoners eating their water-soup (bread boiled in mere water) and heard them say, "We are locked up and almost starved to death." . . .

To their wanting necessary food, I must add not only the demands of gaolers, &c. for fees; but also the extortion of bailiffs. These detain in their houses (properly enough denominated *spunging-houses*) at an enormous expence, prisoners who have money. I know there is a legal provision against this oppression; but the mode of obtaining redress (like that of recovering the groats) is attended with difficulty: and the abuse continues. The rapine of these extortioners needs some more effectual and easy check: no bailiff should be suffered to keep a public house; the mischiefs occasioned by their so doing, are complained of in many parts of the kingdom. . . .

Felons have in some Gaols two pennyworth of bread a day; in some three halfpennyworth; in some a pennyworth; in some a shilling a week: the particulars will be seen hereafter in their proper places. I often weighed the bread in different prisons, and found the penny loaf 7½ to 8½ ounces, the other loaves in proportion. It is probable that when this allowance was fixed by its value, near double the quantity that the money will now purchase, might be bought for it: yet the allowance continues unaltered: and it is not uncommon to see the whole purchase, especially of the smaller sums, eaten at breakfast: which is sometimes the case when they receive their pittance but once in two days; and then on the following day they must fast.

This allowance being so far short of the cravings of nature, and in some prisons lessened by farming to the gaoler, many criminals are half starved: such of them as at their commitment were in health, come out almost famished, scarce able to move, and for weeks incapable of any labour.

Many prisons have NO WATER. This defect is frequent in Bridewells, and Town-Gaols. In the felons courts of some County-Gaols there is no water: in some places where there is water, prisoners are always locked up within doors, and have no more than the keeper or his servants think fit to bring them: in one place they are limited to three pints a day each—a scanty provision for drink and cleanliness!

And as to AIR, which is no less necessary than either of the two preceding articles, and given us by Providence quite *gratis,* without any care or labour of our own; yet, as if the bounteous goodness of Heaven excited our envy, methods are contrived to rob prisoners of this *genuine cordial of life,* as Dr. Hales very properly calls it: I mean by preventing that circulation and change of the salutiferous fluid, without which animals cannot live and thrive. It is well known that air which has performed its office in the lungs, is seculent and noxious. Writers upon the subject shew, that a hogshead of it will last a man only an hour: but those who do not choose to consult philosophers, may judge from a notorious fact. In 1756, at Calcutta in Bengal, out of 170 persons who were confined in a hole there one night, 154 were taken out dead. The few survivors ascribed the mortality to their want of fresh air, and called the place, from what they suffered there, *Hell in miniature!*

Air which has been breathed, is made poisonous to a more intense degree by the effluvia from the sick; and what else in prisons is offensive. My reader will judge of its malignity, when I assure him, that my cloaths were in my first journeys so offensive, that in a post-chaise I could not bear the windows drawn up: and was therefore often obliged to travel on horseback. The leaves of my memorandum-book were often so tainted, that I could not use it till after spreading it an hour or two before the fire: and even my antidote, a vial of vinegar, has after using it in a few prisons, become intolerably disagreeable. I did not wonder that in those journies many gaolers made excuses; and did not go with me into the felons' wards.

From hence any one may judge of the probability there is against the health and life of prisoners, crowded in close rooms, cells, and subterraneous dungeons, for fourteen or sixteen hours out of the four and twenty. In some of those caverns the floor is very damp: in others there is sometimes an inch or two of water; and the straw, or bedding is laid on such floors, seldom on barrack bedsteads. Where prisoners are not kept in underground cells, they are often confined to their rooms, because there is no court belonging to the prison, which is the case in most City and Town-Gaols: or because the walls round the yard are ruinous, or too low for safety: or because the goaler has the ground for his own use. Prisoners confined in this manner, are generally unhealthy. Some Gaols have no SEWERS; and in those that have, if they be not properly attended to, they are, even to a visitant, offensive beyond expression: how noxious then to people constantly confined in those prisons!

One cause why the rooms in some prisons are so close, is perhaps the window-tax, which the gaolers have to pay: this tempts them to stop the windows, and stifle their prisoners.

In many Gaols, and in most Bridewells, there is no allowance of STRAW for prisoners to sleep on; and if by any means they get a little, it is not changed for months together, so that it is almost worn to dust. Some lie upon rags, others upon the bare floors. When I have complained of this to the keepers, their justification has been, "The county allows no straw; the prisoners have none but at my cost."

The evils mentioned hitherto affect the *health* and *life* of prisoners: I have now to complain of what is pernicious to their MORALS; and that is, the confining all sorts of prisoners together: debtors and felons; men and women; the young beginner and the old offender: and with all these, in some counties, such as are guilty of misdemeanors only; who should have been committed to Bridewell, to be corrected by diligence and labour; but for want of food, and the means of procuring it in those prisons, are in pity sent to such County-Gaols as afford these offenders prison-allowance.

Few prisons separate men and women in the day-time. In some counties the Gaol is also the Bridewell: in others those prisons are contiguous, and the yard common. There the petty offender is committed for instruction to the most profligate. In some Gaols you see (and who can see it without pain?) boys of twelve or fourteen eagerly listening to the stories told by practised and experienced criminals, of their adventures, successes, stratagems, and escapes.

I must here add, that in some few Gaols are confined idiots and lunatics. These serve for sport to idle visitants at assizes, and other times of general resort. The insane, where they are not kept separate, disturb and terrify other prisoners. No care is taken of them, although it is probable that by medicines, and proper regimen, some of them might be restored to their senses, and to usefulness in life.

I am ready to think, that none who give credit to what is contained in the foregoing pages, will wonder at the havock made by the GAOL-FEVER. From my own observations in 1773 and 1774, I was fully convinced that many more were destroyed by it, than were put to death by all the public executions in the kingdom. This frequent effect of confinement in prison seems generally understood, and shews how full of emphatical meaning is the curse of a severe creditor, who pronounces his debtor's doom to ROT IN GAOL. I believe I have learned the full import of this sentence, from the vast numbers who to my certain knowledge, some of them before my eyes, have perished in our Gaols.

On Crimes and Punishments

I · INTRODUCTION

Men generally abandon the most important regulations either to the care of ordinary common sense or to the discretion of persons who have an interest in opposing the wisest laws—laws, that is, of the kind that naturally promote the universal distribution of advantages while they resist the force that tends to concentrate them in the hands of a few, placing the summit of power and happiness on one side, and on the other, only weakness and misery. It is, therefore, only after they have passed through a thousand errors in matters most essential to life and liberty, after they have arrived at the limits of endurance, exhausted by the wrongs they have suffered, that men are induced to remedy the disorders that oppress them and to acknowledge the most palpable truths, which, precisely because of their simplicity, escape the attention of vulgar minds accustomed not to analyzing things, but to receiving general impressions all of a piece, rather from tradition than through study.

If we glance at the pages of history, we will find that laws, which surely are, or ought to be, compacts of free men, have been, for the most part, a mere tool of the passions of some, or have arisen from an accidental and temporary need. Never have they been dictated by a dispassionate student of human nature who might, by bringing the actions of a multitude of men into focus, consider them from this single point of view: *the greatest happiness shared by the greatest number.* Happy are those few nations that have not waited for the slow succession of coincidence and human vicissitude to force some little turn for the better after the limit of evil has been reached, but have facilitated the intermediate progress by means of good laws. . . .

The true relations between sovereigns and their subjects, and between nations, have been discovered. Commerce has been reanimated by the common knowledge of philosophical truths diffused by the art of printing, and there has sprung up among nations a tacit rivalry of industriousness that is most humane and truly worthy of rational beings. Such good things we owe to the productive enlightenment of this age. But very few persons have studied and fought against the cruelty of punishments and the irregularities of criminal procedures, a part of legislation that is as fundamental as it is widely neglected in almost all of Europe. Very few persons have undertaken to demolish the accumulated errors of centuries by rising to general principles, curbing, at least, with the sole force that acknowledged truths possess, the unbounded course of ill-directed power which has continually produced a long and authorized example of the most cold-blooded barbarity. And yet the groans of the weak, sacrificed to cruel ignorance and to opulent indolence; the barbarous torments, multiplied with lavish and useless severity, for crimes either not proved or wholly imaginary; the filth and horrors of a prison, intensified by that cruelest tormentor of the miserable, uncertainty—all these ought to have roused that breed of magistrates who direct the opinions of men.

The immortal Montesquieu has cursorily touched upon this subject. Truth, which is one and indivisible, has obliged me to follow the illustrious steps of that great man, but the thoughtful men for whom I write will easily distinguish my traces from his. I shall deem myself happy if I can obtain, as he did, the secret thanks of the unknown and peace-loving disciples of reason, and if I can inspire that tender thrill with which persons of sensibility respond to one who upholds the interests of humanity.

Adherence to a strictly logical sequence would now lead us to examine and distinguish the various kinds of crimes and modes of punishment; but these are by their nature so variable, because of the diverse circumstances of time and place, that the result would be a catalogue of enormous and boring detail. By indicating only the most general principles and the most dangerous and commonest errors, I will have done enough to disabuse both those who, from a mistaken love of liberty, would be ready to introduce anarchy, and those who would like to see all men subjected to a monastic discipline.

But what are to be the proper punishments for such crimes?

Is the death penalty really *useful* and *necessary* for the security and good order of society? Are torture and torments *just,* and do they attain the *end* for which laws are instituted? What is the best way to prevent crimes? Are the same punishments equally effective for all times? What influence have they on customary behavior? These problems deserve to be analyzed with that geometric precision which the mist of sophisms, seductive eloquence, and timorous doubt cannot withstand. If I could boast only of having been the first to present to Italy, with a little more clarity, what other nations have boldly written and are beginning to practice, I would account myself fortunate. But if, by defending the rights of man and of unconquerable truth, I should help to save from the spasm and agonies of death some wretched victim of tyranny or of no less fatal ignorance, the thanks and tears of one innocent mortal in his transports of joy would console me for the contempt of all mankind.

II · THE ORIGIN OF PUNISHMENTS, AND THE RIGHT TO PUNISH

No lasting advantage is to be hoped for from political morality if it is not founded upon the ineradicable feelings of mankind. Any law that deviates from these will inevitably encounter a resistance that is certain to prevail over it in the end—in the same way that any force, however small, if continuously applied, is bound to overcome the most violent motion that can be imparted to a body.

Let us consult the human heart, and we shall find there the basic principles of the true right of the sovereign to punish crimes.

No man ever freely sacrificed a portion of his personal liberty merely in behalf of the common good. That chimera exists only in romances. If it were possible, every one of us would prefer that the compacts binding others did not bind us; every man tends to make himself the center of his whole world.

The continuous multiplication of mankind, inconsiderable in itself yet exceeding by far the means that a sterile and uncultivated nature could offer for the satisfaction of increasingly complex needs, united the earliest savages. These first communities of necessity caused the formation of others to resist the first, and the primitive state of warfare thus passed from individuals to nations.

Laws are the conditions under which independent and isolated men united to form a society. Weary of living in a continual state of war, and of enjoying a liberty rendered useless by the uncertainty of preserving it, they sacrificed a part so that they might enjoy the rest of it in peace and safety. The sum of all these portions of liberty sacrificed by each for his own good constitutes the sovereignty of a nation, and their legitimate depositary and administrator is the sovereign. But merely to have established this deposit was not enough; it had to be defended against private usurpations by individuals each of whom always tries not only to withdraw his own share but also to usurp for himself that of others. Some tangible motives had to be introduced, therefore, to prevent the despotic spirit, which is in every man, from plunging the laws of society into its original chaos. These tangible motives are the punishments established against infractors of the laws. I say "tangible motives" because experience has shown that the multitude adopt no fixed principles of conduct and will not be released from the sway of that universal principle of dissolution which is seen to operate in both the physical and the moral universe, except for motives that directly strike the senses. These motives, by dint of repeated representation to the mind, counterbalance the powerful impressions of the private passions that oppose the common good. Not eloquence, not declamations, not even the most sublime truths have sufficed, for any considerable length of time, to curb passions excited by vivid impressions of present objects.

It was, thus, necessity that forced men to give up part of their personal liberty, and it is certain, therefore, that each is willing to place in the public fund only the least possible portion, no more than suffices to induce others to defend it. The aggregate of these least possible portions constitutes the right to punish; all that exceeds this is abuse and not justice; it is fact but by no means right.*

Punishments that exceed what is necessary for protection of the deposit of public security are by their very nature unjust, and punishments are increasingly more just as the safety which the sovereign secures for his subjects is the more sacred and inviolable, and the liberty greater.

III · CONSEQUENCES

The first consequence of these principles is that only the laws can decree punishments for crimes; authority for this can reside only with the legislator who represents the entire society united by a social contract. No magistrate (who is a part of society) can, with justice, inflict punishments upon another member of the same society. But a punishment that exceeds the limit fixed by the laws is just punishment plus another punishment; a magistrate cannot, therefore, under any pretext of zeal or concern for the public good, augment the punishment established for a delinquent citizen.

The second consequence is that the sovereign, who represents the

* Note that the word "right" is not opposed to the word "might"; the first is rather a modification of the second—that modification, to be precise, which is most advantageous to the greater number. And by "justice" I mean nothing more than the bond required to maintain the unity of particular interests which would otherwise dissolve into the original state of insociability.

Care must be taken not to attach to this word "justice" the idea of some real thing, as of a physical force or of an existent being; it is simply a human way of conceiving things, a way that has an enormous influence on everyone's happiness. Much less have I in mind that other kind of justice which emanates from God, and which relates directly to the punishments and rewards of the life to come.

society itself, can frame only general laws binding all members, but he cannot judge whether someone has violated the social contract, for that would divide the nation into two parts, one represented by the sovereign, who asserts the violation of the contract, and the other by the accused, who denies it. There must, therefore, be a third party to judge the truth of the fact. Hence the need for a magistrate whose decisions, from which there can be no appeal, should consist of mere affirmations or denials of particular facts.

The third consequence is this: even assuming that severity of punishments were not directly contrary to the public good and to the very purpose of preventing crimes, if it were possible to prove merely that such severity is useless, in that case also it would be contrary not only to those beneficent virtues that spring from enlightened reason which would rather rule happy men than a herd of slaves in whom a timid cruelty makes its endless rounds; it would be contrary to justice itself and to the very nature of the social contract.

IV · INTERPRETATIONS OF THE LAWS

A fourth consequence: Judges in criminal cases cannot have the authority to interpret laws, and the reason, again, is that they are not legislators. Such judges have not received the laws from our ancestors as a family tradition or legacy that leaves to posterity only the burden of obeying them, but they receive them, rather, from the living society, or from the sovereign representing it, who is the legitimate depositary of what actually results from the common will of all. [The judges] receive them not as obligations of some ancient oath* (null, to begin with, because it pretended to bind wills that were not then existent, and iniquitous, because it reduced men from a social state to that of an animal herd), but as consequences

---

* Each individual is indeed bound to society, but society is, in turn, bound to each individual by a contract which, of its very nature, places both parties under obligation. This obligation, which descends from the throne to the cottage, which binds equally the loftiest and the meanest of men, signifies only that it is in the interests of all that the pacts advantageous to the greatest number be observed.

The word "obligation" is one of those that occur much more frequently in ethics than in any other science, and which are the abbreviated symbol of a rational argument and not of an idea. Seek an adequate idea of the word "obligation" and you will fail to find it; reason about it and you will both understand yourself and be understood by others.

of the tacit or expressed oath of allegiance which the united wills of living subjects have pledged to their sovereign, as bonds necessary for restraining and regulating the internal ferment of private interests. This constitutes the natural and real authority of the laws. Who, then, is to be the legitimate interpreter of the laws? Is it to be the sovereign, that is, the depositary of the actual wills of all, or the judge, whose sole charge is merely to examine whether a particular man has or has not committed an unlawful act?

For every crime that comes before him, a judge is required to complete a perfect syllogism in which the major premise must be the general law; the minor, the action that conforms or does not conform to the law; and the conclusion, acquittal or punishment. If the judge were constrained, or if he desired to frame even a single additional syllogism, the door would thereby be opened to uncertainty.

Nothing can be more dangerous than the popular axiom that it is necessary to consult the spirit of the laws. It is a dam that has given way to a torrent of opinions. This truth, which seems paradoxical to ordinary minds that are struck more by trivial present disorders than by the dangerous but remote effects of false principles rooted in a nation, seems to me to be fully demonstrated. Our understandings and all our ideas have a reciprocal connection; the more complicated they are, the more numerous must the ways be that lead to them and depart from them. Each man has his own point of view, and, at each different time, a different one. Thus the "spirit" of the law would be the product of a judge's good or bad logic, of his good or bad digestion; it would depend on the violence of his passions, on the weakness of the accused, on the judge's connections with him, and on all those minute factors that alter the appearances of an object in the fluctuating mind of man. Thus we see the lot of a citizen subjected to frequent changes in passing through different courts, and we see the lives of poor wretches become the victims of the false ratiocinations or of the momentary seething ill-humors of a judge who mistakes for a legitimate interpretation that vague product of the jumbled series of notions which his mind stirs up. Thus we see the same crimes differently punished at different times by the same court, for having consulted not the constant fixed voice of the law but the erring instability of interpretation.

The disorder that arises from rigorous observance of the letter of a penal law is hardly comparable to the disorders that arise from interpretations. The temporary inconvenience of the former prompts one to make the rather easy and needed correction in the words of the law which are the source of uncertainty, but it curbs that fatal license of discussion which gives rise to arbitrary and venal controversies. When a fixed code of laws, which must be observed to the letter, leaves no further care to the judge than to examine the acts of citizens and to decide whether or not they conform to the law as written; when the standard of the just or the unjust, which is to be the norm of conduct for the ignorant as well as for the philosophic citizen, is not a matter of controversy but of fact; then only are citizens not subject to the petty tyrannies of the many which are the more cruel as the distance between the oppressed and the oppressor is less, and which are far more fatal than those of a single man, for the despotism of many can only be corrected by the depotism of one; the cruelty of a single despot is proportioned, not to his might, but to the obstacles he encounters. In this way citizens acquire that sense of security for their own persons which is just, because it is the object of human association, and useful, because it enables them to calculate accurately the inconveniences of a misdeed. It is true, also, that they acquire a spirit of independence, but not one that upsets the laws and resists the chief magistrates; rather one that resists those who have dared to apply the sacred name of virtue to that weakness of theirs which makes them yield to their self-interested and capricious opinions.

These principles will displease those who have assumed for themselves a right to transmit to their inferiors the blows of tyranny that they have received from their superiors. I would, indeed, be most fearful if the spirit of tyranny were in the least compatible with the spirit of literacy.

V · OBSCURITY OF THE LAWS

If the interpretation of laws is an evil, another evil, evidently, is the obscurity that makes interpretation necessary. And this evil would be very great indeed where the laws are written in a language that is foreign to a people, forcing it to rely on a handful of men because it is unable to judge for itself how its liberty or its members may fare—in a language that transforms a sacred and public book into something very like the private possession of a family. When the number of those who can understand the sacred code of laws and hold it in their hands increases, the frequency of crimes will be found to decrease, for undoubtedly ignorance and uncertainty of punishments add much to the eloquence of the passions. What are we to make of men, therefore, when we reflect that this very evil is the inveterate practice of a large part of cultured and enlightened Europe?

One consequence of this last reflection is that, without writing, a society can never acquire a fixed form of government with power that derives from the whole and not from the parts, in which the laws, which cannot be altered except by the general will, are not corrupted in their passage through the mass of private interests. Experience and reason have shown us that the probability and certainty of human traditions diminish the further removed they are from their source. For, obviously, if there exists no enduring memorial of the social compact, how are the laws to withstand the inevitable pressure of time and of passions?

We can thus see how useful the art of printing is, which makes the public, and not some few individuals, the guardians of the sacred laws. And we can see how it has dissipated the benighted spirit of cabal and intrigue, which must soon vanish in the presence of those enlightened studies and sciences, apparently despised, but really feared, by its adherents. This explains why we now see in Europe a diminishing of the atrocity of the crimes that afflicted our ancestors, who became tyrants and slaves by turns. Any one acquainted with the history of the past two centuries, and of our own time, may observe how from the lap of luxury and softness have sprung the most pleasing virtues, humanity, benevolence, and toleration of human errors. He will see what the real effects were of the so-called simplicity and good faith of old: humanity groaning under implacable superstition; avarice and private ambition staining with blood the golden treasure-chests and thrones of kings; secret betrayals and public massacres; every nobleman a tyrant over the people; ministers of the Gospel truth polluting with blood the hands that daily touched the God of mercy—these, surely, are not the work of this enlightened age that some people call corrupt.

VI · IMPRISONMENT

An error no less common than it is contrary to the purpose of association—which is assurance of personal security—is that of allowing a magistrate charged with administering the laws to be free to imprison a citizen at his own pleasure, to deprive an enemy of liberty on frivolous pretexts, and to leave a friend unpunished notwithstanding the clearest evidences of his guilt. Detention in prison is a punishment which, unlike every other, must of necessity precede conviction for crime, but this distinctive character does not remove the other which is essential—namely, that only the law determines the cases in which a man is to suffer punishment. It pertains to the law, therefore, to indicate what evidences of crime justify detention of the accused, his subjection to investigation and punishment. A man's notoriety, his flight, his nonjudicial confession, the confession of an accomplice, threats and the constant enmity of the injured person, the manifest fact of the crime, and similar evidences, are proofs sufficient to justify imprisonment of a citizen. But these proofs must be determined by the law, not by judges, whose decrees are always contrary to political liberty when they are not particular applications of a general maxim included in the public code. When punishments have become more moderate, when squalor and hunger have been removed from prisons, when pity and mercy have forced a way through barred doors, overmastering the inexorable and obdurate ministers of justice, then may the laws be content with slighter evidences as grounds for imprisonment.

A man accused of a crime, who has been imprisoned and acquitted, ought not to be branded with infamy. How many Romans accused of very great crimes, and then found innocent, were revered by the populace and honored with public offices! For what reason, then, is the fate of an innocent person so apt to be different in our time? It seems to be because, in the present system of criminal law, the idea of power and arrogance prevails over that of justice, because accused and convicted are thrown indiscriminately into the same cell, because imprisonment is rather the torment than the confinement of the accused, and because the internal power that protects the laws and the external power that defends the throne and nation are separated when they ought to be united. By means of the common sanction of the laws, the former [internal power] would be combined with judicial authority, without, however, passing directly under its sway; the glory that attends the pomp and ceremony of a military corps would remove infamy, which, like all popular sentiments, is more attached to the manner than to the thing itself, as is proved by the fact that military prisons are, according to the common opinion, less disgraceful than the civil. Still discernible in our people, in their customs and laws, which always lag several ages behind the actual enlightened thought of a nation —still discernible are the barbaric impressions and savage notions of those people of the North who hunted down our forefathers.

XII · TORTURE

A cruelty consecrated by the practice of most nations is torture of the accused during his trial, either to make him confess the crime or to clear up contradictory statements, or to discover accomplices, or to purge him of infamy in some metaphysical and incomprehensible way, or, finally, to discover other crimes of which he might be guilty but of which he is not accused.

No man can be called *guilty* before a judge has sentenced him, nor can society deprive him of public protection before it has been decided that he has in fact violated the conditions under which such protection was accorded him. What right is it, then, if not simply that of might, which empowers a judge to inflict punishment on a citizen while doubt still remains as to his guilt or innocence? Here is the dilemma, which is nothing new: the fact of the crime is either certain or uncertain; if certain, all that is due is the punishment established by the laws, and tortures are useless because the criminal's confession is useless; if uncertain, then one must not torture the innocent, for such, according to the laws, is a man whose crimes are not yet proved.

What is the political intent of punishments? To instill fear in other men. But what justification can we find, then, for the secret and private tortures which the tyranny of custom practices on the guilty and the innocent? It is important, indeed, to let no known crime pass unpunished, but it is useless to reveal the author of a crime that lies deeply buried in darkness. A wrong already committed, and for which there is no remedy, ought to be punished by political society only because it might otherwise excite false hopes of impunity in others. If it be true that a greater number of men, whether because of fear or virtue, respect the laws than break them, then the risk of torturing an innocent person should be considered greater when, other things being equal, the probability is greater that a man has rather respected the laws than despised them.

But I say more: it tends to confound all relations to require that a man be at the same time accuser and accused, that pain be made the crucible of truth, as if its criterion lay in the muscles and sinews of a miserable wretch.

The law that authorizes torture is a law that says: "Men, resist pain; and if nature has created in you an inextinguishable self-love, if it has granted you an inalienable right of self-defense, I create in you an altogether contrary sentiment: a heroic hatred of yourselves;

and I command you to accuse yourselves, to speak the truth even while muscles are being lacerated and bones disjointed."

This infamous crucible of truth is a still-standing memorial of the ancient and barbarous legislation of a time when trials by fire and by boiling water, as well as the uncertain outcomes of duels, were called "judgments of God," as if the links of the eternal chain, which is in the bosom of the First Cause, must at every moment be disordered and broken by frivolous human arrangements. The only difference between torture and trials by fire and boiling water is that the outcome seems to depend, in the first, on the will of the accused, and in the second, on a purely physical and extrinsic fact; but this difference is only apparent, not real. One is as much free to tell the truth in the midst of convulsions and torments, as one was free then to impede without fraud the effects of fire and boiling water. Every act of our will is invariably proportioned to the force of the sensory impression which is its source; and the sensory capacity of every man is limited. Thus the impression of pain may become so great that, filling the entire sensory capacity of the tortured person, it leaves him free only to choose what for the moment is the shortest way of escape from pain. The response of the accused is then as inevitable as the impressions of fire and water. The sensitive innocent man will then confess himself guilty when he believes that, by so doing, he can put an end to his torment. Every difference between guilt and innocence disappears by virtue of the very means one pretends to be using to discover it. [Torture] is an infallible means indeed—for absolving robust scoundrels and for condemning innocent persons who happen to be weak. Such are the fatal defects of this so-called criterion of truth, a criterion fit for a cannibal, which the Romans, who were barbarous themselves on many counts, reserved only for slaves, the victims of a fierce and overly praised virtue.

Of two men equally innocent or equally guilty, the strong and courageous will be acquitted, the weak and timid condemned, by virtue of this rigorous rational argument: "I, the judge, was supposed to find you guilty of such and such a crime; you, the strong, have been able to resist the pain, and I therefore absolve you; you, the weak, have yielded, and I therefore condemn you. I am aware that a confession wrenched forth by torments ought to be of no weight whatsoever, but I'll torment you again if you don't confirm what you have confessed."

The effect of torture, therefore, is a matter of temperament and calculation that varies with each man according to his strength and sensibility, so that, with this method, a mathematician could more readily than a judge resolve this problem: given the muscular force and nervous sensibility of an innocent person, find the degree of pain that will make him confess himself guilty of a given crime.

The examination of an accused person is undertaken to ascertain the truth. But if this truth is difficult to discover in the air, gesture, and countenance of a man at ease, much more difficult will its discovery be when the convulsions of pain have distorted all the signs by which truth reveals itself in spite of themselves in the countenances of the majority of men. Every violent action confounds and dissolves those little differences in objects by means of which one may occasionally distinguish the true from the false.

A strange consequence that necessarily follows from the use of torture is that the innocent person is placed in a condition worse than that of the guilty, for if both are tortured, the circumstances are all against the former. Either he confesses the crime and is condemned, or he is declared innocent and has suffered a punishment he did not deserve. The guilty man, on the contrary, finds himself in a favorable situation; that is, if, as a consequence of having firmly resisted the torture, he is absolved as innocent, he will have escaped a greater punishment by enduring a lesser one. Thus the innocent cannot but lose, whereas the guilty may gain.

This truth is felt, finally though confusedly, by those very persons who shrink furthest from it in practice. The confession made under torture is of no avail if it be not confirmed with an oath after the torture has stopped, but if the accused does not then confirm the crime, he is again tortured. Some jurists, and some nations, allow this infamous begging of principles to be repeated no more than three times; other nations, and other jurists, leave it to the discretion of the judge.

It would be superfluous to intensify the light, here, by citing the innumerable examples of innocent persons who have confessed themselves criminals because of the agonies of torture; there is no nation, there is no age that does not have its own to cite; but neither will men change nor will they deduce the necessary consequences. Every man who has ever extended his thought even a little beyond the mere necessities of life has at least sometimes felt an urge to run toward Nature, who, with secret and indistinct voices, calls him to her; custom, that tyrant of minds, drives him back and frightens him.

Torture is alleged to be useful, also, as applied to suspected criminals, when they contradict themselves under examination; as if fear of punishment, the uncertainty of the sentence, the pomp and majesty of the judge, the almost universal ignorance of both the wicked and the innocent, were not apt enough to plunge the innocent man who is afraid, as well as the guilty who is seeking to conceal, into contradiction; as if contradictions, which are common enough in men when they are at ease, are not likely to be multiplied in the perturbations of a mind altogether absorbed in the thought of saving itself from imminent peril.

Torture is applied to discover whether the criminal is guilty of crimes other than those of which he is accused; it amounts to this sort of reasoning: "You are guilty of one crime, therefore it is possible that you are guilty also of a hundred others; this doubt weighs on me, and I want to convince myself one way or another by using my criterion of truth: the laws torture you because you are guilty, because you may be guilty, because I insist that you be guilty."

Torture is applied to an accused person to discover his accomplices in the crime. But if it is demonstrated that torture is not an opportune means for discovering the truth, how can it serve to reveal the accomplices, which is one of the truths to be discovered? As if a man who accuses himself would not more readily accuse others. Is it right to torment men for the crime of another? Will not the accomplices be disclosed from the examination of witnesses, from the examination of the accused, from the proofs and from the material fact of the crime—in sum, from all of the very means that should serve to convict the accused of having committed the crime? Accomplices usually fly as soon as their companion is taken; the uncertainty of their lot of itself condemns them to exile, and frees the nation from the danger of further offenses, while the punishment of the criminal who is taken achieves its sole purpose, which is to deter other men, by fear, from committing a similar crime.

Another ridiculous pretext for torture is purgation from infamy; which is to say, a man judged infamous by the laws must confirm his deposition with the dislocation of his bones. This abuse should not be tolerated in the eighteenth century. It is believed that pain, which is a sensation, can purge infamy, which is a purely moral relationship. Is torture perhaps a crucible, and infamy, perhaps, a mixed impure substance? But infamy is a sentiment subject neither to the laws nor to reason, but to common opinion. Torture itself brings real infamy to its victims. Thus, by this method, infamy is to be removed by adding to it.

It is not difficult to trace the origin of this ridiculous law, because the very absurdities that are adopted by an entire nation have always some relation to other common ideas that it respects. The usage seems to have derived from religious and spiritual ideas, which exert a great influence on the thoughts of men, nations, and ages. An infallible dogma assures us that the stains contracted through our human frailty, which have not merited the eternal anger of the Grand Being, must be purged by an incomprehensible fire. Now, infamy is a civil stain, and as suffering and fire remove spiritual and incorporeal stains, why should not spasms of torture remove the civil stain, which is infamy? I believe that the confession of the criminal which is exacted as essential for condemnation in certain tribunals has a similar origin, for in the mysterious tribunal of penance the confession of sins is an essential part of the sacrament. Thus do men abuse the surest lights of Revelation, and as these are the only ones that subsist in times of ignorance, docile humanity turns to them on all occasions and makes of them the most absurd and farfetched applications.

These truths were known to the Roman legislators, among whom one does not encounter the use of torture, except with slaves, who were denied any personality. They are adopted by England, a nation whose glorious attainments in literature, whose superiority in commerce and in wealth, and consequently in power, and whose examples of virtue and of courage, leave no doubt as to the goodness of her laws. Torture has been abolished in Sweden: abolished by one of the wisest monarchs of Europe,* who, having brought philosophy to the throne, a legislator that befriends subjects, has rendered them equal and free in dependence on the laws; this is the sole equality and liberty that reasonable men can desire in the present state of things. Torture is not deemed necessary in the laws that regulate armies, though these are, for the most part, made up of the dregs of nations, which would seem to have more use for it than any other class. How strange a thing, indeed, it must seem to anyone who fails to consider how great is the tyranny of usage that the laws of peace should have to learn a more humane method of judgment from spirits hardened to slaughter and bloodshed!

* [The punctuation suggests that Beccaria is writing of the king responsible for the abolition of torture in Sweden referred to in the first part of the sentence. However, Gustavus III (1746–1792), an enlightened monarch to whom Beccaria's words might well apply, did not attain the throne until 1771, seven years after Beccaria's treatise was published. The reference is perhaps to Frederick II of Prussia (1712–1786).—H. P.]

XV · MILDNESS OF PUNISHMENTS

From simple consideration of the truths thus far presented it is evident that the purpose of punishment is neither to torment and afflict a sensitive being, nor to undo a crime already committed. Can there, in a body politic which, far from acting on passion, is the tranquil moderator of private passions—can there be a place for this useless cruelty, for this instrument of wrath and fanaticism, or of weak tyrants? Can the shrieks of a wretch recall from time, which never reverses its course, deeds already accomplished? The purpose can only be to prevent the criminal from inflicting new injuries on its citizens and to deter others from similar acts. Always keeping due proportions, such punishments and such method of inflicting them ought to be chosen, therefore, which will make the strongest and most lasting impression on the minds of men, and inflict the least torment on the body of the criminal.

Who, in reading history, can keep from cringing with horror before the spectacle of barbarous and useless torments, cold-bloodedly devised and carried through by men who called themselves wise? What man of any sensibility can keep from shuddering when he sees thousands of poor wretches driven by a misery either intended or tolerated by the laws (which have always favored the few and outraged the many) to a desperate return to the original state of nature—when he sees them accused of impossible crimes, fabricated by timid ignorance, or found guilty of nothing other than being true to their own principles, and sees them lacerated with meditated formality and slow torture by men gifted with the same senses, and consequently with the same passions? Happy spectacle for a fanatical multitude!

For a punishment to attain its end, the evil which it inflicts has only to exceed the advantage derivable from the crime; in this excess of evil one should include the certainty of punishment and the loss of the good which the crime might have produced. All beyond this is superfluous and for that reason tyrannical. Men are regulated in their conduct by the repeated impression of evils they know, and not according to those of which they are ignorant. Given, for example, two nations, in one of which, in the scale of punishments proportioned to the scale of crimes, the maximum punishment is perpetual slavery, and in the other the wheel; I say that the first shall have as much fear of its maximum punishment as the second; whatever reason might be adduced for introducing to the first the maximum punishment of the other could similarly be adduced to justify intensification of punishments in the latter, passing imperceptibly from the wheel to slower and more ingenious torments, and at length to the ultimate refinements of a science only too well known to tyrants.

In proportion as torments become more cruel, the spirits of men, which are like fluids that always rise to the level of surrounding objects, become callous, and the ever lively force of the passions brings it to pass that after a hundred years of cruel torments the wheel inspires no greater fear than imprisonment once did. The severity of punishment of itself emboldens men to commit the very wrongs it is supposed to prevent; they are driven to commit additional crimes to avoid the punishment for a single one. The countries and times most notorious for severity of penalties have always been those in which the bloodiest and most inhumane of deeds were committed, for the same spirit of ferocity that guided the hand of the legislators also ruled that of the parricide and assassin. On the throne it dictated iron laws for vicious-spirited slaves to obey, while in private, hiddenly, it instigated the slaughter of tyrants only to make room for new ones.

Two other baneful consequences derive from the cruelty of punishments, interfering with the avowed purpose of preventing crimes. The first is that it is not easy to establish a proper proportion between crime and punishment because, however much an industrious cruelty may have multiplied the variety of its forms, they cannot exceed in force the limits of endurance determined by human organization and sensibility. When once those limits are reached, it is impossible to devise, for still more injurious and atrocious crimes, any additional punishment that could conceivably serve to prevent them. The other consequence is that impunity itself results from the atrocity of penalties. Men are bound within limits, no less in evil than in good; a spectacle too atrocious for humanity can only be a passing rage, never a permanent system such as the laws must be, for if [the laws] are really cruel, they must either be changed or fatal impunity will follow from the laws themselves.

I conclude with this reflection that the scale of punishments should be relative to the state of the nation itself. Very strong and sensible impressions are demanded for the callous spirits of a people that has just emerged from the savage state. A lightning bolt is necessary to stop a ferocious lion that turns upon the shot of a rifle. But to the extent that spirits are softened in the social state, sensibility increases and, as it increases, the force of punishment must diminish if the relation between object and sensory impression is to be kept constant.

XVI · THE DEATH PENALTY

This useless prodigality of torments, which has never made men better, has prompted me to examine whether death if really useful and just in a well-organized government.

What manner of right can men attribute to themselves to slaughter their fellow beings? Certainly not that from which sovereignty and the laws derive. These are nothing but the sum of the least portions of the private liberty of each person; they represent the general will, which is the aggregate of particular wills. Was there ever a man who can have wished to leave to other men the choice of killing him? Is it conceivable that the least sacrifice of each person's liberty should include sacrifice of the greatest of all goods, life? And if that were the case, how could such a principle be reconciled with the other, that man is not entitled to take his own life? He must be, if he can surrender that right to others or to society as a whole.

The punishment of death, therefore, is not a right, for I have demonstrated that it cannot be such; but it is the war of a nation against a citizen whose destruction it judges to be necessary or useful. If, then, I can show that death is neither useful nor necessary I shall have gained the cause of humanity.

There are only two possible motives for believing that the death of a citizen is necessary. The first: when it is evident that even if deprived of liberty he still has connections and power such as endanger the security of the nation—when, that is, his existence can produce a dangerous revolution in the established form of government. The death of a citizen thus becomes necessary when a nation is recovering or losing its liberty or, in time of anarchy, when disorders themselves take the place of laws. But while the laws reign tranquilly, in a form of government enjoying the consent of the entire nation, well defended externally and internally by force, and by opinion, which is perhaps even more efficacious than force, where executive power is lodged with the true sovereign alone, where riches purchase pleasures and not authority, I see no necessity for destroying a citizen, except if his death were the only real way of restraining others from committing crimes; this is the second motive for believing that the death penalty may be just and necessary.

If the experience of all the ages, in which the supreme penalty has never prevented determined men from injuring society, if the example of the Roman citizenry, and twenty years of the reign of Elizabeth of Moscow,* in which she gave to the fathers of the people an illustrious example worth at least as much as many conquests purchased with the blood of children of the fatherland—if all this should fail to persuade men to whom the language of reason is always suspect, and that of authority always efficacious, it suffices merely to consult human nature to perceive the truth of my assertion.

It is not the intensity of punishment that has the greatest effect on the human spirit, but its duration, for our sensibility is more easily and more permanently affected by slight but repeated impressions than by a powerful but momentary action. The sway of habit is universal over every sentient being; as man speaks and walks and satisfies his needs by its aid, so the ideas of morality come to be stamped upon the mind only by long and repeated impressions. It is not the terrible yet momentary spectacle of the death of a wretch, but the long and painful example of a man deprived of liberty, who, having become a beast of burden, recompenses with his labors the society he has offended, which is the strongest curb against crimes. That efficacious idea—efficacious, because very often repeated to ourselves—"I myself shall be reduced to so long and miserable a condition if I commit a similar misdeed" is far more potent than the idea of death, which men envision always at an obscure distance.

The death penalty leaves an impression which, with all its force, cannot make up for the tendency to forget, natural to man even with regard to the most essential things, and readily accelerated by the passions. A general rule: violent passions surprise men, but not for long, and are therefore apt to bring on those revolutions which instantly transform ordinary men into either Persians or Lacedemonians; but in a free and peaceful government the impressions should be frequent rather than strong.

The death penalty becomes for the majority a spectacle and for some others an object of compassion mixed with disdain; these two sentiments rather than the salutary fear which the laws pretend to inspire occupy the spirits of the spectators. But in moderate and prolonged punishments the dominant sentiment is the latter, because it is the only one. The limit which the legislator ought to fix

* [During the reign (1741–1762) of the Empress Elizabeth, capital punishment was not practiced in Russia.—H. P.]

on the rigor of punishments would seem to be determined by the sentiment of compassion itself, when it begins to prevail over every other in the hearts of those who are the witnesses of punishment, inflicted for their sake rather than for the criminal's.

For a punishment to be just it should consist of only such gradations of intensity as suffice to deter men from committing crimes. Now, the person does not exist who, reflecting upon it, could choose for himself total and perpetual loss of personal liberty, no matter how advantageous a crime might seem to be. Thus the intensity of the punishment of a life sentence of servitude, in place of the death penalty, has in it what suffices to deter any determined spirit. It has, let me add, even more. Many men are able to look calmly and with firmness upon death—some from fanaticism, some from vanity, which almost always accompanies man even beyond the tomb, some from a final and desperate attempt either to live no longer or to escape their misery. But neither fanaticism nor vanity can subsist among fetters or chains, under the rod, under the yoke, in a cage of iron, where the desperate wretch does not end his woes but merely begins them. Our spirit resists violence and extreme but momentary pains more easily than it does time and incessant weariness, for it can, so to speak, collect itself for a moment to repel the first, but the vigor of its elasticity does not suffice to resist the long and repeated action of the second.

With the death penalty, every example given to the nation presupposes a new crime; with the penalty of a lifetime of servitude a single crime supplies frequent and lasting examples. And if it be important that men frequently observe the power of the laws, penal executions ought not to be separated by long intervals; they, therefore, presuppose frequency of the crimes. Thus, if this punishment is to be really useful, it somehow must not make the impression on men that it should; that is, it must be useful and not useful at the same time. To anyone raising the argument that perpetual servitude is as painful as death and therefore equally cruel, I will reply that, adding up all the moments of unhappiness of servitude, it may well be even more cruel; but these are drawn out over an entire lifetime, while the pain of death exerts its whole force in a moment. And precisely this is the advantage of penal servitude, that it inspires terror in the spectator more than in the sufferer, for the former considers the entire sum of unhappy moments, while the latter is distracted from the thought of future misery by that of the present moment. All evils are magnified in the imagination, and the sufferer finds compensations and consolations unknown and incredible to spectators who substitute their own sensibility for the callous spirit of a miserable wretch.

This, more or less, is the line of reasoning of a thief or an assassin—men who find no motive weighty enough to keep them from violating the laws, except the gallows or the wheel. I know that cultivation of the sentiments of one's own spirit is an art that is learned through education; but although a thief may not be able to give a clear account of his motives, that does not make them any the less operative: "What are these laws that I am supposed to respect, that place such a great distance between me and the rich man? He refuses me the penny I ask of him and, as an excuse, tells me to sweat at work that he knows nothing about. Who made these laws? Rich and powerful men who have never deigned to visit the squalid huts of the poor, who have never had to share a crust of moldy bread amid the innocent cries of hungry children and the tears of a wife. Let us break these bonds, fatal to the majority and only useful to a few indolent tyrants; let us attack the injustice at its source. I will return to my natural state of independence; I shall at least for a little time live free and happy with the fruits of my courage and industry. The day will perhaps come for my sorrow and repentance, but it will be brief, and for a single day of suffering I shall have many years of liberty and pleasures. As king over a few, I will correct the mistakes of fortune and will see these tyrants grow pale and tremble in the presence of one whom with an insulting flourish of pride they used to dismiss to a lower level than their horses and dogs." Then religion presents itself to the mind of the abusive wretch and, promising him an easy repentance and an almost certain eternity of happiness, does much to diminish for him the horror of that ultimate tragedy.

But he who foresees a great number of years, or even a whole lifetime to be spent in servitude and pain, in sight of his fellow citizens with whom he lives in freedom and friendship, slave of the laws which once afforded him protection, makes a useful comparison of all this with the uncertainty of the result of his crimes, and the brevity of the time in which he would enjoy their fruits. The perpetual example of those whom he actually sees the victims of their own carelessness makes a much stronger impression upon him than the spectacle of a punishment that hardens more than it corrects him.

The death penalty cannot be useful, because of the example of barbarity it gives men. If the passions or the necessities of war have taught the shedding of human blood, the laws, moderators of the conduct of men, should not extend the beastly example, which becomes more pernicious since the inflicting of legal death is attended with much study and formality. It seems to me absurd that the laws, which are an expression of the public will, which detest and punish homicide, should themselves commit it, and that to deter citizens from murder, they order a public one. Which are the true and most useful laws? Those pacts and those conditions which all would observe and propose, while the voice of private interest, which one cannot help hearing, is either silent or in accord with that of the public. What are the sentiments of each and every man about the death penalty? Let us read them in the acts of indignation and contempt with which everyone regards the hangman, who is, after all, merely the innocent executor of the public will, a good citizen contributing to the public good, an instrument as necessary to the internal security of a people as valorous soldiers are to the external. What then is the origin of this contradiction? And why, in spite of reason, is this sentiment indelible in men? Because men, in the most secret recess of their spirits, in the part that more than any other still conserves the original form of their first nature, have always believed that one's own life can be in the power of no one, except necessity alone, which, with its scepter of iron, rules the universe.

What must men think when they see learned magistrates and high ministers of justice, who, with calm indifference, cause a criminal to be dragged, by slow proceedings, to death; and while some wretch quakes in the last throes of anguish, awaiting the fatal blow, the judge who, with insensitive coldness, and perhaps even with secret satisfaction in his personal authority, passes by to enjoy the conveniences and the pleasures of life? "Ah!" they will say, "these laws are but the pretexts of force; the studied and cruel formalities of justice are nothing but a conventional language for immolating us with greater security, like victims destined for sacrifice to the insatiable idol of despotism. Assassination, which is represented to us as a terrible misdeed, we see employed without any repugnance and without excitement. Let us take advantage of the example given us. Violent death seemed to be a terrible spectacle in their descriptions, but we see that it is the affair of a moment. How much less terrible must it be for one who, not expecting it, is spared almost all there is in it of pain!"

Such are the dangerous and fallacious arguments employed, if not with clarity, at least confusedly, by men disposed to crimes, in whom, as we have seen, the abuse of religion is more potent than religion itself.

If one were to cite against me the example of all the ages and of almost all the nations that have applied the death penalty to certain crimes, my reply would be that the example reduced itself to nothing in the face of truth, against which there is no prescription; that the history of men leaves us with the impression of a vast sea of errors; among which, at great intervals, some rare and hardly intelligible truths appear to float on the surface. Human sacrifices were once common to almost all nations, yet who will dare to defend them? That only a few societies, and for a short time only, have abstained from applying the death penalty, stands in my favor rather than against me, for that conforms with the usual lot of great truths, which are about as long-lasting as a lightning flash in comparison with the long dark night that envelops mankind. The happy time has not yet arrived in which truth shall be the portion of the greatest number, as error has heretofore been. And from this universal law those truths only have been exempted which Infinite Wisdom has chosen to distinguish from others by revealing them.

The voice of a philosopher is too weak to contend against the tumults and the cries of so many who are guided by blind custom, but the few wise men who are scattered over the face of the earth shall in their heart of hearts echo what I say; and if the truth, among the infinite obstacles that keep it from a monarch, in spite of himself, should ever reach as far as his throne, let him know that it comes there with the secret approval of all men; let him know that in his worthy presence the bloody fame of conquerors will be silenced, and that posterity, which is just, assigns him first place among the peaceful trophies of the Tituses, of the Antonines, and of the Trajans.

How fortunate humanity would be if laws were for the first time being decreed for it, now that we see on the thrones of Europe monarchs who are beneficent, who encourage peaceful virtues, the sciences, the arts, who are fathers to their peoples, crowned citizens, the increase of whose authority constitutes the happiness of subjects, because it removes that intermediate despotism, the more cruel because less secure, which represses popular expressions of esteem which are ever sincere and ever of good omen when they can reach the throne! If these monarchs, I say, suffer the old laws to subsist, it is because of the infinite difficulties involved in stripping from errors the venerated rust of many centuries. This surely is a reason for enlightened citizens to desire, with greater ardor, the continual increase of their authority.

FURTHER READING

Marcello T. Maestro, *Voltaire and Beccaria as Reformers of Criminal Law* (1942) . Mechanical, brief, but useful comparison.

Coleman Phillipson, *Three Criminal Law Reformers* (1923) . Has an essay on Beccaria; the other two are on Romilly and Bentham.

Paul M. Spurlin, "Beccaria's *Essay on Crimes and Punishments* in Eighteenth-Century America," *Studies on Voltaire and the Eighteenth Century,* Vol. XVII (1963) , 1489–1504. Interesting essay on Beccaria's influence in one country.

Franco Venturi, ed., Beccaria, *Dei delitti e delle pene* (1965) . A brilliant critical edition with fascinating supporting documentation; the French translation (1965) is abridged.

52 ❊ RADISHCHEV

A Journey from St. Petersburg to Moscow

[From A. N. Radishchev, *A Journey from St. Petersburg to Moscow*, translated by Leo Wiener and edited by Roderick P. Thaler, 132–39.*]

The impact of the Enlightenment on eighteenth-century Russia was slight. Catherine of Russia, who ruled her adopted country from 1762 to 1796, made widely publicized obeisances to the Western philosophes: she used Diderot as an agent in Paris to find pictures for her, bought his library and let him keep it during his lifetime. She even allowed herself to be harangued by that spirited philosophe during his exhausting visit to Russia. With Voltaire, perhaps the best-known man of letters in his day, she carried on an extensive correspondence. And for years she professed to be Montesquieu's disciple. Whatever her intentions, her options were limited and her practices authoritarian. If there were any changes at all during her reign, they amounted to fastening the peasant-serfs' yoke more firmly than ever before.

Meanwhile, the Russian nobility avidly copied Western ways without acquiring Western convictions. The state ruled, the nobles and the church served the state, and the vast majority of Russians— the serfs—served the state, the nobles and the church. There was nothing to be done about that. "Much of what the West could offer," a distinguished Russian historian has written, "had only a 'decorative' function, embellishing life and making social intercourse more pleasant and civilized." What was called "Voltairian-

* Cambridge, Mass.: Harvard University Press, © 1958 by the President and Fellows of Harvard College. Reprinted by permission of the publishers.

ism" was widespread in these circles, but it meant "merely superficial and snobbish irreverence for Church ritual and a provocative philosophical rationalism."*

In this atmosphere, Aleksandr Nikolaevich Radishchev (*1749–1802*) represents a striking innovation, a lonely figure pointing to the later alienation of the Russian intelligentsia. His sentimental journey across Russia, with its attacks on serfdom, criticism of bureaucrats, and touching stories idealizing peasants, was published in *1790*. It was a bad time for such books: Catherine was enraged and frightened by the French Revolution and had no use for such enlightened propaganda. Radishchev was tried and condemned to death, but his sentence was commuted to exile in Siberia; Alexander I finally pardoned Radishchev in *1801*. But his life was shattered; in the following year he committed suicide.

My dear city gossips, aunts, sisters, nieces, etc., I had not noticed how long you had detained me. Truly, you are not worth it. On your cheeks there is rouge, on your heart rouge, on your conscience rouge, on your sincerity—soot. Rouge or soot, it's all the same. I shall gallop away from you at full speed to my rustic beauties. True, there are some of them who resemble you, but there are others the likes of whom have not been heard or seen in the cities. See how all my beauties' limbs are round, well-developed, straight, and not contorted. You think it funny that their feet are over eight or even ten inches long. But, my dear niece with your five-inch feet, stand in a row with them and run a race: who will be the first to reach the tall birch tree that stands at the end of the field? Ah—but—you are not up to it! And you, my dear little sister, you, with your three-span waist, you are pleased to make fun of my village nymph, because her abdomen has been allowed to grow naturally. Wait, my dear, I'll have my laugh at you. You have been married these ten months, and your three-span waist is all askew. When it comes to childbirth, you will pipe a different tune. God grant that nothing worse than laughter may ensue. My dear brother-in-law walks about downcast. He has already thrown all your lacings into the fire. He has pulled the stays out of all your dresses, but it is too late. Your

* Marc Raeff, *Origins of the Russian Intelligentsia: The Eighteenth-Century Nobility* (1966), 149–50.

distorted joints can't be straightened out now. Weep, my beloved brother-in-law, weep. Our mother, following the lamentable fashion which often leads to death in childbirth, has for many years been preparing sorrow for you, sickness for her daughter, and feeble bodies for your children. Even now this illness hovers like a deadly weapon over her head, and if it does not cut short your wife's days, thank your lucky stars, and, if you believe that God's Providence was concerned about the matter, thank Him, too, if you wish. But here I am still with the city ladies. That's what custom does: one doesn't feel like leaving them. Indeed I would not leave you if I could persuade you not to paint your faces and your sincerity. And now, goodbye!

While I was watching the village nymphs washing their clothes, my carriage drove off. I was about to start after it, when a girl who looked to be about twenty, but was really only seventeen, put her wet clothes on a yoke and started off the same way I was going. When I caught up with her, I spoke to her.

"Isn't it hard for you to carry such a heavy load, my dear—? I don't know your name."

"My name is Anna, and my load isn't heavy. And even if it were, I would not ask you, sir, to help me."

"Why so stern, Annushka dear? I mean you no harm."

"All right, all right! We've seen gallants like you before. Please go your way!"

"Truly, Anyutushka, I'm not the man you take me for and not the sort you're talking about. I understand that they start by kissing a girl, not by talking with her; but if I were to kiss you, it would be just as though I were kissing my own sister."

"Don't sidle up to me, if you please. I've heard such talk before. If you really mean no harm, what is it you want of me?"

"Dear Annushka, I wanted to know whether your father and mother are still alive, what your circumstances are, whether you're rich or poor, whether you're happy, whether you have a fiancé?"

"What's that to you, sir? This is the first time in my life I've heard such talk."

"From which you may judge, Anyuta, that I'm not a scoundrel and do not mean to insult or dishonor you. I love women because they embody my ideal of tenderness; but most of all I love village or peasant women, because they are innocent of hypocrisy, do not put on the mask of pretended love, and when they do love, love sincerely and with their whole hearts."

While I was saying this, the girl looked at me with eyes wide open with amazement. How, indeed, could it have been otherwise, for who does not know the impudence, the crude, unchaste, and offensive jests, with which the audacious gentry assail the village maidens? In the eyes of old and young nobles alike, they are simply creatures for their lordly pleasure. And they treat them accordingly, especially those unfortunate ones subject to their commands. During the recent Pugachev Rebellion, when all the serfs rose up in arms against their masters, some peasants (this story is not an invention) had tied up their master and started to carry him off to certain death. What was the reason for this? In everything else he was a good and charitable master, but neither the wives nor the daughters of his peasants were safe from him. Every night his emissaries brought him his chosen victim for that day's sacrifice to dishonor. It was known in the village that he had dishonored sixty maidens, robbing them of their purity. A detachment of soldiers that happened to pass by rescued this barbarian from the hands of those who were raging against him. Stupid peasants, you looked for justice from an imposter! But why did you not report your grievance to your rightful judges? They would have condemned the offender to civil death, and you would have remained innocent. But now this evildoer is saved. Happy he if the sight of imminent death has changed his way of thinking and given a new direction to his vital humors. But, we said, the peasant is dead to the law? No, no, he lives, he will live, if he wishes to!

"If you are not jesting, sir," Anyuta said to me, "I will tell you. I have no father; he died two years ago. I have a mother and a little sister. Father left us five horses and three cows. And there are plenty of small animals and fowl, but there is no man in the house to do the farm work. They were going to marry me off into a rich house, to a ten-year-old lad, but I didn't want that. What could I do with such a child? I could not love him. And by the time he was grown up, I would have been an old woman, and he would have been running after others. They say that his father sleeps with his young daughters-in-law until his sons grow up. That's why I didn't want to marry into his family. I want someone my own age. I shall love my husband, and he will love me; I've no doubt of that. I don't want to gallivant with the boys, but I do want to get married, sir. And do you know why?" Anyuta said, letting her eyes droop.

"Tell me, dear Anyutushka, don't be bashful; every word from the lips of innocence is pure."

"Well, then, I'll tell you. A year ago last summer our neighbor's son married my friend with whom I always used to go to quilting parties. Her husband loves her, and she loves him so much that in the tenth month after their wedding she bore him a little son. Every evening she takes him out by the gate to give him an airing. She can't get to see her fill of him. And it looks as though the little fellow already loves his mother. Whenever she says to him 'Agoo, agoo,' he laughs. Tears come to my eyes every day I see him; I should love to have a child like that myself."

At this point I could no longer refrain from embracing Anyuta, and kissed her with all my heart.

"See what a deceiver you are, sir! You are already playing with me," said Anyuta, bursting into tears. "Go away and leave a poor orphan alone. If my father were alive and saw this, he would give you a good beating in spite of your being a nobleman."

"Don't be offended, dear Anyutushka, don't be offended! My kiss does not sully your virtue, which is sacred in my eyes. My kiss is a token of my respect for you, and it was the joyous response of my deeply moved soul. Do not be afraid of me, dear Anyuta, for I am not a rapacious animal like our young noblemen who think nothing of robbing a maiden of her purity. If I had known that my kiss would offend you, I swear in God's name that I would not have dared to kiss you."

"You can see yourself, sir, that I could not help being offended by your kiss, since all mine are meant for another. I have promised them in advance, and I am not free to dispose of them."

"How charming! You have already learned how to love. You have found another heart for your own, a fitting mate. You will be happy. Nothing will sever your union. You will not be surrounded by busybodies who will be watching for a chance to lure you into the nets of destruction. Your true lover's ear will not be open to the voice of temptation, inciting him to violate his troth to you. But why, my dear Anyuta, are you deprived of the pleasure of enjoying happiness in your dear friend's arms?"

"O sir, because they won't let him off to come to us. They demand a hundred rubles. And my mother won't let me go, because I'm her only helper."

"But does he love you?"

"Indeed he does. Every evening he comes to our house and together we watch my friend's baby. He'd love to have a little fellow just like that one. It will be hard for me, but I shall have to stand it. My Vanyukha wants to go to Petersburg to work on the boats, and he will not come back until he has earned a hundred rubles to buy his release."

"Do not let him go, dear Anyutushka, do not let him go! He will be going to his ruin. There he will learn to drink, to waste his money, to eat dainties, despise farm work, and worst of all, he will stop loving you."

"O sir, don't frighten me," said Anyuta, almost in tears.

"And it would be even worse, Anyuta, if he should take service in a nobleman's house. The example of the masters infects the higher servants, these infect the lower, and from them the pestilence of debauchery spreads to the villages. The bad example is the real plague, for everybody does what he sees others do."

"Then what will become of me? I'll never be able to marry him. It's time for him to get married; he's not one to go running about with other girls. They won't let me go into his household; they'll marry him to someone else, and I, poor girl, shall die of grief." Saying this, she shed bitter tears.

"No, my dear Anyutushka, you shall marry him tomorrow. Take me to your mother."

"Here is our house," she said, as she stopped. "Please go away, for if Mother sees me with you, she'll think ill of me. Though she doesn't strike me, her mere words hurt me more than blows."

"No, Anyuta, I'll go with you." And, without waiting for her answer, I walked right through the gate, up the stairs, and into the hut. Anyuta cried after me, "Wait, sir, wait!" But I paid no attention to her. In the hut I found Anyuta's mother, who was kneading dough; near her, on a bench, sat her future son-in-law. I told her, without beating about the bush, that I wanted her daughter to marry Ivan, and that I had brought the means to remove the obstacle thereto.

"Thank you, sir," said the old woman, "but there is no longer any need for it. Vanyukha has just come to tell us that his father has agreed to let him off, to come to us. So we'll have the wedding on Sunday."

"Then let my promised gift be Anyuta's dowry."

"Thank you, no. Gentlemen do not give girls a dowry for nothing. If you have wronged my Anyuta and are giving her a dowry to make up for it, God will punish you for your misdeed, but I will not take the money. If you are a good man and do not hurt the poor, then malicious people would think the worst of me for taking money from you."

I could not sufficiently admire the noble dignity which I had found in these simple country people. Meanwhile Anyuta had come into the hut, and sang my praises to her mother. I tried again to give them the money, offering it to Ivan toward setting up his house, but he said to me: "I have two hands, sir, and with them I will set up my house." Seeing that my presence was not very pleasant for them, I left them and returned to my carriage.

As I drove on from Edrovo, I could not put Anyuta out of my mind. Her innocent sincerity pleased me beyond measure. Her mother's noble act enchanted me. I compared this noble mother, with her sleeves rolled up over the dough or over her milking pail near the cow, with urban mothers. The peasant woman refused to accept my honest, well-intended hundred rubles, which, in proportion to her means and status, would correspond to five, ten, fifteen thousand, or more, for the wife of a colonel, privy councilor, major, or general. Now if a distinguished magnate of the seventieth or— God forbid!—the seventy-second proof were to offer the wife of a colonel, major, privy councilor, or general, who has a pretty or merely virtuous daughter, five, ten, or fifteen thousand (which would be quite in proportion to my offer to the wife of the Edrovo coachman), or if he hinted that he would give her daughter a handsome dowry, or find her an official for her husband, or secure her an appointment as a lady-in-waiting—I ask you, city mothers, would not your heart give a leap?

FURTHER READING

Michael T. Florinski, *Russia, A History and an Interpretation,* 2 vols. (1953). The relevant chapters are suggestive and impressive.

Geroid Tanqueray Robinson, *Rural Russia in the Old Regime* (1932). An authoritative account.

G. S. Thomson, *Catherine the Great and the Expansion of Russia* (1962). Though short and popular, informative and reliable.

53 ❊ LESSING

Die Juden

[From *The Jews,* in *The Dramatic Works of*
G. E. Lessing, edited by Ernest Bell, 2 vols.
(1878), II, 191, 194–96, 199–202, 205–17.]

For the men of the Enlightenment, the Jews were something of a
problem. I underscore the word "something"; the scourge of mod-
ern anti-Semitism has made us very sensitive, but the philosophes
spent very little time on the "Jewish Question," or expressing their
own views of Jews. This is hardly surprising: for a thousand years,
Jews had been separated from the mainstream of Christian cultural
life, essential to some of its less pleasant occupations and generally
despised as the people that had "killed Christ." To the philosophes,
this myth made no sense; and with their programmatic cosmopoli-
tanism and reforming passion, they might have been thought to be
ready to embrace Jews as human beings whom a superstitious past
had grievously wronged.

Some of the philosophes, in fact, took this logical step toward a
more comprehensive humanity. The English deist Toland called for
toleration; Montesquieu repeatedly took anti-Jewish behavior as a
sign of barbarism. But there were other philosophes, notably Vol-
taire, who treated Jews as the ancestors of the Christian supersti-
tion, and thus hardly lovable. The few passages that Voltaire*
devotes to the Jews, therefore, are in the main reproaches for
foisting on the world so much pernicious nonsense. He always
insisted on the intimate connection between the Jews and the
Christians: "When I see Christians cursing Jews," he wrote in his

---

* Voltaire's "anti-Semitism," if we may so call it, was "confirmed" by personal
experiences with Jewish bankers—experiences to which he did not bring his
usual keen analytical spirit.

notebook, "*methinks I see children beating their fathers.*"* The solution to Jewish isolation in his own day struck Voltaire as eminently obvious: total assimilation. This self-satisfied attitude was shared by many of the other philosophes.

Notable among the exceptions to this cultural chauvinism was Lessing. It can be said of him, without the derisive meaning that this phrase has acquired, that some of his best friends were Jews. Not long after he went to Berlin in 1748, he met Moses Mendelssohn, born, like himself, in 1729; Mendelssohn, philosopher, aesthetician, theologian, was intent on bringing the Jews into the cultural circle of the modern world. Lessing and Mendelssohn became, and remained, friends. Lessing's youthful one-act play Die Juden, completed in 1749, reads like a forecast of his friendship. It is not a great play, or even a good one, but it shows, precisely in its youthfulness, the attempt of one enlightened man to apply the principles in which he believes.

SCENES I AND II

[*Martin Krumm and Michel Stich, two thieves, commiserate with each other about a highway robbery in which they were foiled by the arrival of a stranger. As it turns out, Martin Krumm is the bailiff of the landowner whom he was trying to rob (in disguise). The stranger comes upon Krumm and Stich talking, and Stich quickly leaves. Krumm and the traveler discuss the incident, and Krumm in his capacity as bailiff inquires closely as to what happened. The traveler reports that the landowner believes that the robbers were Jews because they had long beards, but he himself is doubtful: ". . . their language," he says, "was the common dialect used among the peasantry here." In addition he wonders that "Jews should be able to make the roads unsafe, since so few of them are suffered to remain in the country." Krumm answers this with a long and passionate diatribe against the Jews. "If I were king," he says, "I should not leave a single one of them alive." He then leaves, making the traveler very fulsome compliments on his rescue.*]

* *Voltaire's Notebooks*, ed. Besterman (1952), 31 (in English).

SCENE III · THE TRAVELER

Trav. Perhaps this fellow, however stupid he is, or pretends to be, is a more wicked rascal than there ever was among the Jews. If a Jew cheats, at least seven times out of nine he has been driven to it by a Christian. I doubt whether many Christians can boast of having dealt uprightly with a Jew, and they are surprised if he endeavors to render like for like. If good faith and honesty are to prevail between two different races, both must contribute equal shares. But how if the one considers it a point of religion and almost a meritorious work to persecute the other? Yet—

SCENES IV AND V

[*The traveler seeks out his servant, Christoph, whom he orders to pack up their things. Christoph, who is a shrewd and rather impertinent fellow, demurs and suggests that they stay longer and reap the benefit of the gratitude their host feels toward them. In addition, he points out insinuatingly that there is a charming young daughter. The traveler responds with an angry speech in which he observes that "most men are too corrupt not to feel the presence of a benefactor burdensome to them." The daughter then arrives and also attempts to persuade the traveler to stay. But she runs away as she hears her father approaching.*]

SCENE VI · THE BARON, THE TRAVELER

Baron. Was not my daughter with you? Why does the wild child run off?

Trav. To possess such an amiable and so merry a daughter is an inestimable fortune. She enchants one by her conversation, which is full of the sweetest innocence and most unaffected wit.

Baron. You judge her too favorably. She has been little into society, and possesses but in small degree the art of pleasing—an art which can hardly be acquired in the country, yet which is often more powerful than Beauty herself. Untrammelled Nature alone has been her tutor.

Trav. And this, but seldom met with in towns, is so much the more fascinating. There everything is feigned, forced, and acquired.

Indeed, we have made such progress in this direction, that to be stupid, to be uncouth, and to be natural, are considered as phrases of the same meaning.

BARON. What could be more agreeable to me than to find that our thoughts and opinions harmonize so well? Would that I had had long ago a friend like you!

TRAV. You are unjust toward your other friends.

BARON. Toward my other friends, do you say? I am fifty years of age. Acquaintances I have had, but no friends. And friendship never appeared to me in so charming a garb as during the few hours in which I have been endeavoring to obtain yours. How can I merit it?

TRAV. My friendship is of so little importance that the mere wish for it is a sufficient merit for obtaining it. Your request is of far more value than that which you request.

BARON. Oh, sir! the friendship of a benefactor—

TRAV. Excuse me—is no friendship. If you look at me in this false aspect, I cannot be your friend. Suppose, for a moment, I were your benefactor; should I not have to fear that your friendship was nothing but gratitude?

BARON. But could not the two be united?

TRAV. Hardly. A noble mind considers gratitude its duty; friendship requires voluntary emotions of the soul alone.

BARON. But how ought I . . . Your nice distinctions confuse me entirely.

TRAV. Only esteem me no more than I deserve. At most I am a man who has done his duty with pleasure. Duty itself does not deserve gratitude. But for having done it with pleasure, I am sufficiently rewarded by your friendship.

BARON. This magnanimity only confuses me the more. But I am, perhaps, too bold. I have not dared as yet to inquire your name, your rank. Perhaps I offer my friendship to a man who . . . who, if he despises it, is—

TRAV. Pardon me, sir. You . . . you make . . . you think too highly of me.

BARON (*aside*). Shall I ask him? He might feel offended at my curiosity.

TRAV. (*aside*). If he asks me, what shall I answer him?

BARON (*aside*). If I do not ask him, he may consider it rudeness.

TRAV. (*aside*). Shall I tell him the truth?

BARON (*aside*). But I will take the safest way. I'll first make inquiries of his servant.

TRAV. (*aside*). How can I get out of this perplexity?

BARON. Why so thoughtful?

TRAV. I was just going to put the same question to you.

BARON. I know now and then we forget ourselves. Let us speak of something else. Do you know that they were really Jews who attacked me? Just now my bailiff told me that some days ago he met three of them on the high road. According to his description they must have looked more like rogues than honest people. And why should I doubt it? People so intent on gain care little whether they make money by fair means or foul—by cunning or force. They seem to be born for commerce, or, to speak more plainly, for cheating. Politeness, liberality, enterprise, discretion, are qualities that would render this people estimable, if they did not use them entirely to our disadvantage. (*He pauses a moment.*) The Jews have already been to me a source of no small mischief and vexation. When I was still in military service, I was persuaded to sign a bill in favor of one of my acquaintances, and the Jew on whom it was drawn not only made me pay the bill, but pay it twice. Oh! they are the most wicked, the most base people! What do you say? You seem cast down.

TRAV. What shall I say? I must confess I have often heard similar complaints.

BARON. And is it not true, their countenance has something that prejudices one against them? It seems to me as if one could read in their eyes their maliciousness, unscrupulousness, selfishness of character, their deceit and perjury. But why do you turn away from me?

TRAV. I hear you are very learned in physiognomies; I am afraid, sir, that mine—

BARON. Oh, you wrong me! How could you entertain such a suspicion? Without being learned in physiognomies, I must tell you, I have never met with a more frank, generous, and pleasing countenance than yours.

TRAV. To tell you the truth, I do not approve of generalizations concerning a whole people. You will not feel offended at my liberty. I should think among all nations good and wicked are to be found. And among the Jews—

SCENES VII AND VIII

[*The daughter returns and reveals to the Baron that the traveler intends to leave. Christoph arrives in traveling dress to announce that everything is ready for their departure. The Baron entreats the traveler to stay on and is seconded by his daughter. He consents and the daughter takes him off for a walk in the garden, urging her father not to be in a hurry to accompany them. Enter Lisette, the maid.*]

SCENE IX · LISETTE, CHRISTOPH, THE YOUNG LADY, THE TRAVELER, THE BARON

BARON (*perceiving* LISETTE *coming*). Sir, I shall follow you immediately, if you will be pleased to conduct my daughter to the garden.

LADY. Oh, stay as long as you please. We shall amuse ourselves. Come. (*Exeunt the* YOUNG LADY *and the* TRAVELER.)

BARON. Lisette, I have something to say to you.

LIS. Well?

BARON (*whispering*). I don't know yet who our guest is. For certain reasons I don't like to ask him. Could not you learn from his servant?

LIS. Oh! I know what you want. My own curiosity has already urged me to do that, and I have come here for that very reason.

BARON. Well, try your best and let me know. You will earn my thanks.

LIS. All right; go now.

CHRIS. You will not be offended, then, sir, that we are pleased to stay. But don't inconvenience yourself at all on my account, I beg. I am contented with everything.

BARON. Lisette, I leave him under your care. Let him want for nothing. (*Exit.*)

CHRIS. I recommend myself, then, to your care, mademoiselle, you who are to let me want for nothing. (*Is going.*)

SCENE X · LISETTE, CHRISTOPH

LIS. (*stopping him*). No, sir, I cannot allow you to be so impolite. Am I not woman enough to be worthy of a little conversation?

CHRIS. The deuce, mistress, you take things too literally. Whether you are woman enough, or perhaps too much, I cannot say. But judging from your loquacity I should almost affirm the latter. But be that as it may, I hope you will dismiss me now; you see my hands and arms are full. As soon as I am hungry or thirsty I'll come to you.

LIS. Our watchman does the same.

CHRIS. The deuce! He must be a clever fellow, if he does as I do.

LIS. If you would like to make his acquaintance, he is chained up in the backyard.

CHRIS. The devil! I verily believe you mean the dog. I see, you thought I meant bodily hunger and thirst; but that was not what I meant. I spoke of the hunger and thirst of love. That, mistress, that. Are you satisfied with my explanation?

LIS. Better than with what it explains.

CHRIS. Now, in confidence: do you mean to imply by that, that a declaration of love from me would not be disagreeable to you?

LIS. Perhaps. Will you make me one? Seriously?

CHRIS. Perhaps.

LIS. Ugh! What an answer! "Perhaps"!

CHRIS. And yet there was not a hair's-breadth difference between yours and mine.

LIS. But from my mouth it means something quite different. A woman's greatest pledge is "perhaps." For however bad our cards may be, we must never allow anyone to see them.

CHRIS. Well, if that's the case! But let's come to business. (*He throws the two portmanteaux on the ground.*) I don't know why I troubled myself so long. There they lie. . . . I love you, mistress.

LIS. I call that saying much in a few words. We'll dissect it.

CHRIS. No, we'll rather leave whole. But, that we may acquaint each other with our thoughts at leisure, be good enough to take a seat. Standing fatigues me. Make no ceremony. (*Makes her sit upon the portmanteau.*) I love you, mistress.

LIS. But . . . my seat is desperately hard. I believe there are books in it.

CHRIS. Yes; full of wit and tenderness, and nevertheless you consider it a hard seat. That is my master's traveling library. It consists of comedies moving to tears, and tragedies moving to laughter; of tender epics, and philosophic drinking songs, and I don't know what more novelties. But we'll change. Take my seat; make no ceremony; mine is the softest.

LIS. Pardon me, I will not be so rude.

CHRIS. Make no ceremony, no compliments. Well, if you won't go, I shall carry you.

LIS. Well, if you order it. (*Is going to change her seat.*)

CHRIS. Order! Good gracious, no! Order means a great deal. If you mean to take it so, you had better keep your seat. (*He sits down again.*)

LIS. (*aside*). The uncivil brute! But no matter.

CHRIS. Well, where did we stop? Yes! I have it; we stopped at love. I love you, then, mistress. *Je vous aime,* I should say if you were a French marquise.

LIS. The deuce! Are you a Frenchman, then?

CHRIS. No, I must confess, to my own disgrace, I am only a German. But I had the good luck to be able to associate with some French gentlemen, from whom I have learned how an honest fellow ought to behave. I think, too, that one can see it in me at a glance.

LIS. You have come, then, from France, with your master?

CHRIS. Oh, no.

LIS. Where from, then? Perhaps—

CHRIS. It is some miles farther than France, where we come from.

LIS. Not from Italy?

CHRIS. Not very far from there.

LIS. From England, then?

CHRIS. Almost. England is a province of the country. Our home is more than two hundred miles from here. But, by Jove! my horses; the poor beasts are still in their harness. Pardon me, mistress. Quick! get up! (*He takes the portmanteaux under his arm.*) In spite of my fervent love I must go, and first attend to what is necessary. We have yet the whole day before us, and, what's better still, the whole night. I see we shall get on together. I shall know where to find you again.

SCENES XI, XII, AND XIII

[*Martin Krumm comes to chat with Lisette and shows her a silver snuffbox. She flirts with him and gets him to give it to her as a present. The daughter comes upon them as Martin is kissing Lisette's hand. She begins to make fun of him, and Lisette joins in. He leaves in anger. The daughter confesses to Lisette that she would like to marry the stranger but fears that she is too young.*]

SCENE XIV · LISETTE, CHRISTOPH

LIS. You must be either hungry or thirsty, sir, that you come again already? Eh?

CHRIS. Yes, indeed. But mind how I have explained hunger and thirst. To tell you the truth, my dear young woman, as soon as I dismounted yesterday I cast my eye on you. But thinking to remain here only a few hours, I thought it would not be worthwhile to make your acquaintance. What could we have done in so short a time? We should have had to begin our novel at the wrong end. And it is not safe to pull the cat out of the stove by the tail.

LIS. True enough; but now we can proceed more according to rule. You can make a proposal; I can reply to it. I can raise scruples; you can overcome them. We may deliberate at each step, and need not sell one another a pig in a poke. If you had made me your offer yesterday at once, I must confess, I should have accepted it. But only fancy how much I should have staked, if I had had no time to inquire about your rank, fortune, country, employments, and such like.

CHRIS. The deuce! But would that have been necessary? Such a fuss! You could not make much more if you were going to be married.

LIS. Oh! if it had been a mere marriage, it would be ridiculous to be so conscientious on my part. But a love affair is quite another thing. The least trifle is of the greatest importance. And therefore don't fancy that you will obtain the least favor from me if you do not satisfy my curiosity in every respect.

CHRIS. Well; and how far does it go?

LIS. Since a servant is best judged by his master, before anything else I wish to know—

CHRIS. Who my master is? Ha! ha! that's good. You ask me a question which I should like to ask you, if I thought you knew more about it than I did.

LIS. And do you really think to get off with this miserable subterfuge? In short, I must know who your master is, or there's an end to our friendship.

CHRIS. I have not known my master longer than four weeks. So long it is since I entered his service at Hamburg. I have come with him from that place, but have never taken the trouble to inquire for his rank or name. But so much is quite certain: he must be rich, for he has not let either himself or me want for anything on our journey. And why should I care about anything else?

LIS. What can I hope from your love, if you won't even trust such a trifle to my discretion? I should never treat you in such a way. For example, you see this handsome silver snuffbox—

CHRIS. Really! Well?

LIS. You only need to beg me, and I'll tell you from whom I have got it.

CHRIS. Oh, that is not of much consequence to me. I'd rather know who is to get it from you.

LIS. I have not exactly settled that point yet. But if you don't get it, it will be no one's fault but your own. I certainly should not leave your openness unrewarded.

CHRIS. Or rather my loquacity. But as I am an honest fellow, if I am silent now, it is from necessity, for, indeed, I don't know what I can tell you. Confound it! How willingly I would pour out my secrets if I only had any!

LIS. Goodbye! I'll not assail your virtue any longer. But I wish it may help you soon to a silver snuffbox and a sweetheart, as it has now deprived you of them. (*Is going.*)

CHRIS. Come, come; patience! (*Aside.*) I see I must tell a lie, for I really cannot let such a present escape. Besides, what harm can it do?

LIS. Well, will you explain yourself more frankly? But I see. You do not like it. No, no, I don't want to know anything—

CHRIS. Yes, yes; you shall know everything! (*Aside.*) What would I not give to be able to tell lies. (*Aloud.*) Well, listen, then! My master . . . is a nobleman. He comes—we come together—from Holland. He was obliged, on account of some vexations—a trifle—a murder—to run for it.

LIS. What! on account of a murder?

CHRIS. Yes. But it was an honorable murder—was obliged to escape in consequence of a duel—and just now he is flying—

LIS. And you, my friend?

CHRIS. I am also flying. The dead one—I mean to say, the friends of the dead one—are prosecuting us, and on account of this prosecution . . . But the rest you can easily guess. What the deuce can one do? Consider for yourself: a saucy young monkey—called us names! My master knocked him down. How could it be otherwise? If anyone calls me names, I do the same, or—I give him a good box on the ear. An honest fellow must not put up with such things.

Lis. Bravo! I like people of that sort; for I am a little hasty myself. But see, there's your master coming. Would anyone believe, from his countenance, that he was so fierce and cruel?

Chris. Come, come; let us get out of his way. He might perhaps see that I have betrayed him.

Lis. Just as you please.

Chris. But the silver snuffbox—

Lis. Come on. (*Aside.*) I must first see what I shall get from my master for the secret I have discovered; if that is worth something, he may have the box.

SCENE XV · THE TRAVELER

Trav. I miss my box. It is a trifle, yet the loss of it would grieve me. Could the bailiff, perhaps . . . But no, I have lost it; I may have pulled it out of my pocket unawares. We ought not to injure anyone even by suspicion. Nevertheless—he pressed close up to me—he snatched at my watch. . . . I caught him at it. . . . Might he not have snatched at the box without my having caught him?

SCENE XVI · MARTIN KRUMM, THE TRAVELER

Krumm (*perceiving the stranger, is about to retire*). Holloa!

Trav. Well, well, my friend, approach. (*Aside.*) He is as shy as if he knew my thoughts! Well? come nearer!

Krumm (*defiantly*). I have no time. I know well you wish to chat with me. I have more important business to attend to. I don't wish to hear your heroic deeds for the tenth time. Relate them to somebody else who has not heard them yet.

Trav. What do I hear! Just now the bailiff was simple and polite, now he is insolent and rude. Which is your true mask?

Krumm. Ah! who the deuce taught you to call my face a mask? I don't want to quarrel with you . . . otherwise— (*Is going away.*)

Trav. (*aside*). His insolent behavior increases my suspicion. (*Aloud.*) No, no, wait a moment. I have something important to ask you.

KRUMM. And I shall have nothing to reply, however important it may be. Therefore, spare yourself the trouble of asking.

TRAV. (*aside*). I'll venture it. But I should be very sorry if I did him a wrong. (*Aloud.*) My friend, have you not seen my snuffbox? I miss it.

KRUMM. What a question! Is it my fault that someone has stolen it? What do you take me for—the receiver or the thief?

TRAV. Who spoke of theft? You are betraying yourself.

KRUMM. I betray myself? Then you think I have got it? But do you know, sir, what it is to accuse an honest fellow of such things? Do you know that?

TRAV. Why shout so loud? I have not yet accused you of anything. You are your own accuser. Besides, I don't know whether I should be greatly in the wrong. Who was it whom I caught snatching at my watch?

KRUMM. Oh! you are a man who can't understand a joke. Listen. (*Aside.*) Suppose he has seen it in Lisette's possession? But the girl has surely not been so foolish as to boast of it.

TRAV. Oh, I understand your way of joking so well that I almost believe you would like to joke with my box also. But if one carries a joke too far, it at last becomes earnest. I should be sorry for your reputation. Suppose I was convinced you had had no evil intentions, would other people too—

KRUMM. Oh! other people . . . other people would have long ago been weary of being charged with things of this sort. But if you think I have got it, search me, examine me.

TRAV. That is not my business. Besides, one does not carry everything in one's pocket.

KRUMM. Very well; but that you may see I am an honest fellow, I'll turn out my pockets myself. Look! (*Aside.*) The devil must have a hand in the game if it should tumble out.

TRAV. Oh, don't trouble yourself.

KRUMM. No, no! you shall see, you shall see. (*He turns one of his pockets inside out.*) Is there a box there? Crumbs of bread are in it; that precious food. (*He turns out another.*) There is nothing here either. But stop, a bit of a calendar; I keep it on account of the verses written above the months. They are very amusing. Well, to proceed. Attend now. I'll turn out the third. (*In turning it out, two large beards fall out.*) The devil! what is that? (*He stoops hastily to pick them up, but the traveler is quicker, and snatches one of them.*)

TRAV. What is the meaning of these things?

KRUMM (*aside*). Cursed fate! I thought I had put them away long ago.

TRAV. Why, this is a beard. (*He puts it to his face.*) Do I look like a Jew now?

KRUMM. Give it back to me. Give it back. Who knows what you may be fancying? I sometimes frighten my little boy with it. That is what it is for.

TRAV. You will be kind enough to leave it me. I will also frighten someone with it.

KRUMM. Don't let us quarrel; I must have it back. (*Tries to snatch it from his hand.*)

TRAV. Go, or—

KRUMM (*aside*). The devil! 'Tis time now to look out where the carpenter has left a hole. (*Aloud.*) All right, sir, all right. I see you came here to bring me ill luck. But may all the devils take me if I am not an honest man! I should like to see the man who can say anything bad of me! Bear that in mind. Whatever may come of it, I can swear I have not used that beard for any evil purpose! (*Exit.*)

SCENE XVII · THE TRAVELER

TRAV. This man himself raises suspicions in me which are very prejudicial to himself. Might he not be one of the disguised robbers? But I will follow out my supposition cautiously.

SCENE XVIII · THE BARON, THE TRAVELER

TRAV. Would you not think I had been fighting yesterday with the Jewish robbers and I had torn out one of their beards? (*He shows him the beard.*)

BARON. What do you mean, sir?—But why did you leave me so hastily?

TRAV. Pardon my want of politeness. I intended to be with you again immediately. I only went to look for my snuffbox, which I must have lost somewhere here.

BARON. I am really sorry for that. Should you, after all, have suffered a loss in my house—

TRAV. The loss would not be so very great. But pray just look at this curious beard.

BARON. You showed it to me before. Why?

TRAV. I will explain myself more intelligibly. I believe . . . But no, I will keep my supposition to myself.

BARON. Your supposition? Explain yourself!

TRAV. No, I have been too hasty. I might be mistaken.

BARON. You make me uneasy.

TRAV. What do you think of your bailiff?

BARON. No, no, we won't turn the conversation. I conjure you, by the benefit you have rendered me, to explain to me what you think, what you suppose, and in what you might be mistaken?

TRAV. A reply to my question alone can induce me to acquaint you with the whole matter.

BARON. What do I think of my bailiff? Well, I consider him a thoroughly honest and upright man.

TRAV. Then forget that I had anything to tell you.

BARON. A beard—suppositions—the bailiff . . . How shall I connect these things? Are my entreaties of no avail? You might be mistaken. Suppose you are mistaken, what risk do you run with a friend?

TRAV. You press me too hard. I tell you, then, that your bailiff incautiously dropped this beard; that he had another, which he hastily put back again in his pocket; that his language betrays a man who thinks that people believe as much evil of him as he is capable of doing; that I also have caught him in an attempt not very conscientious, or at least not very prudent.

BARON. It seems as if my eyes were suddenly opened. I am afraid you will not be mistaken. And you hesitated to inform me of it? I shall go at once and try all means in my power to discover the truth. Am I to harbor murderers in my own house?

TRAV. But do not be angry with me if you should happily find my supposition to be false. You forced it from me, otherwise I should have kept it secret.

BARON. True or false, I shall always be grateful to you.

SCENE XIX · THE TRAVELER
AFTERWARD CHRISTOPH

TRAV. I hope he will not proceed too hastily with him; for however well-founded the suspicion is, the man may nevertheless be innocent. I am very uneasy. . . . Indeed, it is no trifle to cause a master to suspect his servants. Even if he finds them to be innocent, yet he loses his confidence in them forever. Certainly, when I consider the matter more fully, I feel I ought to have been silent. And when they hear that I have ascribed my loss to him, will they not conclude that selfishness and revenge are the causes of my suspicion? I would willingly give a good deal to postpone the investigation.

CHRIS. *(approaches laughing)* . Ha! ha! ha! Do you know, sir, who you are?

TRAV. Do you know that you are a fool? What do you want?

CHRIS. Well, if you don't know it, I will tell you. You are a nobleman; you come from Holland, where you got into a scrape and fought a duel; you were so fortunate as to kill a young monkey of a fellow; the friends of the dead man have pursued you hotly; you have taken to flight; I have the honor of accompanying you on your flight.

TRAV. Are you dreaming, or are you mad?

CHRIS. Neither the one nor the other; since for a madman my discourse would be too reasonable, and for a dreamer too mad.

TRAV. Who has imposed upon you with such nonsense?

CHRIS. Oh, you may rest assured that no one imposes upon me. But don't you think it is cleverly invented in the short time they left me for lying? I'm sure I could not have hit upon anything better. So now at least you are secured against further curiosity.

TRAV. But what am I to make of all this?

CHRIS. No more than you please! Leave the remainder to me. Just listen how it happened. I was asked for your name, rank, fatherland, occupations; I did not let them ask twice. I told all I knew; that is, that I knew nothing at all. You can easily understand that this news was hardly sufficient, and that they had little cause to be contented with it. So they pressed me, but in vain; I kept silent, because I had nothing to keep silent about. But at last the offer of a present induced me to tell more than I knew; that is, I told a lie.

TRAV. You scoundrel! I see what excellent hands I am in.

CHRIS. What! I hope I have not accidentally lied the truth?

TRAV. You impudent liar! You have placed me in an embarrassment out of which—

CHRIS. Out of which you can extricate yourself as soon as you like to make further use of the nice epithet you just now were pleased to bestow on me.

TRAV. But I shall then be obliged to disclose myself?

CHRIS. So much the better; then I too shall learn who you are. But judge for yourself whether, with a good conscience, I could have been conscientious in regard to this lie? (*He pulls out the snuffbox.*) Look at this box! Could I have earned it more easily?

TRAV. Let me look at it. (*He takes it into his hand.*) What do I see?

CHRIS. Ha! ha! ha! I thought you would be astonished. Why, I am sure if you could earn such a box you would not mind telling a lie or two yourself.

TRAV. So you have robbed me of it?

CHRIS. How? What?

TRAV. Your faithlessness vexes me less than the overhasty suspicion which I have cast upon an honest man on account of this box. And you can still be so insanely impudent as to want to persuade me that it was a present, obtained, however, hardly less disgracefully. Go! And never come into my presence again.

CHRIS. Are you dreaming, or are . . . But out of respect for you I will not say it. Surely envy cannot have led you to such extravagances? Do you mean to say this box is yours, and I have robbed you of it, *salva venia?* If it were so, I should be a stupid devil to boast of it in your very presence. Well, there is Lisette coming. Quick, come here! Help me to bring my master back to his senses.

SCENE XX · LISETTE, THE TRAVELER, CHRISTOPH

LIS. Oh, sir, what troubles you are making among us! What harm has our bailiff done to you? You have made our master furious with him. They are talking of beards, and snuffboxes, and robberies; the bailiff is crying and swearing that he is innocent, and that you say what is not true. Our master is not to be softened; and, indeed, he has now sent for the magistrate and the police to put the bailiff in irons. What is the meaning of it all?

CHRIS. Oh, all that is nothing at all! Only listen, listen what he intends to do with me.

TRAV. Yes, indeed, my dear Lisette. I have been too hasty. The bailiff is innocent. It is my wicked servant alone who has brought me into this trouble. It is he who has stolen my box, on account of which I suspected the bailiff, and the beard may certainly have been for the children, as he said. I will go and give him satisfaction; I will confess my mistake. I will do whatever he may request.

CHRIS. No, no, stop; you must first give me satisfaction. In the devil's name, Lisette, why don't you speak? Tell him how it is. I wish that you and your box were both at the dickens! Am I to be called a thief for it? Did you not give it to me?

Lis. Yes, indeed, and I don't want it back again.

Trav. What? It is true, then? But the box is mine.

Lis. Yours? I did not know that.

Trav. And you found it? And my negligence is to blame for all this disturbance. (*To* Christoph.) I have wronged you also;—pardon me! I am ashamed of my hastiness.

Lis. (*aside*). The deuce! Now I begin to see. I don't think he has been overhasty, either.

Trav. Come, we will—

SCENE XXI · THE BARON, THE TRAVELER, LISETTE, CHRISTOPH

Baron (*in a great hurry*). Lisette, restore the box to the gentleman immediately! All is discovered; he has confessed all. And you were not ashamed to accept presents from such a rascal?—Well, where is the box?

Trav. Then it is true, after all?

Lis. The gentleman got it back a long time ago. I thought I might take presents at the hands of those from whom you accepted services. I knew as little of him as you.

Chris. And so my present has gone to the deuce again. Lightly come, lightly go.

Baron. But how can I show my gratitude to you, my dearest friend? You have saved me a second time from an equally great danger. I owe my life to you. Without you I should never have discovered this misfortune that threatened me. My agent, whom I considered the most honest man on my whole property, was the bailiff's accomplice. How, then, could I ever have imagined it? Had you departed today—

Trav. True enough . . . then the assistance which I thought to have rendered you yesterday would have been very incomplete. I therefore consider myself happy that Heaven has chosen me to make this unlooked-for discovery. I now rejoice as much as I feared before that I might be mistaken.

Baron. I admire your philanthropy as much as your magnanimity. Oh, may that be true which Lisette has told me!

SCENE XXII · THE YOUNG LADY, THE BARON, THE TRAVELER, LISETTE, CHRISTOPH

Lis. And why should it not be true?

Baron. Come, my daughter, come. Unite your entreaties with mine: request my preserver to accept your hand, and with your hand my fortune. What more costly gift could my gratitude present him with, than you, whom I love as much as him? Do not wonder that I can make you such an offer! Your servant has disclosed to us who you are. Grant me the inestimable pleasure of showing my gratitude. My fortune is equal to my rank, and this is equal to yours. Here you are safe from your enemies, and come among friends who will adore you.—But you seem depressed. How am I to interpret this?

Lady. Can you be distressed on my account? I assure you I shall obey my papa with pleasure.

Trav. Your magnanimity astonishes me. From the greatness of the reward which you offer me, I now perceive how small was my deed. But what shall I reply to you? My servant has told an untruth, and I—

Baron. Would to Heaven you were not what he says! Would to Heaven your rank were lower than mine! Then the value of my requital would be increased a little, and you would, perhaps, feel less inclined to refuse my entreaty.

Trav. (*aside*). Why do I not disclose myself? (*Aloud.*) Sir, your nobility of mind touches my soul. Ascribe it to fate and not to me, that your offer is in vain. I am—

Baron. Perhaps married already?

Trav. No.

Baron. Well? What, then?

Trav. I am a Jew.

Baron. A Jew? Cruel fate!

Chris. A Jew?

Lis. A Jew?

Lady. Oh! what does that matter?

Lis. Hush, miss, hush! I will tell you afterward what it matters.

Baron. And so there are cases where Heaven itself prevents our being grateful.

Trav. Your wish to be so renders it superfluous.

Baron. I will at least do all that fate permits me to do. Accept my whole fortune. I would rather be poor and grateful than rich and thankless.

TRAV. This offer, too, I must decline, for the God of my fathers has given me more than I want. For requital I ask but one thing, that you will henceforth judge of my nation in a kinder and less sweeping way. I did not conceal my race from you because I am ashamed of my religion. No! But I saw that you felt friendship for me, and enmity against my nation. And the friendship of a man, whoever he may be, has always been esteemed by me.

BARON. I am ashamed of my conduct.

CHRIS. I am only just coming to myself again, after my surprise. What, you are a Jew, and have been bold enough to take an honest Christian into your service? You ought to have served me. That would have been right, according to the Bible. By my faith! You have insulted all Christendom in my person. Now I know the reason why the gentleman would eat no pork during our journey, and did a hundred other follies. Don't fancy I shall go with you any farther. I shall bring an action against you, too.

TRAV. I cannot expect of you that you should think more kindly than other Christian people. I will not remind you from what miserable circumstances I took you at Hamburg: nor will I force you to remain any longer with me. But as I am pretty well satisfied with your services, and have just now suspected you unjustly, you may keep the object that caused my suspicion, as a recompense. (*He gives him the box.*) Your wages you shall also have, and now you may go wherever you please.

CHRIS. Deuce take it! there are Jews too, I suppose, who are no Jews. You are a good fellow. Done! I stay with you. A Christian would have given me a kick in the ribs, and not a snuffbox.

BARON. I am charmed with all I have seen of you. Come, let us take steps to have the guilty ones put in safe custody. Oh, how estimable would the Jews be, were they all like you!

TRAV. And how amiable the Christians, if they all possessed your qualities!

(*Exeunt the* BARON, *the* YOUNG LADY, *and the* TRAVELER.)

SCENE XXIII · LISETTE, CHRISTOPH

LIS. And so, my friend, you told me a lie.

CHRIS. Yes; and for two reasons. Firstly, because I did not know the truth; and secondly, because one cannot tell many truths for a box which one is obliged to give back again.

LIS. And perhaps, if one only knew it, you are a Jew yourself, too, however you may disguise it.

CHRIS. You are too inquisitive for a young lady. Come along with me.

(Exeunt arm in arm.)

FURTHER READING

F. A. Brown, *Gotthold Ephraim Lessing* (1971). A brief biography that does not neglect Lessing's ideas and minor plays.

Hanna Emmrich, *Das Judentum bei Voltaire* (1930). Fully documented study of Voltaire's attitude toward Jews in history.

Peter Gay, "Voltaire's Anti-Semitism," in *The Party of Humanity* (1964), 97–108. Attempts to place Voltaire's scattered remarks on Jews in their context.

Arthur Hertzberg, *The French Enlightenment and the Jews* (1968). Perversely seeks to father modern anti-Semitism on the philosophes; no persuasive evidence is adduced. Useful chiefly in its less polemical chapters, which deal with life of Jews in eighteenth-century Metz.

54 ❧ HAMILTON, MADISON, JAY

The Federalist

[From *The Federalist*, 2 vols. (1901), I, 9–13, 62–70, 353–58.]

For the European philosophes, the war of Britain's American colonies for independence held absorbing interest. Some of the leading revolutionaries had clearly been imbued with the ideas of the Enlightenment; one of their number, Benjamin Franklin, whom many of the philosophes had come to know well, seemed Enlightenment incarnate: he was a simple man close to nature, and a sophisticated thinker alert to science; he was a cultivated man impressive in the salon, and an advanced thinker committed to republicanism. In February 1778, when the aged Voltaire came home to Paris after nearly three decades, he and Franklin met in an elaborately staged interview; as twenty spectators shed "tender tears," Voltaire embraced Franklin and blessed Franklin's grandson, in English, with the words "God and liberty."* The European and the American Enlightenments had met. It remained to be seen if the colonies, once they were triumphant on the battlefield, could establish a republic on the American continent that would bring the ideas of the Enlightenment to the test of reality.

The struggle to establish this enlightened American republic was inevitably highly verbal. And the greatest polemic to emerge from it, the eighty-five newspaper articles published in 1787 which, collected, became The Federalist, *was a pure document of the Enlightenment. James Madison (1751–1836), father of the Constitution and fourth President, imitated Addison and admired Voltaire; in politics he was a disciple of Locke, Montesquieu, and Hume. Alexander Hamilton (1775?–1804), later Secretary of the Treasury*

* See Voltaire to the Abbé Gaultier, Feb. 20, 1778, *Correspondence*, ed. Besterman, XCVIII, 110.

under Washington, however much his preference for monarchy would estrange him from his fellow revolutionaries, could boast a similar philosophical ancestry. John Jay (1745–1829), later first Chief Justice of the United States, was, perhaps, slightly different in philosophical orientation from his colleagues; he was, for one thing, a religious man. But his religion was that of the eighteenth century, and, in any event, his share in The Federalist *papers was slight: he wrote only five of them.*

The Federalist *is a characteristic document of the Enlightenment in many ways. It emerged from a practical, immediate concern: the need to persuade the citizens of the state of New York to support a proposed federal constitution. It was a wholly secular book, appealing to the realities of human nature without showing the slightest interest in divine intervention. It was, in its psychology, a rather pessimistic book, insisting that men are weak, seek power, and need control. It was a cultivated book, drawing for examples from the ancient world, the Republic of Venice, the writings of Montesquieu. It was, finally, a libertarian book, devoted to discovering institutions that would allow men to develop their capacities and participate in the making of the laws.*

THE FEDERALIST NO. 1 *
[ALEXANDER HAMILTON]

October 27, 1787

To the People of the State of New York.

After an unequivocal experience of the inefficacy of the subsisting Federal Government, you are called upon to deliberate on a new Constitution for the United States of America. The subject speaks its own importance; comprehending in its consequences, nothing less than the existence of the Union, the safety and welfare of the parts of which it is composed, the fate of an empire, in many respects, the most interesting in the world. It has been frequently remarked, that it seems to have been reserved to the people of this country, by their conduct and example, to decide the important question, whether

* [From *The Independent Journal*, Oct. 27, 1787.]

societies of men are really capable or not, of establishing good government from reflection and choice, or whether they are forever destined to depend, for their political constitutions, on accident and force. If there be any truth in the remark, the crisis, at which we are arrived, may with propriety be regarded as the era in which that decision is to be made; and a wrong election of the part we shall act, may, in this view, deserve to be considered as the general misfortune of mankind.

This idea will add the inducements of philanthropy to those of patriotism to heighten the solicitude, which all considerate and good men must feel for the event. Happy will it be if our choice should be directed by a judicious estimate of our true interests, unperplexed and unbiassed by considerations not connected with the public good. But this is a thing more ardently to be wished, than seriously to be expected. The plan offered to our deliberations, affects too many particular interests, innovates upon too many local institutions, not to involve in its discussion a variety of objects foreign to its merits, and of views, passions and prejudices little favourable to the discovery of truth.

Among the most formidable of the obstacles which the new Constitution will have to encounter, may readily be distinguished the obvious interest of a certain class of men in every State to resist all changes which may hazard a diminution of the power, emolument and consequence of the offices they hold under the State-establishments—and the perverted ambition of another class of men, who will either hope to aggrandise themselves by the confusions of their country, or will flatter themselves with fairer prospects of elevation from the subdivision of the empire into several partial confederacies, than from its union under one government.

It is not, however, my design to dwell upon observations of this nature. I am well aware that it would be disingenuous to resolve indiscriminately the opposition of any set of men (merely because their situations might subject them to suspicion) into interested or ambitious views: Candour will oblige us to admit, that even such men may be actuated by upright intentions; and it cannot be doubted that much of the opposition which has made its appearance, or may hereafter make its appearance, will spring from sources, blameless at least, if not respectable, the honest errors of minds led astray by preconceived jealousies and fears. So numerous indeed and so powerful are the causes, which serve to give a false bias to the judgment, that we upon many occasions, see wise and good men on the wrong as well as on the right side of questions, of the first magnitude to society. This circumstance, if duly attended to, would furnish a lesson of moderation to those, who are ever so much persuaded of their being in the right, in any controversy. And a further reason for caution, in this respect, might be drawn from the reflection, that we are not always sure, that those who advocate the truth are influenced by purer principles than their antagonists. Ambition, avarice, personal animosity, party opposition, and many other motives, not more laudable than these, are apt to operate as well upon those who support as upon those who oppose the right side of a question. Were there not even these inducements to moderation, nothing could be more illjudged than that intolerant spirit, which has, at all times, characterised political parties. For, in politics as in religion, it is equally absurd to aim at making proselytes by fire and sword. Heresies in either can rarely be cured by persecution.

And yet however just these sentiments will be allowed to be, we have already sufficient indications, that it will happen in this as in all former cases of great national discussion. A torrent of angry and malignant passions will be let loose. To judge from the conduct of the opposite parties, we shall be led to conclude, that they will mutually hope to evince the justness of their opinions, and to increase the number of their converts by the loudness of their declamations, and by the bitterness of their invectives. An enlightened zeal for the energy and efficiency of government will be stigmatized, as the off-spring of a temper fond of despotic power and hostile to the principles of liberty. An overscrupulous jealousy of danger to the rights of the people, which is more commonly the fault of the head than of the heart, will be represented as mere pretence and artifice; the bait for popularity at the expence of public good. It will be forgotten, on the one hand, that jealousy is the usual concomitant of violent love, and that the noble enthusiasm of liberty is too apt to be infected with a spirit of narrow and illiberal distrust. On the other hand, it will be equally forgotten, that the vigour of government is essential to the security of liberty; that, in the contemplation of a sound and well informed judgment, their interest can never be separated; and that a dangerous ambition more often lurks behind the specious mask of zeal for the rights of the people, than under the forbidding appearance of zeal for the firmness and efficiency of government. History will teach us, that the former has been found a much more certain road to the introduction of despotism, than the latter, and that of those men who have overturned the liberties of republics the greatest number have begun their career, by paying an obsequious court to the people, commencing Demagogues and ending Tyrants.

In the course of the preceeding observations I have had an eye, my Fellow Citizens, to putting you upon your guard against all attempts, from whatever quarter, to influence your decision in a matter of the utmost moment to your welfare by any impressions other than those which may result from the evidence of truth. You will, no doubt, at the same time, have collected from the general scope of them that they proceed from a source not unfriendly to the new Constitution. Yes, my Countrymen, I own to you, that, after having given it an attentive consideration, I am clearly of opinion, it is your interest to adopt it. I am convinced, that this is the safest course for your liberty, your dignity, and your happiness. I effect not reserves, which I do not feel. I will not amuse you with an appearance of deliberation, when I have decided. I frankly acknowledge to you my convictions, and I will freely lay before you the reasons on which they are founded. The consciousness of good intentions disdains ambiguity. I shall not however multiply professions on this head. My motives must remain in the depository of my own breast: My arguments will be open to all, and may be judged of by all. They shall at least be offered in a spirit, which will not disgrace the cause of truth.

I propose in a series of papers to discuss the following interesting particulars—*The utility of the* UNION *to your political prosperity— The insufficiency of the present Confederation to preserve that Union—The necessity of a government at least equally energetic with the one proposed to the attainment of this object—The conformity of the proposed constitution to the true principles of republican government—Its analogy to your own state constitution*—and lastly, *The additional security, which its adoption will afford to the preservation of that species of government, to liberty and to property.*

In the progress of this discussion I shall endeavour to give a satisfactory answer to all the objections which shall have made their appearance that may seem to have any claim to your attention.

It may perhaps be thought superfluous to offer arguments to prove the utility of the UNION, a point, no doubt, deeply engraved on the hearts of the great body of the people in every state, and one, which it may be imagined has no adversaries. But the fact is, that we already hear it whispered in the private circles of those who oppose the new constitution, that the Thirteen States are of too great extent for any general system, and that we must of necessity resort to separate confederacies of distinct portions of the whole.* This doctrine will, in all probability, be gradually propagated, till it has votaries enough to countenance an open avowal of it. For nothing can be more evident, to those who are able to take an enlarged view of the subject, than the alternative of an adoption of the new Constitution, or a dismemberment of the Union. It will therefore be of use to begin by examining the advantages of that Union, the certain evils and the probable dangers, to which every State will be exposed from its dissolution. This shall accordingly constitute the subject of my next address.

PUBLIUS

THE FEDERALIST NO. 10†
[JAMES MADISON]

November 22, 1787

To the People of the State of New York.

Among the numerous advantages promised by a well constructed Union, none deserves to be more accurately developed than its tendency to break and control the violence of faction. The friend of popular governments, never finds himself so much alarmed for their character and fate, as when he contemplates their propensity to this dangerous vice. He will not fail therefore to set a due value on any plan which, without violating the principles to which he is attached, provides a proper cure for it. The instability, injustice and confusion introduced into the public councils, have in truth been the mortal diseases under which popular governments have every where perished; as they continue to be the favorite and fruitful topics from which the adversaries to liberty derive their most specious declamations. The valuable improvements made by the American Constitutions on the popular models, both ancient and modern, cannot certainly be too much admired; but it would be an unwarrantable partiality, to contend that they have as effectually obviated the danger on this side as was wished and expected. Complaints are every where heard from our most considerate and virtuous citizens, equally the friends of public and private faith,

---

* The same idea, tracing the arguments to their consequences, is held out in several of the late publications against the New Constitution. (Publius)

† [From *The New-York Packet*, Nov. 23, 1787.]

and of public and personal liberty; that our governments are too unstable; that the public good is disregarded in the conflicts of rival parties; and that measures are too often decided, not according to the rules of justice, and the rights of the minor party; but by the superior force of an interested and over-bearing majority. However anxiously we may wish that these complaints had no foundation, the evidence of known facts will not permit us to deny that they are in some degree true. It will be found indeed, on a candid review of our situation, that some of the distresses under which we labor, have been erroneously charged on the operation of our governments; but it will be found, at the same time, that other causes will not alone account for many of our heaviest misfortunes; and particularly, for that prevailing and increasing distrust of public engagements, and alarm for private rights, which are echoed from one end of the continent to the other. These must be chiefly, if not wholly, effects of the unsteadiness and injustice, with which a factious spirit has tainted our public administrations.

By a faction I understand a number of citizens, whether amounting to a majority or minority of the whole, who are united and actuated by some common impulse of passion, or of interest, adverse to the rights of other citizens, or to the permanent and aggregate interests of the community.

There are two methods of curing the mischiefs of faction: the one, by removing its causes; the other, by controling its effects.

There are again two methods of removing the causes of faction: the one by destroying the liberty which is essential to its existence; the other, by giving to every citizen the same opinions, the same passions, and the same interests.

It could never be more truly said than of the first remedy, that it is worse than the disease. Liberty is to faction, what air is to fire, an aliment without which it instantly expires. But it could not be a less folly to abolish liberty, which is essential to political life, because it nourishes faction, than it would be to wish the annihilation of air, which is essential to animal life, because it imparts to fire its destructive agency.

The second expedient is as impracticable, as the first would be unwise. As long as the reason of man continues fallible, and he is at liberty to exercise it, different opinions will be formed. As long as the connection subsists between his reason and his self-love, his opinions and his passions will have a reciprocal influence on each other; and the former will be objects to which the latter will attach themselves. The diversity in the faculties of men from which the rights of property originate, is not less an insuperable obstacle to a uniformity of interests. The protection of these faculties is the first object of Government. From the protection of different and unequal faculties of acquiring property, the possession of different degrees and kinds of property immediately results: and from the influence of these on the sentiments and views of the respective proprietors, ensues a division of the society into different interests and parties.

The latent causes of faction are thus sown in the nature of man; and we see them every where brought into different degrees of activity, according to the different circumstances of civil society. A zeal for different opinions concerning religion, concerning Government and many other points, as well of speculation as of practice; an attachment to different leaders ambitiously contending for pre-eminence and power; or to persons of other descriptions whose fortunes have been interesting to the human passions, have in turn divided mankind into parties, inflamed them with mutual animosity, and rendered them much more disposed to vex and oppress each other, than to co-operate for their common good. So strong is this propensity of mankind to fall into mutual animosities, that where no substantial occasion presents itself, the most frivolous and fanciful distinctions have been sufficient to kindle their unfriendly passions, and excite their most violent conflicts. But the most common and durable source of factions, has been the various and unequal distribution of property. Those who hold, and those who are without property, have ever formed distinct interests in society. Those who are creditors, and those who are debtors, fall under a like discrimination. A landed interest, a manufacturing interest, a mercantile interest, a monied interest, with many lesser interests, grow up of necessity in civilized nations, and divide them into different classes, actuated by different sentiments and views. The regulation of these various and interfering interests forms the principal task of modern Legislation, and involves the spirit of party and faction in the necessary and ordinary operations of Government.

No man is allowed to be a judge in his own cause; because his interest would certainly bias his judgment, and, not improbably, corrupt his integrity. With equal, nay with greater reason, a body of men, are unfit to be both judges and parties, at the same time; yet, what are many of the most important acts of legislation, but so many judicial determinations, not indeed concerning the rights of single persons, but concerning the rights of large bodies of citizens;

and what are the different classes of legislators, but advocates and parties to the causes which they determine? Is a law proposed concerning private debts? It is a question to which the creditors are parties on one side, and the debtors on the other. Justice ought to hold the balance between them. Yet the parties are and must be themselves the judges; and the most numerous party, or, in other words, the most powerful faction must be expected to prevail. Shall domestic manufactures be encouraged, and in what degree, by restrictions on foreign manufactures? are questions which would be differently decided by the landed and the manufacturing classes; and probably by neither, with a sole regard to justice and the public good. The apportionment of taxes on the various descriptions of property, is an act which seems to require the most exact impartiality; yet, there is perhaps no legislative act in which greater opportunity and temptation are given to a predominant party, to trample on the rules of justice. Every shilling with which they overburden the inferior number, is a shilling saved to their own pockets.

It is in vain to say, that enlightened statesmen will be able to adjust these clashing interests, and render them all subservient to the public good. Enlightened statesmen will not always be at the helm: Nor, in many cases, can such an adjustment be made at all, without taking into view indirect and remote considerations, which will rarely prevail over the immediate interest which one party may find in disregarding the rights of another, or the good of the whole.

The inference to which we are brought, is, that the *causes* of faction cannot be removed; and that relief is only to be sought in the means of controling its *effects*.

If a faction consists of less than a majority, relief is supplied by the republican principle, which enables the majority to defeat its sinister views by regular vote: It may clog the administration, it may convulse the society; but it will be unable to execute and mask its violence under the forms of the Constitution. When a majority is included in a faction, the form of popular government on the other hand enables it to sacrifice to its ruling passion or interest, both the public good and the rights of other citizens. To secure the public good, and private rights, against the danger of such a faction, and at the same time to preserve the spirit and the form of popular government, is then the great object to which our enquiries are directed: Let me add that it is the great desideratum, by which alone this form of government can be rescued from the opprobrium under which it has so long labored, and be recommended to the esteem and adoption of mankind.

By what means is this object attainable? Evidently by one of two only. Either the existence of the same passion or interest in a majority at the same time, must be prevented; or the majority, having such co-existent passion or interest, must be rendered, by their number and local situation, unable to concert and carry into effect schemes of oppression. If the impulse and the opportunity be suffered to coincide, we well know that neither moral nor religious motives can be relied on as an adequate control. They are not found to be such on the injustice and violence of individuals, and lose their efficacy in proportion to the number combined together; that is, in proportion as their efficacy becomes needful.

From this view of the subject, it may be concluded, that a pure Democracy, by which I mean, a Society, consisting of a small number of citizens, who assemble and administer the Government in person, can admit of no cure for the mischiefs of faction. A common passion or interest will, in almost every case, be felt by a majority of the whole; a communication and concert results from the form of Government itself; and there is nothing to check the inducements to sacrifice the weaker party, or an obnoxious individual. Hence it is, that such Democracies have ever been spectacles of turbulence and contention; have ever been found incompatible with personal security, or the rights of property; and have in general been as short in their lives, as they have been violent in their deaths. Theoretic politicians, who have patronized this species of Government, have erroneously supposed, that by reducing mankind to a perfect equality in their political rights, they would, at the same time, be perfectly equalized and assimilated in their possessions, their opinions, and their passions.

A Republic, by which I mean a Government in which the scheme of representation takes place, opens a different prospect, and promises the cure for which we are seeking. Let us examine the points in which it varies from pure Democracy, and we shall comprehend both the nature of the cure, and the efficacy which it must derive from the Union.

The two great points of difference between a Democracy and a Republic are, first, the delegation of the Government, in the latter, to a small number of citizens elected by the rest: secondly, the greater number of citizens, and greater sphere of country, over which the latter may be extended.

The effect of the first difference is, on the one hand to refine and enlarge the public views, by passing them through the medium of a chosen body of citizens, whose wisdom may best discern the true interest of their country, and whose patriotism and love of justice, will be least likely to sacrifice it to temporary or partial considerations. Under such a regulation, it may well happen that the public voice pronounced by the representatives of the people, will be more consonant to the public good, than if pronounced by the people themselves convened for the purpose. On the other hand, the effect may be inverted. Men of factious tempers, of local prejudices, or of sinister designs, may by intrigue, by corruption or by other means, first obtain the suffrages, and then betray the interests of the people. The question resulting is, whether small or extensive Republics are most favorable to the election of proper guardians of the public weal: and it is clearly decided in favor of the latter by two obvious considerations.

In the first place it is to be remarked that however small the Republic may be, the Representatives must be raised to a certain number, in order to guard against the cabals of a few; and that however large it may be, they must be limited to a certain number, in order to guard against the confusion of a multitude. Hence the number of Representatives in the two cases, not being in proportion to that of the Constituents, and being proportionally greatest in the small Republic, it follows, that if the proportion of fit characters, be not less, in the large than in the small Republic, the former will present a greater option, and consequently a greater probability of a fit choice.

In the next place, as each Representative will be chosen by a greater number of citizens in the large than in the small Republic, it will be more difficult for unworthy candidates to practise with success the vicious arts, by which elections are too often carried; and the suffrages of the people being more free, will be more likely to centre on men who possess the most attractive merit, and the most diffusive and established characters.

It must be confessed, that in this, as in most other cases, there is a mean, on both sides of which inconveniencies will be found to lie. By enlarging too much the number of electors, you render the representative too little acquainted with all their local circumstances and lesser interests; as by reducing it too much, you render him unduly attached to these, and too little fit to comprehend and pursue great and national objects. The Federal Constitution forms a happy combination in this respect; the great and aggregate interests being referred to the national, the local and particular, to the state legislatures.

The other point of difference is, the greater number of citizens and extent of territory which may be brought within the compass of Republican, than of Democratic Government; and it is this circumstance principally which renders factious combinations less to be dreaded in the former, than in the latter. The smaller the society, the fewer probably will be the distinct parties and interests composing it; the fewer the distinct parties and interests, the more frequently will a majority be found of the same party; and the smaller the number of individuals composing a majority, and the smaller the compass within which they are placed, the more easily will they concert and execute their plans of oppression. Extend the sphere, and you take in a greater variety of parties and interests; you make it less probable that a majority of the whole will have a common motive to invade the rights of other citizens; or if such a common motive exists, it will be more difficult for all who feel it to discover their own strength, and to act in unison with each other. Besides other impediments, it may be remarked, that where there is a consciousness of unjust or dishonorable purposes, communication is always checked by distrust, in proportion to the number whose concurrence is necessary.

Hence it clearly appears, that the same advantage, which a Republic has over a Democracy, in controling the effects of faction, is enjoyed by a large over a small Republic—is enjoyed by the Union over the States composing it. Does this advantage consist in the substitution of Representatives, whose enlightened views and virtuous sentiments render them superior to local prejudices, and to schemes of injustice? It will not be denied, that the Representation of the Union will be most likely to possess these requisite endowments. Does it consist in the greater security afforded by a greater variety of parties, against the event of any one party being able to outnumber and oppress the rest? In an equal degree does the encreased variety of parties, comprised within the Union, encrease this security. Does it, in fine, consist in the greater obstacles opposed to the concert and accomplishment of the secret wishes of an unjust and interested majority? Here, again, the extent of the Union gives it the most palpable advantage.

The influence of factious leaders may kindle a flame within their particular States, but will be unable to spread a general conflagration through the other States: a religious sect, may degenerate into a political faction in a part of the Confederacy; but the variety of sects dispersed over the entire face of it, must secure the national Councils against any danger from that source: a rage for paper money, for an abolition of debts, for an equal division of property, or for any other improper or wicked project, will be less apt to pervade the whole body of the Union, than a particular member of it; in the same proportion as such a malady is more likely to taint a particular county or district, than an entire State.

In the extent and proper structure of the Union, therefore, we behold a Republican remedy for the diseases most incident to Republican Government. And according to the degree of pleasure and pride, we feel in being Republicans, ought to be our zeal in cherishing the spirit, and supporting the character of Federalists.

PUBLIUS

THE FEDERALIST NO. 51 *
[PROBABLY BY JAMES MADISON]

February 6, 1788

To the People of the State of New York.

To what expedient then shall we finally resort for maintaining in practice the necessary partition of power among the several departments, as laid down in the constitution? The only answer that can be given is, that as all these exterior provisions are found to be inadequate, the defect must be supplied, by so contriving the interior structure of the government, as that its several constituent parts may, by their mutual relations, be the means of keeping each other in their proper places. Without presuming to undertake a full developement of this important idea, I will hazard a few general observations, which may perhaps place it in a clearer light, and enable us to form a more correct judgment of the principles and structure of the government planned by the convention.

In order to lay a due foundation for that separate and distinct exercise of the different powers of government, which to a certain extent, is admitted on all hands to be essential to the preservation of liberty, it is evident that each department should have a will of its own; and consequently should be so constituted, that the members of each should have as little agency as possible in the appointment of the members of the others. Were this principle rigorously adhered to, it would require that all the appointments for the supreme executive, legislative, and judiciary magistracies, should be drawn from the same fountain of authority, the people, through

---

* [From *The New-York Packet,* Feb. 8, 1788.]

channels, having no communication whatever with one another. Perhaps such a plan of constructing the several departments would be less difficult in practice than it may in contemplation appear. Some difficulties however, and some additional expence, would attend the execution of it. Some deviations therefore from the principle must be admitted. In the constitution of the judiciary department in particular, it might be inexpedient to insist rigorously on the principle; first, because peculiar qualifications being essential in the members, the primary consideration ought to be to select that mode of choice, which best secures these qualifications; secondly, because the permanent tenure by which the appointments are held in that department, must soon destroy all sense of dependence on the authority conferring them.

It is equally evident that the members of each department should be as little dependent as possible on those of the others, for the emoluments annexed to their offices. Were the executive magistrate, or the judges, not independent of the legislature in this particular, their independence in every other would be merely nominal.

But the great security against a gradual concentration of the several powers in the same department, consists in giving to those who administer each department, the necessary constitutional means, and personal motives, to resist encroachments of the others. The provision for defence must in this, as in all other cases, be made commensurate to the danger of attack. Ambition must be made to counteract ambition. The interest of the man must be connected with the constitutional rights of the place. It may be a reflection on human nature, that such devices should be necessary to controul the abuses of government. But what is government itself but the greatest of all reflections on human nature? If men were angels, no government would be necessary. If angels were to govern men, neither external nor internal controuls on government would be necessary. In framing a government which is to be administered by men over men, the great difficulty lies in this: You must first enable the government to controul the governed; and in the next place, oblige it to controul itself. A dependence on the people is no doubt the primary controul on the government; but experience has taught mankind the necessity of auxiliary precautions.

This policy of supplying by opposite and rival interests, the defect of better motives, might be traced through the whole system of human affairs, private as well as public. We see it particularly displayed in all the subordinate distributions of power; where the constant aim is to divide and arrange the several offices in such a manner as that each may be a check on the other; that the private interest of every individual, may be a centinel over the public rights. These inventions of prudence cannot be less requisite in the distribution of the supreme powers of the state.

But it is not possible to give to each department an equal power of self defence. In republican government the legislative authority, necessarily, predominates. The remedy for this inconveniency is, to divide the legislature into different branches; and to render them by different modes of election, and different principles of action, as little connected with each other, as the nature of their common functions, and their common dependence on the society, will admit. It may even be necessary to guard against dangerous encroachments by still further precautions. As the weight of the legislative authority requires that it should be thus divided, the weakness of the executive may require, on the other hand, that it should be fortified. An absolute negative, on the legislature, appears at first view to be the natural defence with which the executive magistrate should be armed. But perhaps it would be neither altogether safe, nor alone sufficient. On ordinary occasions, it might not be exerted with the requisite firmness; and on extraordinary occasions, it might be perfidiously abused. May not this defect of an absolute negative be supplied, by some qualified connection between this weaker department, and the weaker branch of the stronger department, by which the latter may be led to support the constitutional rights of the former, without being too much detached from the rights of its own department?

If the principles on which these observations are founded be just, as I persuade myself they are, and they be applied as a criterion, to the several state constitutions, and to the federal constitution, it will be found, that if the latter does not perfectly correspond with them, the former are infinitely less able to bear such a test.

There are moreover two considerations particularly applicable to the federal system of America, which place that system in a very interesting point of view.

First. In a single republic, all the power surrendered by the people, is submitted to the administration of a single government; and usurpations are guarded against by a division of the government into distinct and separate departments. In the compound republic of America, the power surrendered by the people, is first divided between two distinct governments, and then the portion allotted to each, subdivided among distinct and separate departments. Hence a double security arises to the rights of the people.

The different governments will controul each other; at the same time that each will be controuled by itself.

Second. It is of great importance in a republic, not only to guard the society against the oppression of its rulers; but to guard one part of the society against the injustice of the other part. Different interests necessarily exist in different classes of citizens. If a majority be united by a common interest, the rights of the minority will be insecure. There are but two methods of providing against this evil: The one by creating a will in the community independent of the majority, that is, of the society itself; the other by comprehending in the society so many separate descriptions of citizens, as will render an unjust combination of a majority of the whole, very improbable, if not impracticable. The first method prevails in all governments possessing an hereditary or self appointed authority. This at best is but a precarious security; because a power independent of the society may as well espouse the unjust views of the major, as the rightful interests, of the minor party, and may possibly be turned against both parties. The second method will be exemplified in the federal republic of the United States. Whilst all authority in it will be derived from and dependent on the society, the society itself will be broken into so many parts, interests and classes of citizens, that the rights of individuals or of the minority, will be in little danger from interested combinations of the majority. In a free government, the security for civil rights must be the same as for religious rights. It consists in the one case in the multiplicity of interest, and in the other, in the multiplicity of sects. The degree of security in both cases will depend on the number of interests and sects; and this may be presumed to depend on the extent of country and number of people comprehended under the same government. This view of the subject must particularly recommend a proper federal system to all the sincere and considerate friends of republican government: Since it shews that in exact proportion as the territory of the union may be formed into more circumscribed confederacies or states, oppressive combinations of a majority will be facilitated, the best security under the republican form, for the rights of every class of citizens, will be diminished; and consequently, the stability and independence of some member of the government, the only other security, must be proportionally increased. Justice is the end of government. It is the end of civil society. It ever has been, and ever will be pursued, until it be obtained, or until liberty be lost in the pursuit. In a society under the forms of which the stronger faction can readily unite and oppress the weaker, anarchy may as truly be said to reign, as in a state of nature where the weaker individual is not secured against the violence of the stronger: And as in the latter state even the stronger individuals are prompted by the uncertainty of their condition, to submit to a government which may protect the weak as well as themselves: So in the former state, will the more powerful factions or parties be gradually induced by a like motive, to wish for a government which will protect all parties, the weaker as well as the more powerful. It can be little doubted, that if the state of Rhode Island was separated from the confederacy, and left to itself, the insecurity of rights under the popular form of government within such narrow limits, would be displayed by such reiterated oppressions of factious majorities, that some power altogether independent of the people would soon be called for by the voice of the very factions whose misrule had proved the necessity of it. In the extended republic of the United States, and among the great variety of interests, parties and sects which it embraces, a coalition of a majority of the whole society could seldom take place on any other principles than those of justice and the general good; and there being thus less danger to a minor from the will of the major party, there must be less pretext also, to provide for the security of the former, by introducing into the government a will not dependent on the latter; or in other words, a will independent of the society itself. It is no less certain than it is important, notwithstanding the contrary opinions which have been entertained, that the larger the society, provided it lie within a practicable sphere, the more duly capable it will be of self government. And happily for the *republican cause,* the practicable sphere may be carried to a very great extent, by a judicious modification and mixture of the *federal principle.*

PUBLIUS

FURTHER READING

Douglass Adair, "The Tenth Federalist Revisited," *William and Mary Quarterly,* Third Series, Vol. VIII, No. 1 (January 1951), 48–67. Sets straight the most famous of the papers, and rescues it from Charles Beard's misreading.

————, " 'That Politics May be Reduced to a Science,' David Hume, James Madison, and the Tenth *Federalist*," *The Huntington Library Quarterly*, Vol. XX, No. 4 (August 1957), 343–60. Continues the analysis begun in the previous article.

Cecelia M. Kenyon, "Alexander Hamilton: Rousseau of the Right," *Political Science Quarterly*, Vol. LXXIII, No. 2 (June 1958), 161–78. Intelligent analysis of a complicated man's complicated political ideas.

Ralph L. Ketcham, "James Madison and the Nature of Man," *Journal of the History of Ideas*, Vol. XIX, No. 1 (January 1958), 62–76. Useful, especially in conjunction with Adair's essays.

Alpheus T. Mason, "The *Federalist*—A Split Personality," *American Historical Review*, Vol. LVII, No. 3 (April 1952), 625–43. Important for its careful attempt to distinguish among the three authors.

Benjamin Fletcher Wright, "The *Federalist* on the Nature of Political Man," *Ethics*, Vol. LIX, No. 2, Part II (January 1949), 1–31. Crucial.

55 ❋ KANT

Perpetual Peace

[From Immanuel Kant, *On History,* translated
by Lewis White Beck, 85–105.*]

*Among the values of the philosophes, peace ranked high. It is true
that some among them, especially the Scots, celebrated the martial
virtues as signs of a manly civilization and lamented their absence
as a symptom of decadence; but neither Adam Smith nor Adam
Ferguson proposed aggressive wars. Again and again in the course
of the century, the men of the Enlightenment mourned the devastations of war, exposing the viciousness of rulers who made it and the
stupidity of nations who condoned it.*

*At the same time, the philosophes were not pacifists; they did not
counsel passive resistance, and they were far from confident that
war could be ruled out of human affairs. Voltaire, for one, denounced war as a scourge that no amount of intelligent thinking
would ever eliminate. There were some exceptions to this pessimism, among whom Kant is the most prominent. Still, his suggestions for perpetual peace, though more hopeful than other writings
on this subject by other philosophes, is yet marked by a cool
realism. One cannot just legislate war out of existence; peace requires political, social, and psychological preparation. Yet it was
worth trying. The essay, published in 1795, was Kant's way of
trying.*

Perpetual Peace

Whether this satirical inscription on a Dutch innkeeper's sign upon which a burial ground was painted had for its object mankind in general, or the rulers of states in particular, who are insatiable of war, or merely the philosophers who dream this sweet dream, it is not for us to decide. But one condition the author of this essay wishes to lay down. The practical politician assumes the attitude of looking down with great self-satisfaction on the political theorist as a pedant whose empty ideas in no way threaten the security of the state, inasmuch as the state must proceed on empirical principles; so the theorist is allowed to play his game without interference from the worldly-wise statesman. Such being his attitude, the practical politician—and this is the condition I make—should at least act consistently in the case of a conflict and not suspect some danger to the state in the political theorist's opinions which are ventured and publicly expressed without any ulterior purpose. By this *clausula salvatoria* the author desires formally and emphatically to deprecate herewith any malevolent interpretation which might be placed on his words.

SECTION I
Containing the Preliminary Articles for Perpetual Peace among States

1. *"No Treaty of Peace Shall Be Held Valid in Which There Is Tacitly Reserved Matter for a Future War"*

Otherwise a treaty would be only a truce, a suspension of hostilities but not peace, which means the end of all hostilities—so much so that even to attach the word "perpetual" to it is a dubious pleonasm. The causes for making future wars (which are perhaps unknown to the contracting parties) are without exception annihilated by the treaty of peace, even if they should be dug out of dusty documents by acute sleuthing. When one or both parties to a treaty of peace, being too exhausted to continue warring with each other, make a tacit reservation (*reservatio mentalis*) in regard to old claims to be elaborated only at some more favorable opportunity in the future, the treaty is made in bad faith, and we have an artifice worthy of the casuistry of a Jesuit. Considered by itself, it is beneath the dignity of a sovereign, just as the readiness to indulge in this kind of reasoning is unworthy of the dignity of his minister.

But if, in consequence of enlightened concepts of statecraft, the glory of the state is placed in its continual aggrandizement by whatever means, my conclusion will appear merely academic and pedantic.

2. *"No Independent States, Large or Small, Shall Come under the Dominion of Another State by Inheritance, Exchange, Purchase, or Donation"*

A state is not, like the ground which it occupies, a piece of property (*patrimonium*). It is a society of men whom no one else has any right to command or to dispose except the state itself. It is a trunk with its own roots. But to incorporate it into another state, like a graft, is to destroy its existence as a moral person, reducing it to a thing; such incorporation thus contradicts the idea of the original contract without which no right over a people can be conceived. Everyone knows to what dangers Europe, the only part of the world where this manner of acquisition is known, has been brought, even down to the most recent times, by the presumption that states could espouse one another; it is in part a new kind of industry for gaining ascendancy by means of family alliances and without expenditure of forces, and in part a way of extending one's domain. Also the hiring-out of troops by one state to another, so that they can be used against an enemy not common to both, is to be counted under this principle; for in this manner the subjects, as though they were things to be manipulated at pleasure, are used and also used up.

3. *"Standing Armies* (miles perpetuus) *Shall in Time Be Totally Abolished"*

For they incessantly menace other states by their readiness to appear at all times prepared for war; they incite them to compete with each other in the number of armed men, and there is no limit to this. For this reason, the cost of peace finally becomes more oppressive than that of a short war, and consequently a standing army is itself a cause of offensive war waged in order to relieve the state of this burden. Add to this that to pay men to kill or to be killed seems to entail using them as mere machines and tools in the hand of another (the state), and this is hardly compatible with the rights of mankind in our own person. But the periodic and voluntary military exercises of citizens who thereby secure themselves and their country against foreign aggression are entirely different.

The accumulation of treasure would have the same effect, for, of the three powers—the power of armies, of alliances, and of money—the third is perhaps the most dependable weapon. Such accumulation of treasure is regarded by other states as a threat of war, and if it were not for the difficulties in learning the amount, it would force the other state to make an early attack.

4. *"National Debts Shall Not Be Contracted with a View to the External Friction of States"*

This expedient of seeking aid within or without the state is above suspicion when the purpose is domestic economy (e.g., the improvement of roads, new settlements, establishment of stores against unfruitful years, etc.). But as an opposing machine in the antagonism of powers, a credit system which grows beyond sight and which is yet a safe debt for the present requirements—because all the creditors do not require payment at one time—constitutes a dangerous money power. This ingenious invention of a commercial people [England] in this century is dangerous because it is a war treasure which exceeds the treasures of all other states; it cannot be exhausted except by default of taxes (which is inevitable), though it can be long delayed by the stimulus to trade which occurs through the reaction of credit on industry and commerce. This facility in making war, together with the inclination to do so on the part of rulers—an inclination which seems inborn in human nature—is thus a great hindrance to perpetual peace. Therefore, to forbid this credit system must be a preliminary article of perpetual peace all the more because it must eventually entangle many innocent states in the inevitable bankruptcy and openly harm them. They are therefore justified in allying themselves against such a state and its measures.

5. *"No State Shall by Force Interfere with the Constitution or Government of Another State"*

For what is there to authorize it to do so? The offense, perhaps, which a state gives to the subjects of another state? Rather the example of the evil into which a state has fallen because of its lawlessness should serve as a warning. Moreover, the bad example which one free person affords another as a *scandalum acceptum* is not an infringement of his rights. But it would be quite different if a state, by internal rebellion, should fall into two parts, each of which pretended to be a separate state making claim to the whole. To lend assistance to one of these cannot be considered an interference in the constitution of the other state (for it is then in a state of anarchy). But so long as the internal dissension has not come to this critical point, such interference by foreign powers would infringe on the rights of an independent people struggling with its internal disease; hence it would itself be an offense and would render the autonomy of all states insecure.

6. *"No State Shall, during War, Permit Such Acts of Hostility Which Would Make Mutual Confidence in the Subsequent Peace Impossible: Such Are the Employment of Assassins* (percussores), *Poisoners* (venefici), *Breach of Capitulation, and Incitement to Treason* (perduellio) *in the Opposing State"*

These are dishonorable stratagems. For some confidence in the character of the enemy must remain even in the midst of war, as otherwise no peace could be concluded and the hostilities would degenerate into a war of extermination (*bellum internecinum*). War, however, is only the sad recourse in the state of nature (where there is no tribunal which could judge with the force of law) by which each state asserts its right by violence and in which neither party can be adjudged unjust (for that would presuppose a juridical decision); in lieu of such a decision, the issue of the conflict (as if given by a so-called "judgment of God") decides on which side justice lies. But between states no punitive war (*bellum punitivum*) is conceivable, because there is no relation between them of master and servant.

It follows that a war of extermination, in which the destruction of both parties and of all justice can result, would permit perpetual peace only in the vast burial ground of the human race. Therefore, such a war and the use of all means leading to it must be absolutely forbidden. But that the means cited do inevitably lead to it is clear from the fact that these infernal arts, vile in themselves, when once used would not long be confined to the sphere of war. Take, for instance, the use of spies *(uti exploratoribus)*. In this, one employs the infamy of others (which can never be entirely eradicated) only to encourage its persistance even into the state of peace, to the undoing of the very spirit of peace.

Although the laws stated are objectively, i.e., insofar as they express the intention of rulers, mere prohibitions *(leges prohibitivae)*, some of them are of that strict kind which hold regardless of circumstances *(leges strictae)* and which demand prompt execution. Such are Nos. 1, 5, and 6. Others, like Nos. 2, 3, and 4, while not exceptions from the rule of law, nevertheless are subjectively broader *(leges latae)* in respect to their observation, containing permission to delay their execution without, however, losing sight of the end. This permission does not authorize, under No. 2, for example, delaying until doomsday (or, as Augustus used to say, *ad calendas Graecas*) the reestablishment of the freedom of states which have been deprived of it—i.e., it does not permit us to fail to do it, but it allows a delay to prevent precipitation which might injure the goal striven for. For the prohibition concerns only the manner of acquisition which is no longer permitted, but not the possession, which, though not bearing a requisite title of right, has nevertheless been held lawful in all states by the public opinion of the time (the time of the putative acquisition).

SECTION II
Containing the Definitive Articles for Perpetual Peace among States

The state of peace among men living side by side is not the natural state *(status naturalis)*; the natural state is one of war. This does not always mean open hostilities, but at least an unceasing threat of war. A state of peace, therefore, must be *established*, for in order to be secured against hostility it is not sufficient that hostilities simply be not committed; and, unless this security is pledged to each by his neighbor (a thing that can occur only in a civil state), each may treat his neighbor, from whom he demands this security, as an enemy.*

FIRST DEFINITIVE ARTICLE FOR PERPETUAL PEACE

"The Civil Constitution of Every State Should Be Republican"

The only constitution which derives from the idea of the original compact, and on which all juridical legislation of a people must be based, is the republican.† This constitution is established, firstly, by

* We ordinarily assume that no one may act inimically toward another except when he has been actively injured by the other. This is quite correct if both are under civil law, for, by entering into such a state, they afford each other the requisite security through the sovereign which has power over both. Man (or the people) in the state of nature deprives me of this security and injures me, if he is near me, by this mere status of his, even though he does not injure me actively (*facto*); he does so by the lawlessness of his condition (*statu iniusto*) which constantly threatens me. Therefore, I can compel him either to enter with me into a state of civil law or to remove himself from my neighborhood. The postulate which is basic to all the following articles is: All men who can reciprocally influence each other must stand under some civil constitution.

Every juridical constitution which concerns the person who stands under it is one of the following:

(1) The constitution conforming to the civil law of men in a nation (*ius civitatis*).

(2) The constitution conforming to the law of nations in their relation to one another (*ius gentium*).

(3) The constitution conforming to the law of world citizenship, so far as men and states are considered as citizens of a universal state of men, in their external mutual relationships (*ius cosmopoliticum*).

This division is not arbitrary, being necessary in relation to the idea of perpetual peace. For if only one state were related to another by physical influence and were yet in a state of nature, war would necessarily follow, and our purpose here is precisely to free ourselves of war.

† Juridical (and hence) external freedom cannot be defined, as is usual, by the privilege of doing anything one wills so long as he does not injure another. For what is a privilege? It is the possibility of an action so far as one does not injure anyone by it. Then the definition would read: Freedom is the possibility of those actions by which one does no one an injury. One does another no injury (he may do as he pleases) only if he does another no injury—an empty tautology. Rather, my external (juridical) freedom is to be defined as follows: It is the privilege to lend obedience to no external laws except those to which I could have given consent. Similarly, external (juridical) equality in a state is that relationship among the citizens in which no one can lawfully bind another without at the same time subjecting himself to the law by which he also can be

principles of the freedom of the members of a society (as men) ; secondly, by principles of dependence of all upon a single common legislation (as subjects) ; and, thirdly, by the law of their equality (as citizens). The republican constitution, therefore, is with respect to law, the one which is the original basis of every form of civil constitution. The only question now is: Is it also the one which can lead to perpetual peace?

The republican constitution, besides the purity of its origin (having sprung from the pure source of the concept of law), also gives a favorable prospect for the desired consequence, i.e., perpetual peace. The reason is this: if the consent of the citizens is required in order to decide that war should be declared (and in this constitution it cannot but be the case), nothing is more natural than that they would be very cautious in commencing such a poor game, decreeing for themselves all the calamities of war. Among the latter would be: having to fight, having to pay the costs of war from their own resources, having painfully to repair the devastation war

---

bound. No definition of juridical dependence is needed, as this already lies in the concept of a state's constitution as such.

The validity of these inborn rights, which are inalienable and belong necessarily to humanity, is raised to an even higher level by the principle of the juridical relation of man to higher beings, for, if he believes in them, he regards himself by the same principles as a citizen of a supersensuous world. For in what concerns my freedom, I have no obligation with respect to divine law, which can be acknowledged by my reason alone, except insofar as I could have given my consent to it. Indeed, it is only through the law of freedom of my own reason that I frame a concept of the divine will. With regard to the most sublime reason in the world that I can think of, with the exception of God—say, the great Aeon—when I do my duty in my post as he does in his, there is no reason under the law of equality why obedience to duty should fall only to me and the right to command only to him. The reason why this principle of equality does not pertain to our relation to God (as the principle of freedom does) is that this Being is the only one to which the concept of duty does not apply.

But with respect to the right of equality of all citizens as subjects, the question of whether a hereditary nobility may be tolerated turns upon the answer to the question as to whether the preeminent rank granted by the state to one citizen over another ought to precede merit or follow it. Now it is obvious that, if rank is associated with birth, it is uncertain whether merit (political skill and integrity) will also follow; hence it would be as if a favorite without any merit were given command. The general will of the people would never agree to this in the original contract, which is the principle of all law, for a nobleman is not necessarily a noble man. With regard to the nobility of office (as we might call the rank of the higher magistracy) which one must earn by merit, this rank does not belong to the person as his property; it belongs to his post, and equality is not thereby infringed, because when a man quits his office he renounces the rank it confers and reenters into the class of his fellows.

leaves behind, and, to fill up the measure of evils, load themselves with a heavy national debt that would embitter peace itself and that can never be liquidated on account of constant wars in the future. But, on the other hand, in a constitution which is not republican, and under which the subjects are not citizens, a declaration of war is the easiest thing in the world to decide upon, because war does not require of the ruler, who is the proprietor and not a member of the state, the least sacrifice of the pleasures of his table, the chase, his country houses, his court functions, and the like. He may, therefore, resolve on war as on a pleasure party for the most trivial reasons, and with perfect indifference leave the justification which decency requires to the diplomatic corps who are ever ready to provide it.

In order not to confuse the republican constitution with the democratic (as is commonly done), the following should be noted. The forms of a state (*civitas*) can be divided either according to the persons who possess the sovereign power or according to the mode of administration exercised over the people by the chief, whoever he may be. The first is properly called the form of sovereignty (*forma imperii*), and there are only three possible forms of it: autocracy, in which one, aristocracy, in which some associated together, or democracy, in which all those who constitute society, possess sovereign power. They may be characterized, respectively, as the power of a monarch, of the nobility, or of the people. The second division is that by the form of government (*forma regiminis*) and is based on the way in which the state makes use of its power; this way is based on the constitution, which is the act of the general will through which the many persons become one nation. In this respect government is either republican or despotic. Republicanism is the political principle of the separation of the executive power (the administration) from the legislative; despotism is that of the autonomous execution by the state of laws which it has itself decreed. Thus in a despotism the public will is administered by the ruler as his own will. Of the three forms of the state, that of democracy is, properly speaking, necessarily a despotism, because it establishes an executive power in which "all" decide for or even against one who does not agree; that is, "all," who are not quite all, decide, and this is a contradiction of the general will with itself and with freedom.

Every form of government which is not representative is, properly speaking, without form. The legislator can unite in one and the same person his function as legislative and as executor of his will just as little as the universal of the major premise in a syllogism can also be the subsumption of the particular under the universal in the minor. And even though the other two constitutions are always defective to the extent that they do leave room for this mode of administration, it is at least possible for them to assume a mode of government conforming to the spirit of a representative system (as when Frederick II at least *said* he was merely the first servant of the state).* On the other hand, the democratic mode of government makes this impossible, since everyone wishes to be master. Therefore, we can say: the smaller the personnel of the government (the smaller the number of rulers), the greater is their representation and the more nearly the constitution approaches to the possibility of republicanism; thus the constitution may be expected by gradual reform finally to raise itself to republicanism. For these reasons it is more difficult for an aristocracy than for a monarchy to achieve the one completely juridical constitution, and it is impossible for a democracy to do so except by violent revolution.

The mode of government,† however, is incomparably more important to the people than the form of sovereignty, although much depends on the greater or lesser suitability of the latter to the end of [good] government. To conform to the concept of law, however,

---

* The lofty epithets of "the Lord's anointed," "the executor of the divine will on earth," and "the vicar of God," which have been lavished on sovereigns, have been frequently censured as crude and intoxicating flatteries. But this seems to me without good reason. Far from inspiring a monarch with pride, they should rather render him humble, providing he possesses some intelligence (which we must assume). They should make him reflect that he has taken an office too great for man, an office which is the holiest God has ordained on earth, to be the trustee of the rights of men, and that he must always stand in dread of having in some way injured this "apple of God's eye."

† Mallet du Pan [Jacques Mallet du Pan (1749–1800), in his *Über die französische Revolution und die Ursachen ihrer Dauer* (1794) —L.W.B.] in his pompous but empty and hollow language, pretends to have become convinced, after long experience, of the truth of Pope's well-known saying:

> For forms of government let fools contest:
> Whate'er is best administered, is best.

If that means that the best-administered state is the state that is best administered, he has, to make use of Swift's expression, "cracked a nut to come at a maggot." But if it means that the best-administered state also has the best mode of government, i.e., the best constitution, then it is thoroughly wrong, for examples of good governments prove nothing about the form of government. Whoever reigned better than a Titus and a Marcus Aurelius? Yet one was succeeded by a Domitian and the other by a Commodus. This could never have happened under a good constitution, for their unworthiness for this post was known early enough and also the power of the ruler was sufficient to have excluded them.

government must have a representative form, and in this system only a republican mode of government is possible; without it, government is despotic and arbitrary, whatever the constitution may be. None of the ancient so-called "republics" knew this system, and they all finally and inevitably degenerated into despotism under the sovereignty of one, which is the most bearable of all forms of despotism.

SECOND DEFINITIVE ARTICLE FOR A PERPETUAL PEACE

"The Law of Nations Shall be Founded on a Federation of Free States"

Peoples, as states, like individuals, may be judged to injure one another merely by their coexistence in the state of nature (i.e., while independent of external laws). Each of them may and should for the sake of its own security demand that the others enter with it into a constitution similar to the civil constitution, for under such a constitution each can be secure in his right. This would be a league of nations, but it would not have to be a state consisting of nations. That would be contradictory, since a state implies the relation of a superior (legislating) to an inferior (obeying), i.e., the people, and many nations in one state would then constitute only one nation. This contradicts the presupposition, for here we have to weigh the rights of nations against each other so far as they are distinct states and not amalgamated into one.

When we see the attachment of savages to their lawless freedom, preferring ceaseless combat to subjection to a lawful constraint which they might establish, and thus preferring senseless freedom to rational freedom, we regard it with deep contempt as barbarity, rudeness, and a brutish degradation of humanity. Accordingly, one would think that civilized people (each united in a state) would hasten all the more to escape, the sooner the better, from such a depraved condition. But, instead, each state places its majesty (for it is absurd to speak of the majesty of the people) in being subject to no external juridical restraint, and the splendor of its sovereign consists in the fact that many thousands stand at his command to sacrifice themselves for something that does not concern them and without his needing to place himself in the least danger. The chief difference between European and American savages lies in the fact that many tribes of the latter have been eaten by their enemies, while the former know how to make better use of their conquered enemies than to dine off them; they know better how to use them to increase the number of their subjects and thus the quantity of instruments for even more extensive wars.

When we consider the perverseness of human nature which is nakedly revealed in the uncontrolled relations between nations (this perverseness being veiled in the state of civil law by the constraint exercised by government), we may well be astonished that the word "law" has not yet been banished from war politics as pedantic, and that no state has yet been bold enough to advocate this point of view. Up to the present, Hugo Grotius, Pufendorf, Vattel, and many other irritating comforters have been cited in justification of war, though their code, philosophically or diplomatically formulated, has not and cannot have the least legal force, because states as such do not stand under a common external power. There is no instance on record that a state has ever been moved to desist from its purpose because of arguments backed up by the testimony of such great men. But the homage which each state pays (at least in words) to the concept of law proves that there is slumbering in man an even greater moral disposition to become master of the evil principle in himself (which he cannot disclaim) and to hope for the same from others. Otherwise the word "law" would never be pronounced by states which wish to war upon one another; it would be used only ironically, as a Gallic prince interpreted it when he said, "It is the prerogative which nature has given the stronger that the weaker should obey him."

States do not plead their cause before a tribunal; war alone is their way of bringing suit. But by war and its favorable issue in victory, right is not decided, and though by a treaty of peace this particular war is brought to an end, the state of war, of always finding a new pretext to hostilities, is not terminated. Nor can this be declared wrong, considering the fact that in this state each is the judge of his own case. Notwithstanding, the obligation which men in a lawless condition have under the natural law, and which requires them to abandon the state of nature, does not quite apply to states under the law of nations, for as states they already have an internal juridical constitution and have thus outgrown compulsion from others to submit to a more extended lawful constitution according to their ideas of right. This is true in spite of the fact that reason, from its throne of supreme moral legislating authority, absolutely condemns war as a legal recourse and makes a state of peace a direct duty, even though peace cannot be established or secured except by a compact among nations.

For these reasons there must be a league of a particular kind, which can be called a league of peace (*foedus pacificum*), and which would be distinguished from a treaty of peace (*pactum pacis*) by the fact that the latter terminates only one war, while the former seeks to make an end of all wars forever. This league does not tend to any dominion over the power of the state but only to the maintenance and security of the freedom of the state itself and of other states in league with it, without there being any need for them to submit to civil laws and their compulsion, as men in a state of nature must submit.

The practicability (objective reality) of this idea of federation, which should gradually spread to all states and thus lead to perpetual peace, can be proved. For if fortune directs that a powerful and enlightened people can make itself a republic, which by its nature must be inclined to perpetual peace, this gives a fulcrum to the federation with other states so that they may adhere to it and thus secure freedom under the idea of the law of nations. By more and more such associations, the federation may be gradually extended.

We may readily conceive that a people should say, "There ought to be no war among us, for we want to make ourselves into a state; that is, we want to establish a supreme legislative, executive, and judiciary power which will reconcile our differences peaceably." But when this state says, "There ought to be no war between myself and other states, even though I acknowledge no supreme legislative power by which our rights are mutually guaranteed," it is not at all clear on what I can base my confidence in my own rights unless it is the free federation, the surrogate of the civil social order, which reason necessarily associates with the concept of the law of nations—assuming that something is really meant by the latter.

The concept of a law of nations as a right to make war does not really mean anything, because it is then a law of deciding what is right by unilateral maxims through force and not by universally valid public laws which restrict the freedom of each one. The only conceivable meaning of such a law of nations might be that it serves men right who are so inclined that they should destroy each other and thus find perpetual peace in the vast grave that swallows both the atrocities and their perpetrators. For states in their relation to each other, there cannot be any reasonable way out of the lawless condition which entails only war except that they, like individual men, should give up their savage (lawless) freedom, adjust themselves to the constraints of public law, and thus establish a continuously growing state consisting of various nations *(civitas gentium)*, which will ultimately include all the nations of the world. But under the idea of the law of nations they do not wish this, and reject in practice what is correct in theory. If all is not to be lost, there can be, then, in place of the positive idea of a world republic, only the negative surrogate of an alliance which averts war, endures, spreads, and holds back the stream of those hostile passions which fear the law, though such an alliance is in constant peril of their breaking loose again.* *Furor impius intus . . . fremit horridus ore cruento* (Virgil) .†

THIRD DEFINITIVE ARTICLE FOR A PERPETUAL PEACE

"The Law of World Citizenship Shall Be Limited to Conditions of Universal Hospitality"

Here, as in the preceding articles, it is not a question of philanthropy but of right. Hospitality means the right of a stranger not to be treated as an enemy when he arrives in the land of another. One may refuse to receive him when this can be done without causing his destruction; but, so long as he peacefully occupies his place, one may not treat him with hostility. It is not the right to be a permanent visitor that one may demand. A special beneficent agreement would be needed in order to give an outsider a right to become a

---

* It would not ill become a people that has just terminated a war to decree, besides a day of thanksgiving, a day of fasting in order to ask heaven, in the name of the state, for forgiveness for the great iniquity which the human race still goes on to perpetuate in refusing to submit to a lawful constitution in their relation to other peoples, preferring, from pride in their independence, to make use of the barbarous means of war even though they are not able to attain what is sought, namely, the rights of a single state. The thanksgiving for victory won during the war, the hymns which are sung to the God of Hosts (in good Israelitic manner), stand in equally sharp contrast to the moral idea of the Father of Men. For they not only show a sad enough indifference to the way in which nations seek their rights, but in addition express a joy in having annihilated a multitude of men or their happiness.

† ["Within, impious Rage, sitting on savage arms, his hands fast bound behind with a hundred brazen knots, shall roar in the ghastliness of blood-stained lips" (*Aeneid*, I, 294–96, tr. H. Rushton Fairclough, Loeb Classical Library edn.) —L.W.B.]

fellow inhabitant for a certain length of time. It is only a right of temporary sojourn, a right to associate, which all men have. They have it by virtue of their common possession of the surface of the earth, where, as a globe, they cannot infinitely disperse and hence must finally tolerate the presence of each other. Originally, no one had more right than another to a particular part of the earth.

Uninhabitable parts of the earth—the sea and the deserts—divide this community of all men, but the ship and the camel (the desert ship) enable them to approach each other across these unruled regions and to establish communication by using the common right to the face of the earth, which belongs to human beings generally. The inhospitality of the inhabitants of coasts (for instance, of the Barbary Coast) in robbing ships in neighboring seas or enslaving stranded travelers, or the inhospitality of the inhabitants of the deserts (for instance, the Bedouin Arabs) who view contact with nomadic tribes as conferring the right to plunder them, is thus opposed to natural law, even though it extends the right of hospitality, i.e., the privilege of foreign arrivals, no further than to conditions of the possibility of seeking to communicate with the prior inhabitants. In this way distant parts of the world can come into peaceable relations with each other, and these are finally publicly established by law. Thus the human race can gradually be brought closer and closer to a constitution establishing world citizenship.

But to this perfection compare the inhospitable actions of the civilized and especially of the commercial states of our part of the world. The injustice which they show to lands and peoples they visit (which is equivalent to conquering them) is carried by them to terrifying lengths. America, the lands inhabited by the Negro, the Spice Islands, the Cape, etc., were at the time of their discovery considered by these civilized intruders as lands without owners, for they counted the inhabitants as nothing. In East India (Hindustan), under the pretense of establishing economic undertakings, they brought in foreign soldiers and used them to oppress the natives, excited widespread wars among the various states, spread famine, rebellion, perfidy, and the whole litany of evils which afflict mankind.

China and Japan (Nippon), who have had experience with such guests, have wisely refused them entry, the former permitting their approach to their shores but not their entry, while the latter permit this approach to only one European people, the Dutch, but treat them like prisoners, not allowing them any communication with the inhabitants. The worst of this (or, to speak with the moralist, the best) is that all these outrages profit them nothing, since all these commercial ventures stand on the verge of collapse, and the Sugar Islands, that place of the most refined and cruel slavery, produces no real revenue except indirectly, only serving a not very praiseworthy purpose of furnishing sailors for war fleets and thus for the conduct of war in Europe. This service is rendered to powers which make a great show of their piety, and, while they drink injustice like water, they regard themselves as the elect in point of orthodoxy.

Since the narrower or wider community of the peoples of the earth has developed so far that a violation of rights in one place is felt throughout the world, the idea of a law of world citizenship is no high-flown or exaggerated notion. It is a supplement to the unwritten code of the civil and international law, indispensable for the maintenance of the public human rights and hence also of perpetual peace. One cannot flatter oneself into believing one can approach this peace except under the condition outlined here.

FURTHER READING

Arthur Ch. F. Beales, *The History of Peace* (1931) . Survey of peace plans.

Arthur Nussbaum, *A Concise History of the Law of Nations* (1958) . A helpful study of the instrument that Kant and others thought would make peace possible.

Elizabeth V. Souleyman, *The Vision of World Peace in Seventeenth- and Eighteenth-Century France* (1941) . Though confined to France, very informative on pacific thinking in Europe as a whole.

56 ❈ CONDORCET

Sketch of the Progress of the Human Mind

[From Antoine-Nicolas de Condorcet, *Sketch for a Historical Picture of the Progress of the Human Mind,* translated by June Barraclough 1955) , 167–69, 173–76, 196–202.*]

It is appropriate to end this anthology with Condorcet's ecstatic vision. The essay, written as it was in the midst of the French Revolution, stands at the end of the Enlightenment proper. The movement survived, through Bentham and the Utilitarians, through the positivists, and through all the secular humanitarians who, few as they are, live today. But the French Revolution, which in many ways was the child of the Enlightenment, was also its nemesis. With its purges at home and aggression abroad it awakened a revulsion that came to envelop the ideas of the philosophes in one vast mass of incomprehension.

But in one respect the choice is dangerous: it invites misunderstanding. In his final desperate effort, Condorcet summoned up all the expectations that had animated him and his admired teachers for decades. Hopeful as many of the philosophes were, they were not professional optimists; the theory of progress, as I have insisted before, was by no means widespread among literary men who saw the world soberly and recognized its immense difficulties. Condorcet's Sketch for a Historical Picture of the Progress of the Human Mind *is a dream, not a prediction; an epitaph, not an epitome.†*

* Reprinted by permission of George Weidenfeld and Nicolson.

† Lack of space has compelled me to confine this extract to the most optimistic parts, though Condorcet's reservoir of pessimism becomes evident even in these

Marie-Jean-Antoine-Nicolas Caritat, Marquis de Condorcet, was born in 1743, and established himself as a mathematician while still a young man. By 1769 he was a member of the French Academy of Sciences; by 1782, he was in the writer's heaven, the Académie française. While his professional work led him to the theory of probability, his association with older philosophes and his social conscience, led him to speculate on political institutions. He participated actively in the Revolution, championing reform of education and deploring the free use of violence. Proscribed in 1793, he went into hiding and between July of that year and March 1794 wrote his essay on the progress of the human mind—really a prospectus for a comprehensive history. Then he ventured forth and was arrested; the next morning he was found dead in prison, whether by choice or from exhaustion we shall never know. His end lends his last manuscript a peculiar poignancy.

❊

THE NINTH STAGE
From Descartes to the Foundation of the French Republic

. . . The progress of philosophy and the sciences has favoured and extended the progress of letters, and this in turn has served to make the study of the sciences easier, and that of philosophy more popular. The sciences and the arts have assisted one another despite the efforts of the ignorant and the foolish to separate them and make them enemies. Scholarship, which seemed doomed by its respect for the past and its deference towards authority always to lend its support to harmful superstitions, has nevertheless contributed to their eradication, for it was able to borrow the torch of a sounder criticism from philosophy and the sciences. It already knew how to weigh up authorities and compare them; it now learned how to bring every authority before the bar of Reason. It had already

---

pages. A reading of the whole *Sketch* would show even more clearly that Condorcet, the presumed prophet of progress, had many doubts; he saw the past as a vast struggle between entrenched establishments—priests, lawyers, doctors, politicians—and the forces of decency and progress.

discounted prodigies, fantastic anecdotes, facts contrary to all probability; but after attacking the evidence on which such absurdities
relied, it now learned that all extraordinary facts must always be
rejected, however impressive the evidence in their favour, unless
this can truly turn the scale against the weight of their physical or
moral probability.

Thus all the intellectual activities of man, however different they
may be in their aims, their methods, or the qualities of mind they
exact, have combined to further the progress of human reason.
Indeed, the whole system of human labour is like a well-made
machine, whose several parts have been systematically distinguished
but none the less, being intimately bound together, form a single
whole, and work towards a single end.

Turning now our attention to the human race in general, we
shall show how the discovery of the correct method of procedure in
the sciences, the growth of scientific theories, their application to
every part of the natural world, to the subject of every human need,
the lines of communication established between one science and
another, the great number of men who cultivate the sciences, and
most important of all, the spread of printing, how together all these
advances ensure that no science will ever fall below the point it has
reached. We shall point out that the principles of philosophy, the
slogans of liberty, the recognition of the true rights of man and his
real interests, have spread through far too great a number of
nations, and now direct in each of them the opinions of far too
great a number of enlightened men, for us to fear that they will
ever be allowed to relapse into oblivion. And indeed what reason
could we have for fear, when we consider that the languages most
widely spoken are the languages of the two peoples who enjoy
liberty to the fullest extent and who best understand its principles,
and that no league of tyrants, no political intrigues, could prevent
the resolute defence, in these two languages, of the rights of reason
and of liberty?

But although everything tells us that the human race will never
relapse into its former state of barbarism, although everything combines to reassure us against that corrupt and cowardly political
theory which would condemn it to oscillate forever between truth
and error, liberty and servitude, nevertheless we still see the forces
of enlightenment in possession of no more than a very small portion
of the globe, and the truly enlightened vastly outnumbered by the
great mass of men who are still given over to ignorance and prejudice. We still see vast areas in which men groan in slavery, vast

areas offering the spectacle of nations either degraded by the vices of a civilization whose progress is impeded by corruption, or still vegetating in the infant condition of early times. We observe that the labours of recent ages have done much for the progress of the human mind, but little for the perfection of the human race; that they have done much for the honour of man, something for his liberty, but so far almost nothing for his happiness. At a few points our eyes are dazzled with a brilliant light; but thick darkness still covers an immense stretch of the horizon. There are a few circumstances from which the philosopher can take consolation; but he is still afflicted by the spectacle of the stupidity, slavery, barbarism and extravagance of mankind; and the friend of humanity can find unmixed pleasure only in tasting the sweet delights of hope for the future. . . .

THE TENTH STAGE
The Future Progress of the Human Mind

If man can, with almost complete assurance, predict phenomena when he knows their laws, and if, even when he does not, he can still, with great expectation of success, forecast the future on the basis of his experience of the past, why, then, should it be regarded as a fantastic undertaking to sketch, with some pretence to truth, the future destiny of man on the basis of his history? The sole foundation for belief in the natural sciences is this idea, that the general laws directing the phenomena of the universe, known or unknown, are necessary and constant. Why should this principle be any less true for the development of the intellectual and moral faculties of man than for the other operations of nature? Since beliefs founded on past experience of like conditions provide the only rule of conduct for the wisest of men, why should the philosopher be forbidden to base his conjectures on these same foundations, so long as he does not attribute to them a certainty superior to that warranted by the number, the constancy, and the accuracy of his observations?

Our hopes for the future condition of the human race can be subsumed under three important heads: the abolition of inequality between nations, the progress of equality within each nation, and the true perfection of mankind. Will all nations one day attain that state of civilization which the most enlightened, the freest and the least burdened by prejudices, such as the French and the Anglo-Americans, have attained already? Will the vast gulf that separates these peoples from the slavery of nations under the rule of monarchs, from the barbarism of African tribes, from the ignorance of savages, little by little disappear?

Is there on the face of the earth a nation whose inhabitants have been debarred by nature herself from the enjoyment of freedom and the exercise of reason?

Are those differences which have hitherto been seen in every civilized country in respect of the enlightenment, the resources, and the wealth enjoyed by the different classes into which it is divided, is that inequality between men which was aggravated or perhaps produced by the earliest progress of society, are these part of civilization itself, or are they due to the present imperfections of the social art? Will they necessarily decrease and ultimately make way for a real equality, the final end of the social art, in which even the effects of the natural differences between men will be mitigated and the only kind of inequality to persist will be that which is in the interests of all and which favours the progress of civilization, of education, and of industry, without entailing either poverty, humiliation, or dependence? In other words, will men approach a condition in which everyone will have the knowledge necessary to conduct himself in the ordinary affairs of life, according to the light of his own reason, to preserve his mind free from prejudice, to understand his rights and to exercise them in accordance with his conscience and his creed; in which everyone will become able, through the development of his faculties, to find the means of providing for his needs; and in which at last misery and folly will be the exception, and no longer the habitual lot of a section of society?

Is the human race to better itself, either by discoveries in the sciences and the arts, and so in the means to individual welfare and general prosperity; or by progress in the principles of conduct or practical morality; or by a true perfection of the intellectual, moral, or physical faculties of man, an improvement which may result from a perfection either of the instruments used to heighten the intensity of these faculties and to direct their use or of the natural constitution of man?

In answering these three questions we shall find in the experience of the past, in the observation of the progress that the sciences and civilization have already made, in the analysis of the progress of the human mind and of the development of its faculties, the strongest reasons for believing that nature has set no limit to the realization of our hopes.

If we glance at the state of the world today we see first of all that in Europe the principles of the French constitution are already those of all enlightened men. We see them too widely propagated, too seriously professed, for priests and despots to prevent their gradual penetration even into the hovels of their slaves; there they will soon awaken in these slaves the remnants of their common sense and inspire them with that smouldering indignation which not even constant humiliation and fear can smother in the soul of the oppressed.

As we move from nation to nation, we can see in each what special obstacles impede this revolution and what attitudes of mind favour it. We can distinguish the nations where we may expect it to be introduced gently by the perhaps belated wisdom of their governments, and those nations where its violence intensified by their resistance must involve all alike in a swift and terrible convulsion.

Can we doubt that either common sense or the senseless discords of European nations will add to the effects of the slow but inexorable progress of their colonies, and will soon bring about the independence of the New World? And then will not the European population in these colonies, spreading rapidly over that enormous land, either civilize or peacefully remove the savage nations who still inhabit vast tracts of its land?

Survey the history of our settlements and commercial undertakings in Africa or in Asia, and you will see how our trade monopolies, our treachery, our murderous contempt for men of another colour or creed, the insolence of our usurpations, the intrigues or the exaggerated proselytic zeal of our priests, have destroyed the respect and goodwill that the superiority of our knowledge and the benefits of our commerce at first won for us in the eyes of the inhabitants. But doubtless the moment approaches when, no longer presenting ourselves as always either tyrants or corrupters, we shall become for them the beneficent instruments of their freedom. . . .

The progress of the sciences ensures the progress of the art of education which in turn advances that of the sciences. This reciprocal influence, whose activity is ceaselessly renewed, deserves to be seen as one of the most powerful and active causes working for the perfection of mankind. At the present time a young man on leaving school may know more of the principles of mathematics than Newton ever learnt in years of study or discovered by dint of genius, and he may use the calculus with a facility then unknown. The same observation, with certain reservations, applies to all the sciences. As each advances, the methods of expressing a large number of proofs in a more economical fashion and so of making their comprehension an easier matter, advance with it. So, in spite of the progress of science, not only do men of the same ability find themselves at the same age on a level with the existing state of science, but with every generation, that which can be acquired in a certain time with a certain degree of intelligence and a certain amount of concentration will be permanently on the increase, and, as the elementary part of each science to which all men may attain grows and grows, it will more and more include all the knowledge necessary for each man to know for the conduct of the ordinary events of his life, and will support him in the free and independent exercise of his reason.

In the political sciences there are some truths that, with free people (that is to say, with certain generations in all countries) can be of use only if they are widely known and acknowledged. So the influence of these sciences upon the freedom and prosperity of nations must in some degree be measured by the number of truths that, as a result of elementary instruction, are common knowledge; the swelling progress of elementary instruction, connected with the necessary progress of these sciences, promises us an improvement in the destiny of the human race, which may be regarded as indefinite, since it can have no other limits than that of this same progress.

We have still to consider two other general methods which will influence both the perfection of education and that of the sciences. One is the more extensive and less imperfect use of what we might call technical methods; the other is the setting up of a universal language.

I mean by technical methods the art of arranging a large number of subjects in a system so that we may straightway grasp their relations, quickly perceive their combinations, and readily form new combinations out of them.

We shall develop the principles and examine the utility of this art, which is still in its infancy, and which, as it improves, will enable us, within the compass of a small chart, to set out what could possibly not be expressed so well in a whole book, or, what is still more valuable, to present isolated facts in such a way as to allow us to deduce their general consequences. We shall see how by means of a small number of these charts, whose use can easily be learned, men who have not been sufficiently educated to be able to absorb details useful to them in ordinary life, may now be able to master them when the need arises; and how these methods may likewise be of benefit to elementary education itself in all those branches where it is concerned either with a regular system of truths or with a series of observations and facts.

A universal language is that which expresses by signs either real objects themselves or well-defined collections composed of simple and general ideas, which are found to be the same or may arise in a similar form in the minds of all men, or the general relations holding between these ideas, the operations of the human mind, or the operations peculiar to the individual sciences, or the procedures of the arts. So people who become acquainted with these signs, the ways to combine them and the rules for forming them will understand what is written in this language and will be able to read it as easily as their own language.

It is obvious that this language might be used to set out the theory of a science or the rules of an art, to describe a new observation or experiment, the invention of a procedure, the discovery of a truth or a method; and that, as in algebra, when one has to make use of a new sign, those already known provide the means of explaining its import.

Such a language has not the disadvantages of a scientific idiom different from the vernacular. We have already observed that the use of such an idiom would necessarily divide society into two unequal classes, the one composed of men who, understanding this language, would possess the key to all the sciences, the other of men who, unable to acquire it, would therefore find themselves almost completely unable to acquire enlightenment. In contrast to this, a universal language would be learnt, like that of algebra, along with the science itself; the sign would be learnt at the same time as the object, idea or operation that it designates. He who, having mastered the elements of a science, would like to know more of it, would find in books not only truths he could understand by means of the signs whose import he has learnt, but also the explanation of such further signs as he needs in order to go on to other truths.

We shall show that the formation of such a language, if confined to the expression of those simple, precise propositions which form the system of a science or the practice of an art, is no chimerical scheme; that even at the present time it could be readily introduced to deal with a large number of objects; and that, indeed, the chief obstacle that would prevent its extension to others would be the humiliation of having to admit how very few precise ideas and accurate, unambiguous notions we actually possess.

We shall show that this language, ever improving and broadening its scope all the while, would be the means of giving to every subject embraced by the human intelligence, a precision and a rigour that would make knowledge of the truth easy and error almost impossible. Then the progress of every science would be as sure as that of mathematics, and the propositions that compose it would acquire a geometrical certainty, as far, that is, as is possible granted the nature of its aim and method.

All the causes that contribute to the perfection of the human race, all the means that ensure it, must by their very nature exercise a perpetual influence and always increase their sphere of action. The proofs of this we have given and in the great work they will derive additional force from elaboration. We may conclude then that the perfectibility of man is indefinite. Meanwhile we have considered him as possessing the natural faculties and organization that he has at present. How much greater would be the certainty, how much vaster the scheme of our hopes, if we could believe that these natural faculties themselves and this organization could also be improved? This is the last question that remains for us to ask ourselves.

Organic perfectibility or deterioration amongst the various strains in the vegetable and animal kingdom can be regarded as one of the general laws of nature. This law also applies to the human race. No one can doubt that, as preventive medicine improves and food and housing become healthier, as a way of life is established that develops our physical powers by exercise without ruining them by excess, as the two most virulent causes of deterioration, misery and excessive wealth, are eliminated, the average length of human life will be increased and a better health and a stronger physical constitution will be ensured. The improvement of medical practice, which will become more efficacious with the progress of reason and of the social order, will mean the end of infectious and hereditary diseases and illnesses brought on by climate, food, or working conditions. It is reasonable to hope that all other diseases may likewise disappear as their distant causes are discovered. Would it be absurd then to suppose that this perfection of the human species might be capable of indefinite progress; that the day will come when death will be due only to extraordinary accidents or to the decay of the vital forces, and that ultimately the average span between birth and decay will have no assignable value? Certainly man will not become immortal, but will not the interval between the first breath that he draws and the time when in the natural course of events, without disease or accident, he expires, increase indefinitely? Since we are now speaking of a progress that can be represented with some accuracy in figures or on a graph, we shall take this opportunity of explaining the two meanings that can be attached to the word "indefinite."

In truth, this average span of life which we suppose will increase indefinitely as time passes, may grow in conformity either with a law such that it continually approaches a limitless length but without ever reaching it, or with a law such that through the centuries it reaches a length greater than any determinate quantity that we may assign to it as its limit. In the latter case such an increase is truly indefinite in the strictest sense of the word, since there is no term on this side of which it must of necessity stop. In the former case it is equally indefinite in relation to us, if we cannot fix the limit it always approaches without ever reaching, and particularly if, knowing only that it will never stop, we are ignorant in which of the two senses the term "indefinite" can be applied to it. Such is the present condition of our knowledge as far as the perfectibility of the human race is concerned; such is the sense in which we may call it indefinite.

So, in the example under consideration, we are bound to believe that the average length of human life will for ever increase unless this is prevented by physical revolutions; we do not know what the limit is which it can never exceed. We cannot tell even whether the general laws of nature have determined such a limit or not.

But are not our physical faculties and the strength, dexterity and acuteness of our senses, to be numbered among the qualities whose perfection in the individual may be transmitted? Observation of the various breeds of domestic animals inclines us to believe that they are, and we can confirm this by direct observation of the human race.

Finally may we not extend such hopes to the intellectual and moral faculties? May not our parents, who transmit to us the benefits or disadvantages of their constitution, and from whom we receive our shape and features, as well as our tendencies to certain physical affections, hand on to us also that part of the physical organization which determines the intellect, the power of the brain, the ardour of the soul or the moral sensibility? Is it not probable that education, in perfecting these qualities, will at the same time influence, modify and perfect the organization itself? Analogy, investigation of the human faculties and the study of certain facts, all seem to give substance to such conjectures which would further push back the boundaries of our hopes.

These are the questions with which we shall conclude this final stage. How consoling for the philosopher who laments the errors, the crimes, the injustices which still pollute the earth and of which he is often the victim is this view of the human race, emancipated from its shackles, released from the empire of fate and from that of the enemies of its progress, advancing with a firm and sure step along the path of truth, virtue and happiness! It is the contemplation of this prospect that rewards him for all his efforts to assist the progress of reason and the defence of liberty. He dares to regard these strivings as part of the eternal chain of human destiny; and in this persuasion he is filled with the true delight of virtue and the pleasure of having done some lasting good which fate can never destroy by a sinister stroke of revenge, by calling back the reign of slavery and prejudice. Such contemplation is for him an asylum, in which the memory of his persecutors cannot pursue him; there he lives in thought with man restored to his natural rights and dignity, forgets man tormented and corrupted by greed, fear or envy; there he lives with his peers in an Elysium created by reason and graced by the purest pleasures known to the love of mankind.

FURTHER READING

Léon Cahen, *Condorcet et la Révolution française* (1904). An exhaustive biography; opting, incidentally, for death from exhaustion.

Peter Gay, *The Enlightenment: An Interpretation*, Vol. II, *The Science of Freedom* (1969), Chapter 2. Puts the idea of progress in the Enlightenment in its proper social and cultural context.

Gilles-Gaston Granger, *La Mathématique social du marquis de Condorcet* (1956). Interesting examination of Condorcet's efforts to bring quantitative analysis into the study of voting.

Frank E. Manuel, *The Prophets of Paris: Turgot, Condorcet, Saint-Simon, Fourier and Comte* (1962). Excellent set of essays.

Henry Vyverberg, *Historical Pessimism in the French Enlightenment* (1958). A splendid corrective for those who think of the philosophes as optimists.

❧ Index

Abbas the Great (Shah of Persia),
131, 139
Abu Bakr (first caliph), 126
Abundance, 141–42
Academics, 633
Acting, Diderot on, 465–68
Addison, Joseph, 171, 202, 273–74, 443
on opera, 470
Spectator, 274–82, 693
Aeneid (Virgil), 44
Aesculapius, 636
Aesthetics, 418, 420–21, 441–42
classical, 460–62
Reynolds on, 436–39
Winckelmann on Greek, 421–28
See also Taste
Africa, 138
Agag (King of Amalekites), 242
Agesilaus, 563
Agricola, 37, 623n, 624–25
Agriculture, 579–80
Ahasuerus (King of Persia), 506
Alceste (Gluck opera), 470–71, 473–475
Alcibiades, 423
Alembert, Jean le Rond d', 15–16, 21, 38, 56, 293–94
Encyclopédie and, 285–86
Geneva, 294–302
Alexander the Great 44, 460, 631
Alexander of Hales, 162
Alexander Severus (Roman Emperor), 706–707
Alexandria, 41
Alexandros of Alexandria, 239–40
Algarotti, Francesco, 418
Ali (fourth caliph), 126, 129
Alliances
international law and, 134–35
peace treaties, 135, 785–86, 796
Ambition in monarchies, Montesquieu on, 504

America, 138
Spanish conquest in, 139–40
See also North America
Anabaptists, 151
Analysis of Beauty (Hogarth), 418
Anaxagoras, 161
Anglican Church, 113, 199
in *Letters Concerning the English Nation* (Voltaire), 147–49
Anna Ivanovna (Czarina of Russia), 708
Anne (Queen of England), 147–48
Anthony, Marc, 153
Antiochus Epiphanes, 425
Antipater, 496–97
Antipathy and sympathy, principle of, 668
Anti-Semitism, 746–47
Antitrinitarians, 151–53
Antonines (second-century Roman Emperors)
constitution under, 643–51
military forces under, 621–31
prosperity under, 631–43
Antoninus Pius (Roman Emperor), 625, 628–29, 707
Aquinas, St. Thomas, 162
Arabia Felix, 623
Arabs, 41, 346
Arcadius (Eastern Roman Emperor), 653, 706, 708
Arians, 151–53
Voltaire on, 239–41
Ariosto, Ludovico, 444
Aristides, 492
Aristocracy, 347
Montesquieu on nature of, 491, 493, 495–97
Montesquieu on principles of, 500, 502–503
See also Nobility
Aristodamas, 460

811

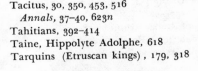